CW00422068

BYRON'S LETTERS AND JOURNALS

Byron's Letters and Journals

A New Selection

From Leslie A. Marchand's
twelve-volume edition

Edited by
RICHARD LANSDOWN

OXFORD
UNIVERSITY PRESS

OXFORD

UNIVERSITY PRESS

Great Clarendon Street, Oxford, OX2 6DP,
United Kingdom

Oxford University Press is a department of the University of Oxford.
It furthers the University's objective of excellence in research, scholarship,
and education by publishing worldwide. Oxford is a registered trade mark of
Oxford University Press in the UK and in certain other countries

First Edition published in 2015

Impression: 1

Published in the United States of America by Oxford University Press
198 Madison Avenue, New York, NY 10016, United States of America

British Library Cataloguing in Publication Data
Data available

Library of Congress Control Number: 2014949666

ISBN 978–0–19–872255–7

Printed in Great Britain by
Clays Ltd, St Ives plc

in memory of Dan Jacobson

1929–2014

'no one has Been & Done like you'

ACKNOWLEDGEMENTS

Two generations of Byron scholars, biographers, students, and readers have acknowledged the debt they owe to Professor Leslie A. Marchand (1900–99), of Rutgers University, and Jock Murray (1909–93), the sixth generation to run the famous London publishing house of that name since it was founded in 1768. Together they established two of the four pillars of contemporary Byron scholarship: Marchand's three-volume *Byron: A Biography*, published in 1957, and the twelve-volume edition of *Byron's Letters and Journals*, published between 1973 and 1982 (with a supplementary volume in 1994). The other two pillars are Jerome McGann's edition of Byron's *Complete Poetical Works*, published in seven volumes by Oxford University Press between 1980 and 1993, and Andrew Nicholson's edition of Byron's *Complete Miscellaneous Prose*, also published by Oxford, in 1991. Without these books, Byron would perhaps still be regarded as he often was in the first half of the 20th century, as the poor cousin of the English Romantic movement.

Marchand's colossal achievement over a lifetime speaks for itself from library shelves around the world. Jock Murray worked closely with him tracking down unpublished Byron letters from all over the world; he also welcomed hundreds of researchers to the Byron archive at Albemarle Street—now held at the National Library of Scotland—and so nurtured the ongoing scholarship that Leslie Marchand inspired. As a result of that scholarship, Byron is now regarded as one of the wonders of English literature, and a creative force to stand alongside Jane Austen and William Wordsworth.

To the current John Murray, the seventh in succession, I owe a more personal debt. His wife Virginia helped me at Albemarle Street when I visited as a doctoral student in the mid-1980s, and I still have copies of letters to Byron from various theatrical types that she pinned together for me all those years ago. More particularly, John inherited the copyright of Leslie A. Marchand's edition of Byron's letters and journals, and he gave me permission to reproduce freely from it in the selection that follows, for which I am profoundly grateful. Without that generous gesture this book would not have been possible. It is a pleasure and a privilege to have helped bring the OUP and the John Murray strands in the Byron publishing story together, and I thank John Murray VII for allowing it to happen.

My thanks also to everybody at Oxford University Press for all their assistance with this project. The commissioning editor was Rachel Platt, the production editor Kizzy Taylor-Richelieu, the copyeditor Jackie Pritchard, and the proofreader the magnificent Jacqueline Harvey. All were models of patience and good humour.

CONTENTS

INTRODUCTION

'Byron's letters appeal on three special grounds to all lovers of English literature,' their editor suggested at the close of the nineteenth century. 'They offer the most suggestive commentary on his poetry; they give the truest portrait of the man; they possess, at their best, in their ease, freshness and racy vigour, a very high literary value.'[1] The great monuments of English Romantic prose are Jane Austen's novels, Hazlitt's essays, Keats's letters, Coleridge's notebooks, and De Quincey's *Confessions of an English Opium Eater*. Byron's letters and journals match these and go further, to provide, taken as a whole, one of the three great informal autobiographies in English, alongside Samuel Pepys's diary and James Boswell's journal.

Like those other two works, the occasionally risqué content of Byron's letters assured them a complex publishing history. (Pepys's diary—deposited by him at Magdalene College, Cambridge after his death in 1703—was first decoded in 1825, but had to wait another 150 years for an unexpurgated edition. Boswell's journal was discovered in Ireland in the 1920s, 130 years after he finished it, and complete publication only came to an end in 1989.) Byron's informal prose has been revealed in three great publishing ventures, stretching over 150 years, all emanating from the English publishing firm of John Murray, with which the poet was associated for almost the whole of his writing life. The first was the *Letters and Journals of Lord Byron: With Notices of his Life*, published in 1830 by his friend and fellow poet Thomas Moore, only six years after the poet's death, which made 561 letters available—albeit in a bowdlerized form. The second was the six volumes of *Letters and Journals*, edited by R. E. Prothero, which supplemented Byron's poems in the great edition of his *Works* published between 1898 and 1904, and which printed nearly 1,200 letters. The treasure was hauled completely into the light in the twelve volumes of *Byron's Letters and Journals*, edited by Leslie Marchand between 1973 and 1982 (a supplementary volume was published in 1994), which brought the total up to 3,000—at last reproduced in

[1] *The Works of Lord Byron: Letters and Journals*, ed. Rowland E. Prothero, vol. i (London: John Murray, 1898), vi.

an unexpurgated text.[2] Three hundred of those letters are reprinted in this selection: about twice as many as Marchand reprinted in his *Selected Letters and Journals* of 1982.

Despite this complex history, each generation of readers has responded to Byron's letters in a strikingly similar way. Moore was certain that the correspondence he printed 'will be found equal, if not superior, in point of vigour, variety, and liveliness, to any that have yet adorned this branch of our literature', and when the historian Thomas Babington Macaulay came to discuss Moore's documentary biography in the *Edinburgh Review* he emphatically concurred. 'The extracts from the journals and correspondence of Lord Byron', he wrote, 'are in the highest degree valuable—not merely on account of the information which they contain respecting the distinguished man by whom they were written, but on account, also, of their rare merit as compositions.' 'If the epistolary style of Lord Byron was artificial,' Macaulay concluded, 'it was a rare and admirable instance of that highest art, which cannot be distinguished from nature.'[3] John Churton Collins reviewed Prothero's edition in similar terms in 1905. 'Byron's letters', he wrote in the *Quarterly Review*,

will probably live as long as his poems. Voluminous as they are, they never weary us. Social sketches dashed off with inimitable happiness; anecdote and incident related as only a consummate *raconteur* can relate them; piquant comments on the latest scandal or the latest book; the gossip and tittle-tattle of the green-room and the boudoir, of the clubs and the salons, so transformed by the humour and the wit of their cynical retailer that they almost rival the dialogue of Congreve and Sheridan; shrewd and penetrating observations on life, on human nature, on politics, on literature, dropped so carelessly that it is only on reflection that we see their wisdom, keep us perpetually amused and entertained.[4]

Collins's attitude to the writer he calls a 'consummate *raconteur*' and a 'cynical retailer' of 'gossip and tittle-tattle'—someone who even drops the penetrating observations on life he has to offer 'carelessly'—is a condescending one. (In the past Byron has frequently suffered from similar forms of literary-critical condescension—his poetry often being regarded as facile and slapdash compared with that of, say, Wordsworth and Keats.) But Collins also set Byron's letters alongside his poems as sources of literary value, and Arthur Symons, writing in 1909, did the same. 'In his letters,' Symons wrote, 'with their brilliant common sense, their wit, their clear and defiant intellect, their intolerant

---

[2] I draw these statistics from Marchand himself: see *Byron's Letters and Journals*, ed. Leslie A. Marchand, 12 vols. (London: John Murray 1973–82), i. 24; cited below as *LJ*.

[3] Thomas Moore, *Letters and Journals of Lord Byron: With Notices of his Life*, 2 vols. (London: John Murray, 1830), i. n.p., and Andrew Rutherford (ed.), *Byron: The Critical Heritage* (London: Routledge and Kegan Paul, 1970), 296.

[4] John Churton Collins, *Studies in Poetry and Criticism* (London: George Bell, 1905), 80.

sincerity, as in his poems, it is not what we call the poet who speaks, it is what we call the natural man. Byron is the supreme incarnation of the natural man...'[5] When the Marchand edition appeared seventy years later, many readers were prepared to go still further in considering the relative merits of Byron's prose and verse. 'No one...need doubt', Michael Ratcliffe wrote in the London *Times*, 'that the letters, perhaps even more than *Don Juan*, are the beginning, middle, and the end of Lord Byron.'[6]

But just what the characteristic qualities of Byron's informal prose are remains difficult to say. 'The letters and journals together give a vivid impression of a fascinating character, who with all his faults, and they were many, insinuates himself into the sympathies of a reader by his transparent humanity,' Leslie Marchand suggested.[7] 'In journals and letters alike,' John Jump commented,

Byron allows his natural mobility of temperament to reveal itself in rapid and sometimes subversive fluctuations of mood; vigorously and racily, he sets down what he has observed; and he comments wittily, sympathetically, humorously, or mockingly upon whatever has excited his interest. He is one of the most versatile and provocative of our letter-writers and diarists; and more than any other he has left us a collection of writings that constitute a brilliant and incisive self-portrait, above all a dramatic self-portrait, of one whom we can never know too well.[8]

No reader is likely to disagree with such views; but they are essentially those of Moore, Macaulay, Prothero, and Collins, with their stress on 'vigour, variety, and liveliness'. The aesthetic features and moral implications of Byron's dramatic self-portrait still await our understanding.

'I have but an indifferent opinion of the prose-style of poets,' Hazlitt wrote in 1822: 'not that it is not sometimes good, nay, excellent; but it is never the better, and generally the worse from the habit of writing verse. Poets are winged animals, and can cleave the air, like birds, with ease to themselves and delight to the beholders; but these "feathered, two-legged things," when they light upon the ground of prose and matter-of-fact, they seem not to have the same use of their feet.'[9] If there is one thing we can say of Byron's letters it is that they are the exception that tests Hazlitt's rule. (To be fair to him, it was probably poets' formal prose Hazlitt had in mind, and he rightly said that Byron's prose of that variety is, as a rule, 'heavy, labored, and coarse'.) 'Their style halts, totters, is

---

[5] Rutherford, *Byron: The Critical Heritage*, 501.
[6] Michael Ratcliffe, 'Byron: Minus the Asterisk', *London Times*, 4 October 1973.
[7] Byron, *Selected Letters and Journals*, ed. Leslie A. Marchand (London: John Murray, 1982), 16.
[8] John D. Jump (ed.), *Byron: A Symposium* (London: Macmillan, 1975), 34.
[9] William Hazlitt, *Complete Works*, ed. P. P. Howe, 21 vols. (London: J. M. Dent, 1930–4), xii. 5.

loose, disjointed, and without expressive pauses or rapid movements,' Hazlitt went on: and perhaps of no prose in English outside Shakespeare's plays is this less true than Byron's in his letters. 'Never, we feel, can written utterance have been less premeditated, less rehearsed, less inhibited, less controlled,' John Jump remarked. Leslie Marchand, too, spoke of the 'bounding spontaneity' of Byron's epistolary style.[10]

Examples of Byron's 'bounding' are never far to seek. 'I am glad you like it,' he wrote to Moore in January 1817 about the recently published third canto of *Childe Harold's Pilgrimage*, the poem that had made him famous overnight in the spring of 1812:

> it is a fine indistinct piece of poetical desolation, and my favourite. I was half mad during the time of its composition, between metaphysics, mountains, lakes, love unextinguishable, thoughts unutterable, and the nightmare of my own delinquencies. I should, many a good day, have blown my brains out, but for the recollection that it would have given pleasure to my mother-in-law; and, even *then*, if I could have been certain to haunt her—but I won't dwell upon these trifling family matters. (*LJ* v. 165)

Unpremeditated this may very well be, but it is 'inhibited'—if that is the word for the poetic employment of language—by Byron's capacity to anticipate, control, and exploit the patterns of speech he is unleashing. In this example (and dozens of parallel passages could be cited from the letters) alliteration begins the process: his 'piece of poetical desolation' introduces the 'mad...metaphysics, mountains' sequence, which gives place to lakes and love, themselves immediately supplanted by a negative-adjectival pattern ('love unextinguishable, thoughts unutterable') itself fused together with an assonantal pattern capped off by 'the nightmare of my own delinquencies'. (Discussing Byron's prose in his autobiography, John Ruskin compared it to 'the serene swiftness of a smith's hammer-strokes on hot iron'.[11]) The bathetic humour in the next sentence, in which Byron resolves to continue his existence if only to plague his wife's mother, is only a different tack in a wonderfully intense form of responsiveness to what preoccupied and distracted him as he wrote—itself an irreverent commentary on the moodily solipsistic and quintessentially Romantic poem ostensibly under discussion. This was exactly the 'same use of his feet' that Byron brought to, and from, his poetry—especially his comic poetry: 'that highest art,' as Macaulay put it, 'which cannot be distinguished from nature.'

Byron's letters exploit dramatic insights as well as linguistic inventions. In November 1818, two and a half years after leaving England in disgrace after the

---

[10] Jump, *Byron: A Symposium*, 17, and *LJ* i. 1.

[11] John Ruskin, *Praeterita*, chapter 8, in *Works*, ed. E. T. Cook and Alexander Wedderburn, 39 vols. (London: George Allen, 1902–12), xxxv. 144; this chapter is one of the most astute critical discussions of the poet that we have.

collapse of his marriage, he was reluctantly visited at Venice by his xenophobic, valetudinarian, and miserly lawyer, John Hanson, on business relating to the sale of Newstead Abbey, the poet's country seat. As if this was not enough, Hanson had forgotten to bring the latest Walter Scott novel and a supply of Byron's favourite toothpaste. 'I'll be revenged on Spooney', Byron wrote to his friend, John Cam Hobhouse:

—five men died of the Plague the other day—in the Lazaretto—I shall take him to ride at the Lido—he hath a reverend care & fear of his health—I will show him the Lazaretto which is not far off you know—& looks nearer than it is—I will tell him of the five men— I will tell him of my contact with [Dr] Aglietti in whose presence they died—& who came into my box at the (St. Benedetto's) Opera the same evening—& shook hands with me;— I will tell him all this—and as he is hypochondriac—perhaps it may kill him.——The Monster left my books—everything—my Magnesia—my tooth powder—&c. &c. and wanted me besides to go to Geneva——but I made him come.—He is a queer fish—the Customs House Officers wanted to examine or have money—he would not pay—they opened every thing.—'Ay—Ay—(said he) look away—Carts Carts' that was his phrase for *papers* with a strong English emphasis & accent on the *s* and he actually made them turn over all the Newstead & Rochdale—& Jew—& Chancery papers exclaiming 'Carts Carts' & came off triumphant with paying a *Centime*—the Officers giving up the matter in despair—finding nothing else—& not being able to translate what they found.——But I have been in a damned passion for all that—for this adventure nearly reconciled me to him. (*LJ* vi. 77–8)

Here is the eternal British citizen submitting obstructively to a continental *douanier*; and the contrast Byron finds between Hanson's 'carts' (that is the French *cartes*, meaning maps or papers), of such powerful but temporary significance, and the parties squabbling over them in so futile but legalistic a spirit, is typical of his appetite for the life going on around him. This appetite for life frequently surprised his acquaintances, who expected to meet Childe Harold in person, and found someone wholly different: 'Byron's suavity of manner surprised and delighted me,' wrote one such witness, who met the poet on his last voyage to Greece; 'my own previous conceptions, supported by common rumour, having prepared me to expect to find in him a man of morose temper and gloomy misanthropy, instead of which, from his fecundity in anecdote, he was a most delightful associate.'[12]

Byron was at least as fecund and sure-footed narrating events as he was analysing characters. 'We have had a deluge here', he wrote to his half-sister from Italy in November 1822:

---

[12] James Hamilton Browne, 'Voyage from Leghorn to Cephalonia with Lord Byron', *Blackwood's Edinburgh Magazine*, 35 (Jan. 1834), 57.

—which has carried away half the country between this and Genoa—(about two miles or less distant) but being on a hill we were only nearly knocked down by the lightning and battered by columns of rain—and our lower floor afloat——with the comfortable view of the whole landscape under water—and people screaming out of their garret windows—*two bridges* swept down—and our next door neighbours—a Cobbler a Wigmaker—and a Gingerbread baker delivering up their whole stock to the elements—which marched away with a quantity of shoes—several perukes—and Gingerbread in all it's branches.—The whole came on so suddenly that there was no time to prepare—think only at the top of the hill—of the road being an impassable cascade—and a child being drowned a few yards from it's own door (as we heard say) in a place where Water is in general a rare commodity. (*LJ* x. 28–9)

Both these passages demonstrate that mobility of temperament John Jump describes: the further Byron goes in humiliating and ridiculing his lawyer, the more likely he is suddenly to forgive him; the more surrealistic his account of a flood, the more likely he is suddenly to remember the human tragedies it might involve.

Nothing seems to miss this alertness to sensation and its corollary expression. Byron was much more interested in art than he pretended to be, for example, but he was as opinionated on the topic as amateurs usually are. 'As for Rubens', he wrote after a visit to Antwerp:

he seems to me (who by the way know nothing of the matter) the most glaring—flaring—staring—harlotry imposter that ever passed a trick upon the senses of mankind—it is not nature—it is not art—with the exception of some linen (which hangs over the cross in one of his pictures) which to do it justice looked like a very handsome table cloth—I never saw such an assemblage of florid night-mares as his canvas contains—his portraits seem clothed in pulpit cushions. (*LJ* v. 73)

As an exercise in criticism, this is wilfully and transparently unfair; but once the reader has been exposed to a tablecloth flipped over a crucifixion, and to this cruel but brilliantly unstudied climactic characterization of the artist's adipose sitters, it is hard to think about Rubens with the reverence he no doubt deserves. The attitude is certainly reductive, but its instinctive antipathy to critical veneration is something that we cannot help but appreciate. Impertinent and intolerantly sincere lines like this about pulpit cushions, it should be noted, are a Byronic speciality: 'I am a length joined to Bologna', Byron wrote to a friend from that city of gourmands in the summer of 1819, 'where I am settled like a Sausage—and shall be broiled like one if this weather continues' (*LJ* vi. 146).

The women in Byron's life were memorialized repeatedly, from what one can only call an unapologetically and intransigently masculine point of view. A long-term Venetian mistress of 1816–18, Marianna Segati, was displayed to readers back in London with proprietorial exhibitionism:

My goddess is only the wife of a 'Merchant of Venice'—but then she is as pretty as an Antelope,—is but two & twenty years old—has the large black Oriental eyes—with the Italian countenance—and dark glossy hair of the curl & colour of Lady Jersey's—then she has the voice of a lute—and the song of a Seraph (though not quite so sacred) besides a long postscript of graces—virtues and accomplishments—enough to furnish out a new Chapter for Solomon's song. (*LJ* v. 133)

This is too full of admiration, *joie de vivre*, and blasphemy to be boorish or coarse, and it is sharpened by Byron's exultant comparison with the women of his native land, whose *'virtues and accomplishments'* (even in the person of a Regency toast like Lady Jersey) can only aspire to this draper's wife from the warm south. What, such a passage asks us, in its ironic fashion, is the difference between a 'grace' and a 'virtue', even if we were to take such terms at face value?

The last and greatest love of Byron's life, Teresa Guiccioli, comes in for the kind of affectionate drollery that is itself testimony to the regard in which he held her. Byron was an excellent horseman, and during his residence in Ravenna of 1820–1, he often rode in the *Pineta* forest outside the town. Teresa sometimes insisted on accompanying him. 'She is an Equestrian too,' he wrote to his half-sister Augusta in July 1819,

—but a bore in her rides—for she can't guide her horse—and he runs after mine—and tries to bite him—and then she begins screaming in a high hat and Sky-blue habit—making a most absurd figure—and embarrassing me and both our grooms—who have the devil's own work to keep her from tumbling—or having her clothes torn off by the trees and thickets of the Pine forest. (*LJ* vi. 186)

Such a picture would be mean-spirited if Byron did not at the same time find the human picture behind the individual one. His mistress screaming in fright is one thing; screaming in fright in the latest *fashion*—'a high hat and Sky-blue habit'—brings her before us as a human just like us, most discomfited when most prepared to appear at our best.

At the other end of the amative scale is the unfortunate Claire Clairmont, who initiated an affair with the poet just before he left London in 1816, and came all the way to Geneva to resume it later that year. 'I am not in love', Byron told Augusta,

nor have any love left for any,—but I could not exactly play the Stoic with a woman—who had scrambled eight hundred miles to unphilosophize me—besides I had been regaled of late with so many 'two courses and a *desert*' (Alas!) of aversion—that I was fain to take a little love (if pressed particularly) by way of novelty. (*LJ* v. 92)

Once more, this seems harsher than it is. Clairmont was something of tragic figure, certainly, but then so was Byron at the time ('I breathe lead' he told his sister earlier in the letter). Furthermore, the notion of someone 'scrambling' half way across Europe to un-philosophize a stoic (which clearly was *not* her primary intention, but rather to show off her lover to Percy Shelley and her stepsister Mary Godwin) when some physical affection was all the 'stoic' ever needed, once again brings their loveless affair back into an emotional realm we cannot help but recognize.

Perhaps it was this alchemical convergence of art and nature, distance and empathy, in Byron's letters that George Wilson Knight had in mind when he commented that 'there is no more Shakespearian writing in England than the prose of Byron's Letters and Journals'.[13] In fact, of all the writings of their era, Byron's letters best deserve the kind of estimation and appreciation that Romantic critics habitually accorded to what the dramatist Coleridge called 'our *myriad-minded* Shakespear', who 'darts himself forth, and passes into all the forms of human character and passion, the one Proteus of the fire and the flood'.[14] 'Nothing is made out by formal inference and analogy, by climax and antithesis', Hazlitt wrote of Shakespeare, as he might have written of Byron's letters had he known them: 'all comes, or seems to come, immediately from nature. Each object and circumstance exists in his mind, as it would have existed in reality: each several train of thought and feeling goes on of itself, without confusion or effort.'[15] Shakespeare 'unites in his soul', the German critic August Wilhelm Schlegel announced, 'the utmost elevation and the utmost depth; and the most opposite and even apparently irreconcilable properties subsist in him peaceably together.'[16] These qualities of sympathy, transparency, and integrity Byron's letters share with Shakespeare, and when Ruskin said that Byron wrote 'as easily as a hawk flies and as clearly as a lake reflects' that is itself to judge him by a Shakespearian standard.[17]

By their nature, letters generally produce a heterogeneous image of their authors, and Byron responded to a collection of Robert Burns's correspondence in terms strikingly similar to those we might employ in considering his own. 'What an antithetical mind!—tenderness, roughness—delicacy, coarseness—sentiment, sensuality—soaring and groveling, dirt and deity—all mixed up in that one compound of inspired clay!' (*LJ* iii. 239). The raciness and vigour that

---

[13] George Wilson Knight, *Byron's Dramatic Prose* (Nottingham: University of Nottingham, 1954), 15. Dryden, Addison, Swift, Johnson, Gibbon, and Burke 'have all gone into the melting pot, like one of Medea's victims', Knight said of Byron's letters, 'and something comes out, young, valiant, resilient…' (*Byron's Dramatic Prose*, 12).

[14] Samuel Taylor Coleridge, *Biographia Literaria*, ed. James Engell and W. Jackson Bate, 2 vols. (Princeton: Princeton University Press, 1983), ii. 19, 27.

[15] Hazlitt, *Complete Works*, v. 50.

[16] August Wilhelm Schlegel, *Lectures on Dramatic Art and Literature*, trans. John Black (1816; London: George Bell, 1909), 368.

[17] Ruskin, *Works*, xxxv. 145.

readers have continually found in Byron's letters—as well as their 'intolerant sincerity'—surely have their origin in this Shakespearian, 'protean' zest for opposite and irreconcilable qualities—ironically enough, given that Byron frequently scorned Shakespeare's achievement even while he was saturated by it. ('That he threw over whatever he did some flashes of genius, nobody can deny', he wrote: 'but this was all'; *LJ* iv. 85.) 'This journal is a relief,' he noted in December 1813:

When I am tired…out comes this, and down goes every thing. But I can't read it over;—and God knows what contradictions it may contain. If I am sincere with myself (but I fear one lies more to one's self than to any one else), every page should confute, refute, and utterly abjure its predecessor. (*LJ* iii. 233)

This is a paradoxical statement from a great Romantic, combining as it does a devout belief in the ultimate incommensurability of human experiences with a rationalist suspicion of intellectual self-sufficiency. 'I have no consistency,' he noted of himself elsewhere, 'except in politics; and *that* probably arises from my indifference on the subject altogether' (*LJ* iii. 242). Consistency *is* indifference for Byron, in prose as in verse, just as in Shakespeare's drama the figures that attracted the playwright's deepest attention, from Falstaff to Cleopatra, and Coriolanus to Malvolio, are ones we can never regard other than ambivalently.

Byron's journals, five in number (in London from November to April 1813; in the Alps in September 1816; at Ravenna during January and February 1821; the 'Detached Thoughts' at Ravenna and Pisa in October and November 1821; and the short journal kept at Cephalonia in September and October 1823), are a comparatively small but vital element in this protean display: whales' backs in a sea of prose, as Keats said of Hazlitt's sentences. Like all correspondents, Byron oriented himself to whoever he was addressing: his mother, wife, half-sister, or last mistress; his publisher, the unfortunate 'Spooney' Hanson, or his intimate friends. The journals, however, are written fundamentally for himself, and so give us a peculiarly intimate sense of revelation. 'A dose of salts has the effect of a temporary inebriation, like light champagne, upon me,' he wrote in the wintry January of 1821 in Ravenna:

But wine and spirits make me sullen and savage to ferocity—silent, however, and retiring, and not quarrelsome, if not spoken to. Swimming also raises my spirits,—but in general they are low, and get daily lower. That is *hopeless*: for I do not think I am so much *ennuyé* [bored] as I was at nineteen. The proof is, that then I must game, or drink, or be in motion of some kind, or I was miserable. At present, I can mope in quietness; and like being alone better than any company—except the lady's whom I serve. But I feel a something, which makes me think that, if I ever reach near to old age, like Swift, 'I shall die at top' first. Only I do not dread idiotism or madness so much as he did. On the contrary, I think some quieter stages of both must be preferable to much of what men think the possession of their senses. (*LJ* viii. 16)

This was written by a person with a preternatural capacity to access not only himself and the compartments of his own mentality but, even as he does so, humanity at large, its need for stimulation, and the pride it takes in its intellectual pre-eminence. A Montaigne-like leisure in self-analysis is another facet of Byron's antithetical mind.

Byron's Alpine journal was intended for Augusta, in the aftermath of his scandalous separation from Lady Byron—in which she herself had played a role as sister and lover combined. But its addressee also gets forgotten at times, as Byron gives vent to his grief and depression:

I am a lover of Nature—and an Admirer of Beauty—I can bear fatigue—& welcome privation—and have seen some of the noblest views in the world.—But in all this—the recollections of bitterness—& more especially of recent & more home desolation—which must accompany me through life—have preyed upon me here—and neither the music of the Shepherd—the crashing of the Avalanche—nor the torrent—the mountain—the Glacier—the Forest—nor the Cloud—have for one moment—lightened the weight upon my heart—nor enabled me to lose my own wretched identity in the majesty & the power and the Glory—around—above—& beneath me. (*LJ* v. 104–5)

Here is a case of Byron's prose as commentary upon or stablemate of his poetry, as Prothero suggested, for clearly this was the mood that inspired *Manfred*, his guilt-ridden but vindicatory drama concerning his relations with Augusta. 'I have kept this record of what I have seen & felt,' he closed to her: 'Love me as you are beloved by me.'

Twice, in Ravenna and Cephalonia, Byron kept journals relating to liberal uprisings, whether against the Austrian or Ottoman empires. Both bring out another level of that moral ambivalence that I have related to Shakespeare in this discussion. Rhetoric has a vital place in politics, and Byron felt this instinctively. The Ravenna journal is a peculiarly downbeat record, though none the less compelling for that. ('Fine day—a few mares' tails portending change, but the sky clear, upon the whole. Rode—fired pistols—good shooting. Coming back, met an old man. Charity—purchased a shilling's worth of salvation'; *LJ* viii. 35.) It memorializes winter slush, lonely rides, solitary dinners, and moody retro-spectives, but it is punctuated by moments of revolutionary excitement and intellectual agitation:

Dined—news come—the *Powers* mean to war with the peoples [that is, the Austrians with the Italians]. The intelligence seems positive—let it be so—they will be beaten in the end. The king-times are fast finishing. There will be blood shed like water, and tears like mist; but the peoples will conquer in the end. I shall not live to see it, but I foresee it. (*LJ* viii. 26)

The nearer Byron got to a real war the more his anticipatory relish became tempered by a humanity that never abandoned him for long. The Greeks were the inheritors of a deeply troubled history, and no one should expect them to constitute a nation of saints:

Whoever goes into Greece at present should do it as Mrs Fry went into Newgate—not in the expectation of meeting with any especial indication of existing probity—but in the hope that time and better treatment will reclaim the present burglariousness and larcenous tendencies which have followed from this General Gaol delivery.—When the limbs of the Greeks are a little less stiff from the shackles of four centuries—they will not march so much 'as if they had gyves on their legs'.——At present the Chains are broken indeed—but the links are still clanking—and the Saturnalia is still too recent to have converted the Slave into a sober Citizen. (*LJ* xi. 32–3)

Among Byron's journals there is a famous empty chair: the memoirs he wrote in Venice in 1819 (and later supplemented), relating to his marriage, which were destroyed in his publisher's fireplace some months after his death in Greece in April 1824. They are a woeful loss, but something in the way Byron described them to the man who would later burn them suggests that they may not have possessed the unpremeditated, uninhibited quality that John Jump valued in the prose that we have. 'You will find many opinions—and some fun', Byron wrote to John Murray, 'with a detailed account of my marriage and it's consequences— as true as a party concerned can make such accounts—for I suppose we are all prejudiced' (*LJ* vi. 236). This does sound like a more rehearsed, studied, or considered kind of writing, concerned with cause and effect, balance, and what Hazlitt called 'formal inference'. At their best, the journals we possess give us a sense of participatory eavesdropping that is rare indeed.

Whether Byron's letters and journals are 'the supreme incarnation of the natural man', as Arthur Symons proposed, is not for me to say; but they are the works of an everyman. Byron was no saint, but then neither did he pose as an apostate, a sinner, or an infidel. He was a reckless and complex individual, but he also exercised a normal degree of temporal self-interest. Far from being the communications of a philosopher, a prophet, a critic, a soldier, or a politician—even a poet: 'what are *they* worth? what have they done' (*LJ* viii. 41)—his letters and journals speak to us all. So it is that Byron's prose is something more than a commentary on his poetry or a self-portrait, and so it is that the value it has for us is deeper than a merely literary one in terms of style and expression— inimitable as those are in his case. Nor does it lie in the statement of ideas or points of view, which in his case are often of a strictly stoical nature. 'All history and experience—and the rest—teaches us that the good and evil are pretty equally balanced in this existence', he wrote: 'and that what is most to be desired is an easy passage out of it.——What can it give us but *years*?' (*LJ* ix. 45). Again: 'What a strange thing is the propagation of life!—A bubble of Seed which may be spilt in a whore's lap — or in the Orgasm of a voluptuous dream—might (for aught we know) have formed a Caesar or a Buonaparte' (*LJ* ix. 47). Again: 'When one subtracts from life infancy (which is vegetation),—sleep, eating, and swilling—buttoning and unbuttoning—how much remains of downright existence? The summer of a dormouse' (*LJ* iii. 235). Such attitudes, being ultimately passive, are ultimately those of a Kent, a Horatio, or an Enobarbus; but Byron's informal prose taken as a whole is Shakespearian in a deeper sense than that, and his response to life more worthy of a Lear, a Hamlet, or an Antony, which is why the claim it makes upon us is fundamentally moral (in the broadest sense of the term) rather than aesthetic—insofar as these factors can be divided from each other. 'No portrait of Byron can equal that which he himself gives in his letters and journals,' John Jump has argued:

Nor is this their only source of interest. They provide glimpses of life in England of his time and in the foreign countries through which he passed; they record his views on literature and politics and religion. But, in so far as they compose a bold and vivid self-portrait, they claim something of the status of a work of art. For they do not merely inform us; they coerce our imaginations as we read, until we seem almost to be in the presence of a living and speaking man.[18]

'The letters are not just conversational and self-revealing,' David Perkins suggests, in terms that complement Jump's discussion peculiarly well:

In the best of them Byron was engaged in vivifying his life by writing it down, reliving his experience under the conditions of art and style—the special art and style he created for his letters. This meant that experience took on an incomparable clearness—character, energy, and idea caught in a bright foreground, the shadowy depths eliminated—accompanied by unpredictable shifts of feeling and ripples of irony.[19]

To vivify life by recording it, and to relive experience under the conditions of art and style, and by such means 'coerce' the imagination of the reader: that, surely, is the fundamental aim of literature. 'How I do delight in observing life as it really is!', Byron wrote, '—and myself, after all, the worst of any' (*LJ* iii. 240). Many other English writers—Keats, the Carlyles (Thomas and Jane), Dickens, Henry James, Robert Louis Stevenson, D. H. Lawrence, and Virginia Woolf, in particular—have left remarkable collections of letters, but the 'special art and style' Byron brought to a life itself far more extensive and various than any lived

---

[18] John Jump, *Byron* (London: Routledge and Kegan Paul, 1972), 48.
[19] David Perkins (ed.), *English Romantic Writers*, 2nd edn. (Fort Worth: Harcourt Brace, 1995), 985.

by these other poets and novelists puts his contribution in a special place. They are the most entertaining and engrossing private documents in the language.

The selection that follows seeks to explore each of Rowland Prothero's observations. It will, hopefully, capture some of the high literary value of Byron's prose, and also produce something like a self-portrait (if not a true portrait, could such a thing ever exist) of this singularly magnetic individual. I have selected the most compelling specimens I could find from the cornucopia Leslie Marchand supplied us with, but always with the aim, also, of telling the story of Byron's life—and each chapter is prefaced with a brief biographical summary to allow the reader to follow that sequence. Furthermore, since Byron's letters on his poetry are some of his most scintillating ('As to "Don Juan"', he wrote to a friend, 'confess—confess—you dog—and be candid—that it is the sublime of *that there* sort of writing—it may be bawdy—but is it not good English?—it may be profligate—but is it not *life*, is it not *the thing?*'; *LJ* vi. 232), what is reprinted here will constitute a commentary on his artistic output, though hardly an objective one. The letters also, of course—as all letters must—shed light on the history and society of their time, from however personal a perspective. In the end, I trust the reader will agree, the elements must overlap: life and art, whether poetic or prosaic, once formed an indivisible experience for the author set at their intersection, and so they always will when we read the record of his creativity—read it, and wonder at it, too.

NOTES ON THE TEXT AND SHORT TITLES

This selection is drawn in its entirety from Marchand's edition of Byron's letters and journals, and basically follows its editorial principles in their entirety, too. Nine principles are stated in full in the Editorial Note added to each volume in the edition, and I summarize them here, using Marchand's own words, and adding a few additional clarifications in square brackets:

1. The place and date of writing is invariably placed at the top right in one line if possible to save space and to follow Byron's general practice.
2. Superior letters such S^r or 30th have been lowered to Sr and 30th. The & has been retained, but $\&^c$ has been printed &c.
3. Byron's spelling has been retained, and [sic] has been avoided except in a few instances when an inadvertent misspelling might change the meaning or be ambiguous.
4. Although Byron was inconsistent and eccentric in his capitalization, Marchand felt it better to have him have his way, to preserve the flavour of his personality and his times. If clarity has seemed to demand a modification, Marchand used square brackets to indicate any departure from the manuscript.
5. Obvious slips of the pen crossed out by the writer have been silently omitted. But crossed out words of any significance to the meaning or emphasis are enclosed in angled brackets <>.
6. Letters undated, or dated with the day of the week only, have been dated, when possible, in square brackets. If the date is conjectural, it is given with a question mark in brackets. Undated letters have been placed within the chronological sequence when from internal or external evidence there are reasonable grounds for a conjectural date. Where a more precise date cannot be established from the context, these letters are placed at the beginning of the month or year in which they seem most likely to have been written.
7. In Marchand's edition the salutation was given on the same line as the text, separated from it by a dash. In order to open up the documents from a reading perspective, I have resorted to the standard letter layout, and entered

a line break after the salutation. The complimentary closing, often on several lines in the manuscript, is given in one line if possible. The PS, wherever it may be written in the manuscript, follows the signature.

8. Byron's punctuation follows no rules of his own or others' making. [His abuse of the apostrophe in expressions like 'wont' and 'it's' will infuriate purists.] He uses dashes and commas freely, but for no apparent reason, other than possibly for natural pause between phrases, or sometimes for emphasis. He is guilty of the 'comma splice', and one can seldom be sure where he intended to end a sentence, or whether he recognized the sentence as a unit of expression. He did at certain intervals place a period and a dash [or two dashes], beginning again with a capital letter. These larger divisions sometimes, though not always, represented what in other writers, particularly in writers of today, correspond to paragraphs. He sometimes used semicolons, but often where we would use commas. Byron himself recognized his lack of knowledge of the logic or rules of punctuation. It is not without reason then that most editors have imposed sentences and paragraphs on him in line with their interpretation of his intended meaning. It was Marchand's feeling, however, that this detracts from the impression of Byronic spontaneity and the onrush of ideas in his letters, without a compensating gain in clarity. In fact, it may arbitrarily impose a meaning or an emphasis not intended by the writer. Marchand felt that there was less danger of distortion if the reader may see exactly how he punctuated and then determine whether a phrase between commas or dashes belongs to one sentence or another. Byron's punctuation seldom if ever makes the reading difficult or the meaning unclear. In rare instances Marchand inserted a comma, or a semicolon, but enclosed it in square brackets. [Note that Marchand did supply some paragraphing in Byron's letters beginning with Volume Seven of his edition, for ease of proof correction and reading: letters of 1820 and afterwards.]

9. Words missing but obvious from the context, such as those lacunae caused by holes in the manuscript, are supplied within square brackets. If they are wholly conjectural, they are followed by a question mark. The same is true of doubtful readings in the manuscript.

The letters to Thomas Moore, first published in his *Letters and Journals of Lord Byron* (1830), were printed with many omissions and the manuscripts have since disappeared. [Marchand noted—but his comment is also true of some letters to other recipients, published by Moore, for which we have no other source.] Moore generally indicated omissions by asterisks * * *, here reproduced as in his text.

Each volume of Marchand's edition listed letters and sources at the end, and included valuable biographical sketches of important figures in the ongoing story, as well as an index. Volume Twelve was first and foremost an index to the edition as a whole.

A modest number of errors did creep into the original edition: Marchand issued corrections in Volume Eleven (incorporated here), which also included some letters of 1809–19 discovered among Scrope Berdmore Davies's papers in 1976, and some additional letters which came to light during the publishing process. The supplementary volume *What Comes Uppermost* (1994) contains new letters discovered to that date.

To all intents and purposes I have left Marchand's text entirely untouched, and only selected from it. Changes—intentional ones, that is; any errors in transcription are another matter, and I hope are not too common—are as follows:

1. I have used single quotation marks where Marchand used double ones.

2. I have glossed short expressions in foreign languages in square brackets, unless I thought an English speaker would recognize them. (Thus I have glossed 'coute qui coute', 'on dit', and 'mirabile dictu', but not 'dama' or 'amante'.) I hope readers will forgive me if I have either insulted their intelligence or left them high and dry. I have also used [*sic*] a little more than Marchand did to indicate occasions on which Byron simply misspelled a word—rather than spelled it in a way we no longer do.

3. Where abbreviated names—'H', 'M', 'DK', or 'Ly B', for example—are clear in context, I have not followed Marchand's custom of always spelling them out; wherever there is any doubt, I have followed his practice.

4. I have employed the ellipse in square brackets […] on as few occasions as possible, in fact only twenty-one times in reproducing 304 letters: where a vital letter drifts off into highly detailed and less interesting matters, or where an extensive PS slows the reading experience. Generally, the principle has been to provide letters in their entirety. Byron hardly used the ellipse at all; the two occasions below are his own, and are not within square brackets.

5. Marchand brought Byron's five journals together, and I have followed suit where his 'Alpine' journal of September 1816, his 'Ravenna' journal of January–February 1821, and his 'My Dictionary' and 'Detached Thoughts' journals of May 1821 and October 1821–May 1822 are concerned. But the November 1813–April 1814 journal and the 'Cephalonia' journal have been broken up amidst and around his letters, with the aim of reflecting their historical presence alongside his correspondence and events at large. The

Alpine journal is kept intact (and reprinted in its entirety) because it was designed as an extended letter to his half-sister. Extracts from the Ravenna journal have been kept together, and so have 'My Dictionary' and 'Detached Thoughts': the Ravenna journal because it occupies a fairly brief period of time, the second two because they are themselves generally undated. The Cephalonia journal is in only two parts anyway (and is reprinted in its entirety); so the 1813–14 journal (much the longest of the five) is the one most significantly re-presented in this way. The reader will decide whether the experiment was worth making.

6. The majority of Byron's letters in Italian were to Teresa Guiccioli, and Marchand reprinted them from Iris Origo's invaluable study *The Last Attachment: The Story of Byron and Teresa Guiccioli*. Other Italian texts were variously translated by Nancy Dersofi, Ricki B. Herzfeld, and Antony Peattie. Sometimes the translators 'tidied up' Byron's punctuation and paragraphing, and I have silently sought to return these letters to their informal state by comparing the translation to the Italian original.

7. All footnotes are my own, but I have of course depended on Marchand a great deal, and sometimes quoted him directly when his comment could not be improved upon. Where a personal identity, historical fact, or literary allusion is unknown to me I have passed it over, rather than say 'unidentified' in each case. The edition of Shakespeare cited is the *Complete Works*, ed. Stanley Wells and Gary Taylor, 2nd edn. (Oxford: Oxford University Press, 2005).

The following short titles are employed:

CMP	Byron, *Complete Miscellaneous Prose*, ed. Andrew Nicholson (Oxford: Oxford University Press, 1991)
CPW	Byron, *Complete Poetical Works*, ed. Jerome J. McGann, 7 vols. (Oxford: Oxford University Press, 1980–93)
Hobhouse Letters	Peter W. Graham (ed.), *Byron's Bulldog: The Letters of John Cam Hobhouse to Lord Byron* (Columbus: Ohio State University Press, 1984)
Life	Leslie A. Marchand, *Byron: A Biography*, 3 vols. (London: John Murray, 1957)
LJ	*Byron's Letters and Journals*, ed. Leslie A. Marchand, 12 vols. (London: John Murray, 1973–82)
Murray Letters	Andrew Nicholson (ed.), *The Letters of John Murray to Lord Byron* (Liverpool: Liverpool University Press, 2007)

A BIOGRAPHICAL BIBLIOGRAPHY

(Place of publication is London unless otherwise noted.)

Leslie Marchand, *Byron: A Biography* (John Murray, 1957) remains the standard, because of its balance and wealth of detail. There is a redaction, *Byron: A Portrait* (John Murray, 1971), which includes later biographical discoveries. Three worthy recent alternatives are Phyllis Grosskurth, *Byron: The Flawed Angel* (Hodder and Stoughton, 1997), Benita Eisler, *Byron: Child of Passion, Fool of Fame* (Hamish Hamilton, 1999), and Fiona MacCarthy, *Byron: Life and Legend* (Faber and Faber, 2002)—though as their titles might suggest, they need to be treated with a degree of caution. Caroline Franklin, *Byron: A Literary Life* (Macmillan, 2000), concentrates on his writing life, and Richard Lansdown, *The Cambridge Introduction to Byron* (Cambridge: Cambridge University Press, 2012), briefly discusses and contextualizes his major works. Norman Page, *A Byron Chronology* (Macmillan, 1988), usefully boils the story down.

Louis Crompton, *Byron and Greek Love* (Faber and Faber, 1985), is a study of his homosexuality, and Michael Foot, *The Politics of Paradise* (Collins, 1988), is a political portrait. William St. Clair, *The Reading Nation in the Romantic Period* (Cambridge: Cambridge University Press, 2004), sheds powerful light on Byron as a publishing phenomenon.

Some older studies retain a great deal of value. See William A. Borst, *Byron's First Pilgrimage* (New Haven: Yale University Press, 1948); C. L. Cline, *Byron, Shelley and their Pisan Circle* (John Murray, 1952); William H. Marshall, *Byron, Shelley, Hunt, and The Liberal* (Philadelphia: University of Pennsylvania Press, 1960); Doris Langley Moore's highly recommended *The Late Lord Byron: Posthumous Dramas* (John Murray, 1961) and *Lord Byron: Accounts Rendered* (John Murray, 1974), which deal engrossingly with his aftermath and his finances, respectively; and Harold Nicholson, *Byron: The Last Journey, April 1823–April 1824* (Constable, 1924), an evocative account of Byron's final trip to Greece.

Figures close to the poet are covered in Margot Strickland, *The Byron Women* (Peter Owen, 1974); Geoffrey Bond, *Lord Byron's Best Friends: From Bulldogs to Boatswain and Beyond* (Nick McCann, 2013); John Beckett, *Byron and Newstead:*

The Aristocrat and the Abbey (Newark: University of Delaware Press, 2001); Paul Elledge, *Lord Byron at Harrow School: Speaking Out, Talking Back, Acting Up, Bowing Out* (Baltimore: Johns Hopkins University Press, 2000); Michael and Melissa Bakewell, *Augusta Leigh, Byron's Half-Sister: A Biography* (Chatto and Windus, 2000); Michael Joyce, *My Friend H.: John Cam Hobhouse* (John Murray, 1948), and Hobhouse's own *Recollections of a Long Life* (John Murray, 1909–11); T. A. J. Burnett, *The Rise and Fall of a Regency Dandy: The Life and Times of Scrope Berdmore Davies* (John Murray, 1981); Terence de Vere White, *Tom Moore: The Irish Poet* (Hamish Hamilton, 1977); Jeffery W. Vail, *The Literary Relationship of Lord Byron and Thomas Moore* (Baltimore: Johns Hopkins University Press, 2001); Paul Douglass, *Lady Caroline Lamb: A Biography* (Macmillan, 2004), and *The Whole Disgraceful Truth: Selected Letters of Lady Caroline Lamb* (Palgrave Macmillan, 2006); Ethel Colburne Mayne, *The Life of Lady Byron* (Constable, 1929); Malcolm Elwin, *Lord Byron's Wife* (Macdonald, 1962), *The Noels and the Milbankes* (Macdonald, 1967), and *Lord Byron's Family: Annabella, Ada and Augusta* (John Murray, 1975); Robert Gittings and Jo Manton, *Claire Clairmont and the Shelleys* (Oxford: Oxford University Press, 1995); Charles E. Robinson, *Shelley and Byron: The Snake and the Eagle Wreathed in Flight* (Baltimore: Johns Hopkins University Press, 1976); Iris Origo, *The Last Attachment: The Story of Byron and Teresa Guiccioli* (John Murray and Jonathan Cape, 1949), and *Allegra* (Hogarth Press, 1935), a life of Byron's natural daughter; Teresa Guiccioli, *Lord Byron's Life in Italy*, trans. Michael Rees (Newark: University of Delaware Press, 2005); and William St. Clair, *Trelawny: The Incurable Romancer* (John Murray, 1977).

The testimony of those who knew Byron has a special value, even if their accounts need to be carefully evaluated. His conversations are recorded in three books edited by Ernest J. Lovell, Jr.: *His Very Self and Voice: Collected Conversations of Lord Byron* (New York: Macmillan 1954), *Medwin's Conversations of Lord Byron* (Princeton: Princeton University Press, 1966), and *Lady Blessington's Conversations of Lord Byron* (Princeton: Princeton University Press, 1969). But see also George Bancroft, 'A Day with Lord Byron', *History of the Battle of Lake Erie and Miscellaneous Papers* (1891); James Hamilton Browne, 'Voyage from Leghorn to Cephalonia with Lord Byron', *Blackwood's Edinburgh Magazine*, 35 (Jan. 1834), 56–67; John William Dudley, *Letters to 'Ivy' from the First Earl of Dudley* (1905); John Galt, *Letters from the Levant* (1813) and *The Life of Lord Byron* (1830); Pryse Lockhart Gordon, *Personal Memoirs*, 2 vols. (1830); Lord Holland, *Further Memoirs of the Whig Party* (1905); Leigh Hunt, *Lord Byron and Some of his Contemporaries*, 2 vols. (1828); James Kennedy, *Conversations on Religion with Lord Byron* (1830); Thomas Moore, *The Life, Letters and Journals of Lord Byron*, 2 vols. (1830); Isaac Nathan, *Fugitive Pieces and Reminiscences of Lord Byron* (1829); William Parry, *The Last Days of Lord Byron* (1825); John William Polidori, *The Diary of John William Polidori* (1911); Stendhal, *Rome,*

Naples and Florence (1854); and Edward John Trelawny, *Records of Shelley, Byron and the Author* (1878).

Letters to Byron can be found in Rowland E. Prothero (ed.), *The Works of Lord Byron: Letters and Journals*, 6 vols. (John Murray, 1898–1901); George Paston and Peter Quennell (eds.), *'To Lord Byron': Feminine Profiles Based on Unpublished Letters* (John Murray, 1939); Peter W. Graham (ed.), *Byron's Bulldog: The Letters of John Cam Hobhouse to Lord Byron* (Columbus: Ohio State University Press, 1984); Marion Kingston Stocking (ed.), *The Clairmont Correspondence*, 2 vols. (Baltimore: Johns Hopkins University Press, 1997); and Andrew Nicholson (ed.), *The Letters of John Murray to Lord Byron* (Liverpool: Liverpool University Press, 2007).

THE LETTERS &
JOURNALS

1

CHILDHOOD, BOYHOOD, YOUTH

January 1788–June 1809

On 9 June 1779 a 23-year-old impecunious army captain, out of the line of succession of an ancient Nottinghamshire barony and disinherited by his father, married his lover, Amelia Osborne, Baroness Conyers, lately divorced from the Marquis of Carmarthen, and wealthy in her own right. Four and a half years later, on 27 January 1784, Amelia Byron was dead, and her husband lost access to her income. The sole surviving issue of the marriage, Augusta Maria, whose mother had died when she was 1 year old, was thereafter raised by relations until she married in 1807.

At a loose end, the charming and unscrupulous 'Mad Jack' Byron found himself another heiress, the 20-year-old Catherine Gordon, descended from the Scottish monarchy, daughter of the twelfth laird of Gight, and inheritor of an estate worth £30,000—a colossal sum in today's money. Three years after their marriage in 12 May 1785 he had again worked his way through most of his wife's income, and she was pregnant in London with their only child. George Gordon Byron was born on 22 January 1788, in a rented room just north of London's Oxford Street, with a single club foot (his right) and no father in attendance. Mad Jack—who on the basis of his actions one would have to say was 'mad' more in the sense of being idiotically self-destructive than impulsive or impetuous—was at risk of arrest for debt if he showed himself in the capital, and soon after his son's birth he decamped to France, where he died in Valenciennes aged 35 in August 1791, in the company of his sister—with whom he had had a sexual affair. That sister's son would marry Augusta Byron in 1807.

Mrs Byron had managed to retain an income of £150 per year from this disaster—not enough to keep her and her son in genteel circles in England. In the summer of 1789, while the French Revolution broke out across the Channel, she returned north of the border, to Aberdeen, where she took lodgings, and where Byron lived for the next nine years. In 1794 'Wee Geordie' entered the town's Grammar School, and in provincial obscurity he might have remained, had not the 22-year-old grandson of the fifth Baron Byron of Rochdale—'the Wicked Lord' (1722–98)—died in an early engagement of the French Revolutionary War, during a British invasion of Corsica in that same year. (Captain Horatio Nelson lost his eye in the same campaign.) The old lord, shut up in solitude and engrossed in feeding the crickets he had tamed and taught to crawl over him,' Leslie Marchand writes, 'had no interest in "the little boy in Aberdeen"' (Life, 10).

Four years later the Wicked Lord himself died, and the 10-year-old Aberdonian schoolboy succeeded to the title and a substantial estate in Nottinghamshire, with some coalfields near Rochdale thrown in (though the land they lay beneath had been let, illegally, before their value was known). Mother and son tried to occupy the ruinous Newstead Abbey—which Henry VIII had given the Byron family during the Dissolution of the Monasteries for services rendered, and which the 'Wicked Lord' had treated with scant regard for years—before renting rooms in Nottingham. Belated attempts were initiated to heal Byron's club foot; more disturbingly, his Scots Calvinist nurse, May Gray, was given the sack for sexually interfering with the 10-year-old boy. At the ripe old age of 8, back in Aberdeen, he had fallen in love with a distant cousin, also 8, Mary Duff. 'How very odd that I should have been so utterly, devotedly fond of that girl,' he wrote in later life (Life, 41), 'at an age when I could neither feel passion, nor know the meaning of the word.'

The future baron needed to gain an English education (not to mention an English accent), and after some local tuition Byron was taken to London by the family lawyer, John Hanson, in July 1799, and entered at Dr Glennie's School in Dulwich in September of that year. In April 1801 he entered Harrow School—alongside Eton College the pre-eminently aristocratic private school of England. Throughout this period Byron holidayed either with the Hansons (who became a surrogate family) or with his mother, depending on the state of their relations. Catherine Byron had been widowed at 26—not that one would know it from her son's references to her. She was superstitious, shrewd, tactless, literal-minded, forthright, proud, obstreperous, and stout; but she also used money to get around her son as she had her husband. Byron's early years at Harrow were stormily unhappy, but his last year or two were marked by a series of intense friendships, often with boys younger than himself. Perhaps he sought vicariously to give the paternal affection he himself had never received—in any event, this emotional pattern recurred frequently in his life. At around this time he also began to correspond with his half-sister Augusta, Amelia's daughter (1783–1851). 'I will cut myself a path through the world,' the 16-year-old told his mother (LJ i. 49), 'or perish in the attempt.'

In late October 1805 Byron took the next step in the nobleman's preparation: he entered the profoundly aristocratic but also profoundly Whiggish Trinity College, at Cambridge University, to read for a Bachelor of Arts. His attendance was as lackadaisical as the standard of tuition in those days—'Nobody here seems to look into an author ancient or modern if they can avoid it' (LJ i. 80)—but though Byron attended only three of the nine terms the university required, aristocratic privilege allowed him to graduate with a Master of Arts in July 1808. An allowance of £500 a year was granted to him from his future estate, but he paid no attention whatever to economy, running up bills freely with furnishers and decorators, booksellers, horse-dealers, tailors, jewellers, and vintners in Cambridge and in London—never mind the high life (and low life) he enjoyed in the capital. His mother and lawyer could only look on; the entail of the estate had broken with the fifth Lord's heir's death, and London moneylenders—'Jews', as Byron, and everybody else, habitually referred to them—were happy to assist a young man with unencumbered prospects. By the end of 1808 the 20-year-old's debts amounted to £12,000. During this period Byron began a lifelong campaign to control his weight, and also publicized his agnosticism.

Another surrogate family, the middle-class Pigots, had taken Byron to its bosom in Southwell, near Nottingham, in 1805, and the young members of it had encouraged the bashful teenaged baron in his first poetic attempts. The result, Fugitive Pieces, was privately printed at Newark in November 1806. The volume's sexual candour caused some affront at Southwell, and Byron bowdlerized the book for reissue as Hours of Idleness the following year. Pleased with himself—but also perhaps a little embarrassed at the emotionally demonstrative nature of his first collection—he presumptuously turned to drafting a satire *after the 18th-century style, called 'British Bards'. In February 1808, long after its release, a withering notice of Hours of Idleness appeared in the great Edinburgh Review, making hay of Byron's callow and gauche self-representation in that book. Byron was profoundly shocked—not least because the Edinburgh was as Whiggish as he was—but yet another iteration of his first collection, Poems Original and Translated, appeared the following month, and Byron combatively reconfigured his satire as English Bards and Scotch Reviewers, eventually published in March 1809. In an important sense, that bad review was the making of him.*

By the spring of 1809 Byron had achieved his majority, fathered a son with a maid at Newstead, and taken his seat in the House of Lords—an affair of only passing interest, according to him, though politics would have been a natural choice of career. 'I am...a solitary animal,' he told a friend, 'miserable enough, & so perfectly a Citizen of the World, that whether I pass my days in Great Britain, or Kamchatka, is to me, a matter of perfect Indifference' (LJ i. 112). His financial position was dreadful; his Rochdale estates could not be sold; the idea of selling Newstead shamed him; and he made reference to other, apparently more scandalous, concerns. After entertaining various plans for Eastern travel during 1808 he borrowed one more pile of money and set off for a tour of the Mediterranean with his Cambridge friend John Cam Hobhouse.

[To Charlotte Augusta Parker[1]]

Newstead Abbey Novr. 8th. 1798

Dear Madam,

My Mamma being unable to write herself desires I will let you know that the potatoes are now ready and you are welcome to them whenever you please—

She begs you will ask Mrs. Parkyns[2] if she would wish the poney to go round by Nottingham or go home the nearest way as it is now quite well but too small to carry me—

I have sent a young Rabbit which I beg Miss Frances will accept off [*sic*] and which I promised to send before—My Mamma desires her best compliments to you all in which I join—I am

Dear Aunt Yours sincerely
Byron

---

[1] 'Mad Jack' Byron's youngest sister (1764–1824). As a 12-year-old, Byron fell in love with her daughter Margaret, who died in 1802; this unrequited affair prompted his first attempt at writing verse.
[2] Byron stayed with his great-aunt's sister Ann Parkyns in Nottingham in 1799, and made an impression on the daughters of the house, including the Miss Frances mentioned below.

—⊗⊗⊗⊗⊚—

I hope you will excuse all blunders as it is the first letter I ever wrote

[To Mrs Catherine Gordon Byron]

Nottingham 13th. March, 1799

Dear Mamma,

I am very glad to hear you are well, I am so myself thank God, upon my word I did not expect so long a Letter from you however I will answer it as well as I can. Mrs. Parkyns & the rest are well and are much obliged to you for the present. Mr. Rogers could attend me every night at a separate hour from the Miss Parkyns's,[3] & I am astonished you do not acquiesce in this scheme which would keep me in mind of what I have almost entirely forgot, I recommend this to you because if some plan of this kind is not adopted I shall be called or rather branded with the name of a dunce which you know I could never bear. I beg you will consider this plan seriously & I will lend it all the assistance in my power. I Shall be very glad to see the letter you talk of & I have time just to say I hope every body is well at Newstead

& remain your affectionate son,
Byron

—⊗⊗⊗⊗⊚—

P. S.—Pray let me know when you are to send in the horses to go to Newstead. May Desires her duty[4] & I also expect an answer By the Miller.

---

[3] Byron was being given tuition in classical languages by a Mr Dummer Rogers, and resented being taught alongside the Parkyns girls. At this stage Mrs Byron was still camping at Newstead.

[4] May Gray, the servant who sexually interfered with Byron, and who is sent 'packing as far as possible' in the next letter. Despite the story of her activities coming out, Mrs Byron did not in fact dismiss her until the end of the year.

[To John Hanson]

[Dulwich, Nov.? 1799]

Sir

I am not a little disappointed at your stay, for this last week I expected you every hour, but however I beg it as a favour that you will come up soon from Newstead as the Holidays commence in three weeks time. I congratulate you on Capt. Hanson's being appointed commander of the Brazen sloop of war, and I congratulate myself on Lord Portsmouth's marriage hoping his lady when he and I meet next will keep him in a little better order.[5] The manner I knew that Capt. Hanson was appointed Commander of the ship before mentioned was this[.] I saw it in the public paper. And now since you are going to Newstead I beg if you meet Gray send her a packing as fast as possible, and give my compliments to Mrs. Hanson and to all my comrades of the Battalions in and out upon different stations,

and remain your little friend
Byron

I forgot to tell you how I was[.] I am at present very well, and my foot goes but indifferently. I cannot perceive any alteration.

[To Mrs Catherine Gordon Byron]

Harrow on the Hill Sunday May 1st. 1803

My Dear Mother

I received your Letter the other day and am happy to hear you are well I hope you will find Newstead in as favourable a state as you can wish. I wish you would write to Sheldrake to tell him to make haste with my Shoes.[6] I am sorry to Say

---

[5] Hanson's brother had been appointed to HMS *Brazen*; Earl Portsmouth, who also resided with the Hansons, had made the mistake of familiarly pulling the younger lord's ears after breakfast one day at the lawyer's house. Portsmouth would make a second marriage with one of Hanson's daughters, and in due course be declared insane. (See letter of 19 March 1823.)

[6] Dr Baillie had inspected Byron's club foot in London, and prescribed a brace to be obtained from Mr Sheldrake.

that Mr. Henry Drury[7] has behaved himself to me in a manner I neither *can* nor *will* bear. He has seized now an opportunity of Showing his resentment towards me. Today in church I was talking to a boy who was sitting next me, *that* perhaps was not right, but hear what followed. after church he spoke not a word to me but he took this boy to his pupil room, where he abused me in a most violent manner, called me *blackguard* said he *would* and *could* have me expelled from the School, & bade me thank his *charity* that *prevented* him, this was the message he sent me, to which I shall return no answer, but submit my case to *you* and those you may think *fit* to *consult*. Is this usage fit for any body [?] had I *stole* or behaved in the most *abominable* way to him his language could not have been more outrageous, what must the boys think of me to hear such a message ordered to be delivered to me by a *master*[?] better let him take away my Life than ruin my *character*. My conscience acquits me of ever *meriting* expulsion at this school, I have been *idle* and I certainly ought not to talk in church, But I have never done a mean action at this school to him or any *one*. If I had done anything so *heinous* why should he allow me to stay at the School, why should he himself be so *criminal* as to overlook faults, which merit the *appellation* of a Blackguard[?] If he had it in his power to have [me] expelled he would long ago have *done* it, as it is, he has done *worse*, if I am treated in this manner, I will not stay at this *school*. [...] If you do not take notice of this I will leave the School myself, but I am sure *you* will not see me *ill treated* better that I should suffer anything than this. I believe you will be tired by this time of reading my Letter but If you love me you will now show it. Pray write me immediately I shall ever remain

your affectionate Son
Byron

P. S.—*Hargreaves Hanson desires his love to you & hopes you are very well. I am not in any want of money so will not ask you for any. God Bless, Bless you.*

---

[7] Byron's tutor at Harrow and son of the headmaster. This tiff soon evaporated: see letter of 25 June 1809.

[To Mrs Catherine Gordon Byron]

[Sept. 15? 1803]

My Dear Mother,

I have sent Mealey to Day to you, before William Came,[8] but now I shall write myself, *I promise* you upon my *honour* I will come over *tomorrow* in the *afternoon,* I was not wishing to resist your *Commands,* and really seriously intended, Coming over tomorrow, ever since I received your Last letter, you know as well as I do that it is not your Company I dislike, but the place you reside in.[9] I know it is time to go to Harrow, It will make me *unhappy,* but I will *obey;* I only *desire, entreat,* this one day, and on my *honour* I will be over tomorrow, in the evening or afternoon. I am Sorry you disapprove my Companions, who however are the first this county affords, and my equals in most respects, but I will be permitted to Chuse for myself, I shall never interfere in yours and I desire you will not molest me in mine; if you Grant me this favour, and allow me this one day unmolested you will eternally oblige your

unhappy Son
Byron

I shall attempt to offer no excuse as you do not desire one. I only entreat you as Governor, not as a Mother, to allow me this one day. Those that I most Love live in this county, therefore in the name of Mercy I entreat this one day to take leave, and then I will Join you again at Southwell to prepare to go to a place where—I will write no more it would only incense you, adieu, Tomorrow I come.

[8] Mealey was the steward at Newstead; perhaps William was William Fletcher, Byron's future manservant (see letter of 26 March 1808). Both had been sent to drag Byron home from nearby Annesley Hall, where he was desperately enamoured of his distant cousin, two years his senior and already engaged, Mary Chaworth. (See letter of 29 November 1813.)

[9] In July 1803 Mrs Byron rented Burgage Manor, at Southwell in Nottinghamsire (a 'sleepy little town of three thousand inhabitants'; *Life,* 75), and Byron restively holidayed there from school.

[To Augusta Byron]

Burgage Manor, March 22d. 1804

Although, My ever Dear Augusta, I have hitherto appeared remiss in replying to your kind and affectionate letters; yet I hope you will not attribute my neglect to a want of affection, but rather to a shyness naturally inherent to my Disposition. I will now endeavour as amply as lies in my power to repay your kindness, and for the Future I hope you will consider me not only as *a Brother* but as your warmest and most affectionate *Friend*, and if ever Circumstances should require it as your *protector*. Recollect, My Dearest Sister, that you are *the nearest relation* I have in *the world both by the ties of Blood* and *Affection*, If there is anything in which I can serve you; you have only to mention it; Trust to your Brother, and be assured he will never betray your confidence. When You see my Cousin and future Brother George Leigh,[10] tell him that I already consider him as my Friend, for whoever is beloved by you, my amiable Sister, will always be equally Dear to me. [...] Also remember me to poor old Murray, tell him we will see that something is to be done for him, for *while I live he shall never be abandoned In his old Age.*[11] Write to me Soon, my Dear Augusta, And do not forget to love me, In the mean time I remain more than words [can] express, your ever sincere, affectionate

Brother and Friend
Byron

P. S.—Do not forget to Knit the purse you promised me, Adieu my beloved Sister.—

[To Augusta Byron]

Burgage Manor April 2d. 1804

I received your present, my beloved Augusta, which was very acceptable, not that it will be of any use as a token of remembrance, No, my affection for you will never permit me to forget you. I am afraid my Dear Girl that you will be

---

[10] Colonel George Leigh (1771–1850), son of 'Mad Jack' Byron's sister, and therefore Augusta's cousin; they married in August 1807, after objections from Leigh's family.

[11] An ancient Byron family retainer, Joe Murray is not to be confused with Byron's later publisher John Murray. He lived on at Newstead until his death in October 1820. 'So—Joe Murray is gathered to his Masters', Byron wrote on hearing the news: 'the very ghosts have died with him' (*LJ* vii. 208).

absent when I am in town[.] I cannot exactly say when I return to Harrow but however it will be in a very short time. I hope you were entertained by Sir Wm. Fawcet's funeral on Saturday, Though I should imagine such spectacles rather calculated to excite Gloomy ideas, But I believe *your motive* was *not quite of so mournful a cast.*[12] You tell me that *you* are tired of London[.] I am rather surprised to hear that for I thought the Gaieties of the Metropolis were particularly pleasing to *young Ladies.*—For my part I detest it, the smoke and the noise feel particularly unpleasant[;] but however it is preferable to this horrid place, where I am oppressed with ennui, and have no amusement of any Kind, except the conversation of my mother which is sometimes very *edifying* but not always very *agreeable.* There are very few books of any Kind that are either instructive or amusing, no society but old parsons and old Maids; I shoot a Good deal, but thank God I have not so far lost my reason as to make shooting my only amusement. There are indeed some of my neighbours whose only pleasures consist in field sports, but in other respects they are only one degree removed from the brute creation. These however I endeavour not to imitate, but I sincerely wish for the company of a few friends about my own age to soften the austerity of the scene, I am an absolute Hermit, in a short time my Gravity which is increased by my solitude will qualify me for an Archbishoprick, I really begin to think that I should become a mitre amazingly well. You tell me to write to you when I have nothing better to do. I am sure writing to you my Dear Sister, must ever form my Greatest pleasure, but especially so, at this time. Your letters and those of one of my Harrow friends form my only resources for driving away *dull care.* For Godsake write me a letter as long as may fill *twenty sheets* of paper, recollect it is my only pleasure. if you won't Give me twenty sheets, at least send me as long an epistle as you can and as soon as possible, there will be time for me to receive one more Letter at Southwell, and as soon as I Get to Harrow I will write to you, excuse my not writing more my Dear Augusta, for I am sure you will be sufficiently tired of reading this complaining narrative[.] God bless you my beloved Sister. Adieu. I remain your sincere and affectionate

Friend and Brother
Byron

---

[12] Augusta attended the funeral of General Sir William Fawcett (1727–1804) on 31 March. Byron implies that her interest would be drawn to Colonel Leigh, presumably (as equerry to the Prince of Wales) a member of the funeral procession.

Remember me kindly to Mrs. Harcourt.

[To Augusta Byron]

Burgage Manor April 9th. 1804

A thousand thanks my dear and Beloved Augusta for your affectionate Letter, and so ready compliance with the request of a peevish and fretful Brother. it acted as a cordial on my drooping spirits and for a while dispelled the Gloom which envelopes me in this uncomfortable place. you see what power your letters have over me, so I hope you will be liberal in your epistolary Consolation.—You will address your next letter to Harrow as I set out from Southwell on wednesday, and am sorry that I cannot contrive to be with you, as I must resume my studies at Harrow directly. If I speak in public at all it will not be till the latter end of June or the beginning of July, you are right in your conjecture for I feel not a little nervous in the anticipation of *my Debut as an orator,*[13] by the bye, I do not dislike Harrow I find *ways* and *means* to amuse *myself very pleasantly* there, the friend whose correspondence I find so amusing is an old sporting companion of mine, whose recitals of Shooting and Hunting expeditions are amusing to me as having often been his companion in them, and I hope to be so still oftener.—My mother Gives a *party* to night at which the principal *Southwell Belles* will be present, with one of which although I don't as yet know whom I shall so far *honour having never seen* them, I intend to *fall violently* in love, it will serve as an amusement pour passer le temps and it will at least have the charm of novelty to recommend it, then you know in the course of a few weeks I shall be quite au desespoir, shoot myself and Go out of the world with eclat, and my History will furnish materials for a pretty little Romance which shall be entitled and denominated the loves of Lord B. and the cruel and Inconstant Sigismunda Cunegunda Bridgetina &c&c princess of Terra Incognita.—Don't you think that I have a very Good Knack for *novel writing?*—I have Just this minute been called away from writing to you by two Gentlemen who have Given me an invitation to Go over to [Screveton?] a village a few miles off and spend a few days, but however I shall not accept it, so you will continue to address your letters to Harrow as usual, write to me as soon as possible and Give me a long letter,

---

[13] In fact Byron's Speech Day effort was a great success: see his later journal, 'Detached Thoughts' (*LJ* ix. 42–3).

Remember me to Mrs. Harcourt and all who enquire after me. Continue to love me and believe me your truly affectionate

Brother and Friend
Byron

———— ∞ ————

P. S.—My Mother's love to you, Adieu.

[To Augusta Byron]

Harrow Saturday 11th. Novr. 1804

I thought my dear Augusta that your opinion of my *meek mamma* would coincide with mine; Her temper is so so variable, and when inflamed, so furious, that I dread our meeting, not but I dare say, that I am troublesome enough, but I always endeavour to be as dutiful as she is possible. She is so very strenuous, and so tormenting in her entreaties and commands, with regard to my reconciliation, with that detestable Lord G[rey][14] that I suppose she has a penchant for his Lordship, but I am confident that he does not return it, for he rather dislikes her, than otherwise, at least as far as I can judge. But she has an excellent opinion of her personal attractions, sinks her age a good six years, avers that when I was born she was only eighteen, when you my dear Sister as well as I know that she was of age when she married my father, and that I was not born for three years afterwards, but vanity is the weakness of *your sex*, and these are mere foibles that I have related to you, and provided she never molested me I should look upon them as follies very excusable in a woman. But I am now coming to what must shock you, as much as it does me, when she has occasion to lecture me (not very seldom you will think no doubt) she does not do it in a manner that commands respect, and in an impressive style. no. did she do that I should amend my faults with pleasure, and dread to offend a kind though just mother. But she flies into a fit of phrenzy upbraids me as if I was the most undutiful

[14] Henry Edward Yelverton, nineteenth Baron Grey de Ruthyn (1780–1810), had taken up a lease on Newstead Abbey in March 1803, when Mrs Byron moved out. At first he and Byron had hit it off; then it seems he had sexually propositioned him during a visit. In any event, Byron would have nothing to do with him thereafter. Lord Grey stayed on at Newstead until the autumn of 1808, when Byron was able to move back in—and redecorate (see letter of 2 November 1808).

wretch in existence, rakes up the ashes of of [sic] my *father*, abuses him, says I shall be a true Byrrone,[15] which is the worst epithet she can invent. Am I to call this woman mother? Because by natures law she has authority over me, am I to be trampled upon in this manner? Am I to be goaded with insult, loaded with obloquy, and suffer my feelings to be outraged on the most trivial occasions? I owe her respect as a Son, But I renounce her as a Friend. What an example does she shew me? I hope in God I shall never follow it. I have not told you all nor can I, I respect you as a female, nor although I ought to confide in you as a Sister, will I shock you with the repetition of Scenes, which you may judge of by the Sample I have given you, and which to all but you are buried in oblivion. Would they were so in my mind. I am afraid they never will. And can I, my dear Sister, look up to this mother, with that respect, that affection I ought. Am I to be eternally subjected to her caprice! I hope not, indeed a few short years will emancipate me from the Shackles I now wear, and then perhaps she will govern her passion better than at present. [...] My mother's precepts, never convey instruction, never fix upon my mind, to be sure they are calculated, to inculcate obedience, so are chains, and tortures, but though they may restrain for a time the mind revolts from such treatment. Not that Mrs. Byron ever injures my *sacred* person. I am rather too old for that, but her words are of that rough texture, which offend more than personal ill usage. 'A talkative woman is like an Adder's tongue,' so says one of the prophets, but which I can't tell, and very likely you don't wish to know, but he was a true one whoever he was.[16] The postage of your letters My dear Augusta don't fall upon me, but if they did it would make no difference, for I am Generally in cash, and should think the trifle I paid for your epistles the best laid out I ever spent in my life. Write Soon. Remember me to Lord Carlisle,[17] and believe me I ever am your affectionate Brother and Friend

Byron

---

[15] Evidently Byron's attempt at his mother's Scottish rhotic r.

[16] The biblical Book of Sirach (26: 27) advises that 'A loud-mouthed, talkative woman is like a trumpet sounding the signal for attack.'

[17] Frederick Howard, fifth Earl of Carlisle (1748–1825), acted as Byron's guardian because his father had married the daughter of the fourth Lord Byron, and his own wife was a sister of the fifth lord. He looked after the poet's and his mother's financial affairs, accordingly. This earned Byron's resentment (see letter of 6 March 1809), but Augusta was in a difficult position as she, too, was a recipient of the family's charity, having lived with them, on and off, and still doing so at the time of writing.

[To Hargreaves Hanson]

Burgage Manor Southwell Notts. Monday April 15th. [1805]

Dear Hargreaves,

As I have been unable to return to town with your Father, I must request that you will take care of my books and a parcel which I expect from my Taylors, and as I understand you are going to pay Farleigh a visit,[18] I would be obliged to you to leave them under the care of one of the Clerks, or a Servant, who may inform me where to find them;—I shall be in town on Wednesday the 24th at farthest; when I shall not hope to see you, or wish it; not but that I should be glad of your *entertaining* and *loquacious* society; (but as I think you will be more amused at Farleigh;) it would be selfish in me to wish that you should forego the pleasures of contemplating *pigs, poultry, pork, pease,* and *potatoes,* together with other *Rural Delights,* for my company.—Much pleasure may you find in your excursion, and I dare say, when you have exchanged *pleadings* for *ploughshares* and *fleecing Clients* for *feeding flocks,* you will be in no hurry to resume your law functions. Remember me to your father and mother; and the Juniors, and if you should find it convenient to dispatch a note in answer to this epistle, it will afford great pleasure to

yours very sincerely & affectionately,
Byron

P. S.—*It is hardly necessary to inform you, that I am heartily tired of Southwell, for I am at this minute experiencing those delights which I have often recapitulated to you, and which are more entertaining to be* talked *of at a distance, than enjoyed at home; I allude to the eloquence of a* near relation *of mine, which is as remarkable as your* taciturnity.

[To John Hanson]

Trin. Coll. Oct 26th. 1805

Dear Sir.

I will be obliged to you to order me down 4 Dozen of Wine, Port—Sherry—Claret, & Madeira, one Dozen of Each; I have got part of my Furniture in, &

---

[18] Farleigh was the Hanson's family estate near Basingstoke, Hampshire.

begin to *admire* a College Life. Yesterday my appearance in the Hall in my State Robes was *Superb*, but uncomfortable to my *Diffidence*.[19] You may order the Saddle & & for Oateater as soon as you please & I will pay for them. I remain Sir

yours truly
Byron

P. S.—Give Hargreaves a hint to be expeditious in sending my valuables which I begin to want. Your Cook had the Impudence to charge my Servant 15 Shillings for 5 days provision which I think is exorbitant, but I hear that in Town *it is but reasonable. Pray is it the Custom to allow your Servants 3 & 6 per Diem, in London? I will thank you for Information on the Subject.*

[To Augusta Byron]

Trin. Coll. Novr. 6th, 1805

My Dear Augusta

As might be supposed I like a College Life extremely, especially as I have escaped the Trammels or rather *Fetters* of my domestic Tyrant Mrs Byron, who continued to plague me during my visit in July and September. I am now most pleasantly situated in *Super*excellent Rooms, flanked on one side by my Tutor, on the other by an old Fellow, both of whom are rather checks upon my *vivacity*. I am allowed 500 a year, a Servant and Horse, so Feel as independent as a German Prince who coins his own Cash, or a Cherokee Chief who coins no Cash at all, but enjoys what is more precious, Liberty. I talk in raptures of that *Goddess* because my amiable Mama was so despotic. I am afraid the Specimens I have lately given her, of my Spirit, and determination to submit to no more unreasonable commands, (or the insults which follow a refusal to obey her implicitly whether right or wrong,) have given high offence, as I had a most *fiery* Letter from the *Court* at *Southwell* on Tuesday, because I would not turn off my Servant, (whom I had not the least reason to distrust, and who had an excellent Character from his last

---

[19] Aristocratic students at Oxford and Cambridge wore more decorative academic robes than commoners. 'Oateater' was clearly a horse; being lame, Byron enjoyed horse riding as a form of exercise throughout his life.

Master) at her suggestion from some caprice she had taken into her head.[20] I sent back to the Epistle which was couched in *elegant* terms a severe answer, which so nettled her Ladyship, that after reading it she returned it in a Cover without *deigning* a Syllable in return. The Letter and my answer you shall behold when you next see me, that you may judge of the Comparative merits of Each. I shall let her go on in the *Heroics*, till she cools, without taking the least notice. Her Behaviour to me for the last two Years neither merits my respect, nor deserves my affection. I am comfortable here, and having one of the best allowances in College, go on Gaily, but not extravagantly. I need scarcely inform you that I am not the least obliged to Mrs. B for it, as it comes off of my property, and She refused to fit out a single thing for me from her own pocket, my Furniture is paid for & she has moreover a handsome addition made to her own income, which I do not in the least regret, as I would wish her to be happy, but by *no means* to live with me in *person*. The sweets of her society I have already drunk to the last dregs, I hope we shall meet on more affectionate Terms, or meet no more. But why do I say? *meet*, her temper precludes every idea of happiness, and therefore in future I shall avoid her *hospitable* mansion, though she has the folly to suppose She is to be Mistress of my house when I come of [age]. I must apologize to you for the [dullness?] Of this letter, but to tell you the [truth, the effects?] of last nights Claret have no[t gone?] out of my head, as I supped with a large party. I suppose that Fool Hanson in his *vulgar Idiom*, by the word Jolly did not mean Fat, but High Spirits, for so far from increasing I have lost one pound in a fortnight as I find by being regularly weighed. Adieu, Dearest Augusta.

[Signature cut out]

[To John Hanson]

Trin. Coll. Cambridge Novr. 23d. 1805

Dear Sir.

Your advice was good but I have not determined whether I shall follow it, this place is the *Devil*, or at least his principal residence, they call it the University, but any other appellation would have suited it much better, for Study is the last pursuit of the Society; the Master eats, drinks, and Sleeps, the Fellows *drink*, *dispute* and *pun*, the *employments* of the under Graduates you will probably

---

[20] Mrs Byron's suspicions were well founded; in 1808 this servant, Francis Boyce, would be transported to Australia for theft.

conjecture without my description.[21] I sit down to write with a head confused with dissipation, which though I hate, I cannot avoid. I have only supped at home 3 times since my arrival, and my table is constantly covered with invitations, after all I am the most *steady* man in the College, nor have I got into *many* Scrapes, and none of consequence. Whenever you appoint a day my Servant shall come up for Oateater, and as the Time of paying my bill now approaches the remaining £50 will be very *agreeable*. You need not make any deduction as I shall want most of it, I will settle with you for the Saddle and accoutrements *next* quarter. The Upholsterer's bill will not be sent in yet, as my Rooms are to be papered and painted at Xmas, when I will procure them; No Furniture has been got except what was absolutely necessary, including some decanters and wine Glasses. Your Cook certainly deceived you, as I know my Servant was in Town 5 days, and she stated 4. I have yet had no reason to distrust him, but we will examine the affair when I come to Town, when I intend Lodging at Mrs. Massingberds.[22] My Mother and I have quarrelled [sic], which I bear with the *patience* of a philosopher, custom reconciles one to every thing. In the hope that Mrs. H. and the *Battalion* are in good Health I remain Sir & &

Byron

[To Mrs Catherine Gordon Byron]

16 Piccadilly Feby. 26th. 1806

Dear Mother,

Notwithstanding your *sage* and economical advice I have paid my *Harrow* Debts, as I can better afford to wait for the Money, than the poor Devils who were my Creditors.—I have also discharged my College Bills, amounting to £231—£75 of which I shall trouble Hanson to repay, being for Furniture, and as my allowance is £500 per annum, I do not chuse to lose the overplus as it makes only £125 per Quarter. I happen to have a few hundreds in ready Cash lying by me, so I have paid the accounts, but I find it inconvenient to remain at College, not for the Expence, as I could live on my Allowance, (only I am naturally extravagant) however the mode of going on does not suit my constitution, improvement at an English University to a Man of Rank is you know impossible, and the very

[21] Each college at Oxford and Cambridge typically has its Master (or Mistress) and its collection of Fellows, often graduates of the university, who constitute a governing body of the college to which they are affiliated.

[22] Byron and his mother had stayed with the mysterious Mrs Massingberd in Piccadilly as long ago as summer 1802. She would later serve as a guarantor for Byron's loans and store the effects of women with whom he consorted (see letter of 20 July 1808).

Idea *ridiculous*. Now I sincerely desire to finish my Education, and having been some Time at Cambridge, the Credit of the University is as much attached to my Name, as if I had pursued my Studies *there* for a Century, but believe me it is nothing more than a Name, which is already acquired; I can now leave it with honour, as I have paid every thing, and wish to pass a couple of Years abroad, where I am certain of employing my Time to far more advantage and at much less expence, than at our English Seminaries. Tis true I cannot enter France, but Germany, and the Courts of Berlin, Vienna, and Petersburg, are still open;[23] I shall lay this Plan before Hanson & Lord C[arlisle] I presume you will all agree, and if you do not, I will if possible get away without your consent, though I should admire it more in the Regular manner and with a Tutor of your furnishing. This is my project, at present I wish *you* to be silent to Hanson, about it, who by the bye, told me he would endeavour to procure your £600 arrears of Income [Tax?], as his Friends are now in possession of the *Treasury*.[24] Let me have your Answer, I intend remaining in Town a month longer, when perhaps I shall bring my Horses and myself down to your residence in that *execrable* Kennel. I hope you have engaged a Man Servant—else it will be impossible for me to visit you, since my Servant must attend chiefly to his horses, at the same Time you must cut an Indifferent Figure with only maids in your habitation,

I remain yours,
Byron

[To John M. B. Pigot]

London, Sunday, Midnight, August 10th, 1806

Dear Pigot,

This *astonishing* packet, will doubtless amaze you, but having an idle hour this evening, I wrote the inclosed Stanza's, which I request you to deliver [to] Ridge to be printed *separate* from my other *Compositions*,[25] as you will perceive them to be *improper* for the perusal of Ladies, of course none of the females of your family

---

[23] Such was the diplomatic state of affairs in the Napoleonic Wars at this time.

[24] The only Whig Government between 1783 and 1827 was the so-called 'Ministry of All the Talents', which ruled from February 1806 until March 1807. The Chancellor of the Exchequer was Lord Henry Petty (see letter of 14 May 1807).

[25] The Nottinghamshire printer John Ridge would privately print Byron's first collection of poems, *Fugitive Pieces*, in November 1806; they were found steamy enough by some of the local womenfolk.

must see them; I offer 1000 apologies for the trouble I have given you in this and other instances.

Yours truly,

[To Dr. T. Falkner]

Janry. 8th. 1807

Sir/[26]

The volume of little pieces, which accompanies this, would have been presented before, had I not been apprehensive, that Miss Falkner's Indisposition, might render such Trifles unwelcome.—There are some Errors of the Printer, which I have not had Time to correct in the Collection, you have it then, with 'all its Imperfections on its head'[27] a heavy weight when joined with the Faults of its Author.—Such 'Juvenilia,' as they can claim no great degree of approbation, I may venture to hope, will also escape the severity of uncalled for, though perhaps *not* undeserved Criticism.—They were written on many, & various Occasions, and are now published merely for the perusal of a friendly Circle. Believe me, Sir, if they afford the slightest amusement, to yourself and the rest of my *social* Readers, I shall have gathered all the '*Bays*' I ever wish to *adorn* the *Head*

of yours very truly,
Byron

P. S.—I hope Miss F. is in a State of Recovery.

[To John Edleston?]

May, 1807

[Note in cipher]
D–R–T [Dearest?]—Why not? With this kiss make me yours again forever
Byron[28]

---

[26] Mrs Byron's landlord at Burgage Manor.   [27] See *Hamlet*, I. v. 79.
[28] John Edlestone, two years younger than Byron, was a choirboy at Trinity Chapel; the exact nature of their relationship remains a mystery. Leslie Marchand writes of this letter (written in code

[To Edward Noel Long]

Southwell May 14th. 1807

My dear Long,

The Spirit of Prophecy certainly animated my pen, when I wrote the *presage* of Petty's Downfall, with his disgrace, at Cambridge, in my 'College Examinations.'[29]—I am sorry I cannot repay the Compliments of your *Sire*, by the requested Copy, all my private volumes are gone, however, my publication will be out in June, & if you are in England at that Time, I shall send a Copy for the purpose.—Not above a dozen of the pieces in my private Copies, will appear '*pro Bono publico* [for the public good]' though the volume will be considerably larger, most of the amatory poems, the Cornelian (which *you* & all the Girls, I know not why think my best) will be omitted,[30] I have lately been brushing up my *Intellects* by Translations from the Greek of Anacreon & Medea, of the former only 2 odes, & a Chorus from the Latter, will make their appearance, I am putting the last touches to a Translation of the Episode of Nisus & Euryalus, (in my opinion the best in point of Versification I have ever written) & now bid an eternal Adieu to the Muse, in an Ode expressive of my Intention to relinquish *Poesy* forever, which will conclude my Volume.—I am tired of versifying, & am irrevocably determined to *rhyme* no more, an employment I merely adopted '*pour passer le Temps*' when this work is accomplished, I shall have obtained all the *Eclat* I desire at present, when it shall be said that I published before I was 20; the merit of the contents is of little Consequence, provided they are not absolutely execrable, the novelty of the *Deed* (which though not *unprecedented*, is at least uncommon, particularly amongst *Patricians*) will secure some share of Credit.— All my Girls are *off*, as I told you in *Rhyme*, consequently I am *dull*. I *swim* when the Weather permits, lately it has been unpropitious to that Amusement. I envy you so noble a *Bath*, as the *Medway*, a small River not above 8 feet in depth, constitutes my [*Lavarium?*; cold bath] here, I have now lost 2 Stone & a half & weigh 12 Stone at '*your Service*' I shall reduce myself to 11. & there stop; if the Skies

with an accompanying key): 'The conjecture that it was addressed to Edleston is based on the fact that it was written a short time before Byron left for Cambridge on June 27, 1807, and on the evidence of his feeling for Edleston in the letters of June 30 and July 5, 1807 [see below], to Elizabeth Pigot' (*LJ* xi. 173).

[29] Long (1788–1809) was a firm friend of Byron's at both Harrow and Cambridge. Lord Henry Petty had just lost his seat, in the collapse of the 'Ministry of All the Talents'. See Byron's poem, 'Thoughts Suggested by a College Examination', published in *Hours of Idleness* (*CPW* i. 92–4).

[30] 'The Cornelian' (*CPW* i. 87–8) was a compliment to Edlestone, but necessarily a private one, given its emotional demonstrativeness. (See letter of 5 July 1807.)

& my Health permit, one Month will effect this, with the assistance of a great coat, 8 Waistcoats, flannel Bandages, daily Physic, no Ale, one meal a Day, & the Hot Bath, in truth, I believe you would not recognize '*George Gordon*,['] at least many of my acquaintance, who have seen me since our meeting, have hardly believed their optics, my visage is lengthened, I appear taller, & somewhat *slim*, & 'mirabile dictu [wonderful to relate]!!' my Hair once black or rather very dark brown, is turned (I know not how but I presume by perpetual perspiration) to a *light Chesnut*, nearly approaching *yellow*, so that I am metamorphosed not a little. You must write previous to your Embarkation, & I hope you will return safe, from 'cutting foreign throats' in company with the *Scum of the Earth*.[31]—Is your Brother at Harrow? if he is I shall *tip* the youth, on my visit to the *Blest Spot*, I see no account of their Speeches in the paper though the speechday is past some time, in our *day* it was different, there has been no mention of a single Speechday since *our departure*, last year or the present.—Wingfield is gone to Marlow,[32] Adieu yours ever

Byron

[To Elizabeth Bridget Pigot]

Trin. Coll. Camb. July 5th. 1807

My dear *Eliza*,

Since my last letter I have determined to reside *another year* at *Granta* as my Rooms &c. &c. are finished in *great Style*, several old friends *come up* again, & many *new* acquaintances made, consequently my Inclination leads me *forward*, & I shall return to College in October if still *alive*. My life here has been one continued *routine* of Dissipation, out at different places every day, engaged to more *dinners* &c. &c. than my *stay* would permit me to *fulfil*, at this moment I write with a *bottle* of *Claret* in my *Head*, & *tears* in my *eyes*, for I have just parted from 'my *Cornelian*' who spent the evening with me; as it was our last Interview, I postponed my engagements to devote the hours of the *Sabbath* to friendship, Edleston & I have separated for the present, & my mind is a *Chaos* of hope & *Sorrow*.—Tomorrow I set out for London, you will address your answer to '*Gordon's*

---

[31] For 'cutting foreign throats' see *Romeo and Juliet*, I. iv. 83. The 'scum of the earth' is the Duke of Wellington's famous remark about allied troops, made in November 1813; it must have been a figure of speech before that time. Long had just joined the Coldstream Guards, and in 1809 he drowned on the way to active service in the Peninsular War.

[32] John Wingfield (1791–1811), also a Harrow friend of Byron's, also joined the Coldstream Guards and died of fever in the Peninsular War.

Hotel' Albemarle Street, where I *sojourn*, during my visit to the *Metropolis*.—I rejoice to hear you are interested in my 'protegè', he has been my *almost constant* associate since October 1805, when I entered Trinity College; his *voice* first attracted my notice, his *countenance* fixed it, & his *manners* attached me to him forever, he departs for a *mercantile house* in *Town*, in October, & we shall probably not meet, till the expiration of my minority, when I shall leave to his *decision*, either *entering* as a *Partner* through my Interest, or residing with me altogether. Of course he *would* in his present *frame* of mind prefer the *latter*, but he may alter his opinion previous to that period, however he shall have his choice, I certainly *love* him more than any human being, & neither *time* or Distance have had the least effect on my (in general) changeable Disposition.—In short, We shall put *Lady E. Butler*, & Miss *Ponsonby* to the *Blush*, *Pylades* & *Orestes* out of countenance, & want nothing but a *Catastrophe* like *Nisus* & *Euryalus*, to give *Jonathan* & *David* the '*go by*'.[33]—He certainly is perhaps more *attached* to *me*, than even I am in *return*, during the whole of my residence at *Cambridge*, we met every day summer & Winter, without passing *one tiresome moment*, & separated *each time* with increasing Reluctance. I hope you will *one day* see *us* together, he is the only *being* I *esteem*, though I *like many*.—The Marquis of *Tavistock* was down the other day, I supped with him at his *Tutor's*, entirely a *whig party*, the opposition *muster* very *strong* here, & Lord Hartington, the Duke of Leinster, &c. &c. are to join us in October, so every thing will be *splendid*.[34]—The *Music* is all over at present, met with another '*accidency*', upset a *Butter Boat* in the *lap* of a *lady*, looked very *blue*, *spectators* grinned, '*curse em*' apropos, sorry to say, been *drunk* every day, & not quite *sober yet*, however touch no meat, nothing but fish, soup & vegetables, consequently does me no harm, sad dogs all the *Cantabs*, mem[orandum], *we mean* to reform next January.—This place is a *Monotony* of *endless variety, like it*, hate Southwell, full of old maids, how is Anne Becher? wants a husband, *men scarce*, wont *bite*, mem[orandum]—tell Anne to fish more cautiously or the *Gudgeons* will be off; catch nothing but *Roach & Dace*.[35]—Write soon has Ridge sold well? or do the Ancients demur? what Ladies have bought? all disappointed I dare say nothing *indecent* in the present publication,[36] <sorry for it> *bad* set at Southwell, no *faces* & dont ever '*mean well*'.—Saw a Girl at

---

[33] Lady Eleanor Butler and Sarah Ponsonby, aristocratic ladies both, lived together as objects of public, even touristic, interest from 1779 to 1829 in the Vale of Llangollen, North Wales. The other names Byron lists are ambiguous male couples from classical and biblical sources.

[34] All these are Whig blue-bloods of Byron's generation.

[35] Anne Becher was perhaps the sister of the Revd John Becher (see letter of 28 March 1808). Of the fish species Byron mentions here, the gudgeon is fast moving and hard to catch; roach and dace are slower and less valued.

[36] The second edition of *Fugitive Pieces*, *Hours of Idleness*, published by Ridge in June 1807.

St. Mary's the Image of Anne Houson, thought it was her, all in the wrong, the Lady stared, so did I, I blushed, so did *not* the Lady, sad thing, wish women, had *more modesty.*—Talking of women brings my *terrier Fanny* into my head[;] how is she? very well I thank you.—Got a Headach, must go to bed, up early in the morning to travel, my 'protegé' breakfasts with me, parting spoils my appetite, excepting from Southwell, mem[orandum]—*I hate Southwell,*

yours ever
Byron

[To Elizabeth Bridget Pigot]

Trinity College Cambridge October 26th. 1807

My dear Elizabeth,

Fatigued with sitting up till four in the morning for these last two days at Hazard, I take up my pen to enquire how your Highness, & the rest of my female acquaintance at the seat of Archiepiscopal Grandeur *Southwell,*[37] go on.—I know I deserve a scolding for my negligence in not writing more frequently, but racing up & down the Country for these last three months, how was it possible to fulfil the Duties of a Correspondent?—Fixed at last for 6 weeks, I write, as *thin* as ever (not having gained an ounce since my Reduction) & rather in better humour, for after all, *Southwell* was a detestable residence; thank St. Dominic I have done with it, I have been twice within 8 miles of it, but could not prevail on myself to *suffocate* in its heavy atmosphere.—This place is wretched enough, a villainous Chaos of Dice and Drunkenness, nothing but Hazard and Burgundy, Hunting, Mathematics and Newmarket, Riot and Racing, yet it is a Paradise compared with the eternal dullness of Southwell, oh! the misery of doing nothing, but make *Love, enemies,* and *Verses.*—Next January, (but this is *entre nous* only, and pray let it be so, or my maternal persecutor will be throwing her Tomahawk at any of my curious projects) I am going to *Sea* for four of [or?] five months, with my Cousin Capt. Bettesworth,[38] who commands the Tartar the finest frigate in the navy. I have seen most scenes, and wish to look at a naval life.—We are going probably to the Mediterranean, or to the West Indies, or to the

---

[37] Southwell is the seat of the Church of England diocese covering Nottinghamshire.
[38] Byron's grandfather Admiral John 'Foulweather Jack' Byron (1723–86) was married to Sophia Trevanion, from whose family George Edmund Byron Bettesworth was descended. He was killed at the battle of Bergen against a Danish-Norwegian force in 1808, commanding HMS *Tartar.*

Devil, and if there is a possibility of taking me to the Latter, Bettesworth will do it, for he has received four and twenty wounds in different places, and at this moment possesses a Letter from the late Ld. Nelson, stating Bettesworth as the only officer of the navy who had more wounds than himself.————I have got a new friend, the finest in the world, a *tame Bear*, when I brought him here, they asked me what I meant to do with him, and my reply was 'he should *sit for a Fellowship*.'[39]—*Sherard* will explain the meaning of the sentence if it is ambiguous.—This answer delighted them not,—we have eternal parties here, and this evening a large assortment of *Jockies*, Gamblers, *Boxers*, *Authors*, *parsons*, and *poets*, sup with me.—A precious Mixture, but they go on well together, and for me, I am a *spice* of every thing except a Jockey, by the bye, I was dismounted again the other day.————Thank your Brother in my name, for his Treatise. I have written 214 pages of a novel, one poem of 380 Lines, to be published (without my name) in a few weeks, with notes, 560 Lines of Bosworth Field, and 250 Lines of another poem in rhyme, besides half a dozen smaller pieces, the poem to be published is a Satire, apropos, I have been praised to the Skies in the Critical Review, and abused equally in another publication, so much the Better, they tell me, for the sale of the Book, it keeps up controversy, and prevents it from being forgotten, besides the first men of all ages have had their share, nor do the humblest escape, so I bear it like a philosopher, it is odd enough the two opposite Critiques came out on the same day, and out of five pages of abuse, [my?] Censor only quotes *two lines*, from different poems, in support of his opinion, now the proper way to *cut* up, is to quote long passages, and make them appear absurd, because simple allegation is no proof.—on the other hand, there are seven pages of praise, and more than *my modesty* will allow, said on the subject.—Adieu yours truly

Byron

P. S.—*Write, Write, Write!!!*

---

[39] This seems unbelievably unlikely, but it seems Byron did indeed find lodgings for a bear at Trinity, or elsewhere in Cambridge. His mother wrote to Hanson on 12 May 1810, while Byron was in Europe: 'The Bear poor Animal died *suddenly* about a fortnight ago' at Newstead (Doris Langley Moore, *Lord Byron: Accounts Rendered* (London: John Murray, 1974), 124).

[To Robert Charles Dallas]

Dorant's. Albemarle St. January 21st. 1808

Sir,[40]

Whenever Leisure and Inclination permit me the pleasure of a visit, I shall feel truly gratified in a personal acquaintance with one, whose mind has been long known to me in his Writings.—You are so far correct in your conjecture, that I am a member of the University of Cambridge, where I shall take my degree of A[rtium]. M[agister]. [Master of Arts] this term, but were Reasoning, Eloquence or Virtue the objects of my search, Granta is not their metropolis, nor is the place of her Situation an 'El Dorado' far less an Utopia, the Intellects of her children are as stagnant as her Cam, and their pursuits limited to the Church,— not of Christ, but of the nearest Benefice.—As to my reading, I believe I may aver without hyperbole, it has been tolerably extensive in the historical department, so that few nations exist or have existed with whose records I am not in some degree acquainted from Herodotus down to Gibbon.—Of the Classics I know about as much as most Schoolboys after a Discipline of thirteen years, of the *Law* of the *Land* as much as enables me to keep 'within the Statute' (to use the Poacher's vocabulary) I did study 'the Spirit of Laws' and the Law of Nations,[41] but when I saw the Latter violated every month, I gave up my attempts at so useless an accomplishment.—Of Geography—I have seen more land on maps than I should wish to traverse on foot, of Mathematics enough to give me the headache without clearing the part affected, of Philosophy Astronomy and Metaphysicks, more than I can comprehend, and of Common Sense, so little, that I mean to leave a Byronian prize at each of our 'Alma Matres' [bountiful mothers: universities] for the first Discovery, though I rather fear that of the Longitude will precede it.—I once thought myself a Philosopher and talked nonsense with great Decorum, I defied pain and preached up equanimity, for some time this did very well, for no one was in *pain* for me but my Friends, and none lost their patience but my hearers, at last a fall from my horse convinced me, bodily suffering was an Evil, and the worst of an argument overset my maxims and my temper at the same moment, so I quitted Zeno for Aristippus,

---

[40] Dallas (1754–1824), a published author, became Byron's literary adviser and editor in his early years, and took the first two cantos of *Childe Harold's Pilgrimage* to the publisher, John Murray, in 1811.
[41] Canonical works of the French Enlightenment, by Baron Montesquieu (1689–1755) and Emerich de Vattel (1714–67), respectively.

and conceive that Pleasure constitutes the '$\tau\sigma$ $K\alpha\lambda o\nu$.'[42]—In Morality I prefer Confucius to the ten Commandments, and Socrates to St. Paul (though the two latter agree in their opinion of marriage) in Religion, I favour the Catholic Emancipation but do not acknowledge the Pope, and I have refused to take the Sacrament because I do not think eating Bread or drinking wine from the hand of an earthly vicar, will make me an Inheritor of Heaven.—I hold virtue in general, or the virtues severally, to be only in the Disposition, each a *feeling* not a principle.—I believe Truth the prime attribute of the Deity, and Death an eternal Sleep, at least of the Body.—You have here a brief compendium of the Sentiments of the *wicked* George Ld. B.—and till I get a new suit you will perceive I am badly cloathed. I remain

yours very truly
Byron

[To William Harness]

Dorant's Hotel Albemarle Street February 16th. 1808

My dear Harness,[43]

Again I trouble you, but I would not do so, did I not hope your Sentiments nearly coincided with mine, on the subject, I am about to mention.—We both seem perfectly to recollect with a mixture of pleasure, and regret, the hours we once passed together, and I assure you most sincerely they are numbered among the happiest of my brief chronicle of enjoyment.—I am now *getting into years*, that is to say, I was *twenty* a month ago, and another year will send me into the World to run my career of Folly with the Rest.—I was *then* just fourteen, you were almost the first of my Harrow friends, certainly the *first* in my esteem, if not in Date, but an absence from Harrow for some time, shortly after, and new Connections on your side, with the difference in our conduct (an advantage decidedly in your favour) from that turbulent and riotous disposition of mine, which impelled me into every species of mischief;—all these circumstances combined to destroy an Intimacy, which Affection urged me to continue, and Memory compels me to regret.—But there is not a circumstance attending that period, hardly a sentence we exchanged, which is not impressed on my mind at

---

[42] Classical (and Platonic) Greek: *to kalon*; 'the beautiful'. Zeno and Aristippus were leading lights of the Eleatic and Cyreniac schools of ancient Greek philosophy, respectively; the former highly intellectual, the latter more hedonistic.
[43] Harness (1790–1869) was a younger schoolfellow at Harrow, whom Byron took under his wing, perhaps because he was also lame. In later life he became curate of All Saints, Knightsbridge.

this moment, I need not say more, this assurance only must convince you, had I considered them as trivial, they would have been less indelible.—How well I recollect the perusal of your *'first flights,'* there is another circumstance you do not know, the *first Lines* I ever attempted at Harrow were addressed to *you,* you were to have seen them, but Sinclair had the copy in his possession when we went home, and on our return *we* were *strangers,* they were destroyed, and certainly no great loss, but you will perceive from this circumstance my opinions at an age, when we cannot be Hypocrites.—I have dwelt longer on this theme, than I intended, and I shall now conclude with what I ought to have begun;—we were once friends, nay, we have always been so, for our Separation was the effect of Chance, not of Disposition, I do not know how far our Destinations in life may throw us together, but if opportunity and Inclination allow you to waste a thought on such a hairbrained being as myself, you will find me at least sincere & not so bigotted to my faults, as to involve others in the Consequence.—Will you sometimes write to me? I do not ask it often, and when we meet, let us be, what we *should* be, and what we *were.* Believe me, my dear William—

yours most truly
Byron

[To John Cam Hobhouse]

Dorant's, February 27th. 1808

Dear Hobhouse,[44]

I write to you to explain a foolish circumstance, which has arisen from some words uttered by me before Pearce and Brown, when I was devoured with Chagrin, and almost insane with the fumes of, not 'last night's Punch'[45] but that evening's wine.—[In] consequence of a misconception of something on my part, I mentioned an intention of withdrawing my name from the Whig Club,[46] this I hear has been broached, and perhaps in a moment of Intoxication and

---

[44] Byron's lifelong best friend and political animal (1786–1859), son of a Whig MP, himself initially a Radical Member of Parliament and later a Whig and Liberal who was raised to the peerage as Baron Broughton de Gyfford in 1851; the poet's fellow traveller and fellow Philhellene; the 'straight man' of their double act but devoted to the poet, to the extent of burning his Memoirs to save his reputation after his death.

[45] See Henry Fielding, *The Tragedy of Tragedies: Tom Thumb the Great* (1730), III. iv. 6.

[46] A Cambridge project dear to Hobhouse's somewhat priggish heart, with fellow members Henry Pearce and Dominick Brown; it seems Byron was letting off steam having just read the critical notice of *Hours of Idleness* in the Whig *Edinburgh Review.*

passion such might be my idea, but *soberly* I have no such design, particularly as I could not abandon my principles, even if I renounced the society with whom I have the honour to be united in sentiments which I never will disavow.—This I beg you will explain to the members as publicly as possible, but should this not be sufficient, and they think proper to erase my name, be it so, I only request that in this case they will recollect, I shall become a *Tory of their own making*. I shall expect your answer on this point with some impatience, now a few words on the subject of my own conduct.—I am buried in an abyss of Sensuality, I have renounced *hazard* however, but I am given to Harlots, and live in a state of Concubinage, I am at this moment under a course of restoration by Pearson's prescription, for a debility occasioned by too frequent Connection.—Pearson sayeth, I have done sufficient with[in?] this last ten days, to undermine my Constitution, I hope however all will soon be well.—As an author, I am cut to atoms in the E Review, it is just out, and has completely demolished my little fabric of fame, this is rather scurvy treatment from a Whig Review, but politics and poetry are different things, & I am no adept in either, I therefore submit in Silence.—Scrope Davies is meandering about London feeding upon Leg of Beef Soup, and frequenting the British Forum, he has given up hazard, as also a considerable sum at the same time.[47]—Altamont is a good deal with me, last night at the Opera Masquerade, we supped with seven whores, a *Bawd* and a *Ballet-master*, in Madame Catalani's apartment behind the Scenes,[48] (of course Catalani was *not* there) I have some thoughts of purchasing D'egville's pupils,[49] they would fill a glorious Harem.—I do not write often, but I like to receive letters, when therefore you are disposed to philosophize, no one standeth more in need of precepts of all sorts than

yours very truly
Byron

---

[47] One of Byron's most attractive cronies and 'One of the cleverest men I ever knew in Conversation' (*LJ* ix. 21), Scrope Berdmore Davies (1782–1852) was an inveterate gambler, eventually ruined by his losses and forced to flee to Bruges in 1820. He lived on in France until his death, and his papers (including letters and poems of Byron) were sensationally discovered in a branch of Barclays Bank in London in 1976.

[48] The diva Angelica Catalani (1780–1849) first appeared in London in 1806. She was a philanthropist as well as a singer, and would never have dined with company of the kind Byron describes.

[49] James D'Egville (1770–1836), English dancer and choreographer: the 'Ballet-master' Byron refers to.

[To John Cam Hobhouse]

Dorant's. March 26th. 1808

Dear Hobhouse,

I have sent Fletcher[50] to Cambridge for various purposes, & he bears this *dispatch* for you.—I am still living with my Dalilah, who has only two faults, unpardonable in a woman,—she can read and write.—Greet in my name the Bilious Birdmore, if you journey this way, I shall be glad to furnish you with Bread and Salt.—The university still chew the Cud of my degree,[51] please God they shall swallow it, though Inflammation be the Consequence.—
I am leading a quiet though debauched life

yours very truly
Byron

[To The Revd John Becher]

Dorant's, March 28, 1808

I have lately received a copy of the new edition from Ridge, and it is high time for me to return my best thanks to you for the trouble you have taken in the superintendence.[52] This I do most sincerely, and only regret that Ridge has not seconded you as I could wish,—at least, in the bindings, paper, &c. of the copy he sent to me. Perhaps those for the public may be more respectable in such articles.

You have seen the Edinburgh Review, of course. I regret that Mrs. Byron is so much annoyed. For my own part, these 'paper bullets of the brain'[53] have only taught me to stand fire; and, as I have been lucky enough upon the whole, my repose and appetite are not discomposed [...]

I am still in or rather near town residing with a nymph, who is now on the sofa vis-a-vis, whilst I am scribbling [...] I have three females (attendants included) in my custody. They accompany me of course.

---

[50] Originally a farmer, then a groom, and finally a valet, William Fletcher (1777–1842) served Byron up until his death in Greece in 1824 and was as devoted to the poet in one way as Hobhouse was in another. Byron's letters are punctuated with references to this exasperating and imperturbably English servant.

[51] Byron's degree was awarded in July 1808, automatically upgraded to a Master's because of his nobility.

[52] Like Dallas, the Revd John Thomas Becher (1770–1848) was happy to serve as Byron's editor and liaison with printers and publishers. Byron knew him through the Pigot family in Southwell.

[53] See *Much Ado About Nothing*, II. iii. 228.

I am *thin* and in exercise. During the spring or summer I trust we shall meet. I hear Lord Ruthyn leaves Newstead in April. * * * As soon as he quits it for ever, I wish much you would take a ride over, survey the mansion, and give me your candid opinion on the most advisable mode of proceeding with regard to the *house. Entre nous*, I am cursedly dipped; my debts, *every* thing inclusive, will be nine or ten thousand before I am twenty-one. But I have reason to think my property will turn out better than general expectation may conceive. Of Newstead I have little hope or care; but Hanson, my agent, intimated my Lancashire property was worth three Newsteads. I believe we have it hollow; though the defendants are protracting the surrender, if possible, till after my majority, for the purpose of forming some arrangement with me, thinking I shall probably prefer a sum in hand to a reversion. Newstead I may *sell*;—perhaps I will not,—though of that more anon. I will come down in May or June.

Yours most truly, &c.

[To John Cam Hobhouse]

Dorant's. April 15th. 1808

My dear Hobhouse,

I proceed as usual turning the twenty four hours to the best account, particularly the nocturnal moiety, my Belles would probably differ, were they together, one is *with* me, and the other *for* me—or any body else, I dare say in my absence.— Besides, I amuse myself with the 'chere amie' of a French Painter in Pall Mall, a lively Gaul;—and occasionally an Opera Girl from the same Meridian.—I have been well about a fortnight, and I trust shall continue so, but I am sadly meagre, and vigilant. Alas! for the Shepherd and his Lambkin![54] how cursedly absurd such proceedings appear compared with your chastity, and my Carnality.——I shall be in Cambridge next month to graduate, the first night I went out after my illness I got into a Row and gave a fellow at the theatre,[55] my address and a black eye, after pugilizing with him and his friend, on their refusing to name their place of Residence, they were kicked out into the Piazzas.—I was very weak and languid, but managed to keep these youths at Bay, till a person whom I dont know engaged one, and I then contended singly with the other till the above consequence ensued. Scrope

---

[54] An irreverent allusion to the first line of 'A Song of Rest' by the German hymnist Phillip Friedrich Hiller (1699–1769), ending 'Let me at last attain that rest, | Which Heaven for me reserveth!'
[55] Given the reference to 'the Piazzas', below, this must be Covent Garden.

Davies is at Portsmouth, I form one of a very sad set, consisting of Capt. Wallace, Sir Godfrey, Sir B. Graham, and other sensual Sinners, we have kept it up, with the most laudable systematic profligacy. Sir G. is with his regiment at present, to the Sorrow of [his] Confederates.—I have given up *play* altogether.—I saw Mahon last night, he made one of a party of ten at a house of Fornication.—

When do you come to town? I long to see you, Adieu

yours very truly
Byron

[To Mrs Elizabeth Massingberd]

May 12th. 1808

I shall call with Mr. Davies and the rest at five to-day to finish the business.[56] I hope you and Miss M will be at home and disengaged.

B

[To Mrs Elizabeth Massingberd]

Brighton July 20th. 1808

Dear Madam,

I have parted with Miss Cameron,[57] & I beg she may have her Clothes & the trunk containing them

yours very truly
Byron

---

[56] Scrope Davies is serving here as the guarantor of a loan arranged by the assiduous Mrs Massingberd. When a loan arranged through Hanson failed to materialize on the eve of Byron's departure from England in June the following year, Davies lent him £4,800 from gambling winnings: a sum not repaid until 1814.

[57] This is Byron's 'Dalilah' mentioned to Hobhouse in the letter of 26 March. Caroline Cameron was around 16 at this time. It seems Byron installed her in boy's clothing as his 'cousin' at his London hotel, where she alarmed the staff by miscarrying, before he took her to Brighton in the same disguise. This would explain the trunkful of women's clothing back in town. (See *Life*, 151, 156.)

[To John Jackson]

Cambridge, [September, 1808]

Dear Jack,[58]

My servants, with their usual acuteness, have contrived to lose my swordstick. Will you get me such another, or as much better as you like, and keep it till I come to town. I also wish you to obtain another bottle of that same Lamb's-Conduit-Street remedy, as I gave the other to a physician to analyze, and I forgot to ask him what he made of it. Keep that also till we meet, which I hope will be soon, and believe me ever yours truly,

B

P. S.—I am this far on my way north, and will write to you again on my arrival.

[To Mrs Catherine Gordon Byron]

Newstead Abbey. Notts. Novr. 2d. 1808

Dear Mother,

If you please we will forget the things you mention, I have no desire to remember them.—When my rooms are finished I shall be happy to see you; as I tell but the truth, you will not suspect me of evasion.—I am furnishing the house more for you than myself, and I shall establish you in it before I sail for India, which I expect to do in March, if nothing particularly obstructive occurs.——I am now fitting up the *green* drawing room, the red (as a bedroom), and the rooms over as sleeping rooms, they will be soon completed, at least I hope so.—I have paid Barnet 182 pounds his whole Bill, I think a *large* one.— I wish you would inquire of Major Watson (who is an old East Indian) what

---

[58] John 'Gentleman' Jackson (1769–1845) was a retired prize fighter, who kept a 'Saloon' (or gym) in Bond Street. The 'remedy' Byron mentions is presumably the 'Pearson's prescription' mentioned to Hobhouse on 27 February, for the treatment of venereal disease. Lamb's Conduit Street, in Bloomsbury, was a 16th-century water source for the City of London: perhaps the name was a jesting reference to an inflamed urethra.

35

things will be necessary to provide for my voyage. I have already procured a friend to write to the *Arabic* Professor at Cambridge,—for some information I am anxious to procure.—I can easily get letters from Government to the Ambassadors Consuls &c. and also to the Governors at Calcutta & Madras; I shall place my *property* and my *will* in the hands of Trustees till my return, and I mean to appoint you one.—From Hanson I have heard nothing; when I do, you shall have the particulars.—After all you must own my project is not a bad one, if I do not travel now, I never shall, and all men should, one day or another. I have at present no connections to keep me at home, no wife, or unprovided sisters Brothers &c.—I shall take care of you, and when I return, I may possibly become a politician, a few years knowledge of other countries than our own will not incapacitate me for that part.—If we see no nation but our own, we do not give mankind a fair chance, it is from *experience* not *Books*, we ought to judge of mankind.—There is nothing like inspection, and trusting to our own senses.

yours very truly
Byron

[To John Hanson]

Newstead Abbey, Notts., November 18th, 1808

Dear Sir,

I am truly glad to hear your health is reinstated. As for my affairs I am sure you will do your best, and, though I should be glad to get rid of my Lancashire property for an equivalent in money, I shall not take any steps of that nature without good advice and mature consideration.

I am (as I have already told you) going abroad in the spring; for this I have many reasons. In the first place, I wish to study India and Asiatic policy and manners. I am young, tolerably vigorous, abstemious in my way of living; I have no pleasure in fashionable dissipation, and I am determined to take a wider field than is customary with travellers. If I return, my judgment will be more mature, and I shall still be young enough for politics. With regard to expence, travelling through the East is rather inconvenient than expensive: it is not like the tour of Europe, you undergo hardship, but incur little hazard of spending money. If I live here I must have my house in town, a separate house for Mrs. Byron; I must keep horses, etc., etc. When I go abroad I place Mrs. Byron at Newstead (there is one great expence saved), I have no horses to keep. A voyage to India will take me six months, and if I had a dozen attendants cannot cost me five hundred pounds; and you will agree with me that a like term of months in England would lead me into four times that expenditure. I have written to Government for letters and permission of the Company,[59] so you see I am *serious*.

You honour my debts; they amount to perhaps twelve thousand pounds, and I shall require perhaps three or four thousand at setting out, with credit on a Bengal agent. This you must manage for me. If my resources are not adequate to the supply I must *sell*, but *not Newstead*. I will at least transmit that to the next Lord. My debts must be paid, if possible, in February. I shall leave my affairs to the care of *trustees*, of whom, with your acquiescence, I shall *name you* one, Mr. Parker another,[60] and two more, on whom I am not yet determined.

Pray let me hear from you soon. Remember me to Mrs. Hanson, whom I hope to see on her return. Present my best respects to the young lady, and believe me, etc.,

Byron

[To John Hanson]

Newstead Abbey, Notts. January 15th. 1809

My dear Sir,

I am much obliged by your kind invitation, but wish you if possible to be here on the 22d.[61] your presence will be of great service, every thing is prepared for your reception exactly as if I remained, & I think Hargreaves will be gratified by the appearance of the place, and the *humours* of the *day*.—I shall on the first opportunity pay my respects to your family, and though I will not trespass on your hospitality on the 22d. my obligation is not less for your agreeable offer, which on any other occasion would be immediately accepted, but I wish you much to be present at the festivities, and I hope you will add *Charles* to the party.—Consider as The Courtier says in the tragedy of 'Tom Thumb'[62]

> This is a day your majesties may boast of it
> 'And since it never can come o'er, tis fit you make the most of it.

I shall take my seat as soon as circumstances will admit, I have not yet chosen my side in politics, nor shall I hastily commit myself with professions, or pledge

---

[59] That is, the East India Company, which ran Britain's Indian colonies as a private concern until 1858, when the Government took direct control.

[60] Byron's cousin Peter Parker, son of the aunt to whom he wrote his first letter, 8 November 1798.

[61] Byron outlines the traditional country-house based celebrations of the heir's coming of age on 22 January, which his legal adviser would be expected to attend. (He did not go himself.)

[62] See Kane O'Hara, *Tom Thumb; a Burletta, Altered from Henry Fielding* (1805), I. i. 18–20.

my support to any man or measures, but though I shall not run headlong into opposition, I will studiously avoid a connection with ministry.—I cannot say that my opinion is strongly in favour of either party, on the one side we have the late underlings of Pitt, possessing all his ill Fortune, without his Talents, this may render their failure more excusable, but will not diminish the public contempt; on the other we have the ill assorted fragments of a worn out minority, Mr. Windham with his Coat *twice* turned, and my Lord Grenville who perhaps has more sense than he can make a good use of;—between the two, and the *Shuttlecock* of both, is Sidmouth & Co. and the general *football* Sir F. Burdett, kicked at by all, and owned by none.[63]————I shall stand aloof, speak what I think, but not often, nor too soon, I will preserve my independence, if possible, but if involved with a party, I will take care not to be the *last* or *least* in the Ranks.—As to *patriotism* The word is obsolete,[64] perhaps improperly so, for all men in this country are patriots, knowing that their own existence must stand or fall with the Constitution, yet every body thinks he could alter it for the better, & govern a people, who are in fact easily governed but always claim the privilege of grumbling.—So much for Politics, of which I at present know little, & care less, by and bye, I shall use the Senatorial privilege of talking, and indeed in such times, and in such a crew, it must be difficult to hold one's tongue.————
Believe me to be with great Sincerity

yours very affectly
Byron

[To John Hanson]

Reddish's Hotel February 4th. 1809

Dear Sir,

I have been thinking of the alteration of my will, & you may *make* the heir at least succeed, but in the event of his demise without issue, the property must go to

---

[63] A fair summary of British politics in 1809, despite Byron's demurral. The early death of William Pitt the Younger (1759–1806) created a political vacuum, not filled by Whig opponents like William Windham (1750–1810; nicknamed 'Weathercock' for his changing view of the war with France) and Baron Grenville (1759–1834). Viscount Sidmouth (1757–1844) eventually became a pronounced Tory, opposed by Radicals in the House of Parliament like Sir Francis Burdett (1770–1844), whom Byron would later support there.

[64] Samuel Johnson's remark of 1775 to the effect that patriotism is 'the last refuge of the scoundrel' is one we tend to misunderstand, being on the other side of the political development Byron describes. For Johnson a 'patriot' was a political radical, who denied the rights of the reigning monarch by appealing to immemorial and inalienable rights of the English citizen.

my Sister's children & the Trevannions, for no Branch of Richard's shall inherit if I can prevent it.—Lucy's annuity may be reduced to fifty pounds, and other fifty go to the Bastard.[65] All the rest may stand.—I remain yours very truly

Byron

[To Mrs Catherine Gordon Byron]

8 St. Ja[mes]'s Street. Mch. 6th. 1809

Dear Mother,

My last Letter was written under great depression of spirits from poor Falkland's death, who has left without a shilling four children and his wife, I have been endeavouring to assist them, which God knows, I cannot do as I could wish from my own embarrassments & the many claims upon me from other quarters.[66]——What you say is all very true, come what may! *Newstead* and I *stand* or fall together, I have now lived on the spot, I have fixed my heart upon it, and no pressure present or future, shall induce me to barter the last vestige of our inheritance; I have that Pride within me, which will enable me to support difficulties, I can endure privations, but could I obtain in exchange for Newstead Abbey the first fortune in the country, I would reject the proposition.—Set your mind at ease on that score. Mr. Hanson talks like a man of Business on the subject, I feel like a man of honour, and I will not sell Newstead.—I shall get my seat on the return of the affidavits from Carhais in Cornwall,[67] and will do something in the house soon, I must dash, or it is all over.—My Satire must be kept secret for a *month*, after that you may say what you please on the subject.— Ld. Carlisle has used me so infamously & refused to state any particular of my family to the Chancellor, I have *lashed* him in my rhymes, and perhaps his Lordship

---

[65] Byron's heir, George Anson Byron (1789–1868), duly succeeded in 1824; he was the son of 'Mad Jack's' younger brother—also called George Anson Byron—whose father, Admiral John 'Foul-weather Jack' Byron (brother to the 'Wicked Lord'), had married into the Cornish Trevanion family. Richard Byron was the younger brother of the admiral. Lucy was a maid at Newstead, pregnant with Byron's illegitimate child. (It proved to be a boy, and inspired his poem 'To My Son'; *CPW* i. 210–11.)

[66] Captain Charles Cary, ninth Lord Falkland (1768–1809), whom Byron had befriended in London, was killed in a drunken quarrel, leaving his pregnant wife destitute. Byron became godfather to the child, and gave £500 to his widow—a sum he left hidden in a teacup after visiting her to prevent embarrassment. She then embarrassingly developed a crush on him.

[67] Because Lord Carlisle had refused to sponsor his entry to the Lords Byron needed to establish his pedigree, which clearly involved some paperwork relating to his Trevanion relatives.

may regret not being more conciliatory.———They tell me it will have a sale, I hope
so for the Bookseller has behaved well as far as publishing well goes.—

Believe me yours truly
Byron

———❦———

P. S.—*You shall have a mortgage on one of the* farms.—

[To John Hanson]

Newstead Abbey. Notts. April 8th. 1809

Dear Sir,

It is of the utmost consequence I should learn whether you have procured me a
mortgage on Newstead, or if not, or if I do not hear from you directly I must
raise money on very bad terms next week.—I have taken the Malta Packet for
May, and if not ready shall forfeit my passage money and Baggage part of which
is sent off.—Pray write

yours truly
Byron

[To John Hanson]

Newstead Abbey. Notts. April 16th. 1809

Dear Sir,

If the consequences of my leaving England, were ten times as ruinous as you
describe, I have no alternative, there are circumstances which render it absolutely indispensible, and quit the country I must immediately.—
My passage is taken, and the 6th of May will be the day of my departure from
Falmouth, I shall be in town on the 22d. of this month, and must raise money on
any terms, all I now look forward [to] is this one object, I have nothing further to
say on the subject.—I had given the Mason the draft,[68] which I am sorry for, but

---

[68] I take this mason's bill to relate to Byron's beloved Newfoundland, Boatswain, who died on 10
November 1808, and who has a memorial in the grounds of Newstead: 'Near this spot are deposited

I trust you will not dishonour it & *me*.—I am pestered to death in country and town, and rather than submit to my present situation, I would abandon every thing, even had I not still stronger motives for urging my departure.—I remain

yours very truly
Byron

[To Mrs Catherine Gordon Byron]

8 St. James's Street. May nineteen 1809

Dear Mother,

I have detected Fletcher in a connection with prostitutes, and of taking to a woman of the town the very boy whom I had committed to his charge,[69] which lad he sent home with a lie in his mouth to screen them both, after the most strict injunctions on my part to watch over his *morals*, & keep him from the *temptations* of this *accursed place*.—I have sent the lad to his father; before this occurrence he was good hearted, honest, and all I could wish him, and would have been so still, but for the machinations of the scoundrel who has not only been guilty of adultery, but of depraving the mind of an innocent stripling, for no other motive, but that which actuates the devil himself, namely, to plunge another in equal infamy.——For his wife's sake he shall have a farm or other provision of some kind, but he quits me the moment I have provided a servant.—I sail on the 16th June.——Break this business to his wife, who will probably hear it from the boy's relatives in another manner.—Did you ever hear any thing so diabolical? he did not even deny it, for I found the address of the strumpet, written in *his own hand*, which I have sent in a letter to Mealey, pray get the paper from M. and *keep* it *carefully*. I have a reason for it.——

Pray write soon, and believe me

yrs ever
Byron

the remains of one who possessed beauty without vanity, strength without insolence, courage without ferocity, and all the virtues of man without his vices', and so forth.

[69] Robert Rushton, whom Byron took to Europe as a sort of page, but soon sent home. See the following letter for Byron's change of heart.

[To Joseph Murray]

8 St. James's Street, June 6, 1809

Mr. Murray, the moment you receive this you will set off for London in some of the coaches with Robert, & take care that he conducts himself properly—Be quick.

[To John Hanson]

Wynn's Hotel. Falmouth June 21st. 1809

Dear Sir,

As it is probable the Packet will not sail for some days, let my Letters of Credit be sent if possible either to the Post office or to this Inn.—Believe me

yrs. &c.
Byron

2
THE GRAND TOUR

June 1809–July 1811

When Byron left London for Falmouth on 20 June 1809 he was setting out on the final phase of an English aristocrat's education: a Grand Tour of the Continent. As a rule, this would have meant a stay in Paris, then a passage of the Alps to Turin, and on to Venice, Florence, Rome, and Naples, as the traveller preferred; but Byron was driven south and east, away from France and Italy and towards the Mediterranean, by war. The prospect should have been a noble one in every respect, but Byron's trip was more a matter of escape than of leisurely opportunity, and was financed by £5,000 borrowed from Scrope Davies, rather than by personal superfluity. England was already problematic for him. He had debts amounting to £10,000, which was an immense sum. (Mr Darcy's annual income in Pride and Prejudice is £10,000: three hundred times the average British per capita income at the time.) His future was unclear—whether parliamentary or poetical. And it seems that something else, more perilous, was preying on his mind. He wrote to Hanson on 16 April 1809 that 'If the consequences of my leaving England, were ten times as ruinous as you describe, I have no alternative, there are circumstances which render it absolutely indispensible, and quit the country I must immediately.' What those circumstances were remains a mystery—or a mystification; but certainly the broad hints he drops to Hobhouse and Charles Skinner Matthews suggest that homosexuality—a capital offence in early 19th-century England—may have been involved.

Whether Byron was running away from or towards forbidden pleasures of this kind, the Mediterranean changed his life completely. From the moment of his arrival at Lisbon on 7 July 1809 there is a note of elation and exultation absent in his correspondence before. A British army had arrived to open a second front in the Napoleonic Wars a year before Byron left England, and scored its first major success at Talavera within weeks of his arrival. Against this background, the poet spent a fortnight in Portugal, then travelled south through scenes of recent conflict to Seville (then headquarters of the Spanish Government) and Cadiz before spending ten days at Gibraltar in early August. By the end of the month he was at Britain's other Mediterranean jewel in the crown, Malta, where he nearly fought a duel, but also had his first love affair with a woman of his own class, Mrs Spencer Smith. By mid-September he was heading east again, and made landfall at Patras, at the western end of the Gulf of Corinth, on 26 September—all this courtesy of the Royal Navy's domination of the Mediterranean since the battle of the Nile in 1798.

Now Byron was free of England in a fuller sense. He and Hobhouse pressed further north-west by ship to the port of Prevesa, thence on horseback through Jannina to 'the glittering minarets of Tepalen' (Child Harold's Pilgrimage, ii. 492), in Albania—among the first Englishmen to visit that province of the Ottoman Empire and its ruler, the Ali Pasha. For Byron, it was a revelation: 'Not even the capital city of the Turks on the Bosporus, with its grander mosques and minarets,' Leslie Marchand remarks, 'nor the palace of the Sultan himself could vie in captivating interest with the absolute little court which Ali Pasha had established in this remote and inaccessible region of Albania' (Life, 208).

45

Having witnessed the festivities associated with the start of Ramadan on 8 October, the Englishmen began to retrace their steps on the 23rd. At Jannina a week later Hobhouse noted in his diary, 'Byron is writing a long poem in the Spenserian stanza' (Life, 212), which would become Childe Harold's Pilgrimage—*the most influential long poem of its age (unless Don Juan is regarded as such). On 20 November he and Hobhouse paused at Missolonghi, a swampy port on the Gulf of Corinth. The poet would die there fifteen years later. 'Thus we lived', Byron wrote in 1813, 'one day in the palace of the Pacha & the next perhaps in the most miserable hut of the Mountains—I confess I preferred the former but never quarrelled with the latter' (LJ iii. 97). On Christmas Day they arrived in Athens, having taken in Parnassus, Delphi, and Thebes en route. A fortnight passed before Byron finally visited the Parthenon, the 'Abode of Gods, whose shrines no longer burn' (Childe Harold's Pilgrimage, ii. 22), where Lord Elgin's agent was busily dismantling the marbles.*

On 5 March Byron and Hobhouse set sail for the epicentre of the Ottoman Empire, Constantinople, travelling at a leisurely pace and taking in Smyrna, Ephesus, the Dardanelles, and Troy before arriving at the capital on 13 May 1810. After an audience with Sultan Mahmoud II—Byron's future opponent in the Greek War of Independence—on 10 July, the pair returned to Athens, and Hobhouse went on for home, somewhat to Byron's relief. ('I feel happier, I feel free'; LJ xi. 157.) Without Hobhouse to restrain him, Byron's homosexuality took off, especially in two tours in the western Peloponnese of late July to early August, and mid-September to early October, when he and his 15-year-old companion Nicolo Giraud were both attacked by a dangerous fever. Back in Athens, and staying at the Capuchin monastery with time on his hands, Byron wrote two more satires, conventional by comparison with his travel poem: Hints from Horace, *and* The Curse of Minerva, *placed on the British as punishment for Elgin's vandalism. Ironically the vessel that carried him away from Athens on 22 April contained the last shipment of Elgin's spoils.*

Stuck in quarantine at Malta for the month of May, and suffering the effects of ongoing illness ('viz. a Gonorrhea a Tertian fever, & the Hemorrhoides, all of which I literally had at once'; LJ ii. 58) Byron reviewed his life thus far in a note headed 'Four or five reasons in favour of a change':

1st At twenty three the best of life is over and its bitters double. 2ndly I have seen mankind in various Countries and find them equally despicable, if anything the Balance is rather in favour of the Turks. 3dly I am sick at heart. (LJ ii. 47)

'Neither maid nor youth delights me now', he quoted despondently from Horace's ode to Venus. 'My affairs at home and abroad are gloomy enough', he went on: 'I have outlived all my appetites and most of my vanities aye even the vanity of authorship' (LJ ii. 47–8). His affairs had many surprises remaining in store, and the travel poem in his luggage—'Childe Burun's Pilgrimage' as it was called—would ensure that the vanities of authorship were far from over for him. Whatever the future held, what he called 'the narrow prejudices of an Islander' had been spirited away.

[To Mrs Catherine Gordon Byron]

Falmouth. June 22, 1809

Dear Mother,

I am about to sail in a few days, probably before this reaches you; Fletcher begged so hard that I have continued him in my service, if he does not behave well abroad, I will send him back in a *transport*.—I have a German servant who has been with Mr. Wilbraham in Persia before, and was strongly recommended to me by Dr. Butler of Harrow, Robert, and William, they constitute my whole suite.[1]—I have letters in plenty.—You shall hear from me at different ports I touch upon, but you must not be alarmed if my letters miscarry.—The Continent is in a fine state! an Insurrection has broken out at Paris, and the Austrians are beating Buonaparte, the Tyrolese have risen.[2]—There is a picture of me in oil to be sent down to Newstead soon, I wish the Miss Parkyns's had something better to do than carry my miniature to Nottingham to copy.[3]——Now they have done it, you may ask them to copy the others, which are greater favourites than my own———As to money matters I am ruined, at least till Rochdale is sold,[4] & if that does not turn out well I shall enter the Austrian or Russian service, perhaps the Turkish, if I like their manners, the world is all before me,[5] and I leave England without regret, and without a wish to revisit any thing it contains, except *yourself*, and your present residence.———
Believe me yours ever sincerely

Byron

---

[1] Of these servants the German, Friese, and young Robert Rushton returned to England from Gibraltar in August; William Fletcher stayed with him. By 'letters' in the following sentence, Byron means letters of credit on foreign banks.

[2] Napoleon suffered his first defeat at Aspern in May 1809, at the hands of the Austrians, but returned the favour at Wagram six weeks later. Tyrolese peasants had rebelled against occupation by French and Bavarian troops, and the introduction of conscription, at the same period. There was no general insurrection in Paris in 1809, but ex-Minister Talleyrand and General Malet were both conspiring against Napoleon at the time, and were disgraced for doing so.

[3] See letter of 8 November 1798. The 'picture of me in oil' is the portrait by George Sanders of Byron landing from a boat, painted in 1807 and now in the Royal Collection.

[4] Resuming and selling this coal-rich property in Yorkshire, leased out by the fifth lord, was a financial pipe dream of Byron's for many years. (See letter of 12 October 1823.)

[5] See Milton, *Paradise Lost*, xii. 646.

P. S.—Pray tell Mr. Rushton his son is well, and doing well, so is Murray, indeed better than I ever saw him, he will be back in about a month, I ought to add leaving Murray to my few regrets, as his age perhaps will prevent my seeing him again;[6] Robert I take with me, I like him, because like myself he seems to be a friendless animal. —

[To Charles Skinner Matthews]

Falmouth June 22 [1809]

My dear Mathieu,[7]

I take up the pen which our friend has for a moment laid down merely to express a vain wish that you were with us in this delectable region, as I do not think Georgia itself can emulate in capabilities or incitements to the 'Plen. and optabil.—Coit.'[8] the port of Falmouth & parts adjacent.——We are surrounded by Hyacinths & other flowers of the most fragrant [na]ture, & I have some intention of culling a handsome Bouquet to compare with the exotics we expect to meet in Asia.—One specimen I shall certainly carry off, but of this here-after.—Adieu Mathieu!——

[To Henry Drury]

Falmouth June 25th. 1809

My dear Drury,[9]

We sail tomorrow in the Lisbon packet having been detained till now by the lack of wind and other necessaries, these being at last procured, by this time tomorrow evening we shall be embarked on the vide world of vaters vor all the vorld like Robinson Crusoe.————The Malta vessel not sailing for some weeks we have determined to go by way of Lisbon, and as my servants term it to

---

[6] For Joe Murray, see letter of 22 March 1804.

[7] Matthews (1785–1811), a talented Cambridge crony of both Hobhouse and Byron, homosexual, brilliant, and a political Radical (Byron nicknamed him 'Citoyen'), drowned in the River Cam soon after Byron's return to England. (See *LJ* vii. 230–4 for a complete portrait.)

[8] 'Coitum plenum and optabilem' (full and perfect intercourse): expression for homosexual sex with a boy in Petronius' *Satyricon* (§86: 4). (On his way home from Greece Byron wrote to Hobhouse: 'Tell M that I have obtained above two hundred pl & opt Cs and am almost tired of them' (*LJ* ii. 23).) Hyacinth was a boy beloved by Apollo, killed in an accident with a discus.

[9] Drury (1778–1841) was Byron's tutor at Harrow; see letter of 1 May 1803.

see 'that there *Portingale*' thence to Cadiz and Gibraltar and so on our old route to Malta and Constantinople, if so be that Capt. Kidd our gallant or rather gallows commander understands plain sailing and Mercator, and takes us on our voyage all according to the Chart.————Will you tell Dr. Butler that I have taken the treasure of a servant Friese the native of Prussia Proper into my service from his recommendation.——He has been all among the worshippers of Fire in Persia and has seen Persepolis and all that.—Hobhouse has made woundy prepar-ations for a book at his return, 100 pens two gallons Japan Ink, and several vols best blank is no bad provision for a discerning Public.—I have laid down my pen, but have promised to contribute a chapter on the state of morals, and a further treatise on the same to be entituled 'Sodomy simplified or Paederasty proved to be praiseworthy from ancient authors and modern practice.'—Hob-house further hopes to indemnify himself in Turkey for a life of exemplary chastity at home by letting out his 'fair bodye'[10] to the whole Divan.—Pray buy his missellingany as the Printer's Devil calls it, I suppose 'tis in print by this time.[11] Providence has interposed in our favour with a fair wind to carry us out of its reach, or he would have hired a Faquir to translate it into the Turcoman Lingo.——

> 'The Cock is crowing
> 'I must be going
> 'And can no more
> *Ghost of Gaffer Thumb*[12]

Adieu believe me yours as in duty bound

Byron

turn over

P. S.—We have been sadly fleabitten at Falmouth.—

---

[10] See 'Clerk Saunders' in Walter Scott, *Minstrelsy of the Scottish Border* (1802–3). The Divan was a council of the sultan of the Ottoman Empire.

[11] For Hobhouse's miscellany see letter of 3 April 1810.

[12] See Kane O'Hara, *Tom Thumb; a Burletta, Altered from Henry Fielding* (1805), I. iv. 23–5.

[To Francis Hodgson]

Falmouth Roads—June 30th 1809

1

Huzza! Hodgson,[13] we are going,
  Our embargo's off at last
Favourable Breezes blowing
  Bend the canvass oer the mast,
From aloft the signal's streaming
  Hark! the farewell gun is fired,
Women screeching, Tars blaspheming,
  Tell us that our time's expired
    Here's a rascal
    Come to task all
  Prying from the custom house,
    Trunks unpacking
    Cases cracking
  Not a corner for a mouse
Scapes unsearched amid the racket,
Ere we sail on board the Packet.—

2

Now our boatmen quit their mooring
  And all hands must ply the oar;
Baggage from the quay is lowering,
  We're impatient—push from shore—
'Have a care! that Case holds liquor
  'Stop the boat—I'm sick—oh Lord!
'Sick, Maam! damme, you'll be sicker
  Ere you've been an hour on board
    Thus are screaming
    Men & women
  Gemmen, Ladies, servants, Jacks,
    Here entangling
    All are wrangling
  Stuck together close as wax,

---

[13] Hodgson (1781–1852) was a tutor at King's College, Cambridge, and a clergyman, whom Byron delighted in teasing, but whom he also helped financially on numerous occasions.

Such the genial noise & racket
Ere we reach the Lisbon Packet,

3

Now we've reached her, lo! the Captain
   Gallant Kidd commands the crew
Passengers *now* their berths are clapt in
   Some to grumble, some to spew,
Heyday! call you that a Cabin?
   Why tis hardly three feet square
Not enough to stow Queen Mab in,
   Who the deuce can harbour there?
     Who Sir? plenty
     Nobles twenty
   Did at once my vessel fill
     Did they—Jesus!
     How you squeeze us
   Would to God, they did so still:
Then I'd scape the heat and racket
Of the good ship, Lisbon Packet.

Note+ Erratum—
   For 'gallant' read 'gallows.'—

4

Fletcher, Murray, Bob, where are you?
   Stretched along the deck like logs
Bear a hand—you jolly tar you!
   Here's a rope's end for the dogs,
Hobhouse muttering fearful curses
   As the hatchway down he rolls
Now his breakfast, now his verses
   Vomits forth & damns our souls,
     Here's a stanza
     On Braganza[14]
   Help!—a couplet—no, a cup
     Of warm water,
     What's the matter?
   Zounds! my liver's coming up,

---

[14] Portuguese royal house, 1640–1908. In 1807 they had fled from Portugal to Brazil in the face of Napoleon's invading army.

I shall not survive the racket
Of this brutal Lisbon Packet.—

5

Now at length we're off for Turkey,
   Lord knows when we shall come back,
Breezes foul, & tempests murkey,
   May unship us in a crack,
But since life at most a jest is
   As Philosophers allow
Still to laugh by far the best is,
   Then laugh on—as I do now,
     Laugh at all things
     Great & small things,
   Sick or well, at sea or shore,
     While we're quaffing
     Let's have laughing
   Who the Devil cares for more?
Some good wine, & who would lack it?
Even on board the Lisbon Packet.

Byron

[To Francis Hodgson]

Lisbon, July 16th, 1809

Thus far have we pursued our route, and seen all sorts of marvellous sights, palaces, convents, &c.—which, being to be heard in my friend Hobhouse's forthcoming Book of Travels, I shall not anticipate by smuggling any account whatsoever to you in a private and clandestine manner. I must just observe that the village of Cintra in Estramadura is the most beautiful, perhaps in the world. * * *

I am very happy here, because I loves oranges, and talk bad Latin to the monks, who understand it, as it is like their own,—and I goes into society (with my pocket-pistols), and I swims in the Tagus all across at once, and I rides on an ass or a mule, and swears Portuguese, and have got a diarrhœa and bites from the mosquitoes. But what of that? Comfort must not be expected by folks that go a pleasuring. * * *

When the Portuguese are pertinacious, I say, 'Carracho!'—the great oath of the grandees, that very well supplies the place of 'Damme,'—and, when dissatisfied with my neighbor, I pronounce him 'Ambra di merdo.'[15] With these two phrases, and a third, 'Avra Bouro,' which signifieth 'Get an ass,' I am universally understood to be a person of degree and a master of languages. How merrily we lives that travellers be!—if we had food and raiment. But, in sober sadness, any thing is better than England, and I am infinitely amused with my pilgrimage as far as it has gone.

To-morrow we start to ride post near 400 miles as far as Gibraltar, where we embark for Melita [Greek name for Malta] and Byzantium. A letter to Malta will find me, or to be forwarded, if I am absent. Pray embrace the Drury and Dwyer and all the Ephesians you encounter. I am writing with Butler's donative pencil, which makes my bad hand worse. Excuse illegibility.[16] * * *

Hodgson! send me the news, and the deaths and defeats and capital crimes and the misfortunes of one's friends; and let us hear of literary matters, and the controversies and the criticisms. All this will be pleasant—'Suave mari magno,' &c.[17] Talking of that, I have been seasick, and sick of the sea. Adieu. Yours faithfully, &c.

[To Mrs Catherine Gordon Byron]

Gibraltar August 11th. 1809

Dear Mother,

I have been so much occupied since my departure from England that till I could address you a little at length, I have forborn writing altogether.—As I have now passed through Portugal & a considerable part of Spain, & have leisure at this place I shall endeavour to give you a short detail of my movements.—We sailed from Falmouth on the 2d. of July, reached Lisbon after a very favourable passage of four days and a half, and took up our abode for a time in that city.—It has been often described without being worthy of description, for, except the view from the Tagus which is beautiful, and some fine churches & convents it contains little but filthy streets & more filthy inhabitants.—To make amends for this the village of Cintra about fifteen miles from the capitol [sic] is perhaps in

---

[15] Perhaps *homem de merda*: 'shit-man' in Portuguese (*hombre de mierda* in Spanish). *Caraljo* translates as 'prick'.

[16] 'Ephesians': friends, companions: a Shakespearian usage. Before Byron left England his Harrow schoolmaster, Dr George Butler, had given him a gold pen.

[17] See Lucretius, *De Rerum Natura*, opening of Book Two, to the effect that it is pleasant to look at a turbulent sea from the safety of the shore.

every respect the most delightful in Europe, it contains beauties of every description natural & artificial, Palaces and gardens rising in the midst of rocks, cataracts, and precipices, convents on stupendous heights a distant view of the sea and the Tagus, and besides (though that is a secondary consideration) is remarkable as the scene of Sir H[ew] D[alrymple]'s convention.[18]—It unites in itself all the wildness of the Western Highlands with the verdure of the South of France. Near this place about 10 miles to the right is the palace of Mafra the boast of Portugal, as it might be of any country, in point of magnificence without elegance, there is a convent annexed, the monks who possess large revenues are courteous enough, & understand Latin, so that we had a long conversation, they have a large Library & asked [me?] if the *English* had *any books* in their country.——I sent my baggage & part of the servants by sea to Gibraltar, and travelled on horseback from Aldea Gallega (the first stage from Lisbon which is only accessible by water) to Seville (one of the most famous cities in Spain where the Government called the Junta is now held) the distance to Seville is nearly four hundred miles & to Cadiz about 90 further towards the Coast.—I had orders from the Government & every possible accommodation on the road, as an English nobleman in an English uniform is a very respectable personage in Spain at present. The horses are remarkably good, and the roads (I assure you upon my honour for you will hardly believe it) very far superior to the best British roads, without the smallest toll or turnpike, you will suppose this when I rode post to Seville in four days, through this parching country in the midst of summer, without fatigue or annoyance.—Seville is a beautiful town, though the streets are narrow they are clean, we lodged in the house of two Spanish unmarried ladies, who possess *six* houses in Seville, and gave me a curious specimen of Spanish manners.—They are women of character, and the eldest a fine woman, the youngest pretty but not so good a figure as Donna Josepha, the freedom of women which is general here astonished me not a little, and in the course of further observation I find that reserve is not the characteristic of the Spanish belles, who are in general very handsome, with large black eyes, and very fine forms.—The eldest honoured your *unworthy* son with very particular attention, embracing him with great tenderness at parting (I was there but 3 days) after cutting off a lock of his hair, & presenting him with one of her own

---

[18] In August 1808, during the first phase of the Peninsular War, the British concluded a disastrous peace treaty with the French army at Cintra, outside Lisbon. The allied commander, Sir Arthur Wellesley (future Duke of Wellington), had defeated General Junot completely, but the negotiations supervised by Sir Hew Dalrymple allowed the French army to be shipped home courtesy of the Royal Navy, with whatever they were carrying. Many in England were scandalized, including William Wordsworth, who wrote a pamphlet on the affair. It is also treated in *Childe Harold's Pilgrimage*, Canto One.

about three feet in length, which I send, and beg you will retain till my return.[19]—Her last words were 'Adio tu hermoso! me gusto mucho' 'Adieu, you pretty fellow you please me much.'—She offered a share of her apartment which my *virtue* induced me to decline, she laughed and said I had some English 'Amante,' (lover) and added that she was going to be married to an officer in the Spanish army.—I left Seville and rode on to Cadiz! through a beautiful country, at Xeres where the Sherry we drink is made I met a great merchant a Mr. Gordon of Scotland, who was extremely polite and favoured me with the Inspection of his vaults & cellars, so that I quaffed at the Fountain head.—Cadiz, sweet Cadiz! is the most delightful town I ever beheld, very different from our English cities in every respect except cleanliness (and it is as clean as London) but still beautiful and full of the finest women in Spain, the Cadiz belles being the Lancashire witches of their land.[20]—Just as I was introduced and began to like the grandees I was forced to leave it for this cursed place, but before I return to England I will visit it again.—The night before I left it, I sat in the box at the opera with Admiral Cordova's family, he is the commander whom Ld. St. Vincent defeated in 1797,[21] and has an aged wife and a fine daughter.——Signorita Cordova the girl is very pretty in the Spanish style, in my opinion by no means inferior to the English in charms, and certainly superior in fascination.—Long black hair, dark languishing eyes, *clear* olive complexions, and forms more graceful in motion than can be conceived by an Englishman used to the drowsy listless air of his country-women, added to the most becoming dress & at the same time the most decent in the world, render a Spanish beauty irresistible. I beg leave to observe that Intrigue here is the business of life, when a woman marries she throws off all restraint, but I believe their conduct is chaste enough before.—If you make a proposal which in England would bring a box on the ear from the meekest of virgins, to a Spanish girl, she thanks you for the honour you intend her, and replies 'wait till I am married, & I shall be too happy.'—This is literally & strictly true.—Miss C & her little brother understood a little French, and after regretting my ignorance of the Spanish she proposed to become my preceptress in that language; I could only reply by a low bow, and express my regret that I quitted Cadiz too soon to permit me to make the progress which would doubtless attend my studies under so charming a directress; I was standing at the back of the box which resembles our opera boxes (the theatre is large and finely decorated, the music admirable) in the

---

[19] Mrs Byron obeyed her son's instruction, and this Spanish keepsake is still preserved in the Byron collection at the National Library of Scotland.

[20] Byron alludes to a famous trial of a dozen witches from Pendle, Lancashire, in 1612—though they were accused of murder, not seduction.

[21] In 1797 the British admiral John Jervis won a famous victory over the Spanish fleet (then allied to France) at Cape St Vincent, off southern Portugal, and was made an earl as a result.

manner which Englishmen generally adopt for fear of incommoding the ladies in front, when this fair Spaniard dispossessed an old women (an aunt or a duenna) of her chair, and commanded me to be seated next herself, at a tolerable distance from her mamma.—At the close of the performance I withdrew and was lounging with a party of men in the passage, when 'en passant' the Lady turned round and called me, & I had the honour of attending her to the Admiral's mansion.—I have an invitation on my return to Cadiz which I shall accept, if I repass through the country on my way from Asia.—I have met Sir John Carr Knight errant at Seville & Cadiz, he is a pleasant man.[22]—I like the Spaniards much, you have heard of the battle near Madrid, & in England they will call it a victory, a pretty victory! two hundred officers and 5000 men killed all English, and the French in as great force as ever.[23]—I should have joined the army but we have no time to lose before we get up the Mediterranean & Archipelago,—I am going over to Africa tomorrow, it is only six miles from this Fortress.—My next stage is Cagliari in Sardinia where I shall be presented to his S[ardinian] Majesty, I have a most superb uniform as a court dress, indispensable in travelling.—

August 13th

I have not yet been to Africa, the wind is contrary, but I dined yesterday at Algesiras with Lady Westmoreland[24] where I met General Castanos the celebrated Spanish leader in the late & present war, today I dine with him, he has offered me letters to Tetuan in Barbary for the principal Moors, & I am to have the house for a few days of one of their great men, which was intended for Lady W, whose health will not permit her to cross the Straits.—

August 15th

I could not dine with Castanos yesterday, but this afternoon I had that honour, he is pleasant, & for aught I know to the contrary, clever,—I cannot go to Barbary, the Malta packet sails tomorrow & myself in it, Admiral Purvis with whom I dined at Cadiz gave me a passage in a frigate to Gibraltar, but we have no ship of war destined for Malta at present, the Packets sail fast & have good accommodations, you shall hear from me on our route, Joe Murray delivers this, I have sent him & the boy back, pray shew the lad any kindness as he is my great

---

[22] Carr (1772–1832) was the author of travel books on France and Holland, gathering materials for *Descriptive Travels in the Southern and Eastern Parts of Spain and the Balearic Isles in the Year 1809* (1811).

[23] Wellesley defeated the French at great cost in allied casualties at the battle of Talavera, 27–8 July 1809. He was made Viscount Wellington after the victory.

[24] Jane Saunders (1779–1857), wife of Conservative politician Lord Westmorland and London socialite, also on her travels.

favourite, I would have taken him on <but you *know boys* are not *safe* among the Turks.—> Say this to his father, who may otherwise think he has behaved ill.— [I hope] This will find you well, believe me yours ever sincerely—

Byron

⟨⟨⟨⟩⟩⟩

P.S.—So Ld. Grey is married to a rustic, well done![25] *if I wed I will bring you home a sultana with half a score cities for a dowry, and reconcile you to an Ottoman daughter in law with a bushel of pearls not larger than ostrich eggs or smaller than Walnuts.——*

[To Captain Cary[26]]

3. Strada di Torni [Valletta, Malta] Sept. 18th. 1809

Sir,

The marked insolence of your behaviour to me the first time I had the honour of meeting you at table, I should have passed over from respect to the General, had I not been informed that you have since mentioned my name in a public company with comments not to be tolerated, more particular after the circumstance to which I allude.—I have only just heard this, or I should not have postponed this letter to so late a period.—As the vessel in which I am to embark must sail the first change of wind, the sooner our business is arranged the better.—Tomorrow morning at 6 will be the best hour, at any place you think proper, as I do not know where the officers and *gentlemen* settle these affairs in your Island.—The favour of an immediate answer will oblige

your obedt. Sert.
Byron

---

[25] For Baron Grey de Ruthyn, see letter of 11 November 1804. In June 1809, a year after his departure from Newstead, Lord Grey married a commoner. In little more than a year he would be dead, aged 30.

[26] Aide-de-camp to the Military Commander of Malta, General Hildebrand Oakes, with whom Byron was dining when some episode had occurred. Since that evening it seems Cary had been spreading gossip about Byron and Mrs Smith. (See letter of 3 May 1810.) Byron left Malta the following day.

[To Mrs Catherine Gordon Byron]

Prevesa. Nov. 12th. 1809

My dear Mother,

I have now been some time in Turkey: this place is on the coast but I have traversed the interior of the province of Albania on a visit to the Pacha.—I left Malta in the Spider a brig of war on the 21st. of Septr. & arrived in eight days at Prevesa.—I thence have been about 150 miles as far as Tepaleen his highness's country palace where I staid three days.—The name of the Pacha is Ali, & he is considered a man of the first abilities, he governs the whole of Albania (the ancient Illyricum) Epirus, & part of Macedonia, his Son *Velly* Pacha to whom he has given me letters governs the Morea & he has great influence in Egypt, in short he is one of the most powerful men in the Ottoman empire.[27]—When I reached Yanina the capital after a journey of three days over the mountains through a country of the most picturesque beauty, I found that Ali Pacha was with his army in Illyricum besieging Ibraham Pacha in the castle of Berat.—He had heard that an Englishman of rank was in his dominions & had left orders in Yanina with the Commandant to provide a house & supply me with every kind of necessary, *gratis*, & though I have been allowed to make presents to the slaves &c. I have not been permitted to pay for a single article of household consumption.—I rode out on the viziers horses & saw the palaces of himself & grandsons, they are splendid but too much ornamented with silk & gold.—I then went over the mountains through Zitza a village with a Greek monastery (where I slept on my return) in the most beautiful Situation (always excepting Cintra in Portugal) I ever beheld.—In nine days I reached Tepaleen, our Journey was much prolonged by the torrents that had fallen from the mountains & intersected the roads. I shall never forget the singular scene on entering Tepaleen at five in the afternoon as the Sun was going down, it brought to my recollection (with some change of *dress* however) Scott's description of Branksome Castle in his lay, & the feudal system.[28]—The Albanians in their dresses (the most magnificent in the world, consisting of a long *white kilt*, gold worked cloak, crimson velvet gold

---

[27] Ali Pasha (1740–1822), the 'Lion of Yannina', a cruel but effective ruler of what is now Albania and northern Greece ('Epirus'), down to the Gulf of Corinth, who played ducks and drakes with Britain and France as it suited him during the Napoleonic Wars. At the time of Byron's visit he was allied with Britain—which accounts for the fulsome welcome he extended to the poet. Later he rebelled against the Ottoman Empire and died in battle at the age of 82; his tomb remains in Ioannina. His son Veli Pasha (whom Byron met in 1810) ruled the Greek province of Morea—nowadays known as the Peloponnese.

[28] See the opening of Walter Scott's *The Lay of the Last Minstrel* (1805).

laced jacket & waistcoat, silver mounted pistols & daggers,) the Tartars with their high caps, the Turks in their vast pelises & turbans, the soldiers & black slaves with the horses, the former stretched in groupes in an immense open gallery in front of the palace, the latter placed in a kind of cloister below it, two hundred steeds ready caparisoned to move in a moment, couriers entering or passing out with dispatches, the kettle drums beating, boys calling the hour from the minaret of the mosque, altogether, with the singular appearance of the building itself, formed a new & delightful spectacle to a stranger.—I was conducted to a very handsome apartment & my health enquired after by the vizier's secretary 'a la mode de Turque.'—The next day I was introduced to Ali Pacha, I was dressed in a full suit of Staff uniform with a very magnificent sabre &c.——The Vizier received me in a large room paved with marble, a fountain was playing in the centre, the apartment was surrounded by scarlet Ottomans, he received me *standing*, a wonderful compliment from a Mussulman, & made me sit down on his right hand.—I have a Greek interpreter for general use, but a Physician of Ali's named [Secularió?] who understands Latin acted for me on this occasion.— His first question was why at so early an age I left my country? (the Turks have no idea of travelling for amusement) he then said the English Minister Capt. Leake[29] had told him I was of a great family, & desired his respects to my mother, which I now in the name of Ali Pacha present to you. He said he was certain I was a man of birth because I had small ears, curling hair, & little white hands, and expressed himself pleased with my appearance & garb.—He told me to consider him as a father whilst I was in Turkey, & said he looked on me as his son.—Indeed he treated me like a child, sending me almonds & sugared sherbet, fruit & sweetmeats 20 times a day.—He begged me to visit him often, and at night when he was more at leisure—I then after coffee & pipes retired for the first time. I saw him thrice afterwards.—It is singular that the Turks who have no heriditary [*sic*] dignities & few great families except the Sultan's pay so much respect to birth, for I found my pedigree more regarded than even my title.—His Highness is 60 years old, very fat & not tall, but with a fine face, light blue eyes & a white beard, his manner is very kind & at the same time he possesses that dignity which I find universal amongst the Turks.—He has the appearance of any thing but his real character, for he is a remorseless tyrant, guilty of the most horrible cruelties, very brave & so good a general, that they call him the Mahometan Buonaparte.—Napoleon has twice offered to make him King of Epirus, but he prefers the English interest & abhors the French as he himself told

---

[29] William Martin Leake (1777–1860), British antiquarian, whose travels in Greece and Asia Minor during the Napoleonic era would be published in the 1820s. He served as British representative at the court of Ali Pasha, and assisted Byron and Hobhouse on the Albanian leg of their journey.

me, he is of so much consequence that he is much courted by both, the Albanians being the most warlike subjects of the Sultan, though Ali is only nominally dependent on the Porte. He has been a mighty warrior, but is as barbarous as he is successful, roasting rebels &c. &c.—Bonaparte sent him a snuffbox with his picture[;] he said the snuffbox was very well, but the picture he could excuse, as he neither liked *it* nor the *original*.—His ideas of judging of a man's birth from ears, hands &c. were curious enough.—To me he was indeed a father, giving me letters, guards, & every possible accommodation.—Our next conversations were of war & travelling, politics & England.—He called my Albanian soldier who attends me, and told him to protect me at all hazards.— His name is Viscillie & like all the Albanians he is brave, rigidly honest, & faithful, but they are cruel though not treacherous, & have several vices, but no mean- nesses.—They are perhaps the most beautiful race in point of countenance in the world, their women are sometimes handsome also, but they are treated like slaves, *beaten* & in short complete beasts of burthen, they plough, dig & sow, I found them carrying wood & actually repairing the highways, the men are all soldiers, & war & the chase their sole occupations, the women are the labourers, which after all is no great hardship in so delightful a climate, yesterday the 11th. Nov. I bathed in the sea, today It is so hot that I am writing in a shady room of the English Consul's with three doors wide open no fire or even *fireplace* in the house except for culinary purposes.—The Albanians [11 lines crossed out] Today I saw the remains of the town of *Actium* near which Anthony lost the world in a small bay where two frigates could hardly manouvre [*sic*], a broken wall is the sole remnant.[30]—On another part of the gulph stand the ruins of Nicopolis built by Augustus in honour of his victory.—Last night I was at a Greek marriage, but this & 1000 things more I have neither time or *space* to describe.—I am going tomorrow with a guard of fifty men to Patras in the Morea, & thence to Athens where I shall winter.—Two days ago I was nearly lost in a Turkish ship of war owing to the ignorance of the captain & crew though the storm was not violent.—Fletcher yelled after his wife, the Greeks called on all the Saints, the Mussulmen on Alla, the Captain burst into tears & ran below deck telling us to call on God, the sails were split, the mainyard shivered, the wind blowing fresh, the night setting in, & all our chance was to make Corfu which is in possession of the French, or (as Fletcher *pathetically* termed it) 'a *watery* grave.'—I did what I could to console Fletcher but finding him incorrigible wrapped myself up in my Albanian capote (an immense cloak) & lay down on deck to wait the worst,

---

[30] A legendary sea battle of 31 BC, at which Mark Antony lost control of the Roman republic to Octavian (later Emperor Augustus). It figures in Shakespeare's *Antony and Cleopatra*, adapted by Dryden in 1677 as *All for Love: or The World Well Lost*.

I have learnt to philosophize on my travels, & if I had not, complaint was useless.—Luckily the wind abated & only drove us on the coast of Suli on the main land where we landed & proceeded by the help of the natives to Prevesa again; but I shall not trust Turkish Sailors in future, though the Pacha had ordered one of his own galleots to take me to Patras, I am therefore going as far as Missolonghi by land & there have only to cross a small gulph to get to Patras.—Fletcher's next epistle will be full of marvels, we were one night lost for *nine* hours in the mountains in a *thunder* storm, & since nearly wrecked, in both cases Fletcher was sorely bewildered, from apprehensions of famine & banditti in the first, & drowning in the second instance.—His eyes were a little hurt by the lightning or crying (I dont know which) but are now recovered.—When you write address to me at Mr. *Strané's* English Consul, Patras, Morea.——I could tell you I know not how many incidents that I think would amuse you, but they crowd on my mind as much as would swell my paper, & I can neither arrange them in the one, or put them down on the other, except in the greatest confusion & in my usual horrible hand.—I like the Albanians much, they are not all Turks, some tribes are Christians, but their religion makes little difference in their manner or conduct; they are esteemed the best troops in the Turkish service.—I lived on my route two days at once, & three days again in a Barrack at Salora, & never found soldiers so tolerable, though I have been in the garrisons of Gibraltar & Malta & seen Spanish, French, Sicilian & British troops in abundance, I have had nothing stolen, & was always welcome to their provision & milk.—Not a week ago, an Albanian chief (every village has its chief who is called Primate) after helping us out of the Turkish Galley in her distress, feeding us & lodging my suite consisting of Fletcher, a Greek, Two Albanians, a Greek Priest and my companion Mr. Hobhouse, refused any compensation but a written paper stating that I was well received, & when I pressed him to accept a few sequins, 'no, he replied, I wish you to love me, not to pay me.' These were his words.—It is astonishing how far money goes in this country, while I was in the capital, I had nothing to pay by the vizier's order, but since, though I have generally had sixteen horses & generally 6 or 7 men, the expence has not been *half* as much as staying only 3 weeks in Malta, though Sir A[lexander]. Ball the governor gave me a house for nothing, & I had only *one servant*.—By the bye I expect Hanson to remit regularly, for I am not about to stay in this province for ever, let him write to me at Mr. Strané's, English Consul, Patras.—The fact is, the fertility of the plains are wonderful, & specie is scarce, which makes this remarkable cheapness.—I am now going to Athens to study modern Greek which differs much from the ancient though radically similar.—I have no desire to return to England, nor shall I unless compelled by absolute want & Hanson's neglect, but I shall not enter Asia for a year or two as I have much to see in Greece & I may perhaps cross into Africa at least the

Ægyptian part.—Fletcher like all Englishmen is very much dissatisfied, though a little reconciled to the Turks by a present of 80 piastres from the vizier, which if you consider every thing & the value of specie here is nearly worth ten guineas English.—He has suffered nothing but from *cold,* heat, & vermin which those who lie in cottages & cross mountains in a wild country must undergo, & of which I have equally partaken with himself, but he is not valiant, & is afraid of robbers & tempests.—I have no one to be remembered to in England, & wish to hear nothing from it but that you are well, & a letter or two on business from Hanson, whom you may tell to write.—I will write when I can, & beg you to believe me,

yr affect. Son
Byron

P. S.—I have some very 'magnifique' Albanian dresses the only expensive articles in this country they cost 50 guineas each & have so much gold they would cost in England two hundred.[31]*—I have been introduced to Hussein Bey, & Mahmout Pacha both little boys grandchildren of Ali at Yanina. They are totally unlike our lads, have painted complexions like rouged dowagers, large black eyes & features perfectly regular. They are the prettiest little animals I ever saw, & are broken into the court ceremonies already, the Turkish salute is a slight inclination of the head with the hand on the breast, intimates always kiss, Mahmout is ten years old & hopes to see me again, we are friends without understanding each other, like many other folks, though from a different cause;—he has given me a letter to his father in the Morea, to whom I have also letters from Ali Pacha.—*

[To John Hanson]

Prevesa. Novr. 12th. 1809

Sir,

I have just written to Mrs. Byron a long letter, she will inform you of my late movements if they chance to interest you.—I write to you pursuant to my intention at every possible convenient opportunity to inform you I am alive, & the reason I write frequently is that some letters probably may not reach their

---

[31] Byron's portrait in Albanian costume, painted by Thomas Phillips in the summer of 1813, now hangs in the National Portrait Gallery, London. In 1814 Byron gave the costume to the socialite Miss Mercer Elphinstone for a fancy-dress party (see *LJ* iv. 112).

destination. I have been travelling in the interior on a visit to the Pacha who received me with great distinction but of this & other matters Mrs. Bn. can inform you, I find Turkey better than Spain or Portugal though I was not displeased with them.—I have been nearly wrecked in a Turkish vessel, the Captain gave all up for lost, but the wind changed & saved us.—I have also been lost in the mountains a whole night in a thunder storm, & if these petty adventures afford you any amusement Mrs. B. (if she receives my letter) can give you a full detail.—I am going to pass a year in Greece before I enter Asia, if you write, address to me at Mr. Strané's English Consul Patras, Morea.—I have no wish to return to England, nor shall I do so unless compelled by necessity.—I am now going to Athens to study the modern Greek which differs from the ancient. Now for my affairs,—I have received not a single letter since I left England,—my copyholds I presume are sold, & my debts in some train, what surplus may be of Rochdale, I should wish to convert into annuities for my own life on good security & tolerable interest, or on good mortgages, if nothing remains, sorry as I should be & much as I should regret it Newstead must go for the sake of justice to all parties, & the surplus be disposed of in like manner in annuities or mortgage.—I still wish to preserve it, though I never may see it again, I never will revisit England if I can avoid it, it is possible I may be obliged to do so lest it should be said I left it to avoid the consequences of my Satire, but I will soon satisfy any doubts on that head if necessary & quit it again, for it is no country for me.—Why I say this is best known to myself, you recollect my impatience to leave it, you also know by what I then & still write that it was not to defraud my creditors, I believe you know me well enough to think no motive of personal fear of any kind would induce me to such a measure; it certainly was none of these considerations, but I never will live in England if I can avoid it, *why* must remain a secret, but the farther I proceed the less I regret quitting it. The country I am now in is extremely cheap from the scarcity of specie & great fertility of the lands in the plains.—I expect to hear from you, & as I have already told you to have fresh remittances as there must be funds long ere now, I also expect some account of my affairs & wish to know what you think Newstead & Rochdale would fetch at a fair price, and what income would accrue from the produce if laid out in the purchase of annuities for my life, or good mortgages.—I beg to be remembered to Mrs. H. & the family

& remain yr. obedt. &c.
Byron

[To Henry Drury]

Salsette frigate. May 3d. 1810
in the Dardanelles off Abydos

My dear Drury,

When I left England nearly a year ago you requested me to write to you.—I will do so.—I have crossed Portugal, traversed the South of Spain, visited Sardinia, Sicily, Malta, and thence passed into Turkey where I am still wandering.—I first landed in Albania the ancient Epirus where we penetrated as far as Mount Tomerit, excellently treated by the Chief Ali Pacha, and after journeying through Illyria, Chaonia, &ctr, crossed the Gulph of Actium with a guard of 50 Albanians and passed the Achelous in our route through Acarnania and Ætolia.—We stopped a short time in the Morea, crossed the gulph of Lepanto and landed at the foot of Parnassus, saw all that Delphi retains and so on to Thebes and Athens at which last we remained ten weeks.—His majesty's ship Pylades brought us to Smyrna but not before we had topographised Attica including of course Marathon, and the Sunian Promontory.—From Smyrna to the Troad which we visited when at anchor for a fortnight off the Tomb of Antilochus, was our next stage, and now we are in the Dardanelles waiting for a wind to proceed to Constantinople.—This morning I *swam* from *Sestos* to *Abydos*, the immediate distance is not above a mile but the current renders it hazardous, so much so, that I doubt whether Leander's conjugal powers must not have been exhausted in his passage to Paradise.[32]—I attempted it a week ago and failed owing to the North wind and the wonderful rapidity of the tide, though I have been from my childhood a strong swimmer, but this morning being calmer I succeeded and crossed the 'broad Hellespont' in an hour and ten minutes.——Well, my dear Sir, I have left my home and seen part of Africa[33] & Asia and a tolerable portion of Europe.—I have been with Generals, and Admirals, Princes and Pachas, Governors and Ungovernables, but I have not time or paper to expatiate. I wish to let you know that I live with a friendly remembrance of you and a hope to meet you again, and if I do this as shortly as possible, attribute it to anything but forgetfulness.—Greece ancient and modern you know too well to require description. Albania indeed I have seen more of than any Englishman

---

[32] The most famous individual to swim from Sestos to Abydos on the Hellespont before Byron was the legendary Leander, who made the trip each night to visit Hero, a priestess of Aphrodite. One night he drowned, and Hero threw herself into the sea in grief. See 'Written after swimming from Sestos to Abydos' (*CPW* i. 281–2).

[33] In fact, Byron never visited Africa; see letter of 11–15 August 1809.

(but a Mr. Leake) for it is a country rarely visited from the savage character of the natives, though abounding in more natural beauties than the classical regions of Greece, which however are still eminently beautiful, particularly Delphi, and Cape Colonna in Attica.—Yet these are nothing to parts of Illyria, and Epirus, where places without a name, and rivers not laid down in maps, may one day when more known be justly esteemed superior subjects for the pencil, and the pen, than the dry ditch of the Ilissus, and the bogs of Bœotia.—The Troad is a fine field for conjecture and Snipe-shooting, and a good sportsman and an ingenious scholar may exercise their feet and faculties to great advantage upon the spot, or if they prefer riding lose their way (as I did) in a cursed quagmire of the Scamander who wriggles about as if the Dardan virgins still offered their wonted tribute. The only vestige of Troy, or her destroyers, are the barrows supposed to contain the carcases of Achilles Antilochus, Ajax , &c. but Mt. Ida is still in high feather, though the Shepherds are nowadays not much like Ganymede.—But why should I say more of these things? are they not written in the *Boke* of Gell?[34] and has not Hobby got a journal? I keep none as I have renounced scribbling.—I see not much difference between ourselves & the Turks, save that we have foreskins and they none, that they have long dresses and we short, and that we talk much and they little.—In England the vices in fashion are whoring & drinking, in Turkey, Sodomy & smoking, we prefer a girl and a bottle, they a pipe and pathic.—They are sensible people, Ali Pacha told me he was sure I was a man of rank because I had *small ears* and hands and *curling hair*.—By the bye, I speak the Romaic or Modern Greek tolerably, it does not differ from the ancient dialects so much as you would conceive, but the pronunciation is diametrically opposite, of verse except in rhyme they have no idea.—I like the Greeks, who are plausible rascals, with all the Turkish vices without their courage.—However some are brave and all are beautiful, very much resembling the busts of Alcibiades, the women not quite so handsome.—I can swear in Turkish, but except one horrible oath, and '*pimp*' and 'bread' and 'water' I have got no great vocabulary in that language.—They are extremely polite to strangers of any rank properly protected, and as I have got 2 servants and two soldiers we get on with great eclât. We have been occasionally in danger of thieves & once of shipwreck but always escaped.—At Malta I fell in love with a married woman and challenged an aid du camp of Genl. Oakes (a rude fellow who grinned at something, I never rightly knew what,) but he explained and apologised, and the lady embarked for

---

[34] According to legend the Scamander at Troy was the site of rituals carried out by local river-nymphs, and certainly the late 19th-century German archaeologist Heinrich Schliemann was convinced that funeral mounds in the region belonged to the heroes of the Trojan War. Sir William Gell (1777–1836) published an early survey, *The Topography of Troy*, in 1804.

Cadiz, & so I escaped murder and adultery.—Of Spain I sent some account to our Hodgson, but I have subsequently written to no one save notes to relations and lawyers to keep them out of my premises.—I mean to give up all connection on my return with many of my best friends as I supposed them, and to snarl all my life, but I hope to have one good humoured laugh with you, and to embrace Dwyer and pledge Hodgson, before I commence Cynicism.—Tell Dr. Butler I am now writing with the gold pen he gave me before I left England, which is the reason my scrawl is more unentelligible [sic] than usual.—I have been at Athens and seen plenty of those reeds for scribbling, some of which he refused to bestow upon me because topographer Gell had brought them from Attica.—But I will not describe, no, you must be satisfied with simple detail till my return, and then we will unfold the floodgates of Colloquoy.—I am in a 36 gun frigate going up to fetch Bob Adair from Constantinople, who will have the honour to carry this letter. And so Hobby's *boke* is out, with some sentimental singsong of mine own to fill up, and how does it take? eh! and where the devil is the 2d Edition of my Satire with additions? and my name on the title page? and more lines tagged to the end with a new exordium and what not, hot from my anvil before I cleared the Channel?— The Mediterranean and the Atlantic roll between me and Criticism, and the thunders of the Hyberborean Review[35] are deafened by the roar of the Helles- pont.—Remember me to Claridge if not translated to College, and present to Hodgson assurances of my high consideration.—Now, you will ask, what shall I do next? and I answer I do not know, I may return in a few months, but I have intents and projects after visiting Constantinople, Hobhouse however will prob- ably be back in September.—On the 2d. of July we have left Albion one year, 'oblitus meorum, obliviscendus et illis,'[36] I was sick of my own country, and not much prepossessed in favour of any other, but I drag on 'my chain' without 'lengthening it at each remove'.—I am like the jolly miller caring for nobody and not cared for.[37] All countries are much the same in my eyes, I smoke and stare at mountains, and twirl my mustachios very independently, I miss no

[35] The *Edinburgh Review*, whose dismissive notice of Byron's *Hours of Idleness* in 1808 inspired *English Bards and Scotch Reviewers*, published anonymously some months before Byron's departure from England. Hobhouse had published *Imitations and Translations* in 1809, bulked out with some poems by Byron himself.

[36] 'Forgetting my friends, and being forgotten by them': a desirable form of life celebrated by Horace in *Epistles*, i. 11. Byron's English quotation is from Oliver Goldsmith's 'The Traveller: or, A Prospect of Society' (1764): 'Where'er I roam, whatever realms to see, | My heart, untravelled, fondly turns to thee: | Still to my brother turns with ceaseless pain, | And drags at each remove a lengthening chain.'

[37] See Isaac Bickerstaffe, *Love in a Village* (1762), I. v. 1–8 (Air 7): 'There was a jolly miller once, | Liv'd on the river Dee; | He work'd, and sung, from morn till night, | No lark more blithe than he. | And this the burthen of his song, | For ever us'd to be, | I care for nobody, not I, | If no one cares for me.'

comforts, and the Musquïtoes that rack the morbid frame of Hobhouse, have luckily for me little effect on mine because I live more temperately.—I omitted Ephesus in my Catalogue, which I visited during my sojourn at Smyrna,—but the temple has almost perished, and St. Paul need not trouble himself to epistolize the present brood of Ephesians who have converted a large church built entirely of marble into a Mosque, and I dont know that the edifice looks the worse for it.—My paper is full and my ink ebbing, Good Afternoon!—If you address to me at Malta, the letter will be forwarded wherever I may be.—Hobhouse greets you, he pines for his poetry, at least some tidings of it.—I almost forgot to tell you that I am dying for love of three Greek Girls at Athens, sisters, two of whom have promised to accompany me to England, I lived in the same house, Teresa, Mariana, and Kattinka are the names of these divinities all of them under 15.[38]—your ταπεινοτατοσ δουλοσ ['most humble servant']

Byron

[To Mrs Catherine Gordon Byron]

Athens. July 20th. 1810

Dear Mother,

I have arrived here in four days from Constantinople which is considered as singularly quick particularly for the season of the year; *you Northern Gentry* can have no conception of a Greek Summer, which however is a perfect Frost compared with Malta, and Gibraltar, where I reposed myself in the *shade* last year after a gentle Gallop of four hundred miles without intermission through Portugal & Spain.—You see by my date that I am at Athens again, a place which I think I prefer upon the whole to any I have seen.—I left Constantinople with Adair at whose audience of leave I saw Sultan Mahmout, and obtained a firman to visit the Mosques of which I think I gave you some description in my last letter, now voyaging towards England in the Salsette frigate in which I visited the plains of Troy, and Constantinople.—My next movement is tomorrow into the Morea, where I shall probably remain a month or two, and then return to winter here if I do not change my plans, which however are very variable as you may suppose, but *none* of them verge to England.—The Marquis of Sligo my old

---

[38] One of Byron's most memorable lyrics, 'Maid of Athens' ('ere we part, | Give, oh give me back my heart!'; *CPW* i. 280–1) was inspired by Teresa Macri, the youngest of these three sisters.

fellow collegian is here, and wishes to accompany me into the Morea, we shall go together for that purpose, but I am already woefully sick of travelling companions after a years experience of Mr. Hobhouse who is on his way to Great Britain.—Ld. S will afterwards pursue his way to the Capitol [sic], and Ld. B. having seen all the wonders in that quarter, will let you know what he does next, of which at present he is not quite certain.—Malta is my perpetual post-office from which my letters are forwarded to all parts of the habitable Globe, by the bye, I have now been in Asia, Africa, and the East of Europe, and indeed made the most of my time, without hurrying over the most interesting scenes of the ancient world.—Fletcher, after having been toasted and roasted, and baked and grilled, and eaten by all sorts of creeping things begins to philosophise, is grown a refined as well as resigned character, and promises at his return to become an ornament to his own parish, and a very prominent person in the future family pedigree of the Fletchers whom I take to be Goths by their accomplishments, Greeks by their acuteness, and ancient Saxons by their appetite.—He (Fletcher) begs leave to send half a dozen sighs to Sally his spouse, and wonders (though I do not) that his ill written and worse spelt letters have never come to hand, as for that matter there is no great loss in either of our letters, saving and except, that I wish you to know we are well and warm enough at this present writing God knows.—You must not expect long letters at present for they are written with the sweat of my brow, I assure you.—It is rather singular that Mr. Hanson has not written a syllable since my departure, your letters I have mostly received, as well as others, from which I conjecture that the man of law is either angry or busy.—I trust you like Newstead and agree with your neighbours, but you know *you* are a *vixen*, is not that a dutiful appellation?—Pray take care of my Books, and several boxes of papers in the hands of Joseph, and pray leave me a few bottles of Champagne to drink for I am very thirsty, but I do not insist on the last article without you like it.—I suppose you have your house full of silly women, prating scandalous things;—have you ever received my picture in oil from Sanders London? it has been paid for these 16 months, why do you not get it?—My Suite consisting of two Turks, two Greeks, a Lutheran, and the nondescript Fletcher, are making so much noise that I am glad to sign myself

yours &c.
Byron

[To John Cam Hobhouse]

Patras. July 29th. 1810

Dear Hobhouse,

The same day, which saw me ashore on Zea [Keos], set me forth once more upon the high seas, where I had the pleasure of seeing the frigate in the *Doldrums* by the light of Sun and Moon.—Before daybreak I got into the Attics at Thaskalio whence I dispatched men to Keratia[39] for horses and in ten hours from landing I was at Athens.—There I was greeted by my Ld. Sligo, and next day Messrs North, Knight, and Fazakerly paid me formal visits.[40]—Sligo has a brig with 50 men who wont work, 12 guns that refuse to go off, and sails that have cut every wind except a contrary one, and then they are as willing as may be.—He is sick of the concern but an Engagement of six months prevents him from parting with this precious Ark.—He *would* travel with me to Corinth, though as you may suppose I was already heartily disgusted with travelling in company.—He has 'en suite' a painter, a captain, a Gentleman misinterpreter (who boxes with the painter) besides sundry idle English Varlets.—We were obliged to have 29 horses in all.—The Captain and the *Drogueman* [*dragoman*: interpreter] were left at Athens to kill bullocks for the crew, and the Marquis & the limner with a ragged Turk by way of Tartar, and the ship's carpenter in the capacity of linguist, with two servants (one of whom had the gripes) clothed both in *leather breeches* (the *Thermometer* 125!!) followed over the hills and far away.—On our route, the poor limner in these gentle latitudes was ever and anon condemned to bask for half an hour that he might produce what he himself termed a 'bellissimo sketche' (pardon the orthography of the last word) of the surrounding country.—You may also suppose that a man of the Marchesa's [Sligo's] kidney was not very easy in his seat, as for the *servants* they and their *leather breeches* were equally immoveable at the end of the first stage.—Fletcher too with his usual acuteness contrived at Megara to ram his damned clumsy foot into a boiling teakettle.—At Corinth we separated, the M[arquis] for Tripolitza, I for Patras. Thus far the ridiculous part of my narrative belongs to others, now comes my turn.—At Vostitza I found my dearly-beloved Eustathius—ready to follow me not only to England, but to Terra Incognita, if so be my compass pointed that way.[41]—This

---

[39] Two harbours near Piraeus, the port of Athens.

[40] Frederick North, fifth Earl of Guilford (1766–1827), Henry Gally Knight (1786–1846), and John Nicholas Fazakerly (1787–1852) were all English philhellenes, travellers, and antiquarians of note.

[41] Eustathius Georgiou, young protégé and—we can assume on the basis of knowing comments elsewhere in Byron's correspondence—lover of the poet. Byron later sent him home: 'he plagued my soul out with his whims, and is besides subject to *epileptic* fits...which made him a perplexing

was four days ago, at present affairs are a little changed.—The next morning I found the dear soul upon horseback clothed very sprucely in Greek Garments, with those ambrosial curls hanging down his amiable back, and to my utter astonishment and the great abomination of Fletcher, a *parasol* in his hand to save his complexion from the heat.—However in spite of the *Parasol* on we travelled very much enamoured, as it should seem, till we got to Patras, where Strané received us into his new house where I now scribble.—Next day he went to visit some accursed cousin and the day after we had a grand quarrel, Strané said I spoilt him, I said nothing, the child was as froward as an unbroken colt, and Strané's Janizary said I must not be surprised, for he was too *true* a *Greek* not to be disagreeable.—I think I never in my life took so much pains to please any one, or succeeded so ill, I particularly *avoided* every thing which *could possibly give* the *least offence* in any *manner*, somebody says that those who try to please will please, this I know not; but I am sure that no one likes to fail in the attempt.—At present he goes back to his father, though he is now become more tractable.—Our *parting* was vastly pathetic, as many kisses as would have sufficed for a boarding school, and embraces enough to have ruined the character of a county in England, besides tears (not on *my* part) and expressions of 'Tenerezza' to a vast amount.— All this and the warmth of the weather has quite overcome me. Tomorrow I will continue, at present 'to bed, 'to bed, 'to bed'.[42]—The youth insists on seeing me tomorrow, the issue of which interview you shall hear.—I wish you a pleasant sleep.—[…]

yours ever
Byron

[To Scrope Berdmore Davies]

Patras, Morea. July 31st. 1810

My dear Davies,

Lord Sligo, who travelled with me a few days ago from Athens to Corinth, informs me that previous to his departure he saw you in London.—Though I do not think you have used me very well in not writing after my very frequent requests to that effect, I shall not give you an opportunity of recriminating, but fill this sheet to remind you of my existence and assure you of my regard, which

companion, in other matters he was very tolerable, I mean as to his *learning*, being well versed in the Ellenics [like 'Greek love', code for homosexuality]' (*LJ* ii. 10).

[42] See *Macbeth*, V. i. 65.

you may accept without scruple, as, God knows, it is no very valuable present.—
As I do suppose that before this time my agents have released you from every
responsibility, I shall say nothing on that head, excepting, that if they have not, it
is proper I should know it immediately, that I may return for that purpose.[43]——Since I left England I have rambled through Portugal, the South of
Spain, touched at Sardinia, Sicily, and Malta, been in the most interesting parts
of Turkey in Europe, seen the Troad and Ephesus, Smyrna, &c. in Asia, *swam* on
the 3d. of May from *Sestos* to Abydos, and finally sojourned at Constantinople,
where I saw the Sultan and visited the interior of the Mosques, went into the
Black Sea, and got rid of Hobhouse. I determined after one years purgatory to
part with that amiable soul, though I like him, and always shall, though I give
him almost as much credit for his good qualities as he does himself, there is
something in his manner &c. in short that will never be any thing but the '*Sow's
Ear*'.——I am also perfectly aware that I have nothing to recommend me as a
Companion, which is an additional reason for voyaging alone.—Besides, I feel
happier, I feel free. 'I can go and I can fly' 'freely to the Green Earths end'[44] and at
present I believe myself to be as comfortable as I ever shall be, and certainly as
I ever have been.—My apparatus for '*flying*' consists of a Tartar, two Albanian
soldiers, a Dragoman, and Fletcher, besides sundry sumpter horses, a Tent, beds
and Canteen.—I have moreover a young Greek in my suite for the purpose of
keeping up and increasing my knowledge of the modern dialect, in which I can
swear fluently, and talk tolerably.—I am almost a Denizen of Athens, residing
there principally when not on the highway.—My next increment from hence is
to visit the Pacha at Tripolitza, and so on to headquarters.—

Hobhouse will arrive in England before this, to him I refer you for all marvels,
he is bursting to communicate, hear him for pity's sake.—He is also in search of
tidings after that bitter 'miscellany', of which we hear nothing, Seaton to be sure
compared him in a letter to Dryden, and somebody else (a Welch physician
I believe) to Pope, and this is all that Hobby has yet got by his book.—I see by the
papers 15th May my Satire is in a third Edition, if I cared much about the matter,
I should say this was poor work, but at present the Thermometer is 125!! and
I keep myself as cool as possible.—In these parts is my Lord of Sligo with a most
innavigable ship, which pertinaciously rejects the addresses of Libs, Notus, and
Auster,[45] talking of ships induces me to inform you that in November last, we
were in peril by sea in a Galliot of the Pacha of Albania, masts by the board, sails

---

[43] See letter of 27 February 1808.

[44] See Milton's *Comus* (1634), 1012–13, where the eponymous spirit boasts: 'I can fly, or I can run |
Quickly to the green earth's end.'

[45] Classical names for the winds: *Lips* (Greek) for the south-west, *Notus* and *Auster* (Greek and
Roman) for the south.

split, captain crying, crew below, wind blowing, Fletcher groaning, Hobhouse despairing, and myself with my upper garments ready thrown open, to swim to a spar in case of accidents; but it pleased the Gods to land us safe on the coast of Suli.—My plans are very uncertain, I may return soon, or perhaps not for another year.—Whenever I do come back it will please me to see you in good plight, I think of you frequently, and whenever Hobhouse unlawfully passed off any of your *good things* as his own, I immediately asserted your claim in all cabins of Ships of war, at tables of Admirals and Generals, Consuls and Ambassadors, so that he has not pilfered a single pun with impunity.—I tell you with great sincerity that I know no person, whom I shall meet with more cordiality.— Address to me at Malta, whence my letters are forwarded to the Levant.—When I was at Malta last,—I fell madly in love with a married woman, and challenged an officer, but the Lady was chaste, and the gentleman explanatory, and thus I broke no commandments.—I desire to be remembered to no one, I have no friends any where, and my acquaintances are I do suppose either incarcerated or made immortal in the Peninsula of Spain.—I lost five guineas by the demise of H. Parker.—Believe me

yours most truly
Byron

P. S.—I believe I have already described my suite, six and myself, as Mr. Wordsworth has it 'we are seven'.[46]*—Tell Mr. E. Ellice that Adair has a letter for him from me to be left at Brookes's.—Adio! I place my name in* modern *Greek on the direction of this letter for your edification.—*

[To John Hanson]

Athens. Novr. 11th. 1810

Dear Sir,

Yours arrived on the first Inst. it tells me I am ruined.—It is in the power of God, the Devil, and Man, to make me poor and miserable, but neither the *second* nor *third* shall make me sell Newstead, and by the aid of the *first* I will persevere in this

---

[46] See Wordsworth's poem of this title in *Lyrical Ballads.*

resolution.—My 'father's house shall *not* be made a den of thieves.'[47]—Newstead shall *not* be sold.—I am some thousand miles from home with few resources, and the prospect of their daily becoming less, I have neither friend nor counsellor, my only English servant departs with this letter, my situation is forlorn enough for a man of my birth and former expectations;—do not mistake this for complaint however, I state the simple fact, and will never degrade myself by lamentations. You have my answer.—Commend me to your family, I perceive Hargreaves is your partner, he always promised to turn out well, and Charles I am sure is a very fine fellow.—As for the others I can't pretend to prophecy, I present my respects to all the ladies, and I suppose I may *kiss* Harriet as you or Mrs. Hanson will be my proxy, provided she is not grown too tall for such a token of remembrance.—I must not forget Mrs. Hanson who has often been a mother to me, and as you have always been a friend I beg you to believe me with all sincerity

yours
Byron

[To Mrs Catherine Gordon Byron]

Athens January 14th. 1811

My dear Madam,

I seize an occasion to write to you as usual shortly but frequently, as the arrival of letters where there exists no regular communication is of course very precarious.—I have received at different intervals several of yours, but generally six months after date, some sooner, some later, and though lately tolerably stationary, the delays appear just the same.—I have lately made several small tours of some hundred or two miles about the Morea, Attica &c. as I have finished my grand Giro by the Troad Constantinople &c. and am returned down again to Athens.—I believe I have mentioned to you more than once that I swam (in imitation of Leander though without his lady) across the Hellespont from Sestos to Abydos. Of this and all other particulars Fletcher whom I have sent home with papers &c. will apprise you.—I cant find that he is any loss, being tolerably master of the Italian & modern Greek languages, which last I am also studying with a master, I can order and discourse more than enough for a reasonable man.—Besides the perpetual lamentations after beef & beer, the stupid bigotted contempt for every thing foreign, and insurmountable incapacity of acquiring even a few words of any language, rendered him like all other

---

[47] See Mark 11: 15–17.

English servants, an incumbrance.—I do assure you the plague of speaking for him, the comforts he required (more than myself by far) the pilaws (a Turkish dish of rice & meat) which he could not eat, the wines which he could not drink, the beds where he could not sleep, & the long list of calamities such as stumbling horses, want of tea!!! &c. which assailed him, would have made a lasting source of laughter to a spectator, and of inconvenience to a Master.—After all the man is honest and in Christendom capable enough, but in Turkey—Lord forgive me, my Albanian soldiers, my Tartars & Janizary worked for him & us too as my friend Hobhouse can testify.—It is probable I may steer homewards in Spring, but to enable me to do that I must have remittances.—My own funds would have lasted me very well, but I was obliged to assist a friend, who I know will pay me, but in the meantime I am out of pocket.—At present I do not care to venture a winter's voyage, even if I were otherwise tired of travelling, but I am so convinced of the advantages of looking at mankind instead of reading about them, and of the bitter effects of staying at home with all the narrow prejudices of an Islander, that I think there should be a law amongst us to set our young men abroad for a term among the few allies our wars have left us.—Here I see and have conversed with French, Italians, Germans, Danes, Greeks, Turks, Armenians, &c. &c. &c. and without losing sight of my own, I can judge of the countries and manners of others.—Where I see the superiority of England (which by the bye we are a good deal mistaken about in many things) I am pleased, and where I find her inferior I am at least enlightened.—Now I might have staid smoked in your towns or fogged in your country a century without being sure of this, and without acquiring anything more useful or amusing at home.—I keep no journal, nor have I any intention of scribbling my travels.—I have done with authorship, and if in my last production I have convinced the critics or the world, I was something more than they took me for, I am satisfied, nor will I hazard *that reputation* by a future effort.—It is true I have some others in manu-script, but I leave them for those who come after me, and if deemed worth publishing, they may serve to prolong my memory, when I myself shall cease to remember.—I have a famous Bavarian Artist taking some views of Athens &c. &c. for me.—This will be better than scribbling, a disease I hope myself cured of.—I hope on my return to lead a quiet and recluse life, but God knows and does best for us all, at least so they say, and I have nothing to object, as on the whole I have no reason to complain of my lot.—I am convinced however that men do more harm to themselves than ever the Devil could do to them. I trust this will find you well and as happy as we can be, you will at least be pleased to hear that I am so &

yours ever
Byron.—

[To John Cam Hobhouse]

Malta. May 15th. 1811

Dear Hobhouse,

Your last 2 letters of 1810 I have just received, they find me on my way homewards, in the beginning of June I sail in the Volage frigate with French prizes and other English ships of war in all I believe 6 or 7 frigates.————I must egotize a little.—I am in bad health & worse spirits, being afflicted in body with what Hostess Quickly in Henry 5th. calls a villainous '*Quotidian Tertian.*' It killed Falstaff & may me. I had it first in the Morea last year, and it returned in Quarantine in this infernal oven, and the fit comes on every other day, reducing me first to the chattering penance of Harry Gill,[48] and then mounting me up to a Vesuvian pitch of fever, lastly quitting me with sweats that render it necessary for me to have a man and horse all night to change my linen.————Of course I am pulled down with a murrain, and as I hear nothing but croaking from H[anson] I am hastening homewards to adjust (if possible) my inadjustable affairs.—*He* wants me to sell N[ewstead]—partly I believe because he thinks it might serve me, and partly I suspect because some of his clients want to purchase it.—I will see them d—d first. I told you I never would sell it in a former letter and I beg to repeat that Negative.—I have told him fifty times to sell Rochdale & he evades and excuses in a very lawyerlike & laudable way.—Tell Davies it is with the greatest regret I see him in such a Situation from which he shall be at all events & at all expence relieved, for if money is not ready I will take the securities on *myself.*————I have looked, asked, and raved after your marbles, and am still looking, asking, & raving, till people think they are my own.[49]—Fletcher was my precursor.—Close, Lander, Mrs. D. have all been examined and declared 'Ignoramus.'—And yet it is so odd that so many packages should have vanished that I shall (in the intervals of my malady) search the surface of the Island.—I am sorry to hear the stationary propensities of your 'Miscellany' and attribute them firstly—to the dead-weight of extraneous productions with which you loaded your own Pegasus, secondly—to the half guinea [price] (one may buy an opera

---

[48] Allusion to Wordsworth's poem, 'Goody Blake and Harry Gill', in which a mean-spirited farmer is cursed with the shivers by an old housewife he catches stealing firewood. For 'quotidian tertian' see *Henry V*, II. i. 114.

[49] Having written *The Curse of Minerva* at the expense of Lord Elgin, Byron was ironically reduced to locating similar souvenirs acquired by his best friend. In fact, Hobhouse's marbles were mixed up with Elgin's and were later traced: see the letter of 15 July.

ticket for less at Hookham's) and thirdly to that 'Walshean' preface[50] from which you & Matttthews predicted such unutterable things. Now what would I do?—cut away the lumber of Ld. Byron, the Honble. G. Lambe, Mr. Bent the Counsellor at Law,[51] and the rest of your contributory friends, castrate that Boccacian tale, expunge the *Walshean* preface (no offence to Matthieu) add some smart things of your own, change the title, and charge only seven & sixpence.——I hear that Jeffrey has promised to review you, this will lift you into life, and seriously speaking, I think your own production would have done much better alone, and the 'Imitations of Juvenal' are certainly as good in their kind as any in our language.——I have completed an Imitation of Horace 'De Arte Poetica' in which you perform the part of *both* the 'Pisos.'[52] I have taken a good deal of pains with it, but wish you to see it before I print, particularly as it is addressed to you.—In one part (I deviate and adapt from the original) I have apostrophized you as a lover of ('Vive la Bagatelle') and it is curious that I should *afterwards* receive a letter from you on the subject of your projected society with that Motto.—I had written the lines without being at all aware of such an intention, and of course am pleased with the coincidence as well as your idea. But more of this in England.—I wish you would fill up your outline with your friends. I have nobody to recommend or to object against, but shall be happy to make a *joint* in the *tail* of your Comet!——I have heard from Matthews, remember me to him most socially, he tells me you have thoughts of betaking shortly to Cambridge, surely this is better than the Militia,—why go abroad again? five and twenty is too late to *ring bells* and write *notes* for a Minister of legation? don't think of such a thing, *read, read, read,* and depend upon it in two years time Fortune or your Father will come round again.——My picture of which you speak is gone to my mother, and if not, it was and is my intention *not* to be *shot* for a long time, and therefore Thou False and foul Insinuator! I repel your surmise, as 'De Wilton' did the Adjuration of the voice from High Cross Edinburgh (see 4th, 5th, or 6th Canto of Marmion),[53] and as it succeeded with him, I trust it will with me, you Unnatural (not Supernatural) Croaker! Avaunt thee Cam! I retort & repel your hint, and hope you yourself will be—shooter of a great many Ptarmigans (or

---

[50] Perhaps Byron is referring to the 'Preface to the Pastorals' included in Dryden's 1697 translation of Virgil's poetical works and ostensibly written by William Walsh, which defends the classic poet from charges of lapsing into vulgarity in his *Eclogues*. Hobhouse made a similar defence of his collection. (See *LJ* vii. 232.)

[51] Jeffrey Hart Bent (1781–1852), Trinity graduate and barrister.

[52] This is *Hints from Horace*, a follow-up to *English Bards and Scotch Reviewers*, not published until 1831. It is based on Horace's *Ars Poetica*, a set of literary-critical observations addressed to his friend Piso and his sons.

[53] Byron is remembering an episode from Walter Scott's *Marmion* (1808), based on the battle of Flodden Field, fought between the Scots and the English in Northumberland in 1513.

men if you like it better), but don't draw me into your parties to shoot or be shotten! for I am determined to come off Conqueror on all such occasions.— I expect letters from you by next packet.—My fantastical adventures I reserve for you and Matthieu and a bottle of Champagne. I parted as I lived friends with all the English & French in Attica, and we had balls, dinners, and amours without number.—I bring you a letter from Cockerell.—Lusieri is also in Malta, and Nicolo whom you remember, who is gone to School here, he was very useful to me at Athens, and it is chiefly through him that I have acquired some knowledge of the Italian & Romaic languages.[54] I was near bringing away Theresa but the mother asked *30 000* piastres!— I had a number of Greek and Turkish women, and I believe the rest of the English were equally lucky, for we were all *clapped.*—I am nearly well again of that distemper, & wish I was as well rid of my 'Quotidian Tertian'——I must go down to Newstead & Rochdale and my mother in a late letter tells me that my property is estimated at above a *hundred thousand pounds* even after all debts &c. are paid off.—And yet I am embarrassed and do not know where to raise a Shilling.———With regard to our acct. dont think of it or let your Father think of it, for I will not hear of it till you are in a state to pay it as easily as so many shillings.—I have fifty resources, & besides my person is parliamentary,[55]—pay your tradesmen,—I am None.—I know your suspicions past & present, but they are ill founded.——Will you meet me in London in July & go down to Rochdale & Notts by way of Cambridge to see Matthieu [?] Leave a direction at Ridgways.—Believe yours

indelibly
B.—

[To Mrs Catherine Gordon Byron]

Volage Frigate. At Sea. June 25th. 1811

Dear Mother,

This letter which will be forwarded on our arrival at Portsmouth (probably about the 4th of July) is begun about 23 days after our departure from Malta.—I have just been two years (to a day on the 2d. of July) absent from England, and

---

[54] Giovanni Battista Lusieri (1755–1821), an Italian painter, served as Lord Elgin's artist and agent in the removal of the Elgin Marbles. His young brother-in-law Nicolo Giraud became Byron's companion (and again, presumably, his lover) on his second excursion to the Peloponnese in September 1810.

[55] Hobhouse had written to Byron on 10 December 1810, listing his debts to the poet, totalling £1,325, and to say that his father had agreed to pay them on his behalf (*Hobhouse Letters*, 61). As a member of the House of Lords, Byron could not be arrested for debt; so, though his financial situation was pressing, Hobhouse's was more so.

I return to it with much the same feelings which prevailed on my departure, viz. indifference, but within that apathy I certainly do not comprise yourself, as I will prove by every means in my power.—You will be good enough to get my apartments ready at Newstead, but don't disturb yourself on any account, particularly mine, nor consider me in any other light than as a visitor.—I must only inform you that for a long time I have been restricted to an entire vegetable diet neither fish or flesh coming within my regimen,[56] so I expect a powerful stock of potatoes, greens, & biscuit, I drink no wine.——I have two servants middle aged men, & both Greeks;—it is my intention to proceed first to town to see Mr. Hanson, & thence to Newstead on my way to Rochdale.—I have only to beg you will not forget my diet, which it is very necessary for me to observe.—I am well in health, as I have generally been, with the exception of two agues, both of which I quickly got over.—My plans will so much depend on circumstances that I shall not venture to lay down an opinion on the subject.—My prospects are not very promising, but I suppose we shall wrestle through life like our Neighbours. Indeed by H[anson]'s last advices I have some apprehensions of finding N——d dismantled by Messrs Brothers &c.[57] and he seems determined to force me into selling it, but he will be baffled.——I dont suppose I shall be much pestered with visitors, but if I am, you must receive them, for I am determined to have nobody breaking in upon my retirement.—You know that I never was fond of society, & I am less so than before.—I have brought you a shawl, & a quantity of Ottar of Roses, but these I must smuggle if possible.—I trust to find my library in tolerable order, Fletcher is no doubt arrived, I shall separate the Mill from Mr. Bowman's farm (for his son is too 'gay a deceiver' to inherit both) & place Fletcher in it, who has served me faithfully, & whose wife is a good woman. Besides, it is necessary to sober young Mr. Bowman, or he will people the parish with bastards.[58]—In a word, if he had seduced a dairy-maid, he might have found something like an apology, but the Girl is his equal, & in high life or low life, reparation is made in such circumstances.——But I shall not interfere further (than like Buonaparte) by diminishing Mr. B's *kingdom*, and erecting part of it into a *principality* for Field Marshal Fletcher!—I hope you govern my little *empire* & it's sad load of national debt, with a wary hand.—To drop my metaphor, I beg leave to subscribe myself

yrs. ever

B.—

---

[56] Byron frequently flirted with vegetarianism as a means of reducing his weight, and his eating habits could alarm his friends, though he was not bulimic.

[57] A Nottingham upholsterers' firm, still owed £1,600 for work carried out at Newstead.

[58] Bowman was a tenant farmer at Newstead who had got a woman pregnant but refused to marry her—an offence Byron had himself been guilty of before leaving England.

[To John Cam Hobhouse]

Reddish's Hotel [London].— July 15th. 1811

My dear Hobhouse,

The day after tomorrow (17th.) I will set out for Sittonbourne [Sittingbourne, Kent], to confabulate, I thank you for your advice, which I shall observe. My *Im[itatio]n* of *Hor[a]ce*, is now transcribing at Cawthorn's,[59] so that I cannot bring the fair Copy, but the moment it is out of his hands you shall have it.—Your marbles are left at the Custom House, Sheerness, as I knew not where to send them, & to smuggle them was impracticable, you will get them on sending a cart or a letter.—I dine with Davies today, he came to me *drunk* last night, & was very friendly, & has got a new set of Jokes, but to you they are doubtless not new.— Drawings I have none, *ready*, but have an excellent Painter in pay in the Levant.— I have brought you *one* (from Cockerell) of Athens, & have in my possession a Romaic Lexicon in three Q[uart]o vols, two or three Greek plays, (i.e. transla- tions from Metastasio & Goldoni) Meletius's Geography (we stole it from the Bishop of Chrysso) a Greek Grammar or two, two live Greeks (both between 30 & 40 yrs. of age & and one of them your old Dragoman Demetrius) & some other Romaic publications (and a manuscript or two which you shall publish as they are very curious if you like) all of which with the owner are as usual very much at your service.—I will bring some books with me

yrs. ever
Byron

[59] The publisher who had issued *English Bards and Scotch Reviewers*. He rejected *Hints from Horace* after a prolonged consideration.

3
CHILDE HAROLD AND CAROLINE LAMB

July 1811–June 1813

When Byron returned to London on Bastille Day, 1811, he in all likelihood felt as many have felt on returning from an extended set of travels away from home: that whereas he had expanded his horizons in almost every direction, everything in England had remained exactly and exasperatingly the same. The same debts; the same circle of cronies from school and university, with nothing much new to report; the same indecision about his career (whether politics or poetry, poetry or politics); the same literary scene, whatever that was worth; the same ineffectual lawyer; the same bothersome mother installed in the same un-remunerative estate in the same provincial county.

All that changed within a matter of weeks. At the end of July Byron heard of his schoolmate John Wingfield's death in the Peninsular War; his mother died from unknown causes, aged 46, on 1 August; his fellow undergraduate and role model, Charles Skinner Matthews, drowned in a pool in Cambridge two days later (whether suicidally or not we do not know); and in October he received news that John Edleston, the Cambridge choirboy he had idolized—'whom I once loved more than I ever loved a living thing, & one who I believe loved me to the last' (LJ ii. 110)—had died as long ago as May. His first letter to his mother from his hotel in Mayfair seems astonishingly formal, but there is no reason to doubt his anguished remark to the housekeeper at Newstead when he came up from London too late to see her still alive: 'Oh, Mrs. By, I had but one friend in the world, and she is gone!' (Life, 285). In response he drew up a preposterous will, charging his executors to bury him in the garden at Newstead alongside his dog Boatswain—it was the first of many theatrical gestures to come.

Still, he had his poems. He thought well of 'Hints from Horace', a tepid satire that might have served as the follow-up to English Bards and Scotch Reviewers, but which remained unpublished until 1831. His proprietorial mentor Robert Charles Dallas, on the other hand, had wit enough to see that 'Childe Burun's Pilgrimage', though a dark horse, had infinitely more running in it, and by the end of August it had found a home under his auspices with the well-established firm of John Murray—then based in the Strand, soon to move to Albemarle Street, Mayfair, where its natural clientele resided. Byron began to add some London literary acquaintance to his Cambridge circle: in particular the 'banker poet' Samuel Rogers, and the Irish bard and bon viveur Thomas Moore. As the fancy took him, he rusticated at Newstead and exercised the droit de seigneur over the maids there, until his heart was well and truly scorched by a Welsh girl, Susan Vaughan, who had the temerity to cheat on him (see letter of 28 January 1812).

On 27 February 1812 Byron gave his maiden speech in the House of Lords (one of only three), opposing a Government bill designed to repress 'frame-breaking' and similar industrial vandalism in the Midlands. The speech was 'full of fancy, wit, and invective', his parliamentary mentor, the Whig Lord Holland recollected, 'but not exempt from affectation nor well reasoned, nor at all suited to our common notions of Parliamentary eloquence' (Life, 322). In that speech he described himself, bleakly, as 'a stranger not only to this house in general, but to almost every individual whose attention I presume to solicit' (CMP 22). Clearly the House was never going to be Byron's home, and just after his speech he anonymously published an even more outspoken poem on the topic, accusing the Parliament of legalized murder (see letter of 1 March 1812).

But politics was forgotten on 10 March 1812, when Childe Harold's Pilgrimage was published and caused an immediate sensation. 'I awoke one morning and found myself famous.' The London elite took up this fascinating misanthrope—a phenomenon in cultural history, it might be said, waiting to happen—with unprecedented alacrity; his beauty, shyness, social unpredictability, and refusal to dance (on account of his crippled foot) only made him more magnetic. One evening in April he was introduced to Lady Caroline Lamb, bored with domesticity, and already infected by Harold-mania. 'I looked earnestly at him, and turned on my heel', she noted; 'My opinion, in my journal was, "mad—bad—and dangerous to know"' (Life, 328). Some time later she added, 'That beautiful pale face is my fate' (Life, 331)—and she never spoke a truer word, remaining infatuated with the poet until her death in 1828.

At first Byron was infatuated in return. His English sexual experience to date, after all, had been restricted to prostitutes and housemaids. Carrying off Lady Caroline (three years older than him, daughter of the Earl of Bessborough, niece of the Duchess of Devonshire, and wife of William Lamb, second son of Lord Melbourne, and future prime minister to Queen Victoria) proved he had arrived as a lord as well as a literary lion. But very soon Lamb's indiscretion—which had been part of her charm when they met—became odious and embarrassing to a man with profoundly traditional views of women and society, and he longed to be free of her importunities and her almost sinister whims. As she became aware of his change of heart her behaviour became increasingly manic and scandalous, until in despair her family dragged her off to Ireland, not before Byron had undertaken to elope with her: a folly from which only John Cam Hobhouse could save him.

In the meantime Byron had found someone much more complaisant and much less complicated: Lady Oxford, fourteen years older than him and a past mistress in the arts of adultery, to whose country house in Hereford he retreated as soon and as frequently as possible. (Lady Oxford was a Whiggish queen bee, too, and fanned what was left of Byron's political ambition.) All these to-ings and fro-ings were set down with novelistic verve in a series of letters to, of all people, Caroline Lamb's mother-in-law, Lady Melbourne—aunt, also, through her own family, to a prudish young lady named Annabella Milbanke, only child of a County Durham baronet, and Byron's future wife. Without his letters to Lady Melbourne this chapter and the next would be greatly impoverished; but it is also true to say that there is something troubling, in its quasi-filial way, about both Byron's attitude to his 60-year-old 'Zia' (auntie) and her attitude to her female relatives.

Affairs with married ladies, pleasant or otherwise, could not help Byron out of his financial predicament. In August 1812 the inevitable was first attempted, and Newstead put up for auction. It sold for £140,000, but the buyer, Thomas Claughton, never made good, and in the end all Byron got was a sacrificed deposit—a handy £25,000. In October, knowing all that she did about Byron's behaviour and his desperation, Lady Melbourne shuffled up some *sort of second-hand proposal to Annabella, which was refused, much to Byron's relief. The following March the plan was for him to escape England with the Oxfords and go to Italy— her husband was notoriously tolerant—but that collapsed. The pressures bearing in on him—financial, sexual, political, and intellectual—found expression in a 400-line poem, 'The Giaour', which broke a three-year writer's block dating back to Greece and early 1810. In May he improved his Whig-cum-Radical political credentials by visiting the editor, journalist, and poet Leigh Hunt, imprisoned for libelling the Prince of Wales. On 1 June Byron gave his last speech in the Lords. His political career was over; his poetic existence was coming back to life; but elsewhere much worse was to come.*

[To Mrs Catherine Gordon Byron]

Reddish's Hotel. July 23d. 1811.
St. James's Street London.

My dear Madam,

I am only detained by Mr. Hanson to sign some Copyhold papers, & will give you timely notice of my approach, it is with great reluctance I remain in town.———

I shall pay a short visit, as we go on to Lancashire on Rochdale business.—I shall attend to your directions of course & am with great respect

yrs. ever
Byron

P. S.—You will consider Newstead as your house not mine, & me as only a visitor.———

[To William Miller]

Reddish's Hotel. July 30th. 1811.

Sir,

I am perfectly aware of the Justice of your remarks, & am convinced that if ever the poem[1] is published the same objections will be made in much stronger

---

[1] That is, *Childe Harold's Pilgrimage*, which Byron offered to Miller at this time.

terms.—But as it is intended to be a poem on *Ariosto's plan* that is to *say* on *no plan* at all,[2] & as is usual in similar cases having a predilection for the worst passages I shall retain those parts though I cannot venture to defend them.—Under these circumstances I regret that you decline the publication, on my own account, as I think the book would have been better in your hands, the pecuniary part you know I have nothing to do with.[3]——But I can perfectly conceive, & indeed *approve* your reasons, & assure you my sensations are not *Archiepiscopal* enough as yet to regard the rejection of my homilies.[4]

I am, Sir, your very obedt. humble Sert.

Byron

[To Scrope Berdmore Davies]

Newstead Abbey, August 7, 1811

My dearest Davies,

Some curse hangs over me and mine. My mother lies a corpse in this house: one of my best friends is drowned in a ditch. What can I say, or think, or do? I received a letter from him the day before yesterday. My dear Scrope, if you can spare a moment, do come down to me. I want a friend. Matthews's last letter was written on *Friday*,—on Saturday he was not. In ability, who was like Matthews? How did we all shrink before him? You do me but justice in saying, I would have risked my paltry existence to have preserved his. This very evening did I mean to write, inviting him, as I invite you, my very dear friend, to visit me. God forgive * * * for his apathy! What will our poor Hobhouse feel! His letters breathe but of Matthews. Come to me, Scrope, I am almost desolate—left almost alone in the world—I had but you and H and M and let me enjoy the survivors whilst I can. Poor M. in his letter of Friday, speaks of his intended contest for Cambridge, and a speedy journey to London. Write or come, but come if you can, or one or both. Yours ever.

---

[2] *Orlando Furioso* (1532), the epic chivalric poem by Ludovico Ariosto, is leisurely in terms of construction, to put it mildly.

[3] Byron took no share in the profits from his poems until *Lara* was published in 1814. Murray paid £600 for the copyright in *Childe Harold*, and a similar sum as regards *The Corsair* (1814)—to Robert Dallas. In 1815 Murray sent Byron cheques for more than £2,500 as part share in receipts—which the poet returned, when his finances were at a complete nadir. (See letter of 2 January 1816.)

[4] See Alain-René Lesage, *Gil Blas* (1735), vii. 4, in which the eponymous hero makes the mistake of frankly criticizing a sermon by his employer, a bishop, and is dismissed for his pains.

[To John Cam Hobhouse]

Newstead Abbey. August 10th. 1811

My dear Hobhouse,

From Davies I had already received the death of Matthews, & from M. a *letter* dated the *day* before his *death*,—In that letter he mentions you, & as it was perhaps the last he ever wrote, you will derive a poor consolation from hearing that he spoke of you with that affectionate familiarity, so much more pleasing from those we love, than the highest encomiums of the World.—My dwelling, you already know, is the House of Mourning, & I am really so much bewildered with the different shocks I have sustained, that I can hardly reduce myself to reason by the most frivolous occupations.—My poor friend J. Wingfield, my Mother, & your best friend, & (surely not the worst of mine) C S M have disappeared in one little month since *my return*, & without my seeing *either*, though I have *heard* from *All*.— There is to me something so incomprehensible in death, that I can neither speak or think on the subject.—Indeed when I looked on the Mass of Corruption which was the being from whence I sprang, I doubted within myself whether I *was*, or She *was not*.—I have lost her who gave me being, & some of those who made that Being a blessing.—I have neither hopes nor fears beyond the Grave, yet if there is within us a 'spark of that Celestial Fire' M has already 'mingled with the Gods'.[5]——In the room where I now write (flanked by the *Skulls* you have seen so often[6]) did you & M. & myself pass some joyous unprofitable evenings, & here we will drink to his Memory, which though it cannot reach the dead, will soothe the Survivors, & to them only death can be an Evil.—I can neither receive or administer Consolation, Time will do it for us, in the Interim let me see or hear from you, if possible both.—I am very lonely, & should think myself miserable, were it not for a kind of hysterical merriment, which I can neither account for, or conquer, but, strange as it is, I do laugh & heartily, wondering at myself while I sustain it.—I have tried reading & boxing, & swimming, & writing, & rising early & sitting late, & water, & wine, with a number of ineffectual remedies, & here I am, wretched, but not 'melancholy or gentlemanlike.'[7]—My dear '*Cam of the Cornish*'

---

[5] See Pope, *Essay on Criticism* (1711), i. 195, and Thomas West's third 'Olympic Ode' (translated from Pindar in 1766), 'To Theron King of Agrigentum', Antistrophe iii.

[6] Newstead contained a collection of skulls, unearthed in its grounds, and thought to be the remains of monks. One had been converted into a wine cup, which Byron's visitors appreciated when visiting the Abbey.

[7] See Ben Jonson, *Every Man in his Humour* (1598), I. ii. 136.

(M's *last* expression![8]) may Man or God give you the happiness, which I wish rather than expect you may attain; believe me none living are more sincerely

yours than
Byron.

Newstead Abbey, Aug. 12th, 1811

DIRECTIONS FOR THE CONTENTS OF A WILL TO BE DRAWN UP IMMEDIATELY.

The estate of Newstead to be entailed (subject to certain deductions) on George Anson Byron,[9] heir at law, or whoever may be the heir at law on the death of Lord B. The Rochdale property to be sold in part or the whole, according to the debts and legacies of the present Lord B.

To Nicolo Giraud of Athens, subject of France, but born in Greece, the sum of seven thousand pounds sterling, to be paid from the sale of such parts of Rochdale, Newstead, or elsewhere, as may enable the said Nicolo Giraud (resident of Athens and Malta in the year 1810) to receive the above sum on his attaining the age of twenty-one years.

To William Fletcher, Joseph Murray, and Demetrius Zograffo (native of Greece), servants, the sum of fifty pounds pr. ann. each, for their natural lives. To Wm. Fletcher, the Mill at Newstead, on condition that he payeth rent, but not subject to the caprice of the landlord. To R[ober]t. Rushton the sum of fifty pounds per ann. for life, and a further sum of one thousand pounds on attaining the age of twenty-five years.

To J[oh]n. Hanson, Esq. the sum of two thousand pounds sterling.

The claims of S. B. Davies, Esq. to be satisfied on proving the amount of the same.

The body of Lord B. to be buried in the vault of the garden of Newstead, without any ceremony or burial-service whatever, or any inscription, save his name and age. His dog not to be removed from the said vault.[10]

---

[8] After his return from the tour to the Mediterranean Hobhouse had been sent into the militia by his father. In 1811 his regiment, the Cornwall and Devon Miners, was ordered to Enniscorthy, County Wexford, Ireland, much to his chagrin; later it would be stationed at Dover.

[9] For Byron's cousin and future seventh lord see letter of 4 February 1809. Byron is formalizing the succession to the estate and title, a process normally carried out in each aristocratic generation, 'subject to certain deductions', should the title-holder want to sell something off in the meantime.

[10] Byron's Nottingham lawyer, Samuel Bolton, noted: 'It is submitted to Lord Byron whether this clause relative to the funeral had better not be omitted. The substance of it can be given in a letter from his lordship to the executors, and accompany the will.' Byron was adamant: 'It must stand', he noted (*LJ* ii. 72).

My library and furniture of every description to my friends Jn. Cam Hobhouse, Esq., and S. B. Davies, Esq., my executors. In case of their decease, the Rev. J. Becher, of Southwell, Notts., and R. C. Dallas, Esq., of Mortlake, Surrey, to be executors.

The produce of the sale of Wymondham in Norfolk, and the late Mrs. B's Scotch property, to be appropriated in aid of the payment of debts and legacies. [...]

[To John Cam Hobhouse]

Newstead Abbey August 30th. 1811

My dear Hobhouse,

Scrope Davies has been here & seemed as much affected by late events as could be expected from one who has lived so much in the world, his society was (as it is always wont to be) very reviving, but now he is gone & I am solitary & sullen.——Not scrap of paper has been found, at Cambridge, which is singular;[11]—I can hardly agree with you in a wish to forget. I love to remember the dead, for we see only their virtues, & when our best friends are thus removed, we become reconciled to our own prospects & 'long to be with them and at Rest.'[12]——I think when your mind is more calm, you ought to write his Epitaph, & we will erect to his memory a monument, in some appropriate place, I do not know any other who would do him justice, indeed it is *your right* & perhaps your *duty*.—Then 'Give his fame to the winds, & let the Harp sigh over his narrow house' you are now in the land of Ossian.[13]———In the poem which I wrote abroad, & is now in the hands of Murray the Bookseller for publication, at the close of the 1st. Canto which treats of Spain, I have two stanzas in commemoration of W[ingfield] who died at Coimbra, & in a note to these having occasion to mention the loss of three persons very dear to me in so very short a time, I have added a very short sentence or two on the subject of our friend, which though they can neither add to his credit or satisfaction, will at least shew my own pride in the acquaintance of such a man.[14]——Your book goes on well & I trust will answer your purpose & my expectations. Demetrius

---

[11] I doubt this is an allusion to Matthews's leaving a suicide note, or similar; but if he cleared his desk, that might be significant.

[12] Hobhouse had written on 25 August, telling Byron, 'do not write so sadly, every line of your last wrings my soul—I strive to forget my lamented friend, do you do the same' (*Hobhouse Letters*, 77). And see Psalm 55: 6: 'Oh that I had wings like a dove! I would fly away and be at rest.'

[13] See Byron's own 'The Death of Calmar and Orla', from *Hours of Idleness* (*CPW* i. 112–16), 'an imitation' of the Gaelic epic imposture by James Macpherson, known as *Ossian* for short (1760).

[14] See *CPW* ii. 189.

has made out a most formidable vocabulary, on which I wait for further orders.[15]—I do not know who is your deputy in town, perhaps Baillie, or Shepherd.—I have had a letter from Bankes, of the patronizing kind, where I am invited to '*one* of *my places* in *Wales*'!![16]——I am going to Lancs. & am in daily expectation of Hanson to back me, & I mean to marry, prudently if possible that is wealthily, I can't afford anything to Love.—I wish you were here, but you *will* be *here*, & we shall laugh again as usual & be very miserable dogs for all that.—My Sister writes me melancholy letters, things are not going on well there, but mismanagement is the hereditary epidemic of our Brood.— Hodgson is battening on 'Lower Moor Herefordshire,' Davies at Harrow-gate.——I am to visit him in Octr. at King's Coll.—Dallas is running to & from Mortlake with his pocket full of proofs of *all* his *friends* who are all Scribblers & make him a Packhorse.——I am here boxing in a Turkish pelise to prevent obesity, & as usual very much yours

Byron

[To Augusta Leigh]

Newstead Abbey August 30th. 1811

My dear Augusta,

The embarrassments you mention in your last letter I never heard of before, but that disease is epidemic in our family.——Neither have I been apprised of any of the changes at which you hint, indeed how should I? on the borders of the Black Sea, we heard only of the Russians.—So you have much to tell, & all will be novelty.——I don't know what Scrope Davies meant by telling you I liked Children, I abominate the sight of them so much that I have always had the greatest respect for the character of *Herod*.——But as my house here is large enough for us all, we should go on very well, & I need not tell you that I long to see *you*.——I really do not perceive any thing so formidable in a journey hither of two days, but all this comes of Matrimony, you have a Nurse & all the &cas. of a family. Well, I must marry to repair the ravages of myself & prodigal ancestry, but if I am ever so unfortunate as to be presented with an Heir, instead of a *Rattle*, he shall be provided with a *Gag*.———I shall perhaps be able to accept

---

[15] Byron's Greek servant Demetrius Zograffo (see letter of 12 August 1811) was doing some translations for Hobhouse; see letter of 16 November 1811. Years later Byron would hear news that he had become a nationalist leader in Athens: 'He was a clever but not *apparently* an enterprizing man,' Byron wrote in the autumn of 1821 (*LJ* ix. 23), 'but Circumstances make men.'

[16] For William Bankes (1786–1855), Byron's Cambridge friend, see letter of 19 February 1820.

D[avies]'s invitation to Cambridge, but I fear my stay in Lancashire will be prolonged, I proceed there in the 2d. week of Septr. to arrange my coal concerns, & then if I can't persuade some wealthy dowdy to ennoble the dirty puddle of her mercantile Blood,—why—I shall leave England & all it's clouds for the East again,—I am very sick of it already.—Joe [Murray] has been getting well of a disease that would have killed a troop of horse, he promises to bear away the palm of longevity from old Parr.[17]—As you wont come, you will write, I long to hear all these unutterable things, being utterly unable to guess at any of them, unless they concern *your* relative the Thane of Carlisle,—though I had great hopes we had done with him.—I have little to add that you do not already know, and being quite alone, have no great variety of incident to gossip with, I am but rarely pestered with visitors, & the few I have I get rid of as soon as possible.——I will now take leave of you in the Jargon of 1794.[18] 'Health & *Fraternity!*'

Yrs. always
B.—

[To John Murray]

Newstead Abbey. Notts. Sept. 5th. 1811

Sir,

The time seems to be past when (as Dr. Johnson said) a man was certain to 'hear the truth from his Bookseller', for you have paid me so many compliments, that, if I was not the veriest scribbler on Earth, I should feel affronted.—As I accept your compliments, it is but fair I should give equal or greater credit to your objections, the more so as I believe them to be well founded.[19]——With regard to the political & metaphysical parts, I am afraid I can alter nothing, but I have high authority for my Errors in that point, for even the *Æneid* was a *political* poem & written for a *political* purpose, and as to my unlucky opinions on Subjects of more importance, I am too sincere in them for recantation.—On Spanish affairs I have said what I saw, & every day confirms me in that notion of the result formed on the Spot, & I rather think honest John Bull is beginning to come round again to that Sobriety which Massena's retreat had begun to reel from it's Centre, the usual consequence of

---

[17] A legendarily long-lived Englishman who, it was said, died at the age of 152 in 1635.

[18] That is, the 'jargon' of the French Revolution: liberté, egalité, fraternité.

[19] Murray had written on 4 September, in flattering terms about *Childe Harold*, but anxious about 'some expressions...concerning Spain and Portugal', and 'some religious feelings which may deprive me of customers among the *Orthodox*' (*Murray Letters*, 3).

unusual success.[20]——So you perceive I cannot alter the Sentiments, but if there are any alterations in the structure of the versification you would wish to be made, I will tag rhymes, & turn Stanzas, as much as you please.—As for the 'Orthodox,' let us hope they will buy on purpose to abuse, you will forgive the one if they will do the other.—You are aware that anything from my pen must expect no quarter on many accounts, & as the present publication is of a Nature very different from the former, we must not be sanguine.—You have given me no answer to my question—tell me fairly did you show the M.S. to some of your Corps?[21]——I sent an introductory Stanza to Mr. Dallas that it might be forwarded to you, the poem else will open too abruptly. The Stanzas had better be numbered in Roman characters; there is a disquisition on the Literature of the modern Greeks, & some smaller poems to come in at the Close.—These are now at Newstead, but will be sent in time.—If Mr. D has lost the Stanza & note annexed to it, write & I will send it myself. —You tell me to add 2 Cantos, but I am about to visit my *Collieries* in Lancashire on the 15th. Inst. which is so *unpoetical* an employment that I need say no more. I am Sir

your most obedt. humble Servt.

B.

[To Francis Hodgson]

Newstead Abbey, Sept. 25, 1811

My dear Hodgson,

I fear that before the latest of October or the first of November, I shall hardly be able to make Cambridge. My everlasting agent puts off his coming like the accomplishment of a prophecy. However, finding me growing serious he hath promised to be here on Thursday, and about Monday we shall remove to Rochdale. I have only to give discharges to the tenantry here (it seems the poor creatures must be raised, though I wish it was not necessary), and arrange the receipt of sums, and the liquidation of some debts, and I shall be ready to enter upon new subjects of vexation. I intend to visit you in Granta, and hope to prevail on you to accompany me here, or there or anywhere.

---

[20] The French general André Masséna had sought to push the allies out of Portugal by invasion in the autumn of 1810, but was repulsed by Wellington's army at the defensive Lines of Torres Vedras in March of the following year.

[21] Murray had an informal editorial board that often vetted literary projects. Its most fearsome member was the poet and satirist William Gifford (1756–1826), for whom Byron had a profound respect.

I am plucking up my spirits, and have begun to gather my little sensual comforts together. Lucy is extracted from Warwickshire; some very bad faces have been warned off the premises, and more promising substituted in their stead; the partridges are plentiful, hares fairish, pheasants not quite so good, and Girls on the Manor * * * * Just as I had formed a tolerable establishment my travels commenced, and on my return I find all to do over again; my former flock were all scattered; some married, not before it was needful. As I am a great disciplinarian, I have just issued an edict for the abolition of caps; no hair to be cut on any pretext; stays permitted, but not too low before; full uniform always in the evening; Lucinda to be commander—*vice* the present, about to be wedded (*mem[orandum]*. she is 35 with a flat face and a squeaking voice), of all the makers and unmakers of beds in the household.

My tortoises (all Athenians), my hedgehog, my mastiff and the other live Greek, are all purely.[22] The tortoises lay eggs, and I have hired a hen to hatch them. I am writing notes for *my* quarto (Murray would have it a *quarto*), and Hobhouse is writing text for *his* quarto; if you call on Murray or Cawthorn you will hear news of either. I have attacked De Pauw, Thornton,[23] Lord Elgin, Spain, Portugal, the *Edinburgh Review*, travellers, Painters, Antiquarians, and others, so you see what a dish of Sour Crout Controversy I shall prepare for myself. It would not answer for me to give way, now; as I was forced into bitterness at the beginning, I will go through to the last. *Væ Victis* [woe to the conquered]! If I fall, I shall fall gloriously, fighting against a host.

Felicissima Notte a Voss. Signoria,[24]

B.

[To John Cam Hobhouse]

8 St. James's Street. Novr. 16th. 1811

My dear H.

That is a most *impudent* simile & incorrect, for the '*vomit*' came to the '*dog*' & not the '*dog*' to the '*vomit*' & if you who meets me today will teach me how to spit in

---

[22] This is the first of many menageries Byron would collect about himself; the largest would be at Palazzo Mocenigo in Venice in 1817 (see *Life*, 741). 'The other live Greek' is Demetrius Zograffo.

[23] See Byron's lengthy set of 'papers' to *Childe Harold*, i. stanza 73, 'Fair Greece! sad relic of departed worth!' (*CPW* ii. 199–217), where he says that 'De Pauw and Thornton have debased the Greeks beyond their merits' (201), referring to Cornelius de Pauw's *Recherches philosophiques sur les Grecs* (1788) and Thomas Thornton's *Present State of Turkey* (1807), and discusses Thornton at length (203–4).

[24] Italian: 'Good night to your ladies'.

any body's face without offence, I will shake off these gentlemen with the greatest good-will, however I have never *called* on either, so am not to blame for the slightest degree of good manners.[25]——I send you Demo's traduzione [translation], & make the most of it, you must orthographize it in both languages as you will perceive. Why have you omitted the earthquake in the night at Libochabo? I will give up the *flatulent* Secretary, but do let us have the Terramoto.[26]—I dine today with Ward to meet the Lord knows whom.[27]—Moore & I are on the best of terms, I answered his letters in an explanatory way, but of course conceded nothing in the shape of an apology, indeed his own letters were an odd mixture of complaint, & a desire of amicable discussion.—Rogers said his behaviour was rather Irish, & that mine was candid & manly, I hope it was at *least* the latter.—I consulted Scrope before I sent off my letter, but now the matter is completely adjusted, as R said 'honourably' to Both. Sotheby, whom I abused in my last, improves, his face is rather against him, & his manner abrupt & dogmatic, but I believe him to be much more amiable than I thought him.—Rogers is a most excellent & unassuming Soul, & Moore an Epitome of all that's delightful, I asked them & Hodgson to dinner. H of course was drunk & Sensibilitous.——Bland (the *Revd*) has been *challenging* an officer of Dragoons, about a *whore*, & my assistance being required, I interfered in time to prevent him from losing his *life* or his *Living*.—The man is mad, Sir, mad, frightful as a Mandrake, & lean as a rutting Stag,[28] & all about a bitch not worth a Bank token.—She is a common Strumpet as his Antagonist assured me, yet he means to marry her, Hodgson meant to marry her, the officer meant to marry her, her first Seducer (seventeen years ago) meant to marry her, and all this is owing to the *Comet*!——During Bland's absence, H was her Dragon, & left his own Oyster wench to offer her his hand, which she *refused*.—Bland comes home in Hysterics, finds her in keeping (not by H however) & loses his wits.—Hodgson gets drunk & cries, & he & Bland (who have been berhyming each other as you know these six past Olympiads) are now the Antipodes of each other.—I saw this *wonder*, & set her down at seven shilling's worth.——Here is gossip for you! as you know some of the parties.—As to self, I am ill with a cough, Demo has tumbled down

---

[25] Hobhouse had replied to a letter from Byron, about the London company he was keeping, to say that he was 'returning, like a dog to his vomit, to every thing before cast up and rejected' (*Hobhouse Letters*, 86).

[26] Hobhouse published *A Journey through Albania and Other Provinces of Turkey in Europe and Asia, to Constantinople, during the Years 1809 and 1810*, in 1813; in October 1809 they had passed the Albanian town of Libochabo (now Libohovë) and felt an earthquake (Italian: *terremoto*) in the district.

[27] There follow various acquaintances of Byron's: John William Ward, the poets Thomas Moore (1779–1852) and Samuel Rogers (1763–1855), and the Revd Robert Bland, erstwhile teacher at Harrow and a friend of Hodgson.

[28] See Isaac D'Israeli, *Flim-Flams! or The Life and Errors of my Uncle, and the Amours of my Aunt* (1805), i. 182.

stairs, scalded his leg, been kicked by a horse, hurt his kidneys, got a terrible 'catchcold' (as he calls it) & now suffers under these accumulated mischances.— Fletcher is fat & facetious.—

yrs. ever
$M\pi\alpha\iota\rho\hat{\omega}\nu$[29]

[To John Cam Hobhouse]

8. St. James's Street. Decr. 9th. 1811

My dear Hobhouse.

At length I am your rival in Good fortune. I this night saw *Robert Coates* perform Lothario at the Haymarket,[30] the house crammed, but bribery (a bank token) procured an excellent place near the Stage.—Before the curtain drew up a performer (all Gemmen) came forward and thus addressed the house, Ladies &c. 'A melancholy accident has happened to the Gentleman who undertook the part of Altamont,—(here a dead stop—then—) this accident has *happened* to *his brother* who fell this afternoon through a *loop hole* into the *London Dock*, & was taken up dead, Altamont has just entered the house *distractedly*, is—now dress-ing!!! & will appear in 5 minutes!!!'—Such were verbatim the words of the Apologist, they were followed by a roar of laughter & Altamont himself, who did not fall short of Coates in absurdity.—Damn me, if ever I saw such a scene in my life, the play was closed in 3d. act, after Bob's demise nobody would hear a syllable, he was interrupted several times before, & made speeches, every soul was in hysterics, & all the actors on his own model.—You can't conceive how I longed for *you*, your taste for the ridiculous would have been gratified to surfeit. A farce followed in dumb show, after Bob had been hooted from the stage for a bawdy address he attempted to deliver between play & farce.—'Love a la mode' was damned, Coates was damned, every thing was damned & damnable.—His enacting I need not describe, you have seen him at Bath.—But never did you see the *others*, never did you hear the *apology*, never did you behold the 'distracted' survivor of a 'brother' neckbroken through a '*loop-hole* in ye. *London Dock*'!!—Like George Faulkner these fellows defied burlesque.[31]—Oh Captain! eye hath not

---

[29] This is a Greek transliteration of 'Byron'.

[30] Coates (1772–1848) was a wealthy eccentric with a penchant for taking unpaid roles on the West End stage. Here he plays Lothario to somebody else's Altamont in Nicholas Rowe's marital tragedy *The Fair Penitent* (1702). As was usual in theatres at that time, the main drama was followed by a farce, Charles Macklin's *Love à la Mode* (1759).

[31] An Irish publisher and associate of Jonathan Swift, Faulkner (1703–75) was such a notorious vendor of pirated editions that he was satirized in Samuel Foote's *The Orators* (1762) as 'Peter

seen, ear hath not heard, nor can the heart of man conceive tonight's performance.[32]—Baron Geramb was in the Stage box,[33] & Coates in his address *nailed*
the *Baron* to the infinite amusement of the audience, & the discomfiture of
Geramb, who grew very wroth indeed.—I meant to write on other topics but
I must postpone, I can think talk & dream only of these buffoons.—'Tis done, tis
numbered with the things that were, would would it were to come.'[34] & you by
my side to see it.—Heigh ho! Good night.—yrs ever

B

[To John Hanson]

Decr. 15th. 1811

Dear Sir,

I have enclosed a letter of Mrs. Massingberd's who is in the usual dilemma.—
In short I must take the securities on myself, & request you will arrange with
the Jews on ye. subject.—There is nothing else left for it, I cannot allow
people to go to Gaol on my account, it is better they should tear my property
to pieces, than make me a scoundrel.—The remedy is desperate but so is
the disease.—I wish to see you & have called for that purpose.—I will call
tomorrow Morning.

yrs. ever
Byron

P. S.—*Cannot Mrs. M. resist on legal grounds? do see & do something for the poor old Soul
immediately.*—

Paragraph'. When Faulkner sued for libel and won with only tiny damages, he pirated Foote's play in
revenge, and so literally 'defied burlesque'.

[32] See 1 Corinthians 2: 9 and *Midsummer Night's Dream*, IV. i. 209, effortlessly combined here.

[33] Francois Ferdinand, 'Baron' de Geramb (1772–1848), passed himself off around Europe in a
number of guises after the French Revolution and was, it seems, temporarily imprisoned
by Napoleon.

[34] See Joanna Baillie, *De Montfort* (1798), IV. iii. 71–2.

[To John Cam Hobhouse]

8. St. James's Street: Decr. 15th. 1811

My dear Hobhouse.

You are silent—I suppose for ye. same reason that George Lambe's Wit in ye. farce said nothing.[35]—But this awful pause gives me hopes of seeing & hearing you in 'these parts.'—I have been living quietly, reading Sir W. Drummond's book on the bible, & seeing Kemble & Mrs. Siddons.[36]—Yesterday Moore went over with me to Sydenham, but did not find Campbell at home.[37]—M said he was probably at home but 'nefariously dirty' & would not be seen in a poetical pickle.—I think you would like Moore, and I should have great pleasure in bringing you together.—Tomorrow I dine with Rogers & go to Coleridge's Lecture. Coleridge has attacked the 'Pleasures of Hope' & all other pleasures whatsoever.—Cawthorn rises in ye. world, he talks of getting a novel of M [adam]e. D'Arblay's for 1000 Gs!!—You and I must hide our diminished heads.[38]——What are you doing?—Dallas is ill, Hodgson going crazy, (I had a woeful letter from him yesterday, full of Phantasmagoria) Bland is half killed by his faithless Trulla, & Scrope at Cambridge, full of pleasant Mirth.—Hodgson passes his Xmas at Newstead, so does Harness, *him* you dont know, he is a *Harrow* man, that will be *enough* for you.—Sir Wm. Ingilby I have frequently seen lately & other returned voyagers.—Bold Webster is preparing Caudle for his spouse,[39] & I am to be a Godfather.—Ward has left town, & Ld. Valentia gone with his son to Arley hall, is there not a *letter* or *two* wanting in the name of his place?—The Alfred does well, but our Cook has absconded in debt & be damned

---

[35] Perhaps the actor George Lambe took the part of Sir Callaghan O'Brallaghan in *Love à la Mode* the week before: Sir Callaghan refuses to discuss his military record when invited, and Hobhouse was still in the militia.

[36] William Drummond's *Oedipus Judaicus*, a commentary on the Old Testament, was published in 1811. John Kemble (1757–1823) and his sister Sarah Siddons (1755–1831) were English dramatic royalty at the time, famous for tragic roles in revivals.

[37] Thomas Campbell (1777–1844), author of the didactic poem *The Pleasures of Hope*, which Byron regarded very highly; resident in this South London suburb from 1804 to 1820.

[38] Samuel Taylor Coleridge (1772–1834) gave lectures on Shakespeare during the winter of 1811–12. Byron went again on 20 January 1811. Madame d'Arblay was the married name of Frances ('Fanny') Burney (1776–1828), a successful novelist of the 1780s and 1790s, and key influence on Jane Austen, who 'returned' with *The Wanderer: or, Female Difficulties* (1814). It was not published by John Cawthorn, but by the firm of Longman, and did not fare well.

[39] We shall hear more about Byron's Cambridge friend James Wedderburn Webster (1788–1840) and his wife in Chapter 4. The 'bold' husband making a bedtime drink for his expectant wife already suggests a figure of fun.

to him, which has thrown the managing Committee into Hysterics.[40]—I presume ye. papers have told of ye. Riots in Notts, breaking of frames & heads, & outmaneouvreing [sic] the military.—Joe Murray has been frightened by dreams & Ghosts, it is singular that he never superstitized for seventy six years before.— All my affairs are going on very badly, & I must rebel too if they don't amend—I shall return to London for the meeting of Parliament—Cambridge stands where it did, but all our acquaintances are gone or superannuated. I have now exhausted my Gossip, & will spare you for the present, believe me

yrs. ever most truly
$M\pi\alpha\iota\rho\hat{\omega}\nu$

[A Memorandum on Annuities & Loans and Mrs Massingberd[41]]

January 16th. 1812

Lord Byron to the best of his knowledge and recollection in Decr. 1805 January 1806 applied to *King* in consequence of an advertisement in ye. papers who acquainted Ld. B. *that his minority* prevented all money transactions without the security of competent persons; *through Mr. K.* he became acquainted with a Mr. Dellvalley another of the tribes of Israel, and *subsequently* with a Mr. *Howard* of Golden Square.—After many delays during which Ld. B. had interviews with Howard, once he thinks in Golden Square, but more frequently in Piccadilly, Mrs. M agreed to become security jointly with her daughter.—Ld. B. knows Howard's person perfectly well, has not seen him subsequent to the transaction, but recollects Howard's mentioning to him that He Ld. B. was acting imprudently, stating that he made it a rule to advise young men against such proceedings.— Ld. B. recollects on *the day on which the money was paid* at Mrs. M's house, *that he remained* in the next room till the papers were signed, Mrs. M. having stated that the parties wished him to be kept out of sight during the business *and wished to avoid even mentioning his name*.—Mrs. M. deducted the interest for two years & a half and 100 £ for Howards papers.—The second annuity was *settled at Worthing*. Ld. B. thinks Mrs. M. has some letters of Ld. B's at that time written.—Ld. B. was not present.—In 1807. Ld. B. through the means of a Mr. Carpentiere or Carpenter then living at Dorant's hotel as manager of the York under Dorant,

---

[40] This was a Mayfair club founded in 1808, to which Byron was elected while abroad. In later life he described it as 'a little too sober and literary', though 'a decent resource on a rainy day' (*LJ* ix. 22).

[41] Byron sent this memorandum to Hanson, presumably as part of the potential legal appeal mentioned in the letter of 15 December 1811.

was made acquainted with Messrs Thomas & Riley who *declined advancing money on* Mrs. & Miss M's security without the addition of another.—Mr. D[42] *on Ld. B's application* consented to lend his name.—The papers were signed by Mr. D in *Ld. B's presence* at *Mr Thomas's* in Hanover Street, *Ld. B. received* [two words illegible] *paid for the papers after some dispute* on the exorbitancy of the charges, and lodged certain sums with Mr. D for the payment of Interest.—Afterwards *proceeded* to the Insurance office in the Strand.—Ld. B. has frequently seen Messrs Thomas & Riley before & since the transaction, at their house, in Brompton, & in St. James's Street.—They perfectly understood at the time, the annuities were taken up by him.—Recollects Riley pointed out *one of the parties* at Mr. T[homas]' saying with a smile, 'this man wishes to see how his money is paid himself.'—

[To Susan Vaughan]

8. St. James's Street January 28th. 1812

I write to bid you farewell, not to reproach you.—The enclosed papers, *one* in *your own handwriting* will explain every thing.—I will not deny that I have been attached to you, & I am now heartily ashamed of my weakness.—You may also enjoy the satisfaction of have deceived me most completely, & rendered me for the present sufficiently wretched.—From the first I told you that the continuance of our connection depended on your own conduct.——All is over.—I have little to condemn on my own part, but credulity; you threw yourself in my way, I received you, loved you, till you have become worthless, & now I part from you with some regret & without resentment.——I wish you well, do not forget that your own misconduct has bereaved you of a friend, of whom nothing else could have deprived you.—Do not attempt explanation, it is useless, I am *determined*, you cannot deny your handwriting; return to your relations, you shall be furnished with the means, but *him*, who now addresses you for the last time, you will never see again.—

Byron
God bless you!

---

[42] Probably Scrope Berdmore Davies, whom we saw in the letter of 12 May 1808 going to Mrs Massingberd's house 'to finish the business'.

[To Lord Holland[43]]

8 St. James's Street February 25th. 1812

My Lord,

With my best thanks I have the honour to return the Notts letter to your Lordship.—I have read it with attention, but do not think I shall venture to avail myself of it's contents, as my view of the question differs in some measure from Mr. Coldham's.—I hope I do not wrong him, but *his* objections to ye. bill appear to me to be founded on certain apprehensions that he & his coadjutors might be mistaken for the '*original advisers*' (to quote him) of the measure.—For my own part, I consider the manufacturers as a much injured body of men sacrificed to ye. views of certain individuals who have enriched themselves by those practices which have deprived the frame workers of employment.—For instance;—by the adoption of a certain kind of frame 1 man performs ye. work of 7 — 6 are thus thrown out of business.—But it is to be observed that ye. work thus done is far inferior in quality, hardly marketable at home, & hurried over with a view to exportation.—Surely, my Lord, however we may rejoice in any improvement in ye. arts which may be beneficial to mankind; we must not allow mankind to be sacrificed to improvements in Mechanism. The maintenance & well doing of ye. industrious poor is an object of greater consequence to ye. community than ye. enrichment of a few monopolists by any improvement in ye. implements of trade, which deprives ye workman of his bread, & renders ye. labourer 'unworthy of his hire.'—My own motive for opposing ye. bill is founded on it's palpable injustice, & it's certain ineffi-cacy.——I have seen the state of these miserable men, & it is a disgrace to a civilized country.—Their excesses may be condemned, but cannot be subject of wonder.—The effect of ye. present bill would be to drive them into actual rebellion.—The few words I shall venture to offer on Thursday will be founded upon these opinions formed from my own observations on ye. spot.—By previous enquiry I am convinced these men would have been restored to employment & ye. county to tranquillity.—It is perhaps not yet too late & is surely worth the trial. It can never be too late to employ force in such circumstances.——I believe your Lordship does not coincide with me entirely on this subject, & most cheerfully & sincerely shall I submit to your superior

---

[43] Henry Vassall-Fox, third Baron Holland (1773–1840), was a senior Whig politician and nephew of Charles James Fox. He mentored Byron in the House of Lords, and he and his wife were also major socialites: the ruins of their famous house are still visible in its grounds, Holland Park, West London. Byron was a frequent caller there before leaving London in 1816.

judgment & experience, & take some other line of argument against ye. bill, or be silent altogether, should you deem it more advisable.——Condemning, as every one must condemn the conduct of these wretches, I believe in ye. existence of grievances which call rather for pity than punishment.——I have the honour to be with great respect, my Lord, yr. Lordship's

most obedt. & obliged Servt.
Byron

P. S.—I am a little apprehensive that your Lordship will think me too lenient towards these men, & half a framebreaker myself.

[To James Perry]

8, St. James's Street, Sunday, March 1st, 1812

Sir,

I take the liberty of sending an alteration of the last two lines of Stanza 2d which I wish to run as follows,

> 'Gibbets on Sherwood will *heighten* the Scenery
> Showing how Commerce, *how* Liberty thrives!'

I wish you could insert it tomorrow for a particular reason; but I feel much obliged by your inserting it at all.[44] Of course, do *not* put *my name* to the thing. Believe me,

Your obliged and very obedt. Servt.,
Byron

[To Lady Caroline Lamb]

Sy. Even [April, 1812?]

I never supposed you artful, we are *all* selfish, nature did that for us, but even when you attempt deceit occasionally, you cannot maintain it, which is all the

---

[44] James Perry (1756–1821) was the editor of the London Whig newspaper the *Morning Chronicle*. On 2 March 1812 it ran Byron's anonymous 'Ode to the Framers of the Frame Bill' (*CPW* iii. 9), which was well and truly to the left of any opinion likely to be held by Lord Holland.

better, want of success will curb the tendency.——Every word you utter, every line you write proves you to be either *sincere* or a *fool*, now as I know you are not the one I must believe you the other. I never knew a woman with greater or more pleasing talents, *general* as in a woman they should be, something of every thing, & too much of nothing, but these are unfortunately coupled with a total want of common conduct.—For instance the *note* to your *page*, do you suppose I delivered it? or did you mean that I should? I did not of course.—Then your heart—my poor Caro, what a little volcano! that pours *lava* through your veins, & yet I cannot wish it a bit colder, to make a *marble slab* of, as you sometimes see (to understand my foolish metaphor) brought in vases tables &c. from Vesuvius when hardened after an eruption.—To drop my detestable tropes & figures you know I have always thought you the cleverest most agreeable, absurd, amiable, perplexing, dangerous fascinating little being that lives now or ought to have lived 2000 years ago.——I wont talk to you of beauty, I am no judge, but our *beauties* cease to be so when near you, and therefore you have either some or something better. And now, Caro, this nonsense is the first and last compliment (if it be such) I ever paid you, you have often reproached me as wanting in that respect, but *others* will make up the deficiency.—Come to Ly. Grey's, at least do not let me keep you away.—All that you so often *say*, I *feel*, can more be said or felt?——This same prudence is tiresome enough but one *must* maintain it, or what can we do to be saved?— Keep to it.—

[written on cover]

If you write at all, write as usual—but do as you please, only as I never see you— Basta [enough]!

[To Thomas Moore]

May 8th, 1812

I am too proud of being your friend to care with whom I am linked in your estimation, and, God knows, I want friends more at this time than at any other.[45] I am 'taking care of myself' to no great purpose. If you knew my situation

---

[45] Byron's friendship with Moore had started off with an awkward *contretemps* over *English Bards and Scotch Reviewers*, which made fun of Moore's abortive duel with Francis Jeffrey, editor of the *Edinburgh Review*. Moore's response was to challenge Byron in turn in January 1810, but correspondence ensued and things settled down. (See letter of 16 November 1811.)

in every point of view, you would excuse apparent and unintentional neglect. * * * * * * * * I shall leave town, I think; but do not you leave it without seeing me. I wish you, from my soul, every happiness you can wish yourself; and I think you have taken the road to secure it. Peace be with you! I fear she has abandoned me. Ever, &c.

[To Lady Caroline Lamb]

Tuesday [May 19, 1812?]

You should answer the note for the writer seems unhappy.—And when we are so a slight is doubly felt.——I shall go at 12, but you must send me a ticket which I shall religiously pay for. I shall not call because I do not see that we are at all improved by it, why did you send your boy? I was out, & am always so occupied in a morning that I could not have seen him as I wished had I been at home. I have seen Moore's wife, she is beautiful, with the darkest eyes, they have left town.—M is in great distress about us, & indeed people talk as if there were no other pair of absurdities in London.—It is hard to bear all this without cause, but worse to give cause for it.—Our folly has had the effect of a fault.—I conformed & could conform, if you would lend your aid, but I can't bear to see you look unhappy, & am always on the watch to observe if you are trying to make me so.—We must make an effort, this dream this delirium of two months must pass away, we in fact do not know one another, a month's absence would make us rational, you do not think so, I know it, we have both had 1000 previous fancies of the same kind, & shall get the better of this & be as ashamed of it according to the maxim of Rochefoucault.[46]—But it is better that I should leave town than you, & I will make a tour, or go to Cambridge or Edinburgh.—Now dont abuse me, or think me altered, it is because I am not, cannot alter, that I shall do this, and cease to make fools talk, friends grieve, and the wise pity.—Ever most affectionately & sincerely yrs.

B.

---

[46] See La Rochefoucauld, *Maxims* (1678), 71: 'There are few of us who are not ashamed of having loved when we have stopped doing so.'

[To Lord Holland]

June 25th. 1812

My dear Lord,

I must appear very ungrateful & have indeed been very negligent, but till last night I was not apprized of Lady Holland's situation & shall call tomorrow to have the satisfaction I trust of hearing that she is well.—I hope that neither Politics nor Gout have assailed your Lordship since I last saw you & that you also are 'as well as could be expected'.—The other night at a Ball I was presented by order to our gracious Regent, who honoured me with some conversation & professed a predilection for Poesy.—I confess it was a most unexpected honour, & I thought of poor Bankes's adventure with some apprehensions of a similar blunder.—I have now great hopes in the event of Mr. Pye's decease, of 'warbling truth at Court' like Mr. Mallet of indifferent memory.—Consider, 100 marks a year! besides the wine & the disgrace, but then remorse would make me drown myself in my own Butt before the year's end, or the finishing of my first dythyrambic.[47]—So that after all I shall not meditate our Laureat's death by pen or poison.—Will you present my best respects to Lady Holland & believe me hers

& yrs very sincerely & obliged
Byron

[To Lady Caroline Lamb]

[August, 1812?]

My dearest Caroline

If tears, which you saw & know I am not apt to shed, if the agitation in which I parted from you, agitation which you must have perceived through the *whole* of this most *nervous* affair, did not commence till the moment of leaving you approached, if all that I have said & done & am still but too ready to say & do,

---

[47] Byron spoke to the Prince Regent (1762–1830) and future George IV (ruling since his father's descent into madness in 1811) 'for more than half an hour' (*Life*, 354) at a party at this time, and was gratified to do so. He regains some ironic distance here by disparaging the courtly position of Poet Laureate, then held by the nonentity Henry James Pye (1745–1813), who was succeeded by Byron's future *bête noire*, the conservative Lake poet Robert Southey (1774–1843). (Remuneration for the laureateship remains stubbornly anachronistic: it traditionally involves a nominal sum of money and a large barrel—a butt—of fortified wine.)

have not sufficiently proved what my real feelings are & must be ever towards you, my love, I have no other proof to offer; God knows I wish you happy, & when I quit you, or rather when you from a sense of duty to your husband & mother quit me, you shall acknowledge the truth of what I again promise & vow, that no other in word or deed shall ever hold the place in my affection which is & shall be most sacred to you, till I am nothing I never knew till *that moment*, the *madness* of—my dearest & most beloved friend—I cannot express myself—this is no time for words—but I shall have a pride, a melancholy pleasure, in suffering what you yourself can hardly conceive—for you do not know me.—I am now about to go out with a heavy heart, because—my appearing this Evening will stop any absurd story which the events of today might give rise to—do you think *now* that I am *cold & stern, & artful*—will even *others* think so, will your *mother* even—that mother to whom we must indeed sacrifice much, *more* much more on my part, than she shall ever know or can imagine.—'Promises not to love you' ah Caroline it is past promising—but I shall attribute all concessions to the proper motive—& never cease to feel all that you have already witnessed—& more than can ever be known but to my own heart—perhaps to yours—May God protect forgive & bless you—ever & even more than ever

yr. most attached
Byron

P. S.—*These taunts which have driven you to this—my dearest Caroline—were it not for your mother & the kindness of all your connections, is there anything on earth or heaven would have made me so happy as to have made you mine long ago? & not less now than then, but more than ever at this time—you know I would with pleasure give up all here & all beyond the grave for you—& in refraining from this—must my motives be misunderstood—? I care not who knows this—what use is made of it—it is to you & to you only that they owe yourself, I was and am yours, freely & most entirely, to obey, to honour, love*[48]—*& fly with you when, where, & how you yourself might & may determine.*

---

[48] The traditional marriage vow in the Church of England was to 'love, honour, and obey'. Clearly Byron is invoking it as he offers himself for an elopement.

[To Lady Melbourne]

Cheltenham Septr. 10th. 1812

Dear Ly. Melbourne

I presume you have heard & will not be sorry to hear *again* that *they* are safely deposited in Ireland & that the sea rolls between you and *one* of your torments; the other you see is still at your elbow.—Now (if you are as sincere as I sometimes almost dream) you will not regret to hear that I wish this to end, & it certainly shall not be renewed on my part.—It is not that I love another, but loving at all is quite out of my way; I am tired of being a fool, & when I look back on the waste of time,—& the destruction of all my plans last winter by this last romance, I am—what I ought to have been long ago.—It is true from early habit, one must make love mechanically as one swims, I was once very fond of both, but now as I never swim unless I tumble into the water, I don't make love till almost obliged, though I fear *that* is not the shortest way out of the troubled waves with which in such accidents we must struggle.—But I will say no more on this topic, as I am not sure of my ground, and you can easily outwit me as you always hitherto have done.—Today I have had a letter from Ld. Holland wishing me to write for the Opening Theatre,[49] but as all Grubstreet seems engaged in the Contest, I have no ambition to enter the lists, & have thrown my few ideas into the fire—I never risk *rivalry* in any thing, you see the very *lowest*—as in this case discourages me from a sort of mixed feeling, I don't know if it be *pride*, but *you* will say it certainly is not *modesty*.—I suppose your friend Twiss will be *one*—I hear there are five hundred—& I wish him success—I really think he would do it well;[50] but few men who have any character to lose would risk it in an anonymous scramble, for the sake of their own feelings.—I have written to Ld. H to thank him & decline the chance.—Betty is performing here, I fear, very ill, his figure is that of a hippopotamus, his face like the Bull and *mouth* on the pannels of a heavy coach, his arms are fins fattened out of shape, his voice the gargling of an Alderman with the quinsey, and his acting altogether ought to be natural for it certainly is like nothing that *Art* has ever yet exhibited on the stage.[51]—Will you

---

[49] Drury Lane Theatre, which had burned down in 1809, reopened in October 1812. A competition was held to write a poetic address to celebrate the event, but eventually Byron was selected for the job—which involved an almost interminable sequence of letters to Lord Holland, in which Byron nervously revised the poem under composition.

[50] Horace Twiss (1787–1849), lawyer and man of literary pretensions.

[51] William Henry West Betty (1791–1874) had been a child prodigy of the London stage around the turn of the century. By 1812 puberty and the theatrical life had clearly had an effect on his elfin charm.

honour me with a line at your leisure? on the most *indifferent* subject you please & believe me

ever yrs very affectly

B.

[To Lady Melbourne]

Cheltenham Septr. 15th 1812

My dear Ly. M.

'If I were looking in your face entre les deux yeux [between the eyes]' I know not whether I should find 'frankness or truth'—but certainly something which looks quite as well if not better than either, & whatever it may be I would not have it changed for any other expression; as it has defied Time, no wonder it should perplex *me*.—'*Manage* her'!—it is impossible—& as to friendship—no—it must be broken off at once, & all I have left is to take some step which will make her hate me effectually, for she must be in extremes.—What you state however is to be dreaded, besides—she presumes upon the weakness & affection of all about her, and the very confidence & kindness which would break or reclaim a good heart, merely lead her own farther from deserving them.—Were this but secure, you would find find yourself mistaken in me; I speak from experience; except in one solitary instance, three months have ever cured me, take an example.—In the autumn of 1809 in the Mediterranean I was seized with an *everlasting* passion considerably more violent on my part than this has ever been[52]—every thing was settled—& *we* (the *we's* of that day) were to set off for the Friuli; but lo! the Peace spoilt every thing, by putting this in possession of the French, & some particular occurrences in the interim determined me to go on to Constantinople.—However we were to meet next year at a certain time, though I told my amica there was no time like the present, & that I could not answer for the future.—She trusted to her power, & I at the moment had certainly much greater doubts of her than myself.—A year sped & on my return downwards, I found at Smyrna & Athens dispatches, requiring the performance of this 'bon billet qu'a la Chatre'[53] & telling me that one of us had returned to the spot on purpose.—But things had altered as I foresaw, & I proceeded very leisurely, not arriving till

---

[52] This is Mrs Constance Spencer Smith, at Malta, in September 1809: see letter of 3 May 1810.

[53] 'The pretty contract La Chatre has': a lover's undertaking between the Marquis de la Châtre and famous French courtesan Ninon de Lenclos (1620–1705) that the lady dismissed with this lighthearted remark: so, proverbially, any amorous promise that is or can be dishonoured.

some months after, pretty sure that in the interim my Idol was in no want of Worshippers.—But she *was* there, & we met—at the Palace & the Governor (ye. most accomodating of all possible chief Magistrates) was kind enough to leave us to come to the most diabolical of explanations.—It was in the Dogdays, during a Sirocco—(I almost perspire now with the thoughts of it) during the intervals of an intermittent fever (my love had also intermitted with my malady) and I certainly feared the Ague & my Passion would both return in full force.—I however got the better of both, & she sailed up the Adriatic & I down to the Straits.——I had certes a great deal to contend against, for the Lady (who was a *select* friend of the Queen of Naples) had something to gain in a few points, & nothing to lose in *reputation*, & was a woman perfectly mistress of herself & every art of intrigue personal or political, not at all in love, but very able to persuade me that she was so, & sure that I should make a most *convenient* & complaisant fellow traveller.——She is now I am told writing her Memoirs at Vienna, in which I shall cut a very indifferent figure; & nothing survives of this most ambrosial amour, which made me on one occasion risk my life, & on another almost drove me mad, but a few Duke of York*ish* letters,[54] & certain baubles which I dare swear by this time have decorated the hands of half Hungary, & all Bohemia.—Cosi finiva la Musica [that's how the music ends].—

[To Lady Melbourne]

Septr. 25th. 1812

My dear Ly. M.

It would answer no purpose to write a syllable on any subject whatever & neither accelerate nor retard what we wish to prevent, she must be left to Chance; conjugal affection and the Kilkenny Theatricals are equally in your favour—for my part it is an accursed business *towards* nor *from* which I shall not move a single step; if she throws herself upon me 'cosi finiva' if not, the sooner it is over the better—from this moment I have done with it, only before she returns allow me to know that I may act accordingly; but there will be nothing to fear before that time, as if a woman & a selfish woman also, would not fill up the vacancy with the first comer?—As to Annabella she requires time & all the cardinal virtues, & in the interim I am a little verging towards one who demands neither, & saves me besides the trouble of marrying by being married

---

[54] Presumably the then Duke, Prince Frederick (1763–1827), second son of George III. He was involved in a political sex scandal with a certain Mrs Mary Clarke, revealed in the press in 1809 with much comment. Perhaps the Duke's love letters emerged in the coverage.

already.——She besides does not speak English, & to me nothing but Italian, a great point, for from certain coincidences the very sound of that language is Music to me, & she has black eyes & *not* a very white skin, & reminds me of many in the Archipelago I wished to forget, & makes me forget what I ought to remember, all which are against me.—I only wish she did not swallow so much supper, chicken wings—sweetbreads,—custards—peaches & *Port* wine—a woman should never be seen eating or drinking, unless it be *lobster sallad & Champagne*, the only truly feminine & becoming viands.—I recollect imploring one Lady not to eat more than a fowl at a sitting without effect, & have never yet made a single proselyte to Pythagoras.—Now a word to yourself—a much more pleasing topic than any of the preceding.—I have no very high opinion of your sex, but when I do see a woman superior not only to all her own but to most of ours I worship her in proportion as I despise the rest.—And when I know that men of the first judgment & the most distinguished abilities have entertained & do entertain an opinion which my own humble observation without any great effort of discern- ment has enabled me to confirm on the same subject, you will not blame me for following the example of my elders & betters & admiring you certainly as much as you ever were admired.—My only regret is that the very awkward circumstances in which we are placed prevents & will prevent the improvement of an acquaintance which I now almost regret having made—but recollect whatever happens that the loss of it must give me more pain than even the *precious* [*previous?*] *acquisition* (& this is saying *much*) which will occasion that loss. Ld. Jersey has reinvited me to M[iddleton] for the 4 Octr. & I will be there if possible, in the mean time whatever step you take to break off this affair has my full concurrence—but *what* you wished me to write would be a little too indifferent; and *that* now would be an insult, & I am much more unwilling to hurt her feelings now than ever, (not from the mere apprehension of a disclosure in her wrath) but I have always felt that one who has given up much, has a claim upon *me* (at least—whatever she deserve from others) for every respect that she may not feel her own degradation, & this is the reason that I have not written at all lately, lest some expression might be misconstrued by her.— When the Lady herself begins the quarrel & adopts a new 'Cortejo' [lover] then my Conscience is comforted.—She has not written to me for some days, which is either a very bad or very good omen.—

yrs. ever

 [55]

---

[55] Byron frequently used this monogram: it combines the μ and π in Greek to form the 'b' sound in English.

I observe that C in her late epistles, lays peculiar stress upon her powers of attraction, upon W[illiam]'s attachment &c. & by way of enhancing the extreme value of her regards, tells me, that she 'could make any one in love with her' an amiable accomplishment—but unfortunately a little too general to be valuable, for was there ever yet a woman, not absolutely disgusting, who could not say or do the same thing? any woman can make a man in love with her, show me her who can keep him so?—You perhaps can show me such a woman but I have not seen her for these—three weeks.—

[To Lady Melbourne]

Septr. 28th. 1812

My dear Lady M.

The *non*-mention of Miss R[awdon] certainly looks very suspicious but your correspondent has fallen into a mistake in which I am sure neither ye. lady nor myself could possibly join.[56]—Since your departure I have hardly entered a single house, the Rawdons & the Oxfords & a family named Macleod are the only persons I know; Ly. C. Rawdon gave me a general retainer to her box at the theatre, where I generally go, which has probably produced the surmise you mention.—Miss R has always been a mighty favourite with me, because she is unaffected, very accomplished, & lived amongst the Greeks of Venice & Trieste consequently well versed in many topics which are common to her & me & would be very stupid to any one else; I moreover think her very pretty though not at all in the style of beauty which I most admire; but she *waltzes*,[57] & is for many reasons the very last woman on earth I should covet (unless she were 'my neighbor's wife' & then the breaking a commandment would go far in her behalf) nor do I think that our acquaintance has extended even to a common flirtation, besides *her* views are in another quarter, & so most assuredly are mine.—I never heard of the report Ly. M[ilbanke?] *starts* from, & I am sure you will do me the justice to believe, I never dreamed of such a thing, & had I heard it should have disbelieved such nonsense as I do now;—I am not at all

---

[56] This is Elizabeth Anne ('Bessy') Rawdon (1793–1874), who married Lord George William Russell in 1817. In *Beppo* Byron would celebrate her as the only woman he had known 'Whose bloom could after dancing dare the dawn' after a ball (*CPW* iv. 155).

[57] Around this time Byron was at work on one of the few poems he had managed to write since *Childe Harold*: a 200-line satire on the Regency dance-craze, imaginatively entitled *Waltz*. He published it anonymously in 1813 and disclaimed it thereafter.

ashamed of my own bias towards your niece, nor should have the least objection to it's being posted up in Charing Cross, though I should never wish to hazard a refusal.——I certainly did wish to cultivate her acquaintance, but C[aroline] told me she was engaged to Eden,[58] so did several others, Mrs. L[amb?], *her* great friend, was of opinion (& upon my honour I believed her) that she neither did could nor ought to *like* me, & was moreover certain that E would be the *best husband* in the world & I it's *Antithesis*, & certainly *her* word deserved to be taken for *one* of us.—Under all these circumstances, & others I need not recapitulate, was I to hazard my heart with a woman I was very much inclined to like, but at the same time sure could be nothing to me?—& then you know my unfortunate manner which always leads me to talk too much to some particular person or not at all.—At present as I told you in my last I am rather captivated with a woman not very beautiful, but very much in the style I like, dark & lively, & neither more nor less than 'La Pucilla' ['the Flea'] of the Opera, whom I see sometimes at Col. Macleod's & whenever Italian is spoken I always strive to repair ye. inroads want of practice make in my memory of that dearest of all languages.——She is very fond of her husband, which is all the better, as thus, if a woman is attached to her husband how much more will she naturally like one who is *not* her husband—in the same manner as a woman does not always dislike a man who is violently in love with another, arguing says Fielding in this way, 'if Mr.——loves Mrs. or Miss so *much*, how much more will he love *me* who am so far the superior not only of Mrs. or Miss but of all other Mistresses or Misses whatsoever?'[59]—You can hardly say I do not trust you when I tell you all these fooleries——AT THIS *moment*, another *express* from Ireland!!! more Scenes!—this woman will never rest till she has made us all—what she & I at least deserve.—I must now write to her—I wrote Ly. B[essborough] a letter, which she was fool enough to shew her, though I addressed it under cover to Ld. B.—that she might not—*her* name was not mentioned in it, but it was easy to discern by the contents, that I was not eager for their return.—

6. o Clock.

So—having now remanded Mr. O Brien (the Irish Cupid on whose wings this despatch was wafted) back to Waterford—I resume merely to say that I see nothing but marriage & a *speedy one* can save me; if your Niece is attainable I should prefer her—if not—the very first woman who does not look as if she would spit in my face, amongst the variety of spouses provided for me by your

---

[58] George Eden (1784–1849), career politician and heir to Lord Auckland, was a conquest of Annabella's, but she turned him down.
[59] See Henry Fielding, *Tom Jones* (1749), xvi. 9.

correspondents &c. I am infinitely amused with my Cameriero's (who has lived with me since I was ten years old & been over the Mediterranean a prey to all the Mosquitoes & Siroccos in the Levant in my service) he is eternally sounding the praises of a *Dutch Widow* now here of great riches & rotundity, & very pretty withal; whose Abigail has made a conquest of him (a married man) & they have agreed how infinitely convenient it would be that as *they* can't marry, their master & mistress should.[60]—We shall meet at Middleton I hope mia carissima *Zia* [my dearest aunt]—I wish my Nepotism was well over—I do not care at all about Sir R[alph]'s involvements,[61] for I think that with the command of floating capital which my late N[ewstead] Business has put in my power, some arrangements might be made with *him* that might be advantageous to both—supposing this marriage could be effected.—When they come here I don't see how we are to meet for I go no-where—Does Annabella *waltz?*—it is an odd question—but a very essential point with me.—I wish somebody, would say at once that I wish to propose to her—but I have great doubts of *her*— it rests with *herself* entirely.—Believe me

dear Ly. M. *ever* yrs. most affectly.

P. S.—I have written you the vilest & most Egotistical letter that ever was scribbled but Caro's courier made me feel selfish & you will pardon my catching the infection.—Your apology for Ly. M[ilbanke]'s appellation was needless—though all my rhymes have got for me is a villainous nickname.—I know her, but latterly we cut—I suppose upon this most stupid rumour. I don't know how I shall manage this same wooing—I shall be like Comus & the Lady;[62] I am sadly out of practice lately, except for a few sighs to a Gentlewoman at supper who was too much occupied with ye. fourth wing of her second chicken to mind anything that was not material.

---

[60] This was Fletcher's practical scheme as Byron's *camarero* (manservant).

[61] Annabella's father Ralph Milbanke, sixth Baronet of Halnaby (1747–1825), had lost money electioneering; he did spend time in Parliament as MP for County Durham.

[62] *Comus* (1634) is a masque by Milton, involving an aristocratic lady lost in the woods, who is kidnapped by a lecherous wizard. She stoutly resists, and in due course is rescued by her brothers.

[To Lady Melbourne]

Cheltenham Octr. 17th. 1812

'*Cut* her!' My dear Ly. M. marry[63]—Mahomet forbid!—I am sure we shall be better friends than before & if I am not embarrassed by all this I cannot see for the soul of me why *she* should—assure *her* con tutto rispetto [with great respect] that The subject shall never be renewed in any shape whatever, & assure yourself my carissima (not *Zia* what then shall it be? chuse your *own* name) that were it not for this embarras [entanglement] with C[aroline] I would much rather remain as I am.——I have had so very little intercourse with the fair Philosopher that if when we meet I should endeavour to improve our acquaintance she must not *mistake* me, & assure her I never shall mistake her.—I *never did* you will allow;—& God knows whether I am right or not, but I do think I am not very apt to think myself encouraged.—She is perfectly right in every point of view, & during the slight suspense I felt something very like remorse for sundry reasons not at all connected with C nor with any occurrences since I knew you or her or hers; finding I must marry however on *that* score, I should have preferred a woman of birth & talents, but such a woman was not at all to blame for not preferring me; my *heart* never had an opportunity of being much interested in the business, further than that I should have very much liked to be *your relation*.—And now to conclude like Ld. Foppington,[64] 'I have lost a thousand women in my time but never had the ill manners to quarrel with them for such a trifle.'—Talking of addresses put me in mind of my *address* which has been murdered (I *hear*) in the delivery & mauled (I *see*) in the newspapers, & you don't tell me whether you heard it recited, I almost wish you may not, if this be the case.—I am asked to Ld. O[xford]'s & Ld. Harrowby's & am wavering between the two.—I cannot sufficiently thank you for all the trouble you have taken on my account, the interest with which you honour me would amply repay for fifty vexations even if I felt any & perhaps I do without knowing it; but I can't tell how it is, but I think C may be managed now as well as if the whole had taken place if she has either *pride* or *principle*, because she *may* now be convinced with a *little* dexterity at *her return* that I am most anxious to end every thing—added to

---

[63] Meaning here not 'to join in matrimony' but the archaic oath: 'indeed!'

[64] A self-proclaimed womanizer in John Vanbrugh's Restoration comedy *The Relapse* (1696), ultimately more interested in maintaining his appearance and demeanour than in successful seduction.

which the present *denial* will lessen me in her estimation as an *article* of *value*, & her Vanity will help marvellously to her conversion.——You talk of my 'religion' *that* rests between Man & his Maker & to *him* only can my feelings be known, for A[nnabella] it had been sufficient not to find me an '*infidel*' in anything else.—I must now conclude for I am pressed by the post—pray let me hear from you often & believe me ever my dear Ly. M.

yrs. most affectly.
B.

[To John Hanson]

Cheltenham Octr. 18th. 1812

Dear Sir

With perfect confidence in you I sign the note, but is not Claughton's delay very strange? let us take care what we are about, I answered his letter which I enclose to you, very *cautiously*, the wines & China &c. I will not demur much upon but the *vase* & cup (not the *skull cup*) & some little coffee things brought from the East, or made for the purpose of containing relics brought from thence, I will not part with, & if he refuses to ratify, I will take such steps as the Law will allow on the [force?] of the contract for compelling him to ratify it.—Pray write, I am invited to Ld. O[xford] & Ld. H[arrowby]'s, but if you wish very much to meet me I can come to town.——I suppose the tithe purchase will be made in my name.—what is to be done with Deardon?[65] Mrs. M[assingberd] is dead, and I should wish something settled for the Daughter who is still responsible. Will you give a glance into that business, and if possible first settle something about the Annuities.

I shall perhaps draw within a £100 next week, but I will delay for your answer on C[laughton]'s business.

Ever yours, sincerely and affectionately,
Byron

---

[65] James Dearden held the lease of Byron's Rochdale estate and would eventually purchase it for £11,000 in November 1823, six months before Byron's death (see letter of 12 October 1823). Hanson's various lawsuits about the legality of the lease collapsed in July 1820.

[To Lady Caroline Lamb]

[November 1812?]

I am no longer your lover;[66] and since you oblige me to confess it, by this truly unfeminine persecution,—learn, that I am attached to another; whose name it would of course be dishonourable to mention. I shall ever remember with gratitude the many instances I have received of the predilection you have shewn in my favour. I shall ever continue your friend, if your ladyship will permit me so to style myself; and, as a first proof of my regard, I offer you this advice, correct your vanity, which is ridiculous; exert your absurd caprices upon others; and leave me in peace.

Your most obedient servant,

[To Lady Melbourne]

Decr. 23d. 1812

My dear Lady M.

Your last anecdote seems to shew that our friend is actually possessed by 'the foul fiend *Flibertigibbet* who presides over mopping & mowing'[67] & if the provincial literati dont insert it in the St. Alban's Mercury, the collectors of extraordinaries ought to be dismissed for malversation & omission.—Seriously though all this forms *my* best justification—I very much fear it will not forward your interests at the next election except amongst ye. ballad-makers.—What will the Lady B[essborough] say? I fear it will go nigh to the recall of Sir W. Farquhar & the ancient disorder.—Was the 'odious book' (which has just attained the *summit* of *fame* by giving a name to a *very slow race horse!*) added to the conflagration? & what might be the pretty piece of eloquence delivered by her right trusty Henchman?[68] My letter would have added very appropriately to ye. combustibles & I regret ye. omission of such exquisite ingredients.—I wrote to you yesterday (franked & directed to B[rocket?] H[all?] not having then received ye. mandate to ye. contrary) & do not know that I can add anything to my details

---

[66] This letter is reproduced from Lady Caroline's novel about her affair with Byron, *Glenarvon* (1816). Byron read the book and made no comment concerning the letter's authenticity, so we may assume it is genuine.

[67] See Quarto *King Lear*, IV. i. 59.

[68] Lady Caroline had recently had a bonfire at her home (Brocket Hall) near St Albans, Hertfordshire, in which she burned Byron's portrait and copies of letters. Local children were brought along to dance around the conflagration, and a page recited some lines she had written for the occasion. Childe Harold had recently lent his name to a racehorse—not for the last time.

in that sheet—we are completely out of the world in this place, & have not even a *difference* to diversify the scene or amuse our correspondents, & you know perhaps that the recapitulation or display of *all good* things is very insipid to auditors or beholders.—I wait the news of the reception of the same ineffable letter now in your hands though (as I tell her) I have no great hopes of it's doing the least good.—It is written a little gravely but very much nevertheless in the usual tone which Ly. B[essborough] is pleased to say is not 'soothing.'——I am really become very indifferent as to her next proceedings, for what can she do worse than she has already done?—I am much amused with ye. tale of Ly. Cowper's little girl—her Mamma has always had a great share of my *most respectful* admiration, but I dont desire to be remembered to any of you as I suppose the best wish you have is to forget me as soon as possible; besides which under ye. impression of C[aroline]'s correspondence Ly. C[owper] must conceive me to be a sucking Catiline only less respectable.[69]—Bankes is going abroad, & as I said in my last it is not very unlikely that I may recommence voyaging amongst the Mussulmen.—If so I claim you as a correspondent; since you *wont* give me up to the reasonable request of the moderate C[aroline] & in truth I don't wish you should.—You know I have obeyed you in everything, in my suit to ye. *Princess of Parallelograms*, my breach with little *Mania*, & my subsequent acknowledgement of the sovereignty of *Armida*[70]—you have been my director & are still for I do not know anything you could not make me do or undo—& m'amie (but this you *wont believe*) has not yet learned the art of *managing* me nor superseded your authority.—You would have laughed a little time ago, when I inadvertantly said talking of you that there was nothing you could not make me do or give up (if you thought it worth while) a sentiment which did not meet with the entire approbation of my audience but which I maintained like a Muscovite enamoured of *Despotism*.—I hear little from London but the lies of the Gazette & will back Buonaparte against the field still.[71]—Pray write—& tell me how your *taming* goes on—I am all acquiescence to you & as much yours as ever dr. Ly. M

B.

---

[69] Emily Lamb, Lady Cowper (1787–1869), was Lady Melbourne's daughter. She had married in 1805, so if marital rumours were circulating about Byron and one of her children, they would certainly have been premature. The Roman senator Lucius Sergius Catilina (108–62 BC) had an unsavoury reputation for uxoricide and fratricide, and was also tried for raping a Vestal Virgin. ('Sucking' means 'budding' in this context.)

[70] That is, the mathematically inclined Annabella; the unpredictable Lady Caroline; and Lady Oxford, compared to the Saracen witch who waylaid the hero Rinaldo in Tasso's epic *Jerusalem Delivered* (1581).

[71] Napoleon had recently returned to Paris from his disastrous invasion of Russia; perhaps the Government newspaper, the *Gazette*, was speculating on his future.

[To John Hanson]

March 6th. 1813

Dear Sir

I must be ready in April at whatever risk—at whatever loss—you will therefore advertize Rochdale—if you decline this—I will sell it for what it will bring even though but a few thousand pounds.—With regard to Claughton I shall only say that if he knew the ruin—the misery he occasions by his delay he would be sorry for his conduct—& I only hope that he & I may not meet or I shall say something he will not like to hear.—I have called often—I shall call today at three or between three & four—again & again I can only beg of you to forward my plans—for here no power on earth shall make me remain six weeks longer.—

ever yrs.
B.—

[To Lord Holland]

March 25th. 1813

My dear Lord

I regret very much the *cause* of my yesterday's loss—& trust that it exists no longer.—I leave town on Sunday—it will not therefore be in my power to have the pleasure of meeting you on Wednesday next—but I will not leave this country without taking you by the hand & thanking you for many kind-nesses.—The fact is I can do no good anywhere—& am too patriotic—not to prefer doing ill in any country rather than my own.—Where I am going—I cannot positively say—& it is no great matter—'there is a world beyond Rome'[72] and all parts of it are much the same to a personage with few friendships & no connections.—My affairs are also not in the most brilliant order—& the sins of my nonage sit heavy upon my majority—I thought the sale of Newstead would relieve these—but it has merely led me within gunshot of a lawsuit.—I have neither the verve nor the 'copia fandi' to rival Ld. Ellenborough in Moloch-like

---

[72] See *Coriolanus*, III. iii. 139.

declamation in the house [of Lords][73]—& without occupation of some kind I cannot exist—travel therefore is the only pursuit left me—though I have some notion of taking orders.—'*Naxos*' I may perhaps visit—but '*Cyprus*'—is an Island I have long been sick of.[74]—I heard today that Ly. Holland is much better & need not say that I hope my information was correct—pray make my best respects acceptable to her.—Believe me

yr. ever obliged & sincere St.
Byron

[To Augusta Leigh]

4 Bennet Street St. James's. March 26th. 1813—

My dearest Augusta

I did not answer your letter—because I could not answer as I wished but expected that every week would bring me some tidings that might enable me to reply better than by apologies.—But Claughton has not—will not—& I think cannot pay his money—& though luckily it was stipulated that he should never have possession till the whole was paid—the estate is still on my hands—& your brother consequently not less embarrassed than ever.—This is the truth & is all the excuse I can offer for inability but not unwillingness to serve you—I am going abroad again in June—but should wish to see you before my departure— you have perhaps heard that I have been fooling away my time with different '*regnantes*' [mistresses] but what better can be expected from me?—I have but one *relative* & her I never see—I have no connections to domesticate with—& for marriage I have neither the talent nor the inclination—I cannot fortune-hunt nor afford to marry without a fortune—my parliamentary schemes are not much to my taste—I spoke twice last Session—& was told it was well enough— but I hate the thing altogether—& have no intention to 'strut another hour' on that stage.[75]—I am thus wasting the best part of life daily repenting & never amending.—On Sunday I set off for a fortnight for Eywood—near Presteign—in

---

[73] *Copia fandi* is from Virgil's *Aeneid*, meaning abundance of talk, prolixity. Edward Law, first Baron Ellenborough (1750–1818), judge and parliamentarian, had moved from a Whig to a Tory position. Moloch is a false god of the Old Testament who demands cruel and excessive sacrifice.

[74] Naxos is an Aegean island in the Cyclades, profoundly entwined with Greek history and myth (particularly its chief god, Zeus). The much larger Mediterranean island of Cyprus is one of the legendary birthplaces of the goddess of love, Aphrodite.

[75] See *Macbeth*, V. v. 24.

Herefordshire—with the *Oxfords*—I see you put on a *demure* look at the name—which is very becoming & matronly in you—but you wont be sorry to hear that I am quite out of a more serious scrape with another singular personage which threatened me last year—& trouble enough I had to steer clear of it I assure you.—I hope all my nieces are well & increasing in growth & number—but I wish you were not always buried in that bleak common near Newmarket.[76]—I am very well in health—but not happy nor even comfortable—but I will not bore you with complaints—I am a fool & deserve all the ills I have met or may meet with—but nevertheless very *sensibly* dearest Augusta

yr. most affec[tionat]e brother
Byron

[To Lady Caroline Lamb]

4 Bennet Street April 29th. 1813

If you still persist in your intention of meeting me in opposition to the wishes of your own friends & of mine—it must even be so—I regret it & acquiesce with reluctance.————I am not ignorant of the very extraordinary language you have held not only to me but others—& your avowal of your determination to obtain what you are pleased to call 'revenge'—nor have I now to learn that an incensed woman is a dangerous enemy.—Undoubtedly those against whom we can make no defence—whatever they say or do—must be formidable—your words & actions have lately been tolerably portentous—& might justify me in avoiding the demanded interview—more especially as I believe you fully capable of performing all your menaces—but as I once hazarded every thing *for* you—I will not shrink *from* you—perhaps I deserve punishment—if so—you are quite as proper a person to inflict it as any other. You say you will '*ruin me*'—I thank you—but I have done that for myself already—you say you will 'destroy me' perhaps you will only save me the trouble.[77]—It is useless to reason with you—to repeat what you already know—that I have in reality saved you from utter & impending destruction.—Every one who knows you—knows this also—but they do not know as yet what you may & will tell them as I now tell you—that it is in a great measure owing to this persecution—to the accursed things you have

---

[76] The Leighs' house, at Six Mile Bottom, was in an isolated area of Cambridgeshire, near the Newmarket racecourse and given over mostly to stables.

[77] Byron had shared confidences with Lady Caroline about his time in Greece. Homosexuality was a civil offence punishable by death in early 19th-century Britain.

said—to the extravagances you have committed—that I again adopt the resolution of quitting this country—In your assertions—you have either *belied* or
betrayed me—take your choice—in your actions—you have hurt only yourself—
but is that nothing to one who wished you well?——I have only one request to
make—which is not to attempt to see Ly. O[xford]—on her you have no
claim.—You will settle—as you please—the arrangement of this conference—
I do not leave England till June—but the sooner it is over the better—I once
wished for your own sake Ly. M[elbourne] to be present—but if you are to fulfil
any of your threats in word or deed—we had better be alone—

yrs. ever

[To Thomas Moore]

May 19th, 1813

Oh you, who in all names can tickle the town,
Anacreon, Tom Little, Tom Moore, or Tom Brown,—
For hang me if I know of which you may most brag,
Your Quarto two-pounds, or your Twopenny Post Bag;[78]

* * * * * * * * * * * * * * * *

But now to my letter—to *yours* 'tis an answer—
To-morrow be with me, as soon as you can, sir,
All ready and dress'd for proceeding to spunge on
(According to compact) the wit in the dungeon—
Pray Phoebus at length our political malice
May not get us lodgings within the same palace![79]
I suppose that to-night you're engaged with some codgers,
And for Sotheby's Blues have deserted Sam Rogers;
And I, though with cold I have nearly my death got,
Must put on my breeches, and wait on the Heathcote.

---

[78] Moore used many pseudonyms and published in many formats from the small and cheap
(octavo) to the large and expensive (quarto). He had just published *Intercepted Letters, or the Twopenny
Post-bag*, by 'Thomas Brown, the Younger': a set of risqué imaginary poetic epistles from high life.
[79] The Radical poet and editor Leigh Hunt (1784–1859) was imprisoned for two years in Surrey Jail
for libelling the Prince Regent. He would figure in Byron's expatriate Italian life as co-editor of the
Liberal magazine project in Genoa, between 1822 and 1823.

But to-morrow, at four, we'll both play the *Scurra*,
And you'll be Catullus, the R[egen]t Mamurra.[80]

Dear M.—having got this far, I am interrupted by * * * * 10 o'clock.
Half-past 11. * * * * is gone. I must dress for Lady Heathcote's.—Addio.

[To John Murray]

May 23d. 1813

Dear Sir

I question whether ever author before received such a compliment from his
master—I am glad you think the thing is tolerably *vamped* & will be *vendible*.—Pray
look over the proof again—I am but a careless reviser—& let me have 12 struck
off & and one or two for yourself to serve as M.S. for the thing when published
in the body of the volume.[81] If Ly.——————— [Caroline Lamb] sends for it—do
not let her have it—till the copies are ready & then you can send her one.—

yrs. truly
Μπαιρῶν

P. S. H[obhouse]'s book is out at last—I have my copy—which I have lent already.

---

[80] See Catullus, *Carmina*, xxix, which mourns the succession of a decadent Roman general (that is,
the Prince Regent) to northern lands once held by worthier warriors. The English 'scurr' is derived
from the Latin *scurra*, meaning a buffoon or jester.
[81] At this stage Byron was planning to add *The Giaour* to a new edition of *Childe Harold*, rather than
publish it separately.

4

THE GIAOUR AND AUGUSTA LEIGH

June 1813–July 1814

Byron's life was set on wholly new courses by his unexpected ascent to the barony, by his travels in the Mediterranean, and by the publication of Childe Harold. Between the appearance of that poem in March 1812 and his marriage in January 1815 his existence became increasingly frantic. In particular he embarked on a series of affairs that seemed positively designed to bring about his social exposure and downfall, even as his literary fame grew. The married Lady Caroline Lamb was the first of these; the married Lady Oxford the second. But in July 1813 he re-encountered his half-sister Augusta Leigh—herself lost in what Byron called an 'abominable marriage' (LJ iii. 70) to a dim-witted colonel even more terminally insolvent than Byron himself. (George Leigh's vice was gambling; one of the few that Byron never really succumbed to.) She and Byron began an affair the following month. For what it was worth, incest only contravened ecclesiastical law in Britain, and was punishable by six months' imprisonment, whereas homosexuality was a civil offence punishable by death. But it was hardly less scandalous. The risks they ran were atrocious.

Then, in October 1813, Byron made a half-hearted attempt at sexual substitution—which had worked, for him at least, where Lady Caroline was concerned. On a visit to a baronet ex-schoolfriend, James Wedderburn Webster, Byron found himself piqued by Webster's bombastic dependence on his wife's chastity, and initiated a seduction that only just failed to come off. The process was recorded in a novelistic set of letters to Lady Melbourne, to whom he had confessed his affair with Augusta months earlier. He wrote to Lady Melbourne on 13 January 1814:

You are quite mistaken however as to *her*—and it must be from some misrepresentation of mine that you throw the blame so completely on the side least deserving and least able to bear it—I dare say I made the best of my own story as one always does from natural selfishness without intending it—but it was not her fault—but my own *folly* (give it what name may suit it better) and her weakness—for—the intentions of both were very different and for some time adhered to—& when *not* it was entirely my own—in short I know no name for my own conduct.—Pray do not speak so harshly of her to me—the cause of all——— (LJ iv. 27–8)

All that Lady Melbourne could advise was that he marry as soon as possible. (He agreed. 'A wife,' he wrote in his journal in January 1814, 'would be my salvation'; LJ iii. 241.) So, at the same time as seeing Augusta and fiddling with Lady Frances Webster, he continued to correspond with Annabella Milbanke in County Durham, ponderously, passionlessly, and exasperatingly picking away at the state of her affections while she asked him in turn about the state of his faith and mind. Various other marriageable females—Elizabeth Rawdon, Charlotte Leveson-Gower, and Adelaide Forbes—were contemplated by him, by Lady Melbourne, or by them both.

Byron had made plans to escape back to Europe with the easygoing Lady Oxford as early as March 1813, but it seems her husband eventually put his foot down, and they went abroad without him a fortnight or so before Byron took up with Augusta. Then plague spread across the Mediterranean, making travel difficult. Intermittently Byron announced that he was simply upping stakes and leaving, no matter where: Holland, Russia, anywhere without the plague. In August 1813 the idea was to escape to Europe with Augusta. His finances continued to deteriorate, despite Claughton's forfeited deposit on the purchase of Newstead, and by 1815 he had debts of £30,000.

Byron's literary fame thrived on this diet of paranoia, dread, and confusion. In March 1813 he had broken a long fallow period by writing a 400-line poetic melodrama, set in the Aegean, 'The Giaour' (that is, 'the infidel'), about a Westerner consumed by an illicit love affair with a harem-girl in Turkish Greece. Abounding in sex and violence, it was published, somewhat nervously, on 5 June, and Byron promptly became the talk of the town again for literary as well as personal reasons. The Giaour was the first and greatest of a series of narrative poems set in the same Mediterranean region, which effectively became his personal literary real estate. Between them these poems made him a sensation, and threw Sir Walter Scott wholly into the shade as Britain's favourite poet. (Scott took up prose fiction with Waverley in 1814.) 'Stick to the East', Byron told his friend Thomas Moore in August 1813: 'the oracle, Staël, told me it was the only poetical policy' (LJ iii. 101), and Byron obeyed the exiled Swiss-French literary intellectual to the letter: The Bride of Abydos, which flirted with incest, was written in a week in November 1813, and published almost immediately; and The Corsair, which involves a hapless pirate choosing between an honourable love and a dagger-toting vamp, was published in February 1814, and sold 10,000 copies in a day. These poems were evidently reflections of Byron's state of mind. 'In the last three days I have been quite shut up', he wrote to Lady Melbourne on 4 November 1813:

my mind has been from late and later events in such a state of fermentation that as usual I have been obliged to empty it in rhyme—& am in the very heart of another Eastern tale—something of the Giaour cast—but not so sombre though rather more villainous— this is my usual resource—if it were not for some such occupation to dispel reflection during inaction—I verily believe I should very often go mad. (LJ iii. 157)

As if to flout the British public as much as possible, Byron added his previously anonymous 'Lines to a Lady Weeping' (about the Prince Regent's treacherous desertion of the Whigs in 1812) to the second edition of The Corsair—then withdrew it from the third—then reissued it in the fourth. His unsavoury political reputation in the eyes of the Tory Government and its allies in the Press and among the English Lake poets was cemented by his 'Ode on Napoleon Bonaparte', written in April 1814 in response to the Emperor's abdication, which went through ten editions during the year before Byron put his name to it. John Murray jibbed and squirmed at all this political scandal, but he also rubbed his hands with glee, and made decent but fruitless attempts to share his profits with his star author. None of this notoriety seems to have given Byron the least pleasure. In his journal on 24 November 1813 he ranked the British poets in a pyramid: Scott at the apex, Rogers below him, Moore and Campbell below Rogers,

Southey, Wordsworth, and Coleridge below them, and 'the many' beneath them. 'Who would write, who any thing better to do?' he asked:

Look at the querulous and monotonous lives of the 'genus;'—except Cervantes, Tasso, Dante, Ariosto, Kleist (who were brave and active citizens), Æschylus, Sophocles, and some other of the antiques also—what a worthless, idle brood it is! (*LJ* iii. 220–1)

At the end of April Byron must have horrified Murray by announcing his retirement as a poet. By the beginning of May normal service had been resumed.

In and amongst these events, Byron and Augusta stayed together for substantial periods, either at Newstead or Six Mile Bottom. When, in April 1814, Byron wrote to Lady Melbourne that Augusta's latest child (she would have seven in the end) was 'not an "Ape" and if it is— that must be my fault' (LJ iv. 104)—alluding to the possibility that Medora Leigh was his daughter—even he must have realized the risks the pair of them were running. In September that year he proposed to Annabella Milbanke.

[To John Hanson]

June 3d. 1813

Dear Sir

When you receive this I shall have left town for a week—& it is perfectly right we should understand each other—I think you will not be surprised at my persisting in my intention of going abroad.—If the Suit can be carried on in my absence—*well*—if not—it must be given up—one word—one letter to C[laughto]n would put an end to it—but this I shall not do—at all events without acquainting you before hand—nor at all—provided I am enabled to go abroad again—but at all hazards at all losses—on this last point I am as determined as I have been for the last six months—& you have always told me that you would endeavour to assist me in that intention—every thing is ordered & ready—now—do not trifle with me—for I am in very solid serious earnest— & if utter ruin *were* or *is* before me—on the one hand—& wealth at home on the other—I have made my choice—& go I will—If you wish to write address a line before Saturday to Salthill—Post office—Maidenhead I believe but am not sure is the Post town—but I shall not be in London till Wednesday next. Believe me

yrs. ever

Bɴ

———⟨∞⟩———

P. S. Let all the books go to Mr. Murray's immediately—& let the plate linen &c. which I find excepted by the contract—be sold—particularly a large silver vase—with the contents not removed as they are curious—& a silver cup—(not the skull) be sold also—both are of value.————

The Pictures also—& every moveable that is mine & can be converted into cash—all I want is a few thousand pounds—& then adieu—you shan't be troubled with me these ten years—if ever.————

[To Lady Melbourne]

June 21st. 1813

My dear Ly. M[elbourn]e

The Devil—who ought to be civil on such occasions has at last persuaded Ld.————[Oxford] to be so too—for on *her* threatening to fill up my 'carte blanche' in her own way—he quietly ate his own words & intentions—& now they are to 'live happy ever after'—& to sail in the pleasing hope of seeing or not seeing me again.—So that the very letter in which I most committed myself to her—has by Good fortune turned out the most successful of peremptory papers.————But on the other hand—your plague & mine has according to her own account been in 'excellent fooling'[.] Mr. L[amb] on his return found her in tears[1]—& was (no wonder) wroth to a degree—& wanted to know if I (the most inoffensive of men) had affronted her &c.—now this is really laughable—if I *speak* to her *he* is insulted—If I *don't* speak to her—*she* is insulted—now if he is to be equally offended at both—I shall not be long in choosing————I had much rather differ about *something* than *nothing*.—All this I only know from her—& probably it is not true—I however must say that it is not to be expected that I shall throw myself *in* or *out* of the way of either—let them amuse themselves in their own way—I may *shut* myself out of society for my own pleasure—but I will not be *put* out of it by any couple in Christendom. With regard to the miseries of this '*correct & animated* Waltzer' as the M[orning] Post entitles her—I wish she would not call in the aid of so many compassionate Countesses—there is Ly. W[estmorland] (with a tongue too) conceives me to be the greatest Barbarian since the days of Bacchus & Ariadne[2]—and all who hate

---

[1] This is Lady Caroline Lamb and her husband William—Lady Melbourne's second son.
[2] For Lady Westmorland, see letter of 11 August 1809. In Greek myth the nymph Ariadne was abandoned on the island of Naxos by Theseus, after helping him defeat the Minotaur in the Cretan maze; there she was discovered by Bacchus (or Dionysus), the god of intoxication and ecstasy. Byron's 'ticket' in the next sentence must be Lord Melbourne's season ticket to the theatre.

Ly. O[xford]—consisting of *one half* the world—and all who abominate me—
that is the *other half*—will tear the last rag of my tattered reputation into shreds—
threads—filaments & atoms.————Where is my ticket?—that I may person-
ify Ld. M—a gentleman whom I should like to have represented for the last—let
me see—how many years has he been your proprietor?————Why wont *you*
go off with me?—I am sure our elopement would have greater effect—cause a
'greater sensation' as our Orators say—than any event of the kind—since Eve
ran away with the Apple. Believe me

ever yrs. most truly—

[To Lady Melbourne (a)]

July 6th. 1813

My dear Ly. M[elbourn]e

God knows what has happened—but at 4 in the morning Ly. Ossulstone
looking angry (& at that moment ugly) delivered to me a confused kind of
message from you of some scene—this is all I know—except that with laudable
logic she drew the usual feminine deduction that I *'must* have behaved very ill'.—
If Ly. C[aroline] is offended it really must be anger at my *not* affronting her—for
one of the few things I said was a request to know her will & pleasure—if there
was anything I could say do or not do to give her the least gratification—she
walked away without answering—& after leaving me in this not very dignified
situation—& showing her independence to twenty people near—I only saw her
dancing—& in the doorway for a moment—where she said something so very
violent—that I was in distress lest Ld. Y[armouth?]. or Ly. Rancliffe overheard
her—I went to Supper—& saw & heard no more till Ly. Ossulstone told me
your words & her own opinion—& here I am in stupid innocence & ignorance
of my offence or her proceedings.——If I am to be haunted with hysterics
wherever I go—& whatever I do—I think she is not the only person to be
pitied.—I should have returned to her after her *doorway whisper*—but I could not
with any kind of politeness leave Ly. Rancliffe to drown herself in wine & water
or be suffocated in a Jelly-dish—without a spoon or a hand to help her—
besides—if there was & I foresaw there would be something ridiculous—surely
I was better absent than present.—This is really insanity—& every body seems

inoculated with the same distemper—Ly. W says 'you must have done something—you know between people in your situation—a word or a look goes a great way' &c. &c.—so it seems indeed—but I never knew that *neither* words nor looks—in short—downright—innocent—vacant—indefinable *Nothing* had the same precious power of producing this perpetual worry. I wait to hear from you—in case I have to answer you—I trust nothing has occurred to spoil your breakfast—for which the Regent has got a fine day.—

[To Lady Melbourne (b)]

[July 6, 1813]

Dear Ly. M[elbourn]e

Since I wrote ye. enclosed I have heard a strange story of C's scratching herself with glass—& I know not what besides—of all this I was ignorant till this Evening.—What I did or said to provoke her—I know not—I told her it was better to *waltze*—'because she danced well—& it would be imputed to *me*—if she did not'—but I see nothing in this to produce cutting & maiming—besides before supper I saw her—& though she said & did even then a foolish thing—I could not suppose her so frantic as to be in earnest.—She took hold of my hand as I passed & pressed it against some sharp instrument—& said—'I mean to use this'—I answered [']against me I presume[']—& passed on with Ly. R[ancliffe] trembling lest Ld. Y. & Ly. R should overhear her—though not believing it possible that this was more than one of her not uncommon *bravadoes*—for *real feeling* does not disclose its intentions—& always shuns display—I thought little more of this—& leaving the table in search of her would have appeared more particular than proper—though of course had I guessed her to be serious or had I been conscious of offending I should have done every thing to pacify or prevent her.——I know not what to say or do—I am quite unaware of what I did to displease—& useless regret is all I can feel on the subject—Can she be in her senses?—yet—I would rather think myself to blame—than that she were so silly without cause.—I really remained at Ly. H[eathcote]'s till 5 totally ignorant of all that passed—nor do I now know where this cursed scarification took place—nor when—I mean the room—& the hour.————

[To Thomas Moore]

Bennet-street, August 22d, 1813

* * * * * * * * * * * * * * *

As our late—I might say, deceased—correspondence had too much of the town-life leaven in it, we will now, 'paulo majora.'[3] prattle a little of literature in all its branches; and first of the first—criticism. The Prince is at Brighton, and Jackson, the boxer, gone to Margate, having, I believe, decoyed [Lord] Yarmouth to see a milling in that polite neighborhood. Mad[am]e. de Staël Holstein[4] has lost one of her young barons, who has been carbonadoed by a vile Teutonic adjutant,—kilt & killed in a coffee-house at Scrawsenhawsen. Corinne is, of course, what all mothers must be,—but will, I venture to prophesy, do what few mothers could—and write an Essay upon it. She cannot exist without a grievance—and somebody to see, or read, how much grief becomes her. I have not seen her since the event; but merely judge (not very charitably) from prior observation.

In a 'mail-coach copy' of the Edinburgh, I perceive the Giaour is 2d article. The numbers are still in the Leith smack—*pray, which way is the wind?* The said article is so very mild and sentimental, that it must be written by Jeffrey *in love;*—you know he is gone to America to marry some fair one, of whom he has been, for several *quarters, éperdument amoureux* [madly in love]. Seriously—as Winifred Jenkins says of Lismahago—Mr. Jeffrey (or his deputy) 'has done the handsome thing by me,'[5] and I say *nothing*. But this I will say,—If you and I had knocked one another on the head in his quarrel, how he would have laughed, and what a mighty bad figure we should have cut in our posthumous works. By the by, I was called *in* the other day to mediate between two gentlemen bent upon carnage, and,—after a long struggle between the natural desire of destroying one's fellow-creatures, and the dislike of seeing men play the fool for nothing,—I got one to make an apology, and the other to take it, and left them to live happy ever after. One was a peer, the other a friend untitled, and both fond of high play;—and one, I can swear for, though very mild, 'not fearful,'[6] and so dead a shot, that, though the other is the thinnest of

---

[3] *Paulo majora canamus:* 'let us sing of greater things'; a tag from Virgil's *Eclogues.*

[4] Anne Louise Germaine de Staël-Holstein, née Necker (1766–1817), Swiss-French author of the sentimental novel *Corinne*, and first popularizer of German Romantic ideas in her *De l'Allemagne* (*On Germany*), translated into English in 1813, during which year she visited England to great acclaim. After the French Revolution she emigrated to Coppet, in Switzerland, where she held a salon; Byron would visit her there in 1816. Her second son Albert died in a duel while serving in the Swedish army.

[5] See Tobias Smollett, *Humphry Clinker* (1771), letter 83. Francis Jeffrey (1773–1850), editor of the *Edinburgh Review*, retail copies of which came to London by coastal freighter from Leith.

[6] See *The Tempest*, I. ii. 471.

men, he would have split him like a cane. They both conducted themselves very well, and I put them out of *pain* as soon as I could.[7]

* * * * * * * * * * * * * * * *

There is an American Life of G. F. Cooke, *Scurra* deceased, lately published.[8] Such a book!—I believe, since Drunken Barnaby's Journal, nothing like it has drenched the press. All green-room and tap-room—drams and the drama— brandy, whisky-punch, and, *latterly*, toddy, overflow every page. Two things are rather marvellous—first, that a man should live so long drunk, and, next, that he should have found a sober biographer. There are some very laughable things in it, nevertheless;—but the pints he swallowed and the parts he performed are too regularly registered.

All this time you wonder I am not gone: so do I; but the accounts of the plague are very perplexing—not so much for the thing itself as the quarantine established in all ports, and from all places, even from England. It is true the forty or sixty days would, in all probability, be as foolishly spent on shore as in the ship; but one likes to have one's choice, nevertheless. Town is awfully empty; but not the worse for that. I am really puzzled with my perfect ignorance of what I mean to do;—not stay, if I can help it, but where to go? Sligo[9] is for the North,—a pleasant place, Petersburgh, in September, with one's ears and nose in a muff, or else tumbling into one's neckcloth or pocket-handkerchief! If the winter treated Buonaparte with so little ceremony, what would it inflict upon your solitary traveller?—Give me a *sun*, I care not how hot, and sherbet, I care not how cool, and *my* Heaven is as easily made as your Persian's. The Giaour is now 1000 and odd lines. 'Lord Fanny spins a thousand such a day,' eh, Moore?[10]—thou wilt needs be a wag, but I forgive it.

Yours ever,
BN.

---

[7] This was Scrope Berdmore Davies, in a potentially fatal quarrel with Lord Foley.

[8] See W. Dunlap, *Memoirs of George Frederick Cooke, late of the Theatre Royal, Covent Garden* (1813). Cooke (1756–1812), innovative, talented, and versatile, saw his talent collapse into alcoholism exactly as Byron describes.

[9] Howe Peter Browne, second Marquis of Sligo (1788–1845), a Cambridge friend of Byron's, had spent time travelling with him in Greece in the summer of 1810, during which time it seems he heard of events that Byron later developed into *The Giaour* (see journal of 5 December 1813).

[10] See Pope, 'First Satire of the Second Book of Horace' (1733), 6. 'Thou wilt needs be a wag' is not a quotation as such, but surely has its origins in Falstaff's repeated use of the word to Hal in 1 *Henry IV*, I. ii.

*P. S. I perceive I have written a flippant and rather cold-hearted letter; let it go, however. I have said nothing, either, of the brilliant sex; but the fact is, I am, at this moment, in a far more serious, and entirely new, scrape than any of the last twelvemonths,—and that is saying a good deal. * * * It is unlucky we can neither live with nor without these women.*

I am now thinking and regretting that, just as I have left Newstead, you reside near it.[11] Did you ever see it? do—but don't tell me that you like it. If I had known of such intellectual neighbourhood, I don't think I should have quitted it. You could have come over so often, as a bachelor.—for it was a thorough bachelor's mansion—plenty of wine and such sordid sensualities—with books enough, room enough, and an air of antiquity about all (except the lasses) that would have suited you, when pensive, and served you to laugh at when in glee. I had built myself a bath and a vault—and now I sha'n't even be buried in it. It is odd that we can't even be certain of a grave, at least a particular one. I remember, when about fifteen, reading your poems there,—which I can repeat almost now,—and asking all kinds of questions about the author, when I heard that he was not dead according to the preface; wondering if I should ever see him—and though, at that time, without the smallest poetical propensity myself, very much taken, as you may imagine, with that volume. Adieu—I commit you to the care of the gods—Hindoo, Scandinavian, and Hellenic!

*P. S. 2d. There is an excellent review of Grimm's Correspondence and Mad[am]e. de Staël in this No. of the E[dinburgh] R[eview][12] * * * * * Jeffrey, himself, was my critic last year; but this is, I believe, by another hand. I hope you are going on with your* grand coup—*pray do—or that damned Lucien Buonaparte will beat us all. I have seen much of his poem in MS., and he really surpasses every thing beneath Tasso. Hodgson is translating him against another bard.[13] You and (I believe, Rogers) Scott, Gifford and myself, are to be referred to as judges between the twain,—that is, if you accept the office. Conceive our different opinions! I think we, most of us (I am talking very impudently, you will think—us, indeed!) have a way of our own,—at least, you and Scott certainly have.*

[To Annabella Milbanke]

4 Bennet Street August 25th 1813

I am honoured with your letter which I wish to acknowledge immediately.— Before I endeavour to answer it—allow me—briefly if possible—to advert to the

---

[11] Moore lived at Mayfield Cottage in Derbyshire, just across the border with Nottinghamshire.

[12] The *Edinburgh* was catching up, not only with *De l'Allemagne*, but also with the *Correspondance littéraire*, a hand-copied magazine of French Enlightenment thought and literature edited by Friedrich Melchior, Baron von Grimm (1723–1807), between 1753 and 1790, and eventually printed, in extracts, in 1812. It became favourite reading for Byron in later years.

[13] Byron's friend Francis Hodgson and Dr Samuel Butler both translated *Charlemagne* (1814), a poem by Lucien Bonaparte, younger brother of the Emperor, once his ally, latterly his enemy, and an *émigré* in England. A poem on the 8th-century Holy Roman Emperor could hardly fail to provoke comparisons with his contemporary avatar.

circumstances which occurred last Autumn.—Many years had [occurred?] since
I had seen any woman with whom there appeared to me a prospect of rational
happiness—I now saw but one—to whom however I had no pretentions—or at
least too slight for even the hope of success.—It was however said that your
heart was disengaged—& it was on that ground that Ly. M[elbourne]. undertook
to ascertain how far I might be permitted to cultivate your acquaintance on the
chance (a slender one I allow) of improving it into friendship and ultimately to a
still kinder sentiment.—In her zeal in my behalf—friendly and pardonable as it
was—she in some degree exceeded my intentions when she made the more
direct proposal—which yet I do not regret except as far as it appeared presump-
tuous on my part.—That is the truth you will allow when I tell you that it was
not till lately I mentioned to her that I thought she had unwittingly committed
me a little too far in the expectation that so abrupt an overture would be
received—but I stated this casually in conversation & without the least feeling
of irritation towards her or pique against yourself.—Such was the result of my
first & nearest approach to that altar—to which in the state of your feelings—I
should only have led another victim.—When I say the *first* it may perhaps appear
irreconcileable with some circumstances in my life to which I conceive you
allude in part of your letter—but such is the fact—I was then too young to
marry though not to love—but this was the *first direct* or *indirect* approach ever
made on my part to a permanent union with any woman & in all probability it
will be the last. Ly. M. was perfectly correct in her statement that I preferred you
to all others—it was then the fact—it is so still—but it was no disappointment—
because it is impossible to impart one drop more to a cup which already
overflows with the waters of bitterness.—We do not know ourselves—yet
I do not think that self love was much wounded by this event—on the contrary
I feel a kind of pride even in *your rejection*—more I believe than I could derive
from the attachment of another—for it reminds me that I once thought myself
worthy of the affection of almost the only one of your sex I ever truly
respected.—To your letter—the first part surprises me—not that you should
feel attachment—but that such attachment should be 'without hope' may you
recover that hope with it's object!—To the part of your letter regarding myself—
I could say much—but I must be brief—if you hear ill of me it is probably not
untrue though perhaps exaggerated—on any point in which you may honour
me with an interest I shall be glad to satisfy you—to confess the truth or refute
the calumny.—I must be candid with you on the score of Friendship—it is a
feeling towards you with which I cannot trust myself—I doubt whether I could
help loving you—but I trust I may appeal to my conduct since our eclaircisse-
ment [understanding] for the proof—that whatever my feelings may be—they
will exempt you from persecution—but I cannot yet profess indifference—and

I fear that must be the first step—at least in some points—from what I feel to that which you wish me to feel.—You must pardon me & recollect that if anything displeases you in this letter—it is a difficult task for me to write to you at all—I have left many things unsaid—& have said others I did not mean to utter.—My intended departure from this country is a little retarded by accounts of Plague &c. in the part of the world to which I was returning, & I must bend my course to some more accessible region—probably to Russia.—I have only left myself space to sign myself

ever your obliged Sert.
Byron

[To Annabella Milbanke]

Septr. 26th. 1813

My dear friend

for such you will permit me to call you—on my return to town I find some consolation for having left a number of pleasant people—in your letter—the more so as I [had] begun to doubt if I should ever receive another.——You ask me some questions—& as they are about myself—you must pardon ye Egotism into which my answers must betray me.—I am glad that you know any 'good deed' that I am supposed ever to have blundered upon—simply—because it proves that you have not heard me *invariably* ill spoken of—if true—I am sufficiently rewarded by a short step towards your good opinion.—You don't like my 'restless' doctrines—I should be very sorry if *you* did—but *I* can't *stagnate* nevertheless—if I must sail let it be on the ocean no matter how stormy—anything but a dull cruise on a level lake without ever losing sight of the same insipid shores by which it is surrounded.—— 'Gay' but not 'content' very true.——You say I never attempt to 'justify' myself. you are right—at times I can't & occasionally I wont defend by explanations—life is not worth having on such terms—the only attempt I ever made at defence was in a poetical point of view—& what did it end in? not an exculpation of me but an attack on all other persons whatsoever—I should make a pretty scene indeed if I went on defending—besides by proving myself (supposing it possible) a good sort of quiet country gentleman—to how many people should I give more pain than pleasure?—do you think accusers like one the better for being confuted?——You have detected a laughter 'false to the heart'—allowed—yet I have been tolerably sincere with you—& I fear sometimes troublesome.—To the charge of Pride—I suspect I must plead guilty—because when a boy & a very young one it was the constant reproach of schoolfellows & tutors—since I grew up I have heard less about it—

135

probably because I have now neither schoolfellows nor Tutor—it was however originally *defensive*—for at that time my hand like Ishmael's was against every one's & every one's against mine.—I now come to a subject of your enquiry which you must have perceived I always hitherto avoided—an awful one 'Religion'——I was bred in Scotland among Calvinists in the first part of my life—which gave me a dislike to that persuasion—since that period I have visited the most bigotted & credulous of countries—Spain—Greece—Turkey—as a spectacle the Catholic is more fascinating than the Greek or ye. Moslem—but the *last* is the only believer who practices the precepts of his Prophet to the last chapter of his creed.—My opinions are quite undecided—I may say so sincerely—since when given over at Patras in 1810—I rejected & ejected three Priest-loads of spiritual consolation by threatening to turn Mussulman if they did not leave me in quiet—I was in great pain & looked upon death as in that respect a relief—without much regret of the past— & few speculations on the future—indeed so indifferent was I to my *bodily* situation—that though I was without any attendant but a young Frenchman as ill as myself—two barbarous Arn[a]outs—and a deaf & desperate Greek Quack— and my English servant (a man now with me) within 2 days journey—I would not allow the last to be sent for—worth all the rest as he would have been in attendance at such a time because—I really don't know why—unless—it was an indifference to which I am certainly not subject when in good health.—I believe doubtless in God—& should be happy to be convinced of much more—if I do not at present place implicit faith on tradition & revelation of any human creed I hope it is not from a want of reverence for the Creator but the created—& when I see a man publishing a pamphlet to prove that Mr. *Pitt* is risen from the dead (as was done a week ago) perfectly positive in the truth of his assertion—I must be permitted to doubt more miracles equally well attested—but the *moral* of Christianity is perfectly beautiful—& the very sublime of Virtue—yet even there we find some of its finer precepts in earlier axioms of the Greeks.—particularly 'do unto others as you would they should do unto you.'—the forgiveness of injuries—& more which I do not remember.—Good Night—I have sent you a long prose—I hope your answer will be equal in length—I am sure it will be more amusing.—You write remarkably well—which you won't like to hear so I shall say no more about it—

ever yrs. most sincerely
Biron

P. S.—I shall post-scribble this half sheet.—When at Aston I sent you a short note—for I began to feel a little nervous about the reception of my last letter.—I shall be down there again next week & merely left them to escape from ye Doncaster races—being very ill adapted for provincial festivities—but I shall rejoin ye party when they are over.—This letter was written last night after a two day's journey with little rest & no refreshment (eating on the road throws me into a fever directly) you will therefore not wonder if it is a meagre performance.—When you honour me with an answer address to London—present my invariable respects to Sir R. and Ly. Mil[bank]e & once more receive them for yourself— Good Morning.—

[To Lady Melbourne]

Septr. 28th. 1813

My dear Lady Melbourne

I sent you a long letter from Aston last week which I hope has been received at *Brocket*.—The Doncaster races (as I *foretold* you) drove me to town but I have an invitation to go down again this week upon which I am pondering—I had reasons of my own some bad & others good for not accompanying the party to D[oncaste]r—my time was passed pleasantly enough—& as innocently at Aston—as during the 'week' of immaculate memory last autumn at Middleton.—If you received my letter you will remember my sketch of the *Astonian* family—when I return I shall complete it—at present I doubt about the colours—I have been observing & have made out one conclusion which is that my friend W[ebster] will run his head against a wall of his own building.—There are a Count & Countess—somebody—(I forget the name of the exiles)—the last of whom made a desperate attack on W. at Ld. Waterpark's a few weeks ago—& W. in gratitude invited them to his house—there I suppose they now are—(they had not arrived when I set out) to me it appears from W's own narrative—that he will be detected & bullied by the husband into some infernal compromise—& I told him as much—but like *others* of our acquaintance he is deaf as an adder.—I have known him several years & really wish him well—for which reason I overlooked his interference in some concerns of my own where he had no business—perhaps because also they had ceased to interest me—(for we are all selfish & I no more trust myself than others with a good motive) but be that as it may—I wish he would not indulge in such freaks—for which *he* can have no excuse—& the example will turn out none of the best for Ly. F[ann]y.—She seems pretty & intelligent—as far as I observed which was very little—I had &

have other things to reflect upon.—Your opinion of ye. Giaour or rather ye. *additions* honours me highly—you who know how my thoughts were occupied when these last were written—will perhaps perceive in parts a coincidence in my own state of mind with that of my hero—if so you will give me credit for feeling—though on the other hand I lose in your esteem.[14]—I have tried & hardly too to vanquish my demon—but to very little purpose—for a resource that seldom failed me before—did in this instance—I mean *transferring* my regards to another—of which I had a very fair & not *discouraging* opportunity at one time—I willingly would—but the feeling that it was an effort spoiled all again—& *here* I am—*what* I am you know already.—As I have never been accustomed to parade my thoughts before you in a larmoyante [tearful] strain I shall not begin now.—The epistles of your mathematician (A would now be ambiguous) continue—& the last concludes with a repetition of a desire that none but Papa & Mamma should know it—why *you* should not seems to me quite ludicrous & is now past praying for—but—observe—here is the strictest of St. Ursula's 11000 what do you call 'ems?[15]—a wit—a moralist—& religionist—enters into a clandestine correspondence with a personage generally presumed a great Roué—& drags her aged parents into this secret treaty—it is I believe not usual for single ladies to risk such brilliant adventures—but this comes of *infallibility*—not that she ever says anything that might not be said by the Town cryer—still it is imprudent—if I were rascal enough to an unfair advantage.—Alas! poor human nature—here is your niece writing—& doing a foolish thing—*I lecturing* Webster!—& forgetting the tremendous 'beam in my own eye'[16] no—I *do* feel but cannot pluck it out.—These various absurdities & inconsistencies may amuse you—but there is a fate in such small as great concerns or how came Moreau by the loss of his legs? I saw an extract from his last letter to his wife (in M.S. not published) he says—that '*Coquin de Bonaparte est toujours heureux!*'[17] Good night.

ever yrs.

B

[14] When first drafted *The Giaour* was only 344 lines long. By the seventh edition it had become 1,000 lines longer; many of these additions reflected the hero's guilty state of mind. (See *CPW* iii. 411.)

[15] St Ursula is associated with the mythical massacre of her attendant group of 11,000 virgins at the German city of Cologne, in the 4th century.

[16] See Matthew 7: 3: 'And why beholdest thou the mote that is in thy brother's eye, but considerest not the beam that is in thine own eye?'

[17] Jean Victor Marie Moreau, originally a supporter of Napoleon, defected to the allies and was mortally wounded at the battle of Dresden in 1813. 'That scamp Bonaparte,' he wrote, 'always has luck on his side.'

[To Lady Melbourne]

Septr.—Octr. 1st. 1813

My dear Ly. M[elbourn]e

You will have received two letters of mine to atone for my late portentous silence & this is intended as a further expiation—I have just been dining at Holland house—the Queen is grown thin & gracious both of which become her royalty—I met Curran[18] there who electrified me with his imagination—& delighted me with his humour—he is a man of a million—the Irish *when* good are perfect—the little I have seen of him has less *leaven* than any mortal compound I have lately looked into.—Today I heard from my friend W[ebster] again—his *Countess* is he says 'inexorable' what a lucky fellow! happy in his obstacles[19]—in his case I should think them very pleasant—but I don't lay this down as a general proposition.——All my prospect of amusement is clouded— for Petersham has sent an excuse—& there will be no one to make him jealous of but the Curate & the Butler—& I have no thoughts of setting up for myself—I am not exactly cut out for the Lady of the mansion—but I think a stray Dandy would have a chance of preferment[20]—she evidently expects to be attacked—& seems prepared for a brilliant defence—my character as a Roué had gone before me—& my careless & quiet behaviour astonished her so much that I believe she began to think herself ugly—or me blind—if not worse.—They seemed surprised at my declining the races in particular—but for this I had good reasons— firstly—I wanted to go elsewhere—secondly—if I had gone I must have paid some attention to some of them—which is troublesome unless one has something in memory or hope to induce it—& then mine host is so marvelous greeneyed that he might have included me in his Calenture—which I don't deserve—& probably should not like it a bit the better if I did—I have also

---

[18] John Philpot Curran (1750–1817), Irish politician, orator, and wit, and Charlotte of Mecklenburg-Strelitz (1744–1818), wife of George III (by this time lost in insanity).

[19] Webster clearly anticipated something with this French countess. In Byron's next report to Lady Melbourne, on 5 October, he would write that 'W has lost his Countess—his time—& his temper—(I would advise who finds the *last* to return it immediately—as it is of no use to any but the owner—)' (*LJ* iii. 132).

[20] Byron told Lady Melbourne on 5 October that Lady Frances 'is pretty but not surpassing—too thin—& not very animated—but good tempered—& a something interesting enough in her manner & figure—but I never should think of her nor anyone else—if left to my own cogitations—as I have neither the patience nor presumption to advance till met halfway' (*LJ* iii. 133). Charles Stanhope (1780–1851), who styled himself Lord Petersham (and later became the fourth Earl of Harrington), was a notorious dandy and womanizer, who could be expected to flirt with the lady of the house.

reason for returning there on Sunday—with which they have nothing to do[21]—but if C[aroline] takes a suspicious twist *that way*—let her—it will keep her in darkness—but I hope however she won't take a fit of scribbling as she did to Ly. Oxford last year—though Webster's face on the occasion would be quite a Comet—& delight me infinitely more than O[xford]'s which was comic enough.—

Friday Morn.

Yours arrived I will answer on the next page. [...] To return to the W[ebster]'s—I am glad they amuse you—anything that confirms or extends one's observations on life & character delights me even when I don't know people—for this reason—I would give the world to pass a month with Sheridan or any lady or gentleman of the old school—& hear them talk every day & all day of themselves &, acquaintance—& all they have heard & seen in their lives.—W seems in no present peril—I believe the woman is mercenary—& I happen to know that he can't at present bribe her—I told him that it would be known—& that he must expect reprisals—& what do you think was his answer?—'I think any woman fair game—because I can *depend* upon Ly. F's principles—she can't go wrong—& therefore I may[']—[']then why are you jealous of her?[']——[']because—because—zounds I am not jealous—why the devil do you suppose I am?—['] I then enumerated some very gross symptons [*sic*] which he had displayed even before her face—& his servants—which he could not deny—but persisted in his determination to add to his 'bonnes fortunes'—it is a strange being—when I came home in 1811—he was always saying—[']B—do marry—it is the happiest &c.—['] the first thing he said on my arrival at A[ston] was 'B—whatever you do *don't marry*' which considering he had an unmarried sister in law in the house was a very *un*necessary precaution.——Every now & then he has a fit of fondness—& kisses her hand before his guests—which she receives with the most lifeless indifference—which struck me more than if she had appeared pleased or annoyed—her brother told me last year that she married to get rid of her family—(who are ill tempered) & had not been *out* two months so that to use a foxhunting phrase she was 'killed in covert'.—You have enough of them & me for ye present.

yrs. ever

B

---

21 At Byron's request, Lady Frances had invited Augusta to Aston, but she could not come.

[To Lady Melbourne]

Octr. 8th. 1813

My dear Ly. M[elbourn]e

I have volumes—but neither time nor space—I have already trusted too deeply to hesitate now—besides for certain reasons you will not be sorry to hear that I am anything but what I was.—Well then—to begin—& first a word of mine host—he has lately been talking *at* rather than *to* me before the party (with the exception of the women) in a tone—which as I never use it myself I am not particularly disposed to tolerate in others—what *he* may do with impunity—it seems—but not suffer—till at last I told him that the whole of his argument involved the interesting contradiction that 'he might love where he liked but that no one else might like what he ever thought proper to love' a doctrine which as the learned Partridge observed—contains a 'non sequitur' from which I for one begged leave as a general proposition to dissent.[22]—This nearly produced a scene—with me as well as another guest who seemed to admire my sophistry the most of the two—& as it was after dinner & debating time—might have ended in more than wineshed—but that the Devil for some wise purpose of his own thought proper to restore good humour—which has not as yet been further infringed.————In these last few days I have had a good deal of conversation with an amiable person—whom (as we deal in *letters*—& initials only) we will denominate *Ph.* [Frances]—well—these things are dull in detail—take it once—I have made love—& if I am to believe mere *words* (for there we have hitherto stopped) it is returned.—I must tell you the place of declaration however—a billiard room!—I did not as C[aroline] says 'kneel in the middle of the room' but like Corporal Trim to the Nun 'I made a speech'[23]—which as you might not listen to it with the same patience—I shall not transcribe.—We were before on very amiable terms—& I remembered being asked an odd question—'how a woman who liked a man could inform him of it—when he did not perceive it'—I also observed that we went on with our game (of billiards) without *counting* the *hazards*—& supposed that—as mine certainly were not—the thoughts of the other party also were not exactly occupied by what was our ostensible pursuit.—Not quite though pretty well satisfied with my progress—I took a very imprudent step—with pen & paper—in tender & tolerably turned *prose* periods (no *poetry* even when in earnest) here were risks certainly—first

---

[22] See Fielding, *Tom Jones* (1749), ix. 6.
[23] See Sterne, *Tristram Shandy* (1765), viii. 22, in which a war hero has an affair with a nun who dresses his wounds.

how to convey—then how it would be received—it was received however &
deposited not very far from the heart which I wished it to reach—when who
should enter the room but the person who ought at that moment to have been
in the Red sea if Satan had any civility—but *she* kept her countenance & the
paper—& I my composure as well as I could.—It was a risk—& *all* had been lost
by failure—but then recollect—how much more I had to gain by the
reception—if not declined—& how much one always hazards to obtain anything worth having.—My billet prospered—it did more—it even (I am this
moment interrupted by the *Marito* [husband]—& write this before him—he
has brought me a political pamphlet in M.S. to decypher & applaud—I shall
content myself with the last—Oh—he is gone again)—my billet produced an
answer—a very unequivocal one too—but a little too much about virtue—&
indulgence of attachment in some sort of etherial process in which the soul is
principally concerned—which I don't very well understand—being a bad
metaphysician—but one generally *ends* & *begins* with Platonism—& as my
proselyte is only twenty—there is time enough to materialize—I hope nevertheless this spiritual system won't last long—& at any rate must make the
experiment.—I remember my last case was the reverse—as Major O'Flaherty
recommends 'we fought first & explained afterwards.'[24]—This is the present
state of things—much mutual profession—a good deal of melancholy—which
I am sorry to say was remarked by 'the Moor' & as much love as could well be
made considering the time place & circumstances.——I need not say that the
folly & petulance of——[Webster] have tended to all this—if a man is not
contented with a pretty woman & not only runs after any little country girl he
meets with but absolutely boasts of it—he must not be surprised if others admire
that which he knows not how to value—besides he literally provoked & goaded
me into it—by something not unlike bullying—*indirect* to be sure—but tolerably
obvious—'he *would* do this—& he would do that—if any man['] &c. &c.—& *he*
thought that every woman 'was *his* lawful prize nevertheless[']—Oons! who is this
strange monopolist?—it is odd enough but on other subjects he is like other
people but on this he seems infatuated—if he had been rational—& not prated of
his pursuits—I should have gone on very well—as I did at Middleton—even now
I shan't quarrel with him—if I can help it—but one or two of his speeches
has blackened the blood about my heart—& curdled the milk of kindness—if
put to the proof—I shall behave like other people I presume.—I have heard from
A[nnabella]—but her letter to me is *melancholy*—about her old friend Miss
M[ontgomer]y's departure &c.—&c.—I wonder who will have her at last—her

---

[24] A character in Richard Cumberland's comedy, *The West Indian* (1771). Below Byron refers to
Webster as 'the Moor': the archetypal jealous husband in *Othello*.

letter to you is *gay*—you say—that to me must have been written at the same time the little demure Nonjuror!————I wrote to C[aroline] the other day—for I was afraid she might repeat the last year's epistle—& make it *circular* among my friends.————Good evening—I am now going to *billiards.*—

P. S. 6 *o'clock—This business is growing serious—& I think* Platonism *in some peril—There has been very nearly a scene—almost an* hysteric *& really without cause for I was conducting myself with (to me) very irksome decorum—her expressions astonish me—so young & cold as she appeared—but these professions must end as usual—& would—I think—now—had 'l'occasion' been not wanting—had any one come in during the tears & consequent consolation all had been spoiled—we must be more cautious or less larmoyante.*—

   P. S. second—10 o'clock—I write to you just escaped from Claret & vociferation—on G–d knows what paper—my Landlord is a rare gentleman—he has just proposed to me a bet 'that he for a certain sum wins any given woman—against any given homme including all friends present[']—which I declined with becoming deference to him & the rest of the company—is not this at this moment a perfect comedy?—I forgot to mention that on his entrance yesterday during the letter scene—it reminded me so much of an awkward passage in 'the Way to keep him' between Lovemore—Sir Bashful—& my Lady[25]—*that embarrassing as it was I could hardly help laughing—I hear his voice in the passage—he wants me to go to a ball at Sheffield—& is talking to me as I write—Good Night. I am in the act of praising his pamphlet.—I don't half like your story of* Corinne—*some day I will tell you why—If I can—but at present—Good Night.*

[To Lady Melbourne]

Newstead Abbey Octr. 10th. 1813

My dear Ly. M[elbourn]e

I write to you from the melancholy mansion of my fathers—where I am dull as the longest deceased of my progenitors—I hate reflection on irrevocable things & won't now turn sentimentalist. W alone accompanied me here (I return tomorrow to Aston) he is now sitting opposite—& between us are Red & white Champ[agn]e—Burgundy—two sorts of Claret—& lighter vintages—the relics of my youthful cellar which is yet in formidable number & famous

---

[25] Characters in Arthur Murphy's comedy (1760).

order—but I leave the wine to him—& prefer conversing soberly with you.—
Ah! if you knew what a quiet Mussulman life (except in wine) I led here for a few
years—but no matter.—Yesterday I sent you a long letter & must now recur to
the same subject which is uppermost in my thoughts.—I am as much astonished but I hope not so much mistaken as Lord Ogleby at the denouement or
rather commencement of the last week[26]—it has changed my views—my
wishes—my hopes—my everything—& will furnish you with additional proof
of my weakness.—Mine guest (late host) has just been congratulating himself on
possessing a partner without *passion*—I don't know—& cannot yet speak with
certainty—but I never yet saw more decisive preliminary symptoms.———
As I am apt to take people at their word—on receiving my answer—that
whatever the weakness of her heart might be—I should never derive further
proof of it than the confession—instead of pressing the point—I told her that
I was willing to be hers on her own terms & should never attempt to infringe
upon the conditions—I said this without pique—& believing her perfectly in
earnest for the time—but in the midst of our mutual professions or to use her
own expression 'more than mutual' she burst into an agony of crying—& at
such a time & in such a place as rendered such a scene particularly perilous to
both—her sister in the next room—&—[Webster] not far off—of course I said
& did almost everything proper on the occasion—& fortunately we restored
sunshine in time to prevent anyone from perceiving the cloud that had darkened
our horizon.—She says—she is convinced that my own declaration was produced solely because I perceived her previous penchant—which by the bye—as
I think I said to you before—I neither perceived nor expected—I really did not
suspect her of a predilection for anyone—& even now in public with the
exception of those little indirect yet mutually understood—I don't know how
& it is unnecessary to name or describe them—her conduct is as coldly correct
as her still—fair—Mrs. L[amb] like aspect.—She however managed to give me a
note—& to receive another & a ring before——[Webster]'s very face—& yet she
is a thorough devotee—& takes prayers morning and evening—besides being
measured for a new bible once a quarter.—The only alarming thing—is that—
[Webster] complains of her aversion from being beneficial to population &
posterity—if this is an invariable maxim—I shall lose my labour.—Be this as it
may—she *owns* to more—than I ever heard from any woman within the time—
& I shan't take——[Webster]'s word any more for her feelings than I did for that
celestial comparison which I once mentioned.—I think her eye—her change of

---

[26] The superannuated Lord Ogleby figures in George Colman the Elder and David Garrick's *The
Clandestine Marriage* (1766), and is grievously disappointed at the close of the drama when Miss Fanny
is stolen from him by her fiancé, Lovewell.

colour—& the trembling of her hand—& above all her devotion tell a different tale.—Good night—we return tomorrow—& now I drink your health—you are my only correspondent & I believe friend—

ever yrs.
B

[To Augusta Leigh]

October 10th. 1813

My dearest Augusta

I have only time to say that I am not in the least angry—& that my silence has merely arisen from several circumstances which I cannot now detail—I trust you are better—& will continue *best*—ever my dearest

yrs.
B

[To John Hanson]

Octr. 10th. 1813

Dear Sir

I am disposed to advance a loan of 1000£ to James Webster Wedderburne Webster Esqre. of Aston Hall York County—& request you will address to me *there* a *bond & judgement* to be signed by the said as soon as possible.—Of Claughton's payments I know nothing further—and the demands on myself I know also—but W is a very old friend of mine—& a man of property—& as I can command the money he shall have it—I do not at all wish to inconveni- ence you—& I also know that when we balance accounts it will be much in your favour—but if you could replace the sum at Hoares from my advance of thousand eight hundred in July—it would be a favour—or still better if C[laughton] makes further payments—which will render it unnecessary.— Don't let the first part of the last sentence embarrass you at all—the last part about Claughton I could wish you to attend to—I have written this day—about his opening the cellar.—Pray send bond & judgement to Aston as directed—

ever dr. Sir
B

P. S.—Many thanks for your kind invitation—but it was too late—I was in this county before it arrived—My best remembrances to Mrs. H. & all the family.————

[To Lady Melbourne]

Newstead Abbey—Octr. 17th. 1813

My dear Ly. M[elbourn]e

The whole party are here—and now to my narrative.—But first I must tell you that I am rather unwell owing to a folly of last night—About midnight after deep and drowsy potations I took it into my head to empty my *skull cup* which holds rather better than a bottle of Claret at *one draught*—and nearly died the death of Alexander—which I shall be content to do when I have achieved his conquests—I had just sense enough left to feel that I was not fit to join the ladies—& went to bed—where my Valet tells me that I was first convulsed & afterwards so motionless that he thought 'Good Night to Marmion.'[27]—I don't know how I came to do so very silly a thing—but I believe my guests were boasting—& 'company villainous company hath been the spoil of me' I detest drinking in general—& beg your pardon for this excess—I *can't* do so any more.———To my theme—you were right—I have been a little too sanguine— as to the *conclusion*—but hear.—One day left entirely to ourselves was nearly fatal—another such *victory* & with Pyrrhus we were lost————it came to this—'I am entirely at your *mercy*—I own it—I give myself up to you—I am not *cold*— whatever I seem to others—but I know that I cannot bear the reflection hereafter—do not imagine that these are mere words—I tell you the truth— now act as you will[']—was I wrong?—I spared her.—There was a something so very peculiar in her manner—a kind of mild decision—no scene—not even a struggle—but still I know not what that convinced me she was serious—it was not the mere 'No' which one has heard forty times before—& always with the same accent—but the *tone*—and the aspect—yet I sacrificed much—the hour *two* in the morning———[Webster?] away—the Devil whispering that it was mere *verbiage* &c.—& yet I know not whether I can regret it—she seems so very thankful for my forbearance—a proof at least that she was not playing merely

---

[27] Legend says that Alexander the Great died of drink after an immense celebration in Babylon. The hero of Walter Scott's poem *Marmion* (1808) died at the battle of Flodden Field. Byron next alludes to *1 Henry IV*, III. iii. 9–10.

the usual decorous reluctance which is sometimes so tiresome on these occasions.——You ask if I am prepared to go 'all lengths' if you mean by 'all lengths' any thing including duel or divorce—I answer *yes*—I love her—if I did not and much too—I should have been more *selfish* on the occasion before mentioned—I have offered to go away with her—& her answer whether sincere or not is 'that on *my account* she declines it'—in the mean time we are all as wretched as possible—*he* scolding on *account* of *unaccountable* melancholy—the sister very suspicious but rather amused—the friend very suspicious too but (why I know not) not at all amused—il Marito something like Lord Chesterfield in De Grammont[28]—putting on a martial physiognomy—prating with his worthy ally—swearing at servants—sermonizing both sisters—& buying sheep—but never quitting her side now—so that we are in despair—*I* very feverish—restless—and silent—as indeed seems to be the *tacit* agreement of every one else—in short I can foresee nothing—it may end in nothing—but here are half a dozen persons very much occupied—& two if not three in great perplexity—& as far as I can judge—so we must continue.——She *don't* & *won't* live with him—& they have been so far separate for a long time—therefore—I have nothing to answer for on that point—poor thing—she is either the most *artful* or *artless* of her age (20) I ever encountered—she *owns* to so much—and perpetually says—'rather than you should be *angry*' or—'rather than you should like anyone else I will do whatever you please' [']I won't speak to this that or the other if you dislike it—['] & throws or seems to throw herself so entirely upon my direction in every respect—that it disarms me quite—but I am really wretched with the perpetual conflict with myself.—Her health is so very delicate—she is so thin & pale—& seems to have lost her appetite so entirely—that I doubt her being much longer—this is also her own opinion—but these fancies are common to all who are not very happy——if she were once my wife or likely to be so—a warm climate should be the first resort nevertheless for her recovery.—The most perplexing—& yet I can't prevail on myself to give it up—is the *caressing* system—in her it appears perfectly childish—and I do think innocent—but it really puzzles all the Scipio[29] about me to confine myself to the laudable portion of these endearments.————What a cursed situation I have thrust myself into—Potiphar (it used to be O[xford]'s name) putting some stupid question to me the other day—I told him that I rather admired the *sister*—& what does he? but tell *her* this & his *wife* too—who a little too hastily asked him 'if he was *mad*'? which

[28] The second Earl of Chesterfield (1634–1714) is depicted in a state of dreadful jealousy regarding his second wife in the *Memoirs* (1713) of the Comte de Gramont.

[29] The Roman general Scipio Africanus (236–183 BC) restored a captive Iberian woman to her fiancé during his Spanish campaign. The wife of the Egyptian Potiphar tempted the Old Testament patriarch Joseph, who stoutly resisted her (see Genesis 39).

put him to demonstration that a man ought not to be asked if he was mad—for relating that a friend thought his wife's sister a pretty woman—upon this topic he held forth with great fervour for a customary period—I wish he had a quinsey. [...] Heigh ho!—Good Night—address to *Aston*.—

ever yrs.
B

[Journal]

[November 14, 1813]

If this had been begun ten years ago, and faithfully kept!!!—heigho! there are too many things I wish never to have remembered, as it is. Well,—I have had my share of what are called the pleasures of this life, and have seen more of the European and Asiatic world than I have made a good use of. They say 'virtue is its own reward,'—it certainly should be paid well for its trouble. At five-and-twenty, when the better part of life is over, one should be *something*;—and what am I? nothing but five-and-twenty—and the odd months. What have I seen? the same man all over the world,—ay, and woman too. Give *me* a Mussulman who never asks questions, and a she of the same race who saves one the trouble of putting them. But for this same plague—yellow fever—and Newstead delay, I should have been by this time a second time close to the Euxine. If I can overcome the last, I don't so much mind your pestilence; and, at any rate, the spring shall see me there,—provided I neither marry myself nor unmarry any one else in the interval. I wish one was—I don't know what I wish. It is odd I never set myself seriously to wishing without attaining it—and repenting. I begin to believe with the good old Magi, that one should only pray for the nation and not for the individual;—but, on my principle, this would not be very patriotic.

No more reflections.—Let me see—last night I finished 'Zuleika,' my second Turkish Tale [*The Bride of Abydos*]. I believe the composition of it kept me alive—for it was written to drive my thoughts from the recollection of—

'Dear sacred name, rest ever unreveal'd'[30]

At least, even here, my hand would tremble to write it. This afternoon I have burnt the scenes of my commenced comedy. I have some idea of expectorating a romance, or rather a tale in prose;—but what romance could equal the events—

---

[30] See Alexander Pope, *Eloisa to Abelard* (1717), 9–10; below Byron quotes from Virgil's *Aeneid*, ii. 5–6, 'I saw these things in all their horror, | And I bore a great part in them.'

'quaeque ipse.....vidi,
Et quorum pars magna fui' [...]

Nov. 17th

[...] Mr. Murray has offered me one thousand guineas for the 'Giaour' and the 'Bride of Abydos.' I won't—it is too much, though I am strongly tempted, merely for the *say* of it. No bad price for a fortnight's (a week each) what?—the gods know—it was intended to be called Poetry.

I have dined regularly to-day, for the first time since Sunday last—this being Sabbath, too. All the rest, tea and dry biscuits—six *per diem*. I wish to God I had not dined now!—It kills me with heaviness, stupor, and horrible dreams;—and yet it was but a pint of bucellas [Portuguese white wine], and fish. Meat I never touch,—nor much vegetable diet. I wish I were in the country, to take exercise,—instead of being obliged to *cool* by abstinence, in lieu of it. I should not so much mind a little accession of flesh,—my bones can well bear it. But the worst is, the devil always came with it,—till I starve him out,—and I will *not* be the slave of *any* appetite. If I do err, it shall be my heart, at least, that heralds the way. Oh my head—how it aches?—the horrors of digestion! I wonder how Buonaparte's dinner agrees with him? [...]

I remember the effect of the *first* Edinburgh Review on me. I heard of it six weeks before,—read it the day of its denunciation,—dined and drank three bottles of claret, (with S. B. Davies, I think,) neither ate nor slept the less, but, nevertheless, was not easy till I had vented my wrath and my rhyme, in the same pages against every thing and every body. Like George, in the *Vicar of Wakefield*, 'the fate of my paradoxes'[31] would allow me to perceive no merit in another. I remembered only the maxim of my boxing-master, which, in my youth, was found useful in all general riots,—'Whoever is not for you is against you—*mill* away right and left,' and so I did;—like Ishmael, my hand was against all men, and all men's anent me. I did wonder, to be sure, at my own success—

'And marvels so much wit is all his own.'

as Hobhouse sarcastically says of somebody (not unlikely myself, as we are old friends);[32]—but were it to come over again, I would *not*. I have since redde the cause of my couplets, and it is not adequate to the effect. C[aroline?] told me that it was believed I alluded to poor Lord Carlisle's nervous disorder

---

[31] See Oliver Goldsmith's novel (1766), ii. 1.
[32] See Hobhouse's poem 'From Boileau' in his collection *Imitations and Translations* (1809).

in one of the lines.[33] I thank Heaven I did not know it—and would not, could not, if I had. I must naturally be the last person to be pointed on defects or maladies. [...]

Nov. 23d

[...] If I had any views in this country, they would probably be parliamentary. But I have no ambition; at least, if any, it would be 'aut Caesar aut nihil' [either Caesar or nothing]. My hopes are limited to the arrangement of my affairs, and settling either in Italy or the East (rather the last), and drinking deep of the languages and literature of both. Past events have unnerved me; and all I can do now is to make life an amusement, and look on, while others play. After all—even the highest game of crowns and sceptres, what is it? *Vide* Napoleon's last twelve-month. It has completely upset my system of fatalism. I thought, if crushed, he would have fallen, when '*fractus illabitur orbis*,'[34] and not have been pared away to gradual insignificance;—that all this was not a mere *jeu* [game] of the gods, but a prelude to greater changes and mightier events. But Men never advance beyond a certain point;—and here we are, retrograding to the dull, stupid old system,—balance of Europe—poising straws upon king's noses, instead of wringing them off! Give me a republic, or a despotism of one, rather than the mixed government of one, two, three. A republic!—look in the history of the Earth—Rome, Greece, Venice, France, Holland, America, our short (*eheu*! [alas]) Commonwealth, and compare it with what they did under masters. The Asiatics are not qualified to be republicans, but they have the liberty of demolishing despots, which is the next thing to it. To be the first man—not the Dictator—not the Sylla, but the Washington or the Aristides—the leader in talent and truth—is next to the Divinity! Franklin, Penn, and, next to these, either Brutus or Cassius—even Mirabeau—or St. Just.[35] I shall never be any thing, or rather always be nothing. The most I can hope is, that some will say, 'He might, perhaps, if he would.' [...]

---

[33] Feeling that Lord Carlisle had not supported his entry into the House of Lords, Byron took revenge in *English Bards and Scotch Reviewers* (725–6; *CPW* i. 252) by referring to *Tragedies and Poems* (1801) as 'paralytic puling'. It was an unfortunate comment, made in ignorance. (See postscript to letter of 27 December 1813, and Journal of 28 March 1814.)

[34] See Horace's *Odes*, III. iii. 7–8, translated by Philip Francis (1750): 'Let the loud Winds, that rule the Seas, | Their wild tempestuous Horrours raise; | Let Jove's dread Arm with Thunders rend the Spheres, | Beneath the Crush of Worlds undaunted he appears.' This classic statement of a Stoic position is one Byron hoped Napoleon would share.

[35] A long list of selfless leaders (Americans George Washington, Benjamin Franklin, and George Penn; the Greek Aristides; Romans Brutus and Cassius; and French Revolutionaries Count Mirabeau and the more ambivalent architect of the Terror Louis Antoine de Saint-Just) compared to the 2nd-century Roman dictator Lucius Cornelius Sulla.

Thursday, 26th November

[...] I have been thinking lately a good deal of Mary Duff. How very odd that I should have been so utterly, devotedly fond of that girl, at an age when I could neither feel passion, nor know the meaning of the word. And the effect! My mother used always to rally me about this childish amour; and, at last, many years after, when I was sixteen, she told me one day, 'Oh, Byron, I have had a letter from Edinburgh, from Miss Abercromby, and your old sweetheart Mary Duff is married to a Mr. Coe.' And what was my answer? I really cannot explain or account for my feelings at that moment; but they nearly threw me into convulsions, and alarmed my mother so much, that after I grew better, she generally avoided the subject—to *me*—and contented herself with telling it to all her acquaintance. Now, what could this be? I had never seen her since her mother's faux pas at Aberdeen had been the cause of her removal to her grand-mother's at Banff; we were both the merest children. I had and have been attached fifty times since that period; yet I recollect all we said to each other, all our caresses, her features, my restlessness, sleeplessness, my tormenting my mother's maid to write for me to her, which she at last did, to quiet me. Poor Nancy thought I was wild, and, as I could not write for myself, became my secretary. I remember, too, our walks, and the happiness of sitting by Mary, in the children's apartment, at their house not far from Plainstones at Aberdeen, while her lesser sister Helen played with the doll, and we sat gravely making love, in our way.

How the deuce did all this occur so early? where could it originate? I certainly had no sexual ideas for years afterwards; and yet my misery, my love for that girl were so violent, that I sometimes doubt if I have ever been really attached since. Be that as it may, hearing of her marriage several years after was like a thunder-stroke—it nearly choked me—to the horror of my mother and the astonishment and almost incredulity of every body. And it is a phenomenon in my existence (for I was not eight years old) which has puzzled, and will puzzle me to the latest hour of it; and lately, I know not why, the *recollection* (*not* the attachment) has recurred as forcibly as ever. I wonder if she can have the least remembrance of it or me? or remember her pitying sister Helen for not having an admirer too? How very pretty is the perfect image of her in my memory—her brown, dark hair, and hazel eyes; her very dress! I should be quite grieved to see her now; the reality, however beautiful, would destroy, or at least confuse, the features of the lovely Peri which then existed in her, and still lives in my imagination, at the distance of more than sixteen years. I am now twenty-five and odd months....

[To Annabella Milbanke]

Novr. 29th. 1813

No one can *assume* or *presume* less than you do though very few with whom I am acquainted possess half your claims to that 'Superiority,' which you are so fearful of affecting—nor can I recollect one expression since the commencement of our correspondence which has in any respect diminished my opinion of your talents—my respect for your virtues.—My only reason for avoiding the discussion of *sacred* topics—was the sense of my own ignorance & the fear of saying something that might displease—but I *have listened* & will listen to you with not merely patience but pleasure.—When we meet—if we do meet—in Spring—you will find me ready to acquiesce in all your notions upon the point merely personal between ourselves—you will act according to circumstances— it would be premature in us both to anticipate reflections which may never be made—& if made at all—are certainly unfounded.—You wrong yourself very much in supposing that 'the charm' has been broken by our nearer acquaintance—on ye. contrary—that very intercourse convinces me of the value of what I have lost—or rather never found—but I will not deny that circumstances have occurred to render it more supportable.—You will think me very capricious & apt at sudden fancies—it is true I could not exist without some object of attachment—but I have shown that I am not quite a slave to impulse— no man of tolerable situation in life who was quite without self command could have reached the age of 26 (which I shall be—I grieve to speak it—in January) without marrying & in all probability foolishly.—But however weak—(it may merit a harsher term) in my disposition to attach myself—(and as society is now much the same in this as in all other European countries—it were difficult to avoid it) in my search for the 'ideal' the being to whom I would commit the whole happiness of my future life—I have never yet seen but two approaching to the likeness—the first I was too young to have a prospect of obtaining[36]—& subsequent events have proved that my expectations might not have been fulfilled had I ever proposed to & secured my early idol—the *second*—the *only* woman to whom I ever seriously pretended as a wife—had disposed of her heart already—and I think it too late to look for a third.—I shall take ye. world as I find it—& I have seen it much the same in most climates—(a little more fiery perhaps in Greece & Asia—for there they are a strange mixture of languid habits &

---

[36] This is Mary Chaworth; see letter of 15 September 1803. She married, but sought a re-acquaintance with Byron in 1814 after separating from her husband. Nothing came of it, and after a nervous breakdown she and her husband patched things up. (See letter of 12 January 1814.)

stormy passions) but I have no confidence & look for no constancy in affections founded in caprice—& preserved (if preserved) by accident—& lucky conformity of disposition without any fixed principles.—How far this may be my case at present—I know not—& have not had time to ascertain—I can only say that I never was cured of loving any one but by the conduct—by the change—or the violence of the object herself—and till I see reason for distrust I shall flatter myself as heretofore—& perhaps with as little cause as ever.——I owe you some apology for this disquisition—but the singularity of *our* situation led me to dwell on this topic—& your friendship will excuse it.—I am anxious to be candid with you though I fear sometimes I am betrayed into impertinence.—They say that a man never *forgives* a woman who stands in the relation which you do towards me—but to *forgive*—we must first be offended—& I think I cannot recall—even a moment of pique at the past to my memory—I have but *2 friends* of your sex— yourself & Ly. Melbourne—as different in years as in disposition—& yet I do not know which I prefer—believe me a better-*hearted* woman does not exist—and in talent I never saw her excelled & hardly equalled—her kindness to me has been uniform—and I fear severely & ungratefully tried at times on my part—but as it cannot be so again—at least in the same manner—I shall make what atonement I can—if a regard which my own inclination leads me to cultivate—can make any amends for my trespasses on her patience.——The word *patience* reminds me of ye. book I am to send you—it shall be ordered to Seaham tomorrow.[37]— I shall be most happy to see any thing of your writing—of what I have already seen you once heard my favourable & sincere opinion.—I by no means rank poetry or poets high in the scale of intellect—this may look like Affectation— but it is my real opinion—it is the lava of the imagination whose eruption prevents an earth-quake—they say Poets never or rarely go *mad*—Cowper & Collins are instances to the contrary—(but Cowper was no poet)—it is however to be remarked that they rarely do—but are generally so near it—that I cannot help thinking rhyme is so far useful in anticipating & preventing the disorder.—I prefer the talents of *action*—of war—or the Senate—or even of Science—to all the speculations of these mere dreamers of another existence (I don't mean *religiously* but *fancifully*) and spectators of this.——Apathy—disgust—& perhaps incapacity have rendered me now a mere spectator—but I have occasionally mixed in the active & tumultuous departments of existence—& on these alone my *recollection* rests with any satisfaction—though not the *best* parts of it. [...] Mr. Ward & I have talked (I fear it will be only talk as things look undecided in that quarter) of an excursion to Holland—if so—I shall be able to compare a

---

[37] Presumably *The Bride of Abydos*, published a few days later.

Dutch canal with the Bosphorus.—I never saw a Revolution transacting—or at least completed—but I arrived just after the last Turkish one & the *effects* were visible—& had all the grandeur of desolation in their aspect——Streets in ashes—immense barracks (of a very fine construction) in ruins—and above all Sultan Selim's favourite gardens round them in all the wildness of luxurient [*sic*] neglect—his fountains waterless—& his kiosks defaced but still glittering in their decay.—They lie between the city & Buyukderé on the hills above the Bosphorus—& the way to them is through a plain with the prettiest name in the world—'the Valley of Sweet Waters'—But I am sending a volume not a letter.

ever yrs. most truly

B

[Journal]

Sunday, December 5th. [1813]

[...] Galt called.—Mem[orandum].—to ask some one to speak to Raymond in favour of his play. We are old fellow-travellers, and, with all his eccentricities, he has much strong sense, experience of the world, and is, as far as I have seen, a good-natured philosophical fellow. I showed him Sligo's letter on the reports of the Turkish girl's *aventure* at Athens soon after it happened. He and Lord Holland, Lewis, and Moore, and Rogers, and Lady Melbourne have seen it. Murray has a copy. I thought it had been *unknown*, and wish it were; but Sligo arrived only some days after, and the *rumours* are the subject of his letter. That I shall preserve,—*it is as well.* Lewis and Galt were both *horrified*; and L. wondered I did not introduce the situation into 'the Giaour'. He *may* wonder;—he might wonder more at that production's being written at all. But to describe the *feelings* of *that situation* were impossible—it is *icy* even to recollect them.[38] [...]

---

[38] See letter of 22 August 1813. John Galt, the novelist (1779–1839), had encountered Byron during his Mediterranean tour, and would write a biography of the poet in 1830. It seems Byron encountered a Turkish girl on her way to an 'honour killing' by drowning in Athens (whether he was the source of her dishonour is unclear) and managed to negotiate her release. So Matthew Lewis, Gothic novelist (1775–1818), misunderstood: the incident (if it ever took place) was the *source* of *The Giaour*, which involves a killing of just that kind.

[To Lord Holland]

Decr. 7th 1813

My dear Lord

Will you have ye. goodness to present ye. petition which accompanies this billet for me—you will think it an odd thing after the impudence with which I supported Cartwright's & and the variety of impudencies I have uttered in our august house—but I really have not nerves even to present a pet[itio]n far less say a word upon it—at this moment[39]—I can't tell why but so it is—either indolence—or hippishness—or incapacity—or all three.—Pray pardon me this & all other intrusions (*past* at least) from

yrs. very truly
B

[Journal]

Monday, December 13, 1813.

Called at three places—read, and got ready to leave town to-morrow. Murray has had a letter from his brother Bibliopole of Edinburgh, who says 'he is lucky in having such a *poet*'—something as if one was a pack-horse, or 'ass, or any thing that is his;'[40] or, like Mrs. Packwood, who replied to some inquiry after the Odes on Razors,—'Laws, sir, we keeps a Poet.' The same illustrious Edinburgh bookseller once sent an order for books, poesy, and cookery, with this agreeable postscript—'The *Harold* and *Cookery* are much wanted.' Such is fame, and, after all, quite as good as any other 'life in others' breath.'[41] 'Tis much the same to divide purchasers with Hannah Glasse or Hannah More.[42]

---

[39] Byron's last speech in the Lords, on 1 June 1813, was in support of a petition from Major John Cartwright to be allowed to continue circulating another petition calling for parliamentary reform. Only the 'Jacobin' Earl Stanhope supported him. Now a certain W. J. Baldwin was petitioning for release from debtors' prison.

[40] See the Tenth Commandment (Exodus 20: 16): 'Thou shall not covet thy neighbour's house, thou shalt not covet thy neighbour's wife, nor his manservant, nor his maidservant, nor his ox, nor his ass, nor any thing that is thy neighbour's.'

[41] See Pope, *An Essay on Man* (1734), iv. 237.

[42] Mrs Packwood was the wife of a razor strop manufacturer who employed poets to write advertising material for his company. Murray was the publisher of Mrs Rundell's *New System of Domestic Cookery*, which dominated the market for the first half of the 19th century. Hannah Glasse was the author of its 18th-century equivalent, *The Art of Cookery Made Plain and Simple*.

Some editor of some Magazine has *announced* to Murray his intention of abusing the thing '*without reading it.*' So much the better; if he redde it first, he would abuse it more.

Allen (Lord Holland's Allen—the best informed and one of the ablest men I know—a perfect Magliabecchi—a devourer, a Helluo of books, and an observer of men,[43]) has lent me a quantity of Burns's unpublished, and never-to-be-published, Letters. They are full of oaths and obscene songs. What an antithetical mind!—tenderness, roughness—delicacy, coarseness—sentiment, sensuality—soaring and grovelling, dirt and deity—all mixed up in that one compound of inspired clay!

It seems strange; a true voluptuary will never abandon his mind to the grossness of reality. It is by exalting the earthly, the material, the *physique* of our pleasures, by veiling these ideas, by forgetting them altogether, or, at least, never naming them hardly to one's self, that we alone can prevent them from disgusting. [...]

[To John Murray]

January 22d. 1814

Dear Sir/

You will be glad to hear of my safe arrival here [Newstead]—the time of my return will depend upon the weather—which is so impracticable that this letter has to advance through more Snows than ever opposed the Emperor's retreat.— The roads are impassable—and return impossible—for ye. present—which I do not regret as I am much at my ease and *six* and *twenty* complete this day—a very pretty age if it would always last.——Our coals are excellent—our fire places large—my cellar full—and my head empty—and I have not yet recovered my joy at leaving London—if any unexpected turn occurred with my purchaser—I believe I should hardly quit the place at all—but shut my doors & let my beard grow.——I forgot to mention—(& I hope it is unnecessary) that the lines beginning '*Remember him*' &c. must *not* appear with the *Corsair*—you may slip them in with the smaller pieces newly annexed to C[hild]e H[arol]d—but on *no* account permit them to be appended to the Corsair—have the goodness to recollect this particularly.[44]—The books I have brought with me are a great

---

[43] John Allen MD was an associate of Lord Holland and a star turn in the Holland House circle. Antonio Magliabecchi was a 17th-century librarian at the Court of Tuscany. In the second of Pope's *Moral Essays*, 'Of the Characters of Women' (79–82), 'Helluo' is satirized as a dilettante.

[44] This poem (*CPW* iii. 92–3) is a tormented reflection of Byron's abortive affair with Lady Frances Webster: 'Oh, god! that we had met in time— | Our hearts as fond—thy hand more free', and so forth.

consolation for the confinement—& I bought more as we came along—in short—I never consult the thermometer—and shall not put up prayers for a *thaw* unless I thought it would sweep away the rascally invaders of France—was ever such a thing as Blucher's proclamation?[45]—Just before I left town Kemble paid me the compliment of desiring me to write a *tragedy*—I wish I could—but I find my scribbling mood subsiding—not before it was time—but it is lucky to check it at all.—If I lengthen my letter you will think it is coming on again—so Good bye—

yrs. alway
B<small>N</small>

P. S.—If you hear any news of Battle or retreat on ye. part of the Allies (as they call them) pray send it—he has my best wishes to manure the fields of France with an invading army—I hate invaders of all countries—& have no patience with the cowardly cry of exultation over him at whose name you all turned whiter than the Snow to which (under Providence and that special favourite of Heaven Prince Regency) you are indebted for your triumphs.———I open my letter to thank [you] for yours just received.—The lines 'to a Lady weeping' must go with the Corsair—I care nothing for consequences on this point—my politics are to me like a young mistress to an old man the worse they grow the fonder I become of them.—As Mr. G[ifford] likes the 'Portuguese translation' pray insert it as an Ad[ditio]n to the Corsair—Lady West[morlan]d thought it so bad—that after making me translate it she gave me her own version—which is for aught I know the best of the two.[46]—But—I cannot give up my weeping lines—and I do think them good & don't mind what 'it looks like.'———In all points of difference between Mr. G[ifford] & Mr. D[allas]—let the first, keep his place—& in all points of difference between Mr. G[ifford] & Mr. anybody else I shall abide by the former—if I am wrong—I can't help it—but I would rather not be right with any other person—so there is an end of that matter.—After the trouble he has taken about me & mine—I should be very ungrateful to feel or act otherwise—besides in point of judgement he is not to be lowered by a comparison.———In politics he may be right too—but that with me is a feeling and I can't torify my nature.

---

[45] On 1 January 1814 the Prussian marshal Gebhard von Blücher (1742–1819) issued a proclamation to the inhabitants of the left bank of the Rhine, telling them to await an allied invasion and to cooperate thereafter, or to join Napoleon. In due course the War of the Sixth Coalition would end with the allies' arrival at Paris in March; Napoleon abdicated on 4 April.

[46] See 'From the Portuguese' (*CPW* iii. 34).

[Journal]

Feb. 18. [1814]

Better than a month since I last journalised:—most of it out of London, and at Notts., but a busy one and a pleasant, at least three weeks of it. On my return, I find all the newspapers in hysterics, and town in an uproar, on the avowal and republication of two stanzas on Princess Charlotte's weeping at Regency's speech to Lauderdale in 1812. They are daily at it still;—and some of the abuse good, all of it hearty. They talk of a motion in our House upon it—be it so.

Got up—redde the Morning Post containing the battle of Buonaparte, the destruction of the Custom-house, and a paragraph on me as long as my pedigree, and vituperative, as usual. * * * * *

Hobhouse is returned to England.[47] He is my best friend, the most lively, and a man of the most sterling talents extant.

'The Corsair' has been conceived, written, published, &c., since I last took up this Journal. They tell me it has great success;—it was written *con amore*, and much from *existence*. Murray is satisfied with its progress; and if the public are equally so with the perusal, there's an end of the matter. [...]

Midnight

Began a letter, which I threw into the fire. Redde—but to little purpose. Did not visit Hobhouse, as I promised and ought. No matter, the loss is mine. Smoked cigars.

Napoleon!—this week will decide his fate. All seems against him; but I believe and hope he will win—at least, beat back the Invaders. What right have we to prescribe sovereigns to France? Oh for a Republic! 'Brutus, thou sleepest.'[48] Hobhouse abounds in continental anecdotes of this extraordinary man; all in favour of his intellect and courage, but against his *bonhommie*. No wonder;—how should he, who knows mankind well, do other than despise and abhor them?

The greater the equality, the more impartially evil is distributed, and becomes lighter by the division among so many—therefore, a Republic!

More notes from Madame de [Staël] unanswered—and so they shall remain. I admire her abilities, but really her society is overwhelming—an avalanche that buries one in glittering nonsense—all snow and sophistry.

---

[47] Hobhouse travelled in Germany, the Baltic, Austria, the Adriatic, and Holland from June 1813 to February 1814.

[48] See *Julius Caesar*, II. i. 46.

Shall I go to Mackintosh's on Tuesday? um!—I did not go to Marquis Lansdowne's, nor to Miss Berry's, though both are pleasant. So is Sir James's,—but I don't know—I believe one is not the better for parties; at least, unless some *regnante* [mistress] is there.

I wonder how the deuce any body could make such a world; for what purpose dandies, for instance, were ordained—and kings—and fellows of colleges—and women of 'a certain age'—and many men of any age—and myself, most of all!

> 'Divesne prisco et natus ab Inacho
> Nil interest, an pauper et infimâ
> De gente, sub dio [*sic*] moreris,
> Victima nil miserantis Orci.
> * * * * * * * * * * * * * * * *
> Omnes eodem cogimur,'[49]

Is there any thing beyond?—*who* knows? *He* that can't tell. Who tells that there *is*? He who don't know. And when shall he know? perhaps, when he don't expect, and, generally when he don't wish it. In this last respect, however, all are not alike: it depends a good deal upon education,—something upon nerves and habits—but most upon digestion. [...]

[To Annabella Milbanke]

Feby 19th 1814

Many thanks for your answer which has cut the knot—but I had no right to interrogate you on such a subject—& had I been at all aware that my question would have led to any explanation of feelings to which you would not like to recur—of course I should have remained in silence & in darkness.————Still it is not [to] be regretted in one point of view even on your own account—it sets all apprehension of the revival of a subject already discussed long ago between us—at rest:—it is true that it was not in any great peril of revival before—but it is now more completely 'numbered with the things that were', and never can be again.—Ignorant as I am of the person & the circumstances to whom & which you allude—I can form no opinion—except—that if he has put it out of his power to avail himself of such a disposition in his favour—he is fortunate in not knowing that it ever existed.——I was rather sorry (though probably *they* would not believe me) for Bankes & Douglas—who are both very clever & excellent

---

[49] See Horace, *Odes*, II. iii. 21ff., translated by Philip Francis (1750): 'Though you could boast a Monarch's Birth, | Though Wealth unbounded round Thee flows, | Though poor, and sprung from vulgar Earth, | No Pity for his Victim Pluto knows, | For all must tread the Paths of Fate...'

men—& attached to you—and as I had contrived to make my own fortune like Sir Francis Wronghead[50]—I confess that (that terrible pronoun *I* being put out of the question) I should have been glad to have seen one of them in a fair way for happiness but I shall grow impertinent which will do them no good—& me some harm—& so Adieu to the subject.————Since my last letter I believe I have sent another of *omitted* replies to part of your own—and I must shorten this—or you will think me more tedious than usual.—I am at present a little feverish.—I mean mentally—and as usual—on the brink of something or other—which will probably crush me at last—& cut our correspondence short with every thing else—till then—I take as much of it as I can get—& as to my own epistolary offerings—you will only find them too profuse. Besides these domestic stimulants—I have the further satisfaction of still finding the P[rinc]e Regent's friends & Newspapers in gallant array against me—the latter very loud—the former I don't see—if I did our dialogue would probably be very short—but more to the purpose.—I am told also that I am 'out of Spirits' which is attributed to the said paragraphs—he must however be a happy man who has nothing deeper to disturb him.—Ly. M[elbourn]e. I have not yet seen— but I believe she is well—and I hope to find her so shortly.—Pray how old are you?—it is a question one may ask safely for some years to come—I begin to count my own—a few weeks ago I became six & twenty in summers—six hundred in heart—and in head and pursuits about six.

ever yrs very truly
BN

Pray make my best respects acceptable to Sir R and Ly. Milbanke.—

[Journal]

February 20th. [1814]

[…] An invitation to dine at Holland-house to meet Kean.[51] He is worth meeting; and I hope by getting into good society, he will be prevented from falling like Cooke. He is greater now on the stage, and off he should never be less.

---

[50] See John Vanbrugh, *The Provoked Husband* (1728).
[51] Actor Edmund Kean (1787–1833), identified with the Romantic age of the English theatre in reaction to the neoclassical work of Kemble and Siddons. He burst onto the London stage as Shylock

There is a stupid and under-rating criticism upon him in one of the newspapers. I thought that, last night, though great, he rather under-acted more than the first time. This may be the effect of these cavils; but I hope he has more sense than to mind them. He cannot expect to maintain his present eminence, or to advance still higher, without the envy of his green-room fellows, and the nibbling of their admirers. But, if he don't beat them all, why, then—merit hath no purchase in 'these coster-monger days.'[52]

I wish that I had a talent for the drama; I would write a tragedy *now*. But no,— it is gone. Hodgson talks of one,—he will do it well;—and I think M[oor]e should try. He has wonderful powers, and much variety; besides, he has lived and felt. To write so as to bring home to the heart, the heart must have been tried,— but, perhaps, ceased to be so. While you are under the influence of passions, you only feel, but cannot describe them,—any more than, when in action, you could turn round and tell the story to your next neighbour! When all is over,—all, all, and irrevocable,—trust to memory—she is then but too faithful.

Went out, and answered some letters, yawned now and then, and redde the Robbers. Fine,—but Fiesco is better; and Alfieri, and Monti's Aristodemo *best*. They are more equal than the Tedeschi dramatists.[53] [...]

March 7th. [1814]

Rose at seven—ready by half-past eight—went to Mr. Hanson's, Bloomsbury Square—went to church with his eldest daughter, Mary Anne (a good girl), and gave her away to the Earl of Portsmouth.[54] Saw her fairly a countess— congratulated the family and groom (bride)—drank a bumper of wine (wholesome sherris) to their felicity, and all that—and came home. Asked to stay to dinner, but could not. At three sat to Phillips for faces. Called on Lady M[elbourne].—I like her so well, that I always stay too long. (Mem[orandum]. to mend of that.)

Passed the evening with Hobhouse, who has begun a Poem, which promises highly;—wish he would go on with it. Heard some curious extracts from a life of Morosini, the blundering Venetian, who blew up the Acropolis at Athens with a

---

in *The Merchant of Venice* on 26 January 1814 and became famous overnight much as Byron had done some two years before.

[52] See 2 *Henry IV*, I. ii. 170.

[53] *The Robbers* (1781), a *Sturm und Drang* drama by Friedrich Schiller (1759–1805), and his republican history drama, *Fiesco's Conspiracy at Genoa* (1783). Two Italian and neoclassical dramatists (as opposed to German Romantic ones) are Vittorio Alfieri (1749–1803) and Vincenzo Monti (1754–1828). The Italians would remain important models for Byron's own experiments with neoclassical drama in 1820–1.

[54] This was a disastrous marriage; see letter of 19 March 1823.

bomb, and be d[amne]d to him![55] Waxed sleepy—just come home—must go to bed, and am engaged to meet Sheridan to-morrow at Rogers's.

Queer ceremony that same of marriage—saw many abroad, Greek and Catholic—one, at *home*, many years ago. There be some strange phrases in the prorogue (the exhortation) which made me turn away, not to laugh in the face of the surpliceman. Made one blunder, when I joined the hands of the happy— rammed their left hands, by mistake into one another. Corrected it—bustled back to the altar-rail,—and said 'Amen.' Portsmouth responded as if he had got the whole by heart; and, if any thing—was rather before the priest. It is now midnight and * * * * * * * * * * * * * *

[To James Hogg]

Albany, March 24, [1814]

Dear Sir,[56]

I have been out of town, otherwise your letter should have been answered sooner. When a letter contains a request, the said request generally figures towards the *finale*, and so does yours, my good friend. In answering perhaps the other way is the better: so not to make many words about a trifle, (which any thing of mine must be,) you shall have a touch of my quality for your first Number—and if you print that, you shall have more of the same stuff for the successors. Send me a few of your proofs, and I will set forthwith about something, that I at least hope may suit your purposes. So much for the Poetic Mirror, which may easily be, God knows, entitled to hang higher than the prose one.

You seem to be a plain spoken man, Mr. Hogg, and I really do not like you the worse for it. I can't write verses, and yet you want a bit of my poetry for your book. It is for you to reconcile yourself with yourself.—You shall have the *verses*.

You are mistaken, my good fellow, in thinking that I (or, indeed, that any living verse-writer—for we shall sink *poets*) can write as well as Milton. Milton's Paradise Lost is, as a whole, a heavy concern; but the two first books of it are the

---

[55] Francesco Morosini (1619–94), later Doge of Venice, took a highly unfortunate role in the Morean War between Venice and the Ottoman Empire, during which he hit the powder magazine the Turks had established in the Parthenon, causing extensive damage. He attempted to rob sculptures from the building, most of which he broke, and it was after all this vandalism that the Turks began to sell sculptural remains to visitors.

[56] 'The Etterick Shepherd' (1770–1835), autodidact, poet, and novelist, at this stage planning a compilation of contemporary verse. In the end he made a collection of parodies of living poets with the same title, *The Poetic Mirror* (1816). This is Byron's only letter to a working-class intellectual—and it shows.

very finest poetry that has ever been produced in this world—at least since the flood—for I make little doubt Abel was a fine pastoral poet, and Cain a fine bloody poet, and so forth; but we, now-a-days, even we, (you and *I, i.e.)* know no more of their poetry than the *brutum vulgus*—I beg pardon, the swinish multitude, do of Wordsworth and Pye. Poetry must always exist, like drink, where there is a demand for it. And Cain's may have been the brandy of the Antedeluvians, and Abel's the small [?] still.

Shakespeare's name, you may depend on it, stands absurdly too high and will go down. He had no invention as to stories, none whatever. He took all his plots from old novels, and threw their stories into a dramatic shape, at as little expense of thought as you or I could turn his plays back again into prose tales. That he threw over whatever he did write some flashes of genius, nobody can deny: but this was all. Suppose any one to have the *dramatic* handling for the first time of such ready-made stories as Lear, Macbeth, &c. and he would be a sad fellow, indeed, if he did not make something very grand of them. [As] for his historical plays, properly historical, I mean, they were mere re-dressings of former plays on the same subjects, and in twenty cases out of twenty-one, the finest, the very finest things, are taken all but *verbatim* out of the old affairs. You think, no doubt, that *A horse, a horse, my kingdom for a horse!* is Shakespeare's. Not a syllable of it. You will find it all in the old nameless dramatist. Could not one take up Tom Jones and improve it, without being a greater genius than Fielding? I, for my part, think Shakespeare's plays might be improved, and the public seem, and have seemed for to think so too [*sic*], for not one of his is or ever has been acted as he wrote it; and what the pit applauded three hundred years past, is five times out of ten not Shakespeare's, but Cibber's.

Stick you to Walter Scott, my good friend, and do not talk any more stuff about his not being willing to give you real advice, if you really will ask for real advice. You love Southey, forsooth—I am sure Southey loves nobody but himself, however. I hate these talkers one and all, body and soul. They are a set of the most despicable impostors—that is my opinion of them. They know nothing of the world; and what is poetry, but the reflection of the world? What sympathy have this people [*sic*] with the spirit of this stirring age? They are no more able to understand the least of it, than your *lass*—nay, I beg her pardon, *she* may very probably have intense sympathy with both its spirit, (I mean the whisky,) and its body (I mean the bard.) They are mere old wives. Look at their beastly vulgarity, when they wish to be homely; and their exquisite stuff, when they clap on sail, and aim at fancy. Coleridge is the best of the trio—but bad is the best. Southey should have been a parish-clerk, and Wordsworth a man-midwife—both in darkness. I doubt if either of them ever got drunk, and I am of the old creed of Homer the wine-bibber. Indeed I think you and Burns have derived a great advantage from this, that being poets, and drinkers of wine, you have had a new potation to rely upon. Your whisky has made you original. I have always thought it a fine liquor. I back you against beer at all events, gill to gallon.

By the bye, you are a fine hand to cut up the minor matters of verse-writing; you indeed think harmony the all-in-all. My dear sir, you may depend upon it, you never had *name* yet, without making it rhyme to *theme*. I overlook all that sort of thing, however, and so must you, in your turn, pass over my real or supposed ruggedness. The fact is, that I have a theory on the subject, but that I have not time at present for explaining it. The first time all the poets of the age meet—it must be in London, glorious London is the place, after all—we shall, if you please, have a small trial of skill. You shall write seventeen odes for me, anything from Miltonian blank down to Phillupian [*sic*] namby, and I a similar number for you, and let a jury of good men and true be the judges between us. I name Scott for foreman—Tom Campbell may be admitted, and Mrs. Baillie, (though it be not exactly a matron case.) You may name the other nine worthies yourself. We shall, at all events, have a dinner upon the occasion, and I stipulate for a small importation of the peat reek.

Dear sir, believe me sincerely yours,
Byron

[To Harriette Wilson]

Albany [April?] 1814

If my silence has hurt 'your pride or your feelings', to use your own expressions, I am very sorry for it; be assured that such effect was far from my intention.[57] Business, and some little bustle attendant on changing my residence, prevented me from thanking you for your letter as soon as I ought to have done. If my thanks do not displease you, now, pray accept them. I could not feel otherwise than obliged by the desire of a stranger to make my acquaintance.

I am not unacquainted with your name or your beauty, and I have heard much of your talents; but I am not the person whom you would like, either as a lover or a friend. I did not, and do not suspect you, to use your own words once more, of any design of making love to me. I know myself well

---

[57] The courtesan Harriette Wilson (1786–1845) collected men of power and influence, including the Prince Regent and the Duke of Wellington—who famously exploded 'publish and be damned' on hearing of her plans to write her memoirs.

enough to acquit anyone who does not know me, and still more those who do, from any such intention. I am not of a nature to be loved, and so far, luckily for myself, I have no wish to be so. In saying this, I do not mean to affect any particular stoicism, and may possibly, at one time or other, have been liable to those follies, for which you sarcastically tell me, I have now no time: but these, and everything else, are to me, at present, objects of indifference; and this is a good deal to say, at six-and-twenty. You tell me that you wished to know me better, because you liked my writing. I think you must be aware that a writer is in general very different from his productions, and always disappoints those who expect to find in him qualities more agreeable than those of others; I shall certainly not be lessened in my vanity, as a scribbler, by the reflection that a work of mine has given you pleasure; and, to preserve the impression in its favour, I will not risk your good opinion, by inflicting my acquaintance upon you.

Very truly your obliged servant,
B

[Journal]

April 19th. 1814.

There is ice at both poles, north and south—all extremes are the same—misery belongs to the highest and the lowest only,—to the emperor and the beggar, when unsixpenced and unthroned. There is, to be sure, a damned insipid medium—an equinoctial line—no one knows where, except upon maps and measurement.

'And all our *yesterdays* have lighted fools
The way to dusty death.'[58]

I will keep no further journal of that same hesternal torch-light; and, to prevent me from returning, like a dog, to the vomit of memory, I tear out the remaining leaves of this volume, and write, in *Ipecacuanha,*—'that the Bourbons are restored!!!'—'Hang up philosophy,' To be sure, I have long despised myself and man, but I never spat in the face of my species before—'O fool! I shall go mad.'

---

[58] See *Macbeth*, V. v. 21–2. Byron goes on with *Romeo and Juliet*, III. iii. 57, and Folio *King Lear*, II. ii. 459.

[To John Murray]

2 Albany—April 29th. 1814

Dear Sir/

I enclose a draft for the money—when paid send the copyrights—I release you from the thousand pounds agreed on for the Giaour & Bride—and there's an end.———If any accident occurs to me—you may do then as you please—but with the exception of two copies of each for *yourself* only—I expect and request—that the advertisements be withdrawn—and the remaining copies of *all* destroyed—and any expence so incurred I will be glad to defray.———For all this it might be as well to assign some reason—I have none to give except my own caprice, and I do not consider the circumstances of consequence enough to require explanation.———In course I need hardly assure you that they never shall be published with my consent—directly or indirectly by any other person whatsoever, and that I am perfectly satisfied & have every reason so to be with your conduct in all transactions between us as publisher & author.———It will give me great pleasure to preserve your acquaintance—and to consider you as my friend—Believe me very truly and for much attention

yr. obliged & very obedt. St.
Byron

P. S.—*I do not think that I have overdrawn at Hammersley's—but if that be the case I can draw for the superflux on Hoare's—the draft is 5£ short—but that I will make up—on payment—not before—return [of?] the copyright papers.—*

[To John Murray]

May 1st. 1814

Dear <Murray> Sir/

If your present note is serious—and it really would be inconvenient—there is an end of the matter—tear my draft—& go on as usual—in that case we shall recur to our former basis.—That *I* was perfectly *serious* in wishing to suppress all future publication is true—but certainly not to interfere with the convenience of others—& more particularly your own.—Some day I will tell you the reason for this apparently strange resolution—at present it may be enough to say that I recall it at your suggestion—and as it appears to have annoyed you I lose no time in saying so

yrs. truly
B

[To John Hanson]

July 19th. 1814

Dear Sir/

I called in the hope of seeing you before I left town tomorrow—& to say that if Mr. C[laughto]n will give 25–000—or even 20–000—I will close with him—& take back the estate—so much am I convinced that he is a man of neither property nor credit.—He has never *once* kept his word since the sale was concluded—and at all events I will do anything to be rid of him—so tell him in what words you please—for such I appeal to you if he has not proved himself—without faith—& as far as I can perceive without funds.—*You* will cling & cling to the fallacious hope of the fulfilment—already shown to be so—till I am ruined entirely—in short it was a pity to let him go out of town again—without a conclusion—it was only to gain time—*close* with him on any terms—and let us have done with the equivocator.——Pray think of Rochdale—it is the delay which drives me mad—I declare to God—I would rather have but ten thousand pounds clear & out of debt—than drag on the cursed existence of expectation & disappointment which I have endured for these last 6 years—for 6 months longer—though a million came at the end of the them.—Address me at *Hastings House*—Hastings[59]—& believe me

very truly yours
B

P. S.—I hope Charles is better—tell Lord & Lady P[ortsmouth] that Mrs. Chaworth is in town—I believe the Countess knows her is it not so?———

[59] The Sussex seaside town where Byron was staying with Augusta.

5
MARRIAGE AND SEPARATION

August 1814–April 1816

On 9 September 1814 Byron took his life in his hands and proposed to a woman he had not set eyes on for ten months. He wrote from Newstead, and Augusta was with him. Nine days later he received not one but two letters of acceptance from Annabella Milbanke, and a welcoming letter from her father, Sir Ralph. 'It never rains but it pours,' he commented to his half-sister (Life, 474). On 26 September he asked Annabella to 'forgive my weaknesses' and 'love what you can of me & mine—and I will be—I am whatever you please to make me' (LJ iv. 184): the kind of unwise statement that encouraged her belief that she alone could restore and redeem him.

It took six weeks for Byron to visit his fiancée, via London and Augusta's home, by which time the Milbanke family was rigid with nerves. He blamed this delay on Hanson's sloth in drawing up the financial statements necessary for a marriage settlement. Byron's attitude seems to have been genuinely unworldly: 'Her expectations, I am told, are great,' he wrote to Thomas Moore (LJ iv. 202); 'but what, I have not asked.' 'She is an only child,' he reported again on 15 October (LJ iv. 208), 'and Sir R's estates, though dipped by electioneering, are considerable. Part of them are settled on her, but whether that will be dowered now, I do not know.' Annabella's real prospective wealth lay with her maternal uncle Earl Wentworth, whose early death no one would have predicted. A week later he wrote to Annabella herself, to ask, 'Do you think—my love—that happiness depends upon similarities or differences in character?' (LJ iv. 221). It would be hard to imagine an affianced couple more dangerously maladjusted, and Annabella sent Byron away from Seaham a fortnight after his arrival; the tension of being engaged was too much for the pair of them, and Byron found he could only resolve it through physical advances that caused her anguish and concern. Six weeks later he was back, and the couple married on 2 January 1815.

Essentially, the only records we have of this singularly unhappy marriage are those of parties to a legal proceeding, and this is not the place to wade through the piles of testimony regarding Byron's behaviour. It seems he treated his wife with mental cruelty, paraded his affection for Augusta (whom the couple visited, and who visited them for weeks at a time in the extravagant Piccadilly Terrace mansion Byron had rented from the Duchess of Devonshire) in ambiguous terms, was moody and violent (though not to her directly), imparted details of his Eastern adventures, and, perhaps, requested anal sex from her. Priggish and sanctimonious in the extreme, Annabella felt that he laid siege to her morals by claiming 'that morality was one thing in Constantinople, another in London'.[1] It is clear that Byron became increasingly depressed through 1815, mainly because of his deteriorating financial situation, and that she became increasingly concerned at his state of mind—having their doctor observe him to diagnose his condition. Some sort of decision was taken in January 1816 that she and their daughter Ada, born on 10 December, should get some respite with her family at Kirkby Mallory, her uncle's estate in Leicestershire. From there on 16 January she wrote in loving terms to her 'Dearest

---

[1] See Doris Langley Moore, Lord Byron: Accounts Rendered (London: John Murray, 1974), 443.

Duck', saying that she, 'Dad', and 'Mam' looked forward to his joining them, giving a maternal update on Ada's increasing weight, sending love to 'the good goose' (Augusta), and signing herself 'Ever thy most loving/Pippin . . . Pip . . . Ip'.

Then something happened that changed the whole complexion of events' (Life, 565). Perhaps Annabella discussed things that her parents made clear were unforgivable offences (incest, sodomy, sexual perversion). A bout of confessions and statements ensued, legal and medical advice was sought, and on 2 February Byron received a letter from Sir Ralph:

Very recently, circumstances have come to my knowledge, which convince me, that with your opinions it cannot tend to your happiness to continue to live with Lady Byron, and I am yet more forcibly convinced that after her dismissal from your house and the treatment she experienced whilst in it, those on whose protection she has the strongest natural claims could not feel themselves justified in permitting her return thither. (Life, 571)

There is no reason to doubt Byron's shock at receiving such a letter. It would have been an unusual communication, to say the least, in his era, in which husbands took total responsibility for their wives upon marriage—so that Sir Ralph's evocation of 'natural claims' was a moral as well as a legal nullity.

In retrospect we would have to say that the reality of the situation dawned upon him very quickly. By the middle of February, though he totally rejected her father's interference and insisted he had no idea what he was accused of, Byron was already addressing his wife in these terms:

I can only say in the truth of affliction—& without hope—motive—or end in again saying what I have lately but vainly repeated—that I love you:—good or bad—mad or rational—miserable or content—I love you—& shall do to the dregs of my memory & existence.—If I can feel thus for you now—under every possible aggravation & exasperating circumstance that can corrode the heart—& inflame the brain—perhaps you may one day know—or think at least—that I was not all you have persuaded yourself to believe me— (LJ v. 27)

Annabella steadfastly refused an interview, and bunkered down with her legal team, going so far as to interview Lady Caroline Lamb, of all people, on 27 March. (Lady Caroline, of course, had lots to tell, and was eager to impart it.) On 21 April Byron signed a deed of separation amidst the ruins of his household—bailiffs having been in residence since the previous November, and his library having been sold at the beginning of the month. Rumours surrounded him: 'if they were true', he wrote from Venice later (see letter of 7 December 1818), 'I was unfit for England, if false England is unfit for me.' 'All my relations (save one) fell from me—like leaves from the tree in Autumn winds,' he wrote five years later (CMP 171), 'and my few friends became still fewer.' On 8 April the loyal Lady Jersey invited him and his sister to a party where he was egregiously snubbed by the very London socialites who had once lionized him. Only the hostess and the independently wealthy Miss Mercer Elphinstone *were polite, and legend has it that the latter told him, 'You should have married me, and then this would not have happened to you!' (Life, 599). On 14 April he farewelled his sister from London; nine days later his preposterous 'Napoleonic' coach (cost, £500, unpaid for) rolled out of London for Dover. On 25 April he sailed for Ostend, never to see England again.*

An unhappy marriage and a legal separation do not leave much else in a person's life, and it is hardly surprising that Byron's literary output slackened during this period. The murkily melodramatic tale Lara was published in August 1814, and that, apart from an interesting collection of biblical poems, Hebrew Melodies, was all that John Murray had to sell until The Siege of Corinth *and* Parisina *were issued in February 1816. Byron found it hard not to compare his own downfall to that of Napoleon Bonaparte, and his disgust with British politics—'The barking of the wardogs for their carrion' (LJ iv. 295)—became complete. 'If you knew what a hopeless & lethargic den of dullness & drawling our hospital is,' he told Leigh Hunt about the House of Lords in January 1816, 'you would wonder—not that—I very seldom speak—but that I ever attempted it' (LJ v. 19). One avenue for his talent was his membership of the managerial sub-committee of Drury Lane Theatre, which he joined in May 1815. With that business (which he undertook in good earnest), his friends there, the great actor Edmund Kean, and various actresses who came his way, he sought and found some relief from misery at home. In the dying days of his London life Claire Clairmont, the stepdaughter of William Godwin (the anarchist philosopher whom Byron had tried to benefit with some of his literary earnings), threw herself at him. They would meet again at Geneva, which Byron told Hanson would be his* poste restante

[To Thomas Moore]

Hastings, August 3d, 1814

By the time this reaches your dwelling, I shall (God wot) be in town again probably. I have been here renewing my acquaintance with my old friend Ocean; and I find his bosom as pleasant a pillow for an hour in the morning as his daughter's of Paphos could be in the twilight.[2] I have been swimming and eating turbot, and smuggling neat brandies and silk handkerchiefs,—and listening to my friend Hodgson's raptures about a pretty wife-elect of his,—and walking on cliffs, and tumbling down hills, and making the most of the 'dolce far-niente' for the last fortnight. I met a son of Lord Erskine's, who says he has been married a year, and is the 'happiest of men;' and I have met the aforesaid H, who is also the 'happiest of men;' so, it is worth while being here, if only to

---

[2] In Greek myth Aphrodite was born of the ocean, and came ashore at Paphos, on Cyprus.

witness the superlative felicity of these foxes, who have cut off their tails, and would persuade the rest to part with their brushes to keep them in countenance.

It rejoiceth me that you like 'Lara.' Jeffrey is out with his 45th Number, which I suppose you have got. He is only too kind to me, in my share of it, and I begin to fancy myself a golden pheasant, upon the strength of the plumage wherewith he hath bedecked me. But then, 'surgit amari,' &c.—the gentlemen of the Champion, and Perry, have got hold (I know not how) of the condolatory address to Lady J[ersey] on the picture-abduction by our R * * * [Regent]. and have published them—with my name, too, smack—without even asking leave, or inquiring whether or no! D—n their impudence, and d—n every thing. It has put me out of patience, and so, I shall say no more about it.[3]

You shall have Lara and Jacque (both with some additions) when out; but I am still demurring and delaying, and in a fuss, and so is R[ogers] in his way.

Newstead is to be mine again. Claughton forfeits twenty-five thousand pounds; but that don't prevent me from being very prettily ruined. I mean to bury myself there—and let my beard grow—and hate you all.

Oh! I have had the most amusing letter from Hogg, the Ettrick minstrel and shepherd. He wants me to recommend him to Murray, and, speaking of his present bookseller, whose 'bills' are never 'lifted,' he adds, *totidem verbis* [in so many words], 'God d—n him and them both.' I laughed, and so would you too, at the way in which this execration is introduced. The said Hogg is a strange being, but of great, though uncouth, powers. I think very highly of him, as a poet; but he, and half of these Scotch and Lake troubadours, are spoilt by living in little circles and petty societies. London and the world is the only place to take the conceit out of a man—in the milling phrase. Scott, he says, is gone to the Orkneys in a gale of wind;—during which wind, he affirms, the said Scott, 'he is sure, is not at his ease,—to say the best of it.' Lord, Lord, if these home-keeping minstrels had crossed your Atlantic or my Mediterranean, and tasted a little open boating in a white squall—or a gale in 'the Gut'[4]—or the 'Bay of Biscay,' with no gale at all—how it would enliven and introduce them to a few of the sensations!—to say nothing of an illicit amour or two upon shore, in the way of

---

[3] Murray published Byron's *Lara* with Samuel Rogers's *Jacqueline* on 6 August, to the approval of the all-powerful Francis Jeffrey at the *Edinburgh Review*. But in late July and early August the *Champion* and the *Morning Chronicle* published Byron's anonymous satirical poem 'Condolatory Address to Sarah, Countess of Jersey, On the Prince Regent's Returning her Picture to Mrs Mee' (*CPW* iii. 272–3), and named him when doing so. '*Surgit amari aliquid*' is from Lucretius, *De Rerum Natura*, iv. 1133: approximately translated by Byron himself in *Childe Harold's Pilgrimage*, i. 817–18 (*CPW* ii. 38): 'Still from the fount of joy's delicious springs | Some bitter o'er the flowers its bubbling venom flings.'

[4] A naval term for the straits of Gibraltar. The 'Scotch and Lake troubadours' are Walter Scott (1771–1832), William Wordsworth (1770–1850), Samuel Taylor Coleridge (1772–1834), and Robert Southey (1774–1843). Moore had crossed the Atlantic to take an Admiralty post in Bermuda in 1803 and thereafter travelled in North America until his return to England in November 1804.

essay upon the Passions, beginning with simple adultery, and compounding it as they went along.

I have forwarded your letter to Murray,—by the way, you had addressed it to *Miller*. Pray write to me, and say what art thou doing? 'Not finished!'—Oons! how is this?—these 'flaws and starts' must be 'authorised by your grandam,'[5] and are unbecoming of any other author. I was sorry to hear of your discrepancy with the * *s, or rather your abjuration of agreement. I don't want to be impertinent, or buffoon on a serious subject, and am therefore at a loss what to say.

I hope nothing will induce you to abate from the proper price of your poem, as long as there is a prospect of getting it. For my own part, I have, *seriously*, and *not whiningly* (for that is not my way—at least, it used not to be) neither hopes, nor prospects, and scarcely even wishes. I am, in some respects, happy, but not in a manner that can or ought to last,—but enough of that. The worst of it is, I feel quite enervated and indifferent. I really do not know, if Jupiter were to offer me my choice of the contents of his benevolent cask, what I would pick out of it.[6] If I was born, as the nurses say, with a 'silver spoon in my mouth,' it has stuck in my throat, and spoiled my palate, so that nothing put into it is swallowed with much relish,—unless it be cayenne. However, I have grievances enough to occupy me that way too;—but for fear of adding to yours by this pestilent long diatribe, I postpone the reading them, *sine die* [for good]. Ever, dear M., yours, &c.

P. S.—Don't forget my godson.[7] You could not have fixed on a fitter porter for his sins than me, being used to carry double without inconvenience. * * * * * *

[To Annabella Milbanke]

August 10th 1814

I will answer your question as openly as I can.—I did—do—and always shall love you—and as this feeling is not exactly an act of will—I know no remedy

---

[5] See *Macbeth*, III. iv. 62–5.
[6] In the *Iliad*, xxiv. 527–33, Achilles tells Priam that Zeus dispenses gifts for mortals from one of two urns, full of evils and blessings respectively.
[7] In fact Mrs Moore soon gave birth to a daughter, Olivia Byron Moore; she died in infancy (see letter of 5 January 1816).

and at all events should never find one in the sacrifice of your comfort.—When an acquaintance commenced—it appeared to me from all that I saw and heard—that you were the woman most adapted to render any man (who was neither inveterately foolish nor wicked) happy—but I was informed that you were attached if not engaged[8]—and very luckily—to a person for whose success—all the females of the family—where I received my intelligence— were much interested.——Before such powerful interest—and your supposed inclinations—I had too much humility or pride to hazard importunity or even attention—till I at last learned—almost by accident—that I was misinformed— as to the engagement—the rest you know—and I will not trouble you with 'a twice told tale' 'signifying nothing.'[9]————————What your own feelings and objections were and are I have not the right and scarcely the wish to enquire—it is enough for me that they exist—they excite neither astonishment nor displeasure—it would be a very hard case—if a woman were obliged to account for her repugnance—you would probably like me if you could—and as you cannot—I am not quite coxcomb enough to be surprized at a very natural occurrence.——You ask me how far my peace is—or may be affected by those feelings towards you?——I do not know—not quite enough to invade yours— or request from your pity what I cannot owe to your affection.————I am interrupted—perhaps it is as well upon such a subject.—

ever most truly yrs.

B

[To Annabella Milbanke]

Newstead Abbey. Septr. 9th 1814

You were good enough in your last to say that I might write 'soon'—but you did not add *often*—I have therefore to apologize for again intruding on your time— to say nothing of patience.—There is something I wish to say—and as I may not see you for some—perhaps for a long time—I will endeavour to say it at once.——A few weeks ago you asked me a question—which I answered—I have now one to propose—to which if improper—I need not add that your declining to reply to it will be sufficient reproof.—It is this.—Are the

---

[8] To George Eden (see letter of 28 September 1812).
[9] See *King John*, III. iv. 108 and *Macbeth*, V. v. 27.

'objections'—to which you alluded—insuperable?—or is there any line or change of conduct which could possibly remove them?—I am well aware that all such changes are more easy in theory than practice—but at the same time there are few things I would not attempt to obtain your good opinion—at all events I would willingly know the worst—still I neither wish you to promise or pledge yourself to anything—but merely to learn a *possibility* which would not leave you the less a free agent.——When I believed you attached—I had nothing to urge—indeed I have little now—except that having heard from yourself that your affections are not engaged—my importunities may appear not quite so selfish however unsuccessful—It is not without a struggle that I address you once more on this subject—yet I am not very consistent—for it was to avoid troubling you upon it that I finally determined to remain an absent friend rather than become a tiresome guest—if I offend it is better at a distance.———With the rest of my sentiments you are already acquainted—if I do not repeat them it is to avoid—or at least not increase your displeasure.—

ever yrs. most truly

B

[To John Cam Hobhouse]

Newstead Abbey, Septr. 14th. 1814

My dear Hobhouse

Clau[ghton] has relinquished his purchase and twenty five thousand pounds out of twenty eight d[itt]o. paid on account—and I am Abbot again—it is all signed—sealed and *re*-delivered——So much for your enquiry—he wishes to *renew*—but I will first see an' the monies be palpable and tangible—before I recontract with him or others—though if he could complete I should have no objection, on the old terms.—But now for other matters:—if a circumstance (which may happen—but is as unlikely to happen as Johanna's establishing herself the real Mrs. Trinity[10]) does not occur—I have thoughts of going direct and directly to Italy—if so—will you come with me?—I want your opinion first—your advice afterwards—and your company always:—I am pretty well in funds—having better than £4000 at Hoares—a note of Murray for £700 (the price of *Larry*) at a *year's* date last month—and the Newstead Michaelmas will give me from a thousand to 15—if not 1800—more—I believe it is raised to between

---

[10] The fraudulent mystic Joanna Southcott, who died aged 65 in December 1814, had announced in 1813 that she was about to give birth to a new Messiah.

177

3 & 4000—but then there is land upon *hand* (which of course payeth no rent for the present & be damned to it) altogether I should have somewhere about £5000 tangible[11]—which I am not at all disposed to spend at home—now I would wish to set apart £3000 for the tour—do you think *that* would enable me to see all *Italy* in a gentlemanly way?—with as few servants & luggage (except my aperients) as we can help.—And will you come with me?—you are the only man with whom I could travel an hour except an 'ιατρος' [physician]—in short you know my dear H—that with all my bad qualities—(and d——d bad they *are* to be sure) I like you better than any body—and we have travelled together before—and been old friends and all that—and we have a thorough fellow-feeling & contempt for all things of the sublunary sort—and so do let us go & call the 'Pantheon a cockpit' like the learned Smelfungus.[12]—The Cash is the principal point—do you think that will do—viz £3000 clear from embarkation onwards. I have a world of watches & snuffboxes & telescopes—which would do for the Mussulmans if we liked to cross from Otranto & see our friends again.—— They are all safe at Hammersleys.—would my *coach* do?—*beds* I have & all canteens &c. from *your* Man of Ludgate Hill[13]—with saddles—pistols—tromboni—& what not.—I shall know tomorrow or next day—whether I can go—or not—and shall be in town next week—where I must see you or hear from you—if we set off—it should be in October—and the earlier the better.—Now don't engage yourself— but take up your map—& ponder upon this.—ever dear H.

yrs most affectly.

B

[To Lady Melbourne]

Newstead Abbey—Septr. 18th. 1814

My dear Lady M[elbourn]e.

Miss Milbanke has accepted me:—and her answer was accompanied by a very kind letter from your brother—may I hope for your consent too? without it

---

[11] Byron has money in the bank, his first payment ever from Murray (for *Lara*) in the form of a promissory note, and the prospect of the quarterly rents from tenants at Newstead.

[12] Tobias Smollett's *Travels through France and Italy* (1766) was so given to dyspeptic comments about sites on the Grand Tour (like the Pantheon in Rome) that his fellow novelist Laurence Sterne nicknamed the author 'Smelfungus' in his own *Sentimental Journey* (1768).

[13] On 15 July 1813 Byron spent £400—nearly the equivalent of his annual allowance as a Cambridge undergraduate—at Bryant's Military Warehouse, Ludgate Hill, on what we would call camping equipment: trunks, hammocks, four-poster beds, a stove, kettles, saddles, and so on, and so forth. (See Langley Moore, *Lord Byron: Accounts Rendered*, 201.)

I should be unhappy—even were it not for many reasons important in other points of view—& with it I shall have nothing to require except your good wishes now— and your friendship always.——I lose no time in telling you how things are at present—many circumstances may doubtless occur in this as in other cases to prevent it's completion—but I will hope otherwise.—I shall be in town by thursday—& beg one line to Albany to say you will see me at your own day—hour—& place.——In course I mean to reform most thoroughly & become 'a good man and true'[14] in all the various senses of these respective & respectable appellations— seriously—I will endeavour to make your niece happy not by 'my deserts but what I will deserve'[15]—of my deportment you may reasonably doubt—of her merits you can have none.——I need not say that this must be a *secret*—do let me find a few words from you in Albany & believe me ever most affectly yrs.

B

[To Annabella Milbanke]

Newstead Abbey—Septr. 20th. 1814

There is one point on which—though you have not lately pressed it—I am sure you feel anxious on my behalf—and to this will I speak, I mean—Religion.— When I tell you that I am so convinced of it's importance in fixing the principles—that I could never have had perfect confidence in any woman who was slightly impressed with it's truth—you will hardly believe that I can exact more tolerance than I am willing to grant.—I will not deny that my own impressions are by no means settled—but that they are perverted to the extent which has been imputed to them on the ground of a few passages in works of fiction—I cannot admit to those whose esteem I would secure—although from a secret aversion from explanations & vindications I have hitherto entered into none to those who would never have made the charge but from a wish to condemn rather than convert.—To you—my conduct must be different—as my feelings—I am rather bewildered by the variety of tenets—than inclined to dispute their foundation—in a word—I will read what books you please— hear what arguments you please—and in leaving the choice to your judgment— let it be a proof that my confidence in your understanding & your virtues is equal.—You shall be 'my Guide—Philosopher and friend'[16] my whole heart

---

[14] A widely used expression from the *Golden Sayings* of the 1st-century Greek Stoic philosopher Epictetus.
[15] See *Richard III*, IV. iv. 346.
[16] See Pope, *An Essay on Man* (1734), iv. 390.

is yours—and if possible let me make it not unworthy of her to whom it is bound—& from whom but one event can divide it.—This is my third letter in three days—I will therefore shorten it—I proceed on my way to London tomorrow.—With every sentiment of respect—and—may I add the word?— Love—

ever yours
Byron

[To John Hanson]

Octr. 5th. 1814

My dear Sir/

I do not wish to hurry or to plague you but I cannot help saying that *delay* in this business may do me great harm—& that it has even done *some* already.—I hope as I [have] ever shewn not only my confidence in you professionally—but I trust my regard for you & yours personally—that you will not lose much time in seeing me—and that in the mean time you are considering & arranging what may best be done on my approaching marriage.—My relatives that are to be are expecting me—& wondering that I do not come—I can only say that nothing detains me but not seeing you first & making the arrangements.—If I could have come to H[urstbourne] I would willingly but it is not in my power.—

ever yrs. truly
Byron

[To Annabella Milbanke]

Octr. 14th. 1814

I have not seen the paragraph you mention—but it cannot *speak* more humbly of me in the comparison than I *think*.—This is one of the lesser evils to which notoriety and a carelessness of fame—in the only good sense of the word—has rendered me liable—a carelessness which I do not now feel since I have obtained something worth caring for.—The truth is that could I have foreseen that your life was to be linked to mine—had I even possessed a distinct hope however distant— I would have been a different and a better being—as it is—I have sometimes doubts—even if I should not disappoint the future nor act hereafter unworthily of you—whether the past ought not to make you still reject me—even that portion of it with which you are not unacquainted.—I did not believe such a woman existed—at least for me—and I sometimes fear I ought to wish that she had not—I must turn from the subject.—Yesterday I answered your letter—will you repeat my thanks to Lady Milbanke for hers—& believe me

yrs. ever

B

P. S.—I am not satisfied with what I have written—but I shall not improve by adding to it— in ten or twelve days the moment I can leave N[ewstea]d we shall meet—till then let me hear from you—I will write tomorrow—my Love—do forgive me—if I have written in a spirit that renders you uncomfortable—I cannot embody my feelings in words—I have nothing to desire—nothing I would see altered in you—but so much in myself—I can conceive no misery equal to mine if I failed in making you happy—& yet how can I hope to do justice to those merits—from whose praise there is not a dissentient voice?——

P. S. 2d.—I have since the morning seen the paragraph—it is just to you—& not very unjust to me—merely the old story of 'the thorny paths of Satire & the gloomy recesses of Misanthropy' from which the writer hopes you will withdraw me—I'm sure so do I.—He adds laughably enough 'we hope so much contradiction will not exist after the ceremony' alluding to the con—& re-contradiction.——There are also some epigrams by no means bad & very complimentary to you in which such a 'Heraclitus'—as I am—is made to leave off melancholy under your auspices—and a long address in the M[ornin]g P[os]t to me—making me responsible for a sentiment in 'the Giaour' though it is in the mouth of a fictitious character—these 'paper bullets of the brain' will not penetrate mine—& I could forgive any censure but of you.[17]——

[To John Cam Hobhouse]

Octr. 17th. 1814

My dear Hobhouse

If I have not answered your very kind letter immediately—do not impute it to neglect—I have expected you would be in town or near it—& waited to thank you in person.————Believe me no change of time or circumstance short of

---

[17] Clearly someone in a newspaper had commented on Byron's forthcoming marriage in a judicatory vein, and compared the poet to the 5th-century BC Greek sceptic and materialist Heraclitus of Ephesus. Another writer in the *Morning Post* newspaper continued the discussion by ascribing views stated in *The Giaour* to Byron himself. For 'paper bullets of the brain', see *Much Ado About Nothing*, II. iii. 228.

insanity can make any difference in my feelings—and I hope in my conduct towards you—I have known you too long & tried you too deeply—a new mistress is nothing to an old friend—the latter can't be replaced in this world—nor—I very much fear—in the next—and neither in this nor the other could I meet with one so deserving of my respect & regard.————— Well—H.—I am engaged—& we wait only for settlements and all that to be married—my intended it seems has liked me very well for a long time—which I am sure her encouragement gave me no reason to suspect—but so it is according to her account—the circumstances which led to the renewal of my proposal I will acquaint you with when we meet—if you think such material concerns worth your enquiry.—Hanson is going down next week to Durham to confabulate with Sir R[alph]'s agents on the score of temporalities—& I suppose I must soon follow to my Sire in law's that is to be—I confess that the character of wooer in this regular way does not sit easy upon me—I wish I could wake some morning & find myself fairly married—I do hate (out of Turkey) all fuss & bustle—& ceremony so much and one can't be married according to what I hear without *some*.————I wish—whenever this same form is muttered over us—that you could make it convenient to be present—I will give you due notice—if you would but take a wife & be coupled then also like people electrified in company through the same chain—it would be still further comfort.—Good-Even—

ever yrs. most truly
B

[To John Hanson]

Oct. 24th. 1814

Dear Sir

I am truly sorry to write to you in any terms but the most friendly—but circumstances compel me.—It is now *five weeks* since I announced to you Miss M's resolution & mine—& since that period little or nothing has been done towards the object of our wishes.—I should not be a very impartial judge doubtless in my own case—but this is not my opinion so much as that of her connections & of mine—who have written to me—and when I state the *fact*— that I am waiting for your return—they express their surprize that in business of so much importance—so much time should be lost—and delays as it were sought for—it looks like trifling on my part—and on yours does not appear very attentive to me as a client or friendly as a man.—I have written to you 3 times to press your departure—but without an answer—I certainly did hope that on an occasion not the least important with regard to my present as well as future prospects & happiness there would not have been so much necessity of urging you in behalf of yours very truly

Byron

P. S.—A very little more delay will settle the business most effectually—in which case I shall have reason to remember Mr. [Viney?][18]*—& your zeal in his cause—all the rest of my life.*

[To Lady Melbourne]

Seaham. Novr. 4th. 1814

My dear Lady M[elbourn]e.

I have been here these two days—but waited to observe before I imparted to you 'my confidential Counsel' as Master Hoar would say—my remarks.——Your brother pleases me much—to be sure his stories are long—but I believe he has told most of them—& he is to my mind the perfect gentleman——but I don't like Lady Mil[bank]e at all—I can't tell why—for we don't differ—but so it is— she seems to be every thing here—which is all very well—and I am & mean to be very conformable & dutiful but nevertheless I wish she & mine aunt could change places as far as regards me & mine.—A's meeting & mine made a kind of scene.—though there was no acting nor even speaking—but the pantomine [*sic*] was very expressive—she seems to have more feeling than we imagined— but is the most *silent* woman I ever encountered—which perplexes me extremely—I like them to talk—because then they *think* less—much cogitation will not be in my favour—besides I can form my judgments better—since unless the countenance is flexible—it is difficult to steer by mere looks—I am studying her but I can't boast of my progress in getting at her disposition—and if the conversation is to be all on one side—I fear committing myself—& those who only listen—must have their thoughts so much about them—as to seize any weak point at once—however the die is cast—neither party can recede—the lawyers are here—mine & all—& I presume the parchment once scribbled I shall become Lord Annabella.——I can't yet tell whether we are to be happy or not—

---

[18] With Byron's marriage yet to be settled from the point of view of financial settlements, Hanson disappeared to Ilfracombe, in Devon, to look after a client there.

I have every disposition to do her all possible justice—but I fear she won't govern me—& if she don't it will not do at all—but perhaps she may mend of that fault.———I have always thought—first that she did not like me at all—& next—that her supposed after liking was *imagination*—this last I conceive that my presence would—perhaps has removed—if so—I shall soon discover it—but mean to take it with great philosophy—and to behave attentively & well—though I never could love but that which *loves*—& this I must say for myself—that my attachment always increases in due proportion to the return it meets with—& never changes in the presence of it's object—to be sure like Mrs. Damer I have 'an opinion of absence.'[19]———Pray write—I think you need not fear that the *answer* to *this* will run any of the risks you apprehend—It will be a great comfort to me in all events to call you Aunt & to know that you are sure of my being

ever yrs.

B

[To Lady Melbourne]

Novr. 13th. 1814

My dear Lady Mel[bourn]e.

I delivered your letters—but have only mentioned ye receipt of your *last* to myself.————Do you know I have great doubts—if this will be a marriage now.—her disposition is—the very reverse of *our* imaginings—she is overrun with fine feelings—scruples about herself & *her* disposition (I suppose in fact she means mine) and to crown all is taken ill once every 3 days with I know not what—but the day before and the day after she seems well—looks & eats well & is cheerful & confiding & in short like any other person in good health & spirits.—A few days ago she made one *scene*—not altogether out of C[aroline]'s style—it was too long & too trifling in fact for me to transcribe—but it did me no good———in the article of conversation however she has improved with a vengeance—but I don't much admire these same agitations upon slight occasions.—I don't know—but I think it by no means impossible you will see me in town soon—I can only interpret these things one way—& merely wait to be certain to make my obeisances and 'exit singly.' I hear of nothing but 'feeling' from morning till night—except from Sir Ralph with whom I go on

---

[19] Anne Seymour Damer (1749–1828) was, despite her plain name, a Whig aristocrat and daughter-in-law of the first Earl of Dorchester, but a widow since 1776. She was also a talented sculptor.

to admiration—Ly. M too is pretty well—but I am never sure of A—for a moment—the least word—and you know I rattle on through thick & thin (always however avoiding anything I think can offend her favourite notions) if only to prevent me from yawning—the least word—or alteration of tone—has some inference drawn from it—sometimes we are too much alike—& then again too unlike—this comes of *system*—& squaring her notions to the Devil knows what—for my part I have lately had recourse to the eloquence of *action* (which Demosthenes calls the first part of oratory) & find it succeeds very well & makes her very quiet which gives me some hopes of the efficacy of the 'calming process' so renowned in *'our* philosophy.'[20]—In fact and entre nous it is really amusing—she is like a child in that respect—and quite *caressable* into kindness and good humour—though I don't think her temper *bad* at any time—but very *self*-tormenting—and anxious—and romantic.————In short—it is impossible to foresee how this will end *now*—anymore than 2 years ago—if there is a break—it shall be *her* doing not mine.—

ever yrs. most truly

B

[To Annabella Milbanke]

Decr. 23d. 1814

Dearest A

If we meet let it be to marry—had I remained at S[eaham] it had probably been over by this time—with regard to our being under the same roof and *not* married—I think past experience has shown us the awkwardness of that situation—I can conceive nothing above purgatory more uncomfortable.————If a postponement is determined upon—it had better have been decided at a distance—I shall however set out tomorrow—but stop one day at Newmarket.————Hobhouse I believe accompanies me—which I rejoice at—for if we don't marry I should not like a 2d. journey back quite alone—and remaining at S[eaham] might only revive a scene like the former and to that I confess myself unequal.————The profile[21]—it is like—but I think more like the *Sphinx*—I am

[20] Perhaps an allusion to *Hamlet*, I. v. 167–8: 'There are more things in heaven and earth, Horatio, | Than are dreamt of in your philosophy.'
[21] Annabella must have sent Byron a silhouette of herself; such pictures were always drawn or cut in profile, and thus very difficult to produce as self-portraits.

puzzling myself to imagine how you could have taken it unless opposite a mirror—or two mirrors—or—or—how?—

ever dearest A—

yrs

B

[To Lady Melbourne]

January 7th. 1815

Dearest Aunt

Bell sent you a few lines yesterday as an accompaniment to an answer of mine to an epistle of Caro's about her present—which of course she will be very glad to receive—I wonder C[aroline] should think it necessary to make such a preface—*we* are very well disposed *towards* her—and can't see why there should not be a peace with her as well as with America.[22]——About this and every thing else I will do as you like—if you prefer that we should quarrel with that branch of the cousinhood—I shall have no objection—but I suppose George & Lord Cowper and I and our female appendages are not to be involved in the like bickering any more now than heretofore.[23]—Bell & I go on extremely well so far without any other company than our own selves as yet—I got a wife and a cold on the same day—but have got rid of the last pretty speedily—I don't dislike this place[24]—it is just the spot for a Moon—there is my only want a *library*—and thus I can always amuse myself—even if alone—I have great hopes this match will turn out well—I have found nothing as yet that I could wish changed for the better—but Time does wonders—so I won't be too hasty in my happiness.——I will tell you all about the ceremony when we meet,—it went off very pleasantly—all but the cushions—which were stuffed with Peach-stones I believe—and made me make a face that passed for piety.—My love to all my relatives—by the way what do they

---

[22] The Anglo-American War of 1812–15—a sideshow of the Napoleonic Wars—was concluded and settled at the Treaty of Ghent, signed at Christmas 1814, and ratified in the United States two months later.

[23] Lady Caroline Lamb's husband William was second son of Lord Melbourne, and became his heir after the first son, Peniston (whom Lord Melbourne in all likelihood actually fathered—Lady Melbourne had many affairs), died. George Lamb was fourth son. The Melbournes' first daughter was Emily Lamb, Lady Cowper. The other branch of the cousinhood would be on Lady Melbourne's side: her brother was Annabella's father.

[24] The Byrons spent what the poet called their 'treaclemoon' at Halnaby Hall, a property belonging to the Milbanke family, near Darlington, County Durham. It was demolished in the 1950s.

mean to give *me?* I will compromise provided they let me choose what I will have instead of their presents—nothing but what they could very well spare.—

> ever Aunt thine dutifully
>
> B

———⊗⊗⊗———

P. S.—Lady Byron sends her love—but has not seen this epistle—recollect—we are to keep our secrets—& correspondence as heretofore—mind that.—

[To John Cam Hobhouse]

Seaham—January 26th. 1815

My dear H[obhous]e

Your packet hath been perused and firstly I am lost in wonder & obligation at your good nature in taking so much trouble with Spooney[25] and my damnable concerns—I would leave to your choice our 'Counsellors at law' as Mrs. Heidelberg calls them—a—Templeman I think stands first on your list—so prithee fix on him—or whom you please—but do *you fix*—for you know *I* never could.[26]— N[ewstead] *must* be sold—without delay—and even at a loss—*out* of *debt* must be my first object—and the sooner the better.—My debts can hardly be less than thirty thousand—there is *six thousand* charged on N[ewstead] to a Mr. Sawbridge[27]—a *thousand*—to Mrs. B[yron] at Nott[ingha]m—a *Jew debt* of which the interest must be more than the principal—& of which H[anson] must get an amount from *Thomas*—another Jew debt—six *hundred* prin[cipal]—and no interest (as I have kept that down) to a man in New Street—I forget his name but shall know on half year's day—a good deal still before majority—in which the 'old women' of former celebrity were concerned[28]—but *one* is defunct—and the debt itself may wait my convenance—since it is not in my name—and indeed the interest has pretty well paid principal & all being transcendantly usurious,—a

---

[25] Byron's nickname for Hanson; it derives from the 'flash' idiom of the late 18th-century criminal class, and means a simple, silly, or foolish person.

[26] Mrs Heidelberg is a character from George Colman the Elder and David Garrick's *The Clandestine Marriage* (1766). Giles Templeman was an eminent London barrister.

[27] Hanson's partner had organized a £6,000 loan from Mr Sawbridge before Byron's Grand Tour in 1809. It was only finalized after his departure, and would not be repaid until Newstead was sold in 1818.

[28] Elizabeth Massingberd and her daughter. (See letter of 15 December 1811.)

good deal of tradesmen &c. &c.—You know I have paid off *Scrope* that is 6000 & more—nearly 3000 to *Hans*. Carvel[29]—then I lent rather more than £1600 to Hodgson—£1000 to 'bold' Webster—and nearly 3000 to George L[eigh] or rather to Augusta   the *last* sums I never *wish* to see again—and others I *may wish*—I have W[ebster]'s bond which is worth a damn or two—but from Hodg I neither asked nor wanted security—but there was 150 lent at Hastings to the same Hod which was punctually *promised* to be paid in six weeks—and has been paid with the usual punctuality—viz—not at all.—I think I have now accounted for a good deal of Clau[ghton]'s disbursements—the rest was swallowed up by duns—necessities—luxuries—fooleries—jewelleries—'whores and fiddlers'.—As for expectations, don't talk to me of 'expects' (as Mr Lofty says to Croaker of 'suspects'[30]) the Baronet is eternal—the Viscount immortal—and my Lady (*senior*) without end.—They grow more healthy every day and I verily believe Sir R[alph] Ly. M[ilbanke] and Lord W[entworth] are at this moment cutting a fresh set of teeth and unless they go off by the usual fever attendant on such children as don't use the 'American soothing syrup' that they will live to have them all drawn again.[31]—

[displaced sheet perhaps belonging here]

'The Melodies'—damn the melodies—I have other tunes—or rather tones—to think of—but—Murray *can't* have them, or *shan't*—or I shall have Kin[nair]d and Braham upon me.[32]——Take the *box* any night or all nights week after *next*—only send to Lady Melbourne—to tell her of your intention for the night or nights—as I have long ago left her paramount during my absence.—

ever d[ea]r H. thine
B

---

[29] 'Hans Carvel', a marital satire by Matthew Prior (1664–1721); *Hans* means John *Hanson* in this case.

[30] Characters in Oliver Goldsmith's *The Good-Natured Man* (1768), v. 475–80: 'Sir, I will not be satisfied—Suspects! [...] Who am I, I say, who am I?'

[31] In fact, Annabella's maternal uncle, the wealthy Lord Wentworth ('the Viscount'), died on 17 April. His property then passed to Lady Milbanke, thenceforth Lady Noel (see letter of 12 June 1815), until she died in January 1821, when her estate passed in turn to Byron himself as her only child's husband, finally making him (on paper at least) a wealthy man. Sir Ralph died in 1825.

[32] In September 1814 Byron's Cambridge friend Douglas Kinnaird (1788–1830) wrote to him, urging the case of the Jewish musician Isaac Nathan, who wanted Byron to compose some poems on Old Testament themes for him to set to music. The result was *Hebrew Melodies*, a melange of earlier and more recent items, some not explicitly biblical at all, published by Murray in May 1815. Nathan and the Jewish singer John Braham published an edition with music beforehand, in April.

[To Samuel Taylor Coleridge]

Piccadilly, March 31st, 1815

Dear Sir,

It will give me great pleasure to comply with your request, though I hope there is still taste enough left among us to render it almost unnecessary, sordid and interested as, it must be admitted, many of 'the trade' are, where circumstances give them an advantage.[33] I trust you do not permit yourself to be depressed by the temporary partiality of what is called 'the public' for the favourites of the moment; all experience is against the permanency of such impressions. You must have lived to see many of these pass away, and will survive many more—I mean personally, for *poetically*, I would not insult you by a comparison.

If I may be permitted, I would suggest that there never was such an opening for tragedy. In Kean, there is an actor worthy of expressing the thoughts of the characters which you have every power of imbodying; and I cannot but regret that the part of Ordonio was disposed of before his appearance at Drury-lane. We have had nothing to be mentioned in the same breath with 'Remorse' for very many years; and I should think that the reception of that play was sufficient to encourage the highest hopes of author and audience.[34] It is to be hoped that you are proceeding in a career which could not but be successful. With my best respects to Mr. Bowles, I have the honour to be

Your obliged and very obedient servant,

Byron

P. S.—*You mention my 'Satire,' lampoon, or whatever you or others please to call it, I can only say, that it was written when I was very young and very angry, and has been a thorn in my side ever since; more particularly as almost all the persons animadverted upon became subsequently my acquaintances, and some of them my friends, which is 'heaping fire upon an*

---

[33] Coleridge had written to Byron at length on 30 March—appealing, as he put it, to 'a sort of pre-established good Will, not unlike that with which the Swan instinctively takes up the weakling Cygnet into the Hollow between its wings'—and seeking his help in placing a new collection of poems with London publishers. (See *Collected Letters of Samuel Taylor Coleridge*, ed. Earl Leslie Griggs, 6 vols. (Oxford: Oxford University Press, 1956–71), iv. 559–63.) Murray published *Christabel and Other Poems* in 1816.
[34] Coleridge had written a tragedy, *Osorio*, in 1797. In late 1812 he revised it as *Remorse*, at the invitation of Samuel Whitbread, manager at the Drury Lane Theatre. It had a run of twenty nights in January 1813, with Alexander Rae taking the part of Ordonio.

enemy's head,'[35] and forgiving me too readily to permit me to forgive myself. The part applied to you is pert, and petulant, and shallow enough;[36] but, although I have long done every thing in my power to suppress the circulation of the whole thing, I shall always regret the wantonness or generality of many of its attempted attacks.

[To Lady Byron]

[April 13–14? 1815]

Dearest

Now your mother is come I won't have you worried any longer—more particularly in your present situation which is rendered very precarious by what you have already gone through.[37] Pray—come home—

ever thine
B

[To Thomas Moore]

13, Piccadilly Terrace, June 12th. 1815

I have nothing to offer in behalf of my late silence, except the most inveterate and ineffable laziness; but I am too supine to invent a lie, or I *certainly* should, being ashamed of the truth. K * * [Kinnaird], I hope, has appeased your magnanimous indignation at his blunders. I wished and wish you were in the Committee, with all my heart.[38] It seems so hopeless a business, that the company of a friend would be quite consoling,—but more of this when we meet. In the mean time, you are entreated to prevail upon Mrs. Esterre to engage herself.[39] I believe she has been written to, but your influence, in person, or proxy, would probably go farther than our proposals. What they are, I know

---

[35] See Proverbs 25: 21–2.

[36] See *English Bards and Scotch Reviewers*, 255–6 (*CPW* i. 237): 'Shall gentle COLERIDGE pass unnoticed here, | To turgid ode, and tumid stanza dear?'

[37] Lord Wentworth fell ill in early April, and Annabella—in the early stages of her first pregnancy—left London to stay with him at Kirkby Mallory until her mother came down from Seaham.

[38] Byron joined the management sub-committee at Drury Lane Theatre in May 1815, at the prompting of Douglas Kinnaird—who had already involved him in the *Hebrew Melodies* project. After Byron's self-imposed exile in 1816 Kinnaird, as senior partner and later manager at Ransom and Morland's bank, would become his financial adviser in England and an important confidant.

[39] The Irish nationalist and Catholic emancipationist Daniel O'Connell (1775–1847) had recently killed a Dublin Protestant politician, John D'Esterre, in a duel. As Moore was in Dublin at the time of writing, Byron suggested his destitute widow might consider a career on the stage.

not; all *my* new function consists in listening to the despair of Cavendish Bradshaw, the hopes of Kinnaird, the wishes of Lord Essex, the complaints of Whitbread, and the calculations of Peter Moore,—all of which, and whom, seem totally at variance.[40] C. Bradshaw wants to light the theatre with *gas*, which may, perhaps (if the vulgar be believed) poison half the audience, and all the *Dramatis Personae*. Essex has endeavoured to persuade K * * [Kinnaird] not to get drunk, the consequence of which is, that he has never been sober since. Kinnaird, with equal success, would have convinced Raymond that he, the said Raymond, had too much salary. Whitbread wants us to assess the pit another sixpence,—a d——d insidious proposition—which will end in an O. P. combustion. To crown all, R * * [Robins], the auctioneer, has the impudence to be displeased because he has no dividend. The villain is a proprietor of shares, and a long-lunged orator in the meetings. I hear he has prophesied our incapacity,— 'a foregone conclusion,' whereof I hope to give him signal proofs before we are done.[41] [...]

To go on with the poetical world, Walter Scott has gone back to Scotland. Murray, the bookseller, has been cruelly cudgelled of misbegotten knaves, 'in Kendal green,' at Newington Butts, in his way home from a purlieu dinner—and robbed,—would you believe it?—of three or four bonds of forty pound apiece, and a seal-ring of his grandfather's, worth a million! This is his version,—but others opine that D'Israeli, with whom he dined, knocked him down with his last publication, 'the Quarrels of Authors,' in a dispute about copyright.[42] Be that as it may, the newspapers have teemed with his 'injuria formae,'[43] and he has been embrocated and invisible to all but the apothecary ever since.

Lady B is better than three months advanced in her progress towards maternity, and, we hope, likely to go well through with it. We have been very little out this season, as I wish to keep her quiet in her present situation. Her father and

---

[40] All fellow members of the sub-committee: Augustus Cavendish Bradshaw, Whig MP for Castle Rising, Norfolk (1768–1832); George Capel-Coningsby, fifth Earl of Essex and Lord Lieutenant of Herefordshire (1757–1839); and Samuel Whitbread, brewer and Whig politician (1764–1815), who restored the Drury Lane Theatre after its destruction by fire in 1809. Raymond, mentioned below, was the Theatre's stage-manager.

[41] Drury Lane's rival, Covent Garden, had endured a season of 'OP' ('Old Prices') riots when it raised admission charges in 1809. George Henry Robins was London's most flamboyant auctioneer; a few years later he would lead the campaign against poor management at Drury Lane, and take his philanthropy up the road to Covent Garden.

[42] Murray had been mugged in the London suburb of Stoke Newington: 'Those lonely fields are at all times dangerous', Byron advised after the fact (*LJ* iv. 294). (His allusion to 1 *Henry IV*, II. v. 236 is wonderfully appropriate, as Falstaff and his cronies were themselves the orchestrators of a farcical robbery in Shakespeare's play.) Isaac D'Israeli (1766–1848), father of future prime minister Benjamin Disraeli, was a literary man in Murray's stable and an acquaintance of Byron's, best known for the anecdotal *Curiosities of Literature* (1791); he published *Quarrels of Authors* in 1814.

[43] A tag from Virgil's *Aeneid*: *spretaeque injuria formae* ('affront offered to [Juno's] neglected beauty').

mother have changed their names to Noel, in compliance with Lord Went-worth's will, and in complaisance to the property bequeathed by him.

I hear that you have been gloriously received by the Irish,—and so you ought. But don't let them kill you with claret and kindness at the national dinner in your honour, which, I hear and hope, is in contemplation. If you will tell me the day, I'll get drunk myself on this side of the water, and waft you an applauding hiccup over the Channel.

Of politics, we have nothing but the yell for war; and C, * * h [Castlereagh] is preparing his head for the pike, on which we shall see it carried before he has done. The loan has made every body sulky. I hear often from Paris, but in direct contradiction to the home statements of our hirelings.[44] Of domestic doings, there has been nothing since Lady D * *. Not a divorce stirring,—but a good many in embryo, in the shape of marriages.

I enclose you an epistle received this morning from I know not whom; but I think it will amuse you. The writer must be a rare fellow.

P. S.—A gentleman named D'Alton (not your Dalton) has sent me a National Poem called 'Dermid.' The same cause which prevented my writing to you operated against my wish to write to him an epistle of thanks. If you see him, will you make all kinds of fine speeches for me, and tell him that I am the laziest and most ungrateful of mortals?

A word more;—don't let Sir John Stevenson (as an evidence on trials for copyright, &c.) talk about the price of your next Poem, or they will come upon you for the Property Tax for it. I am serious, and have heard a long story of the rascally tax-men making Scott pay for his. So, take care. Three hundred is a devil of a deduction out of three thousand.

[To Lady Byron]

Epping. August 31st. 1815

Dearest Pip

The learned Fletcher with his wonted accuracy having forgotten something I must beg you to forward it.——On my dressing table *two phials labelled 'drops'*

---

[44] On 26 May foreign minister Viscount Castlereagh (1769–1822) had seen through the House of Commons a £500,000 loan to the King—that is, to the Prince Regent—to fund Britain's alliances with Russia, Prussia, and Austria. Byron was hearing from Hobhouse, who had travelled to Paris in April and stayed until July, witnessing the 'Hundred Days' of Napoleon's return to power, concluded at Waterloo.

containing certain liquids of I know not what pharmacopoly—(*but white* & clear so you can't mistake I hope) *one* of these I want in my materia medica.[45]—Pray send it carefully packed to me at Goose's per coach on receiving this—and believe me

ever most lovingly thine—
B (not *Frac.*[46])

[To Samuel Taylor Coleridge]

13—Terrace Piccadilly—Oct. 18th. 1815

Dear Sir

Your letter I have just received.[47]—I will willingly do whatever you direct about the volumes in question—the sooner the better—it shall not be for want of endeavour on my part—as a Negociator with the 'Trade' (to talk technically) that you are not enabled to do yourself justice.—Last Spring I saw W[alte]r Scott—he has repeated to me a considerable portion of an unpublished poem of yours—the wildest & finest I ever heard in that kind of composition—the title he did not mention—but I think the heroine's name was Geraldine—at all events—the 'toothless mastiff bitch'—& the 'witch Lady'—the descriptions of the hall—the lamp suspended from the image—& more particularly of the *Girl* herself as she went forth in the evening—all took a hold on my imagination which I never shall wish to shake off.—I mention this—not for the sake of boring you with compliments—but as a prelude to the hope that this poem is or is to be in the volumes you are now about to publish.—I do not know that even 'Love' or the 'Ancient Mariner' are so impressive—& to me there are few things in our tongue beyond these two productions.——Wr Scott is a staunch & sturdy admirer of yours—& with a just appreciation of your capacity—deplored to me the want of inclination & exertion which prevented you from giving full scope to your mind.—I will answer your question as to the 'Beggar's [Bush?]'—tomorrow—or next day—I shall see Rae & Dibdin (the acting M[anage]rs) tonight for that

---

[45] 'Medical substance': a collective name for numerous medical handbooks cataloguing herbal and medicinal treatments, issued by both ancient and modern authorities.

[46] Byron was on his way to visit Augusta ('Goose') at Six Mile Bottom. It seems words had been exchanged before his departure, but he says he is 'not fractious' now.

[47] Coleridge had replied to Byron's letter of 31 March (above) with another lengthy summary of his literary projects, plans for plays and adaptations of plays (including Fletcher's *Beggar's Bush* of 1622), and sundry other theatrical matters. The poem Byron had heard Scott recite was *Christabel*, which Coleridge sent to Byron a few days later. Their correspondence petered out after Byron's departure from England, and Coleridge next wrote to him in September 1819 to complain at finding his name taken in vain in *Don Juan*, i. 1636 (Byron called him a drunk).

purpose.—Oh—your tragedy—I do not wish to hurry you—but I am indeed very anxious to have it under consideration—it is a field in which there are none living to contend against you & in which I should take a pride & pleasure in seeing you compared with the dead—I say this *not* disinterestly but as a *Committee* man—we have nothing even tolerable—except a tragedy of Sotheby's—which shall not interfere with yours—when ready—you can have no idea what trash there is in the four hundred *fallow* dramas now lying on the shelves of D[rury] L[ane]. I never thought so highly of good writers as lately—since I have had an opportunity of comparing them with the bad.—

ever yrs. truly
Byron

[To Thomas Moore]

13, Terrace, Piccadilly, October 28, 1815

You are, it seems, in England again, as I am to hear from every body but yourself; and I suppose you punctilious, because I did not answer your last Irish letter. When did you leave the 'swate country?' Never mind, I forgive you;—a strong proof of—I know not what—to give the lie to—

> 'He never pardons who hath done the wrong.'[48]

You have written to * * . You have written to Perry, who intimates hope of an Opera from you. Coleridge has promised a Tragedy. Now, if you keep Perry's word, and Coleridge keeps his own, Drury-lane will be set up;—and, sooth to say, it is in grievous want of such a lift. We began at speed, and are blown already. When I say 'we.' I mean Kinnaird, who is the 'all in all sufficient.'[49] and can count, which none of the rest of the Committee can.

It is really very good fun, as far as the daily and nightly stir of these strutters and fretters[50] go; and, if the concern could be brought to pay a shilling in the pound, would do much credit to the management. Mr.——[Sotheby] has an accepted tragedy, * * * * [*Ivan*],[51] whose first scene is in his sleep (I don't mean the author's). It was forwarded to us as a prodigious favourite of Kean's; but the said

---

[48] See Dryden's *Conquest of Granada* (1672), 2. I. ii. 5–6: 'Forgiveness to the injured does belong | But they ne'er pardon who hath done the wrong.'

[49] See *Othello*, IV. i. 267.   [50] See *Macbeth*, V. v. 24.

[51] *Ivan*, by the poetaster and translator William Sotheby (1757–1833) was recommended for production by Byron, but eventually withdrawn by the author and performed at Covent Garden instead.

Kean, upon interrogation, denies his eulogy, and protests against his part. How it will end, I know not.

I say so much about the theatre, because there is nothing else alive in London at this season. All the world are out of it, except us, who remain to lie in,—in December, or perhaps earlier. Lady B is very ponderous and prosperous, apparently, and I wish it well over.

There is a play before me from a personage who signs himself 'Hibernicus.' The hero is Malachi, the Irishman and king; and the villain and usurper, Turgesius, the Dane. The conclusion is fine. Turgesius is chained by the leg (*vide* stage direction) to a pillar on the stage; and King Malachi makes him a speech, not unlike Lord Castlereagh's about the balance of power and the lawfulness of legitimacy, which puts Turgesius into a frenzy—as Castlereagh's would, if his audience was chained by the leg. He draws a dagger and rushes at the orator; but, finding himself at the end of his tether, he sticks it into his own carcass, and dies, saying, he has fulfilled a prophecy.

Now, this is *serious, downright matter of fact*, and the gravest part of a tragedy which is not intended for burlesque. I tell it you for the honour of Ireland. The writer hopes it will be represented:—but what is Hope? nothing but the paint on the face of Existence; the least touch of truth rubs it off, and then we see what a hollow-cheeked harlot we have got hold of. I am not sure that I have not said this last superfine reflection before. But never mind;—it will do for the tragedy of Turgesius, to which I can append it.

Well, but how dost thou do? thou bard, not of a thousand, but three thousand! I wish your friend, Sir John Piano-forte, had kept that to himself, and not made it public at the trial of the song-seller in Dublin.[52] I tell you why; it is a liberal thing for Longman to do, and honourable for you to obtain; but it will set all the 'hungry and dinnerless, lank-jawed judges' upon the fortunate author. But they be d——d!—the 'Jeffrey and the Moore together are confident against the world in ink.'[53] By the way, if C * * e [Coleridge]—who is a man of wonderful talent, and in distress, and about to publish two vols. of Poesy and Biography, and who has been worse used by the critics than ever we were—will you, if he comes out, promise me to review him favourably in the E[dinburgh] R[eview]? Praise him, I think you must, but you will also praise him *well*,—of all things the most difficult. It will be the making of him.

---

[52] The London publisher Longman had agreed to pay Moore £3,000 for his Turkish tale *Lalla Rookh*, sight unseen, and Sir John Stevenson, who arranged Moore's popular songs for music, had let the fact slip during a legal process involving copyright. (See letter of 12 June 1815.)

[53] See 1 *Henry IV*, V. i. 116–17.

This must be a secret between you and me, as Jeffrey might not like such a project;—nor, indeed, might C himself like it. But I do think he only wants a pioneer and a sparkle or two to explode most gloriously.

> Ever yours most affectionately,
> B

P. S.—This is a sad scribbler's letter; but the next shall be 'more of this world.'

[To John Murray]

January 2d. 1816

Dear Sir

Your offer is *liberal* in the extreme—(you see I use the *word to & of* you—though I would not consent to your using it of yourself to Mr. H[unt?]) & much more than the two poems can possibly be worth—but I cannot accept it—nor will not.[54]— You are most welcome to them as additions to the collected volumes without any demand or expectation on my part whatever—but I cannot consent to their separate publication.—I do not like to risk my fame (whether merited or not) which I have been favoured with—upon compositions which I do not feel to be at all equal to my own notions of what they should be—(& as I flatter myself some *have been* here & there)—though they may do very well as things without pretension to add to the publication with the lighter pieces.—I am very glad that the hand-writing was a favourable omen of the morale of the piece—but you must not trust to that—for my copyist would write out anything I desired in all the ignorance of innocence—I hope however in this instance with no great peril to either.[55]——

> yrs. very truly
> Byron

[54] Murray had sent Byron a bank draft for 1,000 guineas for the copyrights of *The Siege of Corinth* and *Parisina*; they would be published together on 7 February. A conservative, Murray did not approve of a Radical writer like Leigh Hunt.
[55] Lady Byron herself had copied out Byron's manuscript; in *Parisina* the heroine marries a man with whose illegitimate son she had previously been engaged, thus raising the spectre of incest.

P. S.—I have enclosed your draft torn *for fear of accidents by the way:—I wish you would not throw temptation in mine—it is not from a disdain of the universal idol—nor from a present superfluity of his treasures—I can assure you—that I refuse to worship him—but what is right is right—& must not yield to circumstances.—*

[To Thomas Moore]

January 5th, 1816

I hope Mrs. M is quite re-established. The little girl was born on the 10th of December last: her name is Augusta *Ada* (the second a very antique family name,—I believe not used since the reign of King John). She was, and is, very flourishing and fat, and reckoned very large for her days—squalls and sucks incessantly. Are you answered? Her mother is doing very well, and up again.

I have now been married a year on the second of this month—heigh-ho! I have seen nobody lately much worth noting, except S * * [Sebastiani] and another general of the Gauls, once or twice at dinners out of doors. S * * is a fine, foreign, villainous-looking, intelligent, and very agreeable man; his compatriot is more of the *petit-maître* [dandy], and younger, but I should think not at all of the same intellectual calibre with the Corsican—which S, you know, is, and a cousin of Napoleon's.[56]

Are you never to be expected in town again? To be sure, there is no one here of the 1500 fillers of hot rooms, called the fashionable world. My approaching papa-ship detained us for advice, &c. &c.—though I would as soon be here as any where else on this side of the straits of Gibraltar.

I would gladly—or, rather, sorrowfully—comply with your request of a dirge for the poor girl you mention. But how can I write on one I have never seen or known? Besides, you will do it much better yourself. I could not write upon any thing, without some personal experience and foundation; far less on a theme so peculiar. Now, you have both in this case; and, if you had neither, you have more imagination, and would never fail.

This is but a dull scrawl, and I am but a dull fellow. Just at present, I am absorbed in 500 contradictory contemplations, though with but one object in view—which will probably end in nothing, as most things we wish do. But never mind—as somebody says, 'for the blue sky bends over all'.[57] I only

---

[56] The Corsican Count Sebastiani (1771–1851) was a French soldier and diplomat who managed to serve both the Napoleonic and the Bourbon administrations. He spent a year of exile in Britain after the restoration of Louis XVIII before returning to his political career.

[57] See Coleridge's *Christabel*, i. 330 and *Hamlet*, V. i. 249–50.

could be glad, if it bent over me where it is a little bluer; like the 'skyish top of blue Olympus', which, by the way, looked very white when I last saw it. Ever, &c.

[To Lady Byron]

January 6th 1816

When you are disposed to leave London—it would be convenient that a day should be fixed—& (if possible) not a very remote one for that purpose.—Of my opinion upon that subject—you are sufficiently in possession—& of the circumstances which have led to it—as also—to my plans—or rather—intentions—for the future.——When in the country, I will write to you more fully—as Lady Noel has asked you to Kirkby—there you can be for the present—unless you prefer Seaham.————As the dismissal of the present establishment is of importance to me—the sooner you can fix on the day the better—though of course your convenience & inclination shall be first consulted.——The child will of course accompany you—there is a more easy and safer carriage than the chariot—(unless you prefer it) which I mentioned before—on that you can do as you please.[58]—

[To Sir Ralph Noel]

February 2d. 1816

Sir

I have received your letter.—To the vague & general charge contained in it I must naturally be at a loss how to answer—I shall therefore confine myself to the tangible fact which you are pleased to alledge as one of the motives for your present proposition.—Lady Byron received no 'dismissal' from my house in the sense you have attached to the word—she left London by medical advice—she parted from me in apparent—and on my part—real harmony—though at that particular time rather against my inclination for I begged her to remain with the intention of myself accompanying her when some business necessary to be arranged permitted my departure.——It is true—that previous to this period—I had suggested to her the expediency of a temporary residence with her parents:—

---

[58] Lady Byron left London with her daughter to visit her parents at Kirkby Mallory on 15 January; neither saw Byron again.

my reason for this was very simple & shortly stated—viz—the embarrassment of my circumstances & my inability to maintain our present establishment.—The truth of what is thus stated may be easily ascertained by reference to Lady B—who is Truth itself—if she denies it—I abide by that denial.——My intention of going abroad originated in the same painful motive—& was postponed from a regard to her supposed feelings on that subject.—During the last year I have had to contend with distress without—& disease within:—upon the former I have little to say—except that I have endeavoured to remove it by every sacrifice in my power—& the latter I should not mention if I had not recent & professional authority for saying—that the disorder which I have to combat—without much impairing my apparent health—is such as to induce a morbid irritability of temper—which—without recurring to external causes—may have rendered me little less disagreeable to others than I am to myself.——I am however ignorant of any particular ill treatment which your daughter has encountered:—she may have seen me gloomy—& at times violent—but she knows the causes too well to attribute such inequalities of disposition to herself—or even to me—if all things be fairly considered.——And now Sir—not for your satisfaction—for I owe you none—but for my own—& in justice to Lady Byron—it is my duty to say that there is no part of her conduct—character—temper—talents—or disposition— which could in my opinion have been changed for the better—neither in word nor deed—nor (as far as thought can be dived into) thought—can I bring to recollection a fault on her part—& hardly even a failing—She has ever appeared to me as one of the most amiable of beings—& nearer to perfection than I had conceived could belong to Humanity in it's present existence.——Having said thus much—though more in words—less in substance—than I wished to express——I must come to the point—on which subject I must for a few days decline giving a decisive answer.—I will not however detain you longer than I can help—and as it is of some importance to your family as well as mine—and a step which cannot be recalled when taken—you will not attribute my pause to any wish to inflict pain or vexation on you & yours:—although there are parts of your letter—which—I must be permitted to say—arrogate a right which you do not now possess—for the present at least—your daughter is my wife:—she is the mother of my child—& until I have her express sanction of your proceedings—I shall take leave to doubt the propriety of your interference.—This will be soon ascertained—& when it is—I will submit to you my determination—which will depend very materially on hers.——I have the honour to be

yr. most obedt. & very humble Sert.
Byron

[To Lady Byron]

February 3d. 1816

I have received a letter from your father proposing a separation between us—to which I cannot give an answer without being more acquainted with your own thoughts & wishes—& from *yourself*:—to vague & general charges & exaggerated statements from others I can give no reply:——it is to *you* that I look—& with *you*—that I can communicate on this subject,——when I permit the interference of relatives—it will be as a courtesy to them—& not the admission of a right.——I feel naturally at a loss how to address you—ignorant as I am—how far the letter I have received—has received your sanction—& in the circumstances into which this precipitation has forced me—whatever I might say would be liable to misconstruction—I am really ignorant to what part of Sir Ralph's letter alludes—will you explain?——To conclude—I shall eventually abide by your decision—but I request you most earnestly to weigh well the probable consequences—& to pause before you pronounce.——Whatever may occur—it is but justice to you to say—that you are exempt from all fault whatever—& that neither now nor at any time have I the slightest imputation of any description to charge upon you.——I cannot sign myself other than

yours ever most affectionately
BN

[To Lady Byron]

February 5th. 1816

Dearest Bell

No answer from you yet—perhaps it is as well—but do recollect—that all is at stake—the present—the future—& even the colouring of the past:—The whole of my errors—or what harsher name you choose to give them—you know—but I loved you—and will not part from you without your *own* most express & *expressed* refusal to return to or receive me.——Only say the word—that you are still mine in your heart—and 'Kate!—I will buckler thee against a million'[59]—

ever yours dearest most
B

---

[59] See *The Taming of the Shrew*, III. iii. 111 (not the most diplomatic of Shakespeare's plays to allude to, under the circumstances).

[To John Cam Hobhouse]

F[ebruar]y 8th. 1816

Dear H

I shall be very glad to see you—but it is all vain—& all over.—She has written two letters—one to Mrs. L[eigh] & since—a second to me—quite decisive of her determination on the subject.——However—let me see you—I mean to go abroad the moment packages will permit.——'There is a world beyond Rome'[60]—

ever yrs.
B

[To Lady Byron]

February 8th. 1816

All I can say seems useless—and all I could say—might be no less unavailing—yet I still cling to the wreck of my hopes—before they sink forever.——Were you then *never* happy with me?—did you never at any time or times express yourself so?—have no marks of affection—of the warmest & most reciprocal attachment passed between us?—or did in fact hardly a day go down without some such on one side and generally on both?—do not mistake me—[two lines crossed out] I have not denied my state of mind—but you know it's causes—& were those deviations from calmness never followed by acknowledgement & repentance?— was not the last which occurred more particularly so?—& had I not—had we not—the days before & on the day when we parted—every reason to believe that we loved each other—that we were to meet again—were not your letters kind?— had I not acknowledged to you all my faults & follies—& assured you that some had not—& would not be repeated?—I do not require these questions to be answered to me—but to your own heart.——The day before I received your father's letter—I had fixed a day for rejoining you—if I did not write lately— Augusta did—and as you had been my proxy in correspondence with her—so did I imagine—she might be the same for me to you.—Upon your letter to me—this day—I surely may remark—that it's expressions imply a treatment which I am incapable of inflicting—& you of imputing to me—if aware of their latitude—& the extent of the inferences to be drawn from them.—This is not just——but I have no reproaches—nor the wish to find cause for them.——Will you see

[60] See *Coriolanus*, III. iii. 139: 'There is a world elsewhere.'

me?—when & where you please—in whose presence you please:—the interview shall pledge you to nothing—& I will say & do nothing to agitate either—it is torture to correspond thus—& there are things to be settled & said which cannot be written.——You say 'it is my disposition to deem what I *have worthless*'—did I deem *you* so?—did I ever so express myself to you—or of you—to others?—— You are much changed within these twenty days or you would never have thus poisoned your own better feelings—and trampled upon mine.——

ever yrs. most truly & affectionately
B

[To Lady Byron]

February 26th. 1816

Dearest Pip

I wish you would make it up—for I am dreadfully sick of all this—& cannot foresee any good that can come of it.—If you will—I am ready to make any penitential speech or speeches you please—& will be very good and tractable for the rest of my days—& very sorry for all that have gone before.—At any rate—if you won't comply with this proposition—I beg you to keep this note to yourself—& neither show it to Doctors Bailey nor Lushington nor Commons[61]—nor any other of your present Cabinet—at least the professional part of it.—I am very sure *you* will not mistake it for anything but what it is meant to be—& I am terribly tired of the stately style of our late letters & obliged to take refuge in that which I was used to

yrs. ever & truly
B

Private—

---

[61] Matthew Baillie was a doctor Lady Byron consulted as regards her husband's mental health (just as his mother had consulted him about his club foot in 1799; see letter of 1 May 1803). Stephen Lushington was her barrister. By 'commons' Byron means legal offices.

[To Lady Byron]

March 4th. 1816

Dearest

If I did not believe that you are sacrificing your own happiness—as much—as I know—you are destroying mine:—if I were not convinced—that some rash determination—& it may be—promise—is the root of the bitter fruits we are now at the same time devouring & detesting—I would & could address you no more.——Did I not love you—were I not sure that you still love me—I should not have endured what I have already. I have rejected all propositions of separation—as I would spurn an adder—and from the same motive.—If you or yours conceive that I am activated by mercenary motives—I appeal to the tenor of my past life in such respects—I appeal to my conduct with regard to settlements previous to your marriage—I appeal to all who know me—or who ever will know.—Whatever I may have felt—(& what I feel—I often shew—) in moments of pressure and distress—they were not the privations of Misfortune from which I recoiled—but it's indignities.—I look upon the *manner* & statement of the proposals lately transmitted to me—as the greatest insult I have received from your family—in this struggle for moral existence,—I will not trust myself with the subject.—I desire to see you—I request to be reconciled with you:——recollect I have done all that human being can in such circumstances to effect this object for your sake—for my child's—for mine—even for those who endeavour to prevent it—I will persevere in it—while the shadow of a hope can be distinguished—and when even that is effaced—I shall regret the sufferings—which to more than *one*—or *two*—will be inevitable—there is that which will recoil upon some who may deem themselves secure.—

yrs. ever most attachedly
B

[To Thomas Moore]

March 8th. 1816

I rejoice in your promotion as Chairman and Charitable Steward, &c. &c. These be dignities which await only the virtuous. But then, recollect you are *six* and *thirty* (I speak this enviously—not of your age, but the 'honour—

love—obedience—troops of friends,'[62] which accompany it), and I have eight years good to run before I arrive at such hoary perfection; by which time,—if I *am* at all,—it will probably be in a state of grace or progressing merits.

I must set you right in one point, however, The fault was *not*—no, nor even the misfortune—in my 'choice' (unless in *choosing* at all)—for I do not believe—and I must say it, in the very dregs of all this bitter business—that there ever was a better, or even a brighter, a kinder, or a more amiable and agreeable being than Lady B. I never had, nor can have, any reproach to make her, while with me. Where there is blame, it belongs to myself, and, if I cannot redeem, I must bear it.

Her nearest relatives are a * * * *—my circumstances have been and are in a state of great confusion—my health has been a good deal disordered, and my mind ill at ease for a considerable period. Such are the causes (I do not name them as excuses) which have frequently driven me into excess, and disqualified my temper for comfort. Something also may be attributed to the strange and desultory habits which, becoming my own master at an early age, and scrambling about, over and through the world, may have induced. I still, however, think that, if I had a fair chance, by being placed in even a tolerable situation, I might have gone on fairly. But that seems hopeless,—and there is nothing more to be said. At present—except my health, which is better (it is odd, but agitation or contest of any kind gives a rebound to my spirits and sets me up for the time)—I have to battle with all kinds of unpleasantness, including private and pecuniary difficulties, &c. &c.

I believe I may have said this before to you,—but I risk repeating it. It is nothing to bear the *privations* of adversity, or, more properly, ill fortune; but my pride recoils from its *indignities*. However, I have no quarrel with that same pride, which will, I think, buckler me through every thing. If my heart could have been broken, it would have been so years ago, and by events more afflicting than these.

I agree with you (to turn from this topic to our shop) that I have written too much. The last things were, however, published very reluctantly by me, and for reasons I will explain when we meet. I know not why I have dwelt so much on the same scenes, except that I find them fading, or *confusing* (if such a word may be) in my memory, in the midst of present turbulence and pressure, and I felt anxious to stamp before the die was worn out. I now break it. With those countries, and events connected with them, all my really poetical feelings begin and end. Were I to try, I could make nothing of any other subject,—and that I have apparently exhausted. 'Woe to him,' says Voltaire, 'who says all he could

---

[62] See *Macbeth*, V. iii. 27.

say on any subject.' There are some on which, perhaps, I could have said still more: but I leave them all, and not too soon.

Do you remember the lines I sent you early last year, which you still have? I don't wish (like Mr. Fitzgerald, in the Morning Post) to claim the character of 'Vates' in all its translations, but were they not a little prophetic? I mean those beginning 'There's not a joy the world can,' &c. &c. on which I rather pique myself as being the truest, though the most melancholy, I ever wrote.[63]

What a scrawl I have sent you! You say nothing of yourself, except that you are a Lancastrian churchwarden, and an encourager of mendicants. When are you out? and how is your family? My child is very well and flourishing, I hear; but I must see also. I feel no disposition to resign it to the contagion of its grandmother's society, though I am unwilling to take it from the mother.[64] It is weaned, however, and something about it must be decided.

Ever, &c.

[To Lady Byron]

March 25th. 1816

Dear Lady Byron

I am truly sorry to hear that you have been informed & falsely informed that—since the commencement of the proceedings which are presumed to be drawing towards a conclusion—I have spoken of you harshly or lightly.—Neither are true—and no such terms—if such have been used—have originated from me—or have been sanctioned by me.—I have been out but little—indeed hardly at all—have seen no one with very few exceptions—but my own immediate relatives or connections—and to all these I can & do appeal—for confirmation or refutation of what is here advanced. I might indeed assert—& could prove—(but it matters little)—that the contrary has been the case.——If in the violence & outrageous latitude of accusation which has been indulged beyond all example and all excuse in the present case by those who from friendship to you or aversion from me—or both—have thought proper to proclaim themselves assailants in your cause—any few—(and few they must have been) of those who have known me & judged less severely of me—have been provoked to repel accusation by imputation—and have endeavoured to find a defence for

---

[63] See 'Stanzas for Music' (*CPW* iii. 284–6), written in February 1815, after Byron heard that his Harrow friend, the Duke of Dorset, had been killed in a riding accident.

[64] In Byron's era it was the father's right to do exactly this; he would demand that Claire Clairmont surrender Allegra, her daughter by him, in 1818.

me—in crimination of you—I disavow their conduct—and disclaim them-selves.——I have interfered in no such proceedings—I have raised no party—nor even attempted it—neither should I have succeeded in such an attempt—the World has been with you throughout—the contest has been as unequal to me as it was undesired—and my name has been as completely blasted as if it were branded on my forehead:—this may appear to you exaggeration—it is not so—there are reports which once circulated not even falsehood—or their most admitted & acknowledged falsehood—can neutralize—which no contradiction can obliterate—nor conduct cancel:——such have since your separation been busy with my name—you are understood to say—'that you are not responsible for these—that they existed previous to my marriage—and at most were only *revived* by our differences'—Lady Byron they did not exist—but even if they had—does their *revival* give you no feeling?—are you calm in the contemplation of having (however undesignedly) raised up that which you can never allay?—& which but for you might have never arisen?—is it with perfect apathy you quietly look upon this resurrection of Infamy?—To return to what is the object of my present intrusion upon you—I have little to add— except that I am & have been very much hurt to hear that you could give credit to my having recourse to such unworthy means of defence as recrimination on you:—my first letter to your father is in itself sufficient to have rendered abortive such attempts had I been willing to use them—Few people have attempted to blame you to me—& those who have will not venture to say that they have met With encour-agement.—[…]—Of whomever & whatever I have spoken—I have never blamed you—never attempted to condemn you.—The utmost I may have said—is—that I looked upon the proceedings as extreme and that I had no great faith in your affection for me.—This however was only repeated by me to Augusta:—and it was the conviction of *more* than myself—though *not* of *her*—on the contrary—she always combated the impression.—It is not very wonderful—that such a belief confirmed by events should exist in any mind—even in mine.—

ever yrs. most affectly.

B

P. S.—*If you will name the person or persons who have attributed to me—abuse of you— you will do an act of justice—& so will I.—I shall at least know whom to avoid—surely— there was bitterness enough in my portion without this addition.—*

[To John Murray]

[March 30, 1816?]

Dear Sir/

I send you my last night's dream—and request to have 50 copies (for *private distribution*) struck off—and a proof tomorrow if possible.—I wish Mr. Gifford to look at them—they are from life.[65]—

yrs. &c.
B

[To 'G. C. B.' (Claire Clairmont)]

[March–April? 1816]

Ld. B. is not aware of any 'importance' which can be attached by any person to an interview with him—& more particularly by one with whom it does not appear that he has the honour of being acquainted.————He will however be at home at the hour mentioned.[66]

[To Margaret Mercer Elphinstone]

April 11th. 1816

Dear Miss Mercer/

I thank you truly for yr. kind acceptance of my memorial—more particularly as I felt a little apprehensive that I was taking a liberty of which you might disapprove.——A more useless friend you could not have—but still a very sincere and by no means a new one—although from circumstances you never knew—(nor would it have pleased you to know)—how much.—These having long ceased to exist—I breathe more freely on this point—because *now* no

---

[65] This is 'A Sketch from Private Life' (*CPW* iii. 382–6), Byron's brutal verse accusation of Mrs Mary Anne Clermont, Lady Milbanke's long-established maid (waiting on her in fact at the time of Annabella's birth), who went on to become Annabella's governess and companion. It was Byron's view that this old retainer had hardened Annabella's view of him, and made reconciliation impossible. The poem was published in the press in mid-April, and formed part of the scandalous background to Byron's exile.

[66] Mary Jane 'Claire' Clairmont (1798–1879) was William Godwin's second wife's 17-year-old daughter by a previous marriage. She and Byron became sexual partners, if hardly lovers, before his departure from England, and were reunited in Switzerland in late May.

motive can be attributed to me with regard to you of a selfish nature—at least I hope not.——I know not why I venture to talk thus—unless it be—that the time is come—when whatever I may say—can not be of importance enough to give offence—& that neither my vanity nor my wishes ever induced me at any time to suppose that I could by any chance have become more to you than I now am.——This may account to you for that which—however little worth accounting for—must otherwise appear inexplicable in our former acquaintance—I mean—those 'intermittents' at which you used to laugh—as I did too—although they caused me many a serious reflection.—But this is foolish—perhaps improper—yet it is—or rather—was the truth—and has been a silent one while it could have been supposed to proceed from hope or presumption:—I am now as far removed from both by irrevocable circumstances as I always was by my own opinion & by yours—& I soon shall be still further if further be possible—by distance.——I cannot conclude without wishing you a much happier destiny—not than *mine is*—for that is nothing—but than mine ever could have been—with a little common sense & prudence on my part:—no one else has been to blame—it may seem superfluous to wish *you* all this—& it would be so if our happiness always depended on ourselves—but it does not—a truth which I fear I have taught rather than learned however unintentionally.—

ever most truly yrs.
Byron

P. S.—*This letter was intended as an answer to your note—which however required none—will you excuse it for the sake of the paper on which it is written? it is part of the spoils of Malmaison[67] & the imperial bureau—(as it was told me) and for this reason you will perhaps have the kindness to accept a few sheets of it which accompany this—their stamp is the Eagle.—Adieu—*

---

[67] One-time home of Napoleon and the Empress Josephine, to which the Emperor retreated after his defeat at Waterloo, before surrendering to British authorities. Perhaps Hobhouse supplied Byron with some of the Emperor's stationery: he was in Paris after Napoleon's escape from Elba.

[To John Hanson]

Sunday.—14 Apl. 1816

Dear Sir/

The sooner the deed is ready for signature the better—I shall be at home on any afternoon at three to sign it.[68]——Wharton has written to me to request the naming of a day.—Mr. Hobhouse has written to you—merely to enter on record *his* opinion as to the *meaning* of the paper—which he drew up—but of course I abide by the Solicitor General's present pronunciation upon it.——Pray let us finish this as soon as need be—& believe me

yrs very truly
Byron

P. S.—I want Lady B's letter from Kirkby—the letter—before *this business.*[69]—

[To James Wedderburn Webster]

April 16th. 1816

Dear Webster/

I have no desire to dun or to distress you—but I was surprized at your silence—more especially hearing that you were purchasing lands & tenements.—Hearing this I naturally thought you were in a state of disentanglement—& my own affairs being at present in a very poetical posture—I stated to you my expectation that you would take steps towards the payment—for which I can hardly be considered as very importunate—as it is now the third year without allusion to the subject[70]—nor had it been made now—were I not about to leave England—& anxious to settle my affairs previously.——I now write to mention—that it being inconvenient to you—I will say no more on the subject—you must be

---

[68] Byron signed the deed of separation a week later on 21 April 1816, and Hobhouse, Davies, Kinnaird, and Samuel Rogers stayed with him that evening.
[69] Byron means the 'Dearest Duck, [...] Ever thy most loving Pippin ... Pip ... Ip' letter Annabella wrote on 16 January, when relations still seemed normal.
[70] See letter of 10 October 1813.

aware that it could be no pleasure to me to receive that which it would be disturbing to you to pay:—& as I lent it with a view to prevent difficulties I shall not now render any little advantage it may have been to you useless by plunging you into new ones.—I should & shall of course neither take nor authorize any measure that may be disagreeable to you.—Kinnaird (the Hon[oura]ble D[ougla]s) is kind enough to act for me while I am abroad & I will direct him not to molest you:—I write in the greatest hurry with packages—passports—&c.—but shall not be off for a day or two.—

ever yrs. most truly
Byron

[To Isaac Nathan]

Piccadilly, Tuesday Evening [April 16 or 23? 1816]

My dear Nathan,

I have to acknowledge the receipt of your very seasonable bequest, which I duly appreciate; the unleavened bread shall certainly accompany me in my pilgrimage; and, with a full reliance on their efficacy, the *Motsas* shall be to me a charm against the destroying Angel wherever I may sojourn; his serene highness, however will, I hope, be polite enough to keep at a desirable distance from my person, without the necessity of besmearing my *door posts or upper lintels* with the blood of any animal.[71] With many thanks for your kind attention, believe me, My dear Nathan,

Yours very truly,
Byron

[To Augusta Leigh]

April 22d. 1816

My own Sweet Sis

The deeds are signed—so that is over.—All I have now to beg or desire on the subject is—that you will never mention or allude to Lady Byron's name again in any shape—or on any occasion—except indispensable business.—Of the child you will inform me & write about poor little *Da*—& see it whenever you can.—I

---

[71] Nathan had evidently given Byron a packet of kosher crackers to take abroad, and Byron alludes to Exodus 12—the Passover before the Jews' flight from Egypt—in response.

am all in the *hurries*—we set off tomorrow—but I will write from Dover.—My own dearest—kindest—best Sis—

ever & ever thine
B

[To John Hanson]

Dover—April 24th. 1816

Dear Sir/

Denen[?]⁷² has distrained on the effects left at the house in Piccadilly terrace for the half year's rent:—I know not if this be lawful *without a previous action*—This *you* know best—if it be—there is one trunk of wood with papers—letters &c.— also some *shoes*—and another thing or two which I could wish redeemed from the wreck.——They have seized all the *servants' things* Fletcher's & his wife's &c.—I hope you will see to these poor creatures having *their* property secured— as for *mine* it must be sold. I wish Mr. Hobhouse to confer with you upon it.—— Many thanks for yr. good wishes:——I sail tonight for Ostend—my address had best be (for the present)—A—Milord Byron—Poste—Restante—*à Genève.*—I hope that you will not forget—to seize an early opportunity of bringing Rochdale & Newstead to the hammer—or private contract.——I wish you for yourself & family every possible good—& beg my remembrances to all— particularly Lady P[ortsmout]h & Charles——I am with great sincerity

yrs. very affectly.
Byron

P. S.—Send me some news of my child—*every now & then—I beg as a favour not to hear a word of the rest of that branch of the family.—Of course I do not mean my own immediate relatives.—*

---

⁷² James Denen was the Duchess of Devonshire's agent in collecting rent on her London properties.

6

EXILE

April–November 1816

Byron's disastrous marriage and separation sent him back to Europe, not temporarily, as he imagined before his departure, but for good. It therefore made him a European poet rather than an English one who once travelled abroad. At the time it was a dreadful humiliation and severance from his friends and homeland, even if the Continent had retained its allure as an escape hatch ever since his return to England in 1811.

The ignominy of the Separation had the impact that might be expected on a proud but sensitive and insecure individual: a long period of depression ensued, punctuated by a good deal of defensive self-assertion. But there was also relief at being Childe Harold once more, free from a loveless marriage, a steadily deteriorating financial situation, and a country profoundly pleased with itself at winning the Napoleonic Wars. So from the moment he set foot on the Continent we find a resurgence in Byron's prose—and not in his prose alone. ('As soon as he reached his room' at the Cour Impériale in Ostend, his travelling companion William Polidori recorded, 'Lord Byron fell like a thunderbolt upon the chambermaid'; Life, 610.) From Ostend the poet's horrendously unreliable coach then trundled through Belgium for a fortnight, stopping at Bruges, Ghent, Brussels, and the field of Waterloo, before pressing on to Cologne and the Rhine, where he arrived on 8 May.

By that time he had already been at work for ten days or so on a new canto of Childe Harold's Pilgrimage, a first draft of which would be completed in Geneva on 8 June. (The opening stanzas were in fact written on the ferry from Dover.) This emphatic re-commitment to his art is the most important event of this period of Byron's life, though his letters document it only occasionally. He had told Thomas Moore before his departure that he had 'written too much', especially about the East, and exhausted it as a subject (see letter of 8 March 1816), and it is true that whereas the 'Turkish tales' and their derivatives never fail to be interesting, the sequence could not be continued forever. The new canto of Childe Harold took him back to a different wellspring, and what emerged from it in the next few months was prodigious: that poem in hardly more than a month, The Prisoner of Chillon, Manfred, 'The Dream', 'Prometheus', and 'Darkness' in the weeks that followed. If ever there was a case of depression accompanying artistic creativity, this was one. The Swiss Alps must take a good deal of credit for this, but so must Mary and Percy Shelley, who were neighbours on the shore of Lake Geneva from June to August of 1816. (The two poets were proudly introduced by Claire Clairmont at Sécheron on 27 May.) Their conversation and intellectual curiosity, which engendered Frankenstein, of course, as well as Byron's new output, surely encouraged and confirmed his artistic renaissance. 'And thus I am absorb'd, and this is life', he wrote in Childe Harold, iii. 689–94 (CPW ii. 104); 'I look upon the peopled desart past, | As on some place of agony and strife, | Where, for some sin, to Sorrow I was cast, | To act and suffer, but remount at last | With a fresh pinion'.

The Rhine, and its source in the Alps, gave him a new perspective on England and the Napoleonic Wars. With each step—Bonn, Koblenz, Drachenfels, Mannheim, Karlsruhe,

Basle—towards his arrival at Geneva on 25 May (only a month after leaving England) he went further into an intellectual landscape very different from both the land of his birth and the Mediterranean of his youth. The Shelleys were there, and so was the irrepressible Madame de Stäel, eager to patch up the Byrons' marriage, and holding court at her house in Coppet, where a fellow guest was the great German critic August Wilhelm von Schlegel. But writers far greater than her—namely, Voltaire, Rousseau, and Gibbon—had all lived on the shores of Lake Geneva, and all would find their place in Childe Harold as moral touchstones from the Enlightenment. In the last week of June, while Mary Shelley laboured over her novel, Byron toured the lake with her husband. At the end of August he, Hobhouse, and Scrope Davies made a trip to Chamonix and Mont Blanc (he would never see Davies again); and in the second half of September he and Hobhouse made a more ambitious tour of the Bernese Oberland.

This latter tour, as the journal he kept of it for his sister shows, was a revelation. (The summer of 1816 was an unseasonable one: a 'volcanic winter' caused by the eruption of Mount Tambora near Java the previous year—the largest eruption in history. This alteration of the climate explains the cold and wet conditions of the tour, though Byron never complained.) In twelve days Byron and Hobhouse skirted the north shore of Lake Geneva with its Rousseau-esque associations (Lausanne, Vevey, Clarens, and Chillon), which he had already seen with Shelley. But from Chillon on 19 September they struck north-east into the mountains, seeing Mont Davant and the Dent de Jaman before stopping at the village of Montbovon. From there it seems they followed the modern-day Route de l'Intyamon, passing Klettersteig (Byron's 'Kletsgerberg') and Hockenhorn ('Hockthorn') on their right before arriving at Thun on 21 September, four days after setting out. The following day they were rowed—by women, much to Byron's surprise and admiration—down Lake Thun to Neuhaus, thence to Interlaken, with glorious views of the Jungfrau and the Eiger to the south. Perhaps the climactic day was 23 September, when they hiked (or scrambled, presumably, in Byron's case, though he hardly comments on his abilities as a mountaineer) up the Jungfrau itself—or the Wengen Jungfrau below it—having looked up to the Staubbach Falls from the base of the mountain. After staying the night at Grindenwald they headed north-east once more, to the Reichenbach Falls, and from there down to Brienz (25 September), back through the lakes to Thun and north-west to Bern, south-west to Fribourg (where Byron bought a guard dog), thence to Yverdon at the southern end of Lake Neuchatel (28 September), Aubonne, and back to Geneva on 29 September, in time for Byron to find an ecstatic letter from John Murray about the new instalment of Childe Harold.

Almost directly he returned to his drama Manfred, which he had started in August, inspired, as he later put it, 'by the Staubach & the Jungfrau—and something else' (LJ vii. 113): that 'something else' being his illicit and lost love for Augusta. 'Do not "hate yourself"', he wrote to her in August 1816 (LJ v. 89); 'if you hate either let it be me—but do not—it would kill me; we are the last persons in the world—who ought—or could cease to love one another.' There was also a clinging and pitiful letter from Claire Clairmont, six months pregnant by him and in hiding at Bath. For his legitimate child, he showed a good deal more concern. Hearing that Lady Byron herself contemplated a trip to the Continent he voiced his objections in a letter to Augusta. Whereas he would not 'attempt to withdraw my child from it's mother' ('I think that would be harsh'), 'I must strongly protest at my daughter's leaving England . . . at so early a time of life—& subjected to so many unavoidable risks of health & comfort' (LJ v. 109). On 5 October, six days after his return to Diodati, he and Hobhouse set out once more, for the Simplon Pass and Italy. 'I have no plans', he had told Murray on 30 September (LJ v. 108), '& am nearly as indifferent as to what may come—as where I go.' But Italy was holding a new life-chapter in store for him as he made way from Milan, through Verona, to Venice: '(next to the East) the greenest island of my imagination' (LJ v. 129).

'The proprietor of the villa, a great admirer of Byron's poetry,' Leslie Marchand records, 'coming in immediately after his tenant had departed, asked the caretaker if he had preserved the numerous first drafts which Byron had scattered through all the rooms of the house and which M. Diodati considered as so many precious autographs of the poet. The reply he received was: "I should lie to you, Sir, if I didn't tell you that at least two days were occupied in burning all those scraps of paper"' (Life, 659).

[To John Cam Hobhouse]

Ostend.—April 27th. [26th.?] 1816

My dear Hobhouse

We got in last night very well—though it blew freshly & contrary all the way— but we tacked & tided in about midnight.—All are—and every thing is— landed—& tonight we design for Ghent.[1]—As a veteran I stomached the sea pretty well—till a damned 'Merchant of Bruges'[2] capsized his breakfast close by me—& made me sick by contagion:—but I soon got well—& we were landed at least ten hours sooner than expected—and our Inn (the 'Cure imperial' as Fletcher calls it—) furnished us with beds & a 'flaggon of Rhenish'[3]—which by the blessing of Scrope's absence—the only blessing his absence could confer—

---

[1] Byron's party comprised himself, his doctor, William Polidori (1795–1821), a Swiss guide named Berger, Fletcher, and Robert Rushton, the last two of whom had started out with him on his previous European tour, seven years earlier. Rushton returned home from Geneva, and would not serve Byron again.
[2] Douglas Kinnaird's adaptation of Fletcher's Beggar's Bush (1622), entitled The Merchant of Bruges, played at Drury Lane in 1815. Byron alludes to it again in the letter of 1 May 1816.
[3] See Hamlet, V. i. 175; the preferred drink of the jester Yorick, according to the gravedigger in this famous scene (see letter of 16 May 1816, where Byron compares Scrope Davies to Yorick). Fletcher misunderstood Cour Impériale: imperial court or courtyard.

was not indulged in to the extent of the 'light wine' of our parting potations.——
Don't forget the Cundums—and will you tell Manton that he has put a very bad
brush into the pistol case—& to send me *two* good new ones by your servant
(when you come) for cleaning the *locks* of my pistols.[4]——*You* are in town by
this time—having dined at Canterbury or Sittingbourne—pitying us 'poor
mariners that sail upon the seas'[5]—we are in the agonies of furnishing Berger
with [*stivilli? stivale:* boots?] to march en Courier before us—& the last I saw of
Fletcher was with two eggs in his mouth.——The sick Dutchman set off per
packet for Bruges this morning:——the custom house was very polite—and all
things very fair—I don't know why you vituperated Ostend:—it seems a very
tolerable town—better than Dover—better than the Spanish & Portuguese
ordinary towns—or any of our Oriental—at least in the Caravansera department.—I shall lay to for you at Geneva—you have perhaps examined my late
Piccadilly premises—and I hope recovered your personals.——My best luck—
or rather his own—to Scrope—all remembrances to Kinnaird & the rest of 'us
youth'[6] and ever

yrs. most truly
Byron

P. S.—*If you hear anything of my little daughter tell it me—good I hope.—As to the rest—
as the Irishman said in the Dublin Theatre when Wellesley Pole was there—'Here's three
times three for Lord Wellington and Silence for the rest of the family.'[7]—Tell Scrope that
Mr. Levi did us about the Ducats—by ninepence each—I will thrash him as I come
back.—Mind you write—& fix a time for coming—or 'Sdeath and Pin money!—I shall be
very indignant.—*

---

[4] Condoms in Byron's day were manufactured from animal gut or from linen; rubber alternatives
were invented in the 1850s. Joseph Manton was a London gunsmith, one of whose apprentices, James
Purdey, founded the Mayfair premises still trading to this day.
[5] See 'The Queen's Marie' in Walter Scott's *Minstrelsy of the Scottish Border* (1802).
[6] See 1 *Henry IV*, II. ii. 83.
[7] William Pole-Tylney-Long-Wellesley was a scapegrace nephew of the Duke of Wellington,
dandy, and MP for St Ives, in Cornwall. 'Where's Long Pole Wellesley?' Byron would ask in *Don
Juan* (xi. 617), after he left the country to escape his debts in 1822: 'Diddled.'

[To John Cam Hobhouse]

Bruxelles—May 1st. 1816

My dear H[obhous]e

You will be surprized that we are not more 'en avant' [further on] and so am I—but Mr. Baxter's wheels and springs have not done their duty[8]—for which I beg that you will abuse him like a pickpocket (that is—*He*—the said *Baxter* being the *pickpocket*) and say that I expect a deduction—having been obliged to come out of the way to this place—which was not in my route—for repairs—which however I hope to have accomplished so as to put us in motion in a day or two.——We passed through Ghent—Antwerp—and Mechlin—& thence diverged here—having seen all the sights—pictures—docks—basins[9]—& having climbed up steeples &c. & so forth——the first thing—after the flatness & fertility of the country which struck me—was the beauty of the towns—Bruges first—where you may tell Douglas Kinnaird—on entering at Sunset—I overtook a crew of beggarly looking gentlemen not unlike Oxberry[10]—headed by a Monarch with a Staff the very facsimile of King Clause in the said D K's revived drama.——We lost our way in the dark—or rather twilight—not far from Ghent—by the stupidity of the postilion (*one* only by the way to 4 horses) which produced an alarm of intended robbery among the uninitiated—whom I could not convince—that four or five well-armed people were not immediately to be plundered and anatomized by a single person fortified with a horsewhip to be sure—but nevertheless a little encumbered with large jack boots—and a tight jacket that did not fit him—The way was found again without loss of life or limb:——I thought the learned Fletcher at least would have known better after our Turkish expeditions—and defiles—and banditti—& guards &c. &c. than to have been so valourously alert without at least a better pretext for his superfluous courage. I don't mean to say that they were *frightened* but they were vastly suspicious without any cause.—At Ghent we stared at pictures—& climbed up a steeple 450 steps in altitude—from which I had a good view & notion of these 'paese bassi.' [low countries]——Next day we broke down—by a damned wheel (on which Baxter should be broken) pertinaciously refusing it's stipulated

---

[8] Byron's coach was built by the firm of Charles Frederick Baxter, of Long Acre in London's West End. He kept it till the end of his life, writing to his Genoa banker before he set off for Greece in July 1823: 'I particularly recommend to your Care my own travelling Chariot—which I would not part with for any consideration' (*LJ* x. 214).

[9] Napoleon was quick to recognize the possibilities of Antwerp as a port, and developed facilities there from 1811 to 1813.

[10] The comic actor William Oxberry (1784–1824) was often associated with Drury Lane.

rotation—this becalmed us at Lo-Kristi [Lochristi]—(2 leagues from Ghent)—& obliged us to return for repairs——At Lo Kristi I came to anchor in the house of a Flemish Blacksmith (who was ill of a fever for which Dr. Dori physicked him— I dare say he is dead by now) and saw somewhat of Lo-Kristi—Low-country— low life—which regaled us much—besides it being a Sunday—all the world were in their way to Mass—& I had the pleasure of seeing a number of very ordinary women in extraordinary garments:—we found the 'Contadini' [peas- ants] however very goodnatured & obliging though not at all useful.—At Antwerp we pictured—churched—and steepled again—but the principal Street and *bason* pleased me most—poor dear Bonaparte!!!—and the foundries &c.—as for Rubens—I was glad to see his tomb on account of that ridiculous description (in Smollet's P Pickle) of Pallet's absurdity at his monument[11]—but as for his works—and his superb 'tableaux'—he seems to me (who by the way know nothing of the matter) the most glaring—flaring—staring—harlotry imposter that ever passed a trick upon the senses of mankind—it is not nature—it is not art—with the exception of some linen (which hangs over the cross in one of his pictures) which to do it justice looked like a very handsome table cloth—I never saw such an assemblage of florid night-mares as his canvas contains—his por- traits seem clothed in pulpit cushions.——On the way to Mechlin—a wheel—& a *spring* too gave way—that is—the one went—& the other would not go—so we came off here to get into dock—I hope we shall sail shortly.——On to Geneva.— Will you have the goodness—to get at my account at Hoares—(my bankers) I believe there must be a balance in my favour—as I did not draw a great deal previously to going:—whatever there may be over the two thousand five hundred—they can send by you to me in a further credit when you come out:—I wish you to enquire (for fear any tricks might be played with my drafts) my bankers books left with you—will show you exactly what I have drawn—and you can let them have the book to make out the remainder of the account. All I have to urge to Hanson—or to our friend Douglas K—is to *sell* if possible.—— All kind things to Scrope—and the rest—

ever yrs. most truly & obligedly
B

---

[11] Peter Paul Rubens (1577–1640), Flemish baroque master, is buried in St James' Church, Antwerp. Mr Pallet is a painter and dilettante in Tobias Smollett's *Peregrine Pickle* (1751). In chapter 57 he falls to his knees at Rubens's tomb 'and worshipped with such appearance of devotion, that the attendant, scandalised at his superstition, pulled him up; observing...that the person buried in that place was no saint, but as great a sinner as himself'.

P. S.—If you hear of my child—let me know any good of her health—& well doing.—Will you bring πασανιας *(Taylor's ditto[12]) when you come—I shall bring to for you at Geneva—don't forget to urge Scrope into our crew—we will buy females and found a colony—provided Scrope does not find those ossified barriers to 'the forefended place'—which cost him such a siege at Brighthelmstone[13]—write at your leisure—or 'ipse veni'.[14]——*

[To John Cam Hobhouse]

Carlsruhe—May 16th. 1816

My dear Hobhouse/

We are this far by the Rhenish route on our way to Switzerland—where I shall wait to hear of your intentions as to junction before I go to Italy.——I have written to you three times—and mention the number—in case of any non-arrival of epistles.—We were obliged to diverge from Anvers & Mechlin to Brussels—for some wheel repairs—& in course seized the opportunity to visit Mont St. Jean &c. where I had a gallop over the field on a Cossac horse (left by some of the Don gentlemen at Brussels) and after a tolerably minute investigation—returned by Soignies—having purchased a quantity of helmets sabres &c all of which are consigned to the care of a Mr. Gordon at B[russe]ls (an old acquaintance) who desired to forward them to Mr. Murray—in whose keeping I hope to find them safe some day or other.[15]——Our route by the Rhine has been beautiful—& much surpassing my expectation—though very much answering in it's outlines to my previous conceptions.——The Plain at Waterloo is a fine one—but not much after Marathon & Troy—Cheronea—& Platea.[16]——Perhaps there is something of prejudice in this—but I detest the

---

[12] *The Description of Greece*, by the 2nd-century traveller Pausanius, was translated by Thomas Taylor in 1794.

[13] It seems Davies had been frustrated by a whalebone corset during a sexual encounter in the Sussex seaside town of Brighton, where he had holidayed with Byron in 1808. The quote is from Folio *King Lear*, V. i. 11, where it carries the same implication.

[14] 'Come yourself!', from the fictional letter of Penelope to Odysseus in Ovid's *Heroides*.

[15] Byron visited the field of Waterloo—during which British troops famously resisted French cavalry attacks at the hill of Mont Saint Jean—with an old friend of his mother's, Major Pryce Lockhart Gordon, whom he met by chance in Brussels. It seems his horse had once belonged to a rider from the Russian army, which traditionally drew its mounts from the Cossack region around the River Don.

[16] Legendary battles of the classical world, in Greece and Asia Minor, the sites of which Byron had visited on his Grand Tour.

cause & the victors—& the victory—including Blucher & the Bourbons.——
From Bonn to Coblenz—& Coblenz again to Bingen & Mayence—nothing can
exceed the prospects at every point—not even—any of the old scenes—though
this is in a different style:—what it most reminded me of were parts of Cintra—
& the valley which leads from Delvinachi—by Libochabo and Argyrocastro (on
the opposite mountains) to Tepaleni—the last resemblance struck even the
learned Fletcher—who seems to thrive upon his present expedition & is full of
comparisons & preferences of the present to the last—particularly in the articles
of provision & Caravanseras.[17]——Poor Polidori is devilish ill—I do not know
with what—nor does he—but he seems to have a slight constitution—& is
seriously laid up—if he does not get well soon—he will be totally unfit for
travelling—his complaints are headaches & feverishness:—all the rest are well—
for the present—nor has he had any patients except a Belgian Blacksmith (at
Lo Kristi a village where our wheels stuck) and himself.—At Cologne I had a
ludicrous adventure—the host of our hotel mistook a German Chambermaid—
whose red cheeks & white teeth had made me venture upon her carnally—for
his wife—& stood swearing at the door like a Squadron of Cavalry—to the
amusement of consternation of all his audience—till the mystery was developed
by his wife walking out of her own room—& the girl out of mine.—We have
seen all the sights—churches & so forth—& at Coblentz crossed the Rhine—and
scrambled up the fortress of Ehrenbreitstein now a ruin—we also saw on the
road the sepulchres—& monuments of Generals Marceau & Hoche & went up
to examine them—they are simple & striking—but now much neglected if not
to say defaced by the change of times & this cursed after-crop of rectilignes &
legitimacy.[18]—At Manheim we crossed the Rhine & keep on this side to avoid
the French segment of Territory at Strasburg—as we have not French passports—& no desire to view a degraded country—& oppressed people.—This
town (a very pretty one) is the seat of the court of the Grand Duke of Baden:—
tomorrow I mean to proceed (if Polidori is well enough) on our journey.—At
Geneva I expect to hear from you—tell me of Scrope and his intentions—and of
all or any things or persons—saving and except *one* subject—which
I particularly beg never to have mentioned again—unless as far as regards my
child—& my *child* only.——If Scrope comes out—tell him there are some 'light

---

[17] Or *caravanserai*: an inn in the Ottoman Empire. Byron is remembering his travels in Portugal and
Albania.

[18] The fortress of Ehrenbreitsein, looking down on the confluence of the Moselle and the Rhine at
Koblenz, was demolished by the French when they were forced to abandon it in 1801, and later
rebuilt. Marceau and Hoche were heroic French generals in the French Revolutionary wars, buried
together nearby. *Rectiligne* is an adjective meaning 'straight' or 'rectilinear'; no doubt Byron is referring
to 'legitimate' 'line of succession' re-established in Bourbon France after the fall of Napoleon.

wines' which will bring to his recollection 'the day of Pentecost' & other branches of his vinous thirty nine articles.—I have solaced myself moderately with such 'flaggons of Rhenish' as have fallen in my way—but without our Yorick—they are nothing.—I hope your book of letters is not slack in sale—and I can't see why Ridgway should not pay 'a few paouands' for the 2d. Edition unless it be that I did not pay him his bill & that he thinks therefore *you* should.[19]——I trust that you will give *Spooney* [Hanson] a jog as to selling & so forth—& tell my Potestas [power: of attorney] (Kinnaird) to come the committee over him.—I suppose poor K will be devilishly bothered with his Drury Lane speech this year—how does Mathurin's play go on[20]—or rather go off—of course the prologue has fallen to your lot—& the Comedy eh?—I hope you executed the ten thousand petty commissions I saddled you withal——pray remember me to all the remembering—& not less to the superb Murray—who is now enjoying inglorious ease at his green table—& wishing for somebody to keep him in hot water.——Wishing you all prosperity—I am ever

yrs. most truly
Byron

[To Pryce Gordon]

[Geneva, June? 1816]

I cannot tell you what a treat your gift of Casti has been to me; I have almost got him by heart. I had read his 'Animali Parlanti,' but I think these 'Novelle' much better. I long to go to Venice to see the manners so admirably described[21]

---

[19] Ridgeway published Hobhouse's *Letters by an Englishman Resident at Paris during the Last Reign of Napoleon* in 1815.

[20] Alongside Sotheby's *Ivan*, the only other 'serious' play Byron was able to support at Drury Lane was Robert Maturin's *Bertram*, which opened three weeks after he left the country: it did well by the standards of contemporary tragedies, being acted twenty-two times and being reprinted six times in 1816.

[21] Gordon had done Byron the inestimable favour of giving him the *Novelle galanti* ('Ritzy Stories') by the Italian comic poet Giovanni Battista Casti (1724–1803). These tales in ottava rima would directly inspire *Beppo* and *Don Juan* once Byron got to Venice. (This is all of Byron's letter that survives, quoted by Gordon in his *Personal Memoirs* of 1830.)

[To John Cam Hobhouse]

Evian—June 23d. 1816

My dear H[obhous]e/

Despite of this date—address as usual to the Genevese Poste—which awaits your answers as I await your arrival—with that of Scrope—whose pocket appears (by your late letter of revolutions at the Union) to have become as 'light' as his 'wines'—though I suppose on the whole he is still worth at least 50-000 p[oun]ds—being what is called here a 'Millionaire' that is in Francs & such Lilliputian coinage.[22] I have taken a very pretty villa in a vineyard—with the Alps behind—& Mt. Jura and the Lake before—it is called Diodati—from the name of the Proprietor—who is a descendant of the critical & illustrissimi Diodati[23]—and has an agreeable house which he lets at a reasonable rate per season or annum as suits the lessée—when you come out—don't go to an Inn— not even to Secheron—but come on to head-quarters—where I have rooms ready for you—and Scrope—and all 'appliances & means to boot'.[24]—Bring with you also for me some bottles of *Calcined Magnesia*—a new *Sword cane*— procured by Jackson—he alone knows the sort—(my last tumbled into this lake—[25]) some of Waite's *red* tooth-powder—& tooth-brushes—a Taylor's *Pawrsanias*—and—I forget the other things.—Tell Murray I have a 3d. Canto of Childe Harold finished—it is the longest of the three—being one hundred & eleven Stanzas—I shall send it by the first plausible conveyance.—At the present writing I am on my way on a water-tour round the Lake Leman—and am thus far proceeded in a pretty open boat which I bought & navigate—it is an English one & was brought lately from Bordeaux—I am on shore for the Night—and have just had a row with the Syndic of this town who wanted my passports which I left at Diodati—not thinking they would be wanted except in grand route—but it seems this is Savoy and the dominion of his Cagliari Majesty whom we saw at his own Opera—in his own city—in 1809[26]—however by dint of references to Geneva—& other corroborations—together with being in a

---

[22] Hobhouse had written on 8 June to say that Davies had 'reduced his body pecuniary of late' by gambling at the Union club in London; accordingly, he looked forward to some respite on the Continent, as well as some 'light French wines' of the kind Byron had mentioned on 16 May (*Hobhouse Letters*, 225).

[23] Giovanni Diodati (1576–1649), Swiss-Italian Calvinist theologian and translator of the Bible, sought out for his learning by John Milton as a young man on his European travels.

[24] See 2 *Henry IV*, III. i. 29.

[25] See letter of September 1808.

[26] The Italian Duchy of Savoy, centred on Turin, traditionally occupied territory along the modern Swiss–French–Italian border, and had also ruled the island of Sardinia (from its capital, Cagliari,

very ill humour—Truth has prevailed—wonderful to relate they actually take one's word for a fact—although it is credible and indubitable.—Tomorrow we go to Meillerei—& Clarens—& Vevey—with Rousseau in hand—to see his scenery—according to his delineation in his Heloise now before me.[27]—The views have hitherto been very fine—but I should conceive less so than those of the remainder of the lake.——All your letters (that is *two*) have arrived—thanks & greetings:—what—& who—the devil is 'Glenarvon'.[28] I know nothing—nor ever heard of such a person—and what do you mean by a brother in India?— you have none in India—it is *Scrope* who has a brother in India.—my remembrances to Kinnaird—& Mrs. Kinn[air]d—to all & every body—& Hunt in particular—& Scrope—& Mr. Murray—and believe me

yrs ever most truly

B

P. S.—*I left the Doctor at Diodati—he sprained his ancle. P. S. Will you particularly remember to bring me a largish bottle of the strongest* Pot Ash—*as before—Mr. Le Man will furnish it—that Child and Childish Dr. Pollydolly contrived to find it broken,—or to break it at Carlsruhe—so that I am in a fuss—the Genevese make it badly—it effervesces in the Sulphuric acid, and it ought not—bring me some of a more quiescent character.*[29]

[To John Murray]

Diodati—nr. Geneva. July 22d. 1816

Dear Sir

I wrote to you a few weeks ago—and Dr. P[olidori] received your letter—but ye. packet has not made its appearance nor ye. epistle of which you gave notice

---

visited by Byron and Hobhouse in 1809) since 1720. Evian, in the Haute-Savoie region of Switzerland was under its control, whereas Geneva was part of the newly guaranteed Swiss federation.

[27] Rousseau's epistolary novel *Julie: or the New Héloïse* (1761), one of the publishing sensations of the 18th century, involved the relationships of a young woman with her husband and her erstwhile tutor—and therefore the difference between marital and passionate love.

[28] The first Byron heard of Caroline Lamb's novel about their affair (published in May 1816) was from Hobhouse in a letter of 8 June: 'Glenarvon has done nothing but render the little vicious author more odious if possible than ever' (*Hobhouse Letters*, 226).

[29] Potassium carbonate, like calcium carbonate (baking soda), is an antacid, and so was commonly used to treat indigestion, from which Byron suffered a good deal, due to his irregular diet. Le Mann was the Byrons' doctor in London.

therein.—I enclose you an advertisement—which was copied by Dr. P—& which appears to be about the most impudent imposition that ever issued from Grub Street.—I need hardly say that I know nothing of all this trash—nor whence it may spring—'Odes to St. Helena—Farewells to England—&c. &c.'—and if it can be disavowed—or is worth disavowing you have full authority to do so.—I never wrote nor conceived a line of any thing of the kind—any more than of two other things with which I was saddled—something about 'Gaul' and another about 'Mrs. La Valette'—and as to the 'Lily of France' I should as soon think of celebrating a turnip.——On the 'morning of my Daughter's birth' I had other things to think of than verses—and should never have dreamed of such an invention—till Mr. Johnston and his pamphlet's advertisement broke in upon me with a new light on the Crafts & subtilties of the Demon of printing—or rather publishing.——I did hope that some succeeding lies would have superseded the thousand and one which were accumulated during last winter—I can forgive whatever may be said of or against me—but not what they make me say or sing for myself—it is enough to answer for what I have written—but it were too much for Job himself to bear what one has not—I suspect that when the Arab Patriarch wished that 'his Enemy had written a book'[30] he did not anticipate his own name on the title page.——I feel quite as much bored with this foolery as it deserves—and more than I should be—if I had not a headache.——Of Glenarvon—Madame de Stael told me (ten days ago at Copet) marvellous & grievous things—but I have seen nothing of it but the Motto—which promises amiably 'For us & for our tragedy'—if such be the posy what should the ring be? 'a name to all succeeding &c.'[31]—the generous moment selected for the publication is probably its kindest accompaniment—and truth to say—the time was well chosen,—I have not even a guess at the contents—except for the very vague accounts I have heard—and I know but one thing which a woman can say to the purpose on such occasions and that she might as well for her own sake keep to herself—which by the way they very rarely can—that old reproach against their admirers of 'kiss and tell,' bad as it is—is surely somewhat less than——and *publish*.—I ought to be ashamed of the Egotism of this letter—it is not my fault altogether—and I shall be but too happy to drop the subject when others will allow me.—I am in tolerable plight—and in my last letters told you what I had done in the way of all rhyme—I trust that you prosper—and that your authors are in good

---

[30] See Job 31: 35.
[31] See *Hamlet*, III. ii. 142, and *The Corsair*, iii. 695–6: 'He left a Corsair's name to other times, | Linked with one virtue, and a thousand crimes.' 'As for the likeness,' Byron would later say of Lamb's novel, 'the picture can't be good—I did not sit long enough' (*LJ* v. 131).

condition—I should suppose your Stud has received some increase—by what I hear—Bertram must be a good horse—does he run next meeting? and does the Quarterly cover still at so much the mare and the groom?[32] I hope you will beat the Row—

yrs. alway & [truly?]

[To Samuel Rogers]

Diodati—nr. Geneva July 29th. 1816

Dear Rogers

Do you recollect a book? Mathison's letters—which you lent me—which I have still—& yet hope to return to your library?—well—I have encountered at Copet and elsewhere Gray's Correspondent (in it's Appendix) that same Bonstetten—(to whom I lent ye translation of his Correspondent's epistles for a few days)—but all he could remember of Gray amounts to little—except that he was the most 'melancholy and gentlemanlike' of all possible poets.[33]—Bonstetten himself is a fine & very lively old man—and much esteemed by his Compatriots—he is also a litterateur of good repute—and all his friends have a mania of addressing to him volumes of letters—Mathison—Muller the historian &c. &c. He is a good deal at Copet—where I have met him a few times.—All there are well—except Rocca—who I am sorry to say—looks in a very bad state of health—the Duchess seems grown taller—but—as yet—no rounder since her marriage—Schlegel is in high force—and Madame as brilliant as ever.[34]——I came here by the Netherlands—and the Rhine Route—& Basle—Berne—Morat—& Lausanne—I have circumnavigated the lake—and shall go to Chamouni—with the first fair weather—but really we have had lately such stupid mists—fogs—rains—and perpetual density—that one would think Castlereagh had the foreign affairs of

[32] Murray published the *Quarterly Review*, a Tory rival to the *Edinburgh*, which favoured Murray titles such as *Bertram*. A stallion 'covers' a mare, so the book, the journal, and the editor are parties to a successful publication. 'The Row' is a portmanteau phrase for the London publishing industry, in the 18th century centred on Paternoster Row near St Paul's.

[33] *Letters Written from Various Parts of the Continent, between the Years 1785 and 1794*, by the German poet Friedrich von Matthisson, had been translated into English in 1799. Part of the book's interest for British readers was some correspondence between the poet Thomas Gray and the Swiss writer Charles Victor de Bonstetten (1745–1832), reproduced as an appendix. Another devotee of Bonstetten's was the historian of Switzerland, Johannes von Müller.

[34] Madame de Staël's second husband was the Swiss Albert de Rocca, twenty-three years younger than her. Her daughter Albertine had married the French Duc de Broglie in February 1816. The German critic August Wilhelm von Schlegel was a member of her circle, and the Swiss-French writer Benjamin Constant a lover of long standing up until 1811, whose autobiographical novel, *Adolphe*, is a Romantic masterpiece.

the kingdom of Heaven also—upon his hands.——I need say nothing to you of these parts—you having traversed them already—I do not think of Italy before September.——I have read 'Glenarvon'

'From furious Sappho scarce a milder fate
————by her love—or libelled by her hate.'[35]

& have also seen Ben. Constant's Adolphe—and his preface denying the real people—it is a work which leaves an unpleasant impression—but very consistent with the consequences of not being in love—which is perhaps as disagreeable as anything—except being so—I doubt however whether all such 'liens' (as he calls them) [ties, bonds] terminate so wretchedly as his hero & heroine's.—There is a third Canto (a longer than either of the former) of Ch[il]de Har[ol]d finished—and some smaller things—among them a story on the 'Chateau de Chillon'—I only wait a good opportunity to transmit them to the Grand Murray—who—I hope—flourishes.—Where is Moore?—why aint he out?—my love to him—and my perfect consideration & remembrances to all—particularly to Lord & Lady Holland—& to your Duchess of Somers[e]t.—

ever yrs. very truly

P. S.—I send you a fac simile—a note of Bonstetten's thinking you might like to see the hand of Gray's Correspondent.

[To Augusta Leigh]

[Diodati—Geneva Sept. 8th. 1816]

My dearest Augusta

By two opportunities of private conveyance—I have sent answers to your letter delivered by Mr. H[obhouse].——S[crope] is on his return to England—& may probably arrive before this.—He is charged with a few packets of seals—

---

[35] See Pope's *Imitations of Horace*, II. i. 83–4 (1733): 'poxed' is the word Byron drops.

necklaces—balls &c.—& I know not what—formed of Chrystals—Agates—and other stones—*all of & from Mont Blanc* bought & brought by me on & from the spot—expressly for you to divide among yourself and the children—including also your niece Ada, for whom I selected a ball (of Granite—a soft substance by the way—but the only one there) wherewithall to roll & play—when she is old enough—and mischievous enough—and moreover a Chrystal necklace—and anything else you may like to add for her—the Love!——The rest are for you— & the Nursery—but particularly Georgiana—who has sent me a very nice letter.— I hope Scrope will carry them all safely—as he promised——There are seals & all kinds of fooleries—pray—like them—for they come from a very curious place (nothing like it hardly in all I ever saw)—to say nothing of the giver.——And so— Lady B has been 'kind to you' you tell me—'very kind'—umph—it is as well she should be kind to some of us—and I am glad she has the heart & the discernment to be still *your* friend—you was ever so to her.—I heard the other day—that she was very unwell—I was shocked enough—and sorry enough—God knows—but never mind;—H[obhouse] tells me however that she is *not* ill—that she *had* been indisposed—but is better & well to do.—this is a relief.——As for me I am in good health—& fair—though very unequal—spirits—but for all that—she—or rather—the Separation—has broken my heart—I feel as if an Elephant had trodden on it—I am convinced I shall never get over it—but I try.——I had enough before I ever knew her and more than enough—but time & agitation had done something for me; but this last wreck has affected me very differ-ently,—if it were *acutely*—it would not signify—but it is not that,—I breathe lead.——While the storm lasted & you were all pressing & comforting me with condemnation in Piccadilly—it was bad enough—& violent enough—but it is worse now.—I have neither strength nor spirits—nor inclination to carry me through anything which will clear my brain or lighten my heart.—I mean to cross the Alps at the end of this month—and go—God knows where—by Dalmatia—up to the Arnauts again—if nothing better can be done;—I have still a world before me[36]—this—or the next.——H[obhouse] has told me all the strange stories in circulation of me & mine;—*not* true,—I have been in some danger—on the lake—(near Meillerie) but nothing to speak of; and as to all these 'mistresses'—Lord help me—I have had but one.—Now—don't scold—but what could I do?—a foolish girl—in spite of all I could say or do—would come after me—or rather went before me—for I found her here—and I have had all the plague possible to persuade her to go back again—but at last she went.—Now—

---

[36] See the fallen Adam and Eve in the closing lines of Milton's *Paradise Lost*: 'The world was all before them, where to choose | Their place of rest, and Providence their guide. | They, hand in hand, with wandering steps and slow, | Through Eden took their solitary way.'

dearest—I do most truly tell thee—that I could not help this—that I did all I could to prevent it—& have at last put an end to it.—I am not in love—nor have any love left for any,—but I could not exactly play the Stoic with a woman—who had scrambled eight hundred miles to unphilosophize me—besides I had been regaled of late with so many 'two courses and a *desert*' (Alas!) of aversion—that I was fain to take a little love (if pressed particularly) by way of novelty.———And now you know all that I know of that matter—& it is over. Pray—write—I have heard nothing since your last—at least a month or five weeks ago.———I go out very little—except into the *air*—and on journeys—and on the water—and to Coppet— where M[adam]e. de Stael has been particularly kind & friendly towards me—& (I hear) fought battles without number in my very indifferent cause.—It has (they say) made quite as much noise on this as the other side of 'La Manche'[37]—Heaven knows why—but I seem destined to set people by the ears.———Don't hate me— but believe me ever

yrs. most affectly.
B

[To Augusta Leigh]

Clarens. Septr. 18th. 1816

Alpine journal

Yesterday September 17th. 1816—I set out (with H[obhouse]) on an excursion of some days to the Mountains.—I shall keep a short journal of each day's progress for my Sister Augusta—

Sept. 17th.—

Rose at 5.—left Diodati about seven—in one of the country carriages (a Charaban[38])—our servants on horseback—weather very fine—the Lake calm and clear—Mont Blanc—and the Aiguille of Argentière both very distinct—the borders of the Lake beautiful—reached Lausanne before Sunset—stopped & slept at Ouchy.—H went to dine with a Mr. Okeden—I remained at our Caravansera (though invited to the house of H's friend—too lazy or tired—or something else to go) and wrote a letter to Augusta—Went to bed at nine—sheets damp—swore and stripped them off & flung them—Heaven knows where—wrapt myself up in the blankets and slept like a Child of a month's existence—till 5 o Clock of

---

[37] 'The Ditch': the English Channel.
[38] The English charabanc, from the French *char à banc*: a carriage with bench seats.

Septr. 18th.

Called by Berger (my Courier who acts as Valet for a day or two—the learned Fletcher being left in charge of Chattels at Diodati) got up—H walked on before—a mile from Lausanne—the road overflowed by the lake—got on horseback & rode—till within a mile of Vevey—the Colt young but went very well—overtook H. & resumed the carriage which is an open one—stopped at Vevey two hours (the second time I have visited it) walked to the Church—view from the Churchyard superb—within it General Ludlow (the Regicide's) monument—black marble—long inscription—Latin—but simple—particularly the latter part—in which his wife (Margaret de Thomas) records her long—her tried—and unshaken affection—he was an Exile *two and thirty years*—one of the King's (Charles's) Judges—a fine fellow.—I remember reading his memoirs in January 1815 (at Halnaby—) the first part of them very amusing—the latter less so,—I little thought at the time of their perusal by me of seeing his tomb—near him Broughton (who read King Charles's sentence to Charles Stuart)—is buried with a *queer* and rather *canting*—but still a Republican epitaph—Ludlow's house shown—it retains still his inscription 'Omne Solum forte patria'[39]—Walked down to the Lake side—servants—Carriage—saddle horses—all set off and left us plantés la [abandoned there] by some mistake—and we walked on after them towards Clarens—H ran on before and overtook them at last—arrived the second time (1st time was by water) at Clarens beautiful Clarens!—went to Chillon through Scenery worthy of I know not whom—went over the Castle of Chillon again—on our return met an English party in a carriage—a lady in it fast asleep!—fast asleep in the most anti-narcotic spot in the world—excellent— I remember at Chamouni—in the very eyes of Mont Blanc—hearing another woman—English also—exclaim to her party—'did you ever see any thing more *rural*'—as if it was Highgate or Hampstead—or Brompton—or Hayes.—'Rural' quotha!—Rocks—pines—torrents—Glaciers—Clouds—and Summits of eternal snow far above them—and 'Rural!' I did not know the thus exclaiming fair one—but she was a—very good kind of a woman.——After a slight & short dinner—we visited the Chateau de Clarens—an English woman has rented it recently—(it was not let when I saw it first) the roses are gone with their Summer—the family out—but the servants desired us to walk over the interior—saw on the table of the saloon—Blair's sermons—and somebody else's (I forgot who's—) sermons—and a set of noisy children—saw all worth

[39] Edmund Ludlow (1617–92) was one of the signatories to the warrant for the execution of Charles I in 1649. After the restoration of the Stuart monarchy in 1660 he went abroad and wrote his memoirs in exile in Switzerland. His motto in full is *omne solum forti patria, quia patris*, derived from Ovid: 'every land is a brave man's country, given by God.' As clerk of the High Court of Justice, Andrew Broughton announced Charles's sentence.

seeing and then descended to the 'Bosquet de Julie' &c. &c.[40]—our Guide full of *Rousseau*—whom he is eternally confounding with *St. Preux*—and mixing the man and the book—on the steps of a cottage in the village—I saw a young *paysanne* [peasant]—beautiful as Julie herself—went again as far as Chillon to revisit the little torrent from the hill behind it—Sunset—reflected in the lake— have to get up at 5 tomorrow to cross the mountains on horseback—carriage to be sent round—lodged at my old Cottage—hospitable & comfortable—tired with a longish ride—on the Colt—and the subsequent jolting of the Charaban— and my scramble in the hot sun—shall go to bed—thinking of you dearest Augusta.—Mem[orandum].—The Corporal who showed the wonders of Chillon was as drunk as Blucher—and (to my mind) as great a man.[41]—He was *deaf* also—and thinking every one else so—roared out the legends of the Castle so fearfully that H got out of humour—however we saw all things from the Gallows to the Dungeon (the *Potence* & the *Cachets*) and returned to Clarens with more freedom than belonged to the 15th. Century.[42]—At Clarens—the only book (except the Bible) a translation of '*Cecilia*' (Miss Burney's *Cecilia*[43]) and the owner of the Cottage had also called her dog (a fat Pug ten years old—and hideous as Tip) after Cecilia's (or rather Delville's) dog—Fidde—

Septr. 19th.

Rose at 5—ordered the carriage round.—Crossed the mountains to Montbovon on horseback—and on Mules—and by dint of scrambling on foot also,—the whole route beautiful as a *Dream* and now to me almost as indistinct,—I am so tired—for though healthy I have not the strength I possessed but a few years ago.—At Mont Davant we breakfasted—afterwards on a steep ascent— dismounted—tumbled down & cut a finger open—the baggage also got loose and fell down a ravine, till stopped by a large tree—swore—recovered baggage—horse tired & dropping—mounted Mule—at the approach of the summit of Dent Jamant—dismounted again with H. & all the party.—Arrived at a lake in the very nipple of the bosom of the Mountain.—left our quadrupeds with a Shepherd—& ascended further—came to some snow in patches—upon which my forehead's perspiration fell like rain making the same dints as in a

[40] The heroine of Rousseau's *Julie* favoured a particular grove where her tutor and lover, St Preux, visited her.

[41] The Prussian general and hero of Waterloo, Gebhard von Blücher (1742–1819), was fond of the bottle, as became clear when he visited London during 1814.

[42] *The Prisoner of Chillon*, which Byron wrote in the second half of June after visiting the castle with Shelley, is based on the incarceration of François Bonivard between 1530 and 1536 for opposition to Savoyard rule in this area of Switzerland.

[43] Frances Burney's novel was published in 1782. The eponymous heroine marries Mortimer Delvile, the owner of Fidel, at the end of the story. Augusta's dog was called Tip.

sieve—the chill of the wind & the snow turned me giddy—but I scrambled on & upwards—*H.* went to the highest *pinnacle*—I did not—but paused within a few yards (at an opening of the Cliff)—in coming down the Guide tumbled three times—I fell a laughing & tumbled too—the descent luckily soft though steep & slippery—H. also fell—but nobody hurt. The whole of the Mountain superb— the shepherd on a very steep & high cliff playing upon his *pipe*—very different from Arcadia[44]—(where I saw the pastors with a long Musquet instead of a Crook—and pistols in their Girdles)—our Swiss Shepherd's pipe was sweet—& his time agreeable—saw a cow strayed—told that they often break their necks on & over the crags—descended to Montbovon—pretty scraggy village with a wild river—and a wooden bridge.—H. went to fish—caught one—our carriage not come—our horse—mules &c. knocked up—ourselves fatigued—(but so much the better—I shall sleep). The view from the highest point of today's journey comprized on one side the greatest part of Lake Leman—on the other— the valleys & mountains of the Canton Fribourg—and an immense plain with the Lakes of Neufchatel & Morat—and all which the borders of these and of the Lake of Geneva inherit—we had both sides of the Jura before us in one point of view, with Alps in plenty.—In passing a ravine—the Guide recommended strenuously a quickening of pace—as the stones fall with great rapidity & occasional damage—the advice is excellent—but like most good advice impracticable—the road being so rough in this precise point—that neither mules nor mankind—nor horses—can make any violent progress.—Passed without any fractures or menace thereof.—The music of the Cows' bells (for their wealth like the Patriarchs is cattle) in the pastures (which reach to a height far above any mountains in Britain—) and the Shepherds' shouting to us from crag to crag & playing on their reeds where the steeps appeared almost inaccess- ible, with the surrounding scenery—realized all that I have ever heard or imagined of a pastoral existence—much more so than Greece or Asia Minor—for there we are a little too much of the sabre & musquet order—and if there is a Crook in one hand, you are sure to see a gun in the other—but this was pure and unmixed—solitary—savage and patriarchal—the effect I cannot describe—as we went they played the 'Ranz des Vaches' and other airs by way of farewell.[45]—I have lately repeopled my mind with Nature.[46]

---

[44] Byron means the real Arcadia, a region in the central Peloponnese, rather than the pastoral legend of storytellers.

[45] 'Rows of cows': a tune played on the Alpine horn, rural and nostalgic, related to the dairy industry in Switzerland.

[46] This unusual sentiment is echoed in *Childe Harold*, iii. 707–10 (*CPW* ii. 104): 'Are not the mountains, waves, and skies, a part | Of me and of my soul, as I of them? | Is not the love of these deep in my heart | With a pure passion?' Byron later told Thomas Medwin, 'Shelley, when I was in Switzerland, used to dose me with Wordsworth physic even to nausea: and I do remember then

Septr. 20th.

Up at 6—off at 8—the whole of this days journey at an average of between from two thousand seven hundred to three thousand feet above the level of the Sea. This valley the longest—narrowest—& considered one of the finest of the Alps—little traversed by travellers—saw the Bridge of La Roche—the bed of the river very low & deep between immense rocks & rapid as anger—a man & mule said to have tumbled over without damage—(the mule was lucky at any rate—unless I knew the *man* I should be loth to pronounce *him* fortunate).—The people looked free & happy and *rich* (which last implies neither of the former) the cows superb—a Bull nearly leapt into the Charaban—'agreeable companion in a postchaise'[47]—Goats & Sheep very thriving—a mountain with enormous Glaciers to the right—the Kletsgerberg—further on—the Hockthorn—nice names—so soft—Hockthorn I believe very lofty & craggy—patched with snow only—no Glaciers on it—but some good epaulettes of clouds.—Past the boundaries—out of Vaud—& into Bern Canton—French exchanged for a bad German—the district famous for Cheese—liberty—property—& no taxes.— H. went to fish—caught none—strolled to river—saw a boy [and] a kid—kid followed him like a dog—kid could not get over a fence & bleated piteously— tried myself to help kid—but nearly overset both self & kid into the river.— Arrived here about six in the evening—nine o clock—going to bed—H. in next room—knocked his head against the door—and exclaimed of course against doors—not tired today—but hope to sleep nevertheless—women gabbling below—read a French translation of Schiller—Good Night—Dearest Augusta.——

Septr. 21st.

Off early—the valley of Simmenthal as before—entrance to the plain of Thoun very narrow—high rocks—wooded to the top—river—new mountains—with fine Glaciers—Lake of Thoun—extensive plain with a girdle of Alps—walked down to the Chateau de Schadau—view along the lake—crossed the river in a boat rowed by women—*women* [went?] right for the first time in my recollection.—Thoun a pretty town—the whole day's journey Alpine & proud.—

Septr. 22d.

Left Thoun in a boat which carried us the length of the lake in three hours—the lake small—but the banks fine—rocks down to the water's edge.—Landed

reading some things of his with pleasure' (Thomas Medwin, *Conversations of Lord Byron* [1824], ed. Ernest J. Lovell, Jr. (Princeton: Princeton University Press, 1966), 194).

[47] An expression in common use in Byron's time, by passengers seeking or advertising congenial company on a long public coach journey.

at Neuhause,—passed Interlachen—entered upon a range of scenes beyond all description—or previous conception.—Passed a rock—inscription— 2 brothers—one murdered the other—just the place fit for it.—After a variety of windings came to an enormous rock—Girl with fruit—very pretty—blue eyes—good teeth—very fair—long but good features—reminded me of Fy.[48] bought some of her pears—and patted her upon the cheek—the expression of her face very mild—but good—and not at all coquettish.—Arrived at the foot of the Mountain (the Yung-frau—i.e. the Maiden) Glaciers—torrents—one of these torrents *nine hundred feet* in height of visible descent—lodge at the Curate's—set out to see the Valley—heard an Avalanche fall—like thunder—saw Glacier— enormous—Storm came on—thunder—lightning—hail—all in perfection— and beautiful—I was on horseback—Guide wanted to carry my cane—I was going to give it him when I recollected that it was a Swordstick and I thought that the lightning might be attracted towards him[49]—kept it myself—a good deal encumbered with it & my cloak—as it was too heavy for a whip—and the horse was stupid—& stood still every other peal. Got in—not very wet—the Cloak being staunch—H. wet through—H. took refuge in cottage—sent man— umbrella—& cloak (from the Curate's when I arrived—) after him.—Swiss Cur- ate's house—very good indeed—much better than most English Vicarages—it is immediately opposite the torrent I spoke of—the torrent is in shape curving over the rock—like the *tail* of a white horse streaming in the wind—such as it might be conceived would be that of the '*pale* horse' on which *Death* is mounted in the Apocalypse.[50]—It is neither mist nor water but a something between both—it's immense height (nine hundred feet) gives it a wave—a curve—a spreading here— a condensation there—wonderful—& indescribable.—I think upon the whole— that this day has been better than any of this present excursion.—

Septr. 23d.

Before ascending the mountain—went to the torrent (7 in the morning) again— the Sun upon it forming a *rainbow* of the lower part of all colours—but principally purple and gold—the bow moving as you move—I never saw anything like this—it is only in the Sunshine.——Ascended the Wengren Mountain [Wengen Alp].——at noon reached a valley near the summit—left the horses—took off my coat & went to the summit—7000 feet (English feet)

---

[48] That is, Lady Frances ('Fanny') Wedderburn Webster.
[49] Hobhouse had brought out the 'new *sword cane*' Byron had requested from his old sparring partner John Jackson (letter of 23 June).
[50] The Staubbach Falls. See Revelation 6: 8: 'And I looked, and behold a pale horse: and his name that sat on him was Death, and Hell followed with him. And power was given unto them over the fourth part of the earth, to kill with sword, and with hunger, and with death, and with the beasts of the earth.'

above the level of the *sea*—and about 5000 above the valley we left in the morning—on one side our view comprized the *Yung frau* with all her glaciers—then the *Dent d'Argent*—shining like truth—then the *little Giant* (the Kleiner EIgher) & the great Giant (the Grosser EIgher) and last not least—the Wetterhorn.—The height of the Yung frau is 13000 feet above the sea—and 11000 above the valley—she is the highest of this range,—heard the Avalanches falling every five minutes nearly—as if God was pelting the Devil down from Heaven with snow balls—from where we stood on the *Wengren* Alp—we had all these in view on one side—on the other the clouds rose from the opposite valley curling up perpendicular precipices—like the foam of the Ocean of Hell during a Springtide—it was white & sulphery—and immeasurably deep in appearance—the side we ascended was (of course) not of so precipitous a nature—but on arriving at the summit we looked down the other side upon a boiling sea of cloud—dashing against the crags on which we stood (these crags on one side quite perpendicular);—staid a quarter of an hour—began to descend—quite clear from cloud on that side of the mountain—in passing the masses of snow—I made a snowball & pelted H. with it—got down to our horses again—eat something—remounted—heard the Avalanches still—came to a morass—H. dismounted—H. got well over—I tried to pass my horse over—the horse sunk up [to] the chin—& of course he & I were in the mud together—bemired all over—but not hurt—laughed & rode on.—Arrived at the Grindenwald—dined—mounted again & rode to the higher Glacier—twilight—but distinct—very fine Glacier—like a *frozen hurricane*—Starlight—beautiful—but a devil of a path—never mind—got safe in—a little lightning—but the whole of the day as fine in point of weather—as the day on which Paradise was made.—Passed *whole woods of withered pines*—all withered—trunks stripped & barkless—branches lifeless—done by a single winter—their appearance reminded me of me & my family.—

Septr. 24th.

Set out at seven—up at five—passed the black Glacier—the Mountain Wetterhorn on the right—crossed the Scheideck mountain—came to the Rose Glacier—said to be the largest & finest in Switzerland.—*I* think the Bossons Glacier at Chamouni—as fine—H. does not—came to the Reichenback waterfall—two hundred feet high—halted to rest the horses—arrived in the valley of Oberhasli—rain came on—drenched a little—only 4 hours rain however in 8 days—came to Lake of Brientz—then to town of Brientz—changed—H. hurt his head against door.—In the evening four Swiss Peasant Girls of Oberhasli came & sang the airs of their country—two of the voices beautiful—the tunes also—they sing too that *Tyrolese* air & song which you love—Augusta—because I love it—& I love because you love it—they are still singing—Dearest—you do not know how I should have liked this—were you with me—the airs are so wild & original & at the same time of great sweetness.——The singing is over—but below stairs I hear the notes of a Fiddle which bode no good to my nights rest.—The Lord help us!—I shall go down & see the dancing.—

Septr. 25th.

The whole town of Brientz were apparently gathered together in the rooms below—pretty music—& excellent Waltzing—none but peasants—the dancing much better than in England—the English can't Waltz—never could—nor ever will.[51]—One man with his pipe in his mouth—but danced as well as the others—some other dances in pairs—and in fours—and very good.——I went to bed but the revelry continued below late & early.—Brientz but a village.—Rose early.—Embarked on the Lake of Brientz.—Rowed by women in a long boat—one very young & very pretty—seated myself by her—& began to row also—presently we put to shore & another woman jumped in—it seems it is the custom here for the boats to be *manned by women*—for of five men & three women in our bark—all the women took an oar—and but one man.——Got to Interlachen in three hours—pretty Lake—not so large as that of Thoun.—Dined at Interlachen—Girl gave me some flowers—& made me a speech in German—of which I know nothing—I do not know whether the speech was pretty but as the woman was—I hope so.—Saw another—very pretty too—and *tall* which I prefer—I hate short women—for more reasons than one.—Reembarked on the Lake of Thoun—fell asleep part of the way—sent our horses round—found people on the shore blowing up a rock with gunpowder—they blew it up near our boat—only telling us a minute before—mere stupidity—but they might have broke our noddles.—Got to Thoun in the Evening—the weather has been tolerable the whole day—but as the wild part of our tour is finished, it don't matter to us—in all the desirable part—we have been most lucky in warmth & clearness of Atmosphere—for which 'Praise we the Lord.'——

Septr. 26th.

Being out of the mountains my journal must be as flat as my journey.——From Thoun to Bern good road—hedges—villages—industry—prosperity—and all sorts of tokens of insipid civilization.——From Bern to Fribourg.—Different Canton—Catholics—passed a field of Battle—Swiss beat the French—in one of the late wars against the French Republic.—Bought a dog—a very ugly dog—but 'tres mechant' [very fierce]. this was his great recommendation in the owner's eyes & mine—for I mean him to watch the carriage—he hath no tail—& is called 'Mutz'—

---

[51] See letter of 28 September 1812.

which signifies 'Short-tail'—he is apparently of the Shepherd dog genus![52]—The greater part of this tour has been on horseback—on foot—and on mule;—the Filly (which is one of two young horses I bought of the Baron de Vincy) carried me very well—she is young and as quiet as anything of her sex can be—very goodtempered—and perpetually neighing—when she wants any thing—which is every five minutes—I have called her *Biche*—because her manners are not unlike a little dog's[53]—but she is a very tame—pretty childish quadruped.—

Septr. 28th. [27th.]

Saw the tree planted in honour of the battle of Morat—340 years old—a good deal decayed.[54]—Left Fribourg—but first saw the Cathedral—high tower— overtook the baggage of the Nuns of La Trappe who are removing to Normandy from their late abode in the Canton of Fribourg[55]—afterwards a coach with a quantity of Nuns in it—Nuns old—proceeded along the banks of the Lake of Neufchatel—very pleasing & soft—but not so mountainous—at least the Jura not appearing so—after the Bernese Alps—reached Yverdun in the dusk—a long line of large trees on the border of the lake—fine & sombre—the Auberge nearly full—with a German Princess & suite—got rooms—we hope to reach Diodati the day after tomorrow—and I wish for a letter from you my own dearest Sis—May your sleep be soft and your dreams of me.—I am going to bed—good night.—

Septr. 29th. [28th.]

Passed through a fine & flourishing country—but not mountainous—in the evening reached Aubonne (the entrance & bridge something like that of Durham) which commands by far the fairest view of the Lake of Geneva— twilight—the Moon on the Lake—a grove on the height—and of very noble trees.—Here Tavernier (the Eastern traveller) bought (or built) the Chateau because the site resembled and equalled that of *Erivan* (a frontier city of Persia) here he finished his voyages[56]—and I this little excursion—for I am within a few

---

[52] Mutz was not as dauntless as he appeared. On 22 April 1817 Byron reported to Hobhouse that he came off worse in a battle with 'a moderate-sized Pig on the top of the Pennine Alps—the Pig was first thrown into confusion & compelled to retire with great disorder over a steep stone wall but somehow he faced about in a damned hollow way or defile and drove Mutz from all his positions— with such slaughter that nothing but night prevented a total defeat' (*LJ* v. 217).

[53] This seems to be a bit of 'Franglais': in French *biche* is a doe or a hind; 'bitch' is *chienne*.

[54] For the battle of Morat (1476), in which the Swiss heroically defeated the invading Duke of Burgundy, see *Childe Harold's Pilgrimage*, iii. 599–625 (*CPW* ii. 100–1).

[55] La Valsainte Carthusian charterhouse at Cerniat, in the canton of Fribourg, sheltered French Trappists in the French Revolutionary and Napoleonic periods. The monarchy, Byron might have reflected, was not the only thing restored to France in 1816.

[56] Jean-Baptiste Tavernier (1605–89), intrepid French traveller to Persia, India, and Java, published his *Six Voyages* in 1675, written at an estate in Aubonne he bought in 1669.

hours of Diodati—& have little more to see—& no more to say.—In the weather for this tour (of 13 days) I have been very fortunate—fortunate in a companion (Mr. H[obhous]e) fortunate in our prospects—and exempt from even the little petty accidents & delays which often render journeys in a less wild country— disappointing.—I was disposed to be pleased—I am a lover of Nature—and an Admirer of Beauty—I can bear fatigue—& welcome privation—and—have seen some of the noblest views in the world.—But in all this—the recollections of bitterness—& more especially of recent & more home desolation—which must accompany me through life—have preyed upon me here—and neither the music of the Shepherd—the crashing of the Avalanche—nor the torrent—the mountain—the Glacier—the Forest—nor the Cloud—have for one moment— lightened the weight upon my heart—nor enabled me to lose my own wretched identity in the majesty & the power and the Glory—around—above—& beneath me.—I am past reproaches—and there is a time for all things—I am past the wish of vengeance—and I know of none like for what I have suffered— but the hour will come—when what I feel must be felt—& the——but enough.——To you—dearest Augusta—I send—and *for* you—I have kept this record of what I have seen & felt.—Love me as you are beloved by me.——

[To John Murray]

Diodati. Septr. 29th. 1816

My dear Sir

I am very much flattered by Mr. Gifford's good opinion of the M.S.S.—& shall be more so if it answers your expectations—& justifies his kindness.[57]—I liked it myself—but that must go for nothing—the feelings with which much of it was written need not be envied me.—With regard to the price—*I* fixed *none* but left it to Mr. Kinnaird—& Mr. Shelley & yourself to arrange—of course they would do their best—and as to yourself—I know you would make no difficulties.—But I agree with Mr. K. perfectly that the concluding *five hundred* should be only *conditional*—and for my own sake I wish it to be added only in case of your selling a certain number—*that number* to be fixed by *yourself*—I hope this is fair— in every thing of this kind—there must be risk—and till that be past in one way or the other—I would not willingly add to it—particularly in times like the

---

[57] On 12 September Murray had written in great excitement about *Childe Harold* III: 'never since my intimacy with Mr Gifford did I ever see him so heartily pleased or give one fiftieth part of his commendation with one thousandth part of the warmth. Harold is exquisite...' (*Murray Letters*, 173). He went on to offer £1,500 for the copyright.

present—and pray always recollect that nothing could mortify me more—no failure on my own part—than having made you lose by any purchase from me.——The Monody was written by request of Mr. K. for the theatre—I did as well as I could—but where I have not my choice I pretend to answer for nothing.[58]—Mr. H. & myself are just returned from a journey of lakes & mountains—we have been to the Grindenwald—& the Jung-frau—& stood on the summit of the Wengeren Alp—and seen torrents of nine hundred feet in fall—& Glaciers of all dimensions—we have heard Shepherds' pipes—and Avalanches—and looked on the clouds foaming up from the valleys below us— like the spray of the ocean of hell.——Chamouni and that which it inherits—we saw a month ago—but (though Mont Blanc is higher) it is not equal in wildness to the Jung-frau—the Eighers—the Shreckhorn—& the Rose Glacier.—— We set off for Italy next week—the road is within this month infested with Bandits—but we must take our chance & such precautions as are requisite.——

ever yrs. very truly
Byron

P. S.—My best remembrances to Mr. G[ifford]—pray say all that can be said from me to him.——I am sorry that Mr. M. [Moore?] did not like Phillips picture—I thought it was reckoned a good one—if he had made the speech on the original—perhaps he would have been more readily forgiven by the proprietor & the painter of the portrait.—Do not forget to consult Mrs. Leigh on the lines to her—they must not be published without her full consent & approbation.[59]——

[To Augusta Leigh]

Milan.— Octr. 13th. 1816

My dearest Augusta

You see I have got to Milan.—We came by the Simplon—escaping all perils of precipices and robbers—of which last there was some talk & apprehension—a

[58] Byron's 'Monody on the Death of The Right Honourable R. B. Sheridan' (*CPW* iv. 18–22) was more about the author than the subject.
[59] Byron addressed two poems to his sister from Switzerland: 'Stanzas to [Augusta]' and '[Epistle to Augusta]' (see *CPW* iv. 33–40). Augusta allowed the first to be published alongside *The Prisoner of Chillon* in December 1816; the second, finer and more personal, was eventually published in Thomas Moore's biography of the poet in 1830.

chain of English carriages having been stopped near Cesco a few weeks ago—&
handsomely pilfered of various chattels.—We were not molested.——The Simplon as you know—is the most superb of all possible routes;—so I shall not
describe it—I also navigated the Lago Maggiore—and went over the Borromean
Islands—the latter are fine but too artificial—the lake itself is beautiful—as
indeed is the whole country from Geneva hither—and the Alpine part most
magnificent.——Close to Milan is the beginning of an unfinished triumphal
arch—for Napoleon—so beautiful as to make one regret it's non-comple-
tion.[60]—As we only reached Milan last night—I can say little about it—but
will write again in a few days.—The Jerseys are here—Mad[am]e. de Stael is gone
to Paris (or going) from Coppet.—I was more there than elsewhere during my
stay at Diodati—and she has been particularly kind & friendly towards me the
whole time.—When you write—address to *Geneva*—still—Poste *restante*—and
my banker—(Monsr. Hentsch) will forward your letters.—I have written to you
so often lately—that you will not regret the brevity of this.—I hope that you
received safely my presents for the children (by Scrope) and that you also have
(by the post) a little journal of a journey in & on the Alps which I sent you early
this month—having kept it on purpose for *you*.—

> ever my own dearest yrs. most
>
> B

[To Augusta Leigh]

Milan Octr. 15. 1816

My dearest Augusta

I have been at Churches, Theatres, libraries, and picture galleries. The Cathedral
is noble, the theatre grand, the library excellent, and the galleries I know nothing
about—except as far as liking one picture out of a thousand. What has delighted
me most is a manuscript collection (preserved in the Ambrosian library), of
original love-letters and verses of Lucretia de Borgia & Cardinal Bembo; and a
lock of hair—so long—and fair & beautiful—and the letters so pretty & so
loving that it makes one wretched not to have been born sooner to have at least
seen her. And pray what do you think is one of her *signatures*?—why this + a
Cross—which she says 'is to stand for her name &c.' Is not this amusing?

---

[60] This is the Simplon Gate, built on the foundations of the ancient *Porta Giova*, main gate of Milan.
At the time Byron saw it, the construction of the Napoleonic 'Arch of Peace' had been interrupted by
the collapse of the Kingdom of Italy in 1814. It would be completed in 1838.

I suppose you know that she was a famous beauty, & famous for the use she made of it; & that she was the love of this same Cardinal Bembo (besides a story about her papa Pope Alexander & her brother Cæsar Borgia—which some people don't believe—& others do), and that after all she ended with being Duchess of Ferrara, and an excellent mother & wife also; so good as to be quite an example.[61] All this may or may not be, but the hair & the letters are so beautiful that I have done nothing but pore over them, & have made the librarian promise me a copy of some of them; and I mean to get some of the hair if I can. The verses are Spanish—the letters Italian—some signed—others with a cross—but all in her own hand-writing.

I am so hurried, & so sleepy, but so anxious to send you even a few lines my dearest Augusta, that you will forgive me for troubling you so often; and I shall write again soon; but I have sent you so much lately, that you will have too many perhaps. *A thousand loves to you from me*—which is very generous for I only ask *one* in return

Ever dearest thine
B

[To Augusta Leigh]

Octr. 28th. 1816

My dearest Augusta

Two days ago I wrote you the enclosed but the arrival of your letter of the 12th. has revived me a little, so pray forgive the apparent '*humeur*' [mood] of the other, which I do not tear up—from laziness—and the hurry of the post as I have hardly time to write another at present.

I really do not & cannot understand all the mysteries & alarms in your letters & more particularly in the last. All I know is—that no human power short of destruction—shall prevent me from seeing you when—where—& how—I may please—according to time & circumstance; that you are the only comfort (except the remote possibility of my daughter's being so) left me in prospect in existence, and that I can bear the rest—so that you remain; but anything

---

[61] The + was Byron's private symbol for Augusta in correspondence with her and Lady Melbourne. Lucrezia Borgia (1480–1519), daughter of Pope Alexander VI, and sister of Renaissance power broker Cesare Borgia, was married off three times by them for political advantage, finally (aged only 22) to the Duke of Ferrara. Her love affair with the poet and cardinal Pietro Bembo is well attested, but lurid tales of incest remain unproven. See Richard Smith (ed.), *The Prettiest Love Letters in the World* (New York: Godine, 1987).

which is to divide us would drive me quite out of my senses; Miss Milbanke appears in all respects to have been formed for my destruction; I have thus far—as you know—regarded her without feelings of personal bitterness towards her, but if directly or indirectly—but why do I say this?—You know she is the cause of all—whether intentionally or not is little to the purpose——You surely do not mean to say that if I come to England in Spring, that you & I shall not meet? If so I will never return to it—though I must for many reasons—business &c &c—But I quit this topic for the present.[62]

My health is good, but I have now & then fits of giddiness, & deafness, which make me think like Swift—that I shall be like him & the *withered* tree he saw—which occasioned the reflection and 'die at top' first.[63] My hair is growing grey, & *not* thicker; & my teeth are sometimes *looseish* though still white & sound. Would not one think I was sixty instead of not quite nine & twenty? To talk thus—Never mind—either this must end—or I must end—but I repeat it again & again—*that woman* has destroyed me.

Milan has been made agreeable by much attention and kindness from many of the natives; but the whole tone of Italian society is so different from yours in England; that I have not time to describe it, tho' I am not sure that I do not prefer it. Direct as usual to Geneva—hope the best—& love me the most—as I ever must love you.

B

[To Augusta Leigh]

Verona Novr. 6th. 1816

My dearest Augusta

I am thus far on my way to Venice—and shall stay here a day to see the place—the paintings—the 'tomb of all the Capulets' which they show[64]—(at least a tomb they call so after the story—from which Shakespeare drew the plot of his play) and all the sights & so forth at which it is usual to gape in passing.—I left

---

[62] Ever since the Separation, Lady Byron had campaigned for Augusta's redemption by trying to find out if she had resumed sexual relations with Byron after the marriage, and by shaming her into restricting or ceasing her correspondence with her half-brother. 'Goose', with very little will power of her own, generally succumbed to this pressure, much to Byron's consternation.

[63] On a walk near Dublin in 1717 poet and satirist Jonathan Swift (1667–1745) pointed to a dying tree and told his interlocutor, the poet Edward Young, that like it he would 'die at top': go insane.

[64] Anglo-Irish political philosopher Edmund Burke (1729–97) once wrote to his friend and schoolfellow Matthew Smith saying, 'I would rather sleep in a little corner of a country churchyard than in the tomb of all the Capulets'—alluding to the noble house in *Romeo and Juliet*, set in Verona.

Milan on Sunday & have travelled but slowly—over some celebrated ground—
but Lombardy is not a beautiful country at least in autumn—excepting however
the Lago di Garda & it's outlines which are mountainous on one side—and it is a
very fine stormy lake throughout—never quiet—and I had the pleasure of
seeing it in all its vexation—foaming like a little Sea—as Virgil has described
it—but (thank God) you are not a blue-stocking—and I wont inflict the appropriate bit of Latin upon you[65]—my own dearest Sis.———I wrote you a few scraps of
letterets (I may call them they were so short) from Milan—just to keep you out of (or
in) a fuss about baby B.—Dr. Polidori—whom I parted with before I left Geneva—
(not for any great harm—but because he was always in squabbles—& had no kind
of conduct)—contrived at Milan—which he reached before me—to get into a
quarrel with an Austrian—& to be ordered out of the city by the government.———*I
did not even see his adventure*—nor had anything to do with it—except getting him out
of arrest—and trying to get him altogether out of the scrape.[66]—This I mention—
because I know in England—someone or other will probably transfer his adventures to me—after what has been said already—I have a right to suspect every thing
and every body—so I state all this for your satisfaction—and that you may be able
to contradict any such report.—Mr. Hobhouse & Trevannion—and indeed everybody—Italians & English—then at Milan—can corroborate this if necessary.—It
occurred several days before Mr. H & myself left it.———So much for this.———
When we reach Venice I shall write to you again—I had received your acknowledgement of the journal &c. & the trinkets by Scrope—of which I delight to hear
the reception.———In health I am pretty well—except that the confounded Lombardy rains of this season (the autumn) have given me a flying rheumatism—
which is troublesome at times—and makes me feel ancient.—I am also growing
grey & *giddy*—and cannot help thinking my head will decay;—I wish my memory
would—at least my remembrance—except a parenthesis for *ou* [*sic*]—my dearest
Augusta.—Ada—by the way Ada's name (which I found in our pedigree under
King John's reign) is the same with that of the Sister of Charlemagne—as I read the
other day in a book treating of the Rhine.

ever my own—thy own

[65] See Virgil, *Georgics*, ii. 160: '*Fluctibus and fremitu assurgens, Benace, marino*': translated by James Rhoades
as 'with billowing uproar surging like the main' (Benacus being the Roman name for Lake Garda).
[66] The foolish Polidori, whom Byron had parted from in Switzerland, had managed to get himself
into an argument with some Austrian officers at La Scala opera house. Things got out of hand and
the authorities instructed him to leave the city.

P. S.—I forgot to tell you that my dog (Mutz by name & Swiss by nation) shuts a door when he is told—there—that's more than Tip can do.—Remember me to the childer—*and to Georgiana—who I suppose is grown a prodigious penwoman.—I hope she likes her seals and all her share of Mont Blanc.—I have had so much of mountains that I am not yet reconciled to the plains—but they improve. Verona seems a fine city.*

P. S. Novr. 7th.—I have been over Verona.—The Amphitheatre is superb—& in high preservation. Of the truth *of the story of Juliet they seem very tenacious giving the date (1303) and shewing a tomb.—It is an open granite sarcophagus in a most desolate convent garden—which looks quite wild & withered—and once was a Cimetery since ruined—I brought away four small pieces of it for you & the babes (at least the female part of them) and for Ada & her mother if she will accept it from you. I thought the situation more appropriate to the history than if it had been less blighted.—This struck me more than all the antiquities—more even than the Amphitheatre.—*

7
VENICE AND ROME

November 1816–June 1818

'Thank God I am here!' Ruskin wrote on his second visit to Venice, in 1841: 'It is the Paradise of Cities.' Byron's reaction was similarly instinctive. 'There is a monotony to many people in it's Canals & the comparative silence of it's streets', he wrote in September 1818:

[but] to me who have always been always passionate for Venice—and delight in the dialect & naivete of the people—and the romance of it's old history & institutions & appearance all it's disadvantages are more than compensated by the sight of a single Gondola—The view of the Rialto—of the piazza—& the Chaunt of Tasso (though less frequent than of old) are to me worth all the cities on earth—save Rome & Athens. (LJ vi. 66)

From being the greenest island of his imagination Venice became something far more significant: perhaps the one place on earth where he felt completely (if temporarily) at home, spending 38 months there, on and off, from November 1816 to December 1819. He arrived still itinerant and at a loss, however magnificent an experience the Alps had been. He found a city whose faded glory, theatrical setting, fertile mix of classes, moral tolerance, and mysterious atmosphere combined to unleash in his poetry something that had been in his letters all his life: a comic vision of humanity, sinning, but also sinned against by existence.

Immediately upon his arrival, for example, he fell genuinely in love with a married and middle-class Venetian, Marianna Segati—the polar opposite of 'that virtuous monster Miss Milbanke'. 'You can have no idea of my thorough wretchedness', he wrote in the same letter to Augusta in December 1816, 'from the day of my parting from you till nearly a month ago . . . at present I am better—thank Heaven above—& woman beneath' (LJ v. 141). For two years Segati was in ascendancy over him, though she was eventually supplanted by a baker's wife from the Brenta, Margarita Cogni, in early 1818.

'I have not done a stitch of poetry since I left Switzerland', he told Murray in January 1817 (LJ v. 157); but he still had plenty of unfinished business from the Alpine summer. The third canto of Childe Harold appeared in November 1816, The Prisoner of Chillon and Other Poems was published in December, and Byron completed a first (unsatisfactory) draft of Manfred in the New Year. ('I have no great opinion of this piece of phantasy', he confessed; 'but I have rendered it quite impossible for the stage—for which my intercourse with D[rury] L[ane] had given me the greatest contempt' (LJ v. 170). The dramatic poem would be repaired in May.) He still spoke of returning to England in the spring, but in fact on 17 April he left Venice for Rome, via Ferrara, Bologna, and Florence, where he found Hobhouse, ever the eager guide. 'I was delighted with Rome', he told Murray on 4 June, soon after his return, '& was on horseback all round it many hours daily besides in it the rest of my time—bothering over its marvels' (LJ v. 233). (While in Rome he sat for a bust to the Danish sculptor Bertel Thorvaldsen, on one condition: 'I won't have my head garnished like a Xmas pie with Holly—or a Cod's head and Fennel—or whatever the damned weed is they strew round it', he told Hobhouse; 'I wonder you should want me to be such a mountebank'

(LJ v. 243).) 'You are out about the fourth Canto [of Childe Harold]', he told Murray on 17 June: 'I have not done—nor designed a line of continuation to that poem' (LJ v. 240). Ten days later he started a fourth canto all the same, a complex mediation on Roman and Renaissance Italy, eventually festooned with accompanying historical notes swotted up by Hobhouse. Six weeks later it was done.

Childe Harold IV famously started in Venice—'I stood in Venice, on the Bridge of Sighs; | A palace and prison on each hand'—but quickly left it for a poetic tour of Renaissance Italy. By contrast, it was a piece of social gossip heard at a dinner party that brought to fruition what he had said to Major Gordon in June 1816, in response to his gift of Casti's Novelle galanti: 'I long to go to Venice to see the manners so admirably described.' One such custom was the cavalier servente, or a married woman's semi-official lover-cum-surrogate husband: an institution impossible to imagine in Protestant England. The story Byron heard involved a husband long since given up for lost returning home to find his wife firmly established with such a person. The sublime shaggy dog story in ottava rima, Beppo, was the result, once Byron had seen in a ponderously obscure mock epic by John Hookham Frere what English could do with and learn from the ancient Italian measure.

The return to Venice from Rome ended all ideas of returning to England—at least for a while. 'I tell you very sincerely', he wrote to Douglas Kinnaird on 30 May 1817, 'that if I could or can expatriate myself altogether I would and will' (LJ v. 231). In June that year he did what all Venetian aristocrats did: leased a villa at La Mira, on the Brenta River, to escape the heat. The Carnival became a part of his annual ritual, as did the parties at the Ridotto, and the conversazioni at the houses of grandes dames like the Countess Albrizzi. The arrival of Beppo also signalled another prodigious shift, away from the 'Romantic' world of Childe Harold, and towards something just as innovatory. 'With regard to poetry in general', he wrote to Murray on 15 September,

I am convinced the more I think of it—that he [Thomas Moore] and all of us—Scott—Southey—Wordsworth—Moore—Campbell—I—are all in the wrong—one as much as another—that we are upon a wrong revolutionary poetical system—or systems—not worth a damn in itself—& from which none but Rogers and Crabbe are free—and that the present & next generations will finally be of this opinion. (LJ v. 265)

He was wrong about Romanticism, but his feelings in this regard sent him further out in exploration of his talent, and the poetry and drama that he wrote from 1817 onward—when he transited from the world of Childe Harold towards that of Don Juan—mark a new literary attitude, as well as a miraculous convergence of the poet and the letter-writer.

On 10 December 1817 he heard the news he had awaited since his majority, eight years before: Newstead was finally sold, poignantly to an old Harrow schoolfellow, Thomas Wildman—whose fortune came from a Jamaican sugar plantation. His financial misery was over. On 12 January that year Claire Clairmont gave birth to a girl, Allegra, whom Byron *had brought out to Venice in May 1818, when he also took a three-year lease on the Palazzo Mocenigo, on the Grand Canal. 'I must love something in my old age', he wrote, '& probably circumstances will render this poor little creature a greater (& perhaps my only) comfort than any offspring from that misguided & artificial woman—who bears & disgraces my name' (LJ v. 228). Two women who had supported him when few others would—Madame de Staël and Lady Melbourne—died, on 14 July 1817 and 6 April 1818, respectively. Byron had not written to the latter since the Separation. 'The time is past', he wrote, 'in which I could feel for the dead—or I should feel for the death of Lady Melbourne the best & kindest & ablest female I ever knew—young or old' (LJ vi. 34).*

For later writers Venice would often figure as a place of morbidity. For Byron it was a place of life, coarse and refined. 'The Segati and I have been off these two months—or rather three', he wrote to Hobhouse on 19 May 1818; 'I have a world of other harlotry—besides an offer of the daughter of the Arlechino [Harlequin] of St. Luke's theatre—so that my hands are full——whatever my Seminal vessels may be' (LJ vi. 40). Two months previously he had briefly been introduced to a young countess from provincial Ravenna named Teresa Guiccioli. In time she would save him from Venice.

[To John Murray]

Venice Novr. 25th. 1816

Dear Sir

It is some months since I have heard from or of you—I think—*not* since I left Diodati.—From Milan I wrote once or twice;—but have been here some little time—and intend to pass the winter without removing.—I was much pleased with the Lago di Garda & with Verona—particularly the amphitheatre—and a sarcophagus in a Convent garden—which they show as Juliet's—they insist on the *truth* of her history.—Since my arrival at Venice—the Lady of the Austrian Governor told me that between Verona & Vicenza there are still ruins of the Castle of the *Montecchi*—and a chapel once appertaining to the Capulets— Romeo seems to have been of *Vicenza* by the tradition—but I was a good deal surprized to find so firm a faith in Bandello's novel[1]—which seems really to have been founded on a fact.——Venice pleases me as much as I expected—and I expected much—it is one of those places which I know before I see them—and has always haunted me the most—after the East.——I like the gloomy gaiety of their gondolas—and the silence of their canals—I do not even dislike the evident

---

[1] *Romeo and Juliet* (with its lovers' rival families, the Montagues and the Capulets) is based on an Italian narrative by Luigi da Porto (1530) retold by Matteo Bandello in 1554.

decay of the city—though I regret the singularity of it's vanished costume—
however there is much left still;—the Carnival too is coming.——St. Mark's—and
indeed Venice—is most alive at night—the theatres are not open till *nine*—and
the society is proportionably late   all this is to my taste—but most of your
countrymen miss & regret the rattle of hackney coaches—without which they
can't sleep.——I have got remarkably good apartments in a private house—I see
something of the inhabitants (having had a good many letters to some of them)
I have got my gondola—I read a little—& luckily could speak Italian (more
fluently though than accurately) long ago;—I am studying out of curiosity the
Venetian dialect—which is very naive—soft & peculiar—though not at all classical—I go out frequently—and am in very good contentment.——The *Helen* of
Canova—(a bust which is in the house of M[adam]e the Countess d'Albrizzi whom
I know) is without exception to my mind the most perfectly beautiful of human
conceptions—and far beyond my ideas of human execution.—

In this beloved marble view
   Above the works & thoughts of Man—
What Nature *could*—but *would not* do—
   And Beauty and Canova *can*!
Beyond Imagination's power—
   Beyond the Bard's defeated art,
With immortality her dower—
   Behold the *Helen* of the *heart*![2]

Talking of the 'heart' reminds me that I have fallen in love—which except falling
into the Canal—(and that would be useless as I swim) is the best (or worst) thing
I could do.——I am therefore in love—fathomless love—but lest you should
make some splendid mistake—& envy me the possession of some of those
Princesses or Countesses with whose affections your English voyagers are apt to
invest themselves—I beg leave to tell you—that my Goddess is only the wife of a
'Merchant of Venice'—but then she is pretty as an Antelope,—is but two &
twenty years old—has the large black Oriental eyes—with the Italian
countenance—and dark glossy hair of the curl & colour of Lady Jersey's—
then she has the voice of a lute—and the song of a Seraph (though not quite
so sacred), besides a long postscript of graces—virtues and accomplishments—

---

[2] The bust of Helen of Troy by Italian neoclassical sculptor Antonio Canova (1757–1822) is still at
the Palazzo Albrizzi in Venice.

enough to furnish out a new Chapter for Solomon's song.[3]—But her great merit is finding out mine—there is nothing so amiable as discernment.—Our little arrangement is completed—the usual oaths having been taken—and everything fulfilled according to the 'understood relations' of such liaisons. The general race of women appear to be handsome—but in Italy as on almost all the Continent—the highest orders are by no means a well looking generation— and indeed reckoned by their countrymen very much otherwise.—Some are exceptions but most of them as ugly as Virtue herself.—If you write—address to me *here Poste Restante*—as I shall probably stay the winter over.—I never see a newspaper & know nothing of England—except in a letter now & then from my Sister.—Of the M.S. sent you I know nothing except that you have received it— & are to publish it &c. &c. but when—where—& how—you leave me to guess—. But it don't much matter.—I suppose you have a world of works passing through your process for next year—when does Moore's poem appear?—I sent a letter for him addressed to your care the other day.—So—Mr. *Frere* is married[4]—and you tell me in a former letter that he had 'nearly forgotten that he was so—'—he is fortunate.——

yrs ever & very truly
B

[To Augusta Leigh]

Venice. Decr. 19th. 1816

My dearest Augusta

I wrote to you a few days ago.—Your letter of the 1st. is arrived—and you have 'a *hope*' for me—it seems—what 'hope'—child?—my dearest Sis. I remember a methodist preacher who on perceiving a profane grin on the faces of part of his congregation—exclaimed 'no *hopes* for *them* as *laughs*'[5] and thus it is—with us— we laugh too much for hopes—and so even let them go—I am sick of sorrow—

---

[3] The Song of Solomon or Song of Songs is a unique book of the Old Testament (inserted between Ecclesiastes and Isaiah) in that it comprises a sexually explicit dialogue, by biblical standards, between two lovers.

[4] John Hookham Frere (1769–1846) was a minor poet and translator. His greatest claim to literary fame is his mock-epic Arthurian poem *Prospectus and Specimen of an Intended National Work, by William and Robert Whistlecraft* (or 'Whistlecraft', for short), which Byron came to know of (either through Murray or visitors to Venice) around this time and which provided an English model for *Beppo* and thence *Don Juan*.

[5] In a note to *Hints from Horace*, 380 (*CPW* i. 437) Byron identifies this Methodist as one John Stickles, whom he heard preach at Cambridge. Augusta's language suggests Lady Byron had been at her again.

& must even content myself as well as I can—so here goes—I won't be woeful again if I can help it.—My letter to my moral Clytemnestra[6] required no answer—& I would rather have none—I was wretched enough when I wrote it—& had been so for many a long day & month—at present I am less so—for reasons explained in my late letter (a few days ago) and as I never pretend to *be* what I am not you may tell her if you please that I am recovering—and the reason also if you like it.—I do not agree with you about Ada—there was *equivocation* in the answer—and it shall be settled one way or the other—I wrote to Hanson to take proper steps to prevent such a removal of my daughter—and even the probability of it—you do not know the woman so well as I do—or you would perceive in her *very negative answer*—that she *does intend* to take Ada with her—if she should go abroad.——I have heard of Murray's squabble with one of his brethren—who is an impudent impostor—and should be trounced.——You do not say whether the *true po[em]'s* are out—I hope you like them.—You are right in saying that I like Venice—it is very much what you would imagine it—but I have no time just now for description;—the Carnival is to begin in a week—and with it the mummery of masking.——I have not been out a great deal—but quite as much as I like—I am going out this evening—in my *cloak & Gondola*—there are two nice Mrs. Radcliffe words for you[7]—and then there is the place of St Mark—and conversaziones—and various fooleries—besides many *nau[ghty]*. indeed every body is *nau.* so much so that a lady with only *one lover* is not reckoned to have overstepped the modesty of marriage—that being a regular thing;—some have two—three—and so on to twenty beyond which they don't account—but they generally begin by one.—— The husbands of course belong to any body's wives—but their own.——My present beloved—is aged two & twenty—with remarkably fine black eyes—and very regular & pretty features—figure light & pretty—hair dark—a mighty good singer—as they all are—she is married (of course) & has one child—a girl.—Her temper very good—(as you know it had need to be) and lively—she is a Venetian by birth—& was never further from Venice than Milan in her days—her lord is about five years older than me—an exceeding good kind of a man.—That amatory appendage called by us a lover—is here denominated variously—sometimes an 'Amoroso' (which is the same thing) and sometimes a Cavaliero servente—which I need not tell you—is a serving Cavalier.—I told my fair one—at setting out—that as to the love and the Cavaliership—I was quite of accord—*but as to the servitude*—it would not suit me at all—so I begged to hear no

---

[6] Clytemnestra slew her husband, the Greek king Agamemnon, in a bath after his return from the Trojan War. Byron uses this nickname for his ex-wife frequently in letters hereafter.
[7] Ann Radcliffe's Gothic novel *The Mysteries of Udolpho* (1794) is partly set in Venice.

more about it.—You may easily suppose I should not at all shine in the ceremonious department—so little so—that instead of handing the Lady as in duty bound into the Gondola—I as nearly as possible conveyed her into the Canal—and this at midnight—to be sure it was as dark as pitch—but if you could have seen the gravity with which I was committing her to the waves—thinking all the time of something or other not to the purpose;—I always forget that the streets are canals—and was going to walk her over the water—if the servants & the Gondoliers had not awakened me.——So much for love & all that.——The music here is famous—and there will be a whole tribe of singers & dancers during the Carnival—besides the usual theatres.—The Society here is something like our own—except that the women sit in a semicircle at one end of the room—& the men stand at the other.—I pass my mornings at the Armenian convent studying Armenian. My evenings here & there—tonight I am going to the Countess Albrizzi'-s—one of the noblesse—I have also been at the Governor's—who is an Austrian—& whose wife the Countess Goetz appeared to me in the little I have seen of her a very amiable & pleasing woman—with remarkably good manners—as many of the German women have.——There are no English here—except birds of passage—who stay a day & then go on to Florence—or Rome.—I mean to remain here till Spring.—When you write address *directly* here—as in your present letter.—

ever dearest yrs.

B

[To Thomas Moore]

Venice, December 24th, 1816

I have taken a fit of writing to you, which portends postage—once from Verona—once from Venice, and again from Venice—*thrice* that is. For this you may thank yourself, for I heard that you complained of my silence—so, here goes for garrulity.

I trust that you received my other twain of letters. My 'way of life' (or 'May of life,' which is it, according to the commentators?)[8]—my 'way of life' is fallen into great regularity. In the mornings I go over in my gondola to babble Armenian with the friars of the convent of St. Lazarus, and to help one of them in correcting the English of an English and Armenian grammar which he is publishing. In the evenings I do one of many nothings—either at the theatres, or some of the conversaziones, which are like our routs, or rather worse, for the women sit in

---

[8] See *Macbeth*, V. iii. 24–5: 'My way of life | Is fall'n into the sere, the yellow leaf.' It was Samuel Johnson, in his edition of Shakespeare, who suggested that 'way' was a typesetter's error for 'May'.

a semicircle by the lady of the mansion, and the men stand about the room. To be sure, there is one improvement upon ours—instead of lemonade with their ices, they hand about stiff *rum-punch*—punch, by my palate; and this they think *English*. I would not disabuse them of so agreeable an error,—'no, not for Venice'.[9]

Last night I was at the Count Governor's, which, of course, comprises the best society, and is very much like other gregarious meetings in every country,—as in ours,—except that, instead of the Bishop of Winchester, you have the Patriarch of Venice, and a motley crew of Austrians, Germans, noble Venetians, foreigners and, if you see a quiz, you may be sure he is a Consul. Oh, by the way, I forgot, when I wrote from Verona, to tell you that at Milan I met with a countryman of yours—a Colonel [Fitzgerald], a very excellent, good-natured fellow, who knows and shows all about Milan, and is, as it were, a native there. He is particularly civil to strangers, and this is his history,—at least, an episode of it.

Six-and-twenty years ago, Col. [Fitzgerald], then an ensign, being in Italy, fell in love with the Marchesa [Castiglione], and she with him. The lady must be, at least, twenty years his senior. The war broke out; he returned to England, to serve—not his country, for that's Ireland—but England, which is a different thing; and *she*—heaven knows what she did. In the year 1814, the first annunciation of the Definitive Treaty of Peace (and tyranny) was developed to the astonished Milanese by the arrival of Col. [Fitzgerald], who, flinging himself full length at the feet of Mad. [Castiglione], murmured forth, in half-forgotten Irish Italian, eternal vows of indelible constancy. The lady screamed, and exclaimed, 'Who are you?' The Colonel cried, 'What! don't you know me? I am so and so,' &c., &c., &c.; till, at length, the Marchesa, mounting from reminiscence to reminiscence through the lovers of the intermediate twenty-five years, arrived at last at the recollection of her *povero* [pitiful] sub-lieutenant. She then said, 'Was there ever such virtue?' (that was her very word) and, being now a widow, gave him apartments in her palace, reinstated him in all the rights of wrong, and held him up to the admiring world as a miracle of incontinent fidelity, and the unshaken Abdiel of absence.[10]

Methinks this is as pretty a moral tale as any of Marmontel's.[11] Here is another. The same lady, several years ago, made an escapade with a Swede, Count Fersen (the same whom the Stockholm mob quartered and lapidated not very long since),[12] and they arrived at an Osteria [hotel] on the road to Rome or

---

[9] See *The Merchant of Venice*, IV. i. 227.

[10] The seraph Abdiel figures as the essence of zealous faithfulness in Milton's *Paradise Lost*.

[11] Jean-François Marmontel (1723–99), best known for his *Contes moraux*, published in the 1750s.

[12] Axel, Count Fersen (1750–1810), had provided the carriage for the futile 'flight to Varennes' of 1791, when Louis XVI attempted to escape the French Revolution. He was blamed for the mysterious death of Prince Carl August of Sweden in June 1810, and lynched in a riot in Stockholm.

thereabouts. It was a summer evening, and, while they were at supper, they were suddenly regaled by a symphony of fiddles in an adjacent apartment, so prettily played, that, wishing to hear them more distinctly, the Count rose, and going into the musical society, said, 'Gentlemen, I am sure that, as a company of gallant cavaliers, you will be delighted to show your skill to a lady, who feels anxious,' &c., &c. The men of harmony were all acquiescence—every instrument was tuned and toned, and, striking up one of their most ambrosial airs, the whole band followed the Count to the lady's apartment. At their head was the first fiddler, who, bowing and fiddling at the same moment, headed his troop and advanced up the room. Death and discord!—it was the Marquis himself, who was on a serenading party in the country, while his spouse had run away from town. The rest may be imagined—but, first of all, the lady tried to persuade him that she was there on purpose to meet him, and had chosen this method for an harmonic surprise. So much for this gossip, which amused me when I heard it, and I send it to you in the hope it may have the like effect. Now we'll return to Venice.

The day after to-morrow (to-morrow being Christmas-day) the Carnival begins. I dine with the Countess Albrizzi and a party, and go to the opera. On that day the Phenix, (not the Insurance Office, but) the theatre of that name, opens:[13] I have got me a box there for the season, for two reasons, one of which is, that the music is remarkably good. The Contessa Albrizzi, of whom I have made mention, is the De Stael of Venice; not young, but a very learned, unaffected, good-natured woman; very polite to strangers, and, I believe, not at all dissolute, as most of the women are. She has written very well on the works of Canova, and also a volume of Characters, besides other printed matter. She is of Corfu, but married a dead Venetian—that is, dead since he married.

My flame (my 'Donna' whom I spoke of in my former epistle, my Marianna) is still my Marianna, and I her—what she pleases. She is by far the prettiest woman I have seen here, and the most loveable I have met with any where—as well as one of the most singular. I believe I told you the rise and progress of our *liaison* in my former letter. Lest that should not have reached you, I will merely repeat, that she is a Venetian, two-and-twenty years old, married to a merchant well to do in the world, and that she has great black oriental eyes, and all the qualities which her eyes promise. Whether being in love with her has steeled me or not, I do not know; but I have not seen many other women who seem pretty. The nobility, in particular, are a sad-looking race—the gentry rather better. And now, what art *thou* doing?

---

[13] La Fenice, an 18th-century theatre, destroyed by fire and rebuilt on many occasions. There is every likelihood Byron saw Mozart's *Don Giovanni* there during his stay—with implications for his own *Don Juan*. The Phoenix insurance company was an early 18th-century firm, still trading in Byron's time.

What are you doing now,
  Oh Thomas Moore?
What are you doing now,
  Oh Thomas Moore?
Sighing or suing now,
Rhyming or wooing now,
Billing or cooing now,
  Which, Thomas Moore?

Are you not near the Luddites? By the Lord! if there's a row, but I'll be among ye!
How go on the weavers—the breakers of frames—the Lutherans of politics—
the reformers?

As the Liberty lads o'er the sea
Bought their freedom, and cheaply, with blood,
    So we, boys, we
  Will *die* fighting, or *live* free,
And down with all kings but King Ludd!

When the web that we weave is complete,
And the shuttle exchanged for the sword,
  We will fling the winding-sheet
  O'er the despot at our feet,
And dye it deep in the gore he has pour'd.

Though black as his heart its hue,
Since his veins are corrupted to mud,
    Yet this is the dew
  Which the tree shall renew
Of Liberty, planted by Ludd!

There's an amiable *chanson* for you—all impromptu. I have written it principally
to shock your neighbour,[14] who is all clergy and loyalty—mirth and innocence—
milk and water.

But the Carnival's coming,
  Oh Thomas Moore,
The Carnival's coming,
  Oh Thomas Moore,

---

[14] Byron's old literary mentor, the Revd Francis Hodgson, lived near Moore in Derbyshire.

Masking and humming,
Fifing and drumming,
Guitarring and strumming,
Oh Thomas Moore.

The other night I saw a new play,—and the author. The subject was the sacrifice of Isaac. The play succeeded, and they called for the author—according to continental custom—and he presented himself, a noble Venetian, Mali—or Malapiero, by name. Mala was his name, and *pessima* [dreadful] his production,—at least, I thought so; and I ought to know, having read more or less of five hundred Drury Lane offerings, during my coadjutorship with the sub- and-super Committee.

When does your Poem of Poems come out? I hear that the *E[dinburgh] R[eview]* has cut up Coleridge's Christabel, and declared against me for praising it. I praised it, firstly, because I thought well of it; secondly, because Coleridge was in great distress, and after doing what little I could for him in essentials, I thought that the public avowal of my good opinion might help him further, at least with the booksellers. I am very sorry that J[effrey] has attacked him, because, poor fellow, it will hurt him in mind and pocket. As for me, he's welcome—I shall never think less of J for any thing he may say against me or mine in future.

I suppose Murray has sent you, or will send (for I do not know whether they are out or no) the poem, or poesies, of mine, of last summer. By the mass! They're sublime—'Ganion Coheriza'—gainsay who dares![15] Pray, let me hear from you, and of you, and, at least, let me know that you have received these three letters. Direct right *here, poste restante.*

Ever and ever, &c.

P. S.—I heard the other day of a pretty trick of a bookseller, who has published some d[amne]d nonsense, swearing the bastards to me, and saying he gave me five hundred guineas for them. He lies—I never wrote such stuff, never saw the poems, nor the publisher of them, in my life, nor had any communication, directly or indirectly, with the fellow. Pray say as much for me, if need be. I have written to Murray, to make him contradict the imposter.

---

[15] 'Dhandeon co heirogha', the Gaelic motto of the Macdonald clan, adopted by the British Special Air Service regiment as 'Who dares wins'. Byron found this version in Walter Scott's *Waverley* (1814), chapter 44.

[To Douglas Kinnaird]

Venice—January 20th. 1817

My dear Kinnaird

Your letter and its contents (viz. the circulars & indication for £500[16]) are safely arrived—thanks——I have been up all night at the Opera—& at the Ridotto & it's Masquerade[17]—and the devil knows what—so that my head aches a little—but to business.——My affairs ought to be in a small compass—if Newstead were sold they would be settled without difficulty—and if Newstead & Rochdale both were sold—I should think with ease—but till one or both of these are disposed of—they are in a very unpleasant situation.—It is for this reason I so much urge a sale—even at almost any price.—With regard to Hanson—I know not how to act—& I know not what to think—except that I think he wishes me well—it is certainly not his fault that Claughton could not fulfil the conditions of sale.——Mr. Riley has reason—but he must really wait till something can be done about the property—if he likes he may proceed against *it*,[18]—but as to the produce of my *brain*—my M.S.—my Night mare is my own personalty [*sic*]—& by the Lord as I have earned the sum—so will I expend it upon my own proper pleasances—voyagings & what not—so that I request that you will *not* disburse a ducat save to *me* the *owner*.—You do not say a word about the publication itself—from which I infer that it has failed—if so—you may tell me at once—on Murray's account rather than on mine—for I am not to be perturbed by such matters at this time of day—as the fall of the thermometer of a poetical reputation—but I should be sorry for M who is a very good fellow.—— However—as with one thing or another—he—Murray must have cleared on the whole account—dating from the commencement—I feel less anxious for him than I otherwise should.—Your quotation from Shakespeare—humph—I believe that it is applied by Othello to his *wife*—who by the way was *innocent*— the Moor made a mistake—& so have you.——My desire that Murray should pay in the agreement will not appear singular—when you recollect that the time

---

[16] A 'circular note' which the traveller named in it could present to foreign bankers from their bank at home, was normally accompanied by a 'letter of indication' vouching for the traveller's bona fides.

[17] The Ridotto (from *ridurre*: to close off) was the premier gambling room of Venice, patronized by the rich and the celebrated: ''tis a hall', Byron would write in *Beppo* (458–9), 'Where people dance, and sup, and dance again'.

[18] Mr Riley is clearly one of Byron's many creditors, from the professional rather than the personal sector, to judge by Byron's attitude. (Gentlemen repaid 'debts of honour', incurred amongst themselves or through gambling, before mere tradesmen's bills.)

has elapsed within a few days when three quarters of the whole were to have been disbursed by him.——Since my departure from England I have not spent (in nine months) within some hundreds of two thousand pounds so that neither my pleasures nor my perils—when you consider the ground I have gone over & that I had a physician (now gone thank heaven) to fee & feed out of it—a very extravagant silly gentleman he was into the bargain.—By the way—I should wish to know if Hanson has been able to collect *any rent* at all (but little it can be in these times) from N[*ewstead*]—if he has & there be any balance—it may also come to me in the shape of circulars—the time is also approaching when— there will be something due from that magnificent father *at* law of mine—Sir R[alph] N[oel]—from whom I expect punctuality—& am not disposed to remit him any of his remaining duties—let him keep to his time even in trifles.[19]—— You tell me Shelley's wife has drowned herself—the devil she has—do you mean his *wife*—or his Mistress?—Mary Godwin?—I hope not the last[20]—I am very sorry to hear of anything which can plague poor Shelley—besides I feel uneasy about another of his *menage* [household].—You know—& I believe saw once that odd-headed girl—who introduced herself to me shortly before I left England—but you do not know—that I found her with Shelley & her sister at Geneva—I never loved nor pretended to love her—but a man is a man—& if a girl of eighteen comes prancing to you at all hours—there is but one way—the suite of all this is that she was with *child*—& returned to England to assist in peopling that desolate island.—Whether this impregnation took place before I left England or since—I do not know—the (carnal) connection had com- menced previously to my setting out—but by or about this time she has—or is about to produce.—The next question is is the brat *mine?*—I have reason to think so—for I know as much as one can know such a thing—that she had *not lived* with S during the time of our acquaintance—& that she had a good deal of that same with me.—This comes of 'putting it about' (as Jackson calls it) & be damned to it—and thus people come into the world.——So you wish me to come to England—why? for what?—my affairs—I wish they could be settled without—I repeat that your country is no country for me.—I have neither ambition nor taste for your politics—and there is nothing else among you which may not be had better elsewhere.—Besides—Caroline Lamb—& Lady

---

[19] As his father-in-law had settled property on him as part of the marriage settlement, Byron was owed rent on those properties, despite the Separation.
[20] Shelley's first wife and mother of two children by him, Harriet Westbrook, committed suicide by drowning in the Serpentine in Hyde Park. Her body was found on 10 December.

B—my 'Lucy' & my 'Polly'[21] have destroyed my *moral* existence amongst you—&
I am rather sick of being the theme of their mutual inventions—in ten years
I could unteach myself even to your language—& am very sure that—but I have
no time nor space, for further tirade at present—

ever yrs. very truly
B

P. S.—Pray write soon.——
Venice & I agree very well—in the mornings I study Armenian—& in the evenings I go out
sometimes—& indulge in coition always.——I mentioned my liaison to you in a former
letter—it still continues—& probably will—It has however kept me here instead of gad-
abouting the country.—The Carnival is begun—but the zenith of the masking will not arrive
for some weeks.—There is a famous Opera—& several theatres—Catalani[22] is to be here on
the 20th—Society is like other foreign society—I see as much of it as I wish—& might see
more if I liked it.—

ever yrs. most truly
B

P. S.—My respects to Madame[23]—pray answer my letters—& mention anything or
everything except my—family—I will say—for the other word makes me unwell.——

[To Thomas Moore]

Venice, January 28th, 1817

Your letter of the 8th is before me. The remedy for your plethora is simple—
abstinence. I was obliged to have recourse to the like some years ago, I mean in
point of *diet*, and, with the exception of some convivial weeks and days, (it might

---

[21] Lucy Lockit and Polly Peachum are rivals in love for Macheath, the criminal hero of *The Beggar's Opera* (1728), by John Gay.
[22] For Catalani see letter of 27 February 1808.
[23] Douglas Kinnaird's wife, née Keppel, herself a singer, returned to the stage under her maiden name.

be months, now and then), have kept to Pythagoras ever since. For all this, let me hear that you are better. You must not *indulge* in 'filthy beer,' nor in porter, nor eat *suppers*—the last are the devil to those who swallow dinner. *

I am truly sorry to hear of your father's misfortune—cruel at any time, but doubly cruel in advanced life.[24] However, you will, at least, have the satisfaction of doing your part by him, and, depend upon it, it will not be in vain. Fortune, to be sure, is a female, but not such a b * * as the rest (always excepting your wife and my sister from such sweeping terms); for she generally has some justice in the long run. I have no spite against her, though between her and Nemesis I have had some sore gauntlets to run—but then I have done my best to deserve no better. But to *you*, she is a good deal in arrear, and she will come round—mind if she don't: you have the vigour of life, of independence, of talent, spirit, and character all with you. What you can do for yourself, you have done and will do; and surely there are some others in the world who would not be sorry to be of use, if you would allow them to be useful, or at least attempt it.

I think of being in England in the spring. If there is a row, by the sceptre of King Ludd, but I'll be one; and if there is none, and only a continuance of 'this meek, piping time of peace,'[25] I will take a cottage a hundred yards to the south of your abode, and become your neighbour; and we will compose such canticles, and hold such dialogues, as shall be the terror of the *Times* (including the newspaper of that name), and the wonder, and honour, and praise, of the Morning Chronicle and posterity.

I rejoice to hear of your forthcoming in February[26]—though I tremble for the 'magnificence,' which you attribute to the new Childe Harold. I am glad you like it; it is a fine indistinct piece of poetical desolation, and my favourite. I was half mad during the time of its composition, between metaphysics, mountains, lakes, love unextinguishable, thoughts unutterable, and the nightmare of my own delinquencies. I should, many a good day, have blown my brains out, but for the recollection that it would have given pleasure to my mother-in-law; and, even *then*, if I could have been certain to haunt her—but I won't dwell upon these trifling family matters.

Venice is in the *estro* [height] of her carnival, and I have been up these last two nights at the ridotto and the opera, and all that kind of thing. Now for an adventure. A few days ago a gondolier brought me a billet without a

---

[24] Moore's father, John, had been dismissed from his post as master of the Royal Barracks (now the Collins Barracks) in Dublin.
[25] See *Richard III*, I. i. 24.
[26] Moore's Byronic *Lalla Rookh: An Oriental Romance* was published by Longman in 1817.

subscription, intimating a wish on the part of the writer to meet me either in gondola or at the island of San Lazaro, or at a third rendezvous, indicated in the note. 'I know the country's disposition well'—in Venice 'they do let Heaven see those tricks they dare not show,' &c. &c.;[27] so, for all response, I said that neither of the three places suited me; but that I would either be at home at ten at night *alone*, or at the ridotto at midnight, where the writer might meet me masked. At ten o'clock I was at home and alone (Marianna was gone with her husband to a conversazione), when the door of my apartment opened, and in walked a well-looking and (for an Italian) *bionda* [blonde] girl of about nineteen, who informed me that she was married to the brother of my *amorosa*, and wished to have some conversation with me. I made a decent reply, and we had some talk in Italian and Romaic (her mother being a Greek of Corfu), when lo! in a very few minutes, in marches, to my very great astonishment, Marianna S[egati], *in propria persona*, and after making polite courtesy to her sister-in-law and to me, without a single word seizes her said sister-in-law by the hair, and bestows upon her some sixteen slaps, which would have made your ear ache only to hear their echo. I need not describe the screaming which ensued. The luckless visitor took flight. I seized Marianna, who, after several vain efforts to get away in pursuit of the enemy, fairly went into fits in my arms; and, in spite of reasoning, eau de Cologne, vinegar, half a pint of water, and God knows what other waters beside, continued so till past midnight.

After damning my servants for letting people in without apprizing me, I found that Marianna in the morning had seen her sister-in-law's gondolier on the stairs, and, suspecting that his apparition boded her no good, had either returned of her own accord, or been followed by her maids or some other spy of her people to the conversazione, from whence she returned to perpetrate this piece of pugilism. I had seen fits before, and also some small scenery of the same genus in and out of our island: but this was not all. After about an hour, in comes—who? why, Signor S, her lord and husband, and finds me with his wife fainting upon the sofa, and all the apparatus of confusion, dishevelled hair, hats, handkerchiefs, salts, smelling-bottles—and the lady as pale as ashes without sense or motion. His first question was, 'What is all this?' The lady could not reply—so I did. I told him the explanation was the easiest thing in the world; but in the mean time it would be as well to recover his wife—at least, her senses. This came about in due time of suspiration and respiration.

You need not be alarmed—jealousy is not the order of the day in Venice, and daggers are out of fashion; while duels, on love matters, are unknown—at least,

---

[27] See *Othello*, III. iii. 205–7: 'I know our country disposition well. | In Venice they do let God see the pranks | They dare not show their husbands.'

with the husbands. But, for all this, it was an awkward affair; and though he must have known that I made love to Marianna, yet I believe he was not, till that evening, aware of the extent to which it had gone. It is very well known that almost all the married women have a lover; but it is usual to keep up the forms, as in other nations. I did not, therefore, know what the devil to say. I could not out with the truth, out of regard to her, and I did not choose to lie for my sake;— besides, the thing told itself. I thought the best way would be to let her explain it as she chose (a woman being never at a loss—the devil always sticks by them)— only determining to protect and carry her off, in case of any ferocity on the part of the Signor. I saw that he was quite calm. She went to bed, and next day—how they settled it, I know not, but settle it they did. Well—then I had to explain to Marianna about this never to be sufficiently confounded sister-in-law; which I did by swearing innocence, eternal constancy, &c. &c. * * * But the sister-in-law, very much discomposed with being treated in such wise, has (not having her own shame before her eyes) told the affair to half Venice, and the servants (who were summoned by the fight and the fainting) to the other half. But, here, nobody minds such trifles, except to be amused by them. I don't know whether you will be so, but I have scrawled a long letter out of these follies.

Believe me ever. &c.

[To Thomas Moore]

Venice, February 28th, 1817

You will, perhaps, complain as much of the frequency of my letters now, as you were wont to do of their rarity. I think this is the fourth within as many moons. I feel anxious to hear from you, even more than usual, because your last indicated that you were unwell. At present, I am on the invalid regimen myself. The Carnival—that is, the latter part of it—and sitting up late o'nights, had knocked me up a little. But it is over,—and it is now Lent, with all its abstinence and Sacred Music.

The mumming closed with a masked ball at the Fenice, where I went, as also to most of the ridottos, etc., etc.; and, though I did not dissipate much upon the whole, yet I find 'the sword wearing out the scabbard,' though I have but just turned the corner of twenty-nine.

So we'll go no more a roving
So late into the night,

Though the heart be still as loving,
And the moon be still as bright.[28]

For the sword outwears its sheath,
And the soul wears out the breast,
And the heart must pause to breathe,
And Love itself have rest.

Though the night was made for loving,
And the day returns too soon,
Yet we'll go no more a roving
By the light of the moon.

I have lately had some news of litter*atoor*, as I heard the editor of the Monthly pronounce it once upon a time. I hear that W[edderburn]. W[ebster]. has been publishing and responding to the attacks of the Quarterly, in the learned Perry's Chronicle. I read his poesies last autumn, and amongst them found an epitaph on his bull-dog, and another on *myself*.[29] But I beg to assure him (like the astrologer Partridge) that I am not only alive now but was alive also at the time he wrote it.[30] * * * * Hobhouse has (I hear, also) expectorated a letter against the Quarterly, addressed to me. I feel awkwardly situated between him and Gifford, both being my friends.

And this is your month of going to press—by the body of Diana! (a Venetian oath,) I feel as anxious—but not fearful for you—as if it were myself coming out in a work of humour, which would, you know be the antipodes of all my previous publications. I don't think you have any thing to dread but your own reputation. You must keep up to that. As you never showed me a line of your work, I do not even know your measure; but you must send me a copy by Murray forthwith, and then you shall hear what I think. I dare say you are in a pucker. Of all authors, you are the only really *modest* one I ever met with,—which would sound oddly enough to those who recollect your morals when you were young—that is, when you were *extremely* young—I don't mean to stigmatise you either with years or morality.

I believe I told you that the E[dinburgh] R[eview] had attacked me, in an article on Coleridge (I have not seen it)—'*Et tu*, Jeffrey?'—'there is nothing but

---

[28] This first stanza is adapted from the Scottish ballad, 'The Jolly Beggar', first caught in print in 1769: 'And we'll go no more a roving | Sae late into the night, | And we'll gang nae mair a roving, boys, | Let the moon shine ne'er sae bright.'

[29] Webster published *Waterloo and Other Poems* in 1816. It does indeed contain some 'Lines on a Dog Buried at Newstead Abbey' and some others 'On Lord B—n's Portrait' which anticipate the poet's death in a lugubriously silly fashion.

[30] See Jonathan Swift, 'A Vindication of Isaac Bickerstaffe' (1708), his satirical letter on a contemporary writer of almanacs.

roguery in villanous man.'[31] But I absolve him of all attacks, present and future; for I think he had already pushed his clemency in my behoof to the utmost, and I shall always think well of him. I only wonder he did not begin before, as my domestic destruction was a fine opening for all the world, of which all, who could, did well to avail themselves.

If I live ten years longer, you will see, however, that it is not over with me—I don't mean in literature, for that is nothing; and it may seem odd enough to say, I do not think it my vocation. But you will see that I will do something or other—the times and fortune permitting—that, 'like the cosmogony, or creation of the world, will puzzle the philosophers of all ages.'[32] But I doubt whether my constitution will hold out. I have, at intervals, exorcised it most devilishly.

I have not yet fixed a time of return, but I think of the spring. I shall have been away a year in April next. You never mention Rogers, nor Hodgson, your clerical neighbour, who has lately got a living near you. Has he also got a child yet?—his desideratum, when I saw him last. * * * * * * * *

Pray let me hear from you, at your time and leisure, believing me ever and truly and affectionately, &c.

[To Douglas Kinnaird]

Venice. March 31st. 1817

My dear Kinnaird/

I wrote to you a day or two ago to mention that Siri & Wilhelm had demurred a little because *I* should have had a letter of credit as well as the order of Messrs. M[orland] & R[ansom] on them the last of which they had received.—Perhaps you had better send me one for the £500—as well as the like for Torlonia at Rome—where you have sent the same order.—I will have marked down upon Siri's letter whatever sums may have been drawn for before I leave Venice.— I shall follow your advice & retain the circulars till the orders are drawn upon.——Your letter of ye 14th. is before me.—I have no poem nor thought of a poem called the *Gondola*—nor any similar subject.—I have written nothing but a sort of metaphysical poem which was sent to M[urray] the other day—not for publication—but to show to Mr. Gifford.—Tell him to show it to you,— I would not have it published unless G[iffor]d thought it good for anything—for

---

[31] 'Even you, Brutus?': Julius Caesar's last words, of astonishment at being betrayed by his friend and assassin (see *Julius Caesar*, III. i. 76). And see 1 *Henry IV*, II. iv. 124–5.

[32] See Goldsmith, *The Vicar of Wakefield* (1766), chapter 14.

myself I have really & truly no notion what it is good for.[33] I have nothing else—except a translation from a Spanish & Moorish ballad & an Italian translation or two—As to tragedy, I may try one day, but *never* for the *stage*—don't you see I have no luck there?—my two addresses were not liked—& my Committee-ship did but get me into scrapes—no—no—I shall not tempt the Fates that way—besides I should risk more than I could gain—I have no right to encroach on other men's ground—even if I could maintain my own.—You tell me that Maturin's second tragedy has failed[34]—is not this an additional warning to everybody as well as to me—however if the whim seized me I should not consider that nor anything else—but the fact is that success on the stage is not to me an object of ambition—& I am not sure that it would please me to triumph—although it would doubtless vex me to fail.—For these reasons I never will put it to the test.—Unless I could beat them all—it would be nothing—& who could do that? nor I nor any man—the Drama is complete already—there can be nothing like what has been.—You will say this applies to other poetry also—true—but the range is wider—& I look upon the path I struck out in C Harold as a new one—& therefore there can be no comparisons as yet good or bad—I have done—not much—but enough for me—& having just turned nine & twenty I seriously think of giving up altogether—unless Rome should madden me into a fourth Canto—which it may or may not.—I am sorry for Maturin—but as he had made himself considerable enough to have enemies—this was to be expected—he must not however be discouraged.—Make my remembrances acceptable to L[eigh] Hunt—& tell him I shall be very glad to hear from him.—I have had a fever.—Remember me to Scrope to Moore & everybody—your account of Mrs. K's success is very agreeable

ever & truly yrs. most affect.

B

P. S.—*The* Morning Chronicle *has been taken out of your letter I suppose in France—it is useless to send newspapers—they hardly ever arrive—at least the opposition ones.*

---

[33] This is *Manfred*, a first draft of which Byron completed in early February. Gifford thought the final act problematic, and Byron wrote a new one by early May (see letter of 9 May 1817).

[34] Maturin's *Bertram* had been a reasonable success (see letter of 16 May 1816). His follow-up, *Manuel*, failed utterly in March 1817 (see letter of 21 August 1817).

[To John Murray]

Rome, May 9th. 1817

My Dear Sir/

Address all answers to Venice for there I shall return in fifteen days—God willing.——I sent you from Florence the 'Lament of Tasso'—& from Rome the reformed third act of Manfred—both of which I trust will duly arrive.—The terms of these two—I mentioned in my last—& will repeat in this—it is three hundred for each—or six hundred guineas for the two—that is—if you like—& they are good for any thing.——At last one of the parcels is arrived—in the notes to C[hilde] H[arol]d there is a blunder of yours or mine—you talk of arrival at *St. Gingo* and immediately after add—'on the height is the Chateau of Clarens'—This is sad work—Clarens is on the *other* side of the lake—& it is quite impossible that I should have so bungled—look at the MS., and at any rate rectify this.—The 'Tales of my Landlord' I have read with great pleasure—& perfectly understand now why my Sister & aunt are so very positive in the very erroneous persuasion that they must have been written by me[35]—if you knew me as well as they do—you would have fallen perhaps into the same mistake;—some day or other I will explain to you *why* when I have time—at present it does not matter—but you must have thought this blunder of theirs very odd—& so did I—till I had read the book.—Croker's letter to you is a very great compliment—I shall return it to you in my next.——Southey's Wat Tyler is rather awkward[36]—but the Goddess Nemesis has done well—he is—I will not say what—but I wish he was something else—I hate all intolerance—but most the intolerance of Apostacy—& the wretched vehemence with which a miserable creature who has contradicted himself—lies to his own heart—& endeavours to establish his sincerity by proving himself a rascal—*not* for changing his opinions—but for persecuting those who are of less malleable matter—it is no disgrace to Mr. Southey to have written Wat Tyler—& afterwards to have written his birthday or Victory Odes (I speak only of their *politics*) but it is

[35] Two of Walter Scott's novels, *The Black Dwarf* and *Old Mortality* (both 1816), were given out to be tales told by the owner of the Wallace Inn in Scotland; the authorship was an open secret for some, a literary mystery for many.

[36] Robert Southey (1774–1843), colleague of Wordsworth and Coleridge, had been (like them) a Radical in his youth, but was appointed Poet Laureate in 1813, which position he used to upbraid writers on the left. A pirated version of his republican early play *Wat Tyler* was published in 1817, much to his embarrassment, and because it was seditious a judge refused it the protection of copyright.

something for which I have no words for this man to have endeavoured to bring to the stake (for such would he do) men who think as he thought—& for no reason but because they think so still, when he has found it convenient to think otherwise.—Opinions are made to be changed—or how is truth to be got at? we don't arrive at it by standing on one leg? or on the first day of our setting out— but though we may jostle one another on the way that is no reason why we should strike or trample—*elbowing's* enough.—I am all for moderation which profession of faith I beg leave to conclude by wishing Mr. Southey damned—not as a poet—but as a politician. There is a place in Michael Angelo's last judgment in the Sistine Chapel which would just suit him—and may the like await him in that of our Lord and (*not his*) Saviour Jesus Christ—Amen! I perceive you are publishing a *Life* of Raffael d'Urbino—it may perhaps interest you to hear that a set of German artists here allow their *hair* to grow & trim it into *his fashion*— thereby drinking the cummin of the disciples of the old philosopher,—if they would cut their hair & convert it into brushes & paint like him it would be more 'German to the matter.'[37]——I'll tell you a story.—The other day a man here— an English—mistaking the statues of Charlemagne and Constantine—which are *Equestrian* for those of Peter and Paul—asked another—*which* was Paul of these same horsemen?—to which the reply was, 'I thought Sir that St. Paul had never got on horseback since his *accident?*'[38]—I'll tell you another. Henry Fox writing to some one from Naples the other day after an illness—adds 'and I am so changed that my *oldest creditors* would hardly know me.'[39]——I am delighted with Rome—as I would be with a bandbox—that is it is a fine thing to see—finer than Greece—but I have not been here long enough to affect it as a residence— & I must go back to Lombardy—because I am wretched at being away from M[ariann]a.——I have been riding my saddle horses every day—and been to Albano—it's lakes—& to the top of the Alban mount—& to Frascati—Aricia— &c. &c.—with an &c. &c. &c. about the city & in the city—for all which—vide Guide-book.—As a *whole—ancient & modern*—it beats Greece—Constantin- ople—every thing—at least that I have ever seen.—But I can't describe because

---

[37] Richard Dupa's *Life of Raffaele* was published by Murray in 1816. Somehow Byron had learned of the 'Nazarene' group of German artists (an early version of the English Pre-Raphaelite Brotherhood), which had established itself in Rome in 1810, and which rejected neoclassicism in favour of medieval and early Renaissance art. In his *Natural History* (xx. 57) the 1st-century Roman Pliny the Elder had suggested that the students of the Augustan rhetorician Marcus Porcius Latro drank cumin tea to reproduce his pale complexion, supposedly the result of study.

[38] The Apostle Paul was miraculously converted to Christianity when temporarily blinded and thrown from his horse on the road to Damascus: see Acts 9. Equestrian statues of Charlemagne and Constantine are on the left and right, respectively, inside the entrance to St Peter's basilica in the Vatican.

[39] Henry Stephen Fox (1791–1846), Lord Holland's son, was lame and so something of a favourite of Byron's. He would visit the poet in Genoa in April 1823.

my first impressions are always strong and confused—& my Memory *selects* & reduces them to order—like distance in the landscape—& blends them better— although they may be less distinct—there must be a sense or two more than we have as mortals—which I suppose the Devil has—(or t'other) for where there is much to be grasped we are always at a loss—and yet feel that we ought to have a higher and more extended comprehension.——I have had a letter from Moore—who is in some alarm about his poem—I don't see why.—I have had another from my poor dear Augusta who is in a sad fuss about my late illness— do, pray, tell her—(the truth) that I am better than ever—& in importunate health—growing (if not grown) large & ruddy—& congratulated by impertinent persons on my robustious appearance—when I ought to be pale and interesting.— You tell me that George B[yron] has got a son—and Augusta says—a daughter—which is it?—it is no great matter—the father is a good man—an excellent officer—& has married a very nice little woman—who will bring him more babes than income—howbeit she had a handsome dowry—& is a very charming girl—but he may as well get a ship.——I have no thoughts of coming amongst you yet a while—so that I can fight off business—if I could but make a tolerable sale of Newstead—there would be no occasion for my return & I can assure you very sincerely—that I am much happier—(or at least have been so) out of your island than in it.——

Yours ever truly,
B

P. S.—*There are few English here—but several of my acquaintance—amongst others, the Marquis of Lansdowne with whom I dine tomorrow—I met the Jerseys on the road at Foligno—all well—Oh—I forgot—the Italians have printed Chillon &c. a piracy a pretty little edition prettier than yours and published as I found to my great astonishment on arriving here & what is odd is, that the English is quite correctly printed—why they did it or who did it I know not—but so it is—I suppose for the English people.—I will send you a copy.*

[To John Murray]

Venice May 30th 1817

Dear Sir

I returned from Rome two days ago—& have received your letter but no sign nor tidings of the parcel sent through Sir——Stuart which you mention;[40]—after an interval of months a packet of 'Tales,' &c. found me at Rome—but this is all—& may be all that ever will find me—the post seems to be the only sane conveyance—& *that only for letters.*—From Florence I sent you a poem on Tasso—and from Rome the new third act of 'Manfred,' & by Dr. Polidori two pictures for my sister. I left Rome & made a rapid journey home.—You will continue to direct here as usual.—Mr. Hobhouse is gone to Naples—I should have run down there too for a week—but for the quantity of English whom I heard of there—I prefer hating them at a distance—unless an Earthquake or a good real eruption of Vesuvius were insured to reconcile me to their vicinity.—I know no other situation except Hell which I should feel inclined to participate with them—as a race—always excepting several individuals.—There were few of them in Rome—& I believe none whom you know—except that old Blue-*bore* Sotheby—who will give a fine account of Italy in which he will be greatly assisted by his total ignorance of Italian—& yet this is the translator of Tasso.—The day before I left Rome I saw three robbers guillotined—the ceremony—including the *masqued* priests—the half-naked executioners—the bandaged criminals—the black Christ & his banner—the scaffold—the soldiery—the slow procession—& the quick rattle and heavy fall of the axe—the splash of the blood—& the ghastliness of the exposed heads—is altogether more impressive than the vulgar and ungentlemanly dirty 'new drop' & dog-like agony of infliction upon the sufferers of the English sentence.[41] Two of these men—behaved calmly enough—but the first of the three—died with great terror and reluctance—which was very horrible—he would not lie down—then his neck was too large for the aperture—and the priest was obliged to drown his exclamations by still louder exhortations—the head was off before the eye could trace the blow—but from an attempt to draw back the head—notwithstanding it was held forward by the hair—the first head was cut off close to the ears—the other two were taken off more cleanly;—it is better than the Oriental way—& (I should think) than the axe of our ancestors.—The pain

---

[40] Sir Charles Stuart (later Baron Stuart de Rothesay), British ambassador to France, 1815–24.

[41] The 'New Drop' gallows, which allowed as many as a dozen criminals to be hanged simultaneously, was first demonstrated at London's Newgate Prison in December 1783.

seems little—& yet the effect to the spectator—& the preparation to the criminal—is very striking & chilling.—The first turned me quite hot and thirsty—& made me shake so that I could hardly hold the opera-glass (I was close—but was determined to see—as one should see every thing once—with attention) the second and third (which shows how dreadfully soon things grow indifferent) I am ashamed to say had no effect on me—as a horror—though I would have saved them if I could.——It is some time since I heard from you—the *12th April* I believe.—

yrs. ever truly,

B

[To Augusta Leigh]

Venice.—June 3d.–4th. 1817

Dearest Augusta

I returned home a few days ago from Rome—but wrote to you on the road—at Florence I believe—or Bologna—the last city you know—or do not know—is celebrated for the production of Popes—Cardinals—painters—& sausages—besides a female professor of anatomy—who has left there many models of the art in waxwork—some of them not the most decent.—I have received all your letters—I believe—which are full of woes—as usual—megrims & mysteries—but my sympathies remain in suspense—for—for the life of me I can't make out whether your disorder is a broken heart or the ear-ache—or whether it is *you* that have been ill or the children—or what your melancholy—& mysterious apprehensions tend to—or refer to—whether to Caroline Lamb's novels—Mrs Clermont's evidence—Lady Byron's magnanimity—or any other piece of imposture;—I know nothing of what you are in the doldrums about at present—I should think—all that could affect *you*—must have been over long ago—& as for me—leave me to take care of myself—I may be ill or well—in high or low spirits—in quick or obtuse state of feelings—like every body else—but I can battle my way through better than your exquisite piece of helplessness G[eorge] L[eigh] or that other poor creature George Byron—who will be finely helped up in a year or two with his new state of life—I should like to know what they would do in my situation—or in any situation—I wish well to your George—who is the best of the two a devilish deal—but as for the other I shan't forget him in a hurry—& if ever I forgive or allow an opportunity to escape of evincing my sense of his conduct (& of more than his) on a certain occasion[42]—write me down—what you will—but do not suppose me asleep—'let them look to their bond'—sooner or later time & Nemesis will give me the ascendant—& then 'let them look to their bond.'[43] I do not of course allude only to that poor wretch—but to all—to the 3d. & 4th. generations of these accursed Amalekites—& the woman who has been the stumbling block of my—

June 4th. 1817

I left off yesterday at the stumbling block of my Midianite marriage[44]—but having received your letter of the 20th. May—I will be in good humour for the rest of this letter.—I had hoped you would like the miniatures at least one of them—which is in pretty good health—the other is thin enough to be sure—& so was I—& in the ebb of a fever when I sate for it.—By the 'man of fashion' I suppose you mean that poor piece of affectation and imitation Wilmot—another disgrace to me & mine—that fellow.[45] I regret not having shot him—which the persuasions of others—& circumstances which at that time would have rendered combats presumptions against my cause—prevented.—I wish you well of your indispositions which I hope are slight—or I should lose my senses—

yours ever & very truly

B

[To John Murray]

La Mira—nr. Venice—July 8th. 1817

Dear Sir

If you can convey the enclosed letter to its address—or discover the person to whom it is directed you will confer a favour upon the Venetian Creditor of a deceased Englishman.—This epistle is a dun to his Executor for house rent—the name of the insolvent defunct is or was *Porter Valter* according to the account of the plaintiff which I rather suspect ought to be *Walter Porter* according to our

---

[42] Byron's cousin and heir had supported Lady Byron during the Separation, no doubt reflecting that it made the production of a direct male heir less likely. He succeeded as seventh Baron in 1824, and died in 1868 after a naval career of no particular distinction.

[43] See *Merchant of Venice*, III. iii. 4–5: 'I'll have my bond. Speak not against my bond. | I have sworn an oath that I will have my bond.'

[44] The Amalekites and Midianites are rivals and godless enemies of the Hebrews in the Old Testament.

[45] Robert John Wilmot was a mediator in the Separation, whom Byron came to mistrust (see *LJ* v. 48–50), despite being his cousin.

mode of Collocation—if you are acquainted with any dead man of the like name a good deal in debt—pray dig him up—& tell him that 'a pound of his fair flesh' or the ducats are required—& that 'if you deny them, fie upon your law'[46]— I hear nothing more from you about Moore's poem—Roger[s]'s looks—or other literary phenomena—but tomorrow being post-day will bring perhaps some tidings.—I write to you with people talking Venetian all about—so that you must not expect this letter to be all English.—The other day I had a squabble on the highway as follows.—I was riding pretty quickly from Dolo home about 8 in the Evening—when I passed a party of people in a hired carriage—one of whom poking his head out of the window, began bawling to me in an inarticulate but insolent manner—I wheeled my horse round & over-taking, stopped the coach & said 'Signor have you any commands for me?' He replied impudently as to manner 'No'—I then asked him what he meant by that unseemly noise to the discomfiture of the passers by—he replied by some piece of impertinence—to which I answered by giving him a violent slap in the face.—I then dismounted (for this passed at the window—I being on horseback still) & opening the door desired him to walk out—or I would give him another.—But the first had settled him—except as to words—of which he poured forth a profusion in blasphemies swearing that he would go to the police & avouch a battery sans provocation— I said he lied and was a b— & if he did not hold his tongue should be dragged out & beaten anew—he then held his tongue.—I of course told him my name & residence & defied him to the death if he were a gentleman—or not a gentleman & had the inclination to be genteel in the way of combat.—He went to the police—but there having been bystanders in the road—particularly a soldier— who had seen the business—as well as my servant—notwithstanding the oaths of the Coachman & five insides besides the plaintiff—and a good deal of perjury on all sides—his complaint was dismissed—he having been the aggressor—and I was subsequently informed that had I not given him a blow he might have been had into durance. So set down this 'that in Aleppo once—' I 'beat a Venetian'[47] but I assure you that he deserved it—for I am a quiet man like Candide—though with somewhat of his fortune in being forced to forego my natural meekness every now & then.—

yrs.
B

[46] Byron persists in casting himself as Shylock: see *Merchant of Venice*, I. iii. 148–9 and IV. i. 100.
[47] See *Othello*, V. ii. 361–3.

[To John Murray]

Venice, July 20th. 1817

Dear Sir

I write to give you notice that I have completed the *4th.* and *ultimate* Canto of Childe Harold—it consists of 126 stanzas & is consequently the longest of the four.—It is yet to be copied and polished—& the notes are to come—of which it will require more than the *third* Canto—as it necessarily treats more of works of art than of Nature.—It shall be sent towards Autumn—& now for our barter—what do you bid? eh? you shall have samples an it so please you—but I wish to know what I am to expect (as the saying is) in these hard times—when poetry does not let for half it's value.—If you are disposed to do what Mrs. Winifred Jenkins calls 'the handsome thing'[48] I may perhaps throw you some odd matters to the lot—translations—or slight originals—there is no saying what may be on the anvil between this & the booking Season.—Recollect that it is the *last* Canto—& completes the work—whether as good as the others—I cannot judge in course—least of all as yet—but it shall be as little worse as I can help,—I may perhaps give some little gossip in the notes as to the present state of Italian literati & literature; being acquainted with some of their *Capi* [heads]—men as well as books—but this depends upon my humour at the time;—so now—pronounce—I say nothing.——When you have got the whole 4 cantos—I think you might venture on an edition of the whole poem in quarto—with spare copies of the two last for the purchasers of the old edition of the first two.—There is a hint for you worthy of the Row—& now—perpend—pronounce.—I have not received a word from you of the fate of 'Manfred' or 'Tasso' which seems to me odd—whether they have failed or succeeded. As this is a scrawl of business—& I have lately written at length & often on other subjects I can only add that I am,

Yrs. [ever truly?]
B

---

[48] See letter of 22 August 1813.

[To John Murray]

La Mira—Near Venice—August 21st. 1817

Dear Sir

I take you at your word about Mr. Hanson—& will feel obliged if you will *go* to him—& request Mr. Davies also to visit him by my desire—& repeat that I trust that neither Mr. Kinnaird's absence nor mine will prevent his taking all proper steps to accelerate and promote the sales of Newstead and Rochdale—upon which the whole of my future personal comfort depends—it is impossible for me to express how much any delays upon these points would inconvenience me—& I do not know a greater obligation that can be conferred upon me than the pressing these things upon Hanson—& making him act according to my wishes.—I wish you would *speak out* at least to *me* & tell me what you allude to by your odd way of mentioning him—all mysteries at such a distance are not merely tormenting—but mischievous—& may be prejudicial to my interests—so pray—expound—that I may consult with Mr. Kinnaird when he arrives—& remember that I prefer the most disagreeable certainties to hints & innuendoes—the devil take every body—I never can get any person to be explicit about any thing—or any body—& my whole life is past in conjectures of what people mean—you all talk in the style of Caroline Lamb's novels.——It is not Mr. St. John—but *Mr. St. Aubyn*, Son of Sir John St. Aubyn.—*Polidori* knows him—& introduced him to me—he is of Oxford—& has got my parcel—the Doctor will ferret him out or ought.—The Parcel contains many letters—some of Madame de Stael's and other people's—besides M.S.S., &c.—By G—d—if I find the gentleman & he don't find the parcel—I will say something he won't like to hear.—You want a 'civil and delicate declension' for the medical tragedy?[49] Take it—

> Dear Doctor—I have read your play
> Which is a good one in it's way
> Purges the eyes & moves the bowels
> And drenches handkerchiefs like towels
> With tears that in a flux of Grief
> Afford hysterical relief
> To shatter'd nerves & quickened pulses
> Which your catastrophe convulses.

[49] Murray had written to Byron on 5 August about a drama by Dr Polidori entitled *Ximenes: A Dramatic Action*: 'Polidori has sent me his tragedy!!! do me the kindness to send by return of Post a *delicate declension* of it'—which I engage faithfully to copy' (*Murray Letters*, 234).

I like your moral & machinery
Your plot too has such scope for Scenery!
Your dialogue is apt & smart
The play's concoction full of art—
Your hero raves—your heroine cries
All stab—& every body dies;
In short your tragedy would be
The very thing to hear & see
And for a piece of publication
If I decline on this occasion
It is not that I am not sensible
To merits in themselves ostensible
But—and I grieve to speak it—plays
Are drugs—mere drugs, Sir, nowadays—
I had a heavy loss by 'Manuel'—
Too lucky if it prove not annual—
And Sotheby with his damned 'Orestes'
(Which by the way the old Bore's best is,)
Has lain so very long on hand
That I despair of all demand—
I've advertized—but see my books—
Or only watch my Shopman's looks—
Still Ivan—Ina & such lumber
My back shop glut—my shelves encumber.—
There's Byron—too—who once did better
Has sent me—folded in a letter—
A sort of—it's no more a drama
Than Darnley—Ivan—or Kehama[50]—
So altered since last year his pen is—
I think he's lost his wits at Venice—
Or drained his brains away as Stallion
To some dark-eyed & warm Italian;
In short—Sir—what with one & t'other
I dare not venture on another—
I write in haste, excuse each blunder
The Coaches through the Street so thunder.
My Room's so full—we've Gifford here

---

[50] This is a representative list of Regency tragic failures: Sotheby's *Orestes* (1802), *The Death of Darnley* (1814), and *Ivan* (1816), Mrs Wilmot's *Ina* (1815), and Southey's epic *The Curse of Kehama* (1810).

Reading M.S.S.—with Hookham Frere
Pronouncing on the nouns & particles
Of some of our forthcoming articles,
The Quarterly—Ah Sir! if you
Had but the Genius to review—
A smart Critique upon St. Helena
Or if you only would but tell in a
Short compass what—but, to resume
As I was saying—Sir—the Room—
The Room's so full of wits & bards—
Crabbes—Campbells—Crokers—Freres—& Wards,[51]
And others neither bards nor wits;
My humble tenement admits
All persons in the dress of Gent.
From Mr. Hammond to Dog Dent.[52]
A party dines with me today
All clever men who make their way,
They're at this moment in discussion
On poor De Stael's late dissolution—
'Her book they say was in advance—
Pray Heaven! she tell the truth of France,
'Tis said she certainly was married
To Rocca—& had twice miscarried,
No—not miscarried—I opine—
But brought to bed at forty-nine,
Some say she died a Papist—Some
Are of opinion *that's* a Hum—
I don't know that—the fellow Schlegel
Was very likely to inveigle
A dying person in compunction
To try the extremity of Unction.—
But peace be with her—for a woman
Her talents surely were uncommon.
Her Publisher (& Public too)

---

[51] Literary men, mostly: poets George Crabbe (1754–1832), Thomas Campbell, and John Hookham Frere; lawyer, poet, and politician John Wilson Croker (1780–1857); and politician John William Ward (1781–1833).
[52] George Hammond (1763–1853), diplomat, Under Secretary of State for Foreign Affairs, 1807–9, and erstwhile co-editor of the *Anti-Jacobin*; John Dent (1761?–1826), Tory MP, Fellow of the Royal Society, and promoter of the Dog Tax Bill of 1796.

The hour of her demise may rue—
For never more within his shop he—
Pray—was not she interred at Coppet?[']
Thus run our time and tongues away—
But to return Sir—to your play—
Sorry—Sir—but I can not deal—
Unless 'twere acted by O'Neill[53]—
My hands are full—my head so busy—
I'm almost dead—& always dizzy—
And so with endless truth & hurry—
Dear Doctor—I am yours
                    John Murray.

P. S.—I've done the 4th & last Canto—which mounts 133 Stanzas.—I desire you to name a price—if you don't—*I* will—so I advise you in time.

                                                              yrs.
                                 there will be a good many notes.

[To R. B. Hoppner[54]]

                                          Venice—Nov. 28th. 1817

Dear Sir,

I seem fated to give you trouble. Certain persons (or person) unknown this day walked into my hall and during the sleep or neglect of the Servants carried off a blue great coat—a water proof cloak—and a pair of Silver Candlesticks—of which larceny I have given notice to the Police—but they tell me that my complaint will come with greater weight—if the proofs be transmitted through your office and backed by some forms of which I am incompetent or ignorant.— If I am misinformed I hope you will excuse me and blame the bearer (an Italian in my service who has brought me back this information & whom I have instructed to apprize you of all particulars) and if not may I beg your assistance or instruction—not to recover the Chattels or the thief—for that is hopeless—but to make the degree of objection to such conveyance—requisite to apprize the Venetian public that I would rather not be robbed if I could avoid it.—I should

---

[53] Eliza[beth] O'Neill (1791–1872), Irish actress, at the peak of her five-year London stardom before her marriage in 1819.

[54] Richard Belgrave Hoppner (1786–1872), British consul at Venice, 1814–25, who befriended Byron and did him many services—including looking after his illegitimate daughter after her arrival in Venice in May 1818.

have done myself the honour of waiting on you instead of troubling you with this note had I not been laid up with a Cold which has made me deaf and inarticulate.—I have the honour to be

> very truly your obliged & faith[ful] St.
> Byron

[To John Murray]

Venice, January 8th. 1818

1

My dear Mr. Murray,
You're in a damned hurry
To set up this ultimate Canto,
But (if they don't rob us)
You'll see Mr. Hobhouse
Will bring it safe in his portmanteau.—[55]

2

For the Journal you hint of,
As ready to print off;
No doubt you do right to commend it
But as yet I have writ off
The devil a bit of
Our 'Beppo', when copied—I'll send it.—[56]

3

In the mean time you've 'Gally'
Whose verses all tally,
Perhaps you may say he's a Ninny,
But if you abashed are
Because of 'Alashtar'
He'll piddle another 'Phrosine'.—[57]

---

[55] Hobhouse had spent almost a year in Italy, taking Byron around Rome during his *Childe Harold* visit, and visiting him at Venice and La Mira. On 8 January he set off for home, carrying the fourth canto of *Childe Harold's Pilgrimage* with him.

[56] Murray had plans for a new literary journal, and for his star author to contribute to it. Byron had drafted *Beppo* in two nights in October 1817, but only sent it to Murray on 19 January 1818, warning him 'it won't do for your journal—being full of political allusions' (*LJ* vi. 7).

[57] Poems (both 1817) by Henry Gally Knight (1786–1846). 'Why do you send me such trash', Byron asked Murray in September 1817 on receipt of them in a package containing some toothpaste (*LJ* v. 262); 'I shall clean my teeth with one—and wipe my—not shoes with the other.'

4

Then you've Sotheby's Tour,[58]
No great things, to be sure—
You could hardly begin with a less work,
For the pompous rascallion,
Who don't speak Italian
Nor French, must have scribbled by guesswork.

5

No doubt he's a rare man
Without knowing German
Translating his way up Parnassus,
And now still absurder
He meditates Murder
As you'll see in the trash he calls *Tasso's*.

6

But you've others his betters
The real men of letters—
Your Orators—critics—and wits—
And I'll bet that your Journal
(Pray is it diurnal?)
Will pay with your luckiest hits.—

7

You can make any loss up—
With 'Spence' and his Gossip,
A work which must surely succeed,
Then Queen Mary's Epistle-craft,
With the new 'Fytte' of 'Whistlecraft'
Must make people purchase and read.—[59]

8

Then you've General Gordon
Who 'girded his sword on'
To serve with a Muscovite Master
And help him to polish

[58] William Sotheby's *Farewell to Italy, and Occasional Poems* would be published later in the year; some allude to the 16th-century Italian poet Torquato Tasso.
[59] Upcoming publications from the firm: the *Anecdotes* of Joseph Spence (1699–1768) are chatty recollections of the Augustan age of English literature (1820); George Chalmers's *Life of Mary Queen of Scots* (1819); more cantos of Frere's *Whistlecraft* (1818).

A <people> Nation so *owlish*,
They thought shaving their beards a disaster.[60]

9

For the man, '*poor and shrewd*'*
With whom you'd conclude
A Compact without more delay.
Perhaps some such pen is
            *(Vide your letter)
Still extant in Venice,
But <pray> please Sir to mention *your pay?*—

10

Now tell me some news
Of your friends and the Muse
Of the Bar,—or the Gown—or the House,
From Canning the tall wit
To Wilmot the small wit
Ward's creeping Companion and *Louse.*—[61]

11

<He's> Who's so damnably bit
With fashion and Wit
That <still a> he crawls on the surface like Vermin
But an Insect in both,—
By his Intellect's growth
Of what *size* you may quickly determine.

12

Now, I'll put out my taper
(I've finished my paper
For these stanzas you see on the *brink* stand)
There's a whore on my right
For I rhyme best at Night
When a C—t is tied close to *my Inkstand.*

---

[60] Thomas Gordon (1788–1841) travelled in the East a little after Byron, and served in the Russian army from 1813 to 1815. He would later fight in the Greek War of Independence, a history of which he published in 1832.
[61] For Wilmot, see letter of 8 July 1817; for Ward see letter of 21 August 1817. George Canning (1770–1827), Conservative politician, orator, and wit.

13

It was Mahomet's notion   (See his life in
That comical motion   Gibbon's abstract)[62]
Increased his 'devotion in prayer'—
If that tenet holds good
In a Prophet, it should
In a poet be equally fair.—

14

For, in rhyme or in love
(Which both come from above)
I'll *stand* with our '*Tommy*' or '*Sammy*' ('Moore' and 'Rogers')
But the Sopha and lady
Are both of them ready
And so, here's 'Good Night to you dammee!'

[To Douglas Kinnaird]

Venice January 13th. 1818

Dear Douglas

I have received both your letters, Hobhouse set off last Thursday for England.—
As my potestas of attorney you are entitled and authorized—& further hereby
desired to interfere in the disposal of the purchase money for Newstead,—of
course, the debts must be liquidated—the *Jew annuities* first—(saving the Massingberd ones which may wait till the last as the others are more pressing)[.]
Hanson's bill must come in with the rest, & if the whole surplus of money (after
the settlement is fulfilled)—is not sufficient to settle the claims—I must devote a
portion of the income till they are so—& what <quantity> annual sum, I have no
objection to leave to the discretion of my trustees & Creditors.—As you have
been so lucky with Newstead (which appears to have been very fairly sold)[63]
I wish you would try at *Rochdale* too—I should be then quite clear—& have some
little to boot—which (as it is not settled) I could employ in the purchase of an
annuity for my life & for my sister's—supposing we could get the Manor &
minerals tolerably sold.——I am as you may suppose very well pleased so far
with regard to Newstead, it was & will be a great relief to me—at least I hope

---

[62] Edward Gibbon had discussed Muhammad and the rise of Islam in the third instalment of
Decline and Fall of the Roman Empire (1788–9).

[63] Byron received news of the sale of Newstead (for £94,500) to 'my old schoolfellow and a man of
honour' (*LJ* v. 277), Major Thomas Wildman, on 10 December 1817. (See letter of 18 November 1818.)

so.——I hope it will not be necessary for me to come to England to sign papers &c.—but if it is—I must—but not before Autumn—I would rather have a Clerk sent out. I don't want to go [to] England any more.——About Siri & Will-halm[64]—your people had first given me credit for a thousand £—that was some *hundreds more* than was advanced in cash before you came out in August—and since have sent me a clear account in a letter to *me* but as they have not written to *Siri* &c. my *credit there* falls rather short of the balance due (after all drafts up to this day) according to the letter of Messrs Morlands—so I have sent their epistle to Siri's to warrant my drawing as far [as] it goes—I wish you to apply to Hanson for any balance from Newstead at Michaelmas—& also for Sir R. Noel's money now due—and Murray can or may advance a few hundred pounds of [on?] the copy of the coming canto, (as though I have nine hundred pounds in circular notes Morland & Hammersley included—I don't like to use them *here*—because if I travel—or have occasion to go home I wish to reserve them for my journey and expenses elsewhere—having no *letters* of *credit* but for Venice—only these reserved circulars)[.] I would not break in upon my purchase money principal on any account—besides which it will not be forthcoming till April—and the papers must be signed &c. &c. & so forth.—When you write don't write such damned scraps of letters. I owe you a grudge for the last (which was four lines) and you know how spiteful I am—I'll work you you dog you.——Shelley (from Marlow) has written to me about my Daughter (the last bastard one) who it seems is a great beauty—& wants to know what he is to do about sending her—I think she had better remain till Spring—but will you think of some plan for remitting her here—or placing her in England—I shall acknowledge & breed her myself—giving her the name of *Biron* (to distinguish her from little Legitimacy)—and mean to christen her Allegra—which is a Venetian name.—I hope Scrope is well and prepared to row H[obhouse] who has been a long time in setting off—I have transported my horses to the *Lido*—so that I get a gallop of some miles along the Adriatic beach daily—H's notes are rather lengthy[65]—and you are so damned sincere you will be telling him so—now *don't*—at least till I come I have extended the Canto to 184 Stanzas.—

ever yrs
B

---

[64] These were bankers in Venice. Kinnaird worked for 'your people', Ransom and Morland's in London, where Byron also had an account at the international bankers, Hammersley's. Byron did not want to use up circular notes because they were the 19th-century equivalent of traveller's cheques. His letters of credit, on the other hand, were guarantees from British banks only to particular institutions in Venice.

[65] Hobhouse provided a set of historical notes to the fourth canto of *Childe Harold*: 'rather lengthy' would be an understatement.

P. S.—My respects to Mrs. K. Whatever sum or sums however small may be advanced in future you had better send the credit to Siri's direct (or in circulars to me which perhaps may be best) as I don't like discussions & explanations with those kind of persons.—

[To John Cam Hobhouse]

Venice. March 25th. 1818

My dear Hobhouse

I protest against the 'pints' of your sober Association[66]—not that my prospect of infringing the rule is very great—for I will not return to England as long as I can help it;—but as an honorary member—I use my privilege of protest—the restriction upon Scrope will of course have the usual effect of restrictions;—for my own part I have about the same conception of Scrope's company and a *pint* (of anything but brandy) that the close reflection of my years enables me to entertain of the Trinity; unless it be a Scotch pint—& even then it must be in the plural number.—I greatly fear that Scrope & I would very soon set up for ourselves—in case of my return like 'Marius from banishment to power'.[67]——You will have received by this time some letters—or letter—with ye. returned proofs.—I am anxious to hear from or of Spooney—in the hope of the conclusion of the New[stea]d Sale;—& I want you to spur him if possible into the like for *Rochdale*—a Clerk can bring the papers (& by the bye my *Shild*[68] by Clare at the same time—pray—desire Shelley to pack it carefully) with *tooth powder red only*—Magnesia—Soda powders—*tooth brushes*—Diachylon plaster[69]—and any new novels—good for any thing.——I have taken a Palazzo on the Grand Canal for two years—so that you see I *won't* stir—so pray don't mention that any more—my old 'relazione' is over—but I have got several new ones (and a Clap which is nearly well at present) with regard to the proxy

---

[66] We do not have Hobhouse's letter, but this is the revived version of the Rota Club, originally composed of English 17th-century republicans, which began meeting in February 1818. Hobhouse, Kinnaird, and Davies were all members, and Byron was elected *in absentia*. It seems the club minuted some sort of resolution concerning the consumption of alcohol.

[67] Caius Marius, 2nd-century BC Roman consul, was recalled from exile to serve a seventh term, only to die some days later.

[68] See *LJ* vi. 20, letter to Hobhouse of 3 March 1818, quoting from an unknown literary or theatrical source: '"Ah Coquin! vare is my shild?"'

[69] Essentially, a forerunner of the modern pharmaceutical plaster for everyday cuts and grazes, but often containing lead compounds and sundry herbal elements in Byron's day.

I will renew it with pleasure if it can be done without dragging me to London for it—otherwise *not* till I find it necessary to come on business;[70]—there was no occasion for any body's name with Lord H[olland]—but undoubtedly your own would have greater weight with me than any other—had such been requisite—as for the Whigs I won't leave them though they will me—if ever they get anything to scramble for;—pray do you stand this ensuing election?—I wrote to Augusta the other day.——Remember me to Scrope—why don't he write? whenever you come out pray bring him—but I hope that you will turn parliament man—& stay at home,—I shall have great glee in seeing your speeches in the Venetian Gazette.—As for Doug. don't let him neglect his Potestas as Atturney.—How came Scrope to kneel to his Duck—he who like Rolla[71] never kneels—except to his God.—

yrs [scrawl]

P. S.—*The Man who makes your wig—says—that he sent the wig you made me order to Geneva to Hengo—who I suppose wears it himself—& be damned to him—you ought to pay Holmes—as it is all your doing.——I dined with Hoppner & Rose on Monday—all well.—With regard to my money matters—Murray may pay in his money to Morland's in regular order—as I cannot depend for the present on other remittances—& whether I could or not—I choose to have the cash tangible—the Sum is hardly considerable enough to turn into the annuity you proposed, besides I think I can spend the principal—& I like it.——Spur Doug. & Spooney—& never calculate on my return to England—which I may or may not but never willingly.——*

[To John Murray]

Venice. April 11th. 1818

Dear Sir/

Will you send me by letter, packet, or parcel, half a dozen of the coloured prints from Holmes's Miniature (the latter done shortly before I left your country & the prints about a year ago). I shall be obliged to you as some people here have asked

---

[70] Proxy votes could be given in the House of Lords until 1864.
[71] 'Rollo the Viking' (846–931), first Duke of Normandy, was pacified and Christianized by Charles III of France.

me for the like.——It is a picture of my upright Self—done for Scrope B. D[avie]s Esquire.—When you can reprint 'Beppo'—instead of line

> 'Gorging the little Fame to get all raw'

insert—

> Gorging the slightest slice of Flattery raw,—

because—we have the word 'Fame' in the preceding Stanza—(also as a rhyme too)—perhaps the line is now a little weakened—because *all raw* expresses the Cormorant Cameleon's avidity for air—or inflation of his vicious vanity—but—ask Mr. Gifford—& Mr. Hobhouse—& as they think so let it be—for though repetition is only the 'soul of Ballad singing' & best avoided in describing the Harlequin jacket of a Mountebank—yet anything is better than weakening an expression—or a thought.[72]—I would rather be as bouncing as Nat Lee[73]—than wishy-washy like—like—

> He has twelve thousand pounds a year—
>   I do not mean to rally
> His Songs at sixpence would be dear
>   So give them gratis—Gally.
> And if this statement should seem queer
>   Or set down in a hurry
> Go—ask (if he will be sincere)
>   His Publisher—John Murray—
> Come say—how Many have been sold?
>   And don't stand shilly-shally,
> Of bound & lettered red & gold
>   Well printed works of Gally?
>
> For Astley's Circus Upton writes
>   And also for the Surry—
> Fitzgerald weekly (or *weakly*) still recites—
>   Though grinning Critics worry—
> Miss Holford's Peg—& Sotheby's Saul
>   In fame exactly tally—
> From Stationer's Hall—to Grocer's [stall]
>   They go—& so does Gally.—[74]

---

[72] This wonderful line (*Beppo*, 590; *CPW* iv. 152) refers to William Sotheby.

[73] English dramatist Nathaniel Lee (1653–92), who died an alcoholic and a madman, also wrote some extravagant and powerful historical dramas, reminiscent of the pre-Shakespearian stage.

[74] Byron was still harping on Henry Gally Knight, but also on rival poetasters like William Upton (who wrote for the theatres and Astley's circus), William Thomas Fitzgerald (whom Byron had ridiculed in the

He hath a Seat in Parliament—
 So fat, & passing wealthy—healthy
And surely he should be content
 With these—and being wealthy—
But Great Ambition will misrule
 Men at all risks to sally,—
Now makes a poet—now a fool
 And—*we* know *which*—of Gally.—

Between whom & Sotheby there is the difference of the foam of a washing tub from the froth of a Syllabub.—And *you* talk to me of sparing the Knight— because he probably is—but no matter—I was going to say a good customer— but you are above that—however *don't* I *spare* him?—do I molest him? I laugh at him in my letters to you—& that is all—& to these I would have confined myself with regard to t'other fellow—if *he* had not begun first—but in these at least I may say a coxcomb is a *coxcomb*—so allow me to expectorate the ineffable contempt I have for the genus—of that animal—do you ever find me attack the real men of merit—do I not delight in them?—But—

Some in the playhouse like a *row*—
 Some with the Watch to battle—
Exchanging many a midnight blow
 To music of the Rattle.
Some folk like rowing on the Thames
 Some rowing in an Alley—
But all the Row my fancy claims
 Is *rowing* of my Galley.[75]

If you like the same chorus to another tune—of 'Tally i.o. the Grinder.'

1

Mrs. Wilmot sate scribbling a play—
 Mr. Sotheby sate sweating behind her—
But what are all three to the lay
 Of Gally i. o. the Grinder—
  Gally i. o. i. o.

opening line of *English Bards and Scotch Reviewers*; see letter of 8 March 1816), Margaret Holford (author of *Margaret of Anjou: A Poem* (1816)), and William Sotheby (author of *Saul: A Poem in Two Parts* (1817)).

[75] Byron plays on 'row', its meanings, and pronunciations: to quarrel, to propel a craft, and to berate or abuse.

2

I bought me some books t'other day
   And sent them down stairs to the binder,
But the Pastry Cook carried away—
   My Gally i. o. the Grinder.—

3

I wanted to kindle my taper
   And called to the Maid to remind her,
And what should she bring me for paper?
   But Gally i. o. the Grinder.—

4

Amongst my researches for *Ease*
   I went where one's certain to find her—
The first thing by her throne that one sees
   Is Gally i. o. the Grinder.—[76]

Why have you not sent me an answer & list of Subscribers to the translation of the Armenian *Eusebius*—of which I sent you six copies of the printed prospectus (in French) two months ago.—Have you had this letter? I shall send you another—you must not neglect my Armenians.—Tooth powder—Magnesia—Tincture of Myrrh—tooth brushes—diachylon plaister.——and Peruvian Bark[77]—are my personal demands.—

Strahan—Tonson—Lintot of the times[78]
Patron and Publisher of rhymes
For thee the Bard up Pindus climbs—
   My Murray.—
To thee with hope & terror dumb—
The unfledged M.S. authors come—
Thou printest all—& sellest some—
   My Murray. —
Upon thy tables baize so green
The last new Quarterly is seen
But where is thy new Magazine—
   My Murray.—
Along the sprucest bookshelves shine

---

[76] Uses for waste paper in Byron's age, including lining pastrycooks' baking tins.

[77] Derived from the bark of a tree in Central America, and a remedy for fever.

[78] Eighteenth-century publishers of note: William Strahan, Jacob Tonson, and Bernard Lintot. This poem is a parody of the uxorious dirge 'My Mary' by William Cowper (1731–1800).

The works thou deemest most divine—
The 'Art of Cookery'[79] and Mine
     My Murray.—
Tours—Travels—Essays too—I wist—
And Sermons to thy Mill bring Grist—
And then thou hast the 'Navy List'—
     My Murray.—
And Heaven forbid I should conclude
Without the 'Board of Longitude'[80]
Although this narrow paper would—
     My Murray.—

[To John Cam Hobhouse]

Venice. June 1818

Sir

With great grief I inform you of the death of my late dear Master—my Lord—who died this morning at ten of the Clock of a rapid decline & slow fever—caused by anxiety—sea-bathing—women & riding in the Sun against my advice.—He is a dreadful loss to every body, mostly to me—who have lost a master and a place—also I hope you—Sir—will give me a charakter.—I saved in his service as you know several hundred pounds—God knows how—for I don't, nor my late master neither—and if my wage was not always paid to the day—still it was or is to be paid sometime & somehow—you—Sir—who are his executioner won't see a poor Servant wronged of his little all.—My dear Master had several phisicians and a Priest—he died a Papish but is to be buried among the Jews in the Jewish burying ground—for my part I don't see why—he could not abide them when living nor any other people—bating whores—who asked him for money.—He suffered his illness with great patience—except that when in extremity he twice damned his friends & said they were selfish rascals—you—Sir—particularly & Mr. Kinnaird—who had never answered his letters nor

---

[79] One of Murray's best sellers was Mrs Rundell's *Domestic Cookery*, first published in 1806, and frequently reprinted.
[80] In some of his publications Murray proudly announced himself to be 'Bookseller to the Admiralty, and to the Board of Longitude'. Thus he published the *Navy List*, which annually catalogued officers in the Navy and the ships in which they sailed, and he provided books to the committee charged with solving the puzzle of measuring longitude at sea, which sat from 1714 until 1828.

complied with his repeated requests.—He also said he hoped that your new tragedy would be damned—God forgive him—I hope that my master won't be damned like the tragedy.——His nine whores are already provided for—& the other servants—but what is to become of me—I have got his Cloathes & Carriages—& Cash—& everything—but the Consul quite against law has clapt his seal & taken an inven*tary* & swears that *he* must account to my Lord's heirs— who they are—I don't know—but they ought to consider poor Servants & above all his Vally de Sham. My Lord never grudged me perquisites—my wage was the least I got by him—and if I did keep the Countess (she is or ought to be a Countess although she is upon the town) Marietta—Monetta— Piretta—after passing my word to you and my Lord that I would not never no more—still he was an indulgent master—& only said I was a damned fool—& swore & forgot it again.—What Could I do—she said as how she should die—or kill herself if I did not go with her—& so I did—& kept her out of my Lord's washing & ironing—& nobody can deny that although the charge was high— the linen was well got up.—Hope you are well Sir—am with tears in my eyes

yours faithfoolly to command
Wm. Fletcher

P. S.—*If you know any Gentleman in want of a Wally—hope for a charakter*[81]*—I saw your late Swiss Servant in the Galleys at Leghorn for robbing an Inn—he produced your recommendation at his trial.*——

[To Thomas Moore]

Palazzo Mocenigo, Canal Grande, Venice, June 1st. 1818

Your letter is almost the only news, as yet, of Canto 4th, and it has by no means settled its fate—at least, does not tell me how the 'Poeshie' has been received by the public. But I suspect, no great things,—firstly, from Murray's 'horrid still-ness;'[82] secondly, from what you say about the stanzas running into each other, which I take *not* to be *yours*, but a notion you have been dinned with among

---

[81] 'Fletcher' is looking for a reference to find new work as a *valet de chambre*, or manservant.
[82] See Dryden, *Astraea Redux* (1660), 7.

the Blues.[83] The fact is, that the terza rima of the Italians, which always *runs* on and in, may have led me into experiments, and carelessness into conceit—or conceit into carelessness—in either of which events failure will be probable, and my fair woman, 'superne,' end in a fish; so that Childe Harold will be like the mermaid, my family crest, with the Fourth Canto for a tail thereunto.[84] I won't quarrel with the public, however, for the 'Bulgars' are generally right; and if I miss now, I may hit another time:—and so, the 'gods give us joy.'[85] [...]

Hunt's letter is probably the exact piece of vulgar coxcombry you might expect from his situation. He is a good man, with some poetical elements in his chaos; but spoilt by the Christ-Church Hospital and a Sunday newspaper,—to say nothing of the Surry Jail, which conceited him into a martyr. But he is a good man.[86] When I saw 'Rimini' in MSS., I told him that I deemed it good poetry at bottom, disfigured only by a strange style. His answer was, that his style was a system, or *upon system*, or some such cant; and, when a man talks of system, his case is hopeless: so I said no more to him, and very little to any one else.

He believes his trash of vulgar phrases tortured into compound barbarisms to be *old* English; and we may say of it as Aimwell says of Captain Gibbet's regiment, when the Captain calls it an 'old corps.'—'the *oldest* in Europe, if I may judge by your uniform,'[87] He sent out his 'Foliage' by Percy Shelley * * *, and, of all the ineffable Centaurs that were ever begotten by Selflove upon a Night-mare, I think this monstrous Sagittary the most prodigious. *He* (Leigh H.) is an honest Charlatan, who has persuaded himself into a belief of his own impostures, and talks Punch in pure simplicity of heart, taking himself (as poor Fitzgerald said of *himself* in the Morning Post) for *Vates* in both senses [poet and prophet], or nonsenses, of the word. Did you look at the translations of his own which he refers to Pope and Cowper, and says so?—Did you read his skimble-skamble about [Wordsworth] being at the head of his own *profession*, in the *eyes* of *those* who followed it?[88] I thought that Poetry was an *art*, or an *attribute*, and

[83] That is, the 'bluestockings', a collective name for literary ladies and their gentlemen friends, holding court over new publications.

[84] See Horace, *Ars Poetica*, 4: '*Desinat in piscem mulier formosa superne*' (paints a woman above, a fish below). Byron's crest was a mermaid, with *Crede Byron* ('trust Byron') as the motto.

[85] See *As You Like It*, III. iii. 42.

[86] Byron's assassination of Leigh Hunt surely draws from Antony's famous speech, beginning 'Friends, Romans, countrymen, lend me your ears' (*Julius Caesar*, III. ii. 74–107), snidely repeating the formula, 'Brutus is an honourable man'.

[87] See George Farquhar, *The Beaux' Stratagem* (1707), III. ii. 88–9.

[88] Hunt published *Foliage* in 1818. Wordsworth had not been as popularly successful as Byron and Moore, he commented in his preface: 'but taking everything into consideration, the novelty of his poetical system, and the very unattractive and in my opinion mistaken nature of his moral one, he has succeeded still more; and is generally felt among his own profession to be at the head of it.'

not a *profession*—but be it one, is that * * * * * * at the head of *your* profession in *your* eyes? I'll be curst if he is of *mine*, or ever shall be. He is the only one of us (but of us he is not) whose coronation I would oppose. Let them take Scott, Camp-bell, Crabbe, or you, or me, or any of the living, and throne him;—but not this new Jacob Behmen,[89] this * * * * whose pride might have kept him true, even had his principles turned as perverted as his *soi-disant* poetry.

But Leigh Hunt is a good man, and a good father—see his Odes to all the Masters Hunt;—a good husband—see his Sonnet to Mrs. Hunt;—a good friend—see his Epistles to different people;—and a great coxcomb and a very vulgar person in every thing about him. But that's not his fault, but of circumstances.

* * * * * * * * * * * * * *

* * * * * * * * * * * * * *

I do not know any good model for a life of Sheridan but that of *Savage*.[90] Recollect, however, that the life of such a man may be made far more amusing than if he had been a Wilberforce;—and this without offending the living, or insulting the dead. The Whigs abuse him; however, he never left them and such blunderers deserve neither credit nor compassion. As for his creditors,— remember, Sheridan *never had* a shilling, and was thrown, with great powers and passions, into the thick of the world, and placed upon the pinnacle of success, with no other external means to support him in his elevation. Did Fox * * * *pay his* debts?—or did Sheridan take a subscription? Was the Duke of Norfolk's drunkeness [*sic*] more excusable than his? Were his intrigues more notorious than those of all his contemporaries? and is his memory to be blasted, and theirs respected? Don't let yourself be led away by clamour, but compare him with the coalitioner Fox, and the pensioner Burke, as a man of principle, and with ten hundred thousand in personal views, and with none in talent, for he beat them all *out* and *out*. Without means, without connexion, without character, (which might be false at first, and make him mad afterwards from desperation,) he beat them all, in all he ever attempted. But alas poor human nature! Good night—or, rather, morning. It is four, and the dawn gleams over

---

[89] Jakob Böhme (1575–1624), German theologian and mystic.

[90] Moore was planning a life of the politician and playwright whom he and Byron had come to know in his latter years (it would appear in 1825). Byron proposes Samuel Johnson's ambivalent *Life of Mr Richard Savage* (1744) as a model, perhaps because Sheridan, too, failed to reach his full potential. He goes on to contrast Sheridan with other 18th-century political luminaries, Charles James Fox (1749–1806), Edmund Burke (1729–97), and Charles Howard, eleventh Duke of Norfolk (1746–1815), who was fond of the bottle.

the Grand Canal, and unshadows the Rialto. I must to bed; up all night—but, as George Philpot says, 'it's life, though, damme it's life!'[91]

Ever yours,
B

Excuse errors—no time for revision. The post goes out at noon, and I shan't be up then. I will write again soon about your plan *for a publication.*

[To John Cam Hobhouse]

Venice. June 25th. 1818

Dear Hobhouse

I have received yrs. of the 5th.—& have had no letters from any one else—nor desire any—but *letters of Credit.*—Since my last I have had another *Swim* against Mingaldo—whom both Scott & I beat hollow—leaving him breathless & five hundred yards behind hand before we got from Lido to the entrance of the Grand Canal.[92]—Scott went from Lido as far as the Rialto—& was then taken into his Gondola—I swam from Lido right to the end of the Grand Canal—including it's whole length—besides that space from Lido to the Canal's entrance (or exit) by the statue of Fortune—near the Palace—and coming out finally at the end opposite Fusina and Maestri—staying in half an hour &—I know not what distance more than the other two—& swimming easy—the whole distance computed by the Venetians at four and a half of Italian miles.—I was in the sea from half past 4—till a quarter past 8—without touching or resting.—I could not be much fatigued having had a *piece* in the forenoon—& taking another in the evening at ten of the Clock—The Scott I mention is not the vice-Consul—but a traveler—who lives much at Venice—like My*sen*.—He got as far as the Rialto swimming well—the Italian—miles behind & knocked up—hallooing for the boat.—Pray—make Murray *pay*—& Spooney pay—& send the Messenger—& with the other things the enclosed *Corn rubbers.*—As you are full of politics

---

[91] See Arthur Murphy's farce *The Citizen* (1763), I. ii. 12–18: 'Up all night—stripped of nine hundred pounds...cruel luck! damn me, it's life though; this is life.'

[92] Byron undertook this swimming contest with Cavaliere Angelo Mengaldo, a vain ex-soldier of Napoleon's, and Alexander Scott, a Scottish resident of Venice whom he had met through Consul Hoppner.

I say nothing—except that I wish you more pleasure than such trash could give to me.

yrs. very truly & affectly.

B

———⊗⊗⊗———

P. S.—*The wind and tide were both with me. Corn rubbers two dozen*—recollect *they are light & may come in letters.*—

8

DON JUAN AND TERESA GUICCIOLI

July 1818–December 1819

At the beginning of July 1818 Byron began work on his masterpiece, Don Juan: he had 'two stories', he told Murray (LJ vi. 58–9); 'one serious & one ludicrous (a la Beppo) not yet finished—& in no hurry to be so'. (The 'serious' one, itself a brilliant achievement, was Mazeppa, which Byron worked on for no fewer than six months, from April to September.) The cantos of Don Juan unrolled throughout this period: the first was finished in early September 1818; the second by mid-January the following year; the third and the fourth together by the end of November 1819. Friends in England were rendered intensely nervous by its progress. Hobhouse and Scrope Berdmore Davies read the first instalment together, and agreed 'it will be impossible to publish this' (Hobhouse Letters, 256). Hobhouse went on in pusillanimously censorious tones:

the immoral turn of the whole and the rakish air of the half real hero will really injure your reputation both as a man and a poet. Frere remarked, that as a noble and bold assertor of liberty, such as you have always appeared, a certain strictness in appearance was naturally required from you . . . (Hobhouse Letters, 258)

And so forth. But Byron was well aware that he had found a new métier, and insisted on publication, albeit anonymously.

His Venetian life also became more settled. Margarita Cogni, whom he had met at La Mira the previous summer, left her husband and moved into the Palazzo Mocenigo as resident mistress and housekeeper; Shelley visited twice, and his horse rides on the Lido with Byron are evocatively recorded in the opening of his 'Julian and Maddalo'; Claire Clairmont had what we would call 'access' to the eighteen-month-old Allegra at a summer house in Este; and Hanson unwillingly dragged himself to Venice with the legal papers relating the sale of Newstead (the purchase would be paid in February 1819). When Byron's financial problems were at their height, around the time of his departure from England, he displayed the unworldliness and generosity that had always been his hallmark (see letter of 16 April 1816). The moment his financial problems were solved, he became graspingly avaricious, at least in discussions with Murray (about fees for copyright) and Kinnaird (about debts, investments, and monies owed)—sometimes modelling himself on Shakespeare's Shylock. He threw himself into the Carnival once more in the New Year of 1819, and boasted to Kinnaird and Hobhouse of more than 200 sexual conquests in the previous year (see letter of 19 January 1819).

But Hanson's son Newton reported the physical cost of Byron's way of living: 'Lord Byron could not have been more than thirty, but he looked 40. His face had become pale, bloated, and sallow. He had grown very fat, his shoulders broad and round, and the knuckles of his hands were lost in fat' (Life, 759). Shelley, too (who could be hysterically anti-Italian at times), wrote that Byron 'allows fathers & mothers to bargain with him for their daughters, & though this is common enough in Italy, yet for an Englishman to encourage such sickening vice is a melancholy thing', adding: 'He associates with wretches who seem almost to have lost the gait and phisiognomy of man, & who do not scruple to avow practices which are not only not named but I believe seldom even conceived in England.'[1] (This ambiguous remark, it is worth noting, is almost all the evidence we have for Byron's homosexuality between Greece in 1810 and Greece in 1824.)

Surely Byron himself knew that something had to change. Attending Countess Benzoni's conversazione in early April 1819 he met again the Countess Teresa Guiccioli, 19 years old and married to a man nearly three times her age, whose third wife she was. 'She is a sort of Italian Caroline Lamb,' Byron wrote to Kinnaird, 'except that She is prettier, and not so savage.— But She has the same red-hot head—the same noble disdain of public opinion—with the superstructure of all that Italy can add to such natural dispositions' (LJ vi. 115). Within ten days the Guicciolis had returned to their native Ravenna. Having heard that Teresa had miscarried, Byron set off to follow them on 1 June—though, typically, he stopped off for visits to Bologna and Ferrara on the way. Teresa's miscarriage threatened to bring on consumption, and Byron was seriously concerned. 'I do not know what I should do', he wrote (LJ vi. 168), 'if She died—but I ought to blow my brains out—and I hope that I should.' He stayed two months at Ravenna, and then followed the Guicciolis back to Bologna. The case was plain to everybody involved, and Byron—worried about being trapped, perhaps, but also concerned about the social implications of their affair for Teresa (despite all he knew or claimed to know about the cavalier servente tradition)—began toying with a return to England, or even a new career as a settler in Venezuela. ('Europe is grown decrepit', he announced (LJ vi. 212).) But Teresa's ongoing ill health, and her husband's apparent complaisance, kept the couple together. In September Byron 'escorted' her to Venice to visit doctors, then 'accompanied' her to his house at La Mira. There they were visited by Thomas Moore, to whom Byron gave his famous memoirs—'you will find many opinions', he told Murray, 'and some fun—with a detailed account of my marriage and it's consequences' (LJ vi. 236).

Back in Venice by the end of October, Byron himself fell ill of a fever and was nursed by Teresa. At the beginning of November Count Guiccioli decided to put his foot down, and came up to Venice to bring his wife home. She resisted, an elopement was entertained, but Byron persuaded her to go south with her husband, and began to feel that he was free once more. ('I shall quit Italy', he wrote; 'I have done my duty—but the Country has become sad to me,—I feel alone in it—and as I left England on account of my own wife—I now quit Italy for the wife of another' (LJ vi. 241).) This return to England—from the politics and literary culture of which Byron was growing increasingly distant—was delayed by Allegra's falling sick; Teresa wrote in illness and desperation once more; and at the very last moment Byron left Venice on 21 December—'that now empty Oyster shell—without it's pearl' (LJ vi. 237)— never to return, and took the road south to Ravenna.

'At thirty I feel there is no more to look forward to', he wrote to James Wedderburn Webster in July 1819: 'my personal charms have by no means increased—my hair is half grey—and the Crow's-foot has been rather lavish of it's indelible steps.—My hair though not

---

[1] Frederick L. Jones (ed.), The Letters of Percy Bysshe Shelley, 2 vols. (Oxford: Oxford University Press, 1964), ii. 423.

gone seems going—and my teeth remain by way of courtesy—but I suppose they will soon follow—having been too good to last.' 'I have done with Passion forever', he wrote on the same day: 'it is my last Love.—And as to Libertinism—I sickened myself of that as was natural the way I went on—and I have at least derived that advantage from the Vice—to Love in the better sense of the word' (LJ vi. 173–6). In Teresa he had replaced all his English lovers, including Augusta, in one fell swoop.

[To Augusta Leigh]

Venice. August 3d. 1818

Dearest Augusta

I am not uncomfortable but have been obliged to scold Hobhouse &c. for not doing a thing or two for me in England in the way of business.—At present they are done and I am graciously appeased.—My little girl Allegra (the child I spoke to you of) has been with me these three months; she is very pretty—remarkably intelligent—and a great favourite with every body—but what is remarkable—much more like Lady Byron than her mother—so much so as to stupefy the learned Fletcher—and astonish me—is it not odd? I suppose she must also resemble her sister Ada—she has very blue eyes—and that singular forehead—fair curly hair—and a devil of a Spirit—but that is Papa's.——I am in health—& very much yrs.

B

I have just seen Lord Sidney Osborne[2] who was here a few days ago—very well & in high Spirits.——

[To Augusta Leigh]

Venice. Septr. 21st. 1818

Dearest Augusta

I particularly beg that you will contrive to get the enclosed letter safely delivered to Lady Frances—& if there is an answer to let me have it.—You can write to her

[2] Lord Sidney Godolphin Osborne (1789–1861), son of the fifth Duke of Leeds by his second wife. His first, the Marchioness of Carmarthen, had divorced the Duke to marry Captain John Byron: she was Augusta's mother. Osborne came back into Byron's life in Italy and beyond: see letter of 7 April 1823.

first—& state that you have such a letter—at my request—for there is no occasion for any concealment at least with *her*—& pray oblige me so far—for many reasons.——If the Queen dies you are no more a Maid of Honour—is it not so?[3]——Allegra is well—but her mother (whom the Devil confound) came prancing the other day over the Appenines—to see her *shild*—which threw my Venetian loves (who are none of the quietest) into great combustion—and I was in a pucker till I got her to the Euganean hills where she & the child now are—for the present—I declined seeing her for fear that the consequence might be an addition to the family;—she is to have the child a month with her and then to return herself to Lucca—or Naples where she was with her relatives (she is English you know) & to send Allegra to Venice again.—I lent her my house at Este for her maternal holidays.—As troubles don't come single—here is another confusion.— The chaste wife of a baker—having quarrelled with her tyrannical husband—has run away *to* me—(God knows without being invited) & resists all the tears & penitence & beg-pardons of her disconsolate Lord—and the threats of the police—and the priest of the parish besides—& swears she won't give up her unlawful love (myself) for any body—or anything—I assure you I have begged her in all possible ways too to go back to her husband—promising her all kinds of eternal fidelity into the bargain—but she only flies into a fury—and as she is a very tall and formidable Girl of three and twenty—with the large black eyes and handsome face of a pretty fiend—a correspondent figure—and a carriage as haughty as a Princess—with the violent passions & capacities for mischief of an Italian when they are roused—I am a little embarrassed with my unexpected acquisition;—however she keeps my household in rare order—and has already frightened the learned Fletcher out of his remnant of wits more than once—we have turned her into a housekeeper.[4]——As the morals of this place are very lax—all the women commend her & say she has done right—especially her own relations.—You need not be alarmed—I know how to manage her—and can deal with anything but a cold blooded animal such as Miss Milbanke.——The worst is that she won't let a woman come into the house—unless she is as old & frightful as possible—and has sent so many to the right about—that my former female acquaintances are equally frightened & angry.—She is extremely fond of the child—& is very cheerful & good-natured—when not jealous—but Othello him-self was a fool to her in that respect—her soubriquet in her family—was *la Mora* from her colour—as she is very dark (though clear of complexion) which literally

---

[3] Augusta served as Woman of the Bedchamber to George III's Queen Charlotte, who died on 17 November 1818. She was paid £300 a year for the privilege. Though Augusta lost her post, the Queen had ensured she continued on a pension and retained her rooms at Kensington Palace.

[4] This is Margarita Cogni, 'La Fornarina' (the Baker's Wife): Byron tells the tale of their connection in full in the letter of 1 August 1819.

means *the Moor* so that I have 'the Moor of Venice' in propria persona as part of my houshold—she has been here this month.——I had known her (and fifty others) more than a year—but did not anticipate this escapade which was the fault of her booby husband's treatment—who now runs about repenting & roaring like a bullcalf—I told him to take her in the devil's name—but she would not stir—& made him a long speech in the Venetian dialect which was more entertaining to anybody than to him to whom it was addressed.——You see Goose—that there is no quiet in this world—so be a good woman—& repent of yr. sins.—

yrs [scrawl for signature]

[To John Cam Hobhouse]

Venice Novr. 11th. 1818

Dear Hobhouse/

By the favour of Lord Lauderdale[5] (who tells me by the way that you have made some very good speeches—and are to turn out an Orator—*seriously*) I have sent an 'Oeuvre' of 'Poeshie' which will not arrive probably till some [time] after this letter—though they start together—as the letter is rather the youngest of the two.—It is addressed to you at Mr. Murray's.——I request you to read—& having read—and if possible approved to obtain the largest or (if large be undeserved—) the fairest price from him or any one else.—There are firstly—the first Canto of Don Juan—(in the style of Beppo—and Pulci—forgive me for putting Pulci second it is a slip—'Ego et Rex meus'[6]) containing two *hundred* Octaves—and a dedication in verse of a dozen to Bob Southey—bitter as necessary—I mean the dedication; I will tell you why.—The Son of a Bitch on his return from Switzerland two years ago—said that Shelley and I 'had formed a League of Incest and practiced our precepts with &c.'—he lied like a rascal—for they *were not Sisters*—one being Godwin's daughter by Mary Wollstonecraft—and the other the daughter of the present Mrs. G[odwin] by a *former* husband.—The Attack contains no allusion to the cause—but—some good verses—and all political & poetical.—He lied in another sense—for there was no promiscuous intercourse—my commerce being limited to the carnal knowledge of the Miss C[lairmont]—I had nothing to do with the offspring of Mary Wollstonecraft—

---

[5] James Maitland, eighth Earl of Lauderdale (1759–1839), Whig politician with Radical and French Revolutionary sympathies, and negotiator for peace with Napoleon in 1806.

[6] This insolent expression—'I and my king'—was apparently used by English Tudor cardinal Thomas Wolsey in communications with the Pope (see Shakespeare's *Henry VIII*, III. ii. 314–17), so earning Henry's wrath and contributing to Wolsey's downfall.

which Mary was a former Love of Southey's—which might have taught him to respect the fame of her daughter.——Besides this '*Pome*' there is 'Mazeppa' and an Ode on Venice—the last not very intelligible—and you may omit it if you like—Don Juan—and Mazeppa are perhaps better—you will see.—The Whole consists of between two and three thousand lines—and you can consult Douglas K[innaird] about the price thereof and your own Judgment—& whose else you like about their merits.—As one of the poems is as free as La Fontaine—& bitter in politics—too—the damned Cant and Toryism of the day may make Murray pause—in that case you will take any Bookseller who bids best;—when I say *free*—I mean that freedom—which Ariosto Boiardo and Voltaire—Pulci— Berni—all the best Italian & French—as well as Pope & Prior amongst the English permitted themselves;—but no improper words nor phrases—merely some situations—which are taken from life.—However you will see to all this— when the M.S.S. arrive.——I only request that you & Doug. will see to a fair price—'as the Players have had my Goods too cheap'[7]—if Murray won't— another will.—I name no price—calculate by quantity—and quality—and do you and Doug. pronounce—always recollecting as impartial Judges—that you are my friends—and that he is my Banker.—Spooney arrived here today—but has left in Chancery Lane *all* my *books*—everything in short except a damned— (Something)-SCOPE.[8] I have broke the glass & cut a finger in ramming it together—and the *Cornrubbers* but I have given it him!—I have been blaspheming against Scrope's God—ever since his arrival.——Only think—he has left every thing—every thing except his legal papers.—You must send off a Man on purpose with them on the receipt of this—I will pay anything within *three hundred pounds* for the expence of their transportation—but pray let them be sent without fail—and by a person on purpose—they are all in Chancery— (I mean the *Lane*—not the Court—for they would not come out of that in a hurry) with young Spooney—extract them—and send a man by Chaise on purpose—never mind expence nor weight—I must have books & Magnesia— particularly 'Tales of my Landlord'.——I'll be revenged on Spooney—five men died of the Plague the other day—in the Lazaretto—I shall take him to ride at the Lido—he hath a reverend care & fear of his health—I will show him the Lazaretto which is not far off you know—& looks nearer than it is—I will tell him of the five men—I will tell him of my contact with Aglietti[9] in whose

<hr />

[7] A remark of Dryden's recorded in Samuel Johnson's *Lives of the Poets* (1779–81), when Dryden increased his charge for providing poetic prologues to other dramatists' plays.

[8] John Hanson came to Venice with legal papers relating to the sale of Newstead; he also brought a fashionable toy, patented in 1817: the kaleidoscope.

[9] A successful Venetian doctor, whom Byron consulted on his own behalf and, in time, on Teresa Guiccioli's.

presence they died—& who came into my Box at the (St. Benedetto's) Opera the same evening—& shook hands with me;—I will tell him all this—and as he is hypochondriac—perhaps it may kill him.——The Monster left my books—everything—my Magnesia—my tooth powder—&c. &c. and wanted me besides to go to Geneva——but I made him come.—He is a queer fish—the Customs House Officers wanted to examine or have money—he would not pay—they opened every thing.—'Ay—Ay—(said he) look away—*Carts Carts*' that was his phrase for *papers* with a strong English emphasis & accent on the *s* and he actually made them turn over all the Newstead & Rochdale—& Jew—& Chancery papers exclaiming '*Carts Carts*' & came off triumphant with paying a *Centime*—the Officers giving up the matter in despair—finding nothing else—& not being able to translate what they found.——But I have been in a damned passion for all that—for this adventure nearly reconciled me to him.—Pray remember the man & books—and mind & make me a proper paction with Murray or others—I submit the matter to you and Doug.—and you may show the M.S. to Frere and William Rose—and Moore—& whoever you please.—Forgive the Scrawl & the trouble—& write & believe me

ever & truly yrs.
[scrawl for signature]

P. S.—Lord Lauderdale set off today the 12th. Novr.—& means to be in England in about a Month.—

[To Major Thomas Wildman]

Venice. Novr. 18th. 1818

My dear Wildman

Mr. Hanson is on the Eve of his return so that I have only time to return a few inadequate thanks for your very kind letter.——I should regret to trouble you with any requests of mine in regard to the preservation of any signs of my family which may still exist at Newstead—and leave every thing of that kind to your own feelings, present or future, upon the Subject. The portrait which you flatter me by desiring—would not be worth to you your trouble & expence of such an expedition—but you may rely upon your having the very first that may be painted—& which may seem worth your acceptance.——I trust that Newstead will, being yours—remain so—& that it may see you as happy, as I am very sure that you will make your dependents.[10] With regard to myself—you may be sure that whether in the 4th.—5th.—or sixth form—at Harrow,—or in the fluctuations of after-life—I shall always remember with regard my old Schoolfellow—fellow Monitor—& friend;—and recognize with respect the gallant Soldier—who with all the advantages of fortune and allurements of youth to a life of pleasure—devoted himself to duties of a nobler order—and will receive his reward in the esteem and admiration of his Country.—

ever yours most truly & affectly.
Byron

[To Scrope Berdmore Davies]

Venice. Decr. 7th. 1818

My dear Scrope,

You forget that as a Peer I cannot directly nor indirectly interfere in an Election (unless I were proprietor of a Borough) so as to be of service to our friend Hobhouse.—You forget that my arrival would probably have the very reverse effect by reviving every species of Calumny, against *me* for the Electioneering purpose of injuring *him* by the reflection, and that so far from his connection with me being of use to him on such an occasion—it may possibly even *now* be a principal cause of his failing in the attainment of his object.—I wish him every success, but the more I limit myself to wishes only—the better I shall serve him or any one else in that Country.——You can hardly have forgotten the circumstances under which I quitted England, nor the rumours of which I was the Subject—if *they were true* I was unfit for England, if *false* England is unfit for me.——You recollect that with the exception of a few friends (yourself among the foremost of those who staid by me) I was deserted & blackened by all—that even my relations (except my Sister) with that wretched Coxcomb Wilmot and the able-bodied Seaman George,[11] at their head, despaired of or abandoned me—that even Hobhouse thought the tide so strong against me—that he imagined I should

---

[10] Wildman died childless, and Frederick William Webb bought the Abbey from his widow in 1861. Webb's grandson sold it to the philanthropist Sir Julien Cahn, who gave it to the City of Nottingham in 1931. Wildman was a veteran of Waterloo, had by chance met Byron at Dover when he left England in April 1816, and would attend his interment at Hucknall Torkard in 1824.

[11] For the roles of his cousins Robert John Wilmot and George Anson Byron in the Separation, see letter of 3–4 June 1817.

be 'assassinated';—I am not & never was apprehensive on that point—but I am not at all sure that I should not be tempted to assassinate some of the wretched woman's instruments, at least in an honourable way—(Hobhouse's parliamentary predecessor, one of them, having already proved the existence of Nemesis by cutting his own throat[12]) and this might not much forward his Election.——

That sooner or later I must return to England—if I live—seems inevitable—as I have children—connections—property—and interests political as well as personal to require my presence—but I shall not do so willingly—& nothing short of an imperious duty will recall me,—it is true the service of a friend is the most imperious of duties, but my return would *not* serve our friend Hobhouse in this instance—and this conviction is so strong that I should look upon my presence as an actual injury.—With regard to my more personal & private feelings—you are well aware that there is nothing here nor elsewhere that can make me amends for the absence of the friends I had in England—that my Sister—and my daughter;— that yourself and Hobhouse and Kinnaird and others have always claims & recollections that can attach to no subsequent connections of any description— that I shall always look upon you with the greatest regard, & hear of your welfare with the proudest pleasure.—But having said this much,—& feeling far more than I have said; my opinion upon other points is irrevocable—nothing can ever atone to me for the atrocious caprice—the unsupported—almost unasserted—the kind of *hinted* persecution—and *shrugging* Conspiracy—of which I was attempted to be made the victim,—if the tables were to be turned—if they were to decree me all the columns of the Morning Post—and all the tavern-Signs of Wellington, I would not accept them—or if I could tread upon the necks of those who have attempted to bow down mine—I would not do it—not because I do not abhor them—but there is a something inadequate in any species of revenge that I can figure to my imagination—for the treatment they tried to award me.——

We will talk of something else.——Pray report to me the progress of H[obhouse]'s contest—he is in the right to stand—as even if unsuccessful—it is something to have stood for Westminster—but I trust that he will be brought in.—I have heard from all hands that he speaks uncommonly well, Lord Lauderdale told me so in particular very recently.—He is gone to England—& has [a] whole Cargo of my Poesy addressed to Hobhouse's care for Murray[.] *Hanson* has been here too—he *bears* a letter (about *himself*) addressed from me to *Kinnaird & Hobhouse jointly* to which I hope they will *attend*—that is when they have *leisure*—you will see *why*, by the Contents—if the Attorneo delivers them

---

[12] For lawyer George Romilly, who acted for Lady Byron in the Separation, though having a legal retainer from Byron himself, see letter of 7 July 1819.

safely.——Will you remember me to every body—& assure H of my best wishes, and all our friends of my regards—believing me

ever and most affectionately yours

P. S.—*When I sent Hobhouse the parcel by Lord Lauderdale—I knew nothing of the Suicide and Nomination—of course he cannot nor would I wish him to attend to such trifles now, Murray will get one of his literati perhaps—or if not the M.S.S. will take their chance.—— Pray beg Kinnaird to be sure to get my letter to him, from Hanson.—We have all here been much pleased with Hobhouse's book on Italy—some part of it the best he ever wrote—and as good as anything can be.——*

[To Hobhouse and Kinnaird]

Venice January 19th. 1819

Dear H. and dear K.

I approve and sanction all your legal proceedings with regard to my affairs, and can only repeat my thanks & approbation—if you put off the payments of debts 'till *after* Lady Noel's death'—it is well—if till *after* her damnation—better—for that will last forever—yet I hope not:—for her sake as well as the Creditors'— I am willing to believe in Purgatory.——With regard to the Poeshie—I will have no 'cutting & slashing' as Perry calls it—you may omit the stanzas on Castlereagh—indeed it is better—& the two '*Bobs*' at the end of the 3d. stanza of the dedication—which will leave 'high' & 'dry'—good rhymes without any '*double* (or Single) Entendre'[13]—but no more—I appeal—not 'to Philip fasting' but to Alexander drunk—I appeal to Murray at his ledger—to the people—in short, Don Juan shall be an entire horse or none.—If the objection be to the indecency, the Age which applauds the 'Bath Guide' & Little's poems—& reads Fielding & Smollett still—may bear with that;[14]—if to the poetry—I will take my

[13] The 'Dedication' to the first two cantos of *Don Juan* made reference to the British foreign minister, Viscount Castlereagh, as an 'intellectual eunuch', and suggested that the Poet Laureate, Robert Southey, had trouble ejaculating: a 'dry Bob' in Regency slang. Byron withdrew it, as the poem was published anonymously, and the Dedication was not published until 1832.
[14] This was an argument Byron made many times: see letters of 11 November 1818 and 26 January and 4 December 1819.

chance.—I will not give way to all the Cant of Christendom—I have been cloyed with applause & sickened with abuse;—at present—I care for little but the Copyright,—I have imbibed a great love for money—let me have it—if Murray loses this time—he won't the next—he will be cautious—and I shall learn the decline of his customers by his epistolary indications.——But in no case will I submit to have the poem mutilated.—There is another Canto written—but not copied—in two hundred & odd Stanzas, if this succeeds—as to the prudery of the present day—what is it? are we more moral than when Prior wrote—is there anything in Don Juan so strong as in Ariosto—or Voltaire—or Chaucer?—Tell Hobhouse—his letter to De Breme has made a great Sensation—and is to be published in the Tuscan & other Gazettes—Count R[izzo] came to consult with me about it last Sunday—we think of Tuscany—for Florence and Milan are in literary war—but the Lombard league is headed by Monti—& would make a difficulty of insertion in the Lombard Gazettes—once published in the Pisan—it will find its way through Italy—by translation or reply.[15]——So Lauderdale has been telling a story!—I suppose this is my reward for presenting him at Countess Benzone's—& shewing him—what attention I could.——Which 'piece' does he mean?—since last year I have run the Gauntlet;—is it the Tarruscelli—the Da Mosti—the Spineda—the Lotti—the Rizzato—the Elea-nora—the Carlotta—the Giulietta—the Alvisi—the Zambieri—The Eleanora da Bezzi—(who was the King of Naples' Gioaschino's mistress—at least one of them) the Theresina of Mazzurati—the Glettenheimer—& her Sister—the Luigia & her mother—the Fornaretta—the Santa—the Caligari—the Portiera—the Bolognese figurante [dancer]—the Tentora and her sister—cum multis aliis [with many others]?—some of them are Countesses—& some of them Cobblers wives—some noble—some middling—some low—& all whores—which does the damned old 'Ladro—& porco fottuto' [thief and fucked pig] mean?—I have had them all & thrice as many to boot since 1817—Since *he* tells a story about me—I will tell one about him;—when he landed at the *Custom house* from *Corfu*—he called for '*Post horses—directly*'—he was told that there were no horses except mine nearer than the Lido—unless he wished for the four bronze Coursers of St. Mark—which were at his Service.—

I am yrs. ever—

---

[15] Hobhouse and Byron had met Milanese journalist Ludovico di Breme (1780–1820) in October 1816. He later took offence at an essay about Italian literature in Hobhouse's *Historical Illustrations of the Fourth Canto of Childe Harold* (1818; 'Hobhouse's book on Italy', in the previous letter): an essay in fact written by his expatriate compatriot Ugo Foscolo (1778–1827)—though Byron did not know that. Francesco Rizzo-Patrol was a Venetian aristocrat and man of letters; Vincenzo Monti (1754–1828) the leading Italian poet of the time.

Let me have H's Election immediately—I mention it last *as being what I was least likely to forget.——*

P. S.—Whatever Brain-money—you get on my account from Murray—pray remit me—I will never consent to pay away what I earn—that is mine—& what I get by my brains—I will spend on my b——ks—as long as I have a tester or a testicle remaining.—I shall not live long—& for that Reason—I must live while I can—so—let him disburse—& me receive—'for the Night cometh.'[16]*——If I had but had twenty thousand a year I should not have been living now—but all men are not born with a silver or Gold Spoon in their mouths.——My balance—also—my balance—& a Copyright—I have another Canto—too—ready—& then there will be my half year in June—recollect—I care for nothing but 'monies'.—January 20th. 1819.—You say nothing of Mazeppa—did it arrive—with one other—besides that you mention?——*

[To John Murray]

Venice April 6 1819

Dear Sir

The Second Canto of Don Juan was sent on Saturday last by post in 4 packets—two of 4—& two of three sheets each—containing in all two hundred & seventeen stanzas octave measure.—But I will permit no curtailments except those mentioned about Castlereagh & the two 'Bobs' in the introduction.—You sha'n't make *Canticles* of my Cantos. The poem will please if it is lively—if it is stupid it will fail—but I will have none of your damned cutting & slashing.—If you please you may publish *anonymously*[;] it will perhaps be better;—but I will battle my way against them all—like a Porcupine.—So you and Mr. Foscolo &c. want me to undertake what you call a 'great work' an Epic poem I suppose or some such pyramid.[17]—I'll try no such thing—I hate tasks—and then 'seven or eight years!' God send us all well this day three months—let alone years—if one's years can't be better employed than in sweating poesy—a man had better be a ditcher.—And works too!—is Childe Harold nothing? you have so many 'divine' poems, is it nothing to have written a *Human* one? without any of your

---

[16] See John 9: 4.

[17] Murray had written on 19 March to say 'here is *Foscolo* at my side—deploring that a Man of your genius will not occupy some Six or Eight years in the Composition of a Work & Subject worthy of you' (*Murray Letters*, 267). In the English-speaking world Foscolo is remembered for his Romantic novel *Last Letters of Jacopo Ortis* (1798), and little else beside.

worn out machinery.—Why—man—I could have spun the thought of the four cantos of that poem into twenty—had I wanted to book-make—& it's passion into as many modern tragedies—since you want *length* you shall have enough of *Juan* for I'll make 50 cantos.—And Foscolo too! why does *he* not do something more than the letters of Ortis—and a tragedy—and pamphlets—he has good fifteen years more at his command than I have—what has he done all that time?—proved his Genius doubtless—but not fixed it's fame—nor done his utmost.—Besides I mean to write my best work in *Italian*—& it will take me nine years more thoroughly to master the language—& then if my fancy exists & I exist too—I will try what I *can* do *really*.—As to the Estimation of the English which you talk of, let them calculate what it is worth—before they insult me with their insolent condescension.—I have not written for their pleasure;—if they are pleased—it is that they chose to be so,—I have never flattered their opinions—nor their pride—nor will I.—Neither will I make 'Ladies books' 'al dilettar le femine e la plebe' [to please women and workers]—I have written from the fullness of my mind, from passion—from impulse—from many motives—but not for their 'sweet voices.'[18]—I know the precise worth of popular applause—for few Scribblers have had more of it—and if I chose to swerve into their paths—I could retain it or resume it—or increase it—but I neither love ye—nor fear ye and though I buy with ye—and sell with ye—and talk with ye—I will neither eat with ye—drink with ye—nor pray with ye.[19]—They made me without my search a species of popular Idol—they—without reason or judgement beyond the caprice of their Good pleasure—threw down the Image from it's pedestal—it was not broken with the fall—and they would it seems again replace it—but they shall not. You ask about my health—about the beginning of the year—I was in a state of great exhaustion—attended by such debility of Stomach—that nothing remained upon it—and I was obliged to reform my 'way of life' which was conducting me from the 'yellow leaf' to the Ground with all deliberate speed.[20]—I am better in health and morals—and very much yrs. ever,

[scrawl]

P. S.—Tell Mrs. Leigh I never had 'my Sashes' and I want some tooth-powder—the red—by all or any means.—

---

[18] See *Coriolanus*, II. iii. 112.   [19] See *The Merchant of Venice*, I. iii. 33–5.
[20] See *Macbeth*, V. iii. 24–5.

[To John Cam Hobhouse]

Venice April 6. 1819

My dear Hobhouse

I have not derived from the Scriptures of Rochfoucault that consolation which I expected 'in the misfortunes of our best friends'.[21]——I had much at heart your gaining the Election—but from 'the filthy puddle' into which your Patriotism had run you—I had like Croaker my bodings but like old 'Currycomb' you make so 'handsome a Corpse'—that my wailing is changed into admiration.[22]— With the Burdettites divided—and the Whigs & Tories united—what else could be expected? If I had guessed at your *opponent*——I would have made one among you Certes—and have f——d Caroline Lamb out of her 'two hundred votes'—although at the expence of a testicle.——I think I could have neutralized her zeal with a little management—but alas! who could have thought of that Cuckoldy family's <sitting> *standing* for a *member*—I suppose it is the first time that George Lamb ever *stood* for any thing—& William with his 'Corni Cazzo da Seno!' (as we Venetians say—it means Penis *in earnest*—a sad way of swearing) but that you who know them should have to con*cur* with such dogs—well—did I ever—no I never—&c. &c. &c.[23]——I have sent my second Canto—but I will have no gelding.——Murray has my order of the day.—Douglas Kinnaird with more than usual politeness writes me vivaciously that Hanson or I willed the *three per cents* instead of the five—as if I could prefer *three* to *five* per Cent!—death & fiends!—and then *he* lifts up his leg against the publication of Don Juan—et 'tu *Brute*' (the *e mute* recollect) I shall certainly hitch our dear friend into some d——d story or other—'my dear Mr. Sneer—Mr. Sneer—my dear'[24]——I must write again in a few days—it being now past four in the morning—it is Passion week—& rather dull.—I am dull too for I have fallen in love with a Romagnuola Countess from Ravenna—who is nineteen years old & has a Count of fifty— whom She seems disposed to qualify the first year of marriage being just over.— I knew her a little last year at her starting, but they always wait a year—at least

---

[21] See Rochefoucault, *Maxim* 19: 'Nous avons tous assez de force pour supporter les maux d'autrui.'

[22] See the end of the first act of Oliver Goldsmith's *The Good-Natured Man* (1768), where Croaker says of Ruggins, the curry-comb maker: 'I'm told he makes a very handsome corpse, and becomes his coffin prodigiously.'

[23] Hobhouse had stood for election on a Radical ticket at Westminster, but was defeated by (of all people) Caroline Lamb's brother-in-law George Lamb. He would win the seat in 1820. Sir Francis Burdett (1770–1844) was a Radical politician and second member for Westminster in the poll; Byron had supported him from the House of Lords.

[24] See Sheridan, *The Critic* (1779), I. i. 77–8.

generally.—I met her first at the Albrizzi's, and this Spring at the Benzone's—
and I have hopes Sir—hopes—but She wants me to come to Ravenna—& then
to Bologna—now this would be all very well for certainties—but for mere
hopes—if She should plant me—and I should make a 'fiasco' never could
I show my face on the Piazza.———It is nothing that Money can do—for the
Conte is awfully rich—& would be so even in England—but he is fifty and odd—
has had two wives & children before this his third—(a pretty fair-haired Girl last
year out of a Convent—now making her second tour of the Venetian Conversazioni—) and does not seem so jealous this year as he did last—when he stuck
close to her side even at the Governor's.———She is pretty—but has no tact—
answers aloud—when she should whisper—talks of age to old ladies who want
to pass for young—and this blessed night horrified a correct company at the
Benzona's—by calling out to me 'Mio Byron' in an audible key during a dead
Silence of pause in the other prattlers, who stared & whispered [to] their
respective Serventi.—One of her preliminaries is that I must never leave
Italy;—I have no desire to leave it—but I should not like to be frittered down
into a regular Cicisbeo [lover].—What shall I do! I am in love—and tired of
promiscuous concubinage—& have now an opportunity of settling for life.—

[ever yours]

P. S.—*We have had a fortnight ago the devil's own row with an Elephant who broke loose—
ate up a fruitshop—killed his keeper—broke into a Church—and was at last killed by a
Cannon Shot brought from the Arsenal.—I saw him the day he broke open his own house—
he was standing in the Riva*[25] *& his keepers trying to persuade him with* peck-loaves *to go
on board a sort of Ark they had got.—I went close to him that afternoon in my Gondola—&
he amused himself with flinging great beams that flew about over the water in all
directions—he was then not very angry—but towards midnight he became furious—&
displayed the most extraordinary strength—pulling down every thing before him.—All
Musquetry proved in vain—& when he charged the Austrians threw down their musquets
& ran.—At last they broke a hole & brought a field-piece the first shot missed the second
entered behind—& came out all but the Skin at his Shoulder.—I saw him dead the next
day—a stupendous fellow.—He went mad for want of a She it being the rutting month.—
Fletcher is well.—I have got two monkeys, a fox—& two new mastiffs—Mutz is still in high*

---

[25] The Riva degli Schiavoni, which runs along the waterfront at St Mark's Square and the Ducal
Palace.

old age.—The Monkeys are charming.—Last month I had a business about a Venetian Girl who wanted to marry me—a circumstance prevented like Dr. Blifil's Espousals not only by my previous marriage but by Mr. Allworthy's being acquainted with the existence of Mrs. Dr. Blifil.[26]——I was very honest and gave her no hopes—but there was a scene—I having been found at her window at Midnight and they sent me a Priest and a friend of the family's to talk with me next day both of whom I treated with Coffee.——

[To Countess Teresa Guiccioli]

Venice, April 25th, 1819

My Love,

I hope you have received my letter of the 22nd, addressed to the person in Ravenna of whom you told me, before leaving Venice. You scold me for not having written to you in the country—but—how could I? My sweetest treasure, you gave me no other address but that of Ravenna.—If you knew how great is the love I feel for you, you would not believe me capable of forgetting you for a single instant; you must become better acquainted with me—perhaps one day you will know that although I do not deserve you—I do indeed love you. You want to know whom I most enjoy seeing, since you have gone away, who makes me tremble and feel—not what you alone can arouse in my soul—but something like it?—Well—I will tell you—it is the *old porter* whom Fanny used to send with your notes when you were in Venice—and who now brings your letters—still dear, but not so dear as those which brought the hope of seeing you that same day at the usual time.—My Teresa where are you? Everything here reminds me of you—everything is the same, but you are not here and I still am.—In separation the one who goes away suffers less than the one who stays behind.— The distraction of the journey, the change of scene, the landscape—the movement, perhaps even the separation, distracts the mind and lightens the heart.— But the one who stays behind is surrounded by the same things; tomorrow is like yesterday—while only She is lacking who made him forget that a tomorrow would ever come.—When I go to the Conversazione, I give myself up to Tedium, too happy to suffer ennui rather than grief. I see the same faces— hear the same voices—but no longer dare to look towards the sofa where I shall not see *you* any more—but instead some old crone who might be Calunmy personified. I hear, without the slightest emotion, the opening of that door which I used to watch with so much anxiety when I was there before you,

---

[26] See Henry Fielding, *Tom Jones* (1749), i. 10.

hoping to see you come in. I will not speak of *much dearer* places still, for *there* I shall not go—*until* you return. I have no other pleasure than thinking of you, but I do not see how I could see again the places where we have been together— especially those most consecrated to our love—without dying of grief.—Fanny is now in Treviso—and God knows when I shall have any more letters from you—but meanwhile I have received three; you must by now have arrived in Ravenna—I long to hear of your arrival;—my fate depends upon your deci- sion.—Fanny will be back in a few days—but tomorrow I shall send her a note by a friend's hand to ask her not to forget to send me your news, if she receives any letters before returning to Venice.—My Treasure—my life has become most monotonous and sad—neither books—nor music—nor *horses*—(rare things in Venice—but you know that mine are at the Lido) nor dogs—give me any pleasure;—the society of women does not attract me;—I won't speak of the society of men;—for that I have always despised.—For some years I have been trying systematically to avoid strong passions, having suffered too much from the tyranny of love.—*Never to feel admiration*[27]—and to enjoy myself without giving too much importance to the enjoyment in itself—to feel indifference toward human affairs—contempt for many—but hatred for none, this was the basis of my philosophy. I did [not] mean to love any more—nor did I hope to receive Love.—You have put to flight all my resolutions,—now I am all yours,— I will become what you wish—perhaps happy in your love—but never at peace again.—You should not have re-awakened my heart—for—(at least in my own country) my love has been fatal to those I love—and to myself.—But these reflections come too late. You have been mine—and whatever the outcome—I am, and eternally shall be, entirely yours.—I kiss you a thousand and a thousand times—but—

> 'What does it profit you, my heart to be beloved?
> What good to me to have so dear a lover?
> Why should a cruel fate—
> Separate those whom love has once united?'[28]

Love me—as always your most tender and faithful,

B

---

[27] 'Nil admirari'; a famous Stoical tag from Horace, *Letters*, I. vi. 1–2: 'Nought to admire is all the art we know,' as Pope translated it, 'To make men happy and to keep them so.'
[28] See Giovanni Battista Guarini, *The Faithful Shepherd* (1585), III. iv. 8–11.

[To John Murray]

Venice. May 15th. 1819

Dear Sir

I have received & return by this post under cover—the first proof of 'Don Juan.'—Before the second can arrive it is probable that I may have left Venice—and the length of my absence is so uncertain—that you had better proceed to the publication without boring me with more proofs—I sent by last post an addition—and a new copy of 'Julia's letter,'[29] perceiving or supposing the former one in Winter did not arrive.—Mr. Hobhouse is at it again about indelicacy—there is *no indelicacy*—if he wants *that*, let him read Swift—his great Idol—but his Imagination must be a dunghill with a Viper's nest in the middle— to engender such a supposition about this poem.—For my part I think you are all crazed.—What does he mean about 'G—d damn'—there is '*damn*' to be sure—but no 'G—d' whatever.—And as to what he calls 'a p—ss bucket'—it is nothing but simple water—as I am a Sinner—pray tell him so—& request him not 'to put me in a phrenzy,' as Sir Anthony Absolute says—'though he was not the indulgent father that I am.'[30]—I have got yr. extract, & the 'Vampire'.[31] I need not say it is *not mine*—there is a rule to go by—you are my publisher (till we quarrel) and what is not published by you is not written by me.—The Story of Shelley's agitation is true—I can't tell what seized him—for he don't want courage. He was once with me in a Gale of Wind in a small boat right under the rocks between Meillerie & St. Gingo—we were five in the boat—a servant— two boatmen—& ourselves. The Sail was mismanaged & the boat was filling fast—he can't swim.—I stripped off my coat—made him strip off his—& take hold of an oar—telling him that I thought (being myself an expert swimmer) I could save him if he would not struggle when I took hold of him—unless we got smashed against the rocks which were high & sharp with an awkward Surf on them at that minute;—we were then about a hundred yards from shore—

---

[29] Don Juan's first lover, Donna Julia of Seville, wrote him a letter after their affair was discovered and she was sent to a nunnery; it occupies stanzas 192–7 of the first canto of Byron's poem.

[30] See Sheridan, *The Rivals* (1775), II. i. 351–3.

[31] Dr Polidori published his Gothic novel *The Vampyre: A Tale, By the Right Honourable Lord Byron*, in March 1819. In his preface, he described an episode one night at Diodati when Shelley, who had been telling and hearing ghost stories, suddenly dashed from the room in hysteria. 'The physician and Lord Byron followed, and discovered him leaning against a mantle-piece, with cold drops of perspiration trickling down his face. After having given him something to refresh him, upon enquiring into the cause of his alarm, they found that his wild imagination having pictured to him the bosom of one of the young ladies [Mary Godwin] with eyes ... he was obliged to lave the room in order to destroy the impression.' The famous ghost-story challenge was issued in later conversation.

and the boat in peril.—He answered me with the greatest coolness—'that he had no notion of being saved—& that I would have enough to do to save myself, and begged not to trouble me'.—Luckily the boat righted & baling we got round a point into St. Gingo—where the Inhabitants came down and embraced the boatmen on their escape—the Wind having been high enough to tear up some huge trees from the Alps above us as we saw next day.—And yet the same Shelley who was as cool as it was possible to be in such circumstances— (of which I am no judge myself as the chance of swimming naturally gives self-possession when near shore) certainly had the fit of phantasy which P[olidori] describes—though *not exactly* as he describes it. The story of the agreement to write the Ghost-books is true—but the ladies are *not Sisters*—one is Godwin's daughter by Mary Wolstonecraft—and the other the *present* Mrs. Godwin's daughter by a former husband. So much for Scoundrel Southey's Story of '*incest*'—neither was there *any promiscuous intercourse* whatever—both are an invention of the execrable villain Southey—whom I will term so as publicly as he deserves.—Mary Godwin (now Mrs. Shelley) wrote 'Frankenstein'—which you have reviewed thinking it Shelley's—methinks it is a wonderful work for a Girl of nineteen—*not* nineteen indeed—at that time.—I enclose you the beginning of mine—by which you will see how far it resembles Mr. Colburn's publication.[32]—If you choose to publish it in the Edinburgh Magazine (*Wilsons & Blackwoods*) you may—*stating why*, & with such explanatory proem as you please.—I never went on with it—as you will perceive by the date.—I began it in an old account-book of Miss Milbanke's which I kept because it contains the word '*Household*' written by her twice on the inside blank page of the Covers— being the only two Scraps I have in the world in her writing, except her name to the deed of Separation.—Her letters I sent back—except those of the quarrelling correspondence—and those being documents are placed in possession of a third person (Mr. Hobhouse) with copies of several of my own,—so that I have no kind of memorial whatever of her but these *two* words—and her actions. I have torn the leaves containing the part of the tale out of the book & enclose them with this sheet.—Next week—I set out for Romagna—at least in all probability.—You had better go on with the publications without waiting to hear farther—for I have other things in my head.—'Mazeppa' & 'the Ode'—*separate*—what think you?—*Juan anonymous without the dedication*—for I won't be shabby—& attack Southey under Cloud of night.—What do you mean? first you seem hurt by my letter? & then in your next you talk of it's 'power' & so forth—'this is a d—d blind Story Beck—but never mind—go on.' You may be

---

[32] For Byron's 'Augustus Darvell: A Fragment of a Ghost Story', see *CMP* 58–63. He published it alongside *Mazeppa* in 1819 to disprove his connection with Polidori's fraud.

sure I said nothing *on purpose* to plague you—but if you will put me 'in a phrenzy, I will never call you *Jack* again.'[33]—I remember nothing of the epistle at present.—What do you mean by Polidori's *diary?*—why—I defy him to say any thing about me—but he is welcome[34]—I have nothing to *reproach* me with on his score—and I am much mistaken if that is not his *own* opinion—but why publish the names of the two girls? & in such a manner?—what a blundering piece of exculpation!—He asked Pictet[35] &c. to dinner—and of course was left to entertain them.—I went into *Society solely* to present *him* (as I told him) that he might return into good company if he chose—it was the best thing for his youth & circumstances—for myself I had done with Society—& having presented him—withdrew to my own 'way of life.'[36]—It is true that I returned without entering Lady Dalrymple Hamilton's—because I saw it full.—It is true—that Mrs. Hervey (She writes novels) fainted at my entrance into Coppet—& then came back again; on her fainting—the Duchesse de Broglie exclaimed: 'This is *too much*—at Sixty five years of age!'[37]—I never gave 'the English' an opportunity of 'avoiding' me—but I trust, that if ever I do, they will seize it.—

I am yrs. very truly

B

[To Augusta Leigh]

Venice May 17th. 1819

My dearest Love

I have been negligent in not writing, but what can I say[.] Three years absence—& the total change of scene and habit make such a difference—that we have now nothing in common but our affections & our relationship.—

But I have never ceased nor can cease to feel for a moment that perfect & boundless attachment which bound & binds me to you—which renders me utterly incapable of *real* love for any other human being—what could they be to me after *you?* My own XXXX [short word crossed out] we may have been very wrong—but I repent of nothing except that cursed marriage—& your refusing

---

[33] See Sheridan, *The Rivals*, II. i. 353–5.
[34] *The Diary of John William Polidori* was eventually published in 1911.
[35] Marc-Auguste Pictet (1752–1825), Genevan scientist.
[36] See *Macbeth*, V. iii. 24.
[37] Jane Dalrymple-Hamilton (née Duncan; 1780–1852), touring Switzerland in 1816, whose looks Byron commented on favourably (*LJ* v. 132). Mrs Elizabeth Hervey published *Amabel, or Memoirs of a Woman of Fashion* in 1814.

to continue to love me as you had loved me—I can neither forget nor *quite forgive* you for that precious piece of reformation.—but I can never be other than I have been—and whenever I love anything it is because it reminds me in some way or other of yourself—for instance I not long ago attached myself to a Venetian for no earthly reason (although a pretty woman) but because she was called XXXX [short word crossed out] and she often remarked (without knowing the reason)—how fond I was of the name.—It is heart-breaking to think of our long Separation—and I am sure more than punishment enough for all our sins— Dante is more humane in his 'Hell' for he places his unfortunate lovers (Francesca of Rimini & Paolo whose case fell a good deal short of *ours*—though sufficiently naughty) in company—and though they suffer—it is at least together.[38]—If ever I return to England—it will be to see you—and recollect that in all time—& place—and feelings—I have never ceased to be the same to you in heart—Circumstances may have ruffled my manner—& hardened my spirit—you may have seen me harsh & exasperated with all things around me; grieved & tortured with *your new resolution,*—& the soon after persecution of that infamous fiend who drove me from my Country & conspired against my life— by endeavouring to deprive me of all that could render it precious—but remember that even then *you* were the sole object that cost me a tear? and *what tears!* do you remember *our* parting? I have not spirits now to write to you upon other subjects—I am well in health—and have no cause of grief but the reflection that we are not together—When you write to me speak to me of yourself—& say that you love me—never mind common-place people & topics—which can be in no degree interesting—to me who see nothing in England but the country which holds *you*—or around it but the sea which divides us.—They say absence destroys weak passions—& confirms strong ones—Alas! *mine* for you is the union of all passions & of all affections—Has strengthened itself but will destroy me—I do not speak of *physical* destruction—for I have endured & can endure much—but of the annihilation of all thoughts feelings or hopes—which have not more or less a reference to you & to *our recollections*—

Ever dearest
[Signature erased]

---

[38] Two of the most fêted illicit lovers in world literature, who are punished in the second circle of Dante's *Inferno* (Canto 5).

[To John Murray]

Venice, May 21st. 1819

Dear Sir

I should be glad to know why Mr. Hobhouse has not yet seen the second Canto?—and why you took no notice—nor gave any answer to Mr. Kinnaird, when he read to you a passage from my letter to him—requesting *him* to adjust with you some business?—Let me know the *precise time* of your coming here that I may be in the way to receive you, and pray bring me some '*Macassar*' or '*Russia Oil*', as I begin to get venerable.—You talk of 'approximations to indelicacy'— this reminds me of George Lamb's quarrel at Cambridge with Scrope Davies— 'Sir—said George—he *hinted at my illegitimacy*.' 'Yes,' said Scrope—'I called him a damned adulterous bastard'—the approximation and the hint are not unlike.[39]—What think you of Canto second? *there's* a Gale of Wind for you! all nautical—and true to the vocabulary;—Ask the 'Navy List'.—

yrs. [scrawl]
B

[To Countess Teresa Guiccioli]

[Venice, May 28, 1819]

[Interpolated in Fanny Silvestrini's letter[40]]

My Love—I hear with the greatest distress of your illness, and all the more because I had hoped to hear by today's post that you were completely recovered. However, in spite of what you write I shall leave here on Saturday the 29th. I shall go to Bologna and there wait for the letter which you say you are sending me, which Fanny will not fail to forward.—My desire is equal to yours, to see you, to embrace you—and to say a thousand times that I love you.—I kiss you with all my soul, and am always yours.

[scrawl for signature]

---

[39] Murray had written nervously about the second canto of *Don Juan* on 3 May: 'the enquiries after its appearance are not a few—pray use your most tasteful discression <in> an [*sic*] wrap up or leave out certain approximations to indelicacy' (*Murray Letters*, 272).

[40] Silvestrini was a friend of Teresa's, who allowed Byron to add to her letters, and generally aided communication between the lovers. She would later marry Byron's steward Lega Zambelli.

[To John Murray]

Bologna. June 7th. 1819

Dear Sir

Tell Mr. Hobhouse that I wrote to him a few days ago from Ferrara.—It will therefore be idle in him or you to wait for any further answers or returns of proofs from Venice—as I have directed that no English letters be sent after me. The publication can be proceeded in without, and I am already sick of your remarks—to which I think not the least attention ought to be paid. Tell Mr. Hobhouse that since I wrote to him—that I had availed myself of my Ferrara Letters & found the Society much younger and better there than at Venice. I was very much pleased with the little the shortness of my stay permitted me to see of the Gonfaloniere Count Mosti, and his family and friends in general.——I have been picture-gazing this morning at the famous Domenichino and Guido—both of which are superlative.[41]—I afterwards went to the beautiful Cimetery of Bologna—beyond the Walls—and found besides the Superb Burial Ground—an original of a Custode who reminded me of the grave-digger in Hamlet.[42]——He has a collection of Capuchins' Skulls labelled on the forehead—and taking down one of them—said 'this was Brother Desiderio Berro who died at forty—one of my best friends—I begged his head of his Brethren after his decease and they gave it me—I put it in lime and then boiled it—here it is teeth and all in excellent preservation—He was the merriest—cleverest fellow I ever knew, whereever he went he brought joy, and when any one was melancholy the sight of him was enough to make him cheerful again—He walked so actively you might have taken him for a Dancer—he joked—he laughed—oh! he was such a Frate [monk]—as I never saw before nor ever shall again'.—He told me that he had himself planted all the Cypresses in the Cimetery—that he had the greatest attachment to them and to his dead people—that since 1801—they had buried fifty three thousand persons.—In showing some older monuments, there was that of a Roman Girl of twenty—with a bust by Bernini[43] She was a Princess Barberini—dead two centuries ago—he said that on opening her Grave they had

---

[41] For a man who professed to hate art, Byron sometimes went out of his way to inspect it. Both Domenichino (1581–1641) and Guido Reni (1575–1642) were native to Bologna, and are well represented in the Pinacoteca Nazionale there.

[42] See *Hamlet*, V. i.

[43] Gian Lorenzo Bernini (1598–1680), baroque sculptor and architect, who worked for the Barberini family in Rome. The Certosa di Bologna, opened in 1801, is one of Europe's most lavishly appointed neoclassical cemeteries. The bust of Maria Barberini Duglioli by Bernini's student Giuliano Finelli is now in the Louvre; a copy by Giuseppe Giorgetti was incorporated with her tomb in Bologna.

found her hair complete—and 'as yellow as Gold.' Some of the epitaphs at Ferrara pleased me more than the more splendid monuments of Bologna—for instance

> 'Martini Luigi
>> Implora pace.'
> 'Lucrezia Picini
>> Implora eterna quiete.'[44]

Can any thing be more full of pathos! those few words say all that can be said or sought—the dead had had enough of life—all they wanted was rest—and this they 'implore.' there is all the helplessness—and humble hope and deathlike prayer that can arise from the Grave—'implora pace.' I hope, whoever may survive me and shall see me put in the foreigners' burying-Ground at the Lido—within the fortress by the Adriatic—will see those two words and no more put over me I trust they won't think of 'pickling and bringing me home to Clod or Blunderbuss Hall'[45] I am sure my Bones would not rest in an English grave—or my Clay mix with the earth of that Country:—I believe the thought would drive me mad on my death-bed could I suppose that any of my friends would be base enough to convey my carcase back to your soil—I would not even feed your worms—if I could help it.——So—as Shakespeare says of Mowbray the banished Duke of Norfolk—who died at Venice (see Richard 2d.) that he after fighting

> 'Against black Pagans—Turks and Saracens
> And toil'd with works of war, retired himself
> To Italy; and there, at *Venice*, gave
> His body to that *pleasant* Country's Earth,
> And his pure Soul unto his Captain Christ
> Under whose colours he had fought so long.'[46]

Before I left Venice—I had returned to you your late—and Mr. Hobhouse's sheets of Juan—don't wait for further answers from me—but address yours to Venice as usual. I know nothing of my own movements—I may return there in a few days—or not for some time—all this depends on circumstances—I left Mr. Hoppner very well—as well as his son—and Mrs. Hoppner.—My daughter Allegra was well too and is growing pretty—her hair is growing darker and her eyes are blue.—Her temper and her ways Mr. Hoppner says are like mine—as well as her features.—She will make in that case a manageable young lady.——I never hear anything of Ada—the little Electra of my Mycenae—the moral Clytemnestra is not very communicative of her tidings—but there will come a day of reckoning—even if I should not live to see it;—I have at least seen

---

[44] 'Implores peace'; 'implores eternal tranquillity'.
[45] See Sheridan, *The Rivals*, V. iii. 124–5.   [46] See *Richard II*, IV. i. 86–91.

Romilly shivered—who was one of the assassins.[47]——When that felon, or Lunatic—(take your choice—he must be one and might be both) was doing his worst to uproot my whole family tree, branch, and blossoms; when after taking my retainer he went over to them—when he was bringing desolation on my hearth—and destruction on my household Gods—did he think that in less than three years a natural event—a severe domestic—but an expected and common domestic Calamity would lay his Carcase in a Cross road or stamp his name in a Verdict of Lunacy?—Did he (who in his drivelling sexagenary dotage had not the courage to survive his Nurse—for what else was a wife to him at his time of life?—) reflect or consider what my feelings must have been—when wife—and child—and Sister—and name—and fame—and Country were to be my sacrifice on his legal altar—and this at a moment when my health was declining—my fortune embarrassed—and my Mind had been shaken by many kinds of disappointment—while I was yet young and might have reformed what might be wrong in my conduct—and retrieved what was perplexing in my affairs. But the wretch is in his grave,—I detested him living and I will not affect to pity him dead—I still loathe him as much as we can hate dust—but that is nothing. What a long letter I have scribbled

yrs. [scrawl]
B

P. S.—*Here as in Greece they strew flowers on the tombs—I saw a quantity of rose-leaves and entire roses scattered over the Graves at Ferrara—it has the most pleasing effect you can imagine.—*

[To Countess Teresa Guiccioli]

[Ravenna] June 11th, 1819

My Love:

Pray instruct me how I am to behave in these circumstances.—I am not clear as to what it is best to do.—I think of staying here until you go—and then finding a

---

[47] Byron had a particular loathing for the barrister Sir Samuel Romilly (1757–1818), for the reason he explains. Romilly committed suicide on 2 November, shattered by his wife's death a few days before.

way of meeting in Bologna—and then in Ferrara.—But all these plans depend upon your wishes.—I have no life now, except in you.—My peace is lost in any case,—but I should prefer death to this uncertainty.—Pray forgive and pity me. Remember that I am here because you ordered me to come—and that every moment in which I do not——but it is useless to write—I feel inexpressibly unhappy, I do see you—but how? and in what a state!!——I have tried to distract myself with this farce of visiting antiquities—it seems quite intolerably tedious—but at the moment everything else is equally displeasing.—The little that interests me, Dante's tomb—and a few things in the library—I have already seen with an indifference made pardonable by the state of my heart.—You see that I do not go into Society—and that I only seek ways of being near to you—but how?—you are so surrounded;—I am a foreigner in Italy—and still more a foreigner in Ravenna—and naturally little versed in the customs of the country—I am afraid of compromising you—for myself there is little more to fear— my fate is already decided.—It is impossible for me to live long in this state of torment—I am writing to you in tears—and I am not a man who cries easily— when I cry my tears come from the heart, and are of blood.—At this point— (midnight) I have received your letters—and the handkerchief—and I am a little calmer.—I shall study to do all that you command.—I am continuing this note without changing a word—to show you what sort of an inferno I have carried in my heart since my arrival.—If you knew what it costs me to control myself in your presence!—but I will not say more,—let us hope—that time will teach me hypocrisy.—You speak of 'my sacrifices &c.'—don't say any more—my heart is already sacrificed—and after that victim, I can offer no other—A sign from you will suffice to lead me or send me—not only to Bologna, but to the grave.—Do not mistrust me—I do not mistrust you—but the difficulties of our circumstances—I should like to hope—but—but—always a *But!*—meanwhile *you* hope—and that is enough.——I thank you—I embrace you—I kiss you a thousand times

B

P. S.—Why send me back my *handkerchief?—I see from the mark that it is the one I gave you on the evening before your departure—I would not give you back a thread of yours (which I always keep by me) to obtain an empire.——*

[To Richard Belgrave Hoppner]

Ravenna. June 20th. 1819

My dear Hoppner

I wrote to you a week ago (particularly begging a line in answer by return of post) to request you would send off Augustine with the two Grey saddle horses—and the Carriage & Carriage horses—saddles &c. to wait for me at the Pelegrino—(the Inn there) in *Bologna*.—To this letter & one of the same purport to Mr. Scott I have had no answer—which makes me uneasy as I shall probably not return to Venice for some time.—I wished my English letters also to be forwarded with Augustine to Bologna.—If there was any want of Money—Siri & Willhalm would equip him.——Pray write to me here (*Ravenna*) by next post—it will reach me in time,—and do not let Augustine delay a moment for the nonsense of that son of a b—h Edgecombe—who may probably be the cause of his dawdling. I wrote to you from Padua—and from Bologna—& since from Ravenna.——I find my situation very agreeable—but want my horses very much—there being good riding in the environs.—I can fix no time for my return to Venice—it may be soon or late—or not at all—it all depends on the *Dama*, whom I found very seriously in *bed* with a cough and spitting of blood &c.—all of which has subsided—and something else has recommenced.—Her miscarriage has made her a good deal thinner;—and I found all the people here firmly persuaded that she would never recover;—they were mistaken however.—My letters were useful as far as I employed them—and I like both the place and people—though I don't trouble the latter more than I can help.—*She* manages very well—though the *local[e]* is inconvenient—(no *bolts* and be d—d to them) and we run great risks—(were it not at sleeping hours—after dinner)—and *no* place—but the great Saloon of his own palace—so that if I come away with a Stiletto in my gizzard some fine afternoon—I shall not be astonished.—I can't make *him* out at all—he visits me frequently—and takes me out (like Whittington the Lord Mayor[48]) in a coach and *six* horses—the fact appears to be that he is completely *governed* by her—for that matter—so am I.—The people here don't know what to make of us—as he had the character of Jealousy with all his wives—this is the third.—He is the richest of the Ravennese by their own account—but is not popular among them.——By the aid of a Priest—a Chambermaid—a young Negro-boy and a female friend—we are enabled to

---

[48] Richard Whittington (1354–1423), six times Lord Mayor of London, and inspiration for the legend of Dick Whittington and his Cat.

carry on our unlawful loves as far as they can well go—though generally with some peril—especially as the female friend and priest are at present out of town for some days—so that some of the precautions devolve upon the Maid and Negro.——Now do pray—send off Augustine—& carriage—and cattle to Bologna without fail or delay—or I shall lose my remaining Shred of senses.—— Don't forget this.—My coming—going—and every thing depends upon *her* entirely just as Mrs. Hoppner—(to whom I remit my reverences) said, in the true spirit of female prophecy.——You are but a shabby fellow not to have written before—and I am truly

yours [scrawl]

⸺⸺⸺ ⧜ ⸺⸺⸺

P. S.—Address by return of Post to me—at Ravenna.

[To Countess Teresa Guiccioli]

[June–July 1819?]

'My thoughts cannot find rest in me'[49] I was right then—what is that man doing every evening for so long beside you in your box?—'*so we are agreed*'—fine words! '*you are agreed*', it appears,—I have noticed that every time I turned my head toward the stage you turned your eyes to look at that man—and this, after all that had happened today!——But do not fear, tomorrow evening I shall leave the field clear to him.——I have no strength to bear a fresh torment every day— you have made me despicable in my own eyes and perhaps soon in those of others.—Have you not seen my torments? have you not pitied them? I forgive you what you have made me suffer—but I can never forgive myself the weakness of heart which has prevented me until now from taking the only honourable step in such circumstances—that of—bidding you good-bye—for ever——

Midnight——

My time for sleep before I knew you.——Let me go—it is better to die from the pain of separation—than from that of betrayal—my life now is a constant agony—I have enjoyed a unique and final happiness in your arms—but—Oh

---

[49] '*I suoi pensieri in lui dormir non ponno*', last line of the tenth canto of Torquato Tasso's epic, *Jerusalem Delivered* (1581). Byron used the line as the epigraph to *The Corsair* in 1814.

God!—how much more those moments are costing me!—and *they* [cost] *this!*—now that I am writing to you—alone—completely alone;—I had no one but you in the world—and now not having you any more (without the heart what is the rest?) solitude has become as tedious as society—for that image which I pictured as so pure, so dear—is now nothing but a perfidious and menacing shadow,—and yet always *yours.*——

[To John Murray]

Ravenna. August 1st. 1819

Address yr. answer to Venice however

Dear Sir

Don't be alarmed.—You will see me defend myself gaily—that is—if I happen to be in Spirits—and by *Spirits* I don't mean your meaning of the word—but the spirit of a bull-dog when pinched—or a bull when pinned—it is then that they make best sport—and as my Sensations under an attack are probably a happy compound of the united energies of those amiable animals—you may perhaps see what Marrall calls 'rare sport'[50]—and some good tossing and goring in the course of the controversy.—But I must be in the right cue first—and I doubt I am almost too far off to be in a sufficient fury for the purpose—and then I have effeminated and enervated myself with love and the summer in these last two months.—I wrote to Mr. Hobhouse the other day—and foretold that Juan would either fall entirely or succeed completely—there will be no medium—appearances are not favourable—but as you write the day after publication—it can hardly be decided what opinion will predominate.—You seem in a fright—and doubtless with cause.[51]—Come what may—I never will flatter the Million's canting in any shape—circumstances may or may not have placed me at times in a situation to lead the public opinion—but the public opinion—never led nor ever shall lead me.—I will not sit on 'a degraded throne'[52] so pray put Messrs. Southey—or Sotheby—or Tom Moore—or Horace Twiss upon it—they will all of them be transported with their coronation.——You have bought Harlow's

---

[50] See Philip Massinger, *A New Way to Pay Old Debts* (1625), V. i. 399.

[51] Murray wrote on 16 July, the day after the publication of *Don Juan*, about the rumblings of disapproval coming in his direction: 'as soon as these beratings find their way in words & vent in newspapers and reviews—by the Lord you shall have them all—that you may repel them & those who are calling every half hour, I understand—sorry that Mr Murray has "had anything to do with it".... ' (*Murray Letters*, 275).

[52] Byron quotes himself: see [Stanzas ('Could Love for ever')], 45 (*CPW* iv. 244).

drawings of Margarita and me rather dear methinks[53]—but since you desire the story of Margarita Cogni—you shall be told it—though it may be lengthy.——Her face is of the fine Venetian cast of the old Time—and her figure though perhaps too tall not less fine—taken altogether in the national dress.——In the summer of 1817, Hobhouse and myself were sauntering on horseback along the Brenta one evening—when amongst a group of peasants we remarked two girls as the prettiest we had seen for some time.—About this period there had been great distress in the country—and I had a little relieved some of the people.— Generosity makes a great figure at very little cost in Venetian livres—and mine had probably been exaggerated—as an Englishman's——Whether they remarked us looking at them or no—I know not—but one of them called out to me in Venetian—'Why do not you who relieve others—think of us also?'—I turned round and answered her—'Cara—tu sei troppo bella e giovane per aver' bisogno del' soccorso mio' ['sweetheart, you are too young and pretty to need my help']—she answered—[']if you saw my hut and my food—you would not say so[']—All this passed half jestingly—and I saw no more of her for some days—A few evenings after—we met with these two girls again—and they addressed us more seriously—assuring us of the truth of their statement.— They were cousins—Margarita married—the other single.—As I doubted still of the circumstances—I took the business up in a different light—and made an appointment with them for the next evening.—Hobhouse had taken a fancy to the single lady—who was much shorter—in stature—but a very pretty girl also.——They came attended by a third woman—who was cursedly in the way—and Hobhouse's charmer took fright (I don't mean at Hobhouse but at not being married—for here no woman will do anything under adultery), and flew off—and mine made some bother—at the propositions—and wished to consider of them.—I told her 'if you really are in want I will relieve you without any conditions whatever—and you may make love with me or no just as you please—that shall make no difference—but if you are not in absolute necessity— this is naturally a rendezvous—and I presumed that you understood this—when you made the appointment'.—She said that she had no objection to make love with me—as she was married—and all married women did it—but that her husband (a baker) was somewhat ferocious—and would do her a mischief.—In short—in a few evenings we arranged our affairs—and for two years—in the course of which I had <almost two> more women than I can count or recount—she was the only one who preserved over me an ascendancy—

---

[53] English artist George Henry Harlow (1787–1819) had died in London in February, having just returned from Venice, where he drew both Byron and Margarita Cogni. There was a sale of his work after his death, and Murray paid forty guineas each for the drawings (*Murray Letters*, 276).

which was often disputed & never impaired.—As she herself used to say publicly—'It don't matter—he may have five hundred—but he will always come back to me'.——The reasons of this were firstly—her person—very dark—tall—the Venetian face—very fine black eyes—and certain other qualities which need not be mentioned.—She was two & twenty years old—and never having had children—had not spoilt her figure—nor *anything else*—which is I assure you—a great desideration in a hot climate where they grow relaxed and doughy and *flumpity* in a short time after breeding.—She was besides a thorough Venetian in her dialect—in her thoughts—in her countenance—in every thing—with all their naïveté and Pantaloon humour.—Besides she could neither read nor write—and could not plague me with letters—except twice that she paid sixpence to a public scribe under the piazza—to make a letter for her— upon some occasion when I was ill and could not see her.——In other respects she was somewhat fierce and 'prepotente' that is—overbearing—and used to walk in whenever it suited her—with no very great regard to time, place, nor persons—and if she found any women in her way she knocked them down.— When I first knew her I was in 'relazione' (liaison) with la Signora Segati—who was silly enough one evening at Dolo—accompanied by some of her female friends—to threaten her—for the Gossips of the Villeggiatura [holiday let]—had already found out by the neighing of my horse one evening—that I used to 'ride late in the night' to meet the Fornarina.——Margarita threw back her veil (fazziolo) and replied in very explicit Venetian—'You are *not* his *wife*: I am *not* his *wife*—you are his Donna—and I am his *donna*—your husband is a cuckold— and mine is another;—for the rest, what *right* have you to reproach me?—if he prefers what is mine—to what is yours—is it my fault? if you wish to secure him—tie him to your petticoat-string—but do not think to speak to me without a reply because you happen to be richer than I am.'——Having delivered this pretty piece of eloquence (which I translate as it was related to me by a byestander) she went on her way—leaving a numerous audience with Madame Segati—to ponder at her leisure on the dialogue between them.—When I came to Venice for the Winter she followed:—I never had any regular *liaison* with her—but whenever she came I never allowed any other connection to interfere with her—and as she found herself out to be a favourite she came pretty often.—But She had inordinate Self-love—and was not tolerant of other women—except of the Segati—who was as she said my regular 'Amica'—so that I being at that time somewhat promiscuous—there was great confusion— and demolition of head dresses and handkerchiefs—and sometimes my servants in 'redding the fray'[54] between her and other feminine persons—received more

---

[54] See Walter Scott, *Waverley* (1814), chapter 14.

knocks than acknowledgements for their peaceful endeavours.——At the 'Cavalchina' the masqued ball on the last night of the Carnival—where all the World goes—she snatched off the mask of Madame Contarini—a lady noble by birth—and decent in conduct—for no other reason but because she happened to be leaning on my arm.—You may suppose what a cursed noise this made—but this is only one of her pranks.—At last she quarrelled with her husband—and one evening ran away to my house.—I told her this would not do—she said she would lie in the street but not go back to him—that he beat her (the gentle tigress) spent her money—and scandalously neglected his Oven. As it was Midnight—I let her stay—and next day there was no moving her at all.—— Her husband came roaring & crying—& entreating her to come back, *not* She!— He then applied to the Police—and they applied to me—I told them and her husband to *take* her—I did not want her—she had come and I could not fling her out of the window—but they might conduct her through that or the door if they chose it——She went before the Commissary—but was obliged to return with that 'becco Ettico' (consumptive cuckold), as she called the *poor* man who had a P[h]t[h]isick.—In a few days she ran away again.—After a precious piece of work she fixed herself in my house—really & truly without my consent—but owing to my indolence—and not being able to keep my countenance—for if I began in a rage she always finished by making me laugh with some Venetian pantaloon-ery or other—and the Gipsy knew this well enough—as well as her other powers of persuasion—and exerted them with the usual tact and success of all She-things—high and low—they are all alike for that.—Madame Benzone also took her under her protection—and then her head turned.—She was always in extremes either crying or laughing—and so fierce when angered that she was the terror of men women and children—for she had the strength of an Amazon with the temper of Medea.[55] She was a fine animal—but quite untameable. *I* was the only person that could at all keep her in any order—and when she saw me really angry—(which they tell me is rather a savage sight), she subsided.—But she had a thousand fooleries—in her fazziolo—the dress of the lower orders— she looked beautiful—but alas! she longed for a hat and feathers and all I could say or do (and I said much) could not prevent this travestie.—I put the first into the fire—but I got tired of burning them before she did of buying them—so that she made herself a figure—for they did not at all become her.—Then she would have her gowns with a *tail*—like a lady forsooth—nothing would serve her—but 'l'abito colla *coua*', or *cua*, (that is the Venetian for 'la *Coda*' the tail or train) and as

---

[55] Women warriors of Greek legend; and wife of the Greek hero Jason, who slaughtered her children when he abandoned her, and escaped to Athens in a chariot, carrying the bodies with her: an archetype of a jealously possessive and murderous woman.

her cursed pronunciation of the word made me laugh—there was an end of all controversy—and she dragged this diabolical tail after her every where.——In the mean time she beat the women—and stopped my letters.—I found her one day pondering over one—she used to try to find out by their shape whether they were feminine or no—and she used to lament her ignorance—and actually studied her Alphabet—on purpose (as she declared) to open all letters addressed to me and read their contents.——I must not omit to do justice to her house-keeping qualities—after she came into my house as 'donna di governo' [house-keeper] the expences were reduced to less than half—and every body did their duty better—the apartments were kept in order—and every thing and every body else except herself.——That she had a sufficient regard for me in her wild way I had many reasons to believe—I will mention one.——In the autumn one day going to the Lido with my Gondoliers—we were overtaken by a heavy Squall and the Gondola put in peril—hats blown away—boat filling—oar lost—tumbling sea—thunder—rain in torrents—night coming—& wind increasing.—On our return—after a tight struggle: I found her on the open steps of the Mocenigo palace on the Grand Canal—with her great black eyes flashing though her tears and the long dark hair which was streaming drenched with rain over her brows & breast;—she was perfectly exposed to the storm—and the wind blowing her hair & dress about her tall thin figure—and the lightning flashing round her—with the waves rolling at her feet—made her look like Medea alighted from her chariot—or the Sibyl of the tempest that was rolling around her—the only living thing within hail at that moment except ourselves.—On seeing me safe—she did not wait to greet me as might be expected—but calling out to me—'Ah! Can' della Madonna xe esto il tempo per andar' al' Lido?' (ah! Dog of the Virgin!—is this a time to go to Lido?) ran into the house—and solaced herself with scolding the boatmen for not foreseeing the 'temporale' [storm].—I was told by the servants that she had only been prevented from coming in a boat to look after me—by the refusal of all the Gondoliers of the Canal to put out into the harbour in such a moment and that then she sate down on the steps in all the thickest of the Squall—and would neither be removed nor comforted. Her joy at seeing me again—was moderately mixed with ferocity—and gave me the idea of a tigress over her recovered Cubs.——But her reign drew near a close.—She became quite ungovernable some months after—and a concurrence of complaints some true and many false—'a favourite has no friend'[56]—determined me to part with her.—I told her quietly that she must return home—(she had acquired a sufficient provision for herself and mother,

---

[56] See Thomas Gray (1716–71), 'Ode on the Death of a Favourite Cat, Drowned in a Tub of Gold Fishes', 36.

&c. in my service,) and She refused to quit the house.—I was firm—and she went—threatening knives and revenge.—I told her—that I had seen knives drawn before her time—and that if she chose to begin—there was a knife— and fork also at her service on the table and that intimidation would not do.— The next day while I was at dinner—she walked in, (having broke open a glass door that led from the hall below to the staircase by way of prologue) and advancing strait up to the table snatched the knife from my hand—cutting me slightly in the thumb in the operation.—Whether she meant to use this against herself or me I know not—probably against neither—but Fletcher seized her by the arms—and disarmed her.—I then called my boatmen—and desired them to get the Gondola ready and conduct her to her own house again—seeing carefully that she did herself no mischief by the way.—She seemed quite quiet and walked down stairs.—I resumed my dinner.—We heard a great noise— I went out—and met them on the staircase—carrying her up stairs.—She had thrown herself into the Canal.—That she intended to destroy herself I do not believe—but when we consider the fear women and men who can't swim have of deep or even of shallow water—(and the Venetians in particular though they live on the waves) and that it was also night—and dark—& very cold—it shows that she had a devilish spirit of some sort within her.—They had got her out without much difficulty or damage except the salt water she had swallowed and the wetting she had undergone.—I foresaw her intention to refix herself, and sent for a Surgeon—enquiring how many hours it would require to restore her from her agitation, and he named the time.—I then said—'I give you that time— and more if you require it—but at the expiration of the prescribed period—if *She* does not leave the house—*I* will'.——All my people were consternated— they had always been frightened at her—and were now paralyzed—they wanted me to apply to the police—to guard myself—&c. &c.—like a pack of sniveling servile boobies as they were——I did nothing of the kind—thinking that I might as well end that way as another—besides—I had been used to savage women and knew their ways.—I had her sent home quietly after her recovery—and never saw her since except twice at the opera—at a distance amongst the audience.—She made many attempts to return—but no more violent ones.— And this is the story of Margharita Cogni—as far as it belongs to me.—I forgot to mention that she was very devout and would cross herself if she heard the prayer-time strike—sometimes—when that ceremony did not appear to be much in unison with what she was then about.—She was quick in reply—as for instance;—one day when she had made me very angry with beating some-body or other—I called her a *Cow* (*Cow* in Italian is a sad affront and tantamount to the feminine of dog in English) I called her 'Vacca' she turned round— curtsied—and answered 'Vacca *tua* 'Celenza' (i.e. Eccelenza) *your* Cow—please your Excellency.—In short—she was—as I said before—a very fine Animal—of considerable beauty and energy—with many good & several amusing qualities—but wild as a witch—and fierce as a demon.—She used to boast publicly of her ascendancy over me—contrasting it with that of other women—and assigning for it sundry reasons physical and moral which did more credit to her person than her modesty.——True it was that they all tried to get her away—and no one succeeded—till her own absurdity helped them.—Whenever there was a competition, and sometimes—one would be shut in one room and one in another—to prevent battle—she had generally the preference.——

yrs. very truly and affectly
B

P. S.—*The Countess G is much better than she was.—I sent you before leaving Venice—a letter containing the real original sketch—which gave rise to the 'Vampire' &c. did you get it?—*

[To John Murray]

Bologna. August 12th. 1819

Dear Sir

I do not know how far I may be able to reply to your letter—for I am not very well today.—Last night I went to the representation of Alfieri's Mirra—the two last acts of which threw me into convulsions.[57]—I do not mean by that word—a lady's hysterics—but the agony of reluctant tears—and the choaking shudder which I do not often undergo for fiction.—This is but the second time for anything under reality, the first was on seeing Kean's Sir Giles Overreach.[58]—The worst was that the 'dama' in whose box I was—went off in the same way—I really believe more from fright—than any other sympathy—at least with the players—but she has been ill—and I have been ill and we are all languid &

---

[57] This tragedy, by the neoclassical playwright Vittorio Alfieri (1749–1803), whom Byron much admired, involved a story from Ovid's *Metamorphoses* of incestuous love between a father and daughter.

[58] Character from *A New Way to Pay Old Debts*, which Kean triumphantly revived at Drury Lane in 1816. Massinger's is a highly realistic 'villain play' in which Sir Giles Overreach descends into lunacy at the climax.

pathetic this morning—with great expenditure of Sal Volatile.—But to return to your letter of the 23d. of July.——You are right—Gifford is right—Crabbe is right—Hobhouse is right—you are all right—and I am all wrong—but do pray let me have that pleasure.—Cut me up root and branch—quarter me in the Quarterly—send round my 'disjecti membra poetae' like those of the Levite's Concubine—make—if you will—a spectacle to men and angels—but don't ask me to alter for I can't—I am obstinate and lazy—and there's the truth.[59]—But nevertheless—I will answer your friend C. V. who objects to the quick succession of fun and gravity—as if in that case the gravity did not (in intention at least) heighten the fun.[60]—His metaphor is that 'we are never scorched and drenched at the same time!'—Blessings on his experience!—Ask him these questions about 'scorching and drenching'.—Did he never play at Cricket or walk a mile in hot weather?—did he never spill a dish of tea over his testicles in handing the cup to his charmer to the great shame of his nankeen breeches?—did he never swim in the sea at Noonday with the Sun in his eyes and on his head—which all the foam of ocean could not cool? did he never draw his foot out of a tub of too hot water damning his eyes & his valet's? did he never inject for a Gonorrhea?—or make water through an ulcerated Urethra?—was he ever in a Turkish bath—that marble paradise of sherbet and sodomy?—was he ever in a cauldron of boiling oil like St. John?—or in the sulphureous waves of hell? (where he ought to be for his 'scorching and drenching at the same time') did he never tumble into a river or lake fishing—and sit in his wet cloathes in the boat—or on the bank afterwards 'scorched and drenched' like a true sportsman?——'Oh for breath to utter'[61]——but make him my compliments—he is a clever fellow for all that—a very clever fellow.——You ask me for the plan of Donny Johnny—I *have* no plan—I *had* no plan—but I had or have materials—though if like Tony Lumpkin—I am 'to be snubbed so when I am in spirits'[62] the poem will be naught—and the poet turn serious again.—If it don't take I will leave it off where it is with all due respect to the Public—but if continued it must be in my own

---

[59] Murray had written with comments from Gifford and Crabbe, begging him to 'make the few slight alterations which we so anxiously wish...and let us put forth the new Edition with your Lordships name', and so forth (*Murray Letters*, 281). For the 'scattered limbs of the poets' see Horace, *Satires*, I. iv. 62. For the brutal story of a Levite, his concubine, her gang rape, and the division of her body, see Judges 19.

[60] 'C. V.' is Francis Cohen (1788–1861), lawyer and historian, whose initials Byron misread on the letter Murray enclosed with his of 16 July. Cohen complained that 'we are never drenched & scorched *at the same instant while standing on the same spot*' (*Murray Letters*, 279; italics added): that is, that Byron had failed to handle his transitions from tragic to comic decorously.

[61] See 1 *Henry IV*, II. v. 249–50.

[62] See Oliver Goldsmith, *She Stoops to Conquer* (1773), II. i. 776–9: 'I wish you'd let me and my good alone.... Snubbing this way when I'm in spirits. If I'm to have any good, let it come of itself; not to keep dinging it, dinging it into one so.'

way—you might as well make Hamlet (or Diggory[63]) 'act mad' in a strait waistcoat—as trammel my buffoonery—if I am to be a buffoon—their gestures and my thoughts would only be pitiably absurd—and ludicrously constrained.—Why Man the Soul of such writing is it's licence?—at least the *liberty* of that *licence* if one likes—*not* that one should abuse it—it is like trial by Jury and Peerage—and the Habeas Corpus—a very fine thing—but chiefly in the *reversion*—because no one wishes to be tried for the mere pleasure of proving his possession of the privilege.——But a truce with these reflections;—you are too earnest and eager about a work never intended to be serious;—do you suppose that I could have any intention but to giggle and make giggle?—a playful satire with as little poetry as could be helped—was what I meant—and as to the indecency—do pray read in Boswell—what *Johnson* the sullen moralist—says of *Prior* and Paulo Purgante[64] [...] So the Prince has been repealing Lord Ed. Fitzgerald's forfeiture[65]—'Ecco un' Sonnetto!'

> To be the father of the fatherless
> To stretch the hand from the throne's height and raise
> *His* offspring, who expired in other days
> To make thy Sire's Sway by a kingdom less,
> *This* is to be a Monarch, and repress
> Envy into unutterable praise,
> Dismiss thy Guard, and trust thee to such traits,
> For who would lift a hand except to bless?—
> Were it not easy, Sir, and is't not sweet
> To make thyself beloved? and to be
> Omnipotent by Mercy's means? for thus
> Thy Sovereignty would grow but more complete,
> A Despot thou, and yet thy people free,
> And by the Heart not Hand enslaving Us

There you dogs—there's a Sonnet for you—you won't have such as that in a hurray from Mr. Fitzgerald.——You may publish it with my name—an' ye

---

[63] Diggery is a servant who plans to act mad in Isaac Jackman's farce *All the World's a Stage* (1777).

[64] In Boswell's *Life of Johnson* the critic defended poet Matthew Prior (1664–1721), author of 'Paulo Purgante and his Wife', saying his work contained nothing 'that will excite to lewdness'.

[65] Lord Edward Fitzgerald (1763–98) was a member of the Irish Parliament, who eventually conspired with the French Revolutionary Government to invade England, and died from wounds received during his arrest. His property had been confiscated as a traitor, but that decision was reversed in July 1819. 'If I had been a man,' Byron wrote in March 1814, 'I would have made an English Lord Edward Fitzgerald' (*LJ* iii. 249). For the poet William Thomas Fitzgerald, see letters of 11 April and 1 June 1818.

wool—He deserves all praise bad & good—it was a very noble piece of principality.—Would you like an Epigram? <upon a female> a translation.——

> If for silver or for gold—
> You could melt ten thousand pimples
> Into half a dozen dimples
> Then your face we might behold
> Looking doubtless much more smugly
> Yet even then 'twould be damned ugly.

This was written on some French-woman, by Rulhières—I believe.[66]—'And so good morrow t'ye—good Master lieutenant.'——

yrs. [scrawl]

[To Countess Teresa Guiccioli]

Bologna. August 23d. 1819

My dearest Teresa

I have read this book in your garden;[67]—my Love—you were absent—or I could not have read it.—It is a favourite book of yours—and the writer was a friend of mine.—You will not understand these English words—and *others* will not understand them—which is the reason I have not scribbled them in Italian—but you will recognize the hand-writing of him who passionately loved you—and you will divine that over a book which was yours—he could only think of love. In *that word* beautiful in all languages—but most so in yours—*Amor* mio—is comprized my existence here and hereafter.——I feel that I exist here—and I fear that I shall exist hereafter—to *what* purpose—you will decide—my destiny rests with you—& you are a woman nineteen years of age—and two years out of a Convent.——I wish that you had staid there with all my heart—or at least that I had never met you in your married state.—but all this is too late—I love you—and you love me—at least you *say* so—and act as if you *did* so—which last is a great consolation in all events.—But *I* more than love you—and cannot cease to love you.—Think of me sometimes when the Alps and the Ocean divide us—but they never will—unless you wish it.

BN

---

[66] Claude Carloman de Rulhière (1735–91) was a French epigrammatist who often targeted elderly ladies, but it seems this is more in his style than a direct translation. Byron's close might allude to *Othello*, III. i. 40.

[67] Madame de Staël's *Corinna, or Italy* (1807).

[To John Cam Hobhouse]

Venice. Octr. 3d. 1819

Dear Hobhouse

I wrote to Murray last week and begged him to reassure you of my health and sanity—as far as I know at present.—At Bologna I was out of sorts—in health and spirits.—Here—I have health at least.—My South American project of which I believe I spoke to you (as you mention it)—was this.——I perceived by the inclosed paragraphs that advantageous offers were—or are to be held out to settlers in the Venezuelan territory.—My affairs in England are nearly settled—or in prospect of settlement—in Italy I have no debts—and could leave it when I chose.—The Anglo-Americans are a little too coarse for me— and their climate too cold—and I should prefer the others.—I could soon grapple with the Spanish language.——Ellice or others could get me letters to Boliver [*sic*] and his government—and if men of little or of no property are encouraged there—surely with present income—and if I could sell Rochdale— with some capital—I might be suffered as a landholder there—or at least a tenant—and if possible and legal—a Citizen.[68]——I wish you would speak to *Perry* of the M[orning] C[hronicle] who is their *Gazetteer*—about this—and ask like Jeremy Diddler—not for eighteen pence—but information on the subject.[69]—— I assure you that I am very *serious* in the idea—and that the notion has been about me for a long time as you will see by the worn state of the advertisement.— I should go there with my natural daughter Allegra—now nearly three years old—and with me here—and pitch my tent for good and all.—I am not tired of Italy—but a man must be a Cicisbeo and a singer in duets and a Connoisseur of operas—or nothing here—I have made some progress in all these accomplishments—but I can't say that I don't feel the degradation.—Better be a [n] unskilful planter—an awkward settler—better be a hunter—or anything than a flatterer of fiddlers—and a fan-carrier of a woman.—I like women—God he knows—but the more their system here developes upon me—the worse it seems—after Turkey too—here the *polygamy* is all on the female side.——I have been an intriguer, a husband, and now I am a Cavalier Servente.—by the holy!—it is a strange sensation.—After having belonged in my own and other countries—

---

[68] Hobhouse's friend Edward Ellice, MP for Coventry, had American connections. Simón Bolivar (1783–1830), Central American anti-colonialist leader.

[69] James Perry's *Morning Chronicle* carried copy for Central American interests. Jeremy Diddler features in James Kenney's farce *Raising the Wind* (1803): 'you haven't such a thing as tenpence about you, have you?' was an enquiry he explained as one only 'for information'.

to the intriguing—the married—and the keeping—parts of the town—to be sure an honest arrangement is the best—and I have had that too—and have—but they expect it to be for *life*—thereby I presume—excluding longevity.—But let us be serious if possible.——You must not talk to me of England—that is out of the question.—I had a house—and lands—and a wife and child—and a name there—once—but all these things are transmuted or sequestered.—Of the last & best ten years of my life—nearly six have been passed *out* of it.—I feel no love for the soil after the treatment I received before leaving it for the last time—but I do not hate it enough to wish to take a part in it's calamities—as on either side harm must be done before good can accrue—revolutions are not to be made with rose water.[70]——My taste for revolution is abated—with my other passions.——Yet I want a country—and a home—and if possible—a free one—I am not yet thirty two years of age—I might still be a decent citizen and found a *house* and a family,—as good—or better than the former.——I could at all events occupy myself rationally—my hopes are not high—nor my ambition extensive—and when tens of thousands of our Countrymen are colonizing (like the Greeks of old in Sicily and Italy) from as many causes—does my notion seem visionary or irrational?——There is no freedom in Europe—that's certain—it is besides a worn out portion of the globe.—What I should be glad of is *information* as to the encouragement—the means required—and what is accorded & what would be my probable reception—Perry—or Ellice—or many merchants would be able to tell you this for me.—I won't go there to travel but to settle.——Do not laugh at me—you will—but I assure you I am quite in earnest if this thing be practicable. I do not want to have anything to do with the war projects—but to go there as a settler—and if as a Citizen—all the better—my own government would not I think refuse me permission—if they know their own interest—such fellows as I am—are no desideratum for Sidmouth[71] at present—I think.—Address to me at Venice.——I should of course come to Liverpool—or some town on your coast—to take my passage—and receive my credentials—believe me

ever yrs. most truly
Byron

---

[70] See Jean-François Marmontel (1723–99), *Mémoires d'un Père* (1804), xiv: 'Voulez-vous qu'on fasse des revolutions à l'eau rose?'
[71] Henry Addington, first Viscount Sidmouth (1757–1844), was the Tory Home Secretary associated with Government repression, 1812–22.

[To Douglas Kinnaird]

Venice. Octr. 26th. 1819

My dear Douglas

My late expenditure has arisen from living at a distance from Venice and being obliged to keep up two establishments, from frequent journeys—and buying some furniture and books as well as a horse or two—and not from any renewal of the EPICUREAN system as you suspect. I have been faithful to my honest liaison with Countess Guiccioli—and I can assure you that *She* has never cost me directly or indirectly a sixpence—indeed the circumstances of herself and family render this no merit.—I never offered her but one present—a broach of brilliants—and she sent it back to me with her *own hair* in it (I shall *not* say of *what part* but *that* is an Italian custom) and a note to say that she was not in the habit of receiving presents of that value—but hoped that I would not consider her sending it back as an affront—nor the value diminished by the enclosure.—I have not had a whore this half-year—confining myself to the strictest adultery.——Why should you prevent Hanson from making a *peer* if he likes it—I think the '*Garretting*' would be by far the best parliamentary privilege—I know of.——Damn your delicacy.—It is a low commercial quality—and very unworthy a man who prefixes 'honourable' to his nomenclature.[72] If you say that I must sign the bonds—I suppose that I must—but it is very iniquitous to make me pay my debts—you have no idea of the pain it gives one.—Pray do three things—get my property out of the *funds*—get Rochdale sold—get me some information from Perry about *South America*—and 4thly. ask Lady Noel not to live so very long.——As to Subscribing to Manchester—if I do that—I will write a letter to Burdett—for publication—to accompany the Subscription— which shall be more radical than anything yet rooted—but I feel lazy.[73]—I have thought of this for some time—but alas! the air of this cursed Italy enervates— and disfranchises the thoughts of a man after nearly four years of respiration—to say nothing of emission.—As to 'Don Juan'—confess—confess—you dog—and be candid—that it is the sublime of *that there* sort of writing—it may be bawdy— but is it not good English?—it may be profligate—but is it not *life*, is it not *the thing*?—Could any man have written it—who has not lived in the

---

[72] John Hanson's daughter was married to the Earl of Portsmouth (see Journal, 7 March 1814); but Byron's remark is unclear. In Britain the children of viscounts and barons—as well as the holders of certain high offices, particularly in the law—may style themselves as 'the Honourable'.

[73] In his letter Kinnaird had sought a subscription from Byron to aid the suffering of those injured in the Peterloo Massacre in Manchester, August 1819.

world?—and tooled in a post-chaise? in a hackney coach? in a Gondola? against a wall? in a court carriage? in a vis a vis?—on a table?—and under it?—I have written about a hundred stanzas of a third Canto—but it is damned modest—the outcry has frightened me.—I had such projects for the Don—but the *Cant* is so much stronger than *Cunt*—now a days,—that the benefit of experience in a man who had well weighed the worth of both monosyllables—must be lost to despairing posterity.—After all what stuff this outcry is—Lalla Rookh and L-ittle—are more dangerous than my burlesque poem can be—Moore has been here—we got tipsy together—and were very amicable—he is gone on to Rome—I put my life (in M.S.) into his hands—(*not for publication*) you—or any body else may see it—at his return.—It only comes up to 1816.——He is a noble fellow—and looks quite fresh and poetical—nine years (the age of a poem's education) my Senior—he looks younger—this comes of marriage and being settled in the Country. I want to go to South America—I have written to Hobhouse all about it.—I wrote to my wife—three months ago—under care to Murray—has she got the letter—or is the letter got into Blackwood's maga-zine?——You ask after my Christmas pye[74]—Remit it any how—*Circulars* is the best—you are right about *income*—I must have it all—how the devil do I know that I may live a year or a month?—I wish I knew that I might regulate my spending in more ways than one.—As it is one always thinks that there is but a span.—A man may as well break or be damned for a large sum as a small one—I should be loth to pay the devil or any other creditor more than sixpence in the pound.—

[scrawl for signature]

P. S.—I recollect nothing of 'Davies's landlord'—but what ever Davies says—I will swear to—and that's more than he would.—So pray pay—has he a landlady too?—perhaps I may owe her something.——With regard to the bonds I will sign them but—it goes against the grain.——As to the rest—you can't err—so long as you don't pay.——Paying is executor's or executioner's work.——You may write somewhat oftener—Mr. Galignani's messenger gives the outline of your public affairs—but I see no results——you have no man yet—(always excepting Burdett—& you & H[obhouse] and the Gentlemanly leaven of your two-penny loaf of rebellion) don't forget however my charge of horse—and commission for the

[74] Byron refers to rents on his English properties, due at Michaelmas.

Midland Counties and by the holies!—You shall have your account in decimals.—Love to Hobby—but why leave the Whigs?——[75]

[To Countess Teresa Guiccioli]

Venice 25 [November] 1819

My only Treasure

You are and will always be my first thought—but at this moment I am in a terrible state of not knowing what to decide; I am afraid on the one hand of compromising you forever by my return to Ravenna—and its consequences; and on the other hand—of losing you—and myself—and all that I have known or tasted of happiness by not seeing you ever again.——I beg you—I supplicate you—to be calm—and to believe that I cannot cease loving you so long as I live.— I have not gone out of the house since you left—I do not see a living soul of this land, nor do I desire it.—In any case, whether I see you again or not—you are my destiny—the dearest—most loved of women—of beings—for me. Forgive me—I do not know what I say.—I shall not remain *in Venice* after my daughter has recovered her health—but where I shall direct my steps—is, alas, uncertain.—But I love you—I adore you—and you know it well.

B

P. S.—Allegrina and her governess both have double tertian *[fever]—they are very ill— my fever has vanished.—Addio.—Fanny has written to you by every mail delivery—and you should have received a letter from her with a tiny little portrait—which I found and sent immediately for delivery to you.—Greet all the signori Papa—Rasponi &c. and also Alessandro—do not forget Perelli—and Sandri—and all our people.*[76]*——I will write you when I am more calm—and* always *if you permit me—my only and last and best loved friend.*

---

[75] A motif in Byron's letters of this period is his anxiety about Hobhouse deserting the Whigs for the Radical cause. Byron supported reform, but only when introduced by the ruling classes.

[76] That is, to Count Ruggero Gamba Ghiselli (Teresa's father); Count Giulio Rasponi (whom Byron had befriended in Ravenna); Teresa's husband, Count Alessandro Guiccioli; Don Gaspare Perelli (the priest who had passed messages between the lovers); and Sandri (another servant).

[To Countess Teresa Guiccioli]

[Venice, Dec. 2? 1819]

My Love

I am going away in order *to save you*; and I leave a land that has become unbearable without you.—Your letters to Fanny—and also to myself—do wrong to my motives; but in time you will realize your injustice.—You speak of pain—I feel it—but words fail me.——I cannot write to you—but if you could see my heart as you saw it when we were together—you would not speak to me of such cruel abuses.——It is not enough—to leave you for motives of which you were convinced (not very long ago). It is not enough to depart from Italy with a heart that is rent—after having passed all my days since your departure in solitude—sick in body and in spirit—but I must also endure your reproaches—without answering you—and without deserving them.—— Addio—that word—contains the death of my happiness—but even so—let me love you still—let me think of you as the single—ultimate object of so many hopes—and of so much passion;—with whom I have spent moments too sweet—but—perhaps—one day we will again embrace one another—we will again be + + + —what we have been—but—if not—know that no woman will be loved in your stead.——That is said at the beginning of a relationship—I say it at the end.—I love you more than in the first days—of our love—and you know it—even by the sacrifice that I now am making—for your welfare.—Think of A[lessandro]—Think of all that he has done or wanted to do—then you cannot blame me.—Addio—Addio—Love me.—

B

P. S.—*You will hear from me during my trip—and again when Valeriani returns—I will send him upon my arrival.——My address—is L. B.—*

care of Messrs. Ransom
   Bankers—Pall Mall. London England
If it is more convenient for you—address your letters care of the Messrs Siri and Willhalm Bankers *Venice*

[To John Murray]

Venice. Decr. 4th. 1819

My dear Murray

You may do as you please—but you are about an hopeless experiment—Eldon will decide against you—were it only that my name is in the record.[77]——You will also recollect that if the publication is pronounced against on the grounds you mention as *indecent & blasphemous* that *I* lose all right in my daughter's *guardianship* and *education*—in short all paternal authority—and every thing concerning her—except the pleasure I may have chanced to have had in begetting her.—It was so decided in Shelley's case—because he had written—Queen Mab—&c. &c. however you can ask the lawyers—and do as you like—I do not inhibit you trying the question—I merely state one of the consequences to me.——With regard to the Copyright—it is hard that you should pay for a non-entity:——I will therefore refund it—which I can very well do—not having spent it—nor begun upon it—and so we will be quits on that score—it lies at my banker's.——Of the Chancellor's law—I am no judge—but take up Tom Jones & read him [—] Mrs. Waters and Molly Seagrim—or Prior's Hans Carvel—& Paulo Purganti—Smollett's Roderick Random—the chapter of Lord Strutwell—& many others;—Peregrine Pickle the scene of the Beggar Girl——Johnson's *London* for *coarse* expressions—for instance the word '*Clap*' & '*gropes his breeches with a monarch's air*'—Anstey's Bath guide—the 'Hearken Lady Betty Hearken'—take up in short—Pope—Prior—Congreve—Dryden—Fielding—Smollett—& let the Counsel select passages—and what becomes of *their* copyright if his Wat Tyler—decision is to pass into a precedent?[78]——I have nothing more to say—you must judge for yourselves——I wrote to you some time ago—I have had a tertian ague—my daughter Allegra has been ill also—and I have been almost obliged to run away with a married woman.—But with some difficulty—& many internal struggles—I reconciled the lady with her lord—& cured the fever of the Child with bark—& my own with cold water.——I think of setting out for England by the Tyrol in a few days—so that I could wish you to direct yr.

---

[77] Murray had written on 16 November to say that he had met with lawyers in regard to protecting his copyright in *Don Juan*, 'but I am again in a Dilemma about yr Lordships name as my Solicitors say that I must name the Author in my Affadavit' (*Murray Letters*, 301). He did not proceed with the case.

[78] Byron lists a large number of mostly 18th-century morally candid texts, to argue that if the decision as regards Southey's *Wat Tyler* denied him copyright in his work (see letter of 9 May 1817), then large amounts of classic English literature would lose its protection in the same way. In theory, the argument is reasonable; in practice, English moral standards had shifted profoundly since the days of Fielding and Smollett.

next letter to Calais.—Excuse my writing—in great haste—and late in the morning or night—whichever you please to call it.—The third Canto of 'Don Juan' is completed in about two hundred stanzas—very decent—I believe—but do not know—& it is useless to discuss until it can be ascertained if [it] may or may not be a property.—My present determination to quit Italy was unlooked for—but I have explained the reasons in letters to my Sister & Douglas K[innaird]—a week or two ago.—My progress will depend upon the snows of the Tyrol—& the health of my child who is at present quite recovered—but I hope to get on well & am

yrs. ever & truly
B

P. S.—*Many thanks for yr. letters to which you are not to consider this as an answer—but an acknowledgement.—*

[To Countess Teresa Guiccioli]

Venice—Dec. 9, 1819

My Dearest Friend

Your last letter caused me to give up my journey.—I love you—I shall love you, alas,—forever.—Command me—you can arrange my future life—It is enough—that *you do not repent*, whatever the consequences may be.—I thought to save you by leaving—but seeing that you think differently—I await your signal to return to R[avenna].—Regarding A[*lessandro*] I will do as you wish.—

+ + + + +

344

9
RAVENNA

December 1819–October 1821

There is a paradox about Byron's second period in Italy, after his first, Venetian, one. On many levels he was becoming increasingly remote from England. His letters to Moore became less intimate; to Kinnaird more business-like; to Augusta increasingly rare; and to Hobhouse increasingly estranged. John Murray told him that he was losing touch with shifting British moral standards (see letter of 29 March 1820) and Hobhouse told him that he was losing touch with British politics (see letter of 22 April 1820). And he took pride in his intimacy with Italian life, as a friend of the family as well as a lover (see letter of 21 February 1820). His politics moved to the left where the Continent was concerned, towards liberal nationalism; but towards the right where England was concerned, where his passion for reform became tempered by suspicion of reformers—especially working-class ones. ('Low imitations of the Jacobins', he called them in October 1821; LJ viii. 240.)

But where his work was concerned Byron became more completely bound up with Britain than he had ever been—which is why his friends and publisher became increasingly nervous about it. As the years passed, and with the benefit of distance, he opened several related fronts in an all-consuming war on English culture. The most important of these was Don Juan, composed between July 1818 and November 1819 (Cantos I–IV), and October and November 1820 (Canto V), before being suspended for a year (at Teresa's request, Byron said; LJ viii. 147), and resumed in Pisa. Related to the epic was a set of attacks on British literary standards in a set of formal articles (CMP 88–183), the like of which he had never attempted before: 'Some Observations upon an Article in Blackwood's Edinburgh Magazine' (March 1820, but only published in 1833), 'Letter to John Murray Esq.' (February 1821, published in March), and 'Observations upon Observations' (April 1821, but only published in 1832). Out of a review of Don Juan in Blackwood's, and some remarks made about Alexander Pope by the priest and sonneteer William Lisle Bowles (in his 1806 edition of the poet and his Invariable Principles of Poetry of 1819—which might have been so entitled deliberately to attract Byron's odium), Byron spun a set of arguments that came to this eventual proposition:

The truth is that in these days the grand 'primum mobile' of England is Cant—Cant political—Cant poetical—Cant religious—Cant moral—but always Cant—multiplied through all the varieties of life.—It is the fashion—& while it lasts—will be too powerful for those who can only exist by taking the tone of the time.—I say Cant—because it is a thing of words—without the smallest influence on human actions—the English being no wiser—no better—and much poorer—and more divided among themselves—as well as far less moral—than they were before the prevalence of this verbal decorum. (CMP 128)

It was an immense summation, hovering over the literature of the English 19th century like a storm cloud,[1] and many things got swept up in it—including that least offensive English poet John Keats

---

[1] See, for example, Carlyle's Victorian biographer: 'beyond all, his own England appeared to him to be drenched in cant—cant religious, cant political, cant moral, cant artistic, cant everywhere and in everything' (John Clubbe (ed.), Froude's Life of Carlyle (London: John Murray, 1979), 483).

(see letters of 4 November 1820 and 26 April 1821)—whose work Byron described, hysterically, as 'a sort of mental masturbation—he is always f—gg—g his Imagination' (LJ vii. 225).

As early as February 1818 Byron had told Murray that 'the next generation' of English poets would 'tumble and break their necks off our Pegasus, who runs away with us'; 'the next fellows', he continued (LJ vi. 10), 'must go back to the riding-school and the manège, and learn to ride "the great horse."' Related to his war on English cant, therefore, was a smaller battle, with English poetic attitudes as its focus. Keats, English Romantic Shakespearianism, and the feeble efforts of English poets and playwrights inspired an odd set of stablemates for Don Juan: three neoclassical dramas—Marino Faliero (April–July 1820), Sardanapalus (January–May 1821), and The Two Foscari (June–July 1821)—which were every inch the product of the 'riding-school' theory of literature. They were designed in total opposition to the contemporary stage (which he had experienced at first hand at Drury Lane), so Byron was profoundly irritated when Marino Faliero was staged at that very theatre in April 1821.

The rest of his life appeared to be in marked contrast to all this bellicosity. In Ravenna he laboured away at cavalier servitude: 'I am drilling very hard to learn how to double a Shawl, and should succeed to admiration', he wrote in January 1820, 'if I did not always double it the wrong side out' (LJ vii. 28). Then in July of that year the Neapolitans, to some extent inspired and organized by a nationalist, quasi-Masonic secret society, the Carbonari ('charcoal-burners'), rose up against Ferdinand I of the Two Sicilies, and revolution was in the air. (As early as April Byron had told Kinnaird, 'We are in expectation of a row here'; LJ vii. 76.) Teresa's father and brother were highly enthused. Byron offered money to the Neapolitans and bought guns for the Ravennese chapter of the society, then joined it himself. All through autumn and winter plans and rumours circulated, until everything broke down in late February 1821, as Austrian troops passed the city on their way to dealing with the Neapolitans to the south. (The political atmosphere is evoked with intimate precision in the 'Ravenna Journal' he kept at this time.) 'Alas', a lady friend said to Byron, 'the Italians must return to making operas', and Byron was forced to agree that music and making macaroni were their forte (LJ viii. 105). With the benefit of hindsight we can see that the Carbonari was a minor manifestation, but Byron was sure that nothing less than a continental uprising was in prospect, with a financial crisis to match: he told Kinnaird, Lady Byron, and anybody else who would listen to get their money out of Government funds, accordingly.

Domestically, things in the Guiccioli household—where Byron continued to live until finally leaving the city in October 1821, though he was to all intents and purposes a co-respondent in a divorce case—came to head when he and Teresa were discovered 'quasi in the fact' in May 1820 (LJ vii. 102). The following month Teresa's father, Count Ruggero Gamba, appealed to the Pope for a separation, which was granted in July largely because Count Guiccioli had left it too late to argue that he was an innocently duped husband. (Byron meanwhile converted the separation hearing into another potential trigger for a return to England, 'via Switzerland'; LJ vii. 123.) Teresa moved in with her father and charming younger brother Pietro ('he shows character and talent—Big eyebrows!' LJ vii. 146), at the *nearby village of Filetto, and Byron's life fell into another of its daily rounds. In November 1820 the Gambas would return to their Ravenna house, and there things stood until the Government of the Papal States—whether wishing to move Byron on or not we do not know—exiled Ruggero and Pietro in July 1821. Without her father's protection, Teresa might have had to enter a convent, and eventually she was persuaded to join her menfolk in Florence later that month, from whence they moved on to Pisa. It would take Byron no fewer than three months to uproot himself from her husband's house and join her—not that he was idle; he wrote three pieces on loosely biblical themes while biding his time:* Cain, The Vision of Judgment, *and* Heaven and Earth.

A far sadder story played itself out amidst all this adult activity: the life of young Allegra. She had come down to Ravenna with Byron from Venice in January 1820. In late February, mid-March, and late April her mother wrote, concerned about the nature of Byron's household, and asked him either to send the little girl to her or allow a visit, but Byron's attitude to the Shelley household was icily unforgiving. 'I can only say to Claire', he wrote to Hoppner on 22 April 1820,

that I so totally disapprove of the mode of Children's treatment in their family—that I should look upon the Child as going into a hospital.—Is it not so? Have they *reared* one? [...] the Child shall not quit me again—to perish of Starvation, and green fruit—or to be taught to believe there is no Deity.——Whenever there is convenience of vicinity and access—her Mother can always have her with her—otherwise no.—It was so stipulated from the beginning. (*LJ* vii. 80)

In August 1820 he placed Allegra and a nurse in a well-attended house at Filetto. In September he was 'almost tempted to send her back to her atheistical mother', 'were it not for the little child's sake' (LJ vii. 174). The following March he put her in a convent school at Bagnacavallo, twelve miles from Ravenna—which he had not visited beforehand. When his coach rolled out of Ravenna on 29 October 1821 the little girl, nearly 4 years old, was left behind.

[To William Bankes[2]]

Ravenna, February 19th, 1820

I have room for you in the house here, as I had in Venice, if you think fit to make use of it; but do not expect to find the same gorgeous suite of tapestried halls. Neither dangers nor tropical heats have ever prevented your penetrating wherever you had a mind to it, and why should the snow now?—Italian snow—fie

---

[2] Bankes (1786–1855), an early Egyptologist and traveller, had been at Cambridge with Byron. The family house at Kingston Lacey in Devon is full of *objets d'art* collected by him. In 1841 he skipped bail and left England after being charged with homosexual acts, never to return.

on it!—so pray come. Tita's heart yearns for you, and mayhap for your silver broad pieces;[3] and your playfellow, the monkey, is alone and inconsolable.

I forget whether you admire or tolerate red hair, so that I rather dread showing you all that I have about me and around me in this city. Come, nevertheless, you can pay Dante a morning visit, and I will undertake that Theodore and Honoria will be most happy to see you in the forest hard by. We Goths, also, of Ravenna hope you will not despise our arch Goth, Theodoric.[4] I must leave it to these worthies to entertain you all the fore part of the day, seeing that I have none at all myself—the lark, that rouses me from my slumbers, being an afternoon bird. But, then, all your evenings, and as much as you can give me of your nights, will be mine. Ay! and you will find me eating flesh, too, like yourself or any other cannibal, except it be upon Fridays. Then, there are more cantos (and be d—d to them) of what courteous reader, Mr. S[aunders], calls Grub Street, in my drawer, which I have a little scheme to commit to your charge for England;[5] only I must first cut up (or cut down) two aforesaid cantos into three, because I am grown base and mercenary, and it is an ill precedent to let my Mecaenas [sic], Murray, get too much for his money. I am busy, also, with Pulci—translating—servilely translating, stanza for stanza, and line for line, two octaves every night,—the same allowance as at Venice.[6]

Would you call at your banker's in Bologna, and ask him for some letters lying there for me, and burn them?—or I will—so do not burn them, but bring them,—and believe me,

Ever and very affectionately yours,
Byron

[3] Giovanni Battista Falcieri (1798–1874) joined Byron's service in Venice, having once worked for Matthew 'Monk' Lewis, the Gothic novelist. Despite his fearsome appearance he was a gentle and devoted servant, who was with Byron at his death and brought his body back to England. Later in life he was picked up in the Mediterranean by future prime minister Benjamin Disraeli, who found him a job as a messenger at the Foreign Office in London.

[4] This is a brisk round-up of some local sites: Dante's tomb; the mausoleum of Theodoric (471–526), ruler of the Ostrogothic Kingdom of which Ravenna had been the capital; and Theodore and Honoria, figures in a gruesome love story in Boccaccio translated by Dryden, set in the famous pine-wood outside the city.

[5] Bankes had met an Englishman in Venice who told him 'Don Juan was all Grub-street'—that is, hack-work.

[6] Maecenas was a patron of poets in the reign of Roman Emperor Augustus. The polymorphous and multivocal *Morgante Maggiore*, by Luigi Pulci (1432–84), was an important model for Byron's ottava rima poems, and his translation of the first canto of it occupied him from October 1819 until February 1820. It was not published until 1832.

P. S.—I have a particular wish to hear from yourself something about Cyprus, so pray recollect all that you can.—Good night.

[To John Murray]

Ravenna. February 21st. 1820

Dear Murray

The Bulldogs will be very agreeable—I have only those of this country who though good—& ready to fly at any thing—yet have not the tenacity of tooth and Stoicism in endurance of my canine fellow citizens, then pray send them—by the readiest conveyance, perhaps best by Sea.——Mr. Kinnaird will disburse for them & deduct from the amount on your application or on that of Captain Fyler.—I see the good old King is gone to his place—one can't help being sorry—though blindness—and age and insanity are supposed to be draw-backs—on human felicity—but I am not at all sure that the latter at least—might not render him happier than any of his subjects.[7]——I have no thoughts of coming to the Coronation—though I should like to see it—and though I have a right to be a puppet in it—but my division with Lady Byron which has drawn an equinoctial line between me and mine in all other things—will operate in this also to prevent my being in the same procession. [...]

You ask me for a volume of manners &c.—on Italy; perhaps I am in the case to know more of them than most Englishmen—because I have lived among the natives—and in parts of the country—where Englishmen never resided before—(I speak of Romagna and this place particularly) but there are many reasons why I do not choose to touch in print on such a subject—I have lived in their houses and in the heart of their families—sometimes merely as 'amico di casa' [friend of the family] and sometimes as 'Amico di cuore' [lover] of the Dama—and in neither case do I feel myself authorized in making a book of them.——Their moral is not your moral—their life is not your life—you would not understand it—it is not English nor French—nor German—which you would all understand—the Conventual education—the Cavalier Servitude—the habits of thought and living are so entirely different—and the difference becomes so much more striking the more you live intimately with them—that

---

[7] George III died on 29 January 1820, though the Prince Regent had ruled in his stead since 1810. As Poet Laureate, Robert Southey wrote a ridiculous apotheosis for him, *A Vision of Judgement*, the publication of which in April inspired Byron's riposte, *The Vision of Judgment*, eventually published in 1822. (See letter of 6 October 1821.)

I know not how to make you comprehend a people—who are at once temperate and profligate—serious in their character and buffoons in their amusements—capable of impressions and passions which are at once *sudden* and *durable* (what you find in no other nation) and who *actually* have *no society* (what we would call so) as you may see by their Comedies—they have no real comedy not even in Goldoni—and that is because they have no society to draw it from.——

Their Conversazioni are not Society at *all*.—They go to the theatre to talk—and into company to hold their tongues—The *women* sit in a circle and the men gather into groupes—or they play at dreary Faro—or 'Lotto reale'—for small sums.—Their Academie are Concerts like our own—with better music—and more form.—Their best things are the Carnival balls—and masquerades—when every body runs mad for six weeks.——After their dinners and suppers they make extempore verses—and buffoon one another—but it is in a humour which you would not enter into—ye of the North.——

In their houses it is better—I should know something of the matter—having had a pretty general experience among their women—the fisherman's wife—up to the Nobil' Donna whom I serve.——Their system has it's rules—and it's fitnesses—and decorums—so as to be reduced to a kind of discipline—or game at hearts—which admits few deviations unless you wish to lose it.——They are extremely tenacious—and jealous as furies—not permitting their Lovers even to marry if they can help it—and keeping them always close to them in public as in private whenever they can.——In short they transfer marriage to adultery—and strike the *not* out of that commandment.—The reason is that they marry for their parents and love for themselves.—They exact fidelity from a lover as a debt of honour—while they pay the husband as a tradesman—that is not at all.——You hear a person's character—male or female—canvassed—not as depending on their conduct to their husbands or wives—but to their mistress or lover.——And—and—that's all.—If I wrote a quarto—I don't know that I could do more than amplify what I have here noted.——

It is to be observed that while they do all this—the greatest outward respect is to be paid to the husbands—and not only by the ladies but by their Serventi—particularly if the husband serves no one himself—(which is not often the case however) so that you would often suppose them relations—the Servente making the figure of one adopted into the family.—Sometimes the ladies run a little restive—and elope—or divide—or make a scene—but this is at starting generally—when they know no better—or when they fall in love with a foreigner—or some such anomaly—and is always reckoned unnecessary and extravagant.—— […]

By the king's death—Mr. H[obhouse] I hear will stand for Westminster[8]—I shall be glad to hear of his standing any where except in the pillory—which from the company he must have lately kept—(I always except Burdett—and Douglas K. and the genteel part of the reformers) was perhaps to be apprehended. I was really glad to hear it was for libel instead of larceny—for though impossible in his own person he might have been taken up by mistake for another at a meeting.——All reflections on his present case and place are so <very> *Nugatory*—that it would be useless to pursue the subject further.——

I am out of all patience to see my friends sacrifice themselves for a pack of blackguards—who disgust one with their Cause—although I have always been a friend to and a Voter for reform.——If Hunt[9] had addressed the language to me—which he did to Mr. H[obhouse] last election—I would not have descended to call out such a miscreant who won't fight—but have passed my sword-stick through his body—like a dog's and then thrown myself on my Peers—who would I hope—have weighed the provocation;—at any rate—it would have been as public a Service as Walworth's chastisement of Wat. Tyler.——If we must have a tyrant—let him at least be a gentleman who has been bred to the business, and let us fall by the axe and not by the butcher's cleaver.——No one can be more sick of—or indifferent to politics than I am—if they let me alone—but if the time comes when a part must be taken one way or the other—I shall pause before I lend myself to the views of such ruffians—although I cannot but approve of a Constitutional amelioration of long abuses.——Lord George G-ordon—and Wilkes—and Burdett—and Horne Tooke—were all men of education—and courteous deportment—so is Hobhouse—but as for these others—I am convinced—that Robespierre was a Child—and Marat a quaker in comparison of what they would be could they throttle their way to power.[10]——

[scrawl]

---

[8] A general election was required on the death of the British monarch.

[9] Henry 'Orator' Hunt (1773–1835), Radical politician and demagogue, was imprisoned for two years after addressing the crowd at the Peterloo Massacre in Manchester in 1819. (See Byron's reference to 'the Manchester business' in letter of 22 April 1820.) Wat Tyler led the Peasants' Revolt of 1381 and was killed by Sir William Walworth, Lord Mayor of London.

[10] Lord George Gordon (1751–93), instigator of the anti-Catholic Gordon Riots of 1780; John Wilkes (1725–97), Radical journalist and politician; Sir Francis Burdett (1770–1844), reformist member of the House of Commons; Horne Tooke (1736–1812) grammarian and supporter of Wilkes; Maximilien Robespierre (1758–94) and Jean-Paul Marat (1743–93), radical French Revolutionary leaders.

[To John Murray]

Ravenna. March 29th. 1820

Dear Murray,

I sent you yesterday eight sheets of answer to Jack Wilson and the Edin Mag of last August.—Herewith you will receive a note (enclosed) on Pope, which you will find tally with a part of the text of last Post.[11] I have at last lost all patience with the atrocious cant and nonsense about Pope, with which our present blackguards are overflowing, and am determined to make such head against it, as an Individual can by prose or verse—and I will at least do it with good will.——There is no bearing it any longer, and if it goes on, it will destroy what little good writing or taste remains amongst us.——I hope there are still a few men of taste to second me, but if not, I'll battle it alone—convinced that it is in the best cause of English literature.——I have sent you so many packets verse and prose lately, that you will be tired of the postage if not of the perusal.——

I want to answer some parts of your last letter—but I have not time, for I must 'boot and saddle' as my Captain Craigengelt[12] (an officer of the old Napoleon Italian army) is in waiting, and my Groom and cattle to boot.—You have given me a screed of Metaphor and what not about *Pulci*—& manners, '*and going without clothes* like our Saxon ancestors' now the *Saxons did not go* without cloathes and in the next place they are *not* my ancestors, nor yours either, for mine were Normans, and yours I take it by your name were *Gael*.——And in the next I differ from you about the 'refinement' which has banished the comedies of Congreve[13]—are not the Comedies of *Sheridan* acted to the thinnest houses?—I *know* (as *ex-Committed*) that the 'School for Scandal' was the *worst Stock piece* upon record.—I also know that Congreve gave up writing because Mrs. Centlivre's balderdash[14] drove his comedies off—so it is not *decency* but Stupidity—that does all this—for Sheridan is as *decent* a writer as need be—and Congreve no worse than Mrs. Centlivre—of whom Wilkes (the Actor) said—'not only her play would be damned but She too'—he alluded to a 'Bold Stroke for a Wife'.——

---

[11] This is 'Some Observations upon an Article in *Blackwood's Edinburgh Magazine*', in defence of Byron's life abroad (*CMP* 88–119), which in its second half refutes Romantic attacks on Pope.

[12] In Walter Scott's *The Bride of Lammermoor* (1819), a companion of the Laird of Bucklaw.

[13] Murray had written about changing manners in England, which made old ones anachronous ('A man might as well appear without Cloaths——and quote our Saxon ancestors'). He went on to say, 'The Comedies of Charles Seconds days are not tolerated now—and even in my Own time I have gradually seen my favourite Love for Love absolutely pushed by public feeling—from the stage—it is not affectation of morality but the real progress and result of refinement...' (*Murray Letters*, 310).

[14] Susanna Centlivre (*c*.1670–1723) wrote nearly twenty plays, none of which are as brilliant as those by William Congreve (1670–1729), who retired from the stage in 1700, when Centlivre's career was only just beginning.

But last and most to the purpose—Pulci is *not* an *indecent* writer—at least in his first Canto as you will have perceived by this time.——You talk of *refinement*, are you all *more* moral? are you *so* moral?—No such thing,—*I* know what the World is in England by my own proper experience—of the best of it—at least—of the loftiest.—And I have described it every where as it is to be found in all places.—But to return—I should like to see the *proofs* of mine Answer—because there will be something to omit or to alter—but pray let it be carefully printed——When convenient let me have an answer—

yrs.
[scrawl]

[To John Cam Hobhouse]

Ravenna. April 22d. 1820

Dear Hobhouse

By yesterday's post I had yrs. of the 31st. Ulto.——The papers told me that you had got *out*, and got *in*, I am truly glad of both events[15]—though I could have wished the one had had no connection with the other.——I beg your pardon for confounding you with Hunt and Cobbett[16]—but I thought that the Manchester business had effected a reconciliation—at least you all (bating Cobbett) attended one meeting, soon after it—but I am glad to hear you have nothing to do with those scoundrels—I can understand and enter into the feelings of Mirabeau and La Fayette[17]—but I have no sympathy with Robespierre—and Marat—whom I look upon as in no respect worse than those two English ruffians—if they once had the power.——You will hardly suppose that I should deny to you—what I said to another—I *did* use such an expression on the subject of Bristol Hunt—and I repeat it—I do not think the man who would overthrow all laws—should have the benefit of any, he who plays the Tyler or Cade might find the Walworth or Iden—he who enacts the Clodius—the Milo—and what is there in Bristol

---

[15] Hobhouse had been imprisoned for three months for contempt of court (relating to a political pamphlet) from 14 December 1819 up to his release on 28 February ('got *out*'). He had been elected as MP for Westminster directly thereafter ('got *in*').

[16] William Cobbett (1763–1835), pamphleteer and journalist, was a person of more substance than 'Orator' Hunt. He took a variety of radical positions, but was also deeply attached to the English countryside and its traditions. In his letter Hobhouse suggested that the 18th-century times of aristocratic patronage 'are gone by and I am convinced that the proudest of all politicians & the most uncondescending is the man of principle, the real radical Reformer' (*Hobhouse Letters*, 286–7).

[17] Honoré Gabriel Riqueti, Comte de Mirabeau (1749–91), and Gilbert du Motier, Marquis de Lafayette (1757–1834), were on the liberal, aristocratic wing of the French Revolution.

Hunt and Cobbett—*so* honest as the former—or *more* patriotic than the latter?—
'Arcades Ambo' blackguards both.[18]——Why our classical education alone
should teach us to trample on such unredeemed dirt as the *dis*honest
bluntness—the ignorant brutality, the unblushing baseness of these two mis-
creants;—and all who believe in them.——I think I have neither been an illiberal
man nor an unsteady man upon polities—but I think also that if the Manchester
Yeomanry had cut down *Hunt only*—they would have done their duty—as it
was—they committed *murder* both in what they did—and what they did *not*
do,—in butchering the weak instead of *piercing* the wicked, in assailing the
seduced instead of the seducer—in punishing the poor starving populace,
instead of that pampered and dinnered blackguard who is only less contempt-
ible than his predecessor *Orator Henley*[19] because he is more mischievous.——
What I say thus—I say as publicly as you please—if to praise such fellows be the
price of popularity—I spit upon it, as I would in their faces.——

Upon reform you have long known my opinion—but *radical* is a new word
since my time—it was not in the political vocabulary in 1816—when I left
England—and I don't know what it means—is it uprooting?[20]—As to yourself
it is not in the power of political events to change my sentiments—I am rejoiced
to see you in parliament because I am sure you will make a splendid figure in it,
and have fought hard to arrive there—and I esteem and admire Burdett as you
know—but with these and half a dozen more exceptions—I protest, not against
reform—but my most thorough contempt and abhorrence—of all that I have
seen, heard, or heard of the persons calling themselves *reformers, radicals*, and such
other names,—I should look upon being free with such men, as much the same
as being in bonds with felons.——I am no enemy to liberty however, and you
will be glad to hear that there is some chance of it in Italy—the Spanish business
has set the Italians agog,[21] and if there turns up anything as is not unlikely, I may
perhaps 'wink and hold out mine iron' with the rest, or at any rate be a well
wishing spectator of a push against those rascally Austrians who have desolated
Lombardy, and threaten the rest of the bel paese [the beautiful country;
Italy].——I should not like to leave this country in case of a row, but if nothing
occurs, and you could come out during the recess in autumn—I might revert
with you—though only four years of the usual term of transportation are

---

[18] As Tyler was killed by Walworth so Jack Cade, leader of the Kentish Rebellion (1450), was killed
by Alexander Iden, sheriff of the county. Publius Clodius Pulcher, tribune of Rome in the 1st century
BC, unleashed a populist campaign against the statesman Cicero but was killed in a political riot with
his rival, Titus Annius Millo. 'Arcades Ambo' ('countrymen both') is from Virgil's *Eclogues*, vii. 4.

[19] John Henley (1692–1756), flamboyant and populist London preacher.

[20] *OED* first records 'Radical' as a political noun in 1822.

[21] In March 1820 Ferdinand VII of Spain had accepted a liberal constitution after a military
rebellion, but a French army restored absolutism in 1823. Byron's quotation is from *Henry V*, II. i. 6–7.

expired.——I wrote to you last week about my affairs which are puzzling, Dougal says the Irish thing is excellent,[22] Hanson says it is ruinous, decide between them.——I have sent lots of poeshie to Murray who has not condescended to acknowledge but two of half a dozen packets—'*bleed him in the Jugular*' as they did our char a banc driver in the Simmenthal in 1816.——believe me,

yrs ever & truly

B

P. S.—I have written in great haste, and it is bed time—my monkey too has been playing such tricks about the room as Mr. Hunt at his meetings—so that I have hardly had time to be common-sensible but never mind.——

[To Countess Teresa Guiccioli]

[May, 1820?]

M[y] L[ove]

What do you want me to reply?—He has known—or ought to have known, all these things for many months—there is a mystery here that I do not understand, and prefer not to understand.—Is it only *now* that he knows of your *infidelity*? what can he have thought—that we are made of stone—or that I am *more* or *less* than a man? I know of one remedy only—what I have already suggested, *my departure*—it would be a *great sacrifice*, but rather than run into things like this every day it becomes necessary—almost a duty for me—not to remain any longer in these parts.——He says that it is impossible for him to tolerate this relationship any longer—I answer that he *never* should have tolerated it—assuredly it is not the happiest condition, even for me, to be exposed to his scenes, which come too late, now.—But I shall do what a gentleman should do that is not cause disturbance in a family—all this would already be over—if that man—had allowed me to leave in December of last year.—He not only *wished* me to come—but—he said to me with his own lips that I *ought* not to go away 'this being too far-fetched a remedy'. In these circumstances we shall not see each other tonight. Always and *all yours*!

---

[22] Kinnaird had recommended Byron invest in mortgages on Ormond Quay, desirable real estate on the Liffey at Dublin.

[To Countess Teresa Guiccioli]

[May, 1820?]

My Love + + +

The usual inconclusive business—and *inconcludable*—if there be such a word.—
He proposed that I should *go away* (saying that this is the *general desire* and
opinion—and that his friend Marini is surprised that I should stay to cause
trouble in the life of a family) or else that I should use my influence over you to
persuade you to detach yourself from *me* and to *love him*—and also that I should
attach myself, as soon as possible, to *another*.——As to separation—he says that
he does not want it—not being disposed to 'lose the woman[']—to disgust his
relations—and, above all, to *pay* an allowance.—He does not want to cut the
figure, he says, of a 'complacent c[uckold]'—and he charges me to persuade you
that true love is *conjugal* love.—I am using his own words.—He says that my love
not being a first passion—like yours—I should not behave like this, etc. etc. etc.
he does not want this—he does not want that—and does not know what he does
want—but meanwhile he does not want us to love each other—which however
I always shall.

[scrawl]

[To Thomas Moore]

Ravenna, June 1st, 1820

I have received a Parisian letter from W[edderburn] W[ebster], which I prefer
answering through you, if that worthy be still at Paris, and, as he says, an
occasional visitor of yours. In November last he wrote to me a well-meaning
letter, stating, for some reasons of his own, his belief that a reunion might be
effected between Lady B. and myself. To this I answered as usual; and he sent me
a second letter, repeating his notions, which letter I have never answered, having
had a thousand other things to think of. He now writes as if he believed that he
had offended me by touching on the topic; and I wish you to assure him
that I am not at all so,—but on the contrary, obliged by his good-nature. At
the same time acquaint him *the thing is impossible. You know this*, as well as I,—and
there let it end.

I believe that I showed you his epistle in autumn last. He asks me if I have
heard of *my* 'laureat' at Paris,—somebody who has written 'a most sanguinary

Epitre [letter]' against me;[23] but whether in French, or Dutch, or on what score, I know not, and he don't say,—except that (for my satisfaction) he says it is the best thing in the fellow's volume. If there is anything of the kind that I *ought* to know, you will doubtless tell me. I suppose it to be something of the usual sort;—he says, he don't remember the author's name.

I wrote to you some ten days ago, and expect an answer at your leisure.

The separation business still continues, and all the world are implicated, including priests and cardinals. The public opinion is furious against *him,* because he ought to have cut the matter short *at first,* and not waited twelve months to begin. He has been trying at evidence, but can get none *sufficient;* for what would make fifty divorces in England won't do here—there must be the *most decided* proofs. * * *

It is the first cause of the kind attempted in Ravenna for these two hundred years; for, though they often separate, they assign a different motive. You know that the continental incontinent are more delicate than the English and don't like proclaiming their coronation in a court, even when nobody doubts it.

All her relations are furious against him. The father has challenged him—a superfluous valour, for he don't fight, though suspected of two assassinations— one of the famous Monzoni of Forli. Warning was given me not to take such long rides in the Pine Forest without being on my guard; so I take my stiletto and a pair of pistols in my pocket during my daily rides.

I won't stir from this place till the matter is settled one way or the other. She is as femininely firm as possible; and the opinion is so much against him, that the *advocates* decline to undertake his cause, because they say that he is either a fool or a rogue—fool, if he did not discover the liaison till now; and rogue, if he did know it, and waited, for some bad end to divulge it. In short, there has been nothing like it since the days of Guido di Polenta's family, in these parts.[24]

If the man has me taken off, like Polonius 'say he made a good end,'[25]—for a melodrame. The principal security is, that he has not the courage to spend twenty scudi—the average price of a clean-handed bravo—otherwise there is no want of opportunity, for I ride about the wood every evening, with one servant, and sometimes an acquaintance, who latterly looks a little queer in solitary bits of bushes.

Good bye.—Write to yours ever, &c.

---

[23] The French Romantic poet Alphonse de Lamartine (1790–1869) published his ambivalent 'L'Homme—à Lord Byron' in 1820.

[24] Guido di Polenta was the father of Dante's famous illicit lover Francesca da Rimini (see letter of 17 May 1819).

[25] See *Hamlet,* IV. v. 184.

[To Douglas Kinnaird]

Ravenna. July 20th. 1820
11 o'Clock at Night

Dear Douglas

Some weeks ago you will have received my consent to the Mortgage to be lent to Ld. Blessington—what have you done upon it?—my half year's fee from the funds where is it?—Messrs. Hanson write that the Rochdale Cause has been heard—is it decided?—I shall be glad to hear on these and other points at your imperial leisure.[26]——There is a Revolution at Naples and one is expected throughout Italy daily.—I have completed (but have to copy out) a tragedy in five acts—on Marino Faliero Doge of Venice.——The fever has attacked me again but slightly—I caught it riding in the Forest part of which is agueish & marshy.——

Madame Guiccioli has been separated from her husband who has been sentenced (by the Pope) to pay her twelve hundred crowns a year of alimony—a handsome allowance for a lone woman in these parts—almost three hundred pounds sterling a year and worth about a thousand in England.——The story is a long one—he wanted to bully and failed with both lady and gentleman—they say here that he will have me taken off—it is the custom—there were two perished last week—a priest—and a factor—one by a political club—and the other by a private hand for revenge;—nobody fights—but they pop at you from behind trees, and put a knife into you in company—or in turning a corner—while you are blowing your nose—he may do as he pleases—I only recommend to him not to miss—for if such a thing is attempted—and fails—he shan't have another opportunity —'Sauce for the Goose is sauce for the Gander' it would be easy to know the quarter whence it came and I would pistol him on the spot on my return from the escape.——I have taken no precautions (which indeed would be useless)—except taking my pistols when I ride out in the woods every evening— you know I used to be a pretty good shot—and that if the rogues missed that I should probably hit.——All these fooleries are what the people of the place say (who detest him by the way) and whether true or not—I shan't stir a step out of my way;—a man's life is not worth holding on such a tenure as the feat of such fellows and what must be will—if it be decreed but not otherwise.——

---

[26] The Irish first Earl of Blessington was clearly the owner of the Ormond Quay in Dublin: he and his wife visited Byron in Genoa in 1823 (see letters of 5, 14, and 23 April 1823). The lawsuit over Byron's Rochdale collieries had dragged on for fifteen years: Byron would lose in court this very month.

While I am in *the very act of writing* to you—my Steward Lega has come to tell me that this moment—a quarter of an hour past—a brigadier of the Gens d'armes has been shot in the thigh (I heard the pistol and thought it was my servants cleaning, my own and firing them first) by no one knows who—all we know is that they had a quarrel with the populace two weeks ago—who warned them—and had already wounded two before.—They had also a squabble (the Gens d'armes) with my Servants about the lace of my liveries as resembling their uniforms—but they were reduced to order by the decision of the police in favour of the liveries.—I hope none of my ragamuffins have been in this matter.——Here is a state of society for you! it is like the middle ages—Grand Uncertainty—but very dramatic.

yrs. ever

[scrawl]

P. S.—*all fact I assure you. it is Moonlight. A fortnight ago a similar thing happened to these soldiers—but they were only wounded (two of them) with knives—one lost his hat in the Scuffle.*

[To John Murray]

Ravenna. September 7th. 1820

Dear Murray

In correcting the proofs—you must refer to the *Manuscript*—because there are in it *various readings.*—Pray—attend to this—and choose what Gifford thinks best.—Let me know what he thinks of the whole.——You speak of Lady Noel's illness—she is not of those who die—the amiable only do; and they whose death would DO GOOD—live.—Whenever she is pleased to return—it [may] be presumed that She will take her '*divining rod*' along with her— it may be of use to her at home—as well as to the '*rich man*' of the Evangelists.[27]—— Pray do not let the papers paragraph me back to England—they may say what they please—any loathsome abuse—but that.—Contradict it.——My last letters

---

[27] Lady Byron's mother had become Lady Noel by the death of her brother Thomas Noel, Lord Wentworth; she was an enthusiast for divining rods, and died in 1822. I take it Byron refers to the 'eye of the needle' in Matthew 19: 23–6.

will have taught you to expect an explosion here—it was primed & loaded—but they hesitated to fire the train.—One of the Cities shirked from the league.— I cannot write more at large—for a thousand reasons.—Our *'puir hill folk'*[28] offered to strike—and to raise the first banner.—But Bologna paused—and now 'tis Autumn and the season half over—'Oh Jerusalem! Jerusalem!['][29] the Huns are on the Po—but if once they pass it on their march to Naples—all Italy will rise behind them—the Dogs—the Wolves—may they perish like the Host of Sennacherib!—If you want to publish the Prophecy of Dante—you never will have a better time.—Thanks for books—but as yet No 'Monastery' of Walter Scott's the *only* book except Edinburgh & Quarterly which I desire to see.—Why do you send me so much *trash* upon Italy—such tears—&c. which I know *must be false.*—Matthews is good—very good—all the rest—are like Sotheby's *'Good'*[30] or like Sotheby himself—that old rotten Medlar of Rhyme.—The Queen—how is it?—prospers She?—

[To the Neapolitan Insurgents]

[October? 1820]

An Englishman—a friend to liberty—having understood that the Neapolitans permit even foreigners to contribute to the good cause—is desirous that they should do him the honour of accepting a thousand louis—which he takes the liberty of offering.[31]—Having already, not long since, been an oracular witness of the despotism of the Barbarians in the States occupied by them in Italy—he sees, with the enthusiasm natural to a cultivated man, the glorious determination of the Neapolitans to assert their well-won independence. As a member of the English House of Peers, he would be a traitor to the principles which placed the reigning family of England on the throne—if he were not grateful for the noble lesson so lately given both to people and to kings.—The offer which he

---

[28] An expression used repeatedly by Walter Scott in his historical novels to refer to the Scots Presbyterian 'Covenanters' of the seventeenth century, who resisted the monarch and English political interference on religious grounds before being routed by both Oliver Cromwell and the restored Charles II.

[29] See Matthew 23: 37: 'O Jerusalem, Jerusalem, thou that killeth the prophets, and stonest them which are sent unto thee, how often would I have gathered thy children together, even as a hen gathereth her chickens under her wings, and ye would not!' Byron wrote a famous poem, 'The Destruction of Sennacherib' (CPW iii. 309–10) on God's destruction of an Assyrian army outside Jerusalem.

[30] See letter of 8 January 1818.

[31] The Neapolitan Revolution broke out in July 1820, and was put down by Austrian troops from the north in March the following year. (Marching south, they passed Ravenna, which raised the political temperature in the town.) Byron's letter never reached its intended recipients, but was repressed by a double agent in the service of the Papal Government of Romagna.

desires to make is small in itself, as must always be that presented from an individual to a nation but he trusts that it will not be the last they will receive from his countrymen.——

His distance from the frontier, and the feeling of his personal incapacity to contribute efficaciously to the service of the nation, prevents him from proposing himself as worthy of the lowest commission, for which experience and talent might be requisite—but if, as a mere volunteer, his presence were not a burden to whomsoever he might serve under, he would repair to whatever place the N[eapolitan] Government might point out.—there to obey the orders and participate in the dangers—of his commanding officer, without any other motive than that of sharing the destiny of a brave nation, defending itself against the self-called Holy Alliance—which but combines the vice of hypocrisy with despotism.——

[To John Cam Hobhouse]

Ravenna. 8bre [October]. 17.0 1820

My dear Hobhouse

I hope that you have safely received my two late letters—which contained *two* letters from H[oppne]r—relative to the Queen's Concern.——D[ougla]s K[innair]d has written to me but he lets that legal Spooney go on as he pleases—so that the funds will fall & fall—and who knows what thousands of pounds may be lost by his dawdling.——Do pray Stir him up with a long pole—and make him a speech sharp as those you produce in Parliament.—— Recollect that my distance makes me helpless.——Have you seen Murray? and read my '*Tig. and Tiri*[']? have you 'gone again into the Slaughter House Lankey?'[32]——Murray hath projects of publication—about the *prose* too— regarding which I will abide by *your opinion*—which was against publishing the *Blackwood* &c.—I will rest with yr. decision in that matter whatever it be.— Foscolo thinks the tragedy very good Venetian, and Gifford says it is Sterling English.—Now is a good time for the Prophecy of Dante;—Events have acted as

---

[32] In *Anecdotes of the Late Samuel Johnson* (1786; 280), Hester Thrale tells the story of Johnson unwillingly reading the tragedy *Zenobia*, by his friend Arthur Murphy. 'I told him...that there was too much *Tig* and *Tirry* in it.... I looked at nothing but the dramatis, and there was *Tigranes* and *Tiridates*, or *Terbazus*, or such stuff. A man can tell but what he knows, and I never got any further than the first page.' *Marino Faliero* also involves a complex dramatis personae. In his *Life of Johnson* (1791; ii. 339), Boswell describes the critic being read to by a Bennet Langton, the younger. At the end of the first act of a tragedy, against his better judgement, Johnson said, 'Come, let's have some more, let's go into the slaughterhouse again, Lankey. But I am afraid there is more blood than brains.'

an Advertisement thereto.—Egad—I think I am as good a vates (prophet videlicet) as Fitzgerald of the Morning Post.[33]——

On politics I shall say nothing—the post being somewhat suspect.——I see that you are still 'campaigning at the King of Bohemy'[34]—your last Speech is at great length in Galignani—and so you were called to order—but I think that you had the best of it.——You have done your part very well in Parliament to my mind; it was just the place for you—keep it up and go on.—If ever I come home—I will make a speech too—though I doubt my extempore talents in that line—and then *our* house is not animating like the hounds of the commons—when in full cry.—Tis but cold hunting at best in the Lords.——I never could command my own attention to either side of their oratory—but either went away to a ball—or to a beefsteak at Bellamy's—and as there is no answering without listening—nor listening without patience—I doubt whether I should ever make a debater.—— I think I spoke four times in all there—and I did not find my facility encrease with practice.——D[ougla]s K[innair]d did not mention you in his letters—which are always filled with radical politics—all which I can have in the Newspapers.— I wish he was in Parliament again—which I suppose he wishes too.——

We have sad Sirocco weather here at present—and no very bright political horizon.——But on that I shall say nothing—because I *know*—that they have spies upon me—because I sometimes shoot with a rifle.—The exquisite reason!——You will laugh and think of Pope and the Clerks of the Post Office, but a fact I assure you.—They are in such a state of suspicion—as to dread everything and every body—and though I have been a year here—and they know why I came here yet they don't think a woman a sufficing reason for so long a residence.—As for the Scoundrel Austrians they are bullying Lombardy—as usual.—It would be pleasant to see those Huns get their paiks—and it is not off the cards that they may.—

yrs. [scrawl]

They send an order from Rome to disarm my Servants—the best of it is that they were not armed!—

---

[33] See Byron writing to Moore about Leigh Hunt, letter of 1 June 1818.

[34] See Samuel Foote's political comedy *The Mayor of Garratt* (1763), Act II: 'I heard of your tricks at the King of Bohemy when you was campaigning about.'

[To John Murray]

Ravenna. 9bre. [November] 4.0 1820

I have received from Mr. Galignani the enclosed letters—duplicates—and receipts—which will explain themselves.[35]——As the poems are your property, by purchase, right, & justice, *all matters of publication &c. &c. are for you to decide upon.*—I know not how far my compliance with Mr. G's request might be legal, and I doubt that it would not be honest.——In case you choose to arrange with him—I enclose the permits to *you*—& in so doing I wash my hands of the business altogether.—I sign them merely to enable you to exert the power you justly possess more properly.—I will have nothing to do with it further; except in my answer to Mr. Galignani—to state that the letters &c. &c. are sent to you & the causes thereof.——If you can check those foreign Pirates—do;—if not—put the permissive papers in the fire;—*I* can have no view nor object whatever but to secure to you your property—

yrs.
Byron

———∞∞∞———

P. S.—There will be—shortly—'the Devil to pay' here—and as there is no saying that I may not form an Item *in his bill—I shall not now write at greater length;—you have not answered my late letters;—and you have acted foolishly—as you will find out some day.——*
P. S.—I have read part of the Quarterly just arrived.—Mr. Bowles shall be answered—he is not quite correct in his statement about E[nglish] B[ards] & S[cotch] R[eviewers].——They Support Pope I see in the Quarterly—Let them Continue to do so—it is a Sin & a Shame and a damnation—to think that Pope!! should require it—but he does.——Those miserable mountebanks of the day—the poets—disgrace themselves—and deny God—in running down Pope—the most faultless of Poets, and almost of men.——The Edinburgh praises Jack Keats or Ketch or whatever his names are;[36]—why his is the Onanism of Poetry—something like the pleasure an Italian fiddler extracted out of being suspended daily by a Street Walker in Drury Lane—this went on for some weeks—at last the Girl went to get a pint of Gin—met another, chatted too long—and Cornelli was hanged outright before she

---

[35] The entrepreneurial Parisian publisher of the English-language daily newspaper *Galignani's Messenger* wanted the sole right to publish Byron in France.
[36] Jack Ketch was an notoriously unfeeling public executioner, associated with the deaths of aristocratic rebels after the return of English King Charles II in 1660: a moral untouchable, so to speak.

returned. Such like is the trash they praise—and such will be the end of the outstretched poesy of this miserable Self-polluter of the human Mind.—W. Scott's Monastery just arrived—many thanks for that Grand Desideratum of the last Six Months.——

P. S.—You have cut up old Edgeworth it seems amongst you.—You are right—he is a bore.— I met the whole batch—Mr. Mrs. & Miss at a blue breakfast of Lady Davy's in Blue Square—and he proved but bad—in taste and tact & decent breeding.[37]——He began by saying that Parr (Dr. Parr) had attacked—& that he (the father of Miss E) had cut him up in his answer.—Now Parr would have annihilated him—& if he had not—why tell us (a long story) who wanted to breakfast?—I saw them different times in different parties—& I thought him a very tiresome coarse old Irish half and half Gentleman and her a pleasant reserved old woman—with a pencil under her petticoat—however—undisturbed in it's operation by the vicinity of that anatomical part of female humanity—which would have rendered the taking notes neutral or partial in any other she animal above a Cow.—That sort of woman seem to think themselves perfect because they can't get covered; & those who are seem no better for it—the spayed bitches.——

[scrawl]

[To John Murray]

Ravenna. 9bre. [November] 18.0 1820

Dear Moray[38]

The death of Waite is a shock to the—teeth as well as to the feelings of all who knew him.—Good God!—he and *Blake*—both gone!—I left them both in the most robust health—and little thought of the national loss in so short a time as five years.[39]—They were both so much superior to Wellington in rational greatness as he who preserves the hair—& the teeth—is preferable to 'the bloody blustering booby' who gains a name by breaking heads & knocking out grinders.——Who succeeds *him*? where is tooth powder? *mild* & yet efficacious—where is *tincture*? where are cleansing *roots* and *brushes* now to be obtained?—Pray obtain what information you can upon these *Tusculum*

---

[37] The high-minded Edgeworth literary family—particularly the educationist Richard (1744–1817), whom Byron later called 'the worst of bores—a boisterous Bore' (*LJ* ix. 33), and the didactic novelist and children's author Maria (1768–1849)—was not one Byron was likely to warm to. Maria was devoted to her father, completed his memoirs (see letter of 18 November 1820: 'the late *Edgeworth*'), and died unmarried. Samuel Parr (1747–1825) became known as the 'Whig Samuel Johnson' for the rigour of his opinions.

[38] Byron often refers to Murray like this—perhaps with the voracious eel in mind. But Murray and Moray 'were used interchangeably' in Scottish history, Marchand tells us (*LJ* xi. 234), and the name figures in Scott's *Waverley* (1814), chapter 22.

[39] John Waite (dentist) and Benjamin Blake (barber and perfumier), whose services and products Byron greatly depended upon at home and abroad.

questions'—my Jaws ache to think on't.[40]—Poor fellows! I anticipated seeing both—& yet they are gone to that place where both teeth and hair last longer than they do in this life—I have seen a thousand graves opened—and always perceived that whatever was gone—the *teeth and hair* remained of those who had died with them.——Is not this odd?—they go the very first things in youth—& yet last the longest in the dust—if people will but *die* to preserve them?—It is a queer life—and a queer death—that of mortals. I hear that Waite had married—but little thought that the other decease was so soon to overtake him.——Then he was such a delight—such a Coxcomb—such a Jewel of a Man—there is a taylor at Bologna so like him—and also at the top of his profession.——Do not neglect this commission— *who* or *what* can replace him?—what says the public?——

I remand you the preface—*don't forget* that the Italian extract from the Chronicle must be *translated*. With regard to what you say of re-touching the Juans—and the Hints—it is all very well—but I can't *furbish*.—I am like the tyger (in poesy) if I miss my first Spring—I go growling back to my Jungle.—There is no second.—I can't correct—I can't—& I won't.—Nobody ever succeeds in it great or small.—Tasso remade the whole of his Jerusalem but who ever reads that version?—all the world goes to the first.—Pope *added* to the 'Rape of the Lock'—but did not reduce it.——You must take my things as they happen to be—if they are not likely to suit—reduce their *estimate* then accordingly—I would rather give them away than hack & hew them.—I don't say that you are not right—I merely assert that I can not better them.—I must either 'make a spoon or spoil a horn'.—And there's an end.——The parcel of the *second* of June—with the late *Edgeworth*—& so forth—has *never* arrived—parcels of a later date have—of which I have given you my opinions in a late letter.——I remit you what I think a Catholic curiosity—the Pope's brief—authenticating the body of Saint Francis of Assisi,—a town on the road to Rome.——

yrs. ever
[scrawl]

P. S.—*Of the praises of that little dirty blackguard* KEATES *in the Edinburgh—I shall observe as Johnson did when Sheridan the actor got a pension. 'What has he got a pension? then it is time that I should give up* mine.'—*Nobody could be prouder of the praises of the Edinburgh than I was—or more alive to their censure—as I showed in E[nglish] B[ards]*

---

[40] See *Hamlet*, V. i. 90. Cicero, the 1st-century BC Roman politician and orator, wrote his *Tusculan Disputations* at his villa at Tusculum, in the Alban Hills.

and S[cotch] R[eviewe]rs—at present all the men *they have ever praised are degraded by that insane article.*—Why don't they review & praise 'Solomon's Guide to Health' it is better sense—and as much poetry as Johnny Keates.[41] *Bowles must be bowled down*—'tis a sad match at Cricket—if that fellow can get any Notches at Pope's expence.——If he once gets into 'Lord's Ground' (to continue the pun because it is foolish) I think I could beat him in one Innings.[42]——You had not known perhaps—that I was once—(not metaphorically but really) *a good Cricketer*—particularly in batting—and I played in the Harrow match against the Etonians in 1805, gaining more notches (as one of our chosen Eleven) than any except Ld. Ipswich & Brockman on our side.——

[To John Murray]

Ravenna. Decr. 9th. 1820

Dear Murray

I intended to have written to you at some length by this post,—but as the Military Commandant is now lying dead in my house—on Fletcher's bed—I have other things to think of.——He was shot at 8 o Clock this evening about two hundred paces from our door.—I was putting on my great Coat to pay a visit to the Countess G[uiccioli]—when I heard a shot—and on going into the hall—found all my servants on the balcony—exclaiming that 'a Man was murdered'.——As it is the custom here to let people fight it through—they wanted to hinder me from going out—but I ran down into the Street—Tita the bravest of them followed me—and we made our way to the Commandant who was lying on his back with five wounds—of which three in the body—one in the heart.——There were about him—Diego his Adjutant—crying like a Child—a priest howling—a Surgeon who dared not touch him—two or three confused & frightened Soldiers—one or two of the boldest of the mob—and the Street dark as pitch—with the people flying in all directions.—As Diego could only cry and wring his hands—and the Priest could only pray—and nobody seemed able or willing to do anything except exclaim shake and stare—I made my Servant & one of the mob take up the body—sent off Diego crying to the Cardinal—the Soldiers for the Guard—& had the Commandant carried up Stairs to my own quarters.— But he was quite gone.—I made the Surgeon examine him & examined him

---

[41] Dr Samuel Solomon published his successful *Guide to Health* in 1795.

[42] What Byron calls 'notches' we would now call runs in cricket, the spiritual home of which is Lord's Cricket Ground in Marylebone, London. See Byron's letter to a schoolfellow, 4 August 1805 (*LJ* i. 71): 'We have played the Eton and were most confoundedly beat, however it was some comfort to me that I got 11 notches the 1st Innings and 7 the 2nd. which was more than any of our side, except Brockman and Ipswich'.

myself.—He had bled inwardly, & very little external blood was apparent.—One of the Slugs had gone quite through—all but the Skin, I felt it myself.—Two more shots in the body—one in a finger—and another in the arm.—His face not at all disfigured—he seems asleep—but is growing livid.—The Assassin has not been taken—but the gun was found—a gun filed down to half the barrel.——

He said nothing—but 'O Dio!' and 'O Gesu' two or three times. The house was filled at last with Soldiers—officers—police—and military—but they are clearing away—all but the Sentinels—and the [body] is to be removed tomorrow.—It seems if I had not had him taken into my house he might have lain in the Street till morning—for here nobody meddles with such things—for fear of the consequences—either of public suspicion, or private revenge on the part of the Slayers.—They may do as they please—I shall never be deterred from a duty of humanity by all the assassins of Italy—and that is a wide word.——He was a brave officer—but an unpopular man.—The whole town is in confusion.—You may judge better of things here by this detail than by anything which I could add on the Subject—communicate this letter to Hobhouse & Douglas K[innair]d— and believe me

yrs. truly
B

P. S.—The poor Man's wife is not yet aware of his death—they are to break it to her in the morning.—The Lieutenant who is watching the body is smoking with the greatest Sangfroid—a strange people.—

[Ravenna Journal]

[January 4—February 27, 1821][43]

Ravenna, January 4th, 1821

'A sudden thought strikes me.'[44] Let me begin a journal once more. The last I kept was in Switzerland, in record of a tour made in the Bernese Alps, which

---

[43] See *LJ* viii. 11: 'All that we have of this journal is what Moore published [in his biography] as "Extracts from a Diary of Lord Byron, 1821"…. In deference to Hobhouse, who wanted no life of Byron written, he cut out some parts and then apparently destroyed it altogether, for it has not survived.'

[44] See George Canning and John Hookham Frere, *The Rovers, or, The Double Arrangement* (1798), I. i.

I made to send to my sister in 1816, and I suppose that she has it still, for she wrote to me that she was pleased with it. Another, and longer, I kept in 1813–1814, which I gave to Thomas Moore in the same year.

This morning I gat me up late, as usual—weather bad—bad as England—worse. The snow of last week melting to the sirocco of to-day, so that there were two d—d things at once. Could not even get to ride on horseback in the forest. Stayed at home all the morning—looked at the fire—wondered when the post would come. Post came at the Ave Maria, instead of half-past one o'clock, as it ought. Galignani's Messengers, six in number—a letter from Faenza, but none from England. Very sulky in consequence (for there ought to have been letters), and ate in consequence a copious dinner; for when I am vexed, it makes me swallow quicker—but drank very little.

I was out of spirits—read the papers—thought what *fame* was, on reading, in a case of murder, that 'Mr. Wych, grocer, at Tunbridge, sold some bacon, flour, cheese, and, it is believed, some plums, to some gypsy woman accused. He had on his counter (I quote faithfully) a *book*, the Life of *Pamela*, which he was *tearing* for *waste* paper, &c., &c. In the cheese was found, &c., and a *leaf* of *Pamela wrapt round the bacon.*' What would Richardson, the vainest and luckiest of *living* authors (i.e. while alive)—he who, with Aaron Hill, used to prophesy and chuckle over the presumed fall of Fielding (the *prose* Homer of human nature) and of Pope (the most beautiful of poets)—what would he have said, could he have traced his pages from their place on the French prince's toilets (see Boswell's Johnson) to the grocer's counter and the gipsy-murderess's bacon!!![45]

What would he have said? What can anybody say, save what Solomon said long before us? After all, it is but passing from one counter to another, from the bookseller's to the other tradesman's—grocer or pastry-cook. For my part, I have met with most poetry upon trunks; so that I am apt to consider the trunk-maker as the sexton of authorship. [...]

January 5th, 1821

[...] Dined versus six o' the clock. Forgot that there was a plum-pudding, (I have added, lately, *eating* to my 'family of vices,') and had dined before I knew it. Drank half a bottle of some sort of spirits—probably spirits of wine; for what they call brandy, rum, &c. &c., here is nothing but spirits of wine, coloured accordingly. Did *not* eat two apples, which were placed by way of dessert. Fed the two cats,

---

[45] The novelist Samuel Richardson (1689–1761) published *Pamela: Or, Virtue Rewarded* in 1740; Aaron Hill (1685–1750) satirized Pope and flattered Richardson. In his *Life of Johnson* Boswell told the story of a traveller, returned from Paris, who mentioned to Richardson having seen his *Clarissa* on a Crown Prince's table in the French capital. Richardson prompted the traveller to tell this flattering tale to the company at large, but he refused to indulge the author's vanity.

the hawk, and the tame (but *not tamed*) crow. Read Mitford's History of Greece—Xenophon's Retreat of the Ten Thousand. Up to this present moment writing, 6 minutes before eight o' the clock—French hours, not Italian.

Hear the carriage—order pistols and great coat, as usual—necessary articles. Weather cold—carriage open, and inhabitants somewhat savage—rather treacherous and highly inflamed by politics. Fine fellows, though,—good materials for a nation. Out of chaos God made a world, and out of high passions comes a people.

Clock strikes—going out to make love. Somewhat perilous, but not disagreeable. Memorandum—a new screen put up to-day. It is rather antique, but will do with a little repair. […]

January 6th, 1821

[…] What is the reason that I have been, all my lifetime, more or less *ennuyé* [bored]? and that, if any thing, I am rather less so now than I was at twenty, as far as my recollection serves? I do not know how to answer this, but presume that it is constitutional,—as well as the waking in low spirits, which I have invariably done for many years. Temperance and exercise, which I have practiced at times, and for a long time together vigorously and violently, made little or no difference. Violent passions did;—when under their immediate influence—it is odd, but—I was in agitated, but *not* in depressed spirits.

A dose of salts[46] has the effect of a temporary inebriation, like light champagne, upon me. But wine and spirits make me sullen and savage to ferocity—silent, however, and retiring, and not quarrelsome, if not spoken to. Swimming also raises my spirits,—but in general they are low, and get daily lower. That is *hopeless*: for I do not think I am so much *ennuyé* as I was at nineteen. The proof is, that then I must game, or drink, or be in motion of some kind, or I was miserable. At present, I can mope in quietness; and like being alone better than any company—except the lady's whom I serve. But I feel a something, which makes me think that, if I ever reach near to old age, like Swift, 'I shall die at top' first.[47] Only I do not dread idiotism or madness so much as he did. On the contrary, I think some quieter stages of both must be preferable to much of what men think the possession of their senses.

January 7th, 1821, Sunday

Still rain—mist—snow—drizzle—and all the incalculable combinations of a climate, where heat and cold struggle for mastery. Read Spence, and turned over

---

[46] That is, Epsom salts, magnesium sulphate: a mild laxative.
[47] See letter of 28 October 1816.

Roscoe, to find a passage I have not found. Read the 4th vol. of W. Scott's second series of 'Tales of my Landlord'.[48] Dined. Read the Lugano Gazette. Read—I forget what. At 8 went to conversazione. Found there the Countess Geltrude, Betti V. and her husband, and others. Pretty black-eyed woman, that—*only* twenty-two—same age as Teresa, who is prettier, though.

The Count Pietro G[amba] took me aside to say that the Patriots have had notice from Forli (twenty miles off) that to-night the government and its party mean to strike a stroke—that the Cardinal here has had orders to make several arrests immediately, and that, in consequence, the Liberals are arming, and have posted patroles in the streets, to sound the alarm and give notice to fight for it.

He asked me 'what should be done?' I answered, 'Fight for it, rather than be taken in detail;' and offered, if any of them are in immediate apprehension of arrest, to receive them in my house (which is defensible), and to defend them, with my servants and themselves (we have arms and ammunition), as long as we can,—or to try to get them away under cloud of night. On going home, I offered him the pistols which I had about me—but he refused, but said he would come off to me in case of accidents.

It wants half an hour of midnight, and rains;—as Gibbet says, 'a fine night for their enterprise—dark as hell, and blows like the devil.'[49] If the row don't happen *now*, it must soon. I thought that their system of shooting people would soon produce a reaction—and now it seems coming. I will do what I can in the way of combat, though a little out of exercise. The cause is a good one.

Turned over and over half a score of books for the passage in question, and can't find it. Expect to hear the drum and the musquetry momently (for they swear to resist, and are right,)—but I hear nothing, as yet, save the plash of the rain and the gusts of the wind at intervals. Don't like to go to bed, because I hate to be waked, and would rather sit up for the row, if there is to be one.

Mended the fire—have got the arms—and a book or two, which I shall turn over. I know little of their numbers, but think the Carbonari strong enough to beat the troops, even here. With twenty men this house might be defended for twenty-four hours against any force to be brought against it, *now in this place*, for the same time; and, in such a time, the country would have notice, and would rise,—if ever they *will* rise, of which there is some doubt. In the mean time, I may as well read as do any thing else, being alone. [...]

Tuesday, January 9th, 1821

---

[48] That is, *The Heart of Midlothian* (1818).
[49] See George Farquhar, *The Beaux' Stratagem* (1707), IV. i. 568–70: a group of highwaymen share these lines in the original, but Byron's recollection is almost perfect.

[…] Dined. Read Johnson's 'Vanity of Human Wishes,'—all the examples and mode of giving them sublime, as well as the latter part, with the exception of an occasional couplet. I do not so much admire the opening. I remember an observation of Sharpe's (the *Conversationist*, as he was called in London, and a very clever man) that the first line of this poem was superfluous, and that Pope (the best of poets, *I* think,) would have begun at once, only changing the punctuation—

'Survey mankind from China to Peru!'

The former line, 'Let observation.' &c., is certainly heavy and useless. But 'tis a grand poem—and *so true!*—true as the 10th of Juvenal himself.[50] The lapse of ages *changes* all things—time—language—the earth—the bounds of the sea— the stars of the sky, and every thing 'about, around, and underneath' man,[51] *except man himself*, who has always been, and always will be, an unlucky rascal. The infinite variety of lives conduct but to death, and the infinity of wishes lead but to disappointment. All the discoveries which have yet been made have multiplied little but existence. An extirpated disease is succeeded by some new pestilence; and a discovered world has brought little to the old one, except the p[ox]—first and freedom afterwards—the *latter* a fine thing, particularly as they gave it to Europe in exchange for slavery. But it is doubtful whether 'the Sovereigns' would not think the *first* the best present of the two to their subjects.

At eight went out—heard some news. They say the King of Naples has declared, by couriers from Florence, to the *Powers* (as they call now those wretches with crowns) that his Constitution was compulsive, &c., &c., and that the Austrian barbarians are placed again on *war* pay, and will march. Let them—'they come like sacrifices in their trim,'[52] the hounds of hell! Let it still be a hope to see their bones piled like those of the human dogs at Morat, in Switzerland, which I have seen.

Heard some music. At nine the usual visitors—news, *war*, or rumours of war. Consulted with P[ietro]. G[amba]., &c., &c. They mean to *insurrect* here, and are to honour me with a call thereupon. I shall not fall back; though I don't think them in force or heart sufficient to make much of it. But, *onward!*—it is now the time to act, and what signifies *self*, if a single spark of that which would be worthy of the past can be bequeathed unquenchedly to the future? It is not one man, nor a million, but the *spirit* of liberty which must be spread. The waves

[50] Many people besides politician Richard 'Conversation' Sharp (1759–1835) have commented on the tautological nature of the opening of Johnson's poem (1749), imitated from the tenth satire of Roman poet Juvenal: 'Let Observation with extensive View | Survey Mankind from China to Peru.'
[51] See Milton, 'Il Penseroso' (1645), 152.
[52] See 1 *Henry IV*, IV. i. 114. For Morat see Byron's Alpine journal, 27 September 1816.

which dash upon the shore are, one by one, broken, but yet the *ocean* conquers, nevertheless. It overwhelms the Armada, it wears the rock, and, if the *Neptunians* are to be believed,[53] it has not only destroyed, but made a world. In like manner, whatever the sacrifice of individuals, the great cause will gather strength, sweep down what is rugged, and fertilize (for *sea-weed* is *manure*) what is cultivable. And so, the mere selfish calculation ought never to be made on such occasions; and, at present, it shall not be computed by me. I was never a good arithmetician of chances, and shall not commence now. […]

January 13th, 1821, Saturday

Sketched the outline and Dram[ati]s. Pers[onae]. of an intended tragedy of Sardanapalus, which I have for some time meditated. Took the names from Diodorus Siculus, (I know the history of Sardanapalus, and have known it since I was twelve years old), and read over a passage in the ninth vol. octavo of Mitford's Greece, where he rather vindicates the memory of this last of the Assyrians.[54]

Dined—news come—the *Powers* mean to war with the peoples. The intelligence seems positive—let it be so—they will be beaten in the end. The king-times are fast finishing. There will be blood shed like water, and tears like mist; but the peoples will conquer in the end. I shall not live to see it, but I foresee it.

I carried Teresa the Italian translation of Grillparzer's Sappho,[55] which she promises to read. She quarrelled with me, because I said that love was *not the loftiest* theme for true tragedy; and, having the advantage of her native language, and natural female eloquence, she overcame my fewer arguments. I believe she was right. I must put more love into 'Sardanapalus' than I intended. I speak, of course, *if* the times will allow me leisure. That *if* will hardly be a peace-maker.[56] […]

January 15th, 1821

Weather fine. Received visit. Rode out into the forest—fired pistols. Returned home—dined—dipped into a volume of Mitford's Greece—wrote part of a

---

[53] Early 19th-century geologists frequently divided themselves into 'Neptunians' or 'Vulcanists', depending on whether they saw the biblical Flood or volcanic activity as the major influence on the geology of the Earth.

[54] Diodorus Siculus, 1st-century BC author of the *Bibliotheca Historica*, a general history of the Mediterranean region and beyond. William Mitford's multi-volume *History of Greece* was published between 1784 and 1810.

[55] Austrian poet Franz Grillparzer (1791–1872) published his tragedy *Sappho* in 1818; Byron read an Italian translation. It demonstrates a Romantic sensibility within a neoclassical form, which is perhaps why Byron found it of interest.

[56] See *As You Like It*, V. iv. 100.

scene of 'Sardanapalus'. Went out—heard some music—heard some politics. More ministers from the other Italian powers gone to Congress. War seems certain—in that case, it will be a savage one. Talked over various important matters with one of the initiated. At ten and half returned home.

I have just thought of something odd. In the year 1814, Moore ('the poet', *par excellence*, and he deserves it) and I were going together, in the same carriage, to dine with Earl Grey, the Capo Politico [political leader] of the remaining whigs.[57] Murray, the magnificent (the illustrious publisher of that name), had just sent me a Java gazette—I know not why, or wherefore. Pulling it out, by way of curiosity, we found it to contain a dispute (the said Java gazette) on Moore's merits and mine. I think, if I had been there, that I could have saved them the trouble of disputing on the subject. But, there is *fame* for you at six and twenty! Alexander had conquered India at the same age; but I doubt if he was disputed about, or his conquests compared with those of Indian Bacchus, at Java.

It was a great fame to be named with Moore; greater to be compared with him; greatest—*pleasure*, at least—to be *with* him; and, surely, an odd coincidence, that we should be dining together while they were quarrelling about us beyond the equinoctial line.

Well, the same evening, I met Lawrence the painter, and heard one of Lord Grey's daughters (a fine, tall, spirit-looking girl, with much of the *patrician, thorough-bred look* of her father, which I dote upon) play on the harp, so modestly and ingenuously, that she *looked music*. Well, I would rather have had my talk with Lawrence (who talked delightfully) and heard the girl, than have had all the fame of Moore and me put together.

The only pleasure of fame is that it paves the way to pleasure; and the more intellectual our pleasure, the better for the pleasure and for us too. It was, however, agreeable to have heard our fame before dinner, and a girl's harp after. [...]

January 21st, 1821

[...] To-morrow is my birthday—that is to say, at twelve o' the clock, midnight, i.e. in twelve minutes, I shall have completed thirty and three years of age!!!— and I go to my bed with a heaviness of heart at having lived so long, and to so little purpose.

It is three minutes past twelve.—''Tis the middle of the night by the castle clock,'[58] and I am now thirty-three!

---

[57] As well as being associated with the blend of tea, Charles, second Earl Grey, led the Whigs in the Lords through their longest period of opposition, and became prime minister in 1830, when Wellington resigned over the Reform Bill. Thomas Lawrence (1769–1830) was already recognized as Britain's leading portrait painter by 1814.

[58] See Coleridge, *Christabel*, i. 1.

'Eheu, fugaces, Posthume, Posthume,
Labuntur anni;'—[59]

but I don't regret them so much for what I have done, as for what I *might* have
done.

Through life's road, so dim and dirty,
I have dragg'd to three-and-thirty.
What have these years left to me?
Nothing—except thirty-three.

January 22d, 1821

1821.
Here lies
interred in the Eternity
of the Past,
from whence there is no
Resurrection
for the Days—whatever they may be
for the Dust—
the Thirty-Third Year
of an ill-spent Life,
Which, after
a lingering disease of many months
sunk into a lethargy,
and expired,
January 22d, 1821, A. D.
Leaving a successor
Inconsolable
for the very loss which
occasioned its
Existence. [...]

January 28th, 1821

[...] *Memoranda.*
What is Poetry?—The feeling of a Former world and Future.
Thought Second.

---

[59] See Horace, *Odes*, II. xiv. 1–2: 'Ah, Postumus, Postumus, the fleeting years are slipping by.'

Why, at the very height of desire and human pleasure,—worldly, social, amorous, ambitious, or even avaricious,—does there mingle a certain sense of doubt and sorrow—a fear of what is to come—a doubt of what *is*—a retrospect to the past, leading to a prognostication of the future[?] (The best of Prophets of the future is the Past.) Why is this? or these?—I know not, except that on a pinnacle we are most susceptible of giddiness, and that we never fear falling except from a precipice—the higher, the more awful, and the more sublime; and, therefore, I am not sure that Fear is not a pleasurable sensation; at least, *Hope* is; and *what Hope* is there without a deep leaven of Fear? and what sensation is so delightful as Hope? and, if it were not for Hope, where would the Future be?—in hell. It is useless to say *where* the Present is, for most of us know; and as for the Past, *what* predominates in memory?—*Hope baffled*. Ergo, in all human affairs, it is Hope—Hope—Hope. I allow sixteen minutes, though I never counted them, to any given or supposed possession. From whatever place we commence, we know where it all must end. And yet, what good is there in knowing it? It does not make men better or wiser. During the greatest horrors of the greatest plagues, (Athens and Florence, for example—see Thucydides and Machiavelli) men were more cruel and profligate than ever. It is all a mystery. I feel most things, but I know nothing, except ——

———— ———— ———— ————
    ———— ———— ————
———— ———— ———— ————
    ———— ———— ————
———— ———— ———— ————
    ———— ———— ———— 60

Thought for a Speech of Lucifer, in the Tragedy of Cain:—
        Were *Death* an *evil*, would *I* let thee *live*?
        Fool! live as I live—as thy father lives,
        And thy son's sons shall live for evermore. [...]

February 16th, 1821

Last night Il Conte P[ietro]. G[amba]. sent a man with a bag full of bayonets, some muskets, and some hundreds of cartridges to my house, without apprizing me, though I had seen him not half an hour before. About ten days ago, when there was to be a rising here, the Liberals and my brethren C[arbonar]i asked me

---

60 In his biography Moore comments: 'Thus marked, with impatient strokes of the pen by himself, in the original.' Marchand described these marks as: 'two dashes, then six lines of alternating seven- and six-dash lines, with indentations, suggesting that what Byron omitted was a verse of poetry' (*LJ* xi. 234).

to purchase some arms for a certain few of our ragamuffins. I did so immediately, and ordered ammunition, etc., and they were armed accordingly. Well—the rising is prevented by the Barbarians marching a week sooner than appointed; and an *order* is issued, and in force, by the Government, 'that all persons having arms concealed, &c. &c., shall be liable to', &c. &c.—and what do my friends, the patriots, do two days afterwards? Why, they throw back upon my hands, and into my house, these very arms (without a word of warning previously) with which I had furnished them at their own request, and my own peril and expense.

It was lucky that Lega was at home to receive them. If any of the servants had (except Tita and F[letcher] and Lega) they would have betrayed it immediately. In the mean time, if they are denounced, or discovered, I shall be in a scrape.

At nine went out—at eleven returned. Beat the crow for stealing the falcon's victuals. Read 'Tales of my Landlord'—wrote a letter—and mixed a moderate beaker of water with other ingredients. [...]

February 19th, 1821

Came home solus—very high wind—lightning—moonshine—solitary stragglers muffled in cloaks—women in mask—white houses—clouds hurrying over the sky, like spilt milk blown out of a pail—altogether very poetical. It is still blowing hard—the tiles flying, and the house rocking—rain splashing—lightning flashing—quite a fine Swiss Alpine evening, and the sea roaring in the distance.

Visited—conversazione. All the women frightened by the squall: they *won't* go to the masquerade because it lightens—the pious reason!

Still blowing away. A[lborghetti] has sent me some news to-day. The war approaches nearer and nearer. Oh those scoundrel sovereigns! Let us but see them beaten—let the Neapolitans but have the pluck of the Dutch of old, or the Spaniards of now, or of the German protestants, the Scotch presbyterians, the Swiss under Tell, or the Greeks under Themistocles—*all* small and solitary nations (except the Spaniards and German Lutherans), and there is yet a resurrection for Italy, and a hope for the world. [...]

February 24th, 1821

Rode, &c. as usual. The secret intelligence arrived this morning from (the frontier to the C[arbonar]i is as bad as possible. The *plan* has missed—the Chiefs are betrayed, military, as well as civil—and the Neapolitans not only have *not* moved, but have declared to the P[apal] government, and to the Barbarians, that they know nothing of the matter!!!

Thus the world goes; and thus the Italians are always lost for lack of union among themselves. What is to be done *here*, between the two fires, and cut off from the N[orther]n frontier, is not decided. My opinion was,—better to rise than be taken in detail; but how it will be settled now, I cannot tell. Messengers are despatched to the delegates of the other cities to learn their resolutions.

I always had an idea that it would be *bungled*; but was willing to hope, and am so still. Whatever I can do by money, means, or person, I will venture freely for their freedom; and have so repeated to them (some of the Chiefs here) half an hour ago. I have two thousand five hundred scudi, better than five hundred pounds, in the house, which I offered to begin with.

February 25th, 1821

Came home—my head aches—plenty of news, but too tiresome to set down. I have neither read nor written, nor thought, but led a purely animal life all day. I mean to try to write a page or two before I go to bed. But, as Squire Sullen says, 'My head aches consumedly: Scrub, bring me a dram!'[61] Drank some Imola wine, and some punch. [...]

[To John Murray]

Ravenna—Feb[brai]o 160 1821

Dear Moray

In the month of March will arrive from Barcelona—*Signor Curioni* engaged for the Opera.—He is an acquaintance of mine—and a gentlemanly young man— high in his profession.—I must request your personal kindness and patronage in his favour.———Pray introduce him to such of the theatrical people—Editors of Papers—and others, as may be useful to him in his profession publicly and privately.—He is accompanied by the Signora Arpalice Taruscelli—a Venetian lady of great beauty and celebrity and a particular friend of mine—your natural gallantry will I am sure induce you to pay her proper attention.—Tell Israeli— that as he is fond of *literary* anecdotes—she can tell him some of your acquaint- ance abroad.—I presume that he speaks Italian.[62]—Do not neglect this request, but do them and me this favour in their behalf.———I shall write to some others to aid you in assisting them with your countenance.

---

[61] See George Farquhar, *The Beaux' Stratagem*, V. iv. 277, 281.
[62] For Isaac D'Israeli see letter of 12 June 1815. Arpalice Taruscelli is listed among Byron's sexual conquests in the letter of 19 January 1819.

I agree to your request of leaving in abeyance the terms for the three D. J.s till you can ascertain the effect of publication.—If I refuse to alter—you have a claim to so much courtesy in return.—I had let you off your proposal about the price of the Cantos, last year (the 3d. & 4th. always to reckon as *one* only—which they originally were) and I do not call upon you to renew it.—You have therefore no occasion to fight so shy of such subjects as I am not conscious of having given you occasion.——The 5th. is so far from being the last of D. J. that it is hardly the beginning.—I meant to take him the tour of Europe—with a proper mixture of siege—battle—and adventure—and to make him finish as *Anacharsis Cloots*—in the French revolution.[63]—To how many cantos this may extend—I know not—nor whether (even if I live) I shall complete it—but this was my notion.—I meant to have made him a Cavalier Servente in Italy and a cause for a divorce in England—and a Sentimental 'Werther-faced man' in Germany—so as to show the different ridicules of the society in each of those countries——and to have displayed him gradually gaté [spoilt] and blasé as he grew older—as is natural.—But I had not quite fixed whether to make him end in Hell—or in an unhappy marriage,—not knowing which would be the severest.—The Spanish tradition says Hell—but it is probably only an Allegory of the other state.——You are now in possession of my notions on the subject.—

You say 'the Doge' will not be popular—did I ever write for *popularity*?——I defy you to show a work of mine (except a tale or two) of a popular style or complexion.—It appears to me that there is room for a different style of the drama—neither a servile following of the old drama—which is a grossly errornious one—nor yet *too French*—like those who succeeded the older writers.—It appears to me that good English—and a severer approach to the rules—might combine something not dishonourable to our literature.——I have also attempted to make a play without love.——And there are neither rings—nor mistakes—nor starts—nor outrageous ranting villains—nor melodrame—in it.—All this will prevent it's popularity, but does not persuade me that it is *therefore* faulty.—Whatever faults it has will arise from deficiency in the conduct—rather than in the conception—which is simple and severe.—So—you *epigrammatize* upon my *epigram*.——I will *pay you* for *that*—mind if I don't—some day.—I never let anyone off in the long run—*(who first begins)*—remember Sam[64]—

---

[63] Jean-Baptiste du Val-de-Grâce, Baron de Cloots (1755–94), known as 'Anacharsis', was a Prussian freedom lover who joined the French Revolution, only to fall foul of Robespierre and be guillotined as a foreign traitor. Byron's 'Werther-faced man' is from the suicidal eponymous hero of Goethe's iconic Romantic novel (1774).

[64] On 8 January 1821 Byron had sent Murray a squib about the Braziers' Company's support for Queen Caroline (*CPW* vi. 1). Murray acknowledged it, saying that it could be published safely enough: 'there is no such extraordinary wit to betray itself' (*Murray Letters*, 378). On 28 September 1820 Byron had sent Murray a cruelly satirical poem on his old acquaintance Samuel Rogers, called 'Question and

and see if I don't do you as good a turn.—You unnatural publisher!—what—quiz your own authors!—You are a paper Cannibal.—

In the letter on Bowles—(which I sent by Tuesday's post) after the words '*attempts had been made*' (alluding to the republication of 'English Bards')—add the words '*in Ireland*' for I believe that Cawthorn did not begin his attempts till after I had left England the second time.—Pray attend to this.—Let me know what you & your Synod think of the letter on Bowles.——I did not think the second *Seal* so bad—surely it is far better than the Saracen's head with which you have sealed your *last letter*—the larger in *profile* was surely much better than that.—[So] Foscolo says he will get you a [*seal*] *cut* better in Italy—he means a *throat*—that is the only thing they do dexterously.—The Arts—all but Canova's and Morghen's—and Ovid's;—(I don't *mean poetry*)[65] are as low as need be—look at the Seal which I gave to Wm. Bankes—and own it.—How came George Bankes to quote English Bards in the House of Commons? all the World keep flinging that poem in my face.[66]——Belzoni *is* a grand traveller and his English is very prettily broken.——As for News—the Barbarians are marching on Naples——and if they lose a single battle, all Italy will be up.—It will be like the Spanish war if they have any bottom.——'*Letters opened!*' to be sure they are—and that's the reason why I always put in my opinion of the German Austrian Scoundrels;—there is not an Italian who loathes them more than I do—and whatever I could do to scour Italy and the earth of their infamous oppression—would be done 'con amore'.—

yrs. ever & truly
Byron

Recollect that the Hints *must be printed with the* Latin *otherwise there is no sense.—*

Answer' (*CPW* iv. 165–7): 'Mouth which marks the envious Scorner | With a Scorpion in each Corner', and so forth.

[65] For Canova see letter of 25 November 1816; Raffaelo Sanzio Morghen (1758–1833), Italian engraver of note; and see Ovid's 1st-century set of instructional poems on *Ars Amatoria*—the art of love.

[66] George Bankes (1788–1856), long-serving MP for the rotten borough of Corfe Castle, Dorset, and younger brother of Byron's friend William Bankes. Murray published Giovanni Battista Belzoni's *Narrative of the Operations and Recent Discoveries with the Pyramids, Temples, Tombs, and Excavations in Egypt and Nubia* in 1820.

[To Richard Belgrave Hoppner]

Ravenna, April 3d. 1821

My dear Hoppner

Thanks for the translation. I have sent you some books which I do not know whether you have read or not—you need not return them in any case.—I enclose you also a letter from Pisa—on the usual subject—*not* to trouble you as 'umpire' as the person desires—but to enable you to judge whether I do or do not deserve such a piece of objurgation. I have neither spared trouble nor expence in the care of the child—and as she was now four years old complete—and quite above the control of the Servants—& as it was not fit that she should remain with them longer in any case—and as a *man* living without any woman at the head of his house—cannot much attend to a nursery, <as is necessary>—I had no resource but to place her for a time (at a high pension too) in the convent of Bagna-Cavalli (twelve miles off) where the air is good and where she will at least have her learning advanced—& her morals and religion inculcated.—I had also another reason—things were and are in such a state here—that I had no reason to look upon my personal safety as particularly insurable—and I thought the infant best out of harm's way, for the present.——You *know* (perhaps more than I do) that to allow the Child to be with her mother—& with *them* & their principles—would be <like> absolute insanity—if not worse—that even her health would not be attended to properly—to say nothing of the Indecorum.—It is also fit that I should add that I by no means intended nor intend to give a *natural* Child an *English* Education, because with the disadvantages of her birth her after settlement would be doubly difficult.—Abroad—with a fair foreign education—and a portion of five or six thousand pounds—she might and may marry very respectably—in England such a dowry would be a pittance—while <out of it> elsewhere it is a fortune.——It is besides my wish that She should be a R[oma]n *Catholic*—which I look upon as the best religion as it is assuredly the oldest of the various branches of Christianity.——I have no[t?] explained my notions as to the *place* where she now is—it is the best I could find for the present—but I have no prejudices in its favour.—Of 'the promise made at Geneva' of which this person speaks I have no recollection—nor can I conceive it possible to have been entered into—when the child was yet unborn—& might never have been born at all.——You recollect also (*entre nous* for I have not mentioned it as you will perceive by the letter) the pretty story you told me of what occurred at Naples—which I see no reason to doubt in the main points—though Elise might not relate all accurately.—My best respects to Mrs.

Hoppner—and to our acquaintances.——I do not speak of politics because it seems a hopeless subject—as long as these scoundrels are to be permitted to bully States out of their independence.—believe me

yrs. ever & truly
Byron

P. S.—There is a report here of a change in France—but with what truth is not yet known.

[To Percy Bysshe Shelley]

Ravenna, April 26th, 1821

The child continues doing well, and the accounts are regular and favourable. It is gratifying to me that you and Mrs. Shelley do not disapprove of the step which I have taken, which is merely temporary.

I am very sorry to hear what you say of Keats—is it *actually* true? I did not think criticism had been so killing.[67] Though I differ from you essentially in your estimate of his performances, I so much abhor all unnecessary pain, that I would rather he had been seated on the highest peak of Parnassus than have perished in such a manner. Poor fellow! though with such inordinate self-love he would probably have not been very happy. I read the review of 'Endymion' in the Quarterly. It was severe,—but surely not so severe as many reviews in that and other journals upon others.

I recollect the effect on me of the Edinburgh on my first poem; it was rage, and resistance, and redress—but not despondency nor despair. I grant that those are not amiable feelings; but, in this world of bustle and broil, and especially in the career of writing, a man should calculate upon his powers of *resistance* before he goes into the arena.

> 'Expect not life from pain nor danger free,
> Nor deem the doom of man reversed for thee.'[68]

You know my opinion of *that second-hand* school of poetry. You also know my high opinion of your own poetry,—because it is of *no* school. I read Cenci—but,

---

[67] A rumour had circulated to the effect that Keats had died of distress in 1820 from a bad review of his poems in the *Quarterly Review* (published by Murray).

[68] See Samuel Johnson, 'The Vanity of Human Wishes', 155–6.

besides that I think the *subject* essentially *un*-dramatic, I am not an admirer of our old dramatists *as models*. I deny that the English have hitherto had a drama at all. Your Cenci, however, was a work of power, and poetry. As to *my* drama, pray revenge yourself upon it, by being as free as I have been with yours.

I have not yet got your Prometheus, which I long to see. I have heard nothing of mine, and do not know that it is yet published.[69] I have published a pamphlet on the Pope controversy, which you will not like. Had I known that Keats was dead—or that he was alive and so sensitive—I should have omitted some remarks upon his poetry, to which I was provoked by his *attack* upon *Pope*, and my disapprobation of *his own* style of writing.

You want me to undertake a great Poem—I have not the inclination nor the power. As I grow older, the indifference—*not* to life, for we love it by instinct—but to the stimuli of life, increases. Besides, this late failure of the Italians has latterly disappointed me for many reasons,—some public, some personal. My respects to Mrs. S.

Yours ever,

B

P. S.—*Could not you and I contrive to meet this summer? Could not you take a run* alone?

[To Richard Belgrave Hoppner]

Ravenna. July 23d. 1821

My dear Hoppner/

This country being in a state of proscription—and all my friends exiled—or arrested—the whole family of Gamba—obliged to go to Florence for the present—the father & Son for politicians—(& the Guiccioli because menaced with a *Convent*—as her father is *not* here—) I have determined to remove to Switzerland—and they also.—Indeed my life here is not supposed to be particularly safe—but that has been the case for this twelve-month past—and is therefore not the primary consideration.——I have written by the post to Mr. Hentsch Jr. the Banker of Geneva—to provide (if possible) a house for me—and

---

[69] Shelley's *Prometheus Unbound: A Lyrical Drama in Four Acts*, was published in August 1820. Byron's 'Prometheus' was published alongside *The Prisoner of Chillon* in December 1816, but he makes no reference to receiving a copy.

another for Gamba's family (the father son and daughter) on the *Jura* side of the Lake of Geneva—furnished & with stabling (for *me* at least) for eight horses.—I shall bring Allegra with me.—Could you assist me or Hentsch in his researches? The Gambas are at Florence but have authorized me to treat for them.———You know—or do not know that they are great patriots—and both—but the Son in particular very fine fellows.—*This* I know—for I have seen them lately in very awkward situations—*not* pecuniary—but personal—and they behaved like heroes, neither yielding nor retracting.———You have no idea what a state of oppression this country is in—they arrested above a thousand of high & low—throughout Romagna—banished some—& confined others—without *trial*—*process*—or even *accusation*!! Every body says they would [have] done the same by me if they dared proceed openly. My motive however for removing, is because *every one* of my acquaintance to the amount of hundreds almost have been exiled.———Will you do what you can in looking out for a couple of houses—*furnished* and conferring with Hentsch for us? We care nothing about Society—and are only anxious for a temporary and tranquil asylum, and individual freedom.—Believe me

ever & truly yrs.
Byron [...]

[To Percy Bysshe Shelley]

R[avenn]a A[gost]o 26th. 1821

My dear Shelley/

Conclude for the house then forthwith.—I wish that there were two more *stalls*— for I have *eight* horses.—We are in all the agonies of packing.———If my furniture be not sufficient pray engage for some more—and if any money is necessary— draw on me at sight;—you had better *clinch* the Padrone of the palazzo—lest he rise in his price or play some trick with some others of the hectic English.———Do the essential and I will approve and sanction yr. proceedings.

yrs. ever
Byron

P. S.—I mean to send off all furniture before setting out.———My respects to Mrs. S &c. &c. &c. Let me know the road without passing through Florence.———

[To Countess Teresa Guiccioli]

Ravenna September 17. 1821

Gossip Excellency/

We are all preparing—packing—sweating—swearing—and other -*ings*——It has cost me two hours to put in order the archives of your Excellency's letters—being at least five hundred;—a full translation of *Corinne*[70]—that is—*The Gossip*, the romance of Her Excellency Our Lady Countess Teresa Gaspara Domenica Teresa Guiccioli, born Gamba Ghiselli and Respected Gossip.—— Love me always and entirely yours

[scrawl]

P. S.—1000 messages to Papa, and the fraternal Excellency—Go on scolding Lega—who deserves it more every day.

[To John Murray]

Ravenna Septr. 24th. 1821

Dear Murray/

I have been thinking over our late correspondence and wish to propose the following articles for our future.—1stly—That you shall write to me of yourself—of the health wealth and welfare of all friends—but of *me* (*quoad me*) little or nothing.—

2dly—That you shall send me Soda powders—tooth-paste—toothbrushes— or any such anti-odontalgic or chemical articles as heretofore 'ad libitum' upon being re-imbursed for the same.—

3dly—That you shall *not* send me any modern or (as they are called) *new* publications in *English*—*whatsoever*—save and excepting any writing prose or verse of (or reasonably presumed to be of) Walter Scott—Crabbe—Moore— Campbell—Rogers—Gifford—Joanna Baillie—*Irving* (the American) Hogg—

---

[70] For *Corinne*, see letter of 22 August 1813.

Wilson (Isle of Palms Man)[71] or any especial *single* work of fancy which is thought to be of considerable merit.—*Voyages* and *travels*—provided that they are *neither in Greece Spain Asia Minor Albania nor Italy* will be welcome—having travelled the countries mentioned—I know that what is said of them can convey nothing further which I desire to know about them.—No other *English* works whatsoever.——

4thly—That you send me *no periodical works* whatsoever—*no* Edinburgh—Quarterly—Monthly—nor any Review—Magazine—Newspaper English or foreign of any description——

5thly—That you send me *no* opinions whatsoever either *good*—*bad*—or *indifferent*—of yourself or your friends or others—concerning any work or works of mine—past—present—or to come.—

6thly—That all Negotiations in matters of business between you and me pass through the medium of the Hon[oura]ble Douglas Kinnaird—my friend and trustee, or Mr. Hobhouse—as 'Alter Ego' and tantamount to myself during my absence.—or presence.——

Some of these propositions may at first seem strange—but they are founded.—The quantity of trash I have received as books is incalculable, and neither amused nor instructed.—Reviews & Magazines—are at the best but ephemeral & superficial reading—*who thinks* of the *grand article* of *last year* in any *given review*? in the next place—if they regard *myself*—they tend to increase *Egotism,*—if favourable—I do not deny that the praise *elates*—and if unfavourable that the abuse *irritates*—the latter may conduct me to inflict a species of Satire—which would neither do good to you nor to your friends—*they* may smile *now,* and so may *you* but if I took you all in hand—it would not be difficult to cut you up like gourds. I did as much by as powerful people at nineteen years old—& I know little as yet in three & thirty—which should prevent me from making all your ribs—Gridirons for your hearts—if such were my propensity.—But it is *not.*—Therefore let me hear none of your provocations—if anything occurs so very *gross* as to require my notice—I shall hear of it from my personal friends.—For the rest—I merely request to be left in ignorance.—

The same applies to opinions *good*—*bad* or *indifferent* of persons in conversation or correspondence; these do not *interrupt* but they *soil* the *current* of my Mind;—I am sensitive enough—but *not* till I am *touched* & *here* I am beyond the touch of the short arms of literary England—except the few feelers of the

---

[71] Most of these names are now familiar: Joanna Baillie, poet and tragedian (1762–1851), Washington Irving, American essayist and humourist (1783–1859), and John Wilson (aka 'Christopher North', 1785–1854)—the 'Jack Wilson' of the letter of 29 March 1820—essayist and reviewer for *Blackwood's Magazine,* and author of a collection of poems, *The Isle of Palms* (1812).

Polypus that crawl over the Channel in the way of Extract.——All these precautions *in* England would be useless—the libeller or the flatterer would there reach me in spite of all—but in Italy we know little of literary England & think less except what reaches us through some garbled & brief extract in some miserable Gazette.——For *two years* (except two or three articles cut out & sent by *you*—by the post) I never read a newspaper—which was not forced upon me by some accident—& know upon the whole as little of England—as you all do of Italy—& God knows—*that* is little enough with all your travels &c. &c. &c.— The English travellers *know Italy* as *you* know Guernsey—how much is *that?*—If any thing occurs so violently gross or personal as to require notice, Mr. D[ougla]s Kinnaird will let me *know*—but of *praise* I desire to hear *nothing.*——You will say— 'to what tends all this?—' I will answer THAT——to keep my mind *free and unbiased*—by all paltry and personal irritabilities of praise or censure;—To let my Genius take it's natural direction,—while my feelings are like the dead—who know nothing and feel nothing of all or aught that is said or done in their regard.——If you can observe these conditions you will spare yourself & others some pain—let me not be worked upon to rise up—for if I do—it will not be for a little;—if you can *not* observe these conditions we shall cease to be correspond-ents,—but *not friends*—for I shall always be

yrs. ever & truly
Byron

P. S.—I have taken these resolutions not from any irritation against you or yours but simply upon reflection that all reading either praise or censure of myself has done me harm.— When I was in Switzerland and Greece I was out of the way of hearing either—& how I wrote there!—In Italy I am out of the way of it too—but latterly partly through my fault—& partly through your kindness in wishing to send me the newest & most periodical publications—I have had a crowd of reviews &c. thrust upon me—which have bored me with their jargon of one kind or another—& taken off my attention from greater objects.——You have also sent me a parcel of trash of poetry for no reason that I can conceive—unless to provoke me to write a new 'English Bards'—Now this I wish to avoid—for if ever I do—it will be a strong production—and I desire peace as long as the fools will keep their nonsense out of my way.——

[To Thomas Moore]

October 6th, 1821

By this post I have sent my nightmare to balance the incubus of * * * [Southey]'s impudent anticipation of the Apotheosis of George the Third. I should like you to take a look over it, as I think there are two or three things in it which might please 'our puir hill folk.'[72]

By the last two or three posts I have written to you at length. My *ague* bows to me every two or three days, but we are not as yet upon intimate speaking terms. I have an intermittent generally every two years, when the climate is favourable (as it is here), but it does me no harm. What I find worse, and cannot get rid of, is the growing depression of my spirits, without sufficient cause. I ride—I am not intemperate in eating or drinking—and my general health is as usual, except a slight ague, which rather does good than not. It must be constitutional; for I know nothing more than usual to depress me to that degree.

How do *you* manage? I think you told me, at Venice, that your spirits did not keep up without a little claret. I *can* drink, and bear a good deal of wine (as you may recollect in England); but it don't exhilarate—it makes me savage and suspicious, and even quarrelsome. Laudanum has a similar effect; but I can take much of *it* without any effect at all. The thing that gives me the highest spirits (it seems absurd, but true) is a dose of *salts*—I mean in the afternoon, after their effect. But one can't take *them* like champagne.

Excuse this old woman's letter; but my *lemancholy* don't depend upon health, for it is just the same, well or ill, or here or there.

Yours, &c.

[To Countess Teresa Guiccioli]

[Ravenna] October 26th. 1821

M[y] L[ove]

The day after tomorrow I shall start.——The weather is not very favourable, but that does not matter much,—it mattered more for the Dutch horses—which must already be in Pisa.—So let us hope to see each other before long—be reassured and believe me yours

a[mico]. a[mante]. in e[terno]. [scrawl] [...]

---

[72] See letter of 7 September 1820.

10
PISA

October 1821–September 1822

B yron had spent almost two years in Ravenna, immersing himself in an Italian family (his lover's, the Gambas), Italian literature, and Italian dreams of freedom from the post-Napoleonic settlement. Ravenna was a small and provincial city, almost unvisited by the English abroad. Pisa was a large one, and on the tourist route through Tuscany to Rome and Naples. (He would be visited, therefore, by old acquaintances like Samuel Rogers in April 1822, and Hobhouse in September.) Furthermore, when Byron rolled into the city on 1 November 1821, he joined a small but vigorous expatriate circle, of a kind he had not experienced before. The Shelleys were at its head and heart, but the circle also contained Percy's second cousin Thomas Medwin (1788–1869), who would eventually publish a book of conversations with Byron; his friend Edward Williams (1793–1822), a retired lieutenant with literary hankerings; Williams's de facto Jane (1798–1884), to whom Shelley would gravitate in the summer of his death, and who lived with her 'husband' at the Shelleys' only a short walk from Byron's Casa Lanfranchi; Williams's friend, the enigmatic Edward John Trelawny (1792–1881), 'the personification of my Corsair', as Byron told Teresa (Life, 963); and another of Shelley's friends, the Irishman John Taaffe (1767?–1862), also a literary dabbler, and author of A Comment on the Divine Comedy of Dante Alighieri, which Byron touted to John Murray on his behalf. In February 1822 the circle was expanded still more: Byron sent £250 to Leigh Hunt, so that he (and his family) could come out and collaborate with the two established poets in running a new European magazine, provocatively entitled the Liberal. The Hunts arrived in July 1822, accordingly.

But, with all these varying degrees of literary expertise and (it must be said) with all these varying types of liaison—from the Hunts' conventional family, to the Shelleys' almost childless one (Mary had miscarried in June 1822, and had only one surviving child from four previous pregnancies), to the Williamses' arrangement (Jane was married to another man), to Byron's cavalier servitude—tensions were never far from the surface. Shelley had once praised Byron to the skies, saying that 'every word' of the fifth canto of Don Juan 'is pregnant with immortality' (Life, 922); but in May 1822 he despairingly told a friend, 'I do not write—I have lived too long near Lord Byron and the sun has extinguished the glow-worm' (Life, 951).

Of all this, Byron was blissfully unaware. He had 'a very good spacious house upon the Arno' (LJ ix. 66), from which he visited Teresa, and in January 1822 he resumed Don Juan, untouched since November 1819: no fewer than nine cantos were written by February 1823. He had a cruising yacht built for him in Genoa in the same month (undiplomatically called the Bolivar), and in January, too, his mother-in-law died, giving him a half share in an estate worth a good £7,000 a year—though by October 1823 he had in fact only ever received £900 from it (LJ xi. 42). His life settled into a pleasant rhythm of late nights at his poetry, mid-day breakfasts, and rides beyond the town gates with his friends and their ladies in the late afternoon.

Then, on 24 March 1822, on the return from just such a ride, the group fell foul of a short-tempered dragoon named Masi, who rudely rode through the party on his way to report to barracks. Words turned to blows, Masi told the guards at the gate to arrest the English party, then drew his sword, knocked Shelley off his horse and winded Byron's courier. Byron, who had gone on ahead, returned and encountered the furious soldier. He managed to pacify his angry servants on the scene and Masi galloped on, but someone came out of Byron's house and injured him seriously—at first it seemed mortally—in the side. The authorities became involved and four days later Tita Falciere, who was certainly not responsible, was arrested, principally because he looked imposing and habitually went about armed. Byron sought help from the British chargé d'affaires in Florence, Masi thankfully recovered, and Tita was released—albeit into exile. But the affair had caused recriminations within the expatriate circle, and, because Pietro Gamba had been involved, the Tuscan authorities now had the means to move the Gambas on, and their Radical English milord with them. The Shelleys left Pisa for Lerici in late April, and in late May Byron also left the city for the Villa Dupuy at Montenero, near Leghorn (Livorno), where the local authorities proved no more welcoming. Though he returned to Pisa at the beginning of July, the circle was broken.

But worse was to come. On 20 April 1822 Allegra died of a fever at Bagnacavallo. Byron wrote of his painful response to Shelley (see letter of 23 April 1822). By coincidence, Claire Clairmont was up the coast visiting the Shelleys, and they informed her of her daughter's death. Byron sent a portrait and a lock of Allegra's hair to Claire at her request, and she responded with 'a final excoriating letter' (Life, 995), which can hardly have improved Byron's mood. (She would leave to join her brother in Vienna in September.) Then, on 8 July, a mere week after the arrival of the Hunts at Casa Lanfranchi, Shelley and Williams (as well as a boy on board, Charles Vivian) were drowned in the Bay of Spezia, sailing Shelley's 24-foot schooner, the Don Juan. Shelley's body did not wash up for another ten days, and Trelawny was able to identify it only by a volume of Keats in his pocket. Despite the cooling in their relations, Byron was deeply affected. 'You are all brutally mistaken about Shelley', he loyally wrote to Murray (LJ ix. 189–90), 'who was without exception—the best and least selfish man I ever knew.—I never knew one who was not a beast in comparison.' Shelley's remains were kept under lime for a further month before being cremated on the beach at Viareggio, witnessed by Trelawny (who had undertaken arrangements with relish), Hunt, and Byron. The cremation took four hours to complete, and during it Byron took a long swim in the hot sun. The resulting sunburn turned his back into an enormous blister—scorched and drenched at the same time, as he had once said.

Shelley might have been the glue that kept the Liberal project together. As it was, Byron and Hunt never hit it off. Byron did not appreciate Hunt's children under his roof (he called them 'yahoos'), and Mrs Hunt took a petty-bourgeois dislike to him. The pair soldiered on, and the magazine did at least publish The Vision of Judgment in the first issue of October 1822 (and the fragmentary biblical drama Heaven and Earth in January 1823), but Hunt writhed in a state of permanent financial indebtedness and a sense of social ostracism, which he saved up for his memoir, a masterpiece of inverse snobbery, Lord Byron and Some of his Contemporaries, published four years after the poet's death.

Meanwhile a far more important partnership was showing signs of strain: Byron's with John Murray. Murray's lack of attention to the poet's manuscripts, lack of support for Don Juan, and his nervousness regarding Byron's other biblical play, Cain (which caused grievous affront in Church of England circles when it was published in December 1821), gradually infuriated Byron, who resolved to have his friend Kinnaird extend his agency from financial to publishing matters, and negotiate with the publisher on Byron's behalf. Byron's eventual request of 8 July 1822 that the firmly Tory Murray hand over unpublished items in his keeping to the Radical London publisher John Hunt (1775–1848), and the news that such works would probably be used in the Liberal, edited by John's brother Leigh, marked the beginning of the end of Byron's association with him—though as Byron said, 'I cannot keep my resentments' (LJ ix. 120), and the pair managed to keep patching the relationship for some time yet. After publishing Sardanapalus, The Two Foscari, and Cain together in December 1821, Murray would publish only one more Byron text: the turgid Gothic drama Werner in November 1822.

The Gambas had left Montenero for Lucca just as the Hunts arrived in Pisa. But their final destination was Genoa, beyond the reach of the Tuscan authorities, in the Kingdom of Sicily. On 27 September Byron left Pisa to join them. The expatriate experiment was over.

[Journal: 'Detached Thoughts']

[15 October 1821–18 May 1822]

Octr. 15th. 1821

I have been thinking over the other day on the various comparisons good or evil which I have seen published of myself in different journals English and foreign.—This was suggested to me by my accidentally turning over a foreign one lately—for I have made it a rule latterly never to search for anything of the kind—but not to avoid the perusal if presented by Chance.——To begin then— I have seen myself compared personally or poetically—in English French *German* (*as* interpreted to me) Italian and Portuguese within these nine years—to Rousseau—Goethe—Young—Aretine—Timon of Athens—'An Alabaster Vase lighted up within', Satan—Shakespeare—Buonaparte—Tiberius—Æschylus— Sophocles—Euripides—Harlequin—The Clown—Sternhold and Hopkins—to the Phantasmagoria—to Henry the 8th, to Chenier—to Mirabeau—to young R. Dallas (the Schoolboy) to Michael Angelo—to Raphael—to a petit maitre—to Diogenes, to Childe Harold—to Lara—to the Count in Beppo—to Milton—to Pope—to Dryden—to Burns—to Savage—to Chatterton—to 'oft have I heard of thee my Lord Biron' in Shakespeare,[1] to Churchill the poet—to Kean the Actor—to Alfieri &c. &c. &c.—the likeness to Alfieri was asserted very seriously by an Italian who had known him in his younger days—it of course related merely to our apparent personal dispositions——he did not assert it to *me* (for we were not then good friends) but in society.——[2]

The object of so many contradictory comparisons must probably be like something different from them all,—but what *that* is, is more than *I* know, or any body else.——My Mother before I was twenty—would have it that I was like Rousseau—and Madame de Stael used to say so too in 1813—and the Edin[burgh] Review has something of ye sort in it's critique on the 4th Canto of Ch[ild]e Ha[rold]e.——I can't see any point of resemblance—he wrote prose—I verse—he was of the people—I of the Aristocracy—he was a philosopher—I am none—he published his first Work at forty—I mine at eighteen,—his first essay brought him universal applause—mine the contrary—he married his housekeeper—I could not keep house with my wife—he thought all the world in a plot against *him*; my little world seems to think *me* in a plot against it—if I may judge by their abuse in print and coterié—he liked Botany—I like flowers and herbs and trees but know nothing of their pedigrees—he wrote Music—I limit my knowledge of it to what I catch by *Ear*—I never could learn any thing by *study*—not even a language—it was all by rote and ear and memory.—He had a bad memory—I *had* at least an excellent one (ask Hodgson the poet—a good judge for he has an astonishing one) he wrote with hesitation and care—I with rapidity—& rarely with pains—he could never ride nor swim 'nor was cunning of fence'[3]——I was an excellent swimmer—a decent though not at all a dashing rider—(having staved in a rib at eighteen in the course of scampering) & was sufficient of fence—particularly of the Highland broadsword—not a bad boxer—when I could keep my temper—which was difficult—but which I strove to do ever since I knocked down Mr. Purling and put his knee-pan out (with the gloves on) in Angelo's and Jackson's rooms in 1806 during the sparring, and I was besides a very fair Cricketer—one of the Harrow Eleven when we play[ed] against Eton in 1805.——

Besides Rousseau's way of life—his country—his manners—his whole character—were so very different—that I am at a loss to conceive how such a

---

[1] See *Love's Labour's Lost*, V. ii. 827.

[2] Edward Young (1681–1765), English poet; Pietro Aretino (1492–1556), Italian satirist; Thomas Sternhold and John Hopkins, 16th-century setters of the Psalms to music; André Chenier (1762–94), poet and victim of the French Revolution; Count Mirabeau (1749–91), aristocratic French Revolutionary; Richard Savage (1697–1743), English *poète maudit*; Thomas Chatterton (1752–70), English poetical prodigy and suicide; Charles Churchill (1732–64), English satirist; and Vittorio Alfieri (1749–1803), Italian neoclassical dramatist.

[3] See *Twelfth Night*, III. iv. 276.

comparison could have arisen—as it has done three several times and all in rather a remarkable manner. I forgot to say—that *he* was also short-sighted—and that hitherto my eyes have been the contrary to such a degree that in the largest theatre of Bologna—I distinguished and read some busts and inscriptions printed near the stage—from a box so distant—& so *darkly* lighted—that none of the company (composed of young and very bright-eyed people some of them in the same box) could make out a letter—and thought it was a trick though I had never been in that theatre before.—Altogether, I think myself justified in thinking the comparison not well founded. I don't say this out of pique—for Rousseau was a great man—and the thing if true were flattering enough—but I have no idea of being pleased with a chimera.——

13.

Whenever an American requests to see me—(which is *not* unfrequently) I comply—1stly. because I respect a people who acquired their freedom by firmness without excess—and 2dly. because these transatlantic visits 'few and far between'[4] make me feel as if talking with Posterity from the other side of the Styx;—in a century or two the new English & Spanish Atlantides will be masters of the old Countries in all probability—as Greece and Europe overcame their Mother Asia in the older or earlier ages as they are called.

33

I have a notion that Gamblers are as happy as most people—being always *excited*;—women—wine—fame—the table—even Ambition—*sate* now & then—but every turn of the card—& cast of the dice—keeps the Gambler alive—besides one can Game ten times longer than one can do any thing else.—I was very fond of it when young—that is to say of 'Hazard' for I hate all *Card* Games even Faro—When Macco[5] (or whatever they spell it) was introduced I gave up the whole thing—for I loved and missed the *rattle* and *dash* of the box & dice—and the glorious uncertainty not only of good luck or bad luck—but of *any luck at all*—as one had sometimes to throw *often* to decide at all.——I have thrown as many as fourteen mains running and carried off all the cash upon the table occasionally—but I had no coolness or judgement or calculation.—It was the *delight* of the thing that pleased me.—Upon the whole I left off in time without being much a winner or loser.—Since One and twenty years of age—I played but little & then never above a hundred or two—or three.——

---

[4] See Thomas Campbell, *The Pleasures of Hope* (1799), ii. 378.
[5] *OED* records this as the first English usage: a card game normally called 'Macao', similar to baccarat.

48

There was a Madman of the name of Battersby that frequented Steevens's and the Prince of Wales Coffee-houses about the time when I was leading a loose life about town—before I was of age.—One night he came up to some hapless Stranger whose coat was not to his liking and said 'Pray Sir did the tailor cut your coat in that fashion—or did the rats gnaw it?[']

49

The following is—(I believe) better known.—A beau (*dandies* were not then christened) came into the P[rince] of W[ales] and exclaimed—'Waiter bring me a glass of Madeira Negus with a Jelly—and rub my plate with a Chalotte' This in a very soft tone of voice.——A Lieutenant of the Navy who sate in the next box immediately roared out the following rough parody——'Waiter— bring me a glass of d——d stiff Grog—and rub my a—e with a brick-bat.[']

60

No man would live his life over again—is an old & true saying which all can resolve for themselves.—At the same time there are probably *moments* in most men's lives—which they would live over the rest of life to *regain?*—Else why do we live at all? because Hope recurs to Memory—both false—but—but—but— but—and—this *but* drags on till—What? I do not know—& who does?—'He that died o' Wednesday'[6]—by the way—there is a poor devil to be shot tomor- row here—(Ravenna) for murder;—he hath eaten half a Turkey for his dinner— besides fruit & pudding—and he refuses to confess?—shall I go to see him exhale?—No.—And why?—because it is to take place at *Nine;*—Now—could I *save* him—or a fly even from the same catastrophe—I would out-watch years— but as I cannot—I will not get up earlier to see another man shot—than I would to run the same risk in person.—Besides—I have seen more than one die that death (and other deaths) before to-day.—It is not cruelty which actuates mankind—but excitement—on such occasions—at least I suppose so;—it is detestable to *take* life in that way—unless it be to preserve two lives.——

67

When I belonged to the D[rury] L[ane] Committee and was one of the S[ub] C[ommittee] of Management—the number of *plays* upon the shelves were about *five* hundred;—conceiving that amongst these there must be *some* of merit—in person & by proxy I caused an investigation.—I do not think that of those which I saw—there was one which could be conscientiously tolerated.——There never

---

[6] See 1 *Henry IV*, V. i. 136.

were such things as most of them.—Mathurin was very kindly recommended to me by Walter Scott—to whom I had recourse—firstly—in the hope that he would do something for us himself—& secondly—in my despair—that he would point out to us any young (or old) writer of promise.—Mathurin sent his Bertram—and a letter *without* his address—so that at first—I could give him no answer.—When I at last hit upon his residence I sent him a favourable answer and something more substantial.—His play succeeded—but I was at that time absent from England.——I tried Coleridge too—but he had nothing feasible in hand at the time.—Mr. Sotheby obligingly offered *all* his tragedies—and I pledged myself—and notwithstanding many squabbles with my Committe[e]d Brethren—did get 'Ivan' accepted—read—& the parts distributed.—But lo! in the very heart of the matter—upon some *tepid*-ness on the part of Kean—or warmth upon that of the Authour—Sotheby withdrew his play.—— Sir J. B. Burgess did also present four tragedies and a farce—and I moved Green-room & S Committee—but they would not.—Then the Scenes I had to go through!—the authours—and the authoresses——the Milliners—the wild Irishmen—the people from Brighton—from Blackwell—from Chatham—from Cheltenham—from Dublin—from Dundee—who came in upon me!—to all of whom it was proper to give a civil answer—and a hearing—and a reading—— Mrs. Glover's father an Irish dancing Master of Sixty years—called upon me to request to play '*Archer*'—drest in silk stockings on a frosty morning to show his legs—(which were certainly good & Irish for his age—& had been still better)— Miss Emma Somebody with a play entitled the 'Bandit of Bohemia'—or some such title or production—Mr. O'Higgins—then resident at Richmond—with an Irish tragedy in which the unities could not fail to be observed for the protagonist was chained by the leg to a pillar during the chief part of the performance.—He was a wild man of a salvage appearance—and the difficulty of not laughing at him was only to be got over—by reflecting upon the probable consequences of such cachinnation.——As I am really a civil & polite person— and *do* hate giving pain—when it can be avoided—I sent them up to Douglas Kinnaird—who is a man of business—and sufficiently ready with a negative— and left them to settle with him—and as at the beginning of next year—I went abroad—I have since been little aware of the progress of the theatres.

72

When I first went up to College—it was a new and a heavy hearted scene for me.—Firstly—I so much disliked leaving Harrow that though it was time— (I being seventeen) it broke my very rest for the last quarter—with counting the days that remained.—I always *hated* Harrow till the last year and a half—but then I liked it.—2dly. I wished to go to Oxford and not to Cambridge.—3dly. I was so

completely alone in this new world that it half broke my Spirits.—My companions were not unsocial but the contrary—lively—hospitable—of rank—& fortune—& gay far beyond my gaiety—I mingled with—and dined—& supped &c.
with them—but I know not how—it was one of the deadliest and heaviest
feelings of my life to feel that I was no longer a boy. From that moment
I began to grow old in my own esteem—and in my esteem age is not estim-
able.—I took my gradations in the vices—with great promptitude—but they
were not to my taste—for my early passions though violent in the extreme—
were concentrated—and hated division or spreading abroad.—I could have left
or lost the world with or for that which I loved—but though my temperament
was naturally burning—I could not share in the common place libertinism of
the place and time—without disgust.——And yet this very disgust and my heart
thrown back upon itself—threw me into excesses perhaps more fatal than those
from which I shrunk—as fixing upon one (at a time) the passions which spread
amongst many would have hurt only myself.—

73

People have wondered at the Melancholy which runs through my writings.—
Others have wondered at my personal gaiety——but I recollect once after an
hour in which I had been sincerely and particularly gay—and rather brilliant in
company—my wife replying to me when I said (upon her remarking my high
spirits) 'and yet Bell—I have been called and mis-called Melancholy—you must
have seen how falsely frequently.' 'No—B—(she answered) it is not so—at
heart you are the most melancholy of mankind, and often when apparently
gayest.[']——

74

If I could explain at length the *real* causes which have contributed to increase this
perhaps *natural* temperament of mine—this Melancholy which hath made me a
bye-word—nobody would wonder——but this is impossible without doing
much mischief.——I do not know what other men's lives have been—but
I cannot conceive anything more strange than some of the earlier parts of
mine——I have written my memoirs—but omitted *all* the really *consequential*
& *important* parts—from deference to the dead—to the living—and to those who
must be both.—

75

I sometimes think that I should have written the *whole*—as a *lesson*—but it might
have proved a lesson to be *learnt*—rather than *avoided*—for passion is a whirl-
pool, which is not to be viewed nearly without attraction from it's Vortex.——

76

I must not go on with these reflections—or I shall be letting out some secret or other—to paralyze posterity.—

96

Of the Immortality of the Soul—it appears to me that there can be little doubt— if we attend for a moment to the action of Mind.—It is in perpetual activity;—I used to doubt of it—but reflection has taught me better.—It acts also so very independent of body—in dreams for instance incoherently and madly—I grant you;—but still it is *Mind* & much more *Mind*—than when we are awake.—— Now—that *this* should not act *separately*—as well as jointly—who can pro- nounce?—The Stoics Epictetus & Marcus Aurelius call the present state 'a Soul which drags a Carcase'——a heavy chain to be sure, but all chains being material may be shaken off.—How far our future life will be *individual*—or rather—how far it will at all resemble our *present* existence is another question—but that the *Mind* is *eternal*—seems as possible as that the body is not so.—Of course—I have venture[d] upon the question without recurring to Revelation—which however is at least as rational a solution of it—as any other.—A *material* resurrection seems strange and even absurd except for purposes of punishment—and all punishment which is to *revenge* rather than *correct*—must be *morally wrong*—and *when* the *World is at an end*—what moral or warning purpose *can* eternal tortures answer?—human passions have probably disfigured the divine doctrines here— but the whole thing is inscrutable.—It is useless to tell one *not* to *reason* but to *believe*—you might as well tell a man not to wake but *sleep*—and then to *bully* with torments!—and all that!—I cannot help thinking that the *menace* of Hell makes as many devils as the severe penal codes of inhuman humanity make villains.——Man is born *passionate* of body—but with an innate though secret tendency to the love of Good in his Main-spring of Mind.——But God help us all!—It is at present a sad jar of atoms.——

102

What a strange thing is the propagation of life!—A bubble of Seed which may be spilt in a whore's lap—or in the Orgasm of a voluptuous dream—might (for aught we know) have formed a Caesar or a Buonaparte—there is nothing remarkable recorded of their Sires—that I know of.——

118

1

Oh! talk not to me of a name great in story
The days of our Youth, are the days of our Glory,

And the myrtle and ivy of sweet two and twenty
Are worth all your laurels though ever so plenty.

2

What are garlands and crowns to the brow that is wrinkled,
Tis but as a dead flower with May-dew besprinkled,
Then away with all such from the head that is hoary,
What care I for the wreaths that can *only* give Glory?

3

Oh! Fame—if I eer took delight in thy praises—
'Twas less for the sake of thy high-sounding phrases,
Than to see the bright eyes of the dear One discover
She thought that I was not unworthy to love her.

4

There chiefly I sought thee, *there* only I found thee,
Her Glance was the best of the rays that surround thee,
When it sparkled oer aught that was bright in my story,
I knew it was love, and I felt it was Glory.—

I composed these stanzas (except the fourth added now) a few days ago—on the road from Florence to Pisa.—

[To Augusta Leigh]

Pisa. Novr. 4th. 1821

My dearest Augusta/

You will see by the date that I have arrived here safely.—I am writing in a room inconvenient from the extreme heat of the *Sun*—it is like Summer—so fine is the climate.—If the Girls are delicate in health—as you say—you had better bring them out here for a year or two.—The Climate is you know a *medical* one for [?] people.—I have an immense house and could lodge you *all* without the least inconvenience—it would save you expences & you would see your brother.——I recommend this to your thoughts seriously.—Let me know.—I send you some hair *darker* than the other though from the same head—but it is only in parts that it is *so* grey.——Have you sent any to Ada—as requested?

yrs
[scrawl]

P. S.—I am alone *in my house—which is immense—you could bring your drone of a husband with you—it would do him good—and probably save the lives of some of the children, if they are delicate.—As to expences—I will* frank *you* all here[7]*—if you like to take the journey—and I have carriages &c. for you—things don't cost here—what they do amongst you in England.——*

[To John Murray]

Pisa. Decr. 4th. 1821

Dear Sir/

By extracts in the English papers in your holy Ally—Galignani's messenger—I perceive that the 'two greatest examples of human vanity—in the present age'—are firstly 'the Ex-Emperor Napoleon'—and secondly—'his Lordship the noble poet &c.'—meaning your humble Servant—'poor guiltless I'.[8]——Poor Napoleon!—he little dreamed to what 'vile comparisons' the turn of the Wheel would reduce him.—I cannot help thinking however that had our learned brother of the Newspaper Office—seen my very moderate answer to the very scurrile epistle of my radical patron John Hobhouse M.P.—he would have thought the thermometer of my 'Vanity' reduced to a very decent temperature.—By the way, you do not happen to know whether Mrs Fry had commenced her reform of the prisoners at the time when Mr. Hobhouse was in Newgate?[9]——there are some of his phrases—and much of his style (in that same letter) which lead me to suspect that either she had not—or that he had profited less than the others by her instructions.—Last week—I sent back the deed of Mr. Moore signed—and witnessed.—It was inclosed to Mr. Kinnaird with a request to forward it to you.—I have also transmitted to him my opinions upon your proposition &c. &c.—but addressed them to himself.——

I have got here into a famous old feudal palazzo on the Arno—large enough for a garrison—with dungeons below—and cells in the walls—and so full of *Ghosts* that the learned Fletcher (my Valet) has begged leave to change his

---

[7] In Byron's era a Member of Parliament could 'frank' letters: sign them so as to ensure free delivery.

[8] See Pope, 'Epistle to Arbuthnot' (1735), 281.

[9] Elizabeth Fry (1780–1845), Quaker minister and prison reformer, who visited women prisoners at Newgate Prison in 1812, and asked them to mend their language. (See *Don Juan*, x. 673–80; *CPW* v. 463.) (Hobhouse's offensive letter is lost.)

room—and then refused to occupy his *new* room—because there were more Ghosts there than in the other.—It is quite true;—that there are most extraordinary noises (as in all old buildings) which have terrified the servants so—as to incommode me extremely.——There is one place where people were evidently *walled up*—for there is but one possible passage—*broken* through the wall—& then meant to be closed again upon the inmate.—The house belonged to the Lanfranchi family—(the same mentioned by Ugolino in his dream as his persecutor with Sismondi[10]) and had a fierce owner or two in it's t[ime]. The Staircase &c. is said to have been b[uilt] by Michel Agnolo.——It is not yet cold enough for a fire—what a climate!——I am however bothered about the spectres—(as they say the last occupants were too—) of whom I have as yet seen nothing— nor indeed heard (*myself*)—but all the other ears—have been regaled by all kinds of supernatural sounds.——The first night I thought I heard an odd voice—but it has not been repeated.——I have now been here more than a month.—

yrs. & [scrawl]

P. S.—*Pray send me two or three dozen of 'Acton's Corn-rubbers' in a parcel by the post—packed dry & well—if you can.—I have received safely the parcel containing the Seal,—the E[dinburgh] Review—and some pamphlets &c. the others are I presume upon their way.——Are there not designs from Faust? send me some—and a translation of it—if such there is—also of Goethe's life if such there be—if not—the original German.[11]——*

[To Douglas Kinnaird]

Pisa. F[ebruar]y 17th. 1822

My dear Douglas/

I have long ago written to you (in 1818) that in case of mortality on ye. part of Lady Noel, Sir Francis Burdett would be my selection as referee, and I request you with all respect to propose to him the office.[12] If he declines (which I hope

---

[10] See Dante's *Inferno*, Canto 33.

[11] A partial translation of Goethe's masterpiece (recently ascribed to Coleridge) was published in London in 1821, with illustrations by Moritz Retsch (1779–1857). Goethe's autobiography, *Dichtung und Wahrheit* ('Poetry and Truth'), was published in parts between 1811 and 1833.

[12] Lady Noel, Lady Byron's mother, died on 28 January 1822, and her lands and title at Kirkby Mallory, Leicestershire (inherited from her brother Thomas Noel, second Viscount Wentworth),

that he will not)—then Earl Grey.——The next business is my wish that you would *immediately insure Lady Byron's* life for me—for *ten thousand pounds*—or (if the expence seems too great to you) for *six thousand* pounds—that in case of her demise—as the *Marital* is only a *life* interest—there may be some provision to compensate for the diminution of income, and provide for my children—as you will observe that Lady B's daughter only takes in *default* of *male* issue by the Curzons and Shirleys. Do *not* neglect *this*; but act *immediately*;—I will either repay you in your own Circulars (all whilk arrived safely & welcomely) or you may deduct it from our next account. I shall be very uneasy till I hear that you have done this by next post—as otherwise—the whole prospect rests upon the respiration of her Ladyship & my children may be after all no great gainers.—

With regard to the settlement of the property,—I have named my referee, but I have no wish to press Sir Ralph or his offspring hard;—for example—the Mansion-house (which rests in abeyance for the Umpires in this boxing-match to award to time) is no object to me living abroad—and with no wish to return to your agreeable country.—I will wave any pretension to it—or take a moderate equivalent—whichever you think proper—I have no desire but to act as a Gentleman should do—without any real enmity, or affected generosity towards those who have not set me a very violent example of forbearance.—Enclosed are letters from Mr. Hanson (and another Solicitor) on some Rochdale business—by which it seems that I may obtain *two thousand* pounds more or less—for permission to the town to take toll for the new Market place.—I will accept whatever you and he deem fair & reasonable—or I will be as unreasonable as you please.—Will you request Sir Francis Burdett to accept my nomination—he knows Leicestershire—and he knows Lawyers—and he is a man of the loftiest talents and integrity, with whom I have lived a little & for whom I have the highest esteem.—Will not my address through you suffice—without my writing to him in person.——Believe me ever & very truly

yours most affectionately and (since it must be so)
Noel Byron

---

descended to Byron as her daughter's husband—but only for the term of Lady Byron's life, which is why Byron sought to insure it. (A condition of the inheritance, as he says, was that he add the Noel name and crest to his own.) Were Annabella to die, the title would go to the 'male issue', the Honourable Nathaniel Curzon; when he died without issue in 1856 the title returned to her side of the family, and thence to Ada Byron's daughter (the poet's granddaughter) Anne Isabella Noel Blunt. He and Annabella's father each nominated a mediator to settle the estate meanwhile, and Byron nominates his old parliamentary colleague Sir Francis Burdett.

[To Thomas Moore]

Pisa, March 4th, 1822

Since I wrote the enclosed, I have waited another post, and now have your answer acknowledging the arrival of the packet—a troublesome one, I fear, to you in more ways than one, both from weight external and internal.

The unpublished things in your hands, in Douglas K.'s, and Mr. John Murray's, are 'Heaven and Earth, a lyrical kind of Drama upon the Deluge, etc.'; 'Werner,' *now with you;*—a translation of the First Canto of the Morgante Maggiore;—*ditto* of an Episode in Dante;—some stanzas to the Po, June 1st, 1819;—Hints from Horace, written in 1811, but a good deal, *since,* to be omitted; several prose things, which may, perhaps, as well remain unpublished;—'The Vision, &c., of Quevedo Redivivus,'[13] in verse.

Here you see is 'more matter for a May morning;'[14] but how much of this can be published is for consideration. The Quevedo (one of my best in that line) has appalled the Row already, and must take its chance at Paris, if at all. The new Mystery is less speculative than 'Cain,' and very pious; besides, it is chiefly lyrical. The Morgante is the *best* translation that ever was or will be made; and the rest are—whatever you please to think them.

I am sorry you think Werner even *approaching* to any fitness for the stage, which, with my notions upon it, is very far from my present object. With regard to the publication, I have already explained that I have no exorbitant expectations of either fame or profit in the present instances; but wish them published because they are written, which is the common feeling of all scribblers.

With respect to 'Religion,' can I never convince you that *I* have no such opinions as the characters in that drama, which seems to have frightened every body? Yet *they* are nothing to the expressions in Goethe's Faust (which are ten times hardier), and not a whit more bold than those of Milton's Satan. My ideas of a character may run away with me: like all imaginative men, I, of course, embody myself with the character while I *draw* it, but not a moment after the pen is from off the paper.

I am no enemy to religion, but the contrary. As a proof, I am educating my natural daughter a strict Catholic in a convent of Romagna; for I think people can never have *enough* of religion, if they are to have any. I incline, myself, very

---

[13] This is *The Vision of Judgment* (written the previous September–October), by 'Quevedo Redivivus' (Quevedo reborn): an allusion to Francisco Gomez de Quevedo y Villegas (1580–1645), one of whose satires on the Spanish royal family was itself called 'The Vision of the Last Judgement'.

[14] See *Twelfth Night*, III. iv. 140.

much to the Catholic doctrines; but if I am to write a drama, I must make my characters speak as I conceive them likely to argue.

As to poor Shelley, who is another bugbear to you and the world, he is, to my knowledge, the *least* selfish and the mildest of men—a man who has made more sacrifices of his fortune and feelings for others than any I ever heard of. With his speculative opinions I have nothing in common, nor desire to have.

The truth is, my dear Moore, you live near the *stove* of society, where you are unavoidably influenced by its heat and its vapours. I did so once—and too much—and enough to give a colour to my whole future existence. As my success in society was *not* inconsiderable, I am surely not a prejudiced judge upon the subject, unless in its favour; but I think it, as now constituted, *fatal* to all great original undertakings of every kind. I never courted it *then*, when I was young and high in blood, and one of its 'curled darlings;'[15] and do you think I would do so *now*, when I am living in a clearer atmosphere? One thing *only* might lead me back to it, and that is, to try once more if I could do any good in *politics*; but *not* in the petty politics I see now preying upon our miserable country.

Do not let me be misunderstood, however. If you speak your own opinions, they ever had, and will have, the greatest weight with *me*. But if you merely *echo* the 'monde', (and it is difficult not to do so, being in its favour and its ferment,) I can only regret that you should ever repeat any thing to which I cannot pay attention.

But I am prosing. The gods go with you, and as much immortality of all kinds as may suit your present and all other existence.

Yours, &c.

[To Edward J. Dawkins]

Pisa, March 27, 1822

Sir,[16]

I take the liberty of transmitting to you the statements, as delivered to the police, of an extraordinary affair which occurred here on Sunday last. This will not, it is to be hoped, be considered an intrusion, as several British subjects have been insulted and some wounded on the occasion, besides being arrested at the gate of the city without proper authority or reasonable cause.

With regard to the subsequent immediate occurrence of the aggressor's wound, there is little that I can add to the enclosed statements. The testimony

---

[15] See *Othello*, I. ii. 69.
[16] Edward Dawkins (1792–1865), British *chargé d'affaires* at the Tuscan capital, Florence.

of an impartial eye-witness, Dr. Crawford, with whom I had not the honour of a personal acquaintance, will inform you as much as I know myself.

It is proper to add that I conceived the man to have been an officer, as he was well dressed, with scaled epaulettes, and not ill-mounted, and *not* a serjeant-major (the son of a washerwoman, it is said) as he turns out to be.[17]

When I accosted him a second time, on the Lung' Arno, he called out to me with a menacing gesture, 'Are you content?' I (still ignorant of what had passed under the gateway, having ridden through the guard to order my steward to go to the police) answered. 'No; I want your name and address.' He then held out his hand, which I took, not understanding whether he intended it as a pledge of his hostility or of his repentence [*sic*], at the same time stating his name.

The rest of the facts appear to have been as within stated, as far as my knowledge goes. Two of my servants (both Italians) are detained on suspicion of having wounded him. Of this I know no more than the enclosed papers vouch, and can only say that, notwithstanding the atrocious aggression (of the particulars of which I was at the moment ignorant), the act was as completely disapproved of by me as it was totally unauthorized, either directly or indirectly.

It neither is nor has been my wish to prevent or evade the fullest investigation of the business; had it been so, it would have been easy to have either left the place myself or to have removed any suspected person from it, the police having taken no steps whatever till this afternoon—three days after the fact.

I have the honour, etc.
Noel Byron

[To Percy Bysshe Shelley]

April 23d, 1822

The blow was stunning and unexpected; for I thought the danger over, by the long interval between her stated amelioration and the arrival of the express.[18] But I have borne up against it as I best can, and so far successfully, that I can go

---

[17] Byron had mistaken Masi for an officer and challenged him to a duel, which inflamed the situation on the day.

[18] Allegra died on 20 April, under medical attention at the Bagnacavallo convent, perhaps of typhus, perhaps of a malarial infection. Byron's banker in Ravenna, Pellegrino Ghigi, wrote on the 16th to say that she was ill, and Byron sent a courier authorizing the convent to call a doctor from Bologna. Ghigi wrote on the 18th to say she was better. On 22 April news arrived that she was dead. One of the reasons for Byron's lack of concern at Allegra's situation was the fact that Ghigi used the everyday postal system rather than a courier to update him—until it was too late.

about the usual business of life with the same appearance of composure, and even greater. There is nothing to prevent your coming to-morrow; but, perhaps, to-day, and yester-evening, it was better not to have met. I do not know that I have any thing to reproach in my conduct, and certainly nothing in my feelings and intentions toward the dead. But it is a moment when we are apt to think that, if this or that had been done, such event might have been prevented,— though every day and hour shows us that they are the most natural and inevitable. I suppose that Time will do his usual work—Death has done his.

Yours ever,
N. B.

[To Sir Walter Scott]

Pisa, May 4th, 1822

My Dear Sir Walter,

Your account of your family is very pleasing: would that I 'could answer this comfort with the like!'[19] I but I have just lost my natural daughter, Allegra, by a fever. The only consolation, save time, is the reflection that she is either at rest or happy; for her few years (only five) prevented her from having incurred any sin, except what we inherit from Adam.

'Whom the gods love die young.'[20]

I need not say that your letters are particularly welcome, when they do not tax your time and patience; and now that our correspondence is resumed, I trust it will continue.

I have lately had some anxiety, rather than trouble, about an awkward affair here, which you may perhaps have heard of; but our minister has behaved very handsomely, and the Tuscan Government as well as it is possible for such a government to behave, which is not saying much for the latter. Some other English, and Scots, and myself, had a brawl with a dragoon, who insulted one of the party, and whom we mistook for an officer, as he was medalled and well mounted, &c.; but he turned out to be a sergeant-major. He called out the guard at the gates to arrest us (we being unarmed); upon which I and another (an Italian) rode through the said guard; but they succeeded in detaining others of the party. I rode to my house, and sent my secretary to give an account of the

---

[19] See *Macbeth*, IV. iii. 194.
[20] In *Don Juan*, iv. 89 (*CPW* v. 703), Byron ascribes this well-worn expression to Herodotus; its origins are classical, but obscure.

attempted and illegal arrest to the authorities, and then, without dismounting, rode back towards the gates, which are near my present mansion. Half way I met my man, vapouring away, and threatening to draw upon me (who had a cane in my hand, and no other arms). I, still believing him an officer, demanded his name and address, and gave him my hand and glove thereupon. A servant of mine thrust in between us (totally without orders), but let him go on my command. He then rode off at full speed; but about forty paces further was stabbed, and very dangerously (so as to be in peril), by some *callum bog*[21] or other of my people (for I have some rough-handed folks about me), I need hardly say without my direction or approval. The said dragoon had been sabring our unarmed countrymen, however, at the *gate, after they were in arrest*, and held by the guards, and wounded one, Captain Hay, very severely. However, he got his paiks—having acted like an assassin, and being treated like one. *Who* wounded him, though it was done before thousands of people, they have never been able to ascertain, or prove, nor even the *weapon*; some said a *pistol*, an *air-gun*, a stiletto, a sword, a lance, a pitch-fork, and what not. They have arrested and examined servants and people of all descriptions, but can make out nothing. Mr. Dawkins, our minister, assures me that no suspicion is entertained of the man who wounded him having been instigated by me, or any of the party. I enclose you copies of the depositions of those with us, and Dr. Craufurd a canny Scot (*not* an acquaintance), who saw the latter part of the affair. They are in Italian.

These are the only literary matters in which I have been engaged since the publication and row about 'Cain['];—but Mr. Murray has several things of mine in his obstetrical hands. Another Mystery—a Vision—a Drama—and the like. But *you won't* tell me what *you* are doing—however, I shall find you out, write what you will. You say that I should like your son-in-law[22]—it would be very difficult for me to dislike any one connected with you; but I have no doubt that his own qualities are all that you describe.

I am sorry you don't like Lord Orford's new work.[23] My aristocracy, which is very fierce, makes him a favourite of mine. Recollect that those 'little factions' comprised Lord Chatham and Fox, the father; and that *we* live in gigantic and

---

[21] Callum Beg, the suspiciously violent servant of Colonel Mac-Ivor in Scott's *Waverley* (1814); see chapter 58. The guilty party was Byron's coachman, Vincenzo Papi.

[22] John Gibson Lockhart (1794–1854), critic and biographer of Scott. Unbeknownst to Byron (and to Scott, presumably), Lockhart was the author of 'Remarks on *Don Juan*' (August 1819), which Byron had responded to (see letter of 29 March 1820).

[23] Horatio (Horace) Walpole (1717–97), fourth Earl of Orford, Gothic novelist, antiquarian, and second son of George II's great prime minister, Sir Robert Walpole. His *Memoirs of the Last Ten Years of George II* were edited from manuscript by Byron's old parliamentary mentor Lord Holland, and published in 1822.

exaggerated times, which make all under Gog and Magog[24] appear pigmean. After having seen Napoleon begin like Tamerlane and end like Bajazet[25] in our own time, we have not the same interest in what would otherwise have appeared important history. But I must conclude.

Believe me ever and most truly yours,
Noel Byron

[To John Murray]

Montenero. May 26th. 1822 near Leghorn.——

Dear Sir,

The body is embarked—in what ship—I know not—neither could I enter into the details; but the Countess G[amba] G[uiccioli] has had the goodness to give the necessary orders to Mr. Dunn—who superintends the embarkation—& will write to you.——I wish it to be buried in Harrow Church—there is a spot in the Churchyard near the footpath on the brow of the hill looking toward Windsor—and a tomb under a large tree (bearing the name of Peachee—or Peachey) where I used to sit for hours & hours when a boy—this was my favourite spot—but as I wish to erect a tablet to her memory—the body had better be deposited in the Church.—Near the door—on the left as you enter—there is a monument with a tablet containing these words—

> 'When Sorrow weeps o'er Virtue's sacred dust,
> Our tears become us, and our Grief is just,
> Such were the tears she shed, who grateful pays
> This last sad tribute to her love, and praise.'

I recollect them (after seventeen years) not from any thing remarkable in them—but because—from my seat in the Gallery—I had generally my eyes turned towards that monument——as near it as convenient I would wish Allegra to be buried—and on the wall—a marble tablet placed with these words.—

---

[24] A legendary pair of giants in British folklore, obscurely derived from the Old Testament, and guardians of the City of London.
[25] Timur, the 14th-century Mongol warlord, known to English speakers as Tamburlaine the Great, after Marlowe's epic drama (c.1590), and Beyezid I, 14th-century Ottoman sultan massively defeated by Timur in 1402.

> In memory of
> Allegra—
> daughter of G. G. Lord Byron—
> who died at Bagnacavallo
> in Italy April 20th. 1822,
> aged five years and three months.—
> 'I shall go to her, but she shall not return to me.—'
> 2d. Samuel 12.—23.—

The funeral I wish to be as private as is consistent with decency—and I could hope that Henry Drury will perhaps read the service over her.—If he should decline it—it can be done by the usual Minister for the time being.[26]—I do not know that I need add more just now.——I will now turn to other subjects.—

Since I came here I have been invited by the Americans on board of their Squadron where I was received with all the kindness which I could wish, and with *more ceremony* than I am fond of.—I found them finer ships than your own of the same class—well manned & officered.—A number of American gentlemen also were on board at the time & some ladies.—As I was taking leave—an American lady asked for a *rose* which I wore—for the purpose she said of sending to America something which I had about me as a memorial.—I need not add that I felt the compliment properly.—Captain Chauncey showed me an American and very pretty edition of my poems and offered me a passage to the United States—if I would go there.——Commodore Jones was also not less kind and attentive.—I have since received the enclosed letter desiring me to sit for my picture for some Americans.—It is singular that in the same year that Lady Noel leaves by will an interdiction for my daughter to see her father's portrait for many years[27]—the individuals of a nation not remarkable for their liking to the English in particular—nor for flattering men in general, request me to sit for my 'portraicture'—as Baron Bradwardine calls it.—I am also told of considerable literary honours in Germany.——Goëthe I am told is my professed patron and protector.—At Leipsic this year—the highest prize was proposed for a translation of two Cantos of Childe Harold.—I am not sure that this was at *Leipsic*—but Mr. Bancroft was my authority—a good German Scholar (a young

---

[26] In fact, the Vicar of St Mary's in Harrow, J. W. Cunningham, objected to any memorial to Allegra, and she was buried in an unmarked spot near the entrance to the church. The Byron Society installed a memorial plaque in her memory in 1980, incorporating the last line of the letter of 23 April 1822, above.

[27] Marchand comments (*LJ* ix. 127): 'When Lady Noel's will was proved at Doctor's Commons on Feb. 22, 1822, Hanson learned that she left to the Trustees a portrait of Byron with directions that it was not to be shown to his daughter Ada until she was twenty-one, and then only with her mother's consent if Lady Byron was still alive.' Baron Bradwardine is a character in Scott's *Waverley* (1814).

American) and an acquaintance of Goëthe's.——Goëthe and the Germans are particularly fond of Don Juan—which they judge of as a work of Art.—I had heard something like this before through Baron Lutzerode.—The translations have been very frequent of several of the works—and Goëthe made a comparison between Faust and Manfred.——All this is some compensation for your English native brutality so fully displayed this year—(I mean *not your* individually) to it's brightest extent.—I forgot to mention a little anecdote of a different kind—I went over the Constitution (the Commodore's flag ship) and saw among other things worthy of remark a little boy *born* on board of her by a sailor's wife.— They had christened him 'Constitution Jones'—I of course approved the name— and the woman added—'Ah Sir—if he turns out but half as good as his name!'

yrs. ever & truly
N B

[To Edward J. Dawkins]

Monte Nero. Livorno. June 7th. 1822

My dear Sir,

For my sins (I presume) & for your troubles I must intrude upon you again about this business of the Pisans &c.——We are waiting here in a most unpleasant state of suspense——they refuse to give any answer or decision—and the family of the Gambas are without any renewed papers or security of any kind[28]—and all for *what*? what on earth had *they* to do with the matter?—Is it because they are exiles and weak that they are to be persecuted or because they are friends of mine?——I know that *you* can do little for them—as they are not English subjects—but you may perhaps be able to obtain some information.—Of course their fate—must be mine—where they go—I accompany them.—— Madame Guiccioli who is ill was ordered here by Vacca for the benefit of Sea-bathing and we know not whether she will be permitted to remain.—Such conduct is indeed infamous—and can have but one object—viz.—the persecuting *me* through *them*—that when they have driven us from their States—they may tell the Story in their own way.—*This* will I trust at least be prevented—and that you will obtain a *publication* of the conduct of the whole business.—— Whatever personal vexation or inconvenience it may be to give up my house &c.—& remove my furniture before the expiration of the period assigned for

---

[28] The Tuscan authorities had reissued the Gambas' residency permit, but only for a ten-day period: effectively putting them on notice.

their occupation——I care <nothing> little for leaving such a country—but I *do* care for the constructions to which (at this time) my departure may give rise.——The Courier (they may exile him if they like) is in danger from his blow—as the enclosed note will certify.[29]—All that I could wish to know is a *decision* of some kind—that I may know where to go—of course what they decree about the Gambas is decisive with regard to myself.—Collini has had his 100 Sequins—and I hear no more of him.[30]——I have taken the liberty with *you*—to request the elder Count Gamba to present this note—which has swelled into a letter—as he can explain anything you may think worth asking.—— Believe me in all cases and in all places—with much esteem and obligation

ever yrs. faithfully
N B

P. S.—*With regard to the fellow who has (I am now sorry to say) survived the consequences of his cowardly outrage—the other Gentlemen may prosecute—but it would be difficult for me to do so—as I was not one of his victims, except in the bad language which he has sufficiently paid for.——When I say that I am sorry that he has recovered—it is because I see many innocent persons suffering on account of such a miscreant.—*

[To Edward J. Dawkins]

Montenero, June 26th. 1822

Dear Sir,

As a further specimen of the kindness and civility of the Tuscan authorities towards me—I am obliged to inform you that they refuse at Leghorn to accord permission to cruize in sight of the port in my little yacht—which arrived from Genoa last week.—They also refused to let me have a boat from the port (off the Sea-baths which are in *shallow* water—) to undress in when I go out to swim— which I prefer of course in deep water.——My Yacht which was allowed to cruize at Genoa without molestation & which cost me a considerable sum in building &c.—is thus rendered perfectly useless to me—& the expence entirely

---

[29] Giuseppe Strauss, struck in the chest by Masi during the incident of 24 March.
[30] A lawyer recommended by Dawkins to represent Byron in the Masi case.

thrown away.——She is a little thing of about 22 tons—but a model to look at—& sails very fast.—She has nothing obnoxious about her that I know— unless her name ('the Bolivar') should be so—and all her papers are in regular order—& admitted to be so—& no one on board but the Crew.—Tita is still at Spezia.——Thus matters stand with me at present—I only wait for a decision in the affair of the Serjeant to take steps for quitting a country from whose authorities I have experienced every petty vexation and insult—which they could devise—and without cause that I know of. I neither write nor speak [of] them—nor *to* them.——I merely state this to you—(for I have long given up any idea of obtaining [any] species of redress from the Government) to show you the kind of disposition which their authorities uniformly evince in all which regards me.—Believe me

very truly & faithfully yr. obliged Sert.
Noel Byron

[To the Governor of Leghorn]

[July 2, 1822?]

Sir

I write to you in English since I know you do us the honour of understanding our language. There has been issued by you an order of arrest and exile for my courier and an intimation to the family of Count Gamba to leave Tuscany at the end of three days. I am preparing to depart with them as I do not wish to stay any longer in a country where my friends are persecuted and where asylum is denied to the unfortunate. Since I have some affairs to arrange, I beg you to grant them a delay in order that I may depart with them.

[Noel Byron]

[To John Murray]

Pisa. July 8th. 1822

Dear Sir,

Last week I returned you the packet of proofs.—You had perhaps better not publish in the same volume—the *Po*—and *Rimini* translation.—I have consigned a letter to Mr. John Hunt for the 'Vision of Judgement'—which you will hand over to him.—Also the Pulci—original and Italian—and any *prose* tracts of mine—for Mr. Leigh Hunt is arrived here & thinks of commencing a periodical work—to which I shall contribute——I do not propose to you to be the publisher—because I know that you are unfriends——but all things in your care except the volume now in the press—and the M.S.S. purchased of Mr. Moore[31]—can be given for this purpose—according as they are wanted— and I expect that you will show fair play—although with no very good will on your part.——With regard to what you say about your 'want of memory'—I can only remark that you inserted the note to 'Marino Faliero'—against my positive revocation and that you omitted the dedication of 'Sardanapalus' to Goëthe (place it before the volume now in the press) both of which were things not very agreeable to me & which I could wish to be avoided in future as they might be with a very little care—or a simple Memorandum in your pocket book.—It is not impossible that I may have three or four cantos of D Juan ready by autumn or a little later—as I obtained a permission from my Dictatress to continue it— *provided always* it was to be more guarded and decorous and sentimental in the continuation than in the commencement.—How far these Conditions have been fulfilled may be seen perhaps by and bye. But the Embargo was only taken off [upon these] stipulations.——You can answer at yr. leisure.

> yrs. ever
> N B

[To Captain Daniel Roberts]

> Pisa. July 14th. 1822

My dear Sir,

Your opinion has taken from me the slender hope to which I still clung.—I need hardly say that the Bolivar is quite at your disposition as she would have been on a less melancholy occasion—and that I am always

> yr. obliged & faithful friend & Servant
> Noel Byron

---

[31] These are Byron's Memoirs, given by him to Thomas Moore in Venice in October 1819, and sold by him to Murray.

[To Edward J. Dawkins]

July 15th. 1822

Dear Sir

Up to this moment I had clung to a slender hope that Mr. Shelley had still survived the late Gale of Wind.—I sent orders yesterday to the Bolivar to cruize along the coast in search of intelligence—but it seems all over.——I have not waited on you in person being unshaven—unshorn—and uncloathed at this present writing after bathing.——I hope you may do something at Lucca— which has induced me to delay proceeding to Genoa—or addressing Mr. Hill again till this day.—Many thanks.

yrs. ever
N B

[To Douglas Kinnaird]

Pisa. July 19th. 1822

My dear Douglas/

Your letter is dated the 5th. but makes no allusion to the dividend from the funds which I expected and expect still about this time. I regret that you have given up your journey, though I could not have received you very cheerfully, for since the beginning of the year one displeasure has followed another in regular succession. Shelley and Capt. Williams were drowned last week going to Spezia in their boat from Leghorn—supposed to have been swamped in a Squall.—A Boatman was also lost with them.—Shelley's body has been found and identified (though with difficulty) two days ago—chiefly by a book in his Jacket pocket—the body itself being totally disfigured & in a state of putrefaction.—Another body supposed Capt. Williams's also found—with various articles belonging to the boat.—You may imagine the state of their wives and children—& also Leigh Hunt's—who was but just arrived from England.——Yesterday and the day before I made two journeys to the mouth of the Arno and another river (the Serchio) for the purpose of ascertaining the circumstances—and identifications of the bodies—but they were already interred for the present by order of the Sanità or Health Office.

yrs. ever
N B

[To Thomas Moore]

It is boring to trouble you with 'such small gear;'[32] but it must be owned that I should be glad if you would inquire whether my Irish subscription ever reached the committee in Paris from Leghorn.[33] My reasons, like Vellum's,[34] 'are three-fold:'—First, I doubt the accuracy of all almoners, or remitters of benevolent cash; second, I do suspect that the said Committee, having in part served its time to time-serving, may have kept back the acknowledgment of an obnoxious politician's name in their lists; and third, I feel pretty sure that I shall one day be twitted by the government scribes for having been a professor of love for Ireland, and not coming forward with the others in her distresses.

It is not, as you may opine, that I am ambitious of having my name in the papers, as I can have that any day in the week gratis. All I want is to know if the Reverend Thomas Hall did or did not remit my subscription (200 scudi of Tuscany, or about a thousand francs, more of less,) to the Committee at Paris.

The other day at Viareggio, I thought proper to swim off to my schooner (the Bolivar) in the offing, and thence to shore again—about three miles, or better, in all. As it was at mid-day, under a broiling sun, the consequence has been a feverish attack, and my whole skin's coming off, after going through the process of one large continuous blister, raised by the sun and sea together. I have suffered much pain; not being able to lie on my back, or even side; for my shoulders and arms were equally St. Bartholomewed.[35] But it is over,—and I have got a new skin, and am as glossy as a snake in its new suit.

We have been burning the bodies of Shelley and Williams on the sea-shore, to render them fit for removal and regular interment. You can have no idea what an extraordinary effect such a funeral pile has, on a desolate shore, with mountains in the back-ground and the sea before, and the singular appearance the salt and frankincense gave to the flame. All of Shelley was consumed, except his *heart*, which would not take the flame, and is now preserved in spirits of wine.

---

[32] See Folio *King Lear*, III. iv. 13: 'mice and rats and such small deer'.

[33] On 12 July (*LJ* ix. 183) Byron wrote to Moore to say that he had contributed 'two hundred Tuscan crowns to your Irishism committee', founded in Paris in June to aid distressed peasantry in Ireland.

[34] See Joseph Addison's comedy *The Drummer* (1765), in which Sir George Trueman's steward, Vellum, frequently expresses himself in elaborately logical fashion.

[35] St Bartholomew was flayed to death, and the church at Lipari, off Sicily, once claimed miraculously to possess some of his skin.

Your old acquaintance Londonderry has quietly died at North Cray! and the virtuous De Witt was torn in pieces by the populace![36] What a lucky * * the Irishman has been in his life and end. In him your Irish Franklin est mort!

Leigh Hunt is sweating articles for his new Journal; and both he and I think it somewhat shabby in *you* not to contribute. Will you become one of the *proper-rioters*? 'Do, and we go snacks.'[37] I recommend you to think twice before you respond in the negative.

I have nearly (*quite three*) four new cantos of *Don Juan* ready. I obtained permission from the female Censor Morum [moral censor] of *my* morals to continue it, provided it were immaculate; so I have been as decent as need be.[38] There is a deal of war—a siege, and all that, in the style, graphical and technical, of the shipwreck in Canto Second, which 'took' as they say in the Row.

Yours, etc.

—⚬⚬⚬—

P. S.—*That * * * Galignani has about ten lies in one paragraph. It was not a Bible that was found in Shelley's pocket, but John Keats's poems. However, it would not have been strange, for he was a great admirer of Scripture as a composition. I did not send my bust to the academy of New York; but I sat for my picture to young West, an American artist, at the request of some members of that Academy to him that he would take my portrait,—for the Academy, I believe.*

I had, and still have, thought of South America, but am fluctuating between it and Greece. I should have gone, long ago, to one of them, but for my liaison with the Countess G[uicciol]i; for love, in these days, is little compatible with glory. She would be delighted to go too; but I do not choose to expose her to a long voyage, and a residence in an unsettled country, where I shall probably take a part of some sort.

---

[36] Byron was not yet aware that British foreign minister, Irish peer, and Leader of the House of Commons Viscount Castlereagh had committed suicide by cutting his throat with a penknife at his home at North Cray, Kent, on 12 August. Johan de Witt (1625–72), Dutch statesman who was lynched by a royalist mob. The immoral politician died quietly, Byron says; the virtuous one was murdered.

[37] See Pope, 'Epistle to Arbuthnot' (1735), 66.

[38] Byron said this, but in fact had resumed work on *Don Juan* in January. Teresa's interdiction appears to have been a red herring.

[To John Cam Hobhouse]

Pisa. Septr. 2d. 1822

Dear Hobhouse/

I wrote to you as you requested to Geneva but—you have not apparently received the letter.——I am in all the agonies of hiring feluccas—& packing furniture—&c. &c. for *Genoa*—where I have taken a house for a year—and mean to remove shortly—as I told you in my Swiss epistle—and I have not a chair or table—and hardly a stool to sit on—besides the usual confusion attending such operations.——If you come on to Florence—we must contrive a meeting (should I be still here on your arrival) or perhaps you will take Genoa on your way back.—These transient glimpses of old friends are very painful—as I found out the other day after Lord Clare was gone again—however agreeable they make the moment.—They are like a dose of Laudanum and it's subsequent langour.—It is a *lustre* since we met—and I am afraid it is the only *lustre* added to one of us[39]—but you I trust are more resplendent in health & heart.—I have been lately ill—(*all* my Skin peeled off) from swimming three hours in a hot Sun at Via Reggio—but my new Skin is come again—though it is plaguey tender still. Could you not contrive to voyage to Genoa with me—Madame Guiccioli is with me but she will travel with her father—& we could confabulate in the old *imperial* Carriage as heretofore—and squabble away as usual.—I don't know whether your temper is improved—I hear that the hustings have made you somewhat haughty—but that is natural—a man who addresses Senates and Constituents has some right to be so—my own temper is about the same— which is not saying much for it.—However I am always

yrs. truly
N B

[To Douglas Kinnaird]

Pisa. Septr. 12th. 1822

My dear Douglas/

Enclosed, you will find a curious budget of mine for the ensuing year at which the *banker* will laugh—and the *friend* will sigh—the *trustee* however ought to

---

[39] 'Lustre' meaning sheen, gloss; but also from the Latin, *lustrum*, a period of five years. Byron and Hobhouse had not seen each other since January 1818, in Venice. He arrived at Pisa on 15 September.

blush for allowing his trust*ing* or trust*er*—to be overreached by two such scoundrels as Lushington & Colbourne.[40]—As to what regards Murray—that great man ought to be narrowly watched—don't you be talked over by the fellow.—He will prate of piracy—but recollect that he might neutralize this in a great measure by publishing *very cheap* small editions of the *same type with former piracies*—at the same time—reserve his *smooth* octavos—for former publishers [purchasers?]—of the same more expensive Calibre.——Now—do not allow yourself to be carried away by first impressions—which is your grand propensity—so as to make your letters to me a series of contradictions the moment you get off business—though upon *that*—you are very oracular & sensible and of this world.—In short—Doug.—the longer I live—the more I perceive that Money (honestly come by) is the Philosopher's Stone—and therefore do thou be my Man of trust & fidelity—and look after this same— my avarice—or cupidity—is *not* selfish—for my *table* don't cost four shillings a day—and except horses and helping all kinds of patriots—(I have long given up *costly* harlotry) I have no violent expences—but I want to get a sum together to go amongst the Greeks or Americans—and do some good—my great expence this year has been a Schooner which cost me a thousand pounds or better—

yrs. ever
N B

Address to Genoa. *either—poste restante or Villa Saluzzo.*

P. S.—*The four new Cantos will (or* ought *to succeed) for they contain (with poesy intermingled plentifully)—some good sensible practical truths that you don't hear every day in the week;—or at least put so pithily and prudently.*

---

[40] Lady Byron's legal trustees.

11
GENOA

October 1822–July 1823

B yron arrived at Albaro, now a suburb of the great maritime city of Genoa, in early October 1823. He and Teresa were now under the same roof at Casa Saluzzo, though in separate apartments. The bereaved and depressed Mary Shelley, who had miscarried and lost her husband in a matter of four weeks two months earlier, came up from Pisa and lived with Leigh Hunt and his family a mile down the hill, at the forty-room Casa Negroto. Relations with Hunt were frosty beneath the bonhomie; those with Mary Shelley shot through with ambivalence on her side. Byron tried to assist her financially by paying for her copying services. The first edition of the Liberal was published on 15 October, and The Vision of Judgment was in it—without its preface, in which Byron gave grounds for his attack on the Poet Laureate, Robert Southey (CPW vi. 309–12). Byron was convinced John Murray had withheld the preface from John Hunt, and relations with Albemarle Street finally ceased. On 18 November he told Murray, 'I shall withdraw from you as a publisher' (LJ x. 36), and the last business letter he sent was dated 25 December (see below). Ten days earlier, Byron sent Douglas Kinnaird the twelfth canto of Don Juan, which meant that seven cantos of that poem awaited publication.

But—and for the first time in his life, momentously—Byron's appetite for poetry was beginning to wane. His Gothic drama Werner (which he had completed in January 1822, anyway) was the last work of his that Murray published, in November. He worked intermittently on a fascinating Faustian play, The Deformed Transformed, but abandoned it in early 1823. In February 1823 he finished a feeble political satire, The Age of Bronze; in March he completed The Island, on the Bligh Mutiny, and told Kinnaird the Liberal 'was a bad business' (LJ x. 114) with no future in it; in May he finished the last complete canto of Don Juan (the sixteenth) and fourteen stanzas of the seventeenth. At Christmas 1822 he had mentioned the possibility of taking a trip to Naples and writing a fifth canto of Childe Harold; the minute gossip concerning the idea got back to him, through Kinnaird, in February of the following year, he dismissed it: 'I am not going to Naples—nor have any intention of continuing Ch[ild]e H[arold]e' (LJ x. 108). By May 1823 his work as a poet was effectively over.

Just as Greece had ignited his poetic career, so would she end it. In September 1822, while Byron was still at Montenero—hosting John Cam Hobhouse—he was visited by two patriots, the 24-year-old lawyer Nicolas Karvellas (1799–1872) and his brother Francis, whom Byron and Hobhouse had first met in Geneva and later in Milan in 1816. Francis was now a member of the Philiké Hetairia, the Greek equivalent of the Carbonari, and was in correspondence with the western Greek leader, Prince Alexander Mavrocordatos—who had once given Greek lessons to Mary Shelley in Pisa. This coincidence of Hobhouse (his fellow traveller in Greece from years ago) and these two young men from that long-suffering nation surely set Byron's thoughts in motion. If the idea had been stirring before, he made no mention of it. On 16 January 1823 he made the passing remark to Kinnaird: 'I think of going to Greece perhaps to America' (LJ x. 86). Three months later (see letter of 7 April 1823) the decision had been made.

The visit by the Karvellas brothers was an accidental part of a larger development. The death by suicide of the foreign minister Castlereagh in August 1822, and the arrival of his successor, George Canning (with whom Hobhouse had crossed swords in the House, but whom both he and Byron recognized as a civilized Tory), and the failure of the trienio liberal in Spain leading to French invasion in January 1823, between them relaxed British political attitudes to European liberalism, and shifted the focus to Greece, which had pluckily been fighting the Ottoman Empire since 1821. In March 1823 the London Greek Committee was founded by a retired naval officer named Edward Blaquiere, and John Bowring, secretary to the Utilitarian philosopher Jeremy Bentham. Whig politicians (Hobhouse most emphatically included) rallied to the cause. In due course the Committee sent Blaquiere off to Greece with a Greek delegate, Andreas Louriottis, a set of 'Observations' on a Greek constitution drafted by Bentham, and Byron's address in his notebook—with instructions to drop in on the poet on the way; which Blaquiere duly did, on 5 April 1823. Within two days the die was cast, and a week after that Byron wrote to Hobhouse asking him 'please to request Douglas K[innair]d to have the goodness (in case I go up) to let me have credits in the most convenient Italian or Levantine places—for the whole of my disposable funds' (LJ x. 151).

Another set of visitors also disrupted Byron's Italian dolci far niente. Charles John Gardiner, first Earl of Blessington (1782–1829), had joined the House of Lords as a representative peer (from Ireland) the same year as Byron. He and his wife, the exquisite and dashing Marguerite (1789–1849; born plain Margaret Power from Tipperary), were on tour, accompanied by the even more exquisite Frenchman Count Alfred d'Orsay (1801–52), who perhaps had sexual relations with both, and was no count at all, only the son of an illegitimate daughter of one. (In 1827 he would marry Blessington's 15-year-old daughter by his previous wife, and separate a year later.) The party stayed in Genoa during April and May 1823, and visited and socialized with the poet frequently. (Lady Blessington published her louchely atmospheric Conversations with Lord Byron *off the back of this acquaintance in 1834.) The three of them took Byron back to the London he knew before his marriage, of dandies, theatricals, clubs, soirées with Whig hostesses, masked balls, and other adventures— the very world he had been picturing in the 'English' cantos of* Don Juan. *So his Italian life was eroded in two directions: by the glamorous Lady Blessington on the one hand, and by the siren call of Greece on the other.*

Teresa felt her grip on Byron weaken, and reacted much as would be expected: she was still under 25, whereas her lover was verging on middle age. ('His hair has already much of the silver among its dark brown curls,' Lady Blessington pleasantly recorded; Life, 1059.) Her English was not good enough to hold her own with the Blessington party, even if she had shared the cultural references they had in common with Byron. All she could do was sit and stew, apart. Lady Blessington 'has plunged me into a pit of domestic troubles,' Byron told another visitor, his (very remote) relative Lady Hardy: 'for "la mia Dama" M[adam]e La Contesse G.—was seized with a furious fit of Italian jealousy—and was as unreasonable and perverse as can well be imagined'. What Byron went on to say about this 'Goddess of Discord', and Teresa's baseless fear of her—because Byron 'would much rather fall into the Sea than in Love any day of the week' (LJ x. 175)—would hardly have reassured the intensely romantic Teresa. The ebbing of romance, after all, was the source of her anxiety, as she instinctively understood, and to be told that she should not fear another woman because Byron was losing interest in love would have been of no comfort whatever.

Teresa was jealous of Greece, too—and there she was absolutely right. 'She wants to go up to Greece too!', Byron told Kinnaird on 21 May 1823 (LJ x. 178), 'and if she makes a scene—(and she has a turn that way) we shall have another romance—and tale of ill usage and abandonment—and Lady Caroling—and Lady Byroning—and Glenarvoning—all cut and dry.' The 'scenes' he was likely to create in going to Greece were paradoxically the very things, in prospect, that drove him there: 'there never was a man who gave up so much to women', he went on, with ineffably male disingenuousness, 'and all I have gained by it—has been the character of treating them harshly.' He got into just another such 'scene' with Mary Shelley, over financing her return to England. The misunderstanding could not be overcome, and she eventually got help from Trelawny, before leaving Genoa on 23 July 1823.

In May Byron heard that he had been elected to the Greek Committee, and sold the unlucky Bolivar to Lord Blessington, at well below cost. (Blessington's cheque bounced, and it is unclear whether he ever paid for the vessel.) In June he engaged an English ship, the 120-ton brig the Hercules, and began to gather his party: a personal physician (the recently graduated Dr Bruno), Pietro Gamba, and Trelawny. ('How can one spend a year so pleasantly as travelling in Greece, and with an agreeable party?' the Cornish corsair wrote to a friend; Life, 1077.) Byron had uniforms—and even neoclassical helmets—made for himself and these, his aides-de-camp: his helmet flaunted the old Byron crest, with the old motto: 'Crede Byron'—trust Byron.

On 13 July the poet and his party boarded the Hercules. The next day Teresa left for Romagna with her father. The Hercules was becalmed, returned to port, put to sea, encountered a storm, set off again, and pulled in at Livorno, where Byron found a fan letter from none other than Goethe. 'You must ... accept my most sincere acknowledgements in prose,' Byron replied, 'and in hasty prose too—for I am at present on my voyage to Greece once more—and surrounded by hurry and bustle which hardly allow a moment even to Gratitude and Admiration to express themselves.' 'If ever I come back', he concluded (LJ x. 213), 'I will pay a visit to Weimar to offer the sincere homage of one of the many Millions of your admirers.' It was not to be.

[To Mary Shelley]

Octr. 4th. 1822

The Sopha which I request is *not* of your furniture—it was purchased by me at Pisa since you left it.——It is convenient for my room though of little value (about 12 pauls) and I offered to send another (now sent) in it's stead.—I preferred retaining the purchased furniture—but always intended that you should have as good or better in it's place.—I have a particular dislike to any thing of S[helley]'s being within the same walls with Mr. Hunt's children.—They are dirtier and more mischievous than Yahoos[;] what they can['t] destroy with their filth they will with their fingers.—I presume that you received ninety and odd crowns from the wreck of the D[on] J[uan] and also the price of the boat purchased by Capt. R[oberts].[1]—if not you will have *both*—Hunt has these in hand.——With regard to any difficulties about money I can only repeat that I will be your banker till this state of things is cleared up—and you can see what is to be done—so—there is little to trouble you on that score.——I was confined four days to my bed at Lerici.——Poor Hunt with his six little blackguards—are coming slowly up—as usual—he turned back <twice> once—was there ever such a *kraal* [homestead] out of the Hottentot Country before?——

[scrawl]

[To John Murray]

Genoa. Octr. 9th. 1822

Dear Murray,

I have received your letter—and as you explain it—I have no objection on *your* account to omit those passages in the new Mystery—(which were marked in the half sheet sent the other day to Pisa) or the passage in *Cain*—but why not be open and say so at *first*—you should be more strait-forward on every account.[2]—Mr. K[innair]d has four cantos of D[on] J[uan] sent by the post—(or should have)—I have a fifth (the 10th.) finished but not transcribed yet—and the *eleventh*—begun.——With regard to Werner and H[eaven] & E[arth] why are they not published? I should have thought the latitude I gave about terms—might have set you at ease on their account.——I have carried D[on] J[uan] through a siege—to St. Petersburgh—&c. &c. thence to *England*—how do you like that?—I have no wish to break off our connection—but if you are to be

---

[1] Trelawny's friend Captain Daniel Roberts had assisted in the building of both the *Bolivar* and the *Don Juan*. He had lately 'been busy salvaging some of the things found on the *Don Juan*, which had been raised and brought ashore' (*Life*, 1032).

[2] Murray had omitted some lines in which Satan mockingly anticipates Christ's crucifixion (*Cain* I. i. 163–6 (*CPW* vi. 237)). He wrote on 25 September (*Murray Letters*, 442) to say he 'could not venture to give them to the public', and to ask Byron to understand 'those public animadversions which at present fall upon me'. He also objected to John Hunt's ungentlemanly behaviour on a visit to his office: see below.

blown about with every wind—what can I do?—You are wrong—for there will be a *re-action*—you will see that by & bye—and whether there is or not—I cannot allow my opinions—though I am ready to make any allowance in a *trade* point of view—which unpalatable speculations may render necessary to *your* advantage.——

I have been very unwell—four days confined to my bed in 'the worst inn's worst room'[3] at Lerici—with a violent rheumatic and bilious attack—constipation—and the devil knows what—no physician—except a young fellow who however was kind and cautious & that's enough.—Amongst other operations—a *Glyster* [*sic*] was ordered—and administered in such a manner by the performer—that I have ever since been wondering *why* the legislature should punish Bishop Jocelyn and his Soldado?[4]—Since if the episcopal instrument at all resembled the damned squirt of the Ligurian apothecary—the crime will have carried it's own chastisement along with it.——At last I seized Thompson's book of prescriptions—(a donation of yours) and physicked myself with the first dose I found in it—and after undergoing the ravages of all kinds of decoctions—sallied from bed on the fifth day to cross the Gulph to Sestri.—The Sea revived me instantly—and I ate the Sailors cold fish—and drank a Gallon of Country wine—and got to Genoa the same night after landing at Sestri—and have ever since been keeping well—but thinner—and with an occasional cough towards evening.——

With regard to Mr. J. Hunt how could I tell that he insulted you? of course if he did—show him the door—or the window—he had no warrant from me but the letter you received—and I think that was civil enough.——I am afraid the Journal *is* a *bad* business—and won't do—but in it I am sacrificing *myself* for others—*I* can have no advantage in it.—I believe the *brothers* H[unt] to be honest men—I am sure that they are poor ones.—They have not a rap—they pressed me to engage in this work—and in an evil hour I consented—still I shall not repent if I can do them the least service.—I have done all I can for Leigh Hunt—since he came here—but it is almost useless—his wife is ill—his six children not very tractable and In the affairs of this world he himself is a child.—The death of Shelley left them totally aground—and I could not see them in such a state without using the common feelings of humanity—& what means were in my power to set them afloat again.——So D[ouglas] K[innair]d is out of the way?

---

[3] See Pope, *Moral Essays* (1733), iii. 299.
[4] A clyster is any medicine applied via the rectum. Percy Jocelyn (1764–1843), Anglican Bishop of Clogher in Ireland, was apprehended in an indecent act with a Grenadier Guardsman in London in July 1822; he skipped bail and disappeared to Scotland.

he was so the last time I sent him a parcel—and he gives no previous notice—when is he expected again?

yrs.
N B

P. S.—Will you say at once—do you publish Werner & the mystery or not?—You never once allude to them.——That d——d advertisement of Mr. J. Hunt is out of the limits[;][5] *I did not lend him my name to be hawked about in this way.——*

[To Douglas Kinnaird]

Genoa. Novr. 6th. 1822

My dear Douglas

Will you have the goodness to deliver this [6 November 1822, below] yourself?—Mr. Murray has no right to be at once insolent & dishonest.——I have written to you three times lately—(with two Cantos additional of D[on] J[uan]) about the six of which I crave your opinion—and how they may be least disadvantageously published & by *whom.*—You can judge from circumstances—though profit is of course (like Honour) agreeable when it comes reasonably—yet it is not the sole object of

yrs. ever & truly
N B

P. S.—You will let Mr. J. Hunt have such pieces as are mentioned in my letters to him as 'Werner' *&* 'Heaven & Earth' *&c.*

---

[5] See the *Morning Chronicle*, 25 September: 'The long promised periodical work from *Pisa* is nearly ready for publication. Lord BYRON's main portion of it is, we hear, entitled "*The Vision of Judgment*," and is a direct *quiz* upon the Laureate' (*Murray Letters*, 448).

P. S.—You will recollect that you yourself delivered into Murray's hands the preface and carefully corrected copy of the 'Vision &c.' which I transmitted to you—I have your letter stating that you had done so—and another of yours approving the preface and the corrections.—If Murray plays these tricks purposely—he is a villain—& shall be exposed accordingly.

P. S.—If Murray has delivered up the papers in their perfect state the enclosed is unnecessary; if not he deserves it.——

[To John Murray]

Genoa. Novr. 6th. 1822

Sir

I have been again informed by Mr. Hunt that you have not paid the smallest attention to my repeated letters.—Of this you will one day find the consequences.—You will be pleased to deliver into the hands of the Hon[oura]ble Douglas Kinnaird—(who takes charge of this note—) all M.S.S. or printers' proofs of mine whatsoever—and in their corrected state—not omitting Werner—& the other piece which was to have been published with it.——As a publisher I bid you a final farewell.—It would have been my wish to have remained on terms of acquaintance with you—but your recent—& repeatedly rude neglect of my earnest directions to you in matters of business—render that also impracticable.—I had believed you infirm in your purposes occasionally— and not very open in explaining your intentions—but I did *not* believe you capable of the conduct you are now holding—or at least have held up to my latest advices from England.—What *that* is—you may yet be told—by me—as well as by others.—You seem to forget that whether as a tradesman or as a gentleman you are [ever?] bound to be decent and courteous in your intercourse with all classes—and I had hoped that the race of Curl and Osborne was extinct.—Perhaps you wish that of Pope to revive also—[6]

yr. obedt. St.
N B

[6] Edmund Curll (1675–1747) and Thomas Osborne (1704–67), London publishers frequently satirized by Pope.

[To Augusta Leigh]

Albaro. Genoa. Novr. 7th. 1822

My dearest A.

I have yrs. of the 25th.—My Illness is quite gone—it was only at Lerici—on the fourth night, I had got a little sleep and was so wearied that though there were three slight shocks of an Earthquake that frightened the whole town into the Streets——neither they nor the tumult awakened me.—We have had a deluge here—which has carried away half the country between this and Genoa—(about two miles or less distant) but being on a hill we were only nearly knocked down by the lightning and battered by columns of rain—and our lower floor afloat——with the comfortable view of the whole landscape under water— and people screaming out of their garret windows—*two bridges* swept down— and our next door neighbours—a Cobbler a Wigmaker—and a Gingerbread baker delivering up their whole stock to the elements—which marched away with a quantity of shoes—several perukes—and Gingerbread in all it's branches.—The whole came on so suddenly that there was no time to prepare—think only at the top of a hill—of the road being an impassable cascade—and a child being drowned a few yards from it's own door (as we heard say) in a place where Water is in general a rare commodity.——Well— after this comes a preaching Friar—and says that the day of Judgement will take place positively on the *4th*—with all kinds of tempest and what not—in conse-quence of which the whole City—(except some impious Scoffers) sent him presents to avert the wrath of Heaven by his prayers—and even the *public authorities*—had warned the Captains of Ships—who to mend the matter— almost all bought *new Cables* and anchors—by way of weathering the Gale.— But the fourth turned out a very fine day.—All those who had paid their money—are exceptionally angry—and insist either upon having the day of Judgement—or their cash again.—But the Friar's device seems to be 'no money to be returned'—and he says that he merely made a mistake in the time—for the day of Judgement will certainly come for all that either here or in some other part of Italy.—This has a little pacified the expectants—you will think this a fiction—enquire further then—the populace actually used to kiss the fellow's feet in the Streets. His Sermon however had small effect upon some— for they gave a ball on the 3d.—and a tradesman brought me an *over*charge on the same day—upon which I threatened him with the friar—but he said that that was a reason for being paid on the 3d.—as he had a sum to make up for his last account.—There seem to have been all kinds of tempests all over the Globe—

and for my part it would not surprize me—if the earth should get a little tired of the tyrants and slaves who disturb her surface.—

I have also had a love letter from *Pimlico* from a lady whom I never saw in my life—but who hath fallen in love with me for having written *Don Juan!*—I suppose that she is either mad or *nau[ghty]*.—do you remember *Constantia* and *Echo*—and *la Swissesse*[7]—and all my other inamorate—when I was 'gentle and juvenile—curly and gay'[8]—and was myself in love with a certain silly person—[line crossed out]?——But I am grown very good now—and think all such things vanities which is a very proper opinion at thirty four.—I always *say four*—till the five is out.—Since I last wrote—I had written the enclosed letter—which I did not send— thinking it useless—You will please to recollect that you would not be required to know any Italian acquaintance of mine—the Countess G[uiccioli] has a distinct quarter and generally [in a] house with her father and brother—who were exiled on account of politics—and she [was] obliged to go with them or be shut up in a Convent. The Pope gave her a regular separation from her husband like Lady B[yron]'s—three years ago.—We are all in the same house just *now*—only because *our* Ambassador recommended it as safer for *them* in these suspicious times.—As to our *liaison*—you know that *all* foreign ladies & most English have an amitié of the same kind—or not so good perhaps, as *ours* has lasted nearly four years.

[To Lady Hardy]

Albaro. 10bre [December]. 1 o 1822

My dear 'Cousin (*not*) of *Buckingham* and sage grave Woman'[9] it was my intention to have answered yr. letter sooner—but in the interim yr. Chevalier arrived— and calling upon me had not been two minutes in the room (though I had not seen him for these nine years) before he began a long story about you—which I cut short as well as I could by telling him that I *knew* you—and was a *relative* and was not desirous of his confidence on the subject.—He—however—persisted in declaring himself an illused Gentleman—and describing you—as a kind of cold Calypso—who lead astray people of an amatory disposition—without giving

---

[7] Shelley's poem 'To Constantia, Singing' was addressed to Claire Clairmont (perhaps it was a another of her pseudonyms); a woman styling herself 'Echo' wrote Byron explicit fan letters in his years of fame in London; the Swiss Henrietta D'Ussières threw herself at him in 1814 (see *LJ* iv. 122).

[8] See Thomas Moore, *Intercepted Letters; or, The Twopenny Post-Bag* (1813), 74.

[9] See *Richard III*, III. vii. 217. Anne Louisa Emily Hardy (née Berkeley; 1782?–1877), wife of Admiral Sir Thomas Hardy (of 'Kiss me, Hardy' fame), was only remotely related to Byron (see *LJ* x. 30). She had met him in 1814, and was on her travels with her three daughters while her husband was on an expedition to South America. Her 'Chevalier' was none other than Byron's old friend Sir James Wedderburn Webster, still womanizing furiously, and separated from Lady Frances.

them any sort of compensation—contenting yourself it seems—with only making *one* fool—instead of *two*—which is the more approved method of proceeding on such occasions.—For my part—I think you quite right—and be assured from me that a woman who—(as Society is constituted in England—) gives any advantage to a man—may expect a lover—but will sooner or later find a tyrant.—And this may not perhaps be the Man's fault neither—but is the necessary and natural result of the Circumstances of Society which in fact tyrannize over the Man equally with the woman—that is to say—if either of *them* have any feeling or honour.—He (the Chevalier) bored me so upon the subject that I greatly fear (Heaven forgive me for you won't) that I said something about the 'transmutation of hair' but I was surprized into it—by his wanting to [swear?] me out that his black wig—was the shock (or shocking) flaxen poodle furniture with which Nature had decorated his head ten years ago.——

He is gone post to Leghorn in pursuit of you—having (I presume in consequence of your disappearance) actually—(*no* jest I assure you) advertised 'for an agreeable companion in a post-chaise[']¹⁰ in the Genoa Gazette.—I enclose you the paragraph.—Have you found any benefit for your girl from the L[eghorn] Baths? or are you gone to Florence.—You can write to me at yr. own leisure and inclination.—I have always laid it down as a maxim—and found it justified by experience—that a man and a woman—make far better friendships than can exist between two of the same sex—but *then* with the condition—that they never have made—or are to make love with each other.¹¹—Lovers may [be]— and indeed generally are—enemies—but they never can be friends—because there must always be a spice of jealousy—and a something of Self in all their speculations.—Indeed I rather look upon Love altogether as a sort of hostile transaction—very necessary to make—or to break—matches and keep the world a-going—but by no means a sinecure to the parties concerned.—— Now—as *my* Love perils are—I believe pretty well over—and yours by all accounts are never to begin;—we shall be the best friends imaginable—as far as both are concerned—and with this advantage—that we may both fall to loving right and left through all our acquaintance—without either sullenness or sorrow from that amiable passion—which are it's [unnoble?] attributes.—— I address this at hazard to Leghorn—believe me my dear Coz

ever & affectly yrs.
N B

---

¹⁰ See Byron's Alpine journal, 20 September 1816, for this reference.
¹¹ See *Don Juan*, xiv. 743–4 (*CPW* v. 586): 'No friend like to a woman earth discovers, | So that you have not been nor will be lovers.'

[To Douglas Kinnaird]

10bre [December]. 19 o 1822

My dear Douglas

As you are convalescent—that is to say not quite well—but not ill enough to find yourself *not* ennuyè—I have less hesitation in writing frequently—because after having yawned sufficiently over present friends—you can fairly go to sleep over an epistle from the absent.—When you are once abroad again—haranguing—galloping—banking—and prospering—I shall have less chance of attention—but nevertheless I pray you—to 'ride gently over the testicles' as Mrs. Matlock of Cambridge memory was wont in her improvement of language—to direct her Coachman in driving over the Stones.—One would think you had been breaking in my Pegasus—by the falls you have undergone.—Prithee—be careful—after a Man is turned of thirty—why should he ride a mad horse—except in case of war or woman? in all other respects a hackney—or other Coach—is more becoming his age and station.—I have been pondering over the late vicissitudes of our D[on] J[uan]s—I am not quite clear that if we had a proper security for the *accompts* being as correct as Cocker[12]—it would not be the best plan of the two.—As for M[urray]'s intrigues—and R[idgway]'s demons—they are not worth a thought;—I tell you that the two most successful things that ever were written by me—i.e. the E[nglish] B[ards] and the C[hilde] H[arold]—were refused by one half '*the trade*' and reluctantly received by the other.

 There are two or three ways to proceed.——1stly.—You can cast about and see if any proposition is made by these *tanners* of Authors—the Calf-skin and Morocco—and Muscovite publishers.—If eligible—you can decide;—when it is known you will probably have proposals. 2dly.—If not—we have always the option of stamping (an Italic phrase)[13] upon the 'touch and go' own account score——which is only objectionable in as much as it never yet succeeded—but it *may*—as Steam has—and balloons will.——3dly. If so concluded—we must have securities that said publisher or Author & Self's account—shall have his Arithmetic summed up and checked by the skilful in such affairs.—4thly. Are the D Js subject to any laws? that is *your* laws?—which are somewhat of the queerest—and *is* my compact respecting them *binding* to the contracting party?——5thly.—If Mr. J[ohn] H[unt] publishes them eventually—his Son (if

---

[12] See Edward Cocker, *Arithmetick*, first published in 1678, and reprinted constantly as a guide for those doing their own accounts.
[13] That is, *stampare*: to print.

of age) ought to be comprized in the stipulation to render a fair account of 'meum et tuum' [mine and yours] quarterly to persons appointed by the Author for such purposes.—6thly. Some other ought to be bound—*not* for the assetts—but merely in case of nonfulfilment—to see and guarantee that the account (be it good—bad, or indifferent) is a fair and true one—for it is a difficult piece of Antiquarianism to decypher the Hieroglyphic of a publisher's balance—pro—con—or otherwise—or anywise.—I venture to throw out these hints to yr. Honour's Convalescence—but how far they may merit attention in yr. sickness or your health is left to your consideration——'and your petition shall ever &c. &c. &c.[']'[14]——

I am not very well—I suspect worse than you are—at least I hope so.—Ever since the Summer—when I was fool enough to swim some four miles under a boiling Sun at Via Reggio—I have been more or less ailing.——First my Skin peeled off—Well—it came again.—Then I had a fever and a portentious [*sic*] Constipation and inflammation which confined me to my bed in a bad Inn on a worse road.—Well—I thought I was well quit for the winter at least—but lo!—I have within this last month had eruptions and the devil knows what besides—so that I have called in an English Physician—who hath decocted and concocted me—'secundum artem' [according to the art; skillfully] so that I am turned inside out but the malady still continues—and is very troublesome.—I should think that it was the itch—but that it don't infect anybody—and I might think that it was something else—were it not for the same reason.——I am as temperate as an Anchorite—but I suspect that temperance is a more effective medicine at twenty than at thirty and—almost five—Oh Parish Register!—Oh Peerage why?—

Record those years that I would fain deny?[15]

I shall not trouble you further—and I merely, do it now—as a sleeping draught to your Collar-bone.——

You will have seen Hobhouse by this time—with his relations—who I hope returned safely.—I had a letter from his brother dated 1821—introducing an Overland Gentleman from India—whom I wished back again.—However I mounted on 'tit-back for to ride'[16] paid him a visit up four hundred pair of stairs at a Genoese Inn—and came back again half-frozen from politeness to an Equinoctial new acquaintance. Pray—make this a merit to the Demag[og]ue,—it is all out of deference to the M.P. who I hope gets on and neither suffers from Oligarchy—nor that more severe Aristocracy—*Polly*-garchy—I don't mean

---

[14] A traditional form of words used at the end of a petition to an office-holder.

[15] Marchand understandably thought this was an adaptation from Crabbe's *The Parish Register* (1807), but I can find no such line in Crabbe's work; in all likelihood it is original to Byron.

[16] The source of this I cannot find, but a 'tit' is an antique expression for a small horse.

from 'πολλοι' [*polloi*; plebeians]—to recur to the tondapemoibomenosity [?][17] of our Alma [M]ater (with her sour milk) but the regular petticoat regency of all wearers of that magic garment.——I do believe that if women did *not* wear it— their sway would be less—for few C——s come up to the previous preconception—or pre-deception—while the Drapery is floating about them like an Admiral's flag.——Here is a long letter—but you make the reading as short as you like.——

yrs. ever & truly
N B

P. S. *Insure! hast thou? at the Pelican? the Phoenix?—and all life assurances whatsoever?*

[To John Murray]

Genoa. 10bre [December]. 25 o 1822

I had sent you back 'the Quarterly' without perusal—having resolved to read no more reviews good bad or indifferent—but 'who can control his fate?'[18] 'Galignani to whom my English studies are confined' has forwarded a copy of at least one half of it—in his indefatigable Catch-penny weekly compilation—and as 'like Honour it came unlooked for'[19]—I have looked through it.[20]—I must say that upon the *whole*—that is the whole of the *half* which I have read (for the other half is to be the Segment of Gal's next week's Circular) it is extremely handsome & any thing but unkind or unfair.—As I take the good in good part—I must not nor will not quarrel with the bad—what the Writer says of D[on] J[uan] is harsh—but it is inevitable—He must follow—or at least not directly oppose the opinion of a prevailing & yet not very firmly seated party—a review may and will direct or 'turn away' the Currents of opinion—but it must not directly oppose them.—D Juan will be known by and bye for what it is intended a *satire* on *abuses* of the present *states* of Society—and not an eulogy of vice;—it may be now and then voluptuous—I can't help that—Ariosto is worse—Smollett (see Lord Strutwell in vol 2d. of R[oderick] R[andom]) ten times worse—and

---

[17] Marchand notes: 'A jocular compression of a phrase in Homer—"to him in answer spake".'
[18] See *Othello*, V. ii. 272.   [19] See 1 *Henry IV*, V. i. 28.
[20] The Parisian publisher Galignani had reprinted Revd Reginald Heber's ambivalent review of *Sardanapalus, The Two Foscari*, and *Cain* (from the *Quarterly Review* of July 1822) in the *Messenger*.

Fielding no better.——No Girl will ever be seduced by reading D J—no—no—
she will go to Little's poems—& Rousseau's romans [novels]—for that—or even
to the immaculate De Stael——they will encourage her—& not the Don—who
laughs at that—and—and—most other things.—But never mind—'Ca ira!'—
And now to a less agreeable topic, of which 'pars magna es'[21]—you Murray of
Albemarle St.—and the other Murray of Bridge Street—'Arcades Ambo' ('Mur-
rays both') et cant-are pares—ye I say—between you are the Causes of the
prosecution of John Hunt Esqre, on account of the Vision;—you by sending
him an incorrect copy—and the other by his function.[22]——Egad—but
H[unt]'s Counsel will lay it on you with a trowel—for your tergiversifying as
to the M.S.S. &c. whereby poor H[unt] (& for anything I know—myself—I am
willing enough) is likely to be impounded.——

Now—do you see what you and your friends do by your injudicious rude-
ness?—actually cement a sort of connection which you strove to prevent—and
which had the H[unt]s prospered—would not in all probability have continued.—
As it is—I will not quit them in their adversity though it should cost me—
character—fame—money—and the usual et cetera.—My original motives—I
already explained (in the letter which you thought proper to show—[23]) they are
the true ones and I abide by them—as I tell you—and I told L[eig]h H[un]t when
he questioned me on the subject of that letter.——He was violently hurt—&
never will forgive me at bottom—but I can't help that,——I never meant to
make a parade of it—but if he chose to question me—I could only answer the
plain truth—and I confess I did not see anything in that letter to hurt him—
unless I said he was 'a bore' which I don't remember.—Had their Journal gone on
well—and I could have aided to make it better for them—I should then have left
them after my safe pilotage off a lee shore—to make a prosperous voyage by
themselves.—As it is—I can't & would not if I could—leave them amidst the
breakers.—

As to any community of feeling—thought—or opinion between L H & me—
there is little or none—we meet rarely—hardly ever—but I think him a good
principled & able man—& must do as I would be done by.—I do not know what
world he has lived in—but I have lived in three or four—and none of them

<hr />

[21] See Virgil, Aeneid, ii. 5–6: 'All that I saw and part of which I was' in Dryden's translation. 'Ça ira'
(all will be well) is a French Revolutionary song.
[22] For 'Arcades ambo et cantare pares' (countrymen both and singers of equal renown), see letter of
22 April 1820. Charles Murray (no relation) was the secretary of the Constitutional Association
for Opposing the Progress of Disloyal and Seditious Principles, based in Bridge Street, London.
[23] Byron refers to his letter to Murray of 9 October 1822, the part of which referring to Leigh Hunt
Murray admitted (Murray Letters, 455) he had read 'to every gentleman who is in the habit of visiting at
my house'—to demonstrate the purity of Byron's charitable motives, presumably. What Byron said
got back to Hunt, with predictable results, and now it is Murray's motives that are up for scrutiny.

like his Keats and Kangaroo terra incognita—Alas! poor Shelley!—how he would have laughed—had he lived, and how we used to laugh now & then— at various things—which are grave in the Suburbs.—You are all mistaken about Shelley——you do not know—how mild—how tolerant—how good he was in Society—and as perfect a Gentleman as ever crossed a drawing room;—when he liked—& where he liked.—I have some thoughts of taking a run down to Naples—(solus—or at most—*cum sola* [alone together; with Teresa]) this Spring—and writing (when I have studied the Country) a fifth & sixth Canto of Ch[ild]e Harolde—but this is merely an idea for the present—and I have other excursions—& voyages in my mind.——The busts are finished[24]—are you worthy of them?—

yrs. &c.

N B [...]

[To Sir Timothy Shelley]

Genoa, Jan. 7, 1823

Sir,[25]

I trust that the only motive of this letter will be sufficient apology, even from a stranger—I had the honour of being the friend of the late Percy B. Shelley, and am still actuated by the same regard for his memory and the welfare of his family—to which I beg leave to add my respect for yourself and his connections. My Solicitor lately made an application to Mr. Whitton a gentleman in your confidence, in favour of Mr. Shelley's Widow and child by his second marriage both being left by his untimely death entirely destitute.

My intimacy with your late son and the circumstances to me unknown 'till after his decease—of my being named one of the Executors in a will which he left but which is of no avail at present—and may perhaps be always unavailable—seemed to justify this intrusion through a third person. I am unwilling to trouble you personally, for the subject is very painful to my feelings

---

[24] Murray was pitifully eager to come by this pair of busts of Byron and Teresa by Lorenzo Bartolini, which Byron had promised him. ('*Every day of my life*', he wrote to Byron (*Murray Letters*, 450), 'I sit opposite your Lordships Portrait—Pray send me both Busts'.) Byron did not think much of his: 'it exactly resembles a superannuated Jesuit' (*LJ* ix. 213), and in the end Murray got neither: Teresa's is in the Biblioteca Classense in Ravenna; Byron's in the National Portrait Gallery in London.

[25] Relations between Shelley and his father (second Baronet of Castle Goring; 1753–1844) had broken down since the poet's expulsion from Oxford in 1811. Sir Timothy did eventually give Mary Shelley a small allowance after her return to England in 1823, but would have nothing directly to do with her or his grandson.

and must be still more so to yours—I must now, however, respectfully submit to you, the totally destitute state of your daughter-in-law and her child, and I would venture to add—that neither are unworthy your protection. Their wishes are by no means extravagant, a simple provision to prevent them from absolute want now staring them in the face is all that they seek and where can they look for it with propriety—or accept it without bitterness—except from yourself?

I am not sufficiently aware of Mr. Shelley's family affairs to know on what terms he stood with his family, nor if I were so should I presume to address you on that subject. But he is in his grave—he was your Son—and whatever his errors and opinions may have been—they were redeemed by many good and noble qualities.

Might I hope, Sir, that by casting an eye of kindness on his relict and her boy it would be a comfort to them—it would one day be a comfort to yourself, for if ever he had been so unfortunate as to offend you, they are innocent; but I will not urge the topic further and am far more willing to trust to our own feelings and judgement, than to any appeal which may be made to them by others.

Mrs. Shelley is for the present residing near Genoa—indeed she has not the means of taking a journey to England—nor of remaining where she is without some assistance. That this should be derived from other sources than your protection, would be humiliating to you and to her—but she has still hopes from your kindness—let me add from your Justice to her and to your Grandchild.

I beg leave to renew my apology for intruding upon you, which nothing but the necessity of so doing would have induced, and have the honour to be,

Your most obedient, Very humble Servant,
Noel Byron

[To Lady Hardy]

Genoa. F[ebruar]y. 17 o 1823

My dear Cousin

Your letter arrived as I was on the point of answering the former—not forgotten—nor neglected—but my acknowledgement was postponed from day to day till I was afraid that a dilatory reply might look worse than none at all—especially as I thought you might return by the same route—and I could gossip by word of mouth, instead of puzzling you with my hieroglyphics.— That 'your Speech is of broken bones'—I thought that you broke nothing but hearts—but you see how the Gods avenge harmless Flirtation.—The subject however is too serious for buffoonery—I rejoice—that I did not hear of your accident till your recovery—I am enough acquainted with,—and too impatient under pain myself—not to sympathize with sufferings less than what you must have undergone—but women bear these things better than men—an additional proof whereof—is—that you have fought through the Carnival with your arm in a sling—a General would have been carried off the field—and not returned quite so gallantly perhaps.—I hope that your Valour—like Virtue—has been it's own reward—and that the arrival of Lent has found you equally able to sustain its privations.——Your Chevalier errant is here and more errant, though still stationary—than usual—and that is much.—He has embroiled himself with two absent friends—a Sir F. V.—and some Caledonian Chiefs of the race of Diarmid,—Mr. Campbell of Glensaddle—I believe—both of whom have *Cut* him by letter—for reasons—which—as I have nothing to do with—I cannot pretend to explain.—There are also, some high and doubtful questions with his landlord of the [']Croix de Malthe' [Maltese Cross]—his tailor—his shoe-maker—and finally his Valet—also his banker—and two other Bankers—who have manifested an unaccountable aversion from his bills—unless guaranteed by an amicable endorsement—'a *backing* of one's friends' which Pylades himself would probably have avoided.—All these woes—to say nothing of others—he lays to *your* door—for having lured him with deceitful hopes to this mercenary country— where a Man must actually pay for his provisions.——To console himself for your rigour,—on his return he paid his court to a very pretty Madame Quantana—the wife of a rich banker—but his bills seemed no less unacceptable to the Lady than her husband—for neither of them would cash his love or money at whatever discount.—Messrs Gibbs were equally inexorable in the pecuniary part, but we will see what is to be done and get him back to Lausanne, and if possible to his wife—which is an important episode by the way—for he is moving Heaven and Earth—for a reconciliation.—She is at Paris.——I knew her soon after their marriage—and him some years before—when he was in the Hussars—and I was a Collegian.—She was very beautiful—and more romantic than wise—and that unlucky kind of woman—who can do nothing without an Eclât—so that the wonder is that they were not separated before.—He has bored me—into being a Mediator in his behalf—attracted doubtless by my own signal success in amicably arranging my matrimonial affairs.——I have consequently addressed the Lady—in a respectful and conciliatory epistle—representing with all the eloquence of common place—that very trite truism—that all quarrels are bad—but those of holy Matrimony the very worst of all.—I do not know that it will do any good but at least it can only hurt myself—if they make it up—well and good,—if not—they will both fall upon the Pacificator according to the ancient custom.—You ask me as to the prudence of coming by Sea to Genoa—if I had the direction of the Winds like the Philosopher in Rasselas[26]—I should know how to answer.—The passage is made from Leghorn daily and with safety—but I know not how far the presence of an Admiral's Consort—might tempt the Ocean—who was very gallant in the old time.— But you might come by the good (*not* the *new*) road as far as Lerici overland—and embark either from Lerici (on the Gulph) or Spezia—for Sestri or Genoa—and arrive at the former (at least) in a few hours—under sail with a tolerable wind—or by dint of rowing—in a cabin.—There is nothing very formidable in either. I made the passage—after being laid up for four days on a sick bed in a sordid Inn—got to Sestri by twilight—(with oars by the way) and came on to Genoa by land which I reached before dawn—and recovered on—and I believe, *by* the amphibious journey.—But you had better—if you decide on the Sea—avoid the Equinox—which will occur about the period of your proposed departure.— I would send round my Goletta [schooner] for you—but She is laid up in the Arsenal—and is too small for the accommodation of a family—though She is a great 'Summer Bark' as the poets say.—I hope however you will pass this way,— though your Escort is departed—I dare say you have relays upon the road.—— I have not received Lord Dillon's book[27] but am equally obliged—pray—say so.—— I hear very little of Mr. Taaffe—and it would have been as well if that little had been less.—He involved me and some other Englishmen—in a squabble with a drunken dragoon and the Guard on *his* account entirely—and then kept aloof on pretence of having lost his *hat*.——This happened at Pisa.—One was wounded—another arrested—myself and the fourth rode through the Guard—and the affray closed in the Dragoon's being wounded—for some time supposed mortally—but the rascal recovered.—Mr. Taaffe—never made his re-appearance—(after having been the *first* insulted—and the first to complain) till the Squabble was over—and finding that the Pisans took the part of their Scoundrel—(I need not add that he was a *Pisan* himself)—did all he could to shuffle out of any responsibility.—He—Mr. Taaffe—is under some small obligation to me—for I prevented Mr. Trelawny—a truculent Cornish Gentleman— from breaking his bones—for his conduct on this occasion—and I assure you it was no easy matter—I speak of facts sufficiently notorious at the time—to Mr. Dawkins the then Minister at Florence. I am penetrè[?] with the bounties of Lady Jersey though I do not know when I shall be able to avail myself of them,—I was sick of the 'Salons' long before I left England—and I have seen

---

[26] See Samuel Johnson, *The History of Rasselas, Prince of Abyssinia* (1759), chapter 41.
[27] Henry Augustus Dillon-Lee, thirteenth Viscount Dillon (1777–1832), published *The Life and Opinions of Sir Richard Maltravers: An English Gentleman of the Seventeenth Century* in 1822.

enough of the foreign Monde since and before even, to exclaim with Solomon—
that 'all is vanity and that there is nothing new under the Sun'[28]—there may be
something *new* to the *new*—but I am not in that predicament—and I am glad of
it—since it leaves me without ambition or curiosity.——Siate Felice [be
happy]—my Cousin—and let me know that you are so—and I shall be content.—Come this way if you can—or will—or at any rate let me know how far
you are from

yrs. ever and most affectly.
N B

[To Augusta Leigh]

Genoa. F[ebruar]y. 27th. 1823

My dearest Augusta

Your informant was as usual in error—Do not believe all the lies you may
hear.—Hobhouse can tell you that I have *not* lost *any* of my *teeth hitherto*,—since
I was twelve years old—& had a back one taken out by Dumergue to make room
for others growing—and so far from being fatter—at *present* I [am] much thinner
that [sic] when I left England, when I was not very stout, the *latter* you will
regret—the *former* you will be glad to hear—Hobhouse can tell you all
particulars—though I am much reduced since he saw me—and more than *you*
would like.—I write to you these few lines in haste—perhaps we may meet in
Spring—either *here*—or in England.—Hobhouse says your coming out would
be the best thing which you could do, for yourself & me too—

ever yrs. most affectly
N B

[To John Hunt]

Genoa, M[arc]h 17th. 1823

Sir,

Your brother will have forwarded by the post a corrected proof of *The Blues* for
some ensuing number of the journal; but I should think that ye. Pulci translation

---

[28] See Ecclesiastes 1: 2, 9.

had better be preferred for the immediate number, as *The Blues* will only tend further to indispose a portion of your readers.

I still retain my opinion that my connection with the work will tend to any thing but its success. Such I thought from the first, when I suggested that it would have been better to have made a kind of literary appendix to the *Examiner*;[29] the other expedient was hazardous, and has failed hitherto accordingly; and it appears that the two pieces of my contribution have precipitated that failure more than any other. It was a pity to print such a quantity, especially as you might have been aware of my general unpopularity, and the universal run of the period against my productions, since the publication of Mr. Murray's last volume. My talent (if I have any) does not lie in the kinds of composition which is [*sic*] most acceptable to periodical readers. By this time you are probably convinced of this fact. The Journal, if continued (as I see no reason why it should not be), will find much more efficacious assistance in the present and other contributors than in myself. Perhaps also, you should, for the present, reduce the number printed to two thousand, and raise it gradually if necessary. It is not so much against *you* as against me that the hatred is directed; and, I confess, I would rather withstand it *alone,* and grapple with it as I may. Mr. Murray, partly from pique, for he is a Mortal—mortal as his publications, though a bookseller—has done more harm than you are fully aware of, or I either; and you will perceive this probably on my first separate publication, no less than in those connected with *The Liberal.* He has the Clergy, and the Government, and the public with him; I do not much embarrass myself about them when *alone;* but I do not wish to drag others down also. I take this to be the fact, for I do not recollect that so much odium was directed against your family and friends, till your brother, unfortunately for himself, came in literary contact with myself. I will not, however, quit *The Liberal* without mature consideration, though I feel persuaded that it would be for your advantage that I should do so. Time and Truth may probably do away this hostility, or, at least, its effect; but, in the interim, you are the sufferer. Every publication of mine has latterly failed; I am not discouraged by this, because writing and composition are habits of my mind, with which Success and Publication are objects of remoter reference—*not causes* but *effects,* like those of any other pursuit. I have had enough both of praise and abuse to deprive them of their novelty, but I continue to compose for the same reason that I ride, or read, or bathe, or travel—it is a habit.

---

[29] A Radical weekly London newspaper founded by Leigh and John Hunt in 1808, well known for carrying essays by William Hazlitt.

I want sadly *Peveril of the Peak*, which has not yet arrived here, and I will thank you much for a copy;[30] I shall direct Mr. Kinnaird to reimburse you for the price. It will be useless to forward *The Liberal*, the insertion of which will only prevent the arrival of any other books in the same parcel. That work is strictly prohibited, and the packet which came by sea was extracted with the greatest difficulty. Never send by sea, it is a loss of four months; by land a fortnight is sufficient.

Yours ever,

N B

[To John Cam Hobhouse]

G[eno]a M[arc]h 19th. 1823

My dear Hobhouse

Before my affairs can be extracted from the Attorno—Douglas K[innair]d must condescend to complete the negociation with Mr. Deardon of Rochdale.[31]—On the 24th of January I forwarded to K[innair]d a very amicable answer of mine to a letter of Deardon's and also the said letter—the former for him to forward to Mr. D and the latter for his own inspection.—I have since repeatedly pressed him at *least* to *acknowledge* the receipt of these—but not one word of reply on that point.—In the mean time—the suits are going on—and of course expences and anxieties proportionate.—Few of my friends can be more anxious to get rid of law and lawyers than I am.—As to the Portsmouth business—all I know or could know of it was from Mr. H[anson]'s own statement.[32]—He told me that old Lady First Portsmouth was dead—and that Portsmouth's brother wanted him to marry *another old* woman—that he might have no children, but that Lord P wished to marry a *young* woman—and seemed inclined to one of H's daughters.—I saw nothing very unnatural in this—nor lunatical—of Ld. P. himself

---

[30] Walter Scott's novel of 1823, set in the English 17th century.

[31] For James Dearden, see letter of 18 October 1812.

[32] Hobhouse wrote to Byron on 2 March to say that Lord Portsmouth (who had married Hanson's daughter Mary Anne in 1814; see Journal, 7 March 1814) had been declared insane since 1809, and had been abused during the course of the marriage: 'The consummate profligacy brutality & scoundrelism of all the Hansons male & female', he wrote (*Hobhouse Letters*, 325), 'surpass my notions of what occasion and temptation will make of human beings. You recollect what a pretty smockfaced girl Laura Hanson was in our time who looked as if butter would not melt in her mouth—Well it turns out that she used to beat & whip and spit upon this poor crazy creature and joined in all the cruelties against him.' As outcomes of the case, the marriage was annulled, Mary Anne's children (fathered by her lover, the lawyer William Alder) were bastardized, and she escaped to the Continent to avoid imprisonment. Portsmouth was himself sadistic in his lunacy: beating and bleeding his horses, officiating at abattoirs, arranging mock funerals ('black jobs'), and so forth. (See Doris Langley Moore, *Lord Byron: Accounts Rendered* (London: John Murray, 1974), appendix 3.)

I saw nothing till the day of his marriage.——On the evening previous to the ceremony I received an invitation from Mr. H begging me as a friend of many years acquaintance with his family to be present at the marriage—which was to take place next morning.—I went—I saw no appearance of entrapment or compulsion.—The Ladies and other witnesses—went in a Carriage.—The Carriage being full—Lord P and myself walked to the Church.—On the way he told me that he had long liked Miss Hanson—even during the life of the first Lady P—and asked me if I did not think she would make a very good wife.——The Ceremony passed without any thing remarkable—the women cried a little as usual—but Lord P's deportment was quite calm and collected.—After the ceremony I went home—and the family I believe went into the Country.——I did not see the couple again till long afterwards—and then but rarely.—I went as I would do to any other marriage—it was no affair of mine to interfere in—and I thought that if Ld. P. got a good plain quiet homekeeping wife—*young too*—instead of the tough morsel prepared by his brother—it was no bad bargain for either party.—I could not foresee Horsewhipping—and the like of that there.——I could not foretell *Venality*—for I was told that Lord P's property was in *trust*, well secured—and that Lady P. could only have a jointure of a thousand a year.—I could not foresee *Lunacy* in a Man who had been allowed to walk about the world five and forty years as Compos—of voting—franking—marrying—convicting thieves on his own evidence—and similar pastimes which are the privileges of Sanity.—I could have no interest of my own for I never performed with the Miss Hanson's nor whipped Ld. P.——I had nothing to acquire from Mr. Hanson—as the state of his bills do show—being about ten thousand pounds—(most part paid—) since that epoch.—Had my evidence been called for by either party I could have given it impartially.—There is—or was—an affidavit of mine on the subject—before the Chancellor in 1814. I thought—and still think that the Marriage *might* have been like any other marriage.—Of the Courtship which (as far as I can recollect from the time Mr. H first mentioned Ld. P's addresses—and the subsequent day of the ceremony) might be on the tapis [carpet] about ten days—I can say nothing—for I saw nothing—and all I heard was from Mr. Hanson himself—and that I think once only; I had been many years in the habit of seeing my solicitor on my own affairs.—He had been my Attorney—since I was ten years of age.——'Causa scientiae patet'.[33]——It struck me as so little an entrapment for Ld. P that I used to wonder whether the *Girl* would have him—and not whether *he* would take the Girl.—I knew nothing of his ignorance of 'fuff—fuff—fuff'—as Cheeks

---

[33] 'The reason of the knowledge is evident': a legal phrase concerning the evidence of witnesses.

Chester called it——but as he was of a robust[i]ous figure—though not a Solomon—naturally imagined he was not less competent than other people.[34]——We owe to him however the greatest discovery about the blood since Dr. Harvey's;—I wonder if it really hath such an effect—I never was bled in my life—but by leeches—and I thought the leeches d——d bad pieces—but perhaps the tape and lancet may be better.[35]—I shall try on some great emergency.—

I am not very well—from a concoction of humours—for which an English physician prescribes a 'decoction of Woods' (and Forests too I should think from it's varieties of taste)[36] but it seems epidemical in this vicinity—full half a hundred people have got it—in the shape of swelled faces and red faces and all that.—I dined with the B[ritis]h Minister Hill—on Saturday—the Carriage gave way on my return—and I had to walk three miles (about half of the way *up* hill—) in the night—with a bleak wind—which brought on an attack again—otherwise I was better.——I shall be glad to see Blaquiere.—I am *not* going to Naples—I thought of it for an instant—being invited there—and Mr. Murray has set the report afloat—with a story about a New Childe Harold—because I said that *if* I went there—I *might* write another Canto.—All my affairs are going on (in England) not very prosperously—the Noel trustees pay nothing & nobody—we can't get out of the funds—nor accommodate with Deardon—nor publish—(Douglas is afraid—but publish I will—though it were to destroy fame and profit at once—I will not be advised nor dictated to by public or private) I shall have to come home and if I do it shan't be for nothing—for I will bring affairs to a crisis with Henry Brougham directly on my arrival—and one or two more of the same kind—I have nothing on my mind so much as this.[37]—

ever yours & truly & affectly
N B

---

[34] 'Poor devil it seems he was totally impotent and always had been so—being asked what was the difference between adultery & fornication he said one was performed with the thumb the other with the middle finger' (*Hobhouse Letters*, 325).

[35] Langley Moore comments that Portsmouth 'was obsessed by some repulsive notion relating to surgeon's lancets and women' (*Lord Byron: Accounts Rendered*, 461).

[36] Ancient pharmacists often prescribed 'a decoction of the woods': a simmered infusion of various timbers and other products such as hartshorn and sassafras.

[37] Why Byron's hatred of lawyer and politician Henry Brougham (1767–1848), who had supported Lady Byron during the separation, and Robert Southey, who had spread rumours of a 'league of incest' at Diodati in 1816 (see letter of 11 November 1818), should bubble up here is unclear.

P. S.—You are mistaken on one point—I am leading a very chaste *life—and time [too] at thirty five—*

> *'Long may better years arrive!*
> *Better years than thirty five!'—*[38]

[To Douglas Kinnaird]

Genoa. March 31st. 1823

Dear Douglas/

I enclose you the 15th. Canto of D[on] J[uan] and am anxious to know what have become of the others duly sent to you—by the post.—With this there should be *ten* at your disposal for me.——I have only had proofs of the *three* first——and want the others to correct.——I expect that those corrected already are to be published immediately. I care nothing for what may be the consequence—critical or otherwise—all the bullies on earth shall not prevent me from writing what I like—& publishing what I write—'coute qui coute' [cost what it may]—if they had let me alone—I probably should not have continued beyond the five first—as it is—there shall be such a poem—as has not been since Ariosto—in length—in satire—in imagery—and in what I please.—

yrs. ever
N B [...]

[To Thomas Moore]

Genoa, April 2d, 1823

I have just seen some friends of yours, who paid me a visit yesterday, which, in honour of them and of you, I returned to-day;—as I reserve my bear-skin and teeth, and paws and claws, for our enemies.

I have also seen Henry F[ox], Lord H[olland]'s son,[39] whom I had not looked upon since I left him a pretty mild boy, without a neckcloth, in a jacket, and in delicate health, seven long years agone, at the period of mine eclipse—the third, I believe, as I have generally one every two or three years. I think that he has the softest and most amiable expression of countenance I ever saw, and manners

---

[38] See Samuel Johnson, 'To Mrs Thrale, on Completing her Thirty-Fifth Year'.
[39] See letter of 9 May 1817. Fox would have an affair with Teresa Guiccioli in the summer of 1825.

correspondent. If to those he can add hereditary talents, he will keep the name of F in all its freshness for half a century more, I hope. I speak from a transient glimpse—but I love still to yield to such impressions; for I have ever found that those I liked longest and best, I took to at first sight; and I always liked that boy—perhaps, in part, from some resemblance in the less fortunate part of our destinies—I mean, to avoid mistakes, his lameness. But there is this difference, that *he* appears a halting angel, who has tripped against a star; whilst I am *Le Diable Boiteux*,—a soubriquet, which I marvel that, amongst their various *nominis umbrae*, the Orthodox have not hit upon.[40]

Your other allies, whom I have found very agreeable personages, are Milor B[lessington] and *epouse*, travelling with a very handsome companion, in the shape of a 'French Count' (to use Farquhar's phrase in the Beaux Stratagem[41]), who has all the air of a *Cupidon déchaîné* [unleashed Cupid], and is one of the few specimens I have seen of our ideal of a Frenchman *before* the Revolution—an old friend with a new face, upon whose like I never thought that we should look again. Miladi seems highly literary,—to which, and your honour's acquaintance with the family, I attribute the pleasure of having seen them. She is also very pretty, even in a morning,—a species of beauty on which the sun of Italy does not shine so frequently as the chandelier. Certainly, Englishwomen wear better than their continental neighbours of the same sex. Mountjoy seems very good-natured, but is much tamed, since I recollect him in all the glory of gems and snuff-boxes, and uniforms, and theatricals, and speeches in our house—'I mean, of peers,'—(I must refer you to Pope—whom you don't read and won't appreciate—for that quotation, which you must allow to be poetical[42]), and sitting to Stroelling, the painter, (do you remember our visit, with Leckie, to the German?) to be depicted as one of the heroes of Agincourt, 'with his long sword, saddle, bridle, Whack fal de, &c. &c.'[43]

I have been unwell—caught a cold and inflammation, which menaced a conflagration, after dining with our ambassador, Monsieur Hill,—not owing to the dinner, but my carriage broke down in the way home, and I had to walk some miles, up hill partly, after hot rooms, in a very bleak, windy evening, and

---

[40] *The Lame Devil* (1725), a comedy by Alain-René Lesage. *Nominis umbrae*: shadow-name.

[41] See Count Bellair in George Farquhar's comedy (1707).

[42] See Pope, 'On Receiving from the Right Hon. the Lady Frances Shirley a Standish and Two Pens'.

[43] Peter Edward Stroehling (1768–1826), German artist who spent long periods in London from 1803 onwards. Byron visited him with Moore and G. F. Leckie, who had helped settle a contretemps arising from *English Bards and Scotch Reviewers*, in early 1812 (*LJ* ii. 168–9). See the anonymous song 'Mrs Flinn and the Bold Dragoon', about an elderly lady who falls for a soldier, 'with his long sword, saddle, bridle | Whack row de row', and so forth.

over-hotted, or over-colded myself. I have not been so robustious as formerly, ever since the last summer, when I fell ill after a long swim in the Mediterranean, and have never been quite right up to this present writing. I am thin,—perhaps thinner than you saw me, when I was nearly transparent, in 1812,—and am obliged to be moderate of my mouth; which, nevertheless, won't prevent me (the gods willing) from dining with your friends the day after tomorrow.

They give me a very good account of you, and of your nearly 'Emprisoned Angels.' But why did you change your title?—you will regret this some day.[44] The bigots are not to be conciliated; and, if they were—are they worth it? I suspect that I am a more orthodox Christian than you are; and, whenever I see a real Christian, either in practice or in theory, (for I never yet found the man who could produce either, when put to the proof,) I am his disciple. But, till then, I cannot truckle to tithe-mongers,—nor can I imagine what has made *you* circumcise your Seraphs.

I have been far more persecuted than you, as you may judge by my present decadence,—for I take it that I am as low in popularity and bookselling as any writer can be. At least, so my friends assure me—blessings on their benevolence! This they attribute to Hunt; but they are wrong—it must be partly at least, owing to myself; be it so. As to Hunt, I prefer *not* having turned him to starve in the streets to any personal honour which might have accrued from such genuine philanthropy. I really act upon principle in this matter, for we have nothing much in common; and I cannot describe to you the despairing sensation of trying to do something for a man who seems incapable or unwilling to do any thing further for himself,—at least, to the purpose. It is like pulling a man out of a river who directly throws himself in again. For the last three or four years Shelley assisted, and had once actually extricated him. I have since his demise,—and even before,—done what I could: but it is not in my power to make this permanent. I want Hunt to return to England, for which I would furnish him with the means in comfort; and his situation *there*, on the whole, is bettered, by the payment of a portion of his debts, etc.; and he would be on the spot to continue his Journal, or Journals, with his brother, who seems a sensible, plain, sturdy, and enduring person. * * * * *

[44] Moore published *The Loves of the Angels* in December 1822.

[To Edward Blaquiere[45]]

Albaro. April 5th. 1823

Dear Sir

I shall be delighted to see you and your Greek friend—and the sooner the better.—I have been expecting you for some time—you will find me at home—I cannot express to you how much I feel interested in the cause—and nothing but some Italian connections which I had formed in Italy—connections also in some degree referring to the political state of this country—prevented me from long ago—returning to do what little I could as an individual—in that land which is an honour even only to have visited.—

ever yrs. truly
Noel Byron

[To the Earl of Blessington]

April 5th. 1823

My dear Lord B.

How is your Gout?—or rather how are you?—I return the C[ount] D'O[rsay]'s journal which is a very extraordinary production and of a most melancholy truth in all that regards high life in England.—I know or knew personally most of the personages and societies which he describes—and after reading his remarks—have the sensation fresh upon me as if I had seen them yesterday.— I would however plead in behalf of some few exceptions—which I will mention by and bye.—The most singular thing is—how he should have penetrated *not* the *fact*—but the *mystery* of the English Ennui at two and twenty.—I was about the same age when I made the same in almost precisely the same circles (for there is scarcely a person mentioned whom I did not see nightly or daily—and was acquainted more or less intimately with most of them) but I never could have described it so well.[46]—Il faut étre Francais [one must be French]—to effect this.——But he ought also to have been in the Country during the hunting

---

[45] Retired naval officer (1779–1832), author of *Letters from the Mediterranean* (1813), and founder member of the London Greek Committee. He was on his way to Greece with Andreas Luriottis, a Greek Government delegate.

[46] On the contrary, Byron had described English upper-class ennui as well as anyone ever has, in *Don Juan*, xiii. 801–88 (*CPW* v. 554–7), written in February 1823.

season with 'a select party of distinguished guests' as the papers term it.——He ought to have seen the Gentlemen after dinner—(on the hunting days) and the soireè ensuing, thereupon—and the women looking as if they have had [sic] hunted—or rather been hunted—too.——And I could have wished that he had been at a dinner in town—which I recollect at Lord Cowper's small but select—and composed of the most amusing people. The desert was hardly on the table—when out of 12 of the masculine gender—I counted *five asleep*—of these five—three were *Tierney*—Ld. Lansdowne—and Ld. Darnley—I forget the other two—but they were either wits or orators—perhaps poets.[47]——

My residence in the East and in Italy has made me somewhat indulgent of the Siesta—but then they set regularly about it in warm countries—and perform it in Solitude—(or at most in a tete a tete with a proper companion—) and retire quietly to their rooms to get out of the Sun's way for an hour or two.—Altogether your friend's journal is a very formidable production.—Alas! our dearly beloved countrymen have only discovered that they are tired and not that they are tiresome—and I suspect that the communication of the latter unpleasant verity will not be better received than truths usually are.—I have read the whole with great attention—and instruction—I am too good a patriot to say *pleasure*—at least I won't say so—whatever I may think.—I showed it (I hope no breach of confidence) to a young Italian Lady of rank—tres instruite [well educated]—also—and who passes or passed—for being one of the three most celebrated belles in the district of Italy where her family and connections reside in less troublesome times as to politics——(which is *not* Genoa—by the way) and she was delighted with it—and says that she has derived a better notion of English society from it—than from all Madame de Stael's metaphysical dissertations on the same subject in her work on the Revolution.——I beg that you will thank the young Philosopher—and make my compliments to Lady B and her Sister.——Believe me

yr. very obliged and faithful
N B

P. S.—There is a rumour in letters of some disturbance or complot in the French Pyrenean army—Generals suspected or dismissed—and ministers at war travelling to see what's the

---

[47] Peter Leopold Nassau Cowper, fifth Earl Cowper (1778–1837), was a dim bulb, outshone by his wife Emily Lamb (1787–1869), sister-in-law to Lady Caroline Lamb. Other movers and shakers here are the Hon. George Tierney (1761–1830), Henry Petty-Fitzmaurice, third Marquess of Lansdowne (1780–1863), and John Bligh, fourth Earl of Darnley (1767–1831).

matter—'Marry! (as David says) this hath an angry favour'.[48]——Tell C[ount] D'O[rsay] that some of the names are not quite intelligible especially of the Clubs—he speaks of Watt's—perhaps he is right—but in my time Watier's was the Dandy Club—of which (though no Dandy) I was a member at the time too of it's greatest glory—when Brummell and Mildmay—Alvanley and Pierrepoint[49] gave the Dandy balls—and We (the Club i.e.) got up the famous Masquerade at Burlington House and Gardens for Wellington.——He does not speak of the Alfred—which was the most recherché and the most tiresome of any— as I know by being a member of that too.——

[To John Cam Hobhouse]

Genoa April 7th. 1823

My dear H.

I saw Capt. Blaquiere and the Greek Companion of his mission on Saturday.— Of course I entered very sincerely into the object of their journey—and have even offered to go up to the Levant in July—if the Greek provisional Government think that I could be of any use.——It is not that I could pretend to anything in a military capacity—I have not the presumption of the philosopher of Ephesus—who lectured before Hannibal on the art of war—nor is it much that an individual foreigner can do in any other way—but perhaps as a reporter of the actual state of things there—or in carrying on any correspondence between them and their western friends—I might be of use—at any rate I would try.—Capt. Blaquiere (who is to write to you) wishes to have me named a member of the Committee in England—I fairly told him that my name in it's present unpopularity there—would probably do more harm than good—but of this you can judge—and certainly without offence to me—for I have no wish either to *shine*—or to appear officious;—in the mean time he is to correspond with me.—I gave him a letter to Ld. Sydney Osborne at Corfu—but a mere letter of introduction as Osborne will be hampered by his office in any political point of view.[50]—There are some obstacles too to my own going up to the Levant—which will occur to you.—My health—though pretty good—is not

---

[48] See Sheridan, *The Rivals* (1775), V. i. 193: 'favour' meaning look or countenance. In March 1823 a group of senior officers in the Duke of Angoulême's French army were charged with treason.

[49] These are the most celebrated members of the short-lived Dandy circle of Regency London: George Bryan 'Beau' Brummell (1778–1840), Henry Mildmay (1787–1848), Lord Alvanley (1789–1849), and Henry Pierrepoint (1780–1851). The masked ball Watier's members threw for Wellington on 1 July 1814 was a high-water mark for the circle; two years later Brummell fled to France to avoid his debts.

[50] See letter of 3 August 1818. Osborne was Secretary to the Government of the Ionian Islands of western Greece, then under British administration.

quite the same as when it subdued the Olympian Malaria in 1810—and the unsettled state of my lawsuit with Mr. Deardon—and the affairs still in Hanson's hands—tend to keep me nearer home.—Also you may imagine—that the 'absurd womankind' as Monkbarns calls them[51]—are by no means favourable to such an enterprise.—Madame Guiccioli is of course—and naturally enough opposed to my quitting her—though but for a few months—and as she had influence enough to prevent my return to England in 1819—she may be not less successful in detaining me from Greece in 1823.—Her brother Count Gamba the younger—who is a very fine spirited young fellow—as Blaquiere will tell you—is of a very different opinion—and ever since the ruin of Italian hopes in 1820—has been eager to go to Spain or to Greece—and very desirous to accompany me to one or other of those countries—or at any rate to go himself.—I wish you could have seen him—you would have found a very different person from the usual run of young Italians.—

With regard to my peculium—I am pretty well off—I have still a surplus of three thousand pounds of last year's income—a thousand pounds in Exchequer bills in England—and by this time—as also in July—there ought to be further monies paid to my account in Kinnaird's bank.—From literary matters—I know not if any thing will be produced—but even out of my own—K[innair]d will I suppose furnish me with a further credit—if I should require it—since all my receipts will pass through his bank.—I have desired him *not* to pass further sums (except for the Insurances of Ly. B[yron]'s Life) to the payment of what remaining debts (and they are but few) may be extant till the end of the year— when I shall know more precisely what I am to have—and what I may then still owe.

You must be aware that it would not do to go without means into a country where means are so much wanted—and that I should not like to be an incumbrance—go where I would.——Now I wish to know whether *there*—or (if that should not take place—) *here* I can do anything—by correspondence or otherwise to forward the objects of the Well-wishers to the Hellenic struggle.— Will *you* state this to them—and desire them to command me—if they think it could be of any service—of course—I must in no way interfere with Blaquiere— so as to give him umbrage—or to any other person.—I have great doubts—not of my own inclination—but from the circumstances already stated—whether I shall be able to go tip myself—as I fain would do—but Blaquiere seemed to think that I might be of some use—even *here*;—though *what* he did not exactly specify——If there were any things which you wished to have forwarded for the

---

[51] See Walter Scott, *The Antiquary* (1816), chapter 7, where Jonathan Oldbuck, Laird of Monkbarns, says of Sir Arthur Wardour: 'he's as absurd as womankind'.

Greeks—as Surgeons—medicines powder—and swivels &c. of which they tell me that they were in want—you would find me ready to follow any directions—and what is more to the purpose—to contribute my own share to the expence.——Will you let me hear from you—at any rate your opinion—and believe me

Ever yrs.
N B

P. S.—You may show this letter to D[ouglas] K[innair]d—or to any one you please—— including such members of the Committee as you think proper—and explain to them that I shall confine myself to following their directions—if they give me any instructions——my uncertainty as to whether I can so manage as to go personally—*prevents me from being more explicit—(I hear that Strangers are not very welcome to the Greeks—from jealousy) except as far as regards anything I might be able to do here—by obtaining good information—or affording assistance.*

[To the Earl of Blessington]

April 14th, 1823

I am truly sorry that I cannot accompany you in your ride this morning, owing to a violent pain in my face, arising from a wart to which I by medical advice applied a caustic. Whether I put too much, I do not know; but the consequence is, that not only I have been put to some pain, but the peccant part and its immediate environ are as black as if the printer's devil had marked me for an author. As I do not wish to frighten your horses, or their riders, I shall postpone waiting upon you until six o'clock, when I hope to have subsided into a more christianlike resemblance to my fellow-creatures. My infliction has partially extended even to my fingers; for on trying to get the black from off my upper lip at least, I have only transfused a portion thereof to my right hand, and neither lemon-juice nor eau de Cologne, nor any other eau, have been able as yet to redeem it also from a more inky appearance than is either proper or pleasant. But 'out, damn'd spot'[52]—you may have perceived something of the kind yesterday; for on my return, I saw that during my visit it had increased, was increasing, and

---

[52] See *Macbeth*, V. i. 33.

ought to be diminished;[53] and I could not help laughing at the figure I must have cut before you. At any rate, I shall be with you at six, with the advantage of twilight.

Ever most truly, etc.

Eleven o'clock.

P. S.,—I wrote the above at three this morning. I regret to say that the whole of the skin of about an inch square above my upper lip has come off, so that I cannot even shave or masticate, and I am equally unfit to appear at your table, and to partake of its hospitality. Will you therefore pardon me, and not mistake this rueful excuse for a 'make-believe,' as you will soon recognise whenever I have the pleasure of meeting you again, and I will call the moment I am, in the nursery phrase, 'fit to be seen.' Tell Lady B., with my compliments, that I am rummaging in my papers for a MS. worthy of her acceptation. I have just seen the younger Count Gamba; and as I cannot prevail on his infinite modesty to take the field without me, I must take this piece of diffidence on myself also, and beg your indulgence for both.

[To Edward Le Mesurier, RN]

Villa Saluzzo. Albaro. May 5th. 1823

Sir

I have received with great gratitude yr. present of the Newfoundland Dog.[54]— Few gifts could have been more gratifying—as I have ever been partial to the breed.——He shall be taken the greatest care of—and I would not part with him for any consideration;—he is already a chief favourite with the whole house.——I have the honour to be

your much obliged & very faithfl. Servt.
Noel Byron

---

[53] See John Dunning's famous motion in the House of Commons of 3 April 1780: 'That the power of the Crown has increased, is increasing, and ought to be diminished.'

[54] Byron's beloved Boatswain was also a Newfoundland (see letter of 12 August 1811). This one, Lyon, would go to Greece and accompany Byron's body back to England in 1824. See *Life*, 1192.

[John Bowring]

Genoa. May 12th. 1823

Sir,

I have great pleasure in acknowledging your letter and the honour which the Committee have done me.—I shall endeavour to deserve their confidence by every means in my power.—My first wish is to go up into the Levant in person—where I might be enabled to advance—if not the cause—at least the means of obtaining information which the Committee might be desirous of acting upon,—and my former residence in the Country—my familiarity with the Italian language (which is there universally spoken—or at least to the same extent with French in the more polished parts of the Continent) and my *not* total ignorance of the Romaic—would afford me some advantages of experience.— To this project the only objection is of a domestic nature—and I shall try to get over it,—if I fail in this—I must do what I can where I am—but it will be always a source of regret to me—to think—that I might perhaps have done more for the cause on the spot.—Our last information of Capt. Blaquiere—is from Ancona where he embarked with a fair wind for Corfu on the 15th. Ult[i]mo—he is now probably at his destination.—My last letter *from* him personally—was dated Rome—he had been refused a passport through the Neapolitan territory—and returned to strike off through Romagna for Ancona.—Little time however appears to have been lost by the delay.—

The principal material wanted by the Greeks appears to be—1st. a park of field Artillery—light—and fit for Mountain service—2dly. Gunpowder—3dly. hospital or Medical Stores——the readiest mode of transmission is—I hear—by Idra—addressed to Mr. Negri the Minister.[55]—I meant to send up a certain quantity of the two latter—no great deal—but enough for an individual to show his good wishes for the Greek success—but am pausing—because in case I should go myself—I can take them with me.—I do not mean to limit my own contribution to this merely—but—more especially if I can get to Greece myself—I should devote whatever resources I can muster of my own—to advancing the great object.——I am in correspondence with Signor Nicolas Karvellas (well known to Mr. Hobhouse) who is now at Pisa—but his latest advice merely states—that the Greeks are at present employed in organizing their *internal* government—and the details of it's administration—this

---

[55] Theodore Negris, once an Ottoman diplomat, had recently joined the Greek cause. In 1823 he became the adviser of the eastern Greek warlord, Odysseus. I assume Byron refers to the Aegean island of Hydra.

would seem to indicate *security*—but the war is however far from being terminated.—The Turks are an obstinate race—as all former wars have proved them—and will return to the charge for years to come—even if beaten—as it is to be hoped that they will be.——But in no case can the labours of the Committee be said to be in vain—for in the event even of the Greeks being subdued—and dispersed—the funds which could be employed in succouring and gathering together the remnant—so as to alleviate in part their distresses— and enable them to find or make a country (as so many emigrants of other nations have been compelled to do—) would 'bless both those who gave and those who took'[56]—as the bounty both of Justice and of Mercy.—

With regard to the formation of a brigade (which Mr. Hobhouse hints at in his short letter of this day's receipt—enclosing the one to which I have the honour to reply) I would presume to suggest but merely as an opinion—resulting rather from the melancholy experience of the brigades embarked in the Columbian Service—than from any experiment yet fairly tried in *Greece*—that the attention of the Committee had better perhaps be directed to the employment of *Officers* of experience—than the enrolment of raw British Soldiers—which latter are apt to be unruly and not very serviceable—in irregular warfare—by the side of foreigners.——A small body of good officers—especially Artillery—an Engineer—with a quantity (such as the Committee might deem requisite) of stores of the nature which Capt. Blaquiere indicated is most wanted—would I should conceive be a highly useful accession.—Officers who had previously served in the Mediterranean would be preferable—as some knowledge of *Italian* is nearly indispensable.——It would also be as well that they should be aware— that they are not going 'to rough it on a beef steak—and bottle of Port'[57]—but that Greece—never of late years—very plentifully stocked for a *Mess*—is at present the country of all kinds of *privations,*—this remark may seem superfluous—but I have been led to it—by observing that many *foreign* Officers—Italian—French and even German—(but *fewer* of the latter) have returned in disgust—imagining either that they were going up to make a party of pleasure—or to enjoy full pay—speedy promotion and a very moderate degree of duty;—they complain too of having been ill received by the Government or inhabitants, but numbers of these complainants—were mere adventurers—

---

[56] See *The Merchant of Venice*, IV. i. 184, Portia's speech on 'the quality of mercy': 'It blesseth him that gives and him that takes.'

[57] See 'Recollections of a Sea Life' ('by a Midshipman of the Last Century') in the *United Service Journal and Naval and Military Magazine* (1832), 351: 'I think it was here [an amphibious landing at Den Helder, Holland, in 1799, during the War of the Second Coalition] I first heard the old joke about a guardsman roughing it on a beef-steak and a bottle of port.' The expression was immemorial in the British armed services, and perhaps a point of antagonism between the Navy (which often went on short rations) and the Army, which could generally live off the land.

attracted by a hope of command and plunder,—and disappointed of both;—those Greeks that I have seen strenuously deny the charge of inhospitality—and declare that they shared their pittance to the last Crumb with their foreign volunteers.——

I need not suggest to the Committee the very great advantage which must accrue to Great Britain from the success of the Greeks—and their probable commercial relations with England in consequence—because I feel persuaded that the *first* object of the Committee—is their *emancipation*—<[when the?] fruitful and important [boughs?] of the tree of Liberty have been> without any interested views—but the consideration might weigh with the English people in general—in their present passion for every kind of speculation——they need not cross the American Seas—for one much better worth their while—and nearer home.—The resources even for an emigrant population—in the Greek Islands alone—are rarely to be paralleled [*sic*]—and the cheapness of every kind of not *only necessary*—but *luxury*—(that is to say—*luxury of Nature*) fruits—wine— oil—&c.—in a state of peace—are far beyond those of the Cape—and Van Dieman's land—and the other places of refuge—which the English population are searching for over the waters.——I beg that the Committee will command me in any and every way——if I am favoured with any instructions—I shall endeavour to obey them to the letter—whether conformable to my own private opinion or not——I beg leave to add personally my respect for the Gentleman whom I have the honour of addressing—and am Sir—

yr. obliged & very obedt. Sert.
Noel Byron

P. S.—The best refutation of Gell[58]*—will be the active exertions of the Committee;—I am too warm a controversialist—and I suspect that if Mr. Hobhouse has taken him in hand— there will be little occasion for me to 'encumber him with help'.*[59]*—If I go up into the Country—I will endeavour to transmit as accurate and impartial an account as circumstances will permit.——I shall write to Mr. Karvellas;—I expect intelligence from Capt. Blaquiere— who has promised me some early intimation from the seat of the provisional Government.—I gave him a letter of introduction to Lord Sydney Osborne at Corfu—but as Lord S. is in the*

---

[58] In *Narrative of a Journey in the Morea* (1823) Sir William Gell (1777–1836), classical archaeologist and topographer ('that coxcomb'; *Hobhouse Letters*, 329), had argued that were Greece to free itself from the Ottoman Empire it would only fall into the clutches of the Russians.

[59] See Samuel Johnson, 'Letter to Chesterfield' (1755).

Government Service—of course his reception could only be a cautious one—but as he is an old friend of mine—I should hope not an unkind one.——

[To John Cam Hobhouse]

Genoa. May 19th. 1823

My dear H.

I saw yr. speech which did you great credit—at full length—with Canning's civil reply—'Fas est et ab hoste *laudari*'[60]—I have yr. letter of ye. 6th. and enclose one just received from Blaquiere which will 'prate of our whereabouts'[61] to you and all friends to the Cause.—There is no obstacle to my going up—but the 'absurd womankind'[62]—and how absurd they are—as well as those under their dominion—thou knowest by all tale and history—and the experience of several of yr. friends.—It is the more absurd in this case—as the *Pope*—and her Grandfather (the oldest Count Gamba) are extremely desirous of her return to Ravenna—her father has been recalled from his exile (on the late rising account in 1820) but been positively told that he is expected to bring his daughter back with him—her husband—*would* forgive—provided that I (a very reasonable condition) did not continue his Subagent—(as the Irish call a middle man)—and her brother who is a fine bold young fellow—(as he has proved himself more than once) is even more anxious for him and me to go up to Greece than anybody else—being a thorough Liberty boy.—However I hope to prevail upon her to accompany her father to R[avenn]a.—but she has it seems a due share of 'female punctuation'—as Mrs. Malaprop calls it[63]—and stands out upon Sentiment and so forth—against the will of half the families in Romagna—with the Pope at their head—and all this after a liaison of four years and better—besides at present she has a fit of jealousy of Lady Blessington, with whom I have merely a common acquaintance as she is an authoress—and all that.——It is besides against her worldly interest in every way—for they (the Pope that is) have proposed to confirm her separate maintenance from her husband—if she will not make it up with him—but then says the Pope—and the 'Ultra

---

[60] See Ovid, *Metamorphoses*, iv. 428: 'Fas est et ab hoste *doceri*' (one can learn even from an enemy); Byron adapts as 'one can be *praised* even by an enemy': the Radical Hobhouse can be praised by the Tory statesman George Canning (1770–1827). Hobhouse had argued in the House of Commons that France should be prevented from interfering with Spanish liberalism (see letter of 22 April 1820); Canning, as foreign secretary, was sympathetic but pragmatic.

[61] See *Macbeth*, II. i. 58.　　[62] See letter of 7 April 1823.

[63] See Sheridan, *The Rivals*, II. ii. 28. Mrs Malaprop explains that 'there is often a sudden incentive impulse in love, that has a greater induction than years of domestic combination'.

Santissimo' [his holiest] you must not live naughtily with a heretic—and a C-arbonaro—and a foreigner like L[ord] B[yron].——However I *will* go——('d—n my eye—I will go ashore') an' it be possible—or do all I can in the cause—go or not.—I think of about August or earlier—for the voyage—but much would depend on Blaquiere's future letters.—If I go—I presume the Committee will give me some regular instructions of what they wish to be observed—reported or done—I will serve them as humbly as they please—Believe me

ever yrs.
N B

P. S.—I would tell you (were it not per the post) *of some queer things brooding here—I have had some propositions made to me but I answered—you must first show yourselves more capable than you did in the last events before I can take it upon me to answer either for myself—or for any prospect of assistance from the people of England.*

P. S.—Tell Douglas—that when any thing is settled—I will let him know what sum I should like to take in Credit and on what houses.—His answer was as handsome as could possibly be; and as usual with him in such matters—I will try not to abuse either the means—or the purpose for which they are intended.—

[To Edward John Trelawny]

[Genoa] June 15, 1823

My dear T.

You must have heard that I am going to Greece. Why do you not come to me? I want your aid, and am exceedingly anxious to see you. Pray come, for I am at last determined to go to Greece; it is the only place I was ever contented in. I am serious, and did not write before, as I might have given you a journey for nothing; they all say I can be of use in Greece. I do not know how, nor do they; but at all events let us go.

Yours, etc., truly,
N Byron

[To John Bowring]

July 7th. 1823

Dear Sir

We sail on the 12th. for Greece.—I have had a letter from Mr. Blaquiere too long for present transcription but very satisfactory.—The G[ree]k Government expects me without delay.——In conformity to the desire of Mr. B. and other correspondents in Greece—I have to suggest with all deference to the Committee—that a remittance of even '*ten thousand pounds only*' (Mr. B's expression) would be of the greatest service to the G[ree]k Government at present.— I have also to recommend strongly the attempt at a loan—for which there will be offered a sufficient security by deputies now on their way to England.——In the mean time I hope that the Committee will be able to do something effectual.——For my own part—I mean to carry up in cash or credits—above eight and nearly nine thousand pounds sterling—which I am enabled to do by funds which I have in Italy—and Credits from England.—Of this sum I must necessarily reserve a portion for the subsistence of my-self and Suite.—The rest I am willing to apply in the manner which seems most likely to be useful to the cause—having of course some guarantee or assurance that it will not be misapplied to any individual speculation.

If I remain in Greece—which will mainly depend upon the presumed probable utility of my presence there—and the opinion of the Greeks themselves as to it's propriety—in short—if I am welcome to them—I shall continue during my residence at least to apply such portions of my income present and future as may forward the object—that is to say—what I can spare for that purpose.— Privations—I can—or at least could once bear—abstinence I am accustomed to—and as to fatigue—I was once a tolerable traveller—what I may be now—I cannot tell—but I will try.——I await the commands of the Committee— address to Genoa—the letters will be forwarded to me—wherever I may be— by my bankers Messrs Webb and Barry.—It would have given me pleasure to have had some more defined instructions before I went—but these of course rest at the option of the Committee.—I have the honour to be

yr. obedt. and faithl. Sert.
N B

P. S.—Great anxiety is expressed for the printing press and types, &c. I have not the time to provide them, but recommend this to the notice of the Committee. I presume the types must, partly at least, be Greek: they wish to publish papers, and perhaps a Journal, probably in Romaic, with Italian translations.

[To Countess Teresa Guiccioli]

Livorno July 22d. 1823

[Note added to Pietro's letter to Teresa]

My dearest Teresa

I have but a few moments to say that we are all well—and thus far on our way to the Levant—believe that I always *love* you—and that a thousand words could only express the same idea.

ever dearest yrs.
N B

12
GREECE

August 1823–April 1824

On 3 August the Hercules *made landfall at Argostoli, Cephalonia, one of the 'Seven Islands' of Ionia then under a British administration that was hospitable, though also carefully neutral as regarded the Greek uprising. (That administration lasted from 1809 until 1862.) After a week Byron went sightseeing to neighbouring Ithaca, home of Homer's Odysseus. There he met some near-destitute Greeks escaping the mainland conflict, and brought one family, named Chalandritsanos, to Cephalonia. Their 15-year-old son Lukas eventually became a sort of page to Byron, and it is clear that the poet had deeper feelings for him, which went unrequited. (Almost his last poem, '[Love and Death]' (CPW vii. 81–2), is addressed to the boy.) By 17 August Byron was back at Argostoli, and at the beginning of September left the Hercules for a pleasant house at the village of Metaxata, a few miles south, where he would live for four months before shifting his operations to the Greek mainland at Missolonghi in the New Year of 1824.*

For some this hiatus seemed strange, not to say self-indulgent. Certainly, the Cornish corsair Trelawny lost patience, and left Cephalonia on 6 September, making his way to the eastern Greek leader, Odysseus Androutsos, in search of adventure, and taking his Scottish friend Hamilton Browne with him. Prince Alexander Mavrocordatos (1791–1865) was the official leader of the Greek Government, but his power-base was in the west of the country, and the nationalist movement was highly fissiparous. Under such circumstances Byron chose to await 'what Napoleon calls the "March of Events".—These Events however keep their march somewhat secret' (LJ xi. 22). What he waited for was some clarity on Greek leadership, but also three more specific developments: 'the Squadron in relief of Messolonghi' (the nearby port then blockaded by the Turks), the arrival of 'Mr. Parry's detachment' (bringing modern military equipment from England), and 'to receive from Malta or Zante the sum of four thousand pounds sterling' which he had advanced to the Greeks to finance the hoped-for naval squadron (LJ xi. 65). Money, he kept telling his philhellenic friends in London, was the pre-eminent sinew of war; idealism, a poor substitute—and in profoundly short supply locally in any event. He wrote to Mavrocordatos on 2 December to say that:

Greece now faces these three courses—to win her liberty, to become a Colony of the sovereigns of Europe, or to become a Turkish province.——Now she can choose one of the three—but civil war cannot lead to anything but the last two. If she envies the fate of Wallachia or of the Crimea, she can obtain it tomorrow; if that of Italy, the day after tomorrow. But if Greece wants to become forever free, true, and Independent she had better decide now, or never again will she have the chance, never again. (LJ xi. 71)

In the mean time, Byron being Byron, he put down roots. Local British officers were friendly and sympathetic, though the Governor, Charles Napier, needed to be discreet. The future historian of the Greek War, George Finlay, visited in October, as did Byron's kinsman Lord Sidney Osborne, state secretary to the Ionian Islands. (Osborne had a crucial role after Byron's death, ensuring that his body returned to England rather than rest under 'a grey Greek stone' as Byron would have preferred; LJ x. 157.) A young English doctor, Julius Millingen, arrived in November, and Hamilton Browne also came back from the East with two deputies, Andreas Luriottis and Giovanni Orlando D'Silva, for whom Byron wrote letters of introduction to old friends in England, and with whom he signed an agreement to lend the Greek Government £4,000. Later in November Colonel Leicester Stanhope, agent of the London Greek Committee and fervent Benthamite, arrived. In the first fortnight of December 1823 Stanhope and Mavrocordatos met at Missolonghi, the long-awaited squadron arrived and moved some Turkish vessels away, and the invitation came for Byron to move to the mainland. On 29 December he left Cephalonia in a fast-sailing mistico, accompanying Pietro Gamba in a much slower freighter. Adventures with Turkish forces followed, but on 3 January both ships arrived at Missolonghi: 'Crowds of soldiery, and citizens of every rank, sex, and age,' Gamba recorded, 'were assembled on the shore to testify their delight. Hope and content were pictured in every countenance. His Lordship landed in a Speziot boat, dressed in a red uniform' (Life, 1151).

The romance of the occasion brought Byron to his only truly unwise decision: to take on a troop of Souliote ne'er-do-wells as his personal brigade. These men, from the Albanian badlands Byron had visited in 1810, had no particular investment in Greek unity but a powerful interest in Byron's boxes of dollars, and it took many weeks and much wasted energy for him finally to discharge them. At the other end of the scale the Utilitarian Colonel Stanhope was occupied with starting a Greek newspaper, which Byron regarded with some exasperation. By the end of the month the Turks had re-established a blockade of the port ('sixteen sail in all'; LJ xi. 102), and the Greek squadron had turned tail. Mavrocordatos gave Byron the job of a land-based assault on Lepanto (now Naupactus), further east along the northern shore of the gulf of Corinth, in order to pressurize Turkish shipping in the region. The project was delayed and eventually abandoned—in part because Byron's heroic Souliotes refused to fight against 'stone walls', and in part because of the atrocious weather in what Byron called 'this mud-basket': 'the Dykes of Holland when broken down are the Desarts of Arabia for dryness in comparison', he wrote on 5 February (LJ xi. 107), the day on which Captain William Parry at last arrived with his artillery stores. Parry was a 'rough subject', in Byron's own words (LJ xi. 108), but a down-to-earth one by contrast with Mavrocordatos and Stanhope, and Byron came increasingly to depend on him in the months to follow. Certainly he was a welcome change from the earnestly sanctimonious continental philhellenes who clustered at Missolonghi: 'the Lempriere dictionary quotation Gentlemen', as Byron called them (LJ xi. 147).

As the military campaign foundered, George Finlay came back from eastern Greece with letters inviting Mavrocordatos and Byron to a patriotic conference at the fortress town of Salona (now Amfissa), further up the Gulf of Corinth. Byron was unenthusiastic but diplomatic, and on 19 March stated his willingness to attend. 'I have succeeded in supporting the Government of Western Greece for the present', he told Kinnaird on 21 February, 'which would otherwise have been dissolved' (LJ xi. 117), and this was perhaps Byron's greatest contribution to Greek independence: his support for a (somewhat unglamorous) constitutionalist leader rather than a warlord 'eventually made his name a unifying force in Greece' (Life, 1139), but also, of course, carried the financial and moral campaign across the Continent in a way no other person or personality was likely to have done.

On 15 February Byron suffered some kind of extended fit, perhaps brought on by nervous exhaustion. His nervous doctors insisted he be bled and then found it almost impossible to stop the process. His health—or his spirits, at least—never re-established itself, and an earthquake did nothing to settle the tension in the city, what with Turks on the water and almost anarchic Souliotes at loose on land. In March news at last arrived that a British loan to the Greek Government had been finalized in London, which signalled the beginning of the end of Byron's financial exposure: 'The Greek Cause up to this present writing', he told Kinnaird (see letter of 30 March 1824), 'hath cost me of mine own monies about thirty thousand Spanish dollars advanced, without counting my own contingent expences of every kind.'

On 21 February Stanhope went off to Athens, somewhat to Byron's relief; the poet also heard news of Ada from Lady Byron via Augusta—also a relief, as the little girl, now aged 8, had been ill the previous December. But Gamba recorded ongoing health problems: 'vertigos . . . disagreeable nervous sensations', 'frequent oppressions on his chest', and 'a disposition to faint . . . a sort of alarm without any apparent cause' (Life, 1196, 1203, 1210). These were signs of depressive anxiety he had not experienced since London in 1815, and as then, he had no one with whom to share it. As Marchand says, he 'either suppressed from his letters or moulded in the shape of hopefulness all the darker disillusionments of his days in Missolonghi' (Life, 1204). The Salona conference was postponed owing to floods, and on 9 April Byron was soaked to the skin on his daily ride. He became feverish, and within five days was suffering from intermittent delirium. The only thing he stubbornly clung to was an instinctive refusal to be bled, which Messrs Bruno and Millingen insisted was their only avenue, apart from medieval-sounding 'purgatives', 'blisters', and treatments like henbane, cream of tartar, tincture of china, senna, and castor oil. 'Do with me whatever else you please', he initially told his increasingly petrified doctors, 'but bleed me you shall not' (Life, 1215). Eventually, exhausted by lack of sleep and intestinal 'purges', he submitted to some half a dozen bleedings, via lancets and leeches. These undermined what was left of his capacity to resist infection, and he died at six o'clock on the evening of 19 April, in the arms of Tita and Fletcher.

'Let not my body be hacked, or sent to England' was Byron's last request: 'Here let my bones moulder.—Lay me in the first corner without pomp or nonsense' (Life, 1224–5). The following morning his body was subjected to a 'miserably brief' autopsy, even by early nineteenth-century standards (Life, 1233), and his body, heart, brains, and intestines were separately packaged—the lungs, which were left to Missolonghiots as a memento, thereafter disappeared. On 2 May his body left Greece, and arrived in London on 5 July. After lying in state on 9–10 July in a house on Great George Street, near the House of Lords, the body was transported to Nottingham—passing Mary Shelley at her window on Highgate Hill, and Lady Caroline Lamb at the gates of her estate in Hertfordshire. At Nottingham it lay in state *once more, before the poet was buried at St Mary Magdalene, Hucknall Torkard, alongside his mother on 16 July 1824. 'The mighty Pan is dead,' Byron wrote on 10 September 1823, in an eleven-line fragment called 'Aristomenes': 'How much died with him!'*

[To Edward Blaquiere]

Brig Hercules—Capt. Scott—Cephalonia.
August 3d. 1823

Dear Sir,

Here am I—but where are *you?*—at Corfu they say—but *why?*—I have received all yr. letters—with many thanks—what ought I to do?—I have some good will—about nine thousand pounds in Credits or Cash—with the command of more—and all from my own Income.—Of the Committee I only can say that they are full of good <will> intentions—are impatient to hear from you—and that I am a member—the Greek news is here anything but Good.—

ever yrs.
N B

P. S.—*Excuse haste I write on the binnacle of a ship by the light of a lanthorn and a Squall blowing.—*

[To Countess Teresa Guiccioli]

Argostoli de Cefalonia— 10 Agosto 1823

[Added to Pietro Gamba's letter to Teresa]

My dearest T[eres]a

We are here very well and extremely well used by all the English here.——Of Greece and the Greeks—I can say little—for every thing is as yet very uncertain on that point.—I pray you to remain tranquil, and not to believe any nonsense that you may hear; for the present we remain in this island—till we have better intelligence.—Tomorrow we are going to make a tour in the Island—for a day or two—

ever yrs. most affectly. A. A. in e.[1]

N B

[To Charles F. Barry[2]]

Cephalonia. August 10th. 1823

Dear Sir

We have been some days in harbour here to collect information on the state of the neighbouring countries before I proceeded there.—There is great uncertainty in the reports—but on the whole they are unfavourable.—The Turkish fleet is in sight from the heights of these Islands—and the greater part of the nearest coast in a state of declared and partly efficient blockade.—The Greek Government is [word illegible] (it is believed) and the Turks are trying to penetrate into the Morea [the Peloponnese].—The Greeks appear to want every thing—even *union*—for they are divided again it seems among themselves.—All this I state as stated to me—Mr. Blaquiere has left the Morea—and has been at Corfu [on] his way to England.—Notwithstanding all this I shall remain as long as I can to seek an opportunity of reaching the Main—though the hazard is considerable—and perhaps useless.—Every one has been very kind and attentive here—but of course without compromising themselves—which was not to be expected—nor would I wish it.——I speak of the English.——

Of your two Correspondents to whom you gave me letters of Credit—Sr. Carrithi is unwilling—and Mr. Corialegno (is that the name?—) willing—but hardly competent to advance money on even the best bills of exchange. Mr. Carrithi not only declined—but declared that he had no connection with the house of Webb at Genoa—and when referred to the letters for the proof that it was of the *same firm* with that of Leghorn—he replied that it was all the same—he had no connection with either.—As it is probable that the same reply may be made at Zante—and as it is not only extremely inconvenient but even hurtful to the Credit of your house—as well as to myself—I hope that you will take some step to remedy this—otherwise I do not see what is to be done—as my English

---

[1] Byron's old pet greeting: '*amico é amante in eterno*': friend and lover for ever.
[2] Barry was Byron's banker at Livorno: one of a string of bankers who took a shine to him and offered services above and beyond the call of double entry book-keeping. Barry not only found the *Hercules* for Byron, for example, but supervised its supply and outfit. The last letter we have of Byron's (9 April 1824) is to him, and Barry's later letters to Teresa Guiccioli are in the New York Public Library.

letters (which are also very Essential) only refer to Constantinople—Smyrna—Venice—and Trieste—and to your houses at Genoa and Leghorn.——Carrithi made no distinction or difficulty about Messrs Ransom's house—but merely declined acting for your own in any way—and pretended to wonder why you should expect that he should.——This might be remedied by your sending me up my Credits (English and on your house also) in dollars *here*—but with whom here could I trust a sum of thirty five thousand dollars (more or less) with a Greek I could not leave it in safety—and there are no English houses here that I know of—and yet somewhere in these Islands the Credits must be negociated—as being the nearest point to the place where I want them.—The ten thousand dollars which I have on board—are safe—but I have recurred to them—and lucky that I had them—since these fellows would not recognize your firm.—You can address to me here—to the Care of your Correspondent Corialegno (I think the name) who is extremely civil—and will advance what he can—but the truth is—I fancy—that Specie in these islands is nearly as scarce as on the Main—or at any rate that from political or other reasons—they are reluctant to accept your bills—or unused to trade as bankers.——I have engaged about forty Suliotes here (the place and people I knew formerly) but the English Government in violation of a solemn promise on their landing—*now* refuses to restore them their arms.——But nothing can be kinder than the Officers &c. have *been individually* to us—as far as their duty will permit. I say this the more readily as I neither expected—nor had cause to expect it.—Of the Greeks I shall say nothing till I can say something better—except that I am not discouraged—and am

always yrs.
N B

P. S.—If you think any part of this letter worth communicating to Mr. Kinnaird you may—as I have not yet written to England——I shall stay out as long as I can—and do all I can for these Greeks;—but I cannot exaggerate—they must expect only the truth from me both of—and to them. You may also tell Mr. K[innair]d that about the beginning of the year I may probably require an addition to my letters &c. as if these fellows give me an opportunity I will stand by them as I said before.—

[To John Cam Hobhouse]

Metaxata—Isle of Cephalonia Septr. 27th. 1823

My dear Hobhouse/

By the Hercules I wrote at some length—as you probably will know before the arrival of this which will be delivered by Mr. Peacock a Gentleman who has been in the Morea on business respecting a proposed loan to the soi disant [self-proclaimed] Govemment.—I beg you to introduce him to Mr. Bowring—his information may be very useful—as also his influence with the Society which he represented here—he is withal Gentlemanly and intelligent.——Perhaps his friends might combine with the Committee on the score of the loan to the Greeks.—

By the inclosed—(or rather *annexed*) mass of papers—you will see the present state of things.——There is private matter mixed up with the correspondence—but you and Mr. Bowring can extract the useful and public part for the information of those interested on the subject.——The fact is that matters are in great disorder.—No less than three parties—and one conspiracy going on at this moment amongst them—a few steps further and a civil war may ensue.——On all sides they are (as you perceive) trying to enlist me as a partisan—but I have hitherto declared that I can recognize only the Greek Government—without reference to the *persons* who may compose it—and that as a foreigner I have nothing to do with factions or private preferences of individuals.—I have not yet gone to the Main—because to say the truth—it does not appear that I could avoid being considered as a favourer of one party or another—but the moment I can be of any real service I am willing to go amongst them.——Mavrocordato is out—and his friends are mustering people for him wherever they can—he has now agents in the Islands &c.—but the enclosed papers will show you the state of affairs,—without further comment of mine.—When the Committee's stores come out—I will direct them to where they may be *really* wanted—which is no easy point to ascertain—for all the Agents of the G[ree]k Gov[ernmen]t are said to *peculate* to the extent of their opportunities——in short—you will learn from all quarters—but an unfavourable account of their proceedings.—For all this I do not despair—and shall continue up here watching opportunities to serve the cause—but little will be done till there is a regular force of some kind.—

ever yrs.
N B

P. S.—Tell Douglas K—that except the payments to keep up the insurances—*he must not let any monies of mine be converted to Hanson's or others purposes———(the fellow has had thousands already) but to keep everything in bank for the Credits of mine of the present and ensuing year.———Of all things to do anything amongst these fellows* money *is the most essential—and I have no wish to spare mine—though I will not allow a sixpence to be expended except to a public purpose—and under my own eye.*

List of things said to be sent but not yet arrived—and which I am anxious to have.—

Epsom Salts—
Magnesia—Calcined.
Waite's toothpowder.
Smith's tooth brushes—
Acton's Corn rubbers—
Soda powders.—

[Journal]

Metaxata—Cephalonia—Septr. 28th. 1823

On the sixteenth (I think) of July I sailed from Genoa on the English Brig Hercules—Jno. Scott Master—on the 17th. [actually 15th] a Gale of wind occasioning confusion and threatening damage to the horses in the hold—we bore up again for the same port—where we remained four and twenty hours longer and then put to sea—touched at Leghorn—and pursued our voyage by the straits of Messina for Greece—passing within sight of Elba—Corsica—the Lipari islands including Stromboli Sicily Italy &c.—about the 4th of August we anchored off Argostoli, the chief harbour of the Island of Cephalonia.——

Here I had some expectation of hearing from Capt. B[laquiere] who was on a mission from the G[ree]k Committee in London to the Gr[eek] Provisional Gov[ernmen]t of the Morea—but rather to my surprise learned that he was on his way home—though his latest letters to me from the peninsula—after expressing an anxious wish that I should come up without delay—stated further that he intended to remain in the Country for the present.——I have since received various letters from him addrest to Genoa—and forwarded to the Islands—partly explaining the cause of his unexpected return—and also (contrary to his former opinion) requesting me not to proceed to Greece *yet*—for sundry reasons, some of importance.—I sent a boat to Corfu in the hope of finding him still there—but he had already sailed for Ancona.—

In the island of Cephalonia Colonel Napier commanded in chief as Resident—and Col. Duffie the 8th. a King's regiment then forming the Garrison.[3] We were received by both those Gentlemen—and indeed by all the Officers as well as the Civilians with the greatest kindness and hospitality—which if we did not deserve—I still hope that we have done nothing to forfeit—and it has continued unabated—even since the Gloss of new acquaintance has been worn away by frequent intercourse.——We have learned what has since been fully confirmed—that the Greeks are in a state of political dissention amongst themselves—that Mavrocordato was dismissed or had resigned (L'Un vaut bien l'autre [six of one and half a dozen of the other]) and that Colocotroni with I know not what or whose party was paramount in the Morea.[4]—The Turks were in force in Acarnania &c. and the Turkish fleet blockaded the coast from Missolonghi to Chiarenza—and subsequently to Navarino——the Greek Fleet from the want of means or other causes remained in port in Hydra—Ipsara and Spezas[?]—and for aught that is yet certainly known may be there still.[5] As rather contrary to my expectations I had no advices from Peloponnesus—and had also letters to receive from England from the Committee I determined to remain for the interim in the Ionian Islands—especially as it was difficult to land on the opposite coast without risking the confiscation of the Vessel and her Contents—which Capt. Scott naturally enough declined to do—unless I would insure to him the full amount of his possible damage.——

To pass the time we made a little excursion over the mountains to Saint Eufemia—by worse roads than I ever met in the course of some years of travel in rough places of many countries.—At Saint Euphemia we embarked for Ithaca—and made the tour of that beautiful Island—as a proper pendant to the Troad which I had visited several years before.[6]—The hospitality of Capt. Knox (the resident) and his lady was in no respect inferior to that of our military friends of Cephalonia.—That Gentleman with Mrs. K. and some of their friends conducted us to the fountain of Arethusa—which alone would be worth the voyage—but

---

[3] Lieut.-Col. John Duffie was second in command of the 8th (The King's) Regiment of Foot, stationed at Cephalonia.

[4] Theodoros Kolokotronis (1774–1843), a military hero of the Peloponnese, was the leader of one of numerous nationalist factions at this period in the War of Independence.

[5] Acarnania (with Aetolia to its north) is the western shoreline of Greece with the Ionian Sea; Chiarenza is modern-day Elis on the north-western coast of the Peloponnese; Navarino (now Pylos), on the south-western coast of the Peloponnese, would be the site of a crucial naval battle in the War of Greek Independence in 1827; the islands of Idra, Psara, and Spetses are all in the Aegean region of the Mediterranean, east of the Greek mainland and at a great distance from the western end of the Gulf of Corinth.

[6] That is, Troy, where Homer's Greek king of Ithaca, Odysseus, fought the Ten Years War of the *Iliad*: Byron had visited the region in April 1810.

the rest of the Island is not inferior in attraction to the admirers of Nature;—the arts and tradition I leave to the Antiquaries,—and so well have those Gentlemen contrived to settle such questions—that as the existence of Troy is disputed—so that of Ithaca (as *Homer's Ithaca* i.e.) is not yet admitted.—Though the month was August and we had been cautioned against travelling in the Sun—yet as I had during my former experience never suffered from the heat as long as I continued in *motion*—I was unwilling to lose so many hours of the day on account of a sunbeam more or less—and though our party was rather numerous no one suffered either illness or inconvenience as far as could be observed, though one of the Servants (a Negro)[7]—declared that it was as hot as in the West Indies.—I had left our thermometer on board—so could not ascertain the precise degree.—We returned to Saint Eufemia and passed over to the monastery of Samos on the opposite part of the bay and proceeded next day to Argostoli by a better road than the path to Saint Eufemia.—The land Journey was made on Mules.——

Some days after our return, I heard that there were letters for me at Zante— but a considerable delay took place before the Greek to whom they were consigned had them properly forwarded—and I was at length indebted to Col. Napier for obtaining them for me;—*what* occasioned the demur or delay—was never explained.—I learned by my advices from England—the request of the Committee that I would act as their representative near the G[ree]k Gov[ern-men]t and take charge of the proper disposition and delivery of certain Stores &c. &c. expected by a vessel which has not yet arrived up to the present date (Septr. 28th)[8]—Soon after my arrival I took into my own pay a body of forty Suliotes under the Chiefs Photomara—Giavella—and Drako—and would prob-ably have increased the number—but I found them not quite united among themselves in any thing except raising their demands on me—although I had given a dollar per man more each month—than they could receive from the G[ree]k Gov[ernmen]t and they were destitute at the time I took them of every thing.——I had acceded too to their own demand—and paid them a month in advance.——But set on probably by some of the trafficking shopkeepers with whom they were in the habit of dealing on credit—they made various attempts at what I thought extortion—so that I called them together stating my view of the case—and declining to take them on with me—but I offered them another month's pay—and the price of their passage to Acarnania—where they could

---

[7] Byron had inherited Benjamin Lewis from Trelawny: 'his American Negro servant, who spoke French and Italian and understood horses and cooking' (*Life*, 1078).

[8] This was William Parry (1773–1859), who left England on 10 November 1823, but would not arrive at Missolonghi until 5 February 1824.

now easily go as the Turkish fleet was gone—and the blockade removed.—This part of them accepted—and they went accordingly.—Some difficulty arose about restoring their arms by the Septinsular Gov[ernmen]t but these were at length obtained—and they are now with their compatriots in Etolia or Acarnania.——

I also transferred to the resident in Ithaca—the sum of two hundred and fifty dollars for the refugees there—and I had conveyed to Cephalonia—a Moriote family who were in the greatest helplessness—and provided them with a house and decent maintenance under the protection of Messrs. Corgialegno—wealthy merchants of Argostoli—to whom I had been recommended by my Correspondents.——I had caused a letter to be written to Marco Bozzari the acting Commander of a body of troops in Acarnania[9]—for whom I had letters of recommended [sic];—his answer was probably the last he ever signed or dictated—for he was killed in action the very day after it's date—with the character of a good Soldier—and an honourable man—which are not always found together nor indeed separately.——I was also invited by Count Metaxa the Governor of Missolonghi to go over there—but it was necessary in the present state of parties that I should have some communication with the existing Gov[ernmen]t on the subject of their opinion *where* I might be—if not *most* useful—at any rate *least* obnoxious.——

As I did not come here to join a faction but a nation—and to deal with honest men and not with speculators or peculators—(charges bandied about daily by the Greeks of each other) it will require much circumspection <for me> to avoid the character of a partisan—and I perceive it to be the more difficult—as I have already received invitations from more than one of the contending parties— always under the pretext that *they* are the 'real Simon Pure'.[10]——After all—one should not despair—though all the foreigners that I have hitherto met with from amongst the Greeks—are going or gone back disgusted.—

Whoever goes into Greece at present should do it as Mrs. Fry went into Newgate[11]—not in the expectation of meeting with any especial indication of existing probity—but in the hope that time and better treatment will reclaim the present burglarious and larcenous tendencies which have followed this General Gaol delivery.—When the limbs of the Greeks are a little less stiff from the shackles of four centuries—they will not march so much 'as if they had gyves on

---

[9] Markos Botsaris (1788–1823), a Souliote partisan leader in the territory to the north of Missolonghi, died during an attack on the Turkish-held town of Karpenisi in August 1823.

[10] See Susanna Centlivre, *A Bold Stroke for a Wife* (1718), in which Colonel Feignwell pretends to be Simon Pure.

[11] See letter of 4 December 1821.

their legs'.[12]——At present the Chains are broken indeed—but the links are still clanking—and the Saturnalia is still too recent to have converted the Slave into a sober Citizen.—The worst of them is—that (to use a coarse but the only expression that will not fall short of the truth) they are such d——d liars;—there never was such an incapacity for veracity shown since Eve lived in Paradise.—One of them found fault the other day with the English language—because it had so few shades of a Negative—whereas a Greek can so modify a No—to a yes—and vice versa—by the slippery qualities of his language—that prevarication may be carried to any extent and still leave a loop-hole through which perjury may slip without being perceived.——This was the Gentleman's own talk—and is only to be doubted because in the words of the Syllogism— 'Now Epimenides was a Cretan'.[13] But they may be mended by and bye.—

Sept. 30th.

After remaining here some time in expectation of hearing from the G[ree]k G[overnmen]t I availed myself of the opportunity of Messrs B[rowne] and T[relawny] proceeding to Tripolitza—subsequently to the departure of the Turkish fleet to write to the acting part of the Legislature. My object was not only to obtain some accurate information so as to enable me to proceed to the Spot where I might be if not most safe at least more serviceable but to have an opportunity of forming a judgement on the real state of their affairs. In the mean time I hear from Mavrocordato—and the Primate of Hydra—the latter inviting me to that island—and the former hinting that he should like to meet me there or elsewhere.

[To Countess Teresa Guiccioli]

8bre. [October] 7mo. 1823

[Added to Pietro Gamba's letter to Teresa]

My dearest T.

Pietro has told you all the gossip of the Island—our earthquakes—our politics—and present abode in a pretty village.—But he has not told you the result of one of his gallantries—which I leave to him to describe.—As his opinions and mine on the Greeks are nearly similar—I need say little on the subject—I was a fool to come

---

[12] See 1 Henry IV, IV. ii. 40–1.

[13] See Titus 1: 12; source of the 'Cretan paradox', whereby a Cretan states as a fact that Cretans are always liars.

here but being here I must see what is to be done. If we were not at such a distance I could tell you many things that would make you smile—but I hope to do so at no very long period.—Pray keep well—and love me as you are beloved by yrs. ever

a. a. + + + in e.
N B

[To Augusta Leigh]

Cephalonia, 8bre. [October] 12th. 1823

My dearest Augusta

Your three letters on the subject of Ada's indisposition have made me very anxious to hear further of her amelioration.—I have been subject to the same complaint but not at so early an age—nor in so great a degree.—Besides it never affected my eyes—but rather my hearing and that only partially and slightly and for a short time.—I had dreadful and almost periodical headaches till I was fourteen—and sometimes since—but abstinence and a habit of bathing my head in cold water every morning cured me—I think—at least I have been less molested since that period.—Perhaps she will get quite well—when she arrives at womanhood—but that is some time to look forward to, though if she is of so sanguine a habit—it is probable that she may attain to that period earlier than is usual in our colder climate;—in Italy and the East—it sometimes occurs at twelve—or even earlier—I knew an instance in a noble Italian house—at ten—but this was considered uncommon.—You will excuse me touching on this topic *medically* and 'en passant' because I cannot help thinking that the determination of blood to the head so early unassisted—may have some connection with a similar tendency to earlier maturity.—Perhaps it is a phantasy.—At any rate let me know how she is—I need not say how *very* anxious I am (at this distance particularly) to hear of her welfare.——

You ask me why I came up amongst the Greeks?—it was stated to me that my so doing might tend to their advantage in some measure in their present struggle for independence—both as an individual—and as a member for the Committee now in England.—How far this may be realized I cannot pretend to anticipate— but I am willing to do what I can.—They have at length found leisure to quarrel among themselves—after repelling their other enemies—and it is no very easy part that I may have to play to avoid appearing partial to one or other of their factions.—They have turned out Mavrocordato—who was the only *Washington* or *Kosciusko* kind of man amongst them[14]—and they have not yet sent their deputies to London to treat for a loan—nor in short done themselves so much good as they might have done.—I have written to Mr. Hobhouse three several times with a budget of documents on the subject—from which he can extract all the present information for the Committee.—I have written to their Gov[ern-men]t at Tripolizza and Salamis[15]—and am waiting for instructions *where* to proceed—for things are in such a state amongst them—that it is difficult to conjecture where one could be useful to them—if at all.—However I have some hopes that they will see their own interest sufficiently not to quarrel till they have secured their national independence—and then they can fight it out among them in a domestic manner—and welcome.—You may suppose that I have something to *think* of at least—for you can have no idea what an intriguing cunning unquiet generation they are—and as emissaries of all parties come to me at present—and I must act impartially—it makes me exclaim as Julian did at his military exercises—'Oh Plato what a task for a Philosopher!'[16]——

However *you* won't think much of *my philosophy*—nor do I—'entre nous'.——

If you think this epistle or any part of it worth transmitting to Ly B[yron] you can send her a copy—as I suppose—unless she is become I know not what—she cannot be altogether indifferent as to my 'whereabouts' and *what*abouts.

I am at present in a very pretty village (Metaxata in Cephalonia) between the mountains and the Sea—with a view of Zante and the Morea—waiting for some more decisive intelligence from the provisional Gov[ernmen]t in Salamis.—— But here come some visitors.

I was interrupted yesterday—by Col. Napier and the Captain of a King's ship—now in the harbour—Col. N. is resident or Governor here and has been extremely kind and hospitable—as indeed have been all the English here.— When their visit was over a Greek arrived on business about this eternal siege of Mesalonghi (on the coast of Acarnania or Etolia) and some convoys of provisions which we want to throw in—and after this was discussed, I got on horseback (I brought up my horses with me on board and troublesome neighbours they were in blowing weather) and rode to Argostoli and back—and then I had one of my *thunder* headaches (*you* know how my head acts like a barometer when there is electricity in the air) and I could not resume till this morning.— Since my arrival in August I made a tour to Ithaca—(which you will take to be

---

[14] George Washington (1732–99) and Tadeusz Kosciuszko (1746–1817), heroic freedom fighters of the United States and Poland, respectively.

[15] Elements of the Greek Government were sited temporarily in Salamis, north-east of Athens, and Tripoli, in the central Peloponnese.

[16] See Edward Gibbon, *History of the Decline and Fall of the Roman Empire* (1781–9), chapter 19.

Ireland—but if you look into Pope's Odyssey—you will discover to be the antient name of the Isle of Wight) and also over some parts of Cephalonia.——

We are pretty well in health the Gods be thanked! by the way, who is this Dr. Tipperary or Mayo or whatever his name is? I never heard of anything of the name except an Irish County?—Laurence the Surgeon if he be the man who has been persecuted for his metaphysics—is I have heard an excellent professional man—but I wonder Ly. B should employ (so tell her) a Papist or a Sceptic.[17]— I thought that like 'douce David Deans' she would not have allowed 'a Goutte of physic to go through any of the family'[18] unless she was sure that the prescriber was a Cameronian.——

There is a clever but eccentric man here a Dr. Kennedy—who is very pious and tries in good earnest to make converts—but his Christianity is a queer one—for he says that the priesthood of the Church of England are no more Christians than 'Mahmoud or Termagant' are.[19]—He has made some converts I suspect rather to the beauty of his wife (who is pretty as well as pious) than of his theology.—I like what I have seen of him—of *her* I know nothing—nor desire to know—having other things to think about. *He* says that the dozen shocks of an Earthquake we had the other day—are a sign of his doctrine—or a judgement on his audience—but this opinion has not acquired proselytes.— One of the shocks was so prolonged—that though not very heavy—We thought the house would come down—and as we have a staircase to dismount *out* of the house (the buildings here are different from ours), it was judged expedient by the inmates (all *men* please to recollect—as if there had been females we must have helped them out or broken our bones for company) to make an expeditious retreat into the courtyard.—*Who* was *first* out the door I know not—but when I got to the bottom of the stairs I found several arrived before me—which could only have happened by their jumping out of the windows—or down *over* or from the stairs (which had no balustrade or bannisters) rather than in the regular way of descent.—The Scene was ludicrous enough—but we had several more slight shocks in the night but stuck quietly to our beds—for it would have been of no use moving—as the house would have been down first—had it been to come down at all.—

---

[17] Lady Byron had consulted a Dr Mayo about Ada's health; I assume Byron refers to William Lawrence (1783–1867), President of the Royal College of Surgeons, whose *Lectures on Physiology, Zoology and the Natural History of Man* caused a proto-Darwinian scandal when published in 1819.

[18] See Walter Scott, *The Heart of Midlothian* (1818), chapter 11.

[19] See Walter Scott, *Quentin Durward* (1823), chapter 17. Dr James Kennedy (d. 1827) was a Scots evangelical who strove doughtily to talk Byron into sharing his views; he was earnest and intelligent, but sometimes a bore. His pretty wife Hanna edited his invaluable *Conversations with Lord Byron on Religion* (1830).

There was no great damage done in the Island (except an old house or two cracking in the middle), but the soldiers on parade were lifted up as a boat is by the tide—and you could have seen the whole line waving (though no one was in motion) by the heaving of the ground on which they were drawn up.[20]—You can't complain of this being a brief letter.——

I wish you would obtain from Lady B some account of Ada's disposition—habits—studies—moral tendencies—and temper—as well as of her personal appearance for except from the miniature drawn four years ago (and she is now double that age nearly) I have no idea of even her aspect.—When I am advised on these points I can form some notion of her character—and what way her dispositions or indispositions ought [to be] treated—and though I will never interfere with or thwart her mother—yet I may perhaps be permitted to suggest—as she (Lady B.) is not obliged to follow my notions unless she likes—which is not very likely.—Is the Girl imaginative?—at *her* present age— I have an idea that I had many feelings and notions—which people would not believe if I stated them *now*—and therefore I may as well keep them to myself.——Is she social or solitary—taciturn or talkative—fond of reading or otherwise?—and what is her *tic?*—I mean her foible—is she passionate?—I hope that the Gods have made her any thing save *poetical*—it is enough to have one such fool in a family.—You can answer all this at yr. leisure—address to Genoa as usual—the letters will be forwarded better by my Correspondents there.—

yrs. ever

N B

P. S.—Tell Douglas K[innair]d I have only just got his letter of August 14th. and not only approve of his accepting a sum not under ten or twelve thousand pounds for the property in question—but also of his getting as much as can be gotten above that price.[21]

---

[20] Ionia remains prone to earthquakes; the Great Cephalonian Earthquake of 1953 almost levelled the island, and led to a mass exodus of its inhabitants.

[21] Byron's Rochdale property was sold to its leaseholder, James Dearden, for £11,000 in late October 1823.

[Byron's Loan Agreement with the Greek Deputies]

Cephalonia 1/13 November 1823[22]

[Italian text in an unknown hand—signed by Byron and the Deputies—copy of original]

From the precincts of the Magistrate of Health of Argostoli

The prov[isional] Government of Greece, having requested a loan of thirty thousand dollars from his Lordship, Lord Byron, for the sole purpose of providing prompt assistance for the needs of western Greece, as a result of the different offices [*uffizi*: functions] of the qualified authorities meeting with the afore-mentioned praiseworthy Lord, the undersigned Deputies for the loan from London, who have come to Cephalonia expressly to conclude this urgent negotiation, as the most extensive result of the office of the Legislative Body directed to the said Lord 13 October of N. 403.1803 [1823?]. have agreed as follows.——

The Noble Lord pledges himself to pay only four thousand pounds English Sterling in a bill of exchange on London to be negotiated by the Merchants Grant and Co. of Malta.——

This bill of exchange will be made out in the name of Sig[nor]e Giovanni Orlando d'Silva, one of the undersigned Deputies, and endorsed by him to the name of the here present Mr. H[amilton] Browne——Mr. Browne will go in the quickest way possible to Malta, to receive the money, and from thence to return to Cephalonia.——Mr. Browne upon his return in conjunction with the other two subjects will be obliged, as assigned by his Lordship, Lord Byron, and by the Deputies to use the aforementioned money in compliance with the wishes explained by the provisional government of Greece for the various aforementioned offices.——

The undersigned Deputies Orlando and Luriotti pledge on behalf of, and in the name of the prov[isional] Government to repay the said sum of four thousand pounds Sterling to the Noble Lord within six months of the loan from London having taken place. If within this period the sum has not been paid because the said loan has not been realized, they are obliged just the same on behalf of, and in the name of their Government to pay him the interest of four

---

[22] The Greeks still followed the Julian Calendar, twelve days behind the Gregorian Calendar, used in the West since 1582.

per cent a year from today until the loan has been paid off, which will be at his request——

Noel Byron Peer of England
Gio[van]ni Orlando
And[reas] Luriottis

[To Charles F. Barry]

10bre. [December] 11 o 1823

Dear Barry

As I have written to you lately—I shall not now trouble you at length.—The Greek external affairs go on well—the internal so so.——I expect Mavrocordato daily—I hear that I am joined in commission with him by the Gov[ernmen]t— and we are to proceed either against Prevesa or Patras.——But this is merely rumour—for I have no information of the report.—I have advanced four thousand pounds drawn directly on London—to the Greek Govt. to set their Squadron in motion.——The Deputies are gone to England to get the loan.—I have been detained here till now—(and am so *still*—) partly by expecting the approach of their fleet—and partly to negociate their monies—which has been done (or is doing rather) by Messrs Barff and Hancock—and in a handsome manner.[23]—I have not yet received the dollars from Signor Corgialegno—but he has them ready he says—on demand. In my recent letter I abused the said Corgialegno to you pretty handsomely I believe—but rather more than he deserved—I guess—as one always does in a passion.—But I was exceeding wroth with him for behaving not very well to the Greeks.—But let it pass.—

You had better sell off all the things left in Genoa or Albaro—excepting my best travelling carriage—and some few books—presents from the authors— Sylla by Jouy—the life of Gen[era]l Marceau—presented by his sister—a print of the same &c.—you will know the books by the authors' names being written by them on the blank leaves or title pages.—Also reserve a copy of 'the Calyph Vathek[']—and 'Rome Naples and Florence in 1817'[24]—and the two prints of my daughter Ada;—but those of me—and the other furniture may be disposed of.—I pray you state to Mr. K[innair]d that I have written to approve of his

---

[23] Messrs Charles Hancock (at Cephalonia) and Samuel Barff (at neighbouring Zante) were able to meet Byron's financial requirements during his time in Greece, when Charles Barry's contacts failed to come good.

[24] That is, the Gothic novel by William Beckford, *The History of the Caliph Vathek* (published anonymously in 1786), and the travel book by Stendhal (1817).

acceptance of the offer for the Rochdale Manor—and wish to hear how he has arranged the business.——You may also tell him that I expect (through the channel of your house as most convenient for myself) further credits at the beginning of the year—not that I have any *personal* or pressing occasion—but I expect them—because it is likely the expences of part of the war will fall on me chiefly (that is as an *individual*) till the deputies obtain a *national* loan.—As I have embarked in the Cause I won't quit it,—but 'in for a penny in for a pound'— I will do what I can—and all I can—in any way that seems most serviceable.— All this however renders my return rather prolonged and problematical—for who can govern circumstances?—I pray you to be of good cheer and believe me

yrs. ever
N B

[Journal]

1823 10bre. [December] 17th.

My Journal was discontinued abruptly and has not been resumed sooner— because on the day of it's former date I received a letter from my Sister Augusta—that intimated the illness of my daughter—and I had not then the heart to continue it.——Subsequently I had heard through the same channel that she was better—and since that she is well—if so—for me all is well. But although I learned this early in 9bre. [November]—I know not why—I have not continued my journal, though many things which would have formed a curious record have since occurred.—I know not why I resume it even now except that standing at the window of my apartment in this beautiful village—the calm though cool serenity of a beautiful and transparent Moonlight—showing the Islands—the Mountains—the Sea—with a distant outline of the Morea traced between the double Azure of the waves and skies—have quieted me enough to be able to write—from which (however difficult it may seem for one who has written so much publicly—to refrain) is and always has been to me—a task and a painful one——I could summon testimonies were it necessary—but my handwriting is sufficient—it is that of one who thinks much, rapidly—perhaps deeply—but rarely with pleasure.——

But—'En Avant!' [forwards!]—The Greeks are advancing in their public progress—but quarrelling amongst themselves.——I shall probably bon grè mal grè [willy-nilly] be obliged to join one of the factions—which I have hitherto strenuously avoided in the hope to unite them in one common interest.—Mavrocordato—has appeared at length with the Idriote Squadron in these seas—which apparition would hardly have taken place had I not engaged to pay two hundred thousand piastres (10 piastres per dollar being the present value—on the Greek Continent) in aid of Messolonghi—and has commenced operations somewhat successfully but not very prudently.—Fourteen (some say Seventeen) Greek Ships attacked a Turkish vessel of 12 guns—and took her——This is not quite an Ocean-Thermopylæ[25]—but n'importe [never mind]—they (*on dit* [rumour has it]) had found on board 50000 dollars—a sum of great service in their present exigencies—if properly applied.—This prize however has been made within the bounds of Neutrality on the Coast of Ithaca—and the Turks were (it is said) pursued on shore—and some slain.—All this may involve a question of right and wrong with the not very Tolerant Thomas Maitland—who is not very capable of distinguishing either. I have advanced the sum above noted to pay the said Squadron—it is not very large—but it is double that with which Napoleon the Emperor of Emperors—began his campaign in Italy, withal—vide—Las Cases—passim vol 1 (tome premier).[26]

The Turks have retired from before Messolonghi—nobody knows why—since they left provisions and ammunition behind them in quantities—and the Garrison made no sallies or none to any purpose—they never invested Messolonghi this year—but bombarded Anatoliko—(a sort of village which I recollect well having passed through the whole of that country with 50 Albanians in 1809 Messolonghi included) near the Achelous—some say that S[irota?] Pacha heard of an insurrection near Scutari[27]—some one thing some another—for my part I have been in correspondence with the Chiefs—and their accounts are not unanimous.—The Suliotes both there—here—and elsewhere—having taken a kind of liking *to*, or at least formed or renewed a sort of acquaintance *with* me—(as I have aided them and their families in all that I could according to circumstances) are apparently anxious that I should put myself forward as their Chief—(If I may so say) I would rather not for the present—because there are too many divisions and Chiefs already—but if it should appear necessary—why—as they are admitted to be the best and bravest of the present combatants—it might—or may—so happen—that I could would—should—or shall take to me the support of such a body of men—with whose aid—I think something might be done both *in* Greece and *out* of it—(for there is a good deal to put to rights in both)[.] I could maintain them

---

[25] A legendary battle of the Second Persian War (480 BC), in which a small number of Greeks held off a much larger Persian one for seven days at a tiny pass (the 'hot gates') in northern Greece.

[26] That is, Emanuel, Comte de Las Cases (1766–1842), who accompanied Napoleon to St Helena in 1815 and there recorded his (distinctly dubious) *Memorial de Ste Hélène* (1823). Napoleon made his name on his Italian campaign of 1796–7.

[27] Skoutari in Laconia (or Mani), on the extreme south of the Peloponnese.

out of my own present means (always supposing my present income and means to be permanent) they are not above a thousand—and of those not six hundred *real* Suliotes—but they are allowed to be equal (that seems a bravado though but it is in print recently) *one* to 5 European Moslems—and *ten* Asiatics—be it as it may—they are in high esteem—and my very good friends.——

A soldier may be maintained on the Mainland—for 25 piastres (rather better than two dollars a month) monthly—and find his rations out of the Country— or for *five dollars*—including his paying for his rations—therefore for between two and three thousand dollars a month—(and the dollar here is to be had for 4 and 2 pence instead of 4 and 6 pence—the price in England) I could maintain between five hundred and a thousand of these warriors for as long as necessary—and I have more means than are—(supposing them to last) [sufficient] to do so—for my own personal wants are very simple (except in horses for I am no great pedestrian) and my income considerable for any country but England—(being equal to the President's of the United States—the English Secretaries' of State's or the French Ambassador's at Vienna and the greater courts—150000 Francs—I believe) and I have hope to have sold a Manor besides for nearly 3000000 francs more—thus I could (with what We should extract according to the usages of war—also) keep on foot a respectable clan or Sept [*sic*] or tribe or horde—for some time—and as I have not any motive for so doing but the well-wishing to Greece I should hope with advantage.—

[To John Bowring]

10bre. [December] 26th. 1823

Dear Sir

Little need be added to the enclosed Which have arrived this day except that I embark tomorrow for Messolonghi.—The intended operations are detailed in the annexed documents.——I have only to request that the Committee will use every exertion to forward our views—by all it's influence and credit.—I have also to request you *personally* from myself to urge my friend and trustee Douglas Kinnaird (from whom I have not heard these four months nearly) to forward to me all the resources of my *own* we can muster for the ensuing year since it is no time to menager [economize] *purse*—or perhaps—*person*—I *have* advanced—and am advancing all that I have in hand—but I shall require all that can be got together—and (if Douglas has completed the sale of Rochdale—*that* and my years income for next year ought to form a good round sum) as you may perceive that there will be little cash of their own amongst the Greeks—(unless they get the loan) it is the more necessary that those of their friends who have any should risk it.——

The Supplies of the Committee are some useful—and all excellent in their kind—but occasionally hardly *practical* enough—in the present state of Greece—for instance the Mathematical instruments are thrown away—none of the Greeks know a problem from a poker—we must conquer first—and plan afterwards.—The use of the trumpets too may be doubted—unless Constantinople were Jericho—for the Hellenists have no ear for Bugles—and you must send us somebody to listen to them.[28]—We will do our best—and I pray you to stir your English hearts at home to more *general* exertion—for my part—I will stick by the cause while a plank remains which can be honourably clung to—if I quit it—it will be by the Greek's conduct—and not the holy Allies or the holier Mussulmans—but let us hope better things.

ever yrs.
N B

P. S.—As much of this letter as you please is for the Committee—the rest may be 'entre nous'.——

P. S.—I am happy to say that Colonel Leicester Stanhope and myself are acting in perfect harmony together—he is likely to be of great service both to the cause and to the Committee, and is publicly as well as personally a very valuable acquisition to our party on every account. He came up (as they all do who have not been in the country before) with some high-flown notions of the sixth form at Harrow or Eton, &c.; but Col. Napier and I set him to rights on those points, which is absolutely necessary to prevent disgust, or perhaps return; but now we can set our shoulders soberly to the wheel, without quarrelling with the mud which may clog it occasionally.

I can assure you that Col. Napier and myself are as decided for the cause as any German student of them all; but like men who have seen the country and human life, there and elsewhere, we must be permitted to view it in its truth, with its defects as well as beauties,—more especially as success will remove the former gradually.

N B

[28] Byron was part-amused, part-exasperated, by the strange things the London Committee and its Utilitarian brethren thought the Greeks needed—including printing presses and newspapers, as well as mathematical and musical instruments. See his reference to Stanhope's 'high-flown notions', below.

[To Douglas Kinnaird]

10bre. [December] 27th. 1823

Dear Douglas

I am embarking for Missolonghi—Bowring can tell you the rest, for yr. despatches will go together.—I am passing 'the Rubicon'—recollect that for God's sake—and the sake of Greece.—You must let me have all the means and credit of mine that we can *muster* or *master*—and that immediately—and I must do my best to the shirt—and to the skin if necessary.—Stretch my credit and anticipate my means to their fullest extent—if Rochdale sale has been completed I can keep an army *here*, aye, and perhaps command it.

Send me forthwith all the credits you can, and tell the Committee that they should 'enact a man and put money in their purse.'[29] Why, man! if we had but 100,000 *l* sterling in hand, we should now be halfway to the city of Constantine. But the Gods give us joy! 'En avant', or as the Suliotes shout in their war cry— 'Derrah! Derrah!' which being interpreted, means 'On—On—On!'

Yours ever
N B

[To Colonel the Hon. Leicester Stanhope]

Scrofer (or some such name), on board a
Cephaloniote Mistico, Dec. 31st, 1823

My Dear Stanhope,

We are just arrived here, that is, part of my people and I, with some things, &c. and which it may be as well not to specify in a letter (which has a risk of being intercepted, perhaps);—but Gamba, and my horses, negro, steward, and the press, and all the Committee things, also some eight thousand dollars of mine (but never mind, we have more left, do you understand?) are taken by the Turkish frigates, and my party and myself, in another boat, have had a narrow escape last night (being close under their stern and hailed, but we would not answer, and bore away), as well as this morning. Here we are, with the sun and clearing weather, within a pretty little port enough; but whether our Turkish

---

[29] See *Richard III*, V. vi. 2 ('The King enacts more wonders than a man') and *Othello*, I. iii. 339 ('Put money in thy purse').

friends may not send in their boats and take us out (for we have no arms except two carbines and some pistols, and, I suspect, not more than four fighting people on board) is another question, especially if we remain long here, since we are blocked out of Messolonghi by the direct entrance.

You had better send my friend George Drake (Draco), and a body of Suliotes, to escort us by land or by the canals, with all convenient speed. Gamba and our Bombard are taken into Patras, I suppose;[30] and we must take a turn at the Turks to get them out: but where the devil is the fleet gone?—the Greek, I mean; leaving us to get in without the least intimation to take heed that the Moslems were out again.

Make my respects to Mavrocordato, and say, that I am here at his disposal. I am uneasy at being here; not so much on my own account as on that of a Greek boy with me, for you know what his fate would be;[31] and I would sooner cut him in pieces and myself too than have him taken out by those barbarians. We are all very well.

N B

The Bombard was twelve miles out when taken; at least, so it appeared to us (if taken she actually be, for it is not certain); and we had to escape from another vessel that stood right between us and the port.

[To Charles Hancock]

Messolonghi. J[anuar]y. 13th. 1824

Dear S[igno]r. H.

Many thanks for yrs. of ye 5th. ditto to Muir for his.[32]—You will have heard that Gamba and my vessel got out of the hands of the Turks safe and intact—nobody knows well how or why—for there is a mystery in the story somewhat

---

[30] So they were; and because Gamba's ship was flying a neutral flag, the Turks promptly released it—without knowing, presumably, for whom its cargo was intended. See letter of 23 January 1824.

[31] This is Lukas Chalandritsanos; Byron was worried he would be debauched if captured. Apart from that anxiety, Byron thoroughly enjoyed this adventure: 'We are here . . . for the fifth day—without taking our clothes off', he wrote proudly, 'and sleeping on deck in all weathers—but are all very well and in good spirits' (*LJ* xi. 88).

[32] Henry Muir, Health Officer at Argostoli, had also befriended Byron, and shared his scepticism concerning James Kennedy's evangelicalism.

melodramatic—Captain Valsamachi—has I take it spun a long yarn by this time in Argostoli;[33]—I attribute their release entirely to Saint Dionysius of Zante— and the Madonna of the Rock near Cephalonia.—The adventures of my separate bark were also not finished at Dragomestre.—We were conveyed out by some Greek Gunboats—and found the Leonidas brig of war at Sea to look after us.— But blowing weather coming on we were driven on the rocks—*twice*—in the passage of the Scrophes—and the dollars had another narrow escape.[34]—Two thirds of the Crew got ashore over the bowsprit—the rocks were rugged enough—but water very deep close in shore—so that she was after much swearing and some exertion got off again—and away we went with a third of our crew leaving the rest on a desolate island—where they might have been now—had not one of the Gunboats taken them off—for we were in no condition to take them off again.—Tell Muir that Dr. Bruno did not show much fight on the occasion—for besides stripping to the flannel waistcoat— and running about like a rat in an emergency—when I was talking to a Greek boy (the brother of the G[ree]k Girls in Argostoli) and telling him the fact that there was no danger for the passengers whatever there might be for the vessel— and assuring him that I could save both him and myself—without difficulty (though he can't swim) as the water though deep was not very rough—the wind *not* blowing *right* on shore—(it was a blunder of the Greeks who missed stays) the Doctor exclaimed—'Save *him* indeed—by G—d—save *me* rather—I'll be first if I can' a piece of Egotism which he pronounced with such emphatic simplicity—as to set all who had leisure to hear him laughing—and in a minute after—the vessel drove off again after striking twice—she sprung a small leak— but nothing further happened except that the Captain was very nervous after- wards.—To be brief—we had bad weather almost always—though not contrary—slept on deck in the wet generally—for seven or eight nights—but never was in better health (I speak personally) so much so that I actually bathed for a quarter of an hour on the evening of the fourth inst. in the sea—(to kill the fleas and others) and was all the better for it.——We were received at Messo- longhi with all kinds of kindness and honours—and the sight of the fleet saluting &c. and the crowds and different costumes was really picturesque.— We think of undertaking an expedition soon—and I expect to be ordered with

---

[33] Valsamachi skippered Gamba's vessel, and it seems he had once saved the life of a Turkish captain, which perhaps explained their good treatment in Patras.
[34] Dragomestre is the bay below modern Astakos, and Skrofia is a headland coming out to meet the island of Oxeia, approximately 20 miles due west of Missolonghi.

the Suliotes to join the army—all well at present—we found Gamba already arrived—and every thing in good condition.—Remembrance to all friends—

yrs. ever

N B [...]

[To Yusuff Pasha]

J[anuar]y 23d. 1824

Highness—A ship with some of my friends and servants on board was brought under the turrets of a Turkish frigate. It was then released on the order of Your Highness. I thank you, not for having released the ship—since it had a neutral flag and was under English protection—so that no one had the right to detain it—but for having treated my friends with the utmost courtesy—while they were at your disposition.——In the hope of performing an action not displeasing to Your Highness I have asked the Greek Government here—to place four Mussulman prisoners in my hands.—I now release them to Your Highness in recompense, as far as is possible, for your Courtesy.—They are sent without conditions—but if the circumstances could win a place in your memory I would only beg Your Highness to treat with humanity any Greek who may be [captured?] or fall into the hands of the Mussulmans—Since the horrors of war are sufficient in themselves without adding cold-blooded ruthlessness on either side.—

I have the honour to be etc. etc. etc.

[To Prince Alexander Mavrocordatos[35]]

Missolonghi, February 5, 1824

Prince

We have the honour of informing you that the Greek Committee of England has sent a complete laboratory to Greece, with all the necessary craftsmen, which is now being established in Missolonghi. The Committee by this

---

[35] Mavrocordatos (1791–1865) came from a distinguished family of Phanariot (that is, Istanbul-based) Greeks, and carried the courtesy title of Prince as a regional administrator in the Ottoman Empire. In 1818 he went into exile, studied at the University of Padua, and met the Shelley circle in Pisa. He returned to Greece in 1821, and in 1822 was named President of the Executive of the National Assembly. He was identified with the prolonged siege of Missolonghi, and went into temporary retirement when the city finally fell in 1826.

measure, as in all others, hopes to advance the knowledge, and thereby the liberty of Greece.

This laboratory is capable of preparing and manufacturing all war materials for land as well as for maritime service. It can construct ships of every type, cast cannons, mortars, bullets, and Shrapnel bombs, construct [artillery] carriers of every sort, make powder, Congreve rockets, and every sort of incendiary fire.

The Director, or fire master can give instructions for the use of artillery, for throwing bombs and rockets, and for the whole craft of producing every material of war. This laboratory can be considered not only a useful source for all the needs of war, but also a model, and a school.

Having made a sketch of the character of this equipment; we wish to inform you that all of this is only for the public benefit, therefore we beg you to point out to us at once in what way this factory might be of service to you. We also would like to know which articles you consider necessary to prepare for the expedition that is about to take place. And in awaiting your prompt reply, we declare ourselves with the utmost esteem

Your Excellency's most devoted Servants
Noel Byron
Leicester Stanhope

[Note on Suliotes]

Fe[bbrai]o 15 o 1824

Having tried in vain at every expence—considerable trouble—and some danger to unite the Suliotes for the good of Greece—and their own—I have come to the following resolution.—

I will have nothing more to do with the Suliotes—they may go to the Turks or—the devil <but if> they may cut me into more pieces than they have dissensions among them, sooner than change my resolution—[36]

For the rest I hold my means and person at the disposal of the Greek Nation and Government the same as before.

[36] The Souliotes had sought to extort money from Byron by demanding that nearly half their number be raised in rank. (He was bankrolling a brigade of 500 of them.) On 21 February he effectively paid them to leave town, but even then they kept returning.

[Journal]

Upon February 15th—(I write on the 17th. of the same month) I had a strong shock of a Convulsive description but whether Epileptic—Paralytic—or Apoplectic is not yet decided by the two medical men who attend me—or whether it be of some other nature (if such there be) it was very painful and had it lasted a moment longer must have extinguished my mortality—if I can judge by sensations.— I was speechless with the features much distorted—but *not* foaming at the mouth—they say—and my struggles so violent that several persons—two of whom—Mr. Parry the Engineer—and my Servant Tita the Chasseur are very strong men—could not hold me—it lasted about ten minutes—and came on immediately after drinking a tumbler of Cider mixed with cold water in Col. Stanhope's apartments.—This is the first attack that I have had of this kind to the best of my belief. I never heard that any of my family were liable to the same—though my mother was subject to *hysterical* affections. Yesterday (the 16th.) Leeches were applied to my temples. I had previously recovered a good deal—but with some feverish and variable symptoms;—I bled profusely—and as they went too near the temporal Artery—there was some difficulty in stopping the blood—even with the Lunar Caustic—this however after some hours was accomplished about eleven o'clock at night—and this day (the 17th.) though weakly I feel tolerably convalescent.——

With regard to the presumed cause of this attack—as far as I know there might be several—the state of the place and of the weather permits little exercise at present;—I have been violently agitated with more than one passion recently—and a good deal occupied politically as well as privately—and amidst conflicting parties—politics—and (as far as regards public matters) circumstances;—I have also been in an anxious state with regard to things which may be only interesting to my own private feelings—and perhaps not uniformly so temperate as I may generally affirm that I was wont to be—how far any or all of these may have acted on the mind or body of One who had already undergone many previous changes of place and passion during a life of thirty six years I cannot tell—nor——but I am interrupted by the arrival of a report from a party returned from reconnoitring a Turkish Brig of War just stranded on the Coast—and which is to be attacked the moment we can get some guns to bear upon her.—I shall hear what Parry says about it—here he comes.—

[General Orders to the Suliotes]

Messalonghi. 17th Feb[ruar]y 1824

The 1st. Reg[imen]t of Suliotes will parade for service this Morning & march under the orders of the Count Pietro Gamba to their place of destination.

The Artillery Company under the Command of Captain Parry will parade immediately for fatigue Duty & actual Service—

It is expected that every Officer, Non-Commissioned Officer, Soldier, & Civilian, will obey all orders given with promptitude & alacrity—

Generale
Noel Byron
Col. of the 1st Regt. of Suliotes
&
Com[mand]er in Chief of Western Greece

[To Augusta Leigh]

Messolonghi. F[ebruar]y. 23d. 1824

My dearest Augusta

I received a few days ago your and Lady B's report of Ada's health with other letters from England for which I ought to be and am (I hope) sufficiently thankful—as they were of great comfort and I wanted some—having been recently unwell—but am now much better—so that you need not be alarmed.——You will have heard of our journeys—and escapes—and so forth—perhaps with some exaggeration—but it is all very well now—and I have been some time in Greece which is in as good a state as could be expected considering circumstances—but I will not plague you with politics—wars—or *earthquakes*—though we had another very smart one three nights ago which produced a scene ridiculous enough as no damage was done except to those who stuck fast in the scuffle to get first out of the doors or windows—amongst whom some recent importations fresh from England—who had been used to quieter elements—were rather squeezed in the press for precedence.——I have been obtaining the release of about nine and twenty Turkish prisoners—men women and children—and have sent them at my own expence home to their friends—but one a pretty little girl of nine years of age—named Hato or Hatageé has expressed a strong wish to remain with me[37]—or under my care—and I have nearly determined to adopt her—if I thought that Lady B would let her come to England as a Companion to Ada (they are about the same age) and we could easily provide for her—if not I can send her to Italy for education.—She is very lively and quick and with great black Oriental eyes—and Asiatic features— all her brothers were killed in the revolution—her mother wishes to return to her husband who is at Prevesa—but says that she would rather entrust the Child to me—in the present state of the Country——her extreme youth and sex have hitherto saved her life—but there is no saying—what might occur in the course of the *war* (and of *such* a war) and I shall probably commit her to the charge of some English lady in the Islands for the present.—The Child herself has the same wish—and seems to have a decided character for her age;—you can mention this matter if you think it worth while—I merely wish her to be respectably educated and treated—and if my years and all things be considered—I presume it would be difficult to conceive me to have any other views.——

With regard to Ada's health—I am glad to hear that it is so much better—but I think it right that Lady B should be informed and guard against it accordingly—that her description of much of her disposition and tendencies very nearly resembles that of my *own* at a similar age—except that I was much more impetuous.—Her preference of *prose* (strange as it may now seem) *was* and indeed *is* mine—(for I hate *reading* verse—and always did) and I never invented anything but 'boats—ships' and generally something relative to the Ocean—I showed the report to Colonel Stanhope—who was struck with the resemblance of *parts* of it to the *paternal* line—even *now*.—But it is also fit—though unpleasant—that I should mention—that my recent attack and a very severe one—had a strong appearance of *Epilepsy—why*—I know not—for it is late in life—it's first appearance at thirty-six—and as far as *I know*—it is *not hereditary*— and it is that it may not *become* so—that you should tell Lady B to take some precautions in the case of Ada;—my attack has not returned—and I am fighting it off with abstinence and exercise and thus far with success—if merely casual it is all very well.

[No signature in MS.]

[37] Byron discovered this little Turkish girl and her mother being protected by Dr Millingen at his house in Missolonghi.

[To John Murray]

Messolonghi.—F[ebruar]y. 25th. 1824

I have heard from Mr. Douglas K[innair]d that you state 'a report of a satire on Mr. Gifford having arrived from Italy—*said* to be written by *me!*—but that *you* do not believe it.'—I dare say you do not nor any body else I should think— whoever asserts that I am the author or abettor of anything of the kind on Gifford—lies in his throat.—I always regarded him as my literary father—and myself as his prodigal son; if any such composition exists it is none of mine—— *you* know as well as any body upon *whom* I have or have not written—and *you* also know whether they do or did not deserve that same——and so much for such matters.—You will perhaps be anxious to hear some news from this part of Greece—(which is the most liable to invasion) but you will hear enough through public and private channels on that head.—I will however give you the events of a week—mingling my own private peculiar with the public for we are here jumbled a little together at present. On Sunday (the 15th. I believe) I had a strong and sudden convulsive attack which left me speechless though not motionless—for some strong men could not hold me—but whether it was epilepsy—catalepsy—cachexy—apoplexy—or what other *exy*—or *opsy*—the Doctors have not decided—or whether it was spasmodic or nervous &c.—but it was very unpleasant—and nearly carried me off—and all that—on Monday— they put leeches to my temples—no difficult matter—but the blood could not be stopped till eleven at night (they had gone too near the temporal Artery for my temporal safety) and neither Styptic nor Caustic would cauterize the orifice till after a hundred attempts.—

On Tuesday a Turkish brig of war ran on shore—on Wednesday—great preparations being made to attack her though protected by her Consorts—the Turks burned her and retired to Patras—on thursday a quarrel ensued between the Suliotes and the Frank Guard at the Arsenal——a Swedish Officer was killed—and a Suliote severely wounded—and a general fight expected—and with some difficulty prevented—on Friday the Officer buried—and Capt. Parry's English Artificers mutinied under pretence that their lives were in danger and are for quitting the country——they may.—On Saturday we had the smartest shock of an earthquake which I remember (and I have felt thirty slight or smart at different periods—they are common in the Mediterranean) and the whole army discharged their arms—upon the same principle that savages beat drums or howl during an eclipse of the Moon—it was a rare Scene altogether—if you had but seen the English Johnnies who had never been out of a Cockney workshop before! or will again if they can help it—and on Sunday we heard that the Vizir is come down to Larissa with one hundred and odd thousand men.——

In coming here I had two escapes one from the Turks (one of my vessels was taken—but afterwards released) and the other from shipwreck—we drove twice on the rocks near the Scrophes—(Islands near the Coast). I have obtained from the Greeks the release of eight and twenty Turkish prisoners—men women and children—and sent them to Patras and Prevesa—at my own charges—one little Girl of nine years old—who prefers remaining with me—I shall (if I live) send with her mother probably to Italy or to England—and adopt her.—Her name is Hato—or Hatagée—she is a very pretty lively child—all her brothers were killed by the Greeks—and she herself and her mother merely spared by special favour—and owing to her extreme youth—she was then but five or six years old. My health is now better and [I] ride about again—My office here is no sinecure—so many parties—and difficulties of every kind—but I will do what I can—Prince Mavrocordato is an excellent person and does all in his power— but his situation is perplexing in the extreme—still we have great hopes of the success of the contest.—You will hear, however more of public news from plenty of quarters—for I have little time to write—believe me

yrs. &c. &c.
N Bn

[To Countess Teresa Guiccioli]

March 17th, 1824

[At the end of a letter from Pietro Gamba to Teresa[38]]

My dearest T.

The Spring is come—I have seen a Swallow to-day—and it was time—for we have had but a wet winter hitherto—even in Greece.—We are all very well, which will I hope—keep up your hopes and Spirits. I do not write to you letters about politics—which would only be tiresome, and yet we have little else to write about—except some private anecdotes which I reserve for 'viva voce'

---

[38] This is Byron's last letter to Teresa. Her brother would accompany Byron's body to England, attend his funeral, and then return to Greece, where he died of a fever in 1827, aged 26.

when we meet—to divert you at the expense of Pietro and some others.—The Carnival here is curious—though not quite so elegant as those of Italy.——

We are a good many foreigners here of all Nations—and a curious mixture they compose.——I write to you in English without apologies—as you say you have become a great proficient in that language of birds.——To the English and Greeks—I generally write in Italian—from a Spirit of contradiction, I suppose—and to show that I am Italianized by my long stay in your Climate.——Salute Costa[39] and his lady—and Papa and Olimpia and Giulia and Laurina—and believe me—dearest T. t. A. A.—in E.

N Bn

[To Colonel Leicester Stanhope]

Messolonghi. March 19th. 1824

My dear Stanhope

P[rince] Mavrocordato and myself will go to Salona to meet Ulysses—and you may be very sure that P. M. will accept any proposition for the advantage of Greece.—Parry is to answer for himself on his own articles—if I was to interfere with him—it would only stop the whole progress of his exertions—and he is really doing all that can be done without more aid from the Govt. which neither works nor pays.—What can be spared will be sent—but I refer you to Capt. Humphries' report—and to C[ount] Gamba's letter for details upon all subjects.—In the hope of seeing you soon—and deferring much that [will be to?] be said till then—believe me

ever and truly yrs.
N Bn

P. S.—your two letters (to me) are sent to Mr. Barff as you desire—pray Remember me particularly to Trelawny whom I shall be very much pleased to see again.

---

[39] Teresa was staying and studying with Paolo Costa, an academic at the University of Bologna.

[To Samuel Barff]

March 22d. 1824

Dear Sir

Mr. Dunn has received in the course of my stay in Tuscany and the Genoese territory some thousand dollars of mine—always paid without demur or delay—because I made it a rule to have no long accounts in Italy, however high the prices.[40]—His *present* pretension to a much smaller sum is however of a different kind—being an affair (not very creditable to him nor to the persons whom he recommended) of the letting of a house—the demand for which I told him when I saw him at Leghorn—I would certainly not comply with for some time to come at any rate—as I was neither satisfied with the *account* nor the *amount.*—At the same time I then and there paid him a much larger sum on other accounts—which I conceived to be fairer—as I had frequently done before.—I will not accept *this* bill—and I request that you will say as much—and restate what I have stated to you,—as before to *himself* repeatedly.——I will take care however that he shall be no sufferer eventually—but for the present he may wait—as he can well afford; the transaction was one in which he involved me—with a Scoundrel—whom he well knew to be so and whom he ought to have made known as such to me.——He never had to wait for any account of mine *before*—nor should he *now*—had he treated me well in the business,—as it is—he must have patience,—it will be a lesson to him—how he allows men who have used him fairly—and dealt with him considerably—(as I have) to be cheated through his intervention.——You will in consequence remark that I have requested you not to make any advance to him for the present on my accompt.——I appeal to himself—to say whether I have not always dealt with him honourably and readily—and I happen to have his book with me as a voucher.—You will have heard that the Alarm of the Plague has subsided here.——

If the Greek Deputies (as seems probable) have obtained the loan——the sums I have advanced may perhaps be repaid—but it would make no great difference—as I should still spend them in the Cause—and more to boot—— though I should hope to better purpose than paying off arrears of fleets that sail away, and Soldiers that won't march, which, *they say*—what has hitherto been advanced—has been employed in.—But that was not my affair—but of those

---

[40] Henry Dunn (1776–1867), English merchant at Livorno, who carried out various services for Byron, particularly relating to Shelley's cremation. His bills for goods Byron was prepared to meet immediately; bills for house rental (the Villa Dupuy at Montenero) needed further itemization, especially as Byron had entered into a lawsuit against the owner, Francesco Dupuy.

who had the disposal of affairs—and I could not decently say to them—you shall do so and so—because &c. &c. &c.——In a few days—P Mavrocordato and myself—with a considerable escort intend to proceed to Salona at the request of Ulysses and the Chiefs of Eastern Greece—to concert if possible a plan of Union between Western and Eastern Greece—and to take measures offensive and defensive for the ensuing Campaign.——M[avrocordato] is *almost* recalled by the *new* Govt. to the Morea—(to take the lead I rather think) and they have written to propose to me to go either to the Morea with him—or to take the general direction of affairs in this quarter—with General Londo, and any other I may choose to form a Council.—A[ndre]a Londo is my old friend and acquaintance since we were lads in Greece together.[41]—It would be difficult to give a positive answer till the Salona meeting is over—but I am willing to serve them in any capacity they please—either commanding or commanded—it is much the same to me—as long as I can be of any presumed use to them.— Excuse haste.—It is late—and I have been several hours on horseback—in a country so miry after the rains—that every hundred yards brings you to a brook or a ditch—of whose depth—width—colour—and contents—both my horses and their riders have brought away many tokens.—

Yrs. Ever &c.

N Bn [...]

[To Douglas Kinnaird]

Messalonghi, March 30th, 1824

My Dear Douglas,

Signor Zaimi, the third Greek Deputy, will present this to you;[42] and in his behalf I bespeak good hospitality and usual kindness. The other Deputies here can, could or should have presented an introductory epistle to you, as well as to others, on their arrival. The same letter enclosed also a copy of the paper signed by themselves and drawn up in their own way—on my advancing 4000 £ Sterling to the Greek Govt. which was (by their own express wish) to be repaid

---

[41] Byron and Hobhouse had stayed with Andreas Londos (1786–1846), then a governor of the Morea under the Turks, at Vostitza on their way to Athens in December 1809. Despite that position, he joined the Greek cause in 1821 and became a military hero in the early years of the conflict.

[42] Andreas Zaimis (1791–1840) 'was associated', Marchand remarks, 'with Andreas Londos in the so-called second civil war (November, 1824) whose object seemed to be to bring into their own sphere the proceeds of the English loan'. Clearly there was no unified approach in Greece as to the employment of those funds.

in the event of their obtaining a national loan in London, which it should seem that they have accomplished. I have also to apprize you that I have cashed for P Mavrocordato bills to the amount of 550 £ Sterling, which bills are drawn on Mr. Bowring and directed to you. P Mavrocordato says that SS[ignori]. Orlando and Luriotti have assets to supply the needful to the said Mr. Bowring, a fact which you will duly ascertain, or otherwise the 550 £ Sterling, monies advanced by me on the specified bills may be in some sort likely to hitch in their progress to payment.

The Greek Cause up to this present writing hath cost me of mine own monies about thirty thousand Spanish dollars *advanced*, without counting my own contingent expences of every kind. It is true, however, that every thing would have been at a stand still in Messalonghi if I had not done so. Part of this money, more particularly the 4000 £ advanced, and guaranteed by the G[ree]k Deputies is, or ought to be, repaid. To this you will look, but I shall still spend it in the Cause, for I have some hundred men under my command, regularly paid and pretty men enough.

I have written to you repeatedly, imploring you to sell out of the Funds while they are high, and to take four per cent.—or any per cent.—on landed security for the monies.

I have also been, and am, anxious to hear how you have succeeded with Rochdale, the Kirkby Arrears, the new publications, the settling the lawsuits, etc., etc., etc., and always concluding by a request for all possible credits to the extent of my resources, for I must do the thing handsomely.

I have been very unwell, but am supposed to be better, and almost every body else has been ill too—Parry and all, tho' he is a sort of hardworking Hercules. We have had strange weather and strange incidents—natural, moral, physical, martial and political, all which you will hear of perhaps, truly or falsely, from other quarters—I can't gossip just now. I am called to a Congress at Salona with P. Mavrocordato to meet Ulysses and the Eastern Chiefs on State affairs, and on the opening Campaign. What the result is likely to be I cannot say. The General Govt. have assured me the direction of this province, or to join them in the Morea. I am willing to do anything that may be useful.

We were to have besieged Lepanto, but the Suliotes did not like the service 'against Stone walls,' and have had a row besides with some foreigners, in which blood was spilt on both sides, so that that scheme was postponed. Capt. Parry is doing all that circumstances will permit in his department, and indeed in many others, for he does *all* that is done here, without any aid except the Committee's and mine, for the Gk. local Govt. have not a *sou, they* say, and are in debt besides. I have two hundred and twenty five regulars and irregulars in my pay—and had five hundred of the latter, but when they quarrelled amongst themselves, and tried to heighten their pretensions besides, I boomed them off; and by dint of so doing, and turning restive when fair means would not do, the rest are reduced to very good order, and the *regulars* have all along behaved very well, upon the whole—as well as any other troops anywhere. Six Guns belong to this auxiliary Corps of Artillery, which, by the way, is the only *regularly paid* corps in Greece. The Govt. only give them rations—and those reluctantly: they have mutinied twice on account of bad bread, and really with cause, for it was quite unmasticable; but we have gotten a new Commissary, and a Baker, instead of the Bricklayer who furnished the former loaves, apparently,—and with not very good bricks neither. Yesterday there was a Court Martial on a man for stealing; the German Officers wanted to flog, but I positively prohibited anything of the kind: the culprit was dismissed the service—publicly, and conducted through the town to the Police Office to have him punished according to the Civil law. Same day, one amicable officer challenged two others; I had the parties put under arrest until the affair was accommodated: if there is any more challenging, I will call them all out and wafer one half of them.

Matters, however, go on very tolerably, and we expect them to mend still further now that the Greeks have got their loan, and may be organized. Believe me,

Ever your and truly,
N[oe]l B[yro]n

[To the Earl of Clare]

Messolonghi March 31st. 1824

My dearest Clare

This will be presented to you by a live Greek Deputy—for whom I desiderate and solicit your countenance and good will.—I hope that you do not forget that I always regard you as my dearest friend—and love you as when we were Harrow boys together—and if I do not repeat this as often as I ought—it is that I may not tire you with what you so well know.——I refer you to Signor Zaimi the Greek Deputy—for all news public and private.—He will do better than an epistle in this respect.——I was sorry to hear that Dick had exported a married woman from Ireland not only on account of morals but monies—I trust that the Jury will be considerate. I thought that Richard looked sentimental when I saw him at Genoa—but little expected what he was to land in.[43]—Pray

---

[43] Clare's younger brother Richard Hobart Fitzgibbon succeeded Byron's beloved Harrow school friend as third Earl of Clare in 1851. He married in 1825, so clearly this Irish shenanigan was not a lasting one.

who *is* the Lady? the papers merely inform us by dint of Asterisks that she is Somebody's wife—and has Children—and that Dick—(as usual) was 'the intimate friend of the confiding husband[']. It is to be hoped that the jury will be bachelors—pray take care of *yourself*—Clare—my dear—for in some of your letters I had a glimpse of a similar intrigue of yours—have a care of an Eclât—ye Irish Juries lay it on heavy—and then besides you would be fixed for life—with a *second-hand* Epouse—whereas I wish to see you lead a virgin Heiress from Saville Row to Mount-Shannon.—Let me hear from you at your best leisure—and believe me ever and truly my dearest Clare—

yrs.
Noel Byron

[To Charles F. Barry]

April 9th. 1824

[At the end of a letter of Pietro Gamba to Barry]

Dear Barry

The Account up to 11th. July—was 40-541-&c. Genoese livres in my favour—since then I have had a letter of Credit of Messrs Webb for 60.000 Genoese livres—for which I have drawn—but how the account stands *exactly*—you do not state—the balance will of course be replaced by my London Correspondents—referring more particularly to the Hon[oura]ble Douglas Kinnaird who is also my Agent—and trustee—as well as banker—and a friend besides since we were at College together—which is favourable to business—as it gives confidence—or ought to do so.—

I had hoped that you had obtained the price of the Schooner from Ld. Blessington—you must really tell him that I must make the affair public—and take other steps which will be agreeable to neither—unless he speedily pays the money—so long due—and contracted by his own headstrong wish to purchase.—You know how fairly I treated him in the whole affair.——Every thing except the best (i.e. the Green travelling Chariot) may be disposed of—and that speedily—as it will assist to balance our account.——As the Greeks have gotten their loan—they may as well repay mine—which they no longer require—and I request you to forward a copy of the agreement to Mr. Kinnaird and direct him from me to claim the money from the Deputies.—They were welcome to it in their difficulties—and also for Good and all—supposing that they had not got out of them—but as it is—they can afford repayment—and I assure you—that besides *this*—they have had many 'a strong and long pull' at my purse—which

has been (and still is) disbursing pretty freely in their cause—besides—I shall
have to *re-expend* the same monies—having some hundred men under orders—
at my own expence for ye G[ree]k Government and National service.——Of all
these proceedings here, health—politics—plans—acts and deeds—&c. good
or otherwise Gamba or others will tell you—truly or not truly according to
their habits—

yrs. ever
N B_N[44]

[44] This letter, and another to Samuel Barff, Leslie Marchand writes, 'are apparently the last that
Byron wrote. Later that day he went for a ride in the rain and the soaking he got brought on the fever
that resulted in his death ten days later.'

AFTERWORD

News of Byron's death reached London on 14 May, 1824, in letters from Pietro Gamba, William Fletcher, and Lord Sidney Osborne. Three days later, six men met at John Murray's office, and—after a good deal of debate and a great deal of what Doris Langley Moore (in *The Late Lord Byron*) calls 'gentlemanly hysteria'—burned his memoirs in the grate. The key players were Murray, John Cam Hobhouse, and Thomas Moore, but three others had been brought in to represent the interests of Lady Byron, Augusta Leigh, and Moore himself. Byron had given Moore the first instalment of the memoirs in Italy in October 1819, to show around ('you—or any body else may see it—at his return', he told Kinnaird; *LJ* vi. 232) and to profit from as he saw fit; in May 1821 he sent a second group of papers. Moore had sold the entire package to Murray for 2000 guineas later that year—though that arrangement could be interpreted as a secured loan, and that was how Moore now wished the transaction to be seen, as he wanted the document preserved, and he had the money to reclaim it.

Of the six incendiarists only two (Moore and his representative, Thomas Luttrell) had actually read the memoirs, and they argued for their survival. (Murray's literary adviser, William Gifford, not present at the meeting, had read them and pronounced them 'fit only for a brothel'—but he thought that of all Byron's latter-day productions, particularly *Don Juan*.) The four who had not read the papers urged their destruction on the basis of what they understood them to contain. A sensible proposal that the document be put under lock and key with a banker or a lawyer until some future date was rejected. To modern eyes the act of suppression is inexplicable, until we understand the emotional investments involved. None of the three principals was looking at this document at this juncture, alone; all were acting on the basis of their relationship with Byron as a whole. For Murray, who might have made a fortune from the memoirs if published, the aim seems to have been to appear as much the gentleman as all the others, despite his lowly status as a tradesman: less self-interested and more dedicated to the reputation of his beloved author than anybody else. Hobhouse had already petrified Augusta with what the memoirs almost certainly contained, and accordingly took another patch on the moral high ground, to the effect that the decision should be hers and that she had already made it. It was not that he wanted the memoirs destroyed; only that it was her wish, and that therefore he was protecting her interests. Thus, when it came to it, he physically put no papers in the fire: Britain lost a born lawyer when Hobhouse decided on a political career. In reality, Hobhouse was consumed with jealousy that Byron should have put the document into the hands of Moore rather than himself, its rightful and responsible repository. Moore protested, but was tainted by his decision to sell in the first place. It was a thoroughly pathetic affair.

News of Byron's death spread apace. 'And Byron is dead!', Jane Welsh wrote to her future husband, Thomas Carlyle, on 20 May; 'I was told it all at once in a room full of people. My God if they had said that the sun or the moon was gone out of the heavens it could not have struck me with the idea of a more awful and dreary blank in the creation'. In London to consult a doctor, the poet John Clare (who had written a 'Childe Harold's Pilgrimage' and a 'Don Juan' of his own) happened upon Byron's funerary procession making its way up the Tottenham Court Road on 12 July, and was astonished: 'my eye was suddenly arrested by straggling groupes of the common people collected together and talking about a funeral...the train of a funeral suddenly appeard on which a young girl that stood beside me gave a deep sigh and utterd poor Lord Byron'. 'The Reverend the Moral and the fastidious may say what they please about Lord Byrons fame and damn it as they list', Clare went on: 'he has gaind the path of its eternity without them and lives above the blight of their mildewing censure to do him damage.' The future poet laureate, Alfred Tennyson, 15 at the time, went out into the Lincolnshire countryside and simply wrote 'Byron is dead' on a rock. 'The world is rid of Lord Byron,' John Constable less charitably wrote to a friend at the time, 'but the deadly slime of his touch still remains.'

John Murray—who, incidentally, had in 1815 published a novel (*Emma*) by a lady hailing from provincial Hampshire, Jane Austen by name—continued to profit from Byron's deadly slime. So did his firm, which in the years to come would publish authors as different as Charles Darwin and Herman Melville. He died in 1843. With Murray, Moore published the first genuine biography of Byron in 1830–1831—and the last genuine one for a hundred years—where the poet's letters and journals were first introduced to the reading public. He died in 1852, in rural obscurity in Wiltshire, far away from the 'stove' of London society that Byron had accused him of enjoying overmuch, and having buried all five of his children. His puckish charm had waned with the passage of time, as had English high society's general sense of his genius, but he had been a sincere campaigner for the rights of the Irish and of Catholics in Britain. Byron's faithful and long-suffering banker-cum-literary agent and 'sheet anchor' (in the poet's own words), Douglas Kinnaird, died in 1830, aged 42, after a long and obscure illness. He had attempted to buy the memoirs from Murray, as had Byron's old and faithful parliamentary colleague, Sir Francis Burdett. Hobhouse himself, the inveterate bachelor, married in 1828 and became a devoted husband and father of three daughters. His wife died tragically young in 1835 and thereafter he threw himself into politics—progressive rather than radical. (His sole political act remembered today was his invention of the formula, 'His Majesty's loyal Opposition', in the Westminster Parliament.) For his role in turning the Whig party into the Liberal one he was made a baron, like his old friend, in 1851. He died in 1869, aged 82, having fought and lost a long campaign to have a statue of Byron by the Danish sculptor Bertel Thorwaldsen erected in Westminster Abbey; most fittingly, the statue now stands in the library at Trinity College, Cambridge. Westminster Abbey eventually allowed a plaque commemorating Byron in 1974, 20 years after the self-confessed atheist Shelley had been so honoured.

Lady Byron had refused to read the memoirs; on no account whatsoever could she touch pitch. But an outcome the moral majority in Murray's office that day had not anticipated was that once Byron's history of their marriage was destroyed, she need have no fears of meaningful contradiction where her account of the business was concerned. (The destruction of the memoirs also allowed numerous forgeries to circulate in the years that followed, especially as it was understood that Moore had handed them around before selling them to Murray. To this day the hope persists that somebody, somewhere, has an undiscovered copy.) Lady Byron described her life as one of 'undeviating rectitude', and her friends lauded her 'beautiful gift of silence', both of which expressions are woefully far from the truth. In fact, over a lengthily and copiously valetudinarian life—she died in 1860, aged 67—she deployed a poison pen and a network of moral coercion as successfully as anybody in English literary history. Eventually she revealed all, in a manner of speaking, in conversations with her fellow-abolitionist Harriet Beecher Stowe, the author of *Uncle Tom's Cabin*. Stowe's study of the marriage, gallantly and impartially entitled *Lady Byron Vindicated*, appeared in 1870, publicized the Augusta rumours with which Lady Byron had threatened and cajoled everybody with for years, and brought Byron's reputation to a nadir from which it would not recover until André Maurois's and Peter Quennell's biographies of the poet, published in the 1930s. Ironically enough, most of Lady Byron's and therefore Harriet Stowe's testimony originated with a far from neutral witness and a far from model citizen like themselves: Lady Caroline Lamb, who died at Brocket Hall, Hertfordshire, in 1828, having been 'muddled either with Brandy or laudanum' in her later days, and who had separated from her husband in 1825.

Lady Byron's prime victim had been Augusta Leigh, whose crime was that Byron had loved her more than his wife. Augusta died in 1851, and as late as six months before her death Lady Byron was bent on extracting confessions from her, in an interview at the White Hart Inn in Reigate, of all places—with her lawyer in the room. But 'Goose' had put herself in an impossible position, perennially indigent and miserable as she was, and with a brood of children that would have driven any parent to despair, by accepting loans from her 'friend' when her husband's uselessness and her own drove her to request them. She had a good deal to put up with: her son-in-law, for example, seduced another of her daughters, 17 years old at the time, and had two children by her. Augusta stood up to her sister-in-law all too rarely, and Lady Byron never overlooked the opportunity of resuming their correspondence in order further to humiliate her with mental charity.

Byron's devoted servants, William Fletcher and Tita Falcieri, had brought his body home from Greece. Fletcher and Byron's steward, Lega Zambelli, went into business together making pasta in London, but the enterprise came to grief. Fletcher hung on in a state of intermittent dependency on Lady Byron, Murray, Hobhouse, and Augusta. He was still alive in 1847, but when he died we do not know. Fittingly, his son married Zambelli's daughter, and they kept Lega's fascinating papers, now in the British Library. Pietro Gamba had also been on board the *Florida* for that sad voyage, and consequently published his *Narrative of Lord Byron's Last Journey to Greece* in 1825. It is an excellent book, as is the firemaster William Parry's *The Last Days of Lord Byron*, published in the same year. Exiled from Italy, Pietro returned to Greece and died there of typhoid in 1827: his grave is unknown. Lyon, Byron's Newfoundland and companion in Missolonghi ('Lyon, you are no rogue, Lyon.... Thou art more faithful than men, Lyon; I trust thee more...thou art my faithful dog'), also came to England. Hobhouse took him in, but he died within a year, and was buried under a willow tree at Whitton Park, the Twickenham home of Hobhouse's father. ('Hobby' had helped Byron memorialize his first Newfoundland, Boatswain, at Newstead, in 1809.)

Teresa Guiccioli lived a life even longer than Lady Byron, dying the same age as the century, in 1873. After Byron's departure to Greece she returned to Ravenna with her father, and when he was imprisoned as a liberal, she was forced to return to her husband. (She had never accepted anything of monetary value from Byron, and refused to figure in his will; the Gambas were not rich.) She soon left Guiccioli for a second time and had various affairs and liaisons, including one with Lord Holland's son, Henry Fox (whom we saw visiting Byron in Genoa in 1823), and another with the French poet Lamartine. Her husband at last died in 1840, eight years after she had made a pilgrimage to England and Newstead, and had met all the sympathetic members of Byron's old circle. She married the Marquis de Boissy in 1847, published *Lord Byron jugé par les Témoins de sa Vie* in 1868, and also wrote a *Vie de Lord Byron en Italie*, left unfinished at her death: an astute and insightful record. She luxuriated somewhat fulsomely on her relationship with Byron as the years went on, but at least she had earned the right to do so, which Lady Blessington certainly had not.

We last saw Claire Clairmont in the aftermath of Allegra's and Shelley's deaths, leaving Italy for Vienna with her brother. After that she worked as a governess in Moscow from 1825 to 1828 before returning to England and then living in Dresden, Pisa, and Paris at various times before settling in Florence in 1870, where she died in 1879, aged 80. An unscrupulous disciple of Shelley's, the American Edward Silsbee, ingratiated himself into her Florentine existence in the early 1870s, mainly with the aim of getting his hands on Claire's stock of Shelley papers and memorabilia, without success. After her death he was back again, and Claire's niece apparently made marriage with her the price required for the archive, at which point he finally decamped. Henry James heard the story locally eight years after Claire's death, and made it the basis for his novella, *The Aspern Papers*.

Mary Shelley left Genoa for England on 23 July 1823, a week or so after Byron himself had left for Greece. They parted under something of a cloud of misunderstanding about his willingness to pay her travel expenses: a cloud Leigh Hunt was well placed to dispel but did not. (Byron had left funds with his banker for Hunt to deliver to Mary as a third party, but he failed to do so.) Any resentment was short-lived, however. When she heard that the man she called 'the dear capricious fascinating Albe' (a pet-name invented during the *Frankenstein* summer of 1816, perhaps from 'LB') had 'left the desart world', she also wrote, à propos of Shelley's death: 'Can I forget his attentions & consolations to me during my deepest misery?—Never.' She and Augusta were the only two women who visited Byron's body as it lay in state in London in early July. His remains were in a closed casket, and would not have been a pretty sight after a brutal autopsy and two months in a barrel of spirits. In 1826 she published her third novel, *The Last Man*, which contains powerfully idealized portraits of both Byron and her late husband, and she went on to provide important assistance to Thomas Moore in the writing of his biography. She died in 1851.

Mary Shelley's son and only surviving child, Percy Florence (educated at Harrow and Trinity College, Cambridge, coincidentally enough), was bought up in a suffocating atmosphere of reverence for the dead poet, his father. Byron's sole surviving child, Ada, on the other hand, was raised (mostly by her grandmother up until her own death; her mother showed hardly any interest in her) at Kirkby Mallory, Leicestershire, where a portrait of Byron—the most famous, in Albanian costume, now in the British embassy in Athens—was kept hidden from the girl behind a green curtain. Byron heard of this sinister arrangement from his lawyer in 1822. 'I regret what you say of the "Portrait"', he ruefully and placidly wrote to Hanson, 'as some steps must be taken to prevent the Child's mind from being prejudiced against her father—and I beg of you to inform me what *legally* can be done to direct her education so as to prevent her being brought up in a hostile state towards me.' (*LJ* ix. 127.) There could be no legal recourse against this act of needless cruelty, and Ada was not allowed even to see her father's handwriting until after her marriage. A sickly and lonely child, who had inherited her mother's talent for mathematics, Ada was tutored by the scientist Mary Somerville (after whom Somerville College, Oxford is named), through whom she met the inventor of the 'Difference Engine', Charles Babbage, in 1833, when she was aged eighteen. Her father had called Lady Byron a 'Princess of Parallellograms'; Babbage would call Ada 'The Enchantress of Numbers', and her contribution to the history of computer programming was genuine and substantial. The Ada programming language of the 1970s was named after her, as is 'The Ada Initiative', a modern-day pressure group fighting for sexual equality in computer technology. She married in 1835 and had three children in a loveless marriage punctuated by various abortive affairs and her disastrous gambling habit. (Her first child was called Byron, her second Ann Isabella.) She died in 1852, the same age as her father, from cancer of the uterus: her mother 'at her side' and utterly in control of those allowed to visit during her final illness. At her own request, Ada was buried alongside her father at Hucknall Torkard.

* * *

Byron had the misfortune to attract more than his fair share of dysfunctional and humourless admirers, from outright liars like Leigh Hunt, John Trelawny, and Lady Blessington, through self-interested fabricators like Caroline Lamb, Claire Clairmont, and Lady Byron, to devoted friends like Hobhouse, and ambivalent ones like Mary Shelley. No wonder, perhaps, that the people he loved most, Augusta Leigh and Teresa Guiccioli, were ones who made him laugh; and that the superficial Thomas Moore meant more to Byron than the conventional and earnest Hobhouse thought he should have done. Something of a similar competitive psychological desire to know Byron best (proprietorially speaking) and judge him most searchingly (moralistically speaking) has tainted biographies of him from Moore's day to our own. Leslie Marchand's ability to resist both those temptations makes his 1957 biography of the poet still the best that has been published; perhaps it will not be improved upon.

INDEX

Byron's letters to individuals are indexed in bold type.

Maturin, Charles Robert (novelist and playwright) 223, 227, 268, 399

Mavrocordatos, Prince Alexander (Greek political leader) 425, 467, 473, 475, 478–80, 485, **492**, 498, 499, 510

Melbourne, Lady, *see* Lamb

Milbanke, Annabella, *see* Byron

Milbanke, Lady Judith, *née* Noel (afterwards Noel; Lady Byron's mother) 181, 183, 185, 188, 192, 205, 263, 308, 361, 393, 404–5, 412

Milbanke, Sir Ralph (afterwards Noel; Lady Byron's father) 112, 171–2, 178, 183, 184–5, 188, 191–2, **198**, 261, 405

Miller, William (publisher) **85**

Moore, Thomas (poet) 83, 94, 97, **102**, 103, **120**, **131**, 161, **173**, **190**, **194**, **197**, **203**, 250, **255**, **262**, **265**, 292, 340, **358**, 375, **389**, **406**, **448**, 507–508

Murray, Joe (servant) 12, **42**, 48, 51, 56, 88, 91, 98

Murray, John (publisher) 83, 89, **91**, **121**, 126–7, 149, 155, **156**, 158, **166**, 191, **196**, **207**, 223, **225**, **239**, **251**, 260, **269**, **272**, **274**, **276**, 277, **281**, **287**, 304, **310**, **316**, **320**, **321**, **327**, **333**, **343**, **351**, **354**, **361**, **366**, **368**, **379**, **386**, 395, **403**, **411**, **415**, 421, 425, **428**, 430–31, **431**, **437**, 444, **497**, 507–508

Nathan, Isaac (musician and composer) 188, **210**

Newstead Abbey (country seat) 37, 40, 68, 77, 87, 93, 133, 143–4, 156, 304–06; retain 39, 72–3, 75, 78; sell 33, 63, 187, 211, 260, 271, 277; Claughton purchase 84, 112, 114, 117, 118, 127–8, 145, 167, 174, 177, 260; Wildman purchase 250, 284, 286, 299

Noel, Lady Judith, *see* Milbanke

Noel, Sir Ralph, *see* Milbanke

Noel, Thomas, 2nd Viscount Wentworth (Lady Byron's uncle) 171, 188, 190, 192

Osborne, Lord Sydney Godolphin (British diplomat) 301, 453, 459, 467, 507

Oxford, Lady, *see* Harley

Pacha, Ali (Albanian warlord) 58–60, 65

Parker, Mrs Charlotte Augusta (aunt) **7**

Parker, Peter (cousin) 37

Parkyns, Ann (distant relative) 7, 8

Parkyns, Frances 7, 47

Parry, William (artillery expert in Greece) 467, 468, 476, 492–3, 494, 495, 499, 502, 510

Pasha, Yussuf (Turkish potentate in western Greece) **492**

Perry, James (newspaper editor) **101**, 174, 337

'Peterloo Massacre' 339, 355–6

Pigot, Elizabeth Bridget (Southwell friend) **24**, **26**

Pigot, John (Southwell friend) **21**

Polidori, John William (doctor and travelling companion) 215, 217, 220, 222, 225, 244, 277–80, 316–18

Pope, Alexander 354, 365, 370, 449

Portsmouth, Earl, *see* Wallop

Prince Regent (afterwards George IV) 85, 104, 121, 130, 131, 157, 158, 160, 174, 335

Pulci, Luigi (Italian poet) 303, 350

Rawdon, Elizabeth Anne (potential bride) 110

Richardson, Samuel (novelist) 370

Roberts, Captain Daniel (Pisan acquaintance and boat builder) **416**, 428

Rochdale (Lancashire collieries) 5, 33, 36, 47, 63, 75, 77, 85, 91, 92, 117, 167, 211, 260, 277, 284, 286, 337, 405; lawsuit and final sale 360, 445, 482, 487

Rogers, Dummer (tutor) 8

Rogers, Samuel (poet) 83, 94, 97, **227**, 250, 380–81, 393

Romilly, Sir George (barrister) 307, 323

Rousseau, Jean-Jacques 225, 232, 396–7

Rubens, Peter Paul 220

Rushton, Robert (servant), 41–2, 47, 48, 51, 56–7, 88, 217

Schlegel, August Wilhelm (German critic) 216, 279

Scott, Sir Walter 58, 76, 126, 133, 163, 174, 193, 250, 269, 304, 362, 366, **409**, 445

Sebastiani, Count Horace (Napoleonic soldier and diplomat) 197

Segati, Marianna (mistress) 249, 252–3, 254, 257, 264–5, 270, 278, 286,

Shakespeare, William 163, 243, 251, 299; *As You Like It* 293, 374; *Coriolanus* 117, 201, 311; *Hamlet* 22, 185, 197, 217, 226, 321, 359, 367; *1Henry IV* 191, 195, 218, 267, 334, 374, 398, 437, 478; *2Henry IV* 161, 224; *Henry VIII* 303; *Julius Caesar* 158, 267; *King John* 176; *King Lear* 115, 165, 243, 251; *Love's Labour's Lost* 396; *Macbeth* 70, 118, 165, 175, 176, 194, 204, 255, 311, 318, 409, 455, 460; *Merchant of Venice* 256, 274, 275, 311, 458; *Much Ado about Nothing* 32, 181; *Othello* 194, 264, 275, 407, 437, 489; *Richard III* 179, 263, 489; *Romeo and Juliet* 24, 165, 243, 251; *Taming of the Shrew* 200; *The Tempest* 131; *Twelfth Night* 396, 406

Shelley, Mary, *née* Godwin 215–16, 261, 303, 316–17, 382, 425, 427, **427**, 440, 469, 511; *Frankenstein* 317